This given as part [illegible] [illegible]
in [illegible]

PSYCHIC EXPLORATION
A Challenge for Science

Contributors

James B. Beal

E. Douglas Dean

Martin Ebon

Jule Eisenbud

Gerald Feinberg

Willis W. Harman

Charles Honorton

Jean Houston

Stanley Krippner

Lawrence L. LeShan

Robert Masters

Edgar D. Mitchell

Robert L. Morris

Thelma Moss

Brendan O'Regan

Henry K. Puharich

Harold Puthoff

D. Scott Rogo

William G. Roll

Gertrude Schmeidler

Helmut Schmidt

Rex G. Stanford

Russell Targ

Charles T. Tart

William A. Tiller

Montague Ullman

Robert L. Van De Castle

Alan Vaughan

Marcel Vogel

Evan Harris Walker

Rhea A. White

#1 ✓

#2

Secretary to Harmon
→ "Synchronicity"?
Let me borrow
your writing

"Brendon
would be
interested
in this"
never gave
it back
to Joy!

deceased

Plants

EDGAR D. MITCHELL

PSYCHIC EXPLORATION

A Challenge for Science

Edited by JOHN WHITE

G. P. Putnam's Sons, New York

*This book is dedicated to the potential
in humanity which can bring a new age of
understanding, cooperation, and peace*

Contents

II. THE EXPANDING RANGE OF PSYCHIC RESEARCH

III. THE EMERGENCE OF A NEW NATURAL SCIENCE

ON THE METHOD OF SCIENCE

. . . in nature what is absurd, according to our theories, is not always impossible.

. . . facts . . . exist which mean nothing to most minds while they are full of light for others. It even happens that a fact or observation stays a very long time under the eyes of a man of science without in any way inspiring him; then suddenly there comes a ray of light, and the mind interprets the fact quite differently and finds for it wholly new relations. The new idea appears . . . as a kind of sudden revelation. . . .

The experimental method, then, cannot give new and fruitful ideas to men who have none; it can serve only to guide the ideas of men who have them, to direct their ideas and to develop them so as to get the best results.

The idea is a seed; the (experimental) method is the earth furnishing the conditions in which it may develop, flourish and give the best of fruit according to its nature. But as only what has been sown in the ground will ever grow in it, so nothing will be developed by the experimental method except the ideas be submitted to it. The method itself gives birth to nothing.

CLAUDE BERNARD, *Introduction to Experimental Medicine*

ON THE PHILOSOPHY OF SCIENCE

. . . science can only be created by those thoroughly imbued with the aspiration toward truth and understanding. This source of feeling, however, springs from the sphere of religion.

. . . science without religion is lame, religion without science is blind.

ALBERT EINSTEIN, *Ideas and Opinions*

Edgar D. Mitchell

2004 Petaluma

EDGAR D. MITCHELL, Sc.D., is president of the Institute of Noetic Sciences in Palo Alto, California, a nonprofit tax-exempt public corporation dedicated to research and education in the processes of human consciousness to help achieve a new understanding and expanded awareness among all people. He is also chairman of the board of Edgar D. Mitchell & Associates, of Monterey, California.

After graduating from Carnegie Institute of Technology with a bachelor of science degree in 1952, Dr. Mitchell joined the U.S. Navy. He completed flight training in 1954 and served for the next seven years as an aircraft pilot in operational and research posts.

In 1961 Dr. Mitchell attended the U.S. Naval Postgraduate School, earning a second bachelor of science degree. The same year he enrolled in a doctoral program at Massachusetts Institute of Technology. During preparation of his doctoral dissertation, he taught graduate courses in inertial guidance and interplanetary navigation. After receiving a doctor of science degree in 1964, he was assigned as technical director for navy collaboration in the U.S. Air Force Manned Orbiting Laboratory Program and remained in that position until 1965, when he was selected for further training as an aerospace research pilot. This training led to his selection as an astronaut in 1966.

Dr. Mitchell became the sixth man on the moon while serving as lunar module pilot during the Apollo 14 flight in February 1971. He also served as support crew for Apollo 9 and as backup crew for Apollo 10 and Apollo 16.

Upon retirement from the navy with the rank of captain in October 1972, Dr. Mitchell formed Edgar D. Mitchell & Associates. The following March he founded the Institute of Noetic Sciences. Both activities keep him engaged on a full-time basis in the search for solutions to human problems and the release of human potential. During the year following his retirement from the navy, he authored approximately forty articles and lectures dealing with these issues and participated in two major experimental efforts in psychic research.

Dr. Mitchell can be reached at the Institute of Noetic Sciences, 575 Middlefield Road, Palo Alto, Calif. 94301.

John White

JOHN WHITE *is director of education for the Institute of Noetic Sciences in Palo Alto, California.*

Following graduation from Dartmouth College in 1961, Mr. White spent four years as a commissioned naval officer. From 1965 to 1969 he taught English in a Connecticut high school while earning a master's degree in education from Yale University. In 1969 he left full-time teaching to become a writer–editor for the Southern New England Telephone Company. He also began teaching English in the evening division of Quinnipiac College. He maintained both positions until 1972, when he joined Dr. Mitchell in the formation of Edgar D. Mitchell & Associates, Inc.

Mr. White has been Eastern Editor of Psychic *magazine and is presently an associate editor of it. He is also a member of the editorial board of* Journal of Altered States of Consciousness. *His books include* The Highest State of Consciousness (*Doubleday, 1972*), What Is Meditation? (*Doubleday, 1974*) *and* Frontiers of Consciousness (*Julian Press, 1974*). *More than 50 articles and reviews by him have appeared in newspapers and magazines such as* Reader's Digest, Psychic, *and* Fate *and in scholarly journals such as* Journal of Altered States of Consciousness, College Composition and Communication, Fields Within Fields, *and* Jounal for the Study of Consciousness. *Several of them have been reprinted in textbooks on linguistics, education, and biology.*

Acknowledgments

THIS BOOK attempts to provide an authoritative encyclopedic volume on psychic research. Such a collaborative effort requires help from many people who do not appear visibly in its pages. But without their assistance and guidance, the book would be measurably farther from fulfilling its purpose.

First, I want to offer a word of sincere gratitude to Dr. J. B. Rhine and Dr. Louisa E. Rhine of the Foundation for Research on the Nature of Man. As a member of the board of directors of Dr. Rhine's foundation for two years, I have profited immensely from our association and from the help he gave me in my first major research project in extrasensory perception. I regret that he and Mrs. Rhine were unable to participate in this project.

Likewise, I regret that Dr. Gardner Murphy of the Department of Psychology at American University, Dr. Ian Stevenson of the Medical School at University of Virginia, Dr. Shafica Karagulla of the Higher Sense Perception Research Foundation in Los Angeles, and Dr. William E. McGarey of the Association for Research and Enlightenment Clinic in Phoenix, Arizona, had commitments that prevented them from joining us. However, their thoughtful comments have proven useful, and I trust that this book will prove worthy despite their absence from the roster of contributors.

The chapters were read by a four-member editorial review board consisting of three contributors and one outside authority. The contributing members were Dr. William Tiller, Dr. Robert Morris, and Dr. Jean Houston; the fourth member was Dr. Karlis Osis, director of research for the American Society for Psychical Research. Dr. Osis was in India at the time I began this project, and because of previous commitments, he felt unable to contribute a chapter. I am pleased that he could join us in an editorial-review capacity. The board was of incalculable value in strengthening the book, and the authors join me in giving great thanks to the board members for their assistance. That different interpretations and points of view may exist on the basis of the same data is no one's fault, least of all the review board's. It merely indicates that we do not yet have the answers to many problems in psychic research and that we need more experimental work in many areas.

When this book was first conceived, I thought of myself as the sole author. Obviously the conception changed. During late 1971 and 1972, the number of research people working in this field expanded so rapidly, with a consequent increase in new knowledge and developments, that one person could not adequately tell the story in depth. The first shift in the conception involved a major research effort in which Prof. William Braud and Ms. Lyndell Braud of the University of Houston directed a staff that helped me compile information on a variety of topics. The staff consisted of Wallace Domert, Ronald B. Hoffman, Dorothy Lum Wong, Jack B. McMahan, Barry J. Wepman, Ronald Sunderland,

ACKNOWLEDGMENTS

and Leslie Pinter. Their reports are embodied in various chapters of this book.

The initial financial support for this research was granted by the Mind Science Foundation of Los Angeles. I would be remiss if I failed to acknowledge my gratitude to the foundation, especially Dr. J. Wilfred Hahn, its former executive director, and Mr. C. V. Wood of the board of trustees, both of whom shared and encouraged my work in psychic research.

After retiring from the navy in 1972, my continuing effort to study the nature and potential of humanity took the form of a research organization, Edgar D. Mitchell & Associates (EDMA), Inc. Some months later, the research and educational functions of EDMA Corporation were transferred to a new organization, the Institute of Noetic Sciences. My associates in both ventures are scientists, educators, doctors, executives, philanthropists, psychic sensitives, and a variety of other interested parties. Their counsel, guidance, and encouragement during the first difficult months of organizational development was a constant source of inspiration. Without their wisdom and good wishes, the difficulties would certainly have been greater—and perhaps insurmountable.

My wife, Anita, has provided inspiration, encouragement and sparkle to make the efforts of pioneering new ideas less difficult. Her enthusiasm for my endeavors is a continuing source of energy.

My parents, J. T. and Ollidean, have my respect and admiration for their encouragement to academic endeavors and for a heritage of love, productive work and personal discipline. I am always grateful.

Finally, special thanks must be given to my staff. John White, who initially joined me in EDMA Corporation and later took the position of director of education at the Institute of Noetic Sciences, handled the many editorial duties that arise in the production of a work such as this. His devoted efforts, spanning many months of hard work, have more than those of any other single individual made this book possible. Harry Jones, my executive assistant during the initial period of organizational development, ably managed matters in the EDMA Corporation office during my absence. There Ms. June Oldham was for many months my "good right arm," to whose efficient and unstinting efforts I confidently assigned many tasks I might never have otherwise accomplished. And the late Ms. Virginia Meyer gave much-needed secretarial support during our early days. Mr. Chuck Rogers and Ms. Anita Rettig joined our staff later but nevertheless have made contributions that were indispensable.

Ms. Jean Beaulieu provided me with the initial spark that fired my curiosity about this area and eventually launched my investigations in this field. To her I am especially grateful.

All of these people were in a real sense "team members" who helped accomplish "the mission." I am deeply indebted to them all.

For Louise and our daughters, Karlyn and Elizabeth, who served by loving and waiting patiently through years of absence and demanding assignments, there are no words adequate to express my appreciation.

E. D. M.

Preface

THIS VOLUME contains the work of many eminent people, bound together by a common interest in exploring and explaining psychic functioning and its ramifications. They bring knowledge and skill from many disciplines: physical science, medicine, behavioral science, social science, and philosophy. Each approaches the subject from his own field of excellence and together they provide a compelling overview.

I recognize that some portions of the book are more difficult than others. In those chapters where highly technical investigations are reported, the general reader is encouraged to read through quickly, giving greatest attention to the summary, introduction, and conclusion. But you should know that despite the technical material, there are many fascinating studies of anecdotal material that should prove of interest to all.

The more sophisticated reader will notice that this book omits discussion of auras, pharmacology, radionics (a new field that integrates psychic diagnosis and healing with esoteric technology), and astrology and other forms of prophecy. In addition, although some research people claim connections between UFO phenomena and the psychic event, the correlations are not sufficiently established to warrant treatment in this volume. These omissions are not an oversight. Rather, they are due to a paucity of solid research material. That paucity, in turn, is caused primarily by the lack of funding and research support from which this field has generally suffered—a lack, incidentally, that we hope this volume will soon help to change.

A few last words before you start the book. To begin, let me say (without intending to jest): go to the end. You will find an extensive glossary to help the general reader unfamiliar with the terms—old and new—in psychic research, transpersonal psychology, and noetics. And the index can be a useful tool for tracing a subject or idea to get a grasp of it from context.

When reading the book, you will find references cited by an arabic numeral in parentheses thus: (4). References are listed at the end of each chapter. This citation system is designed to minimize disturbance to the general reader's train of thought, while providing adequate material for follow-up by interested scholars and scientists.

Likewise, I asked contributors to minimize use of statistics, probabilities, formulas, and the like. Where such items occur, the author felt it necessary to retain them. The general reader should be able to pass over them without bewilderment; the technically trained reader will, of course, have information the author considers important.

Last of all, I have chosen to use the term "psychic research" rather than the traditional "psychical research." Purists will object that this is improper, it violates custom, it is not the correct adjectival form, etc. I can only answer: language changes constantly, and my intention is to simplify public usage of an otherwise tongue-twisting and sometimes mystifying phrase. In this matter I am following the trend in linguistics to be descriptive, rather than prescriptive. I trust that this encouragement of popular usage will not be offensive to my colleagues and that the research itself—whether termed psychic or psychical—will be encouraged and supported by this volume.

EDGAR D. MITCHELL

Gerald Feinberg

GERALD FEINBERG, *Ph.D., is professor of physics at Columbia University, where he earned his doctorate in 1957. Dr. Feinberg works in the field of elementary particle physics. In 1967 he proposed the existence of tachyons, a hypothetical particle said to travel faster than light. Tachyons have been searched for in experiments but not yet found. Dr. Feinberg has written many articles on physics. His book* The Prometheus Project *(Doubleday, 1969) describes a plan for global participation in the choice of long-range goals for mankind.*

Foreword

MOST NATURAL scientists have paid little attention to reports of that class of phenomena labeled "psychic," although there have been exceptions such as Crookes and Lord Rayleigh. The reasons for this neglect are doubtless diverse. Skepticism about the occurrence of such phenomena, the belief that they lie outside the subject matter of science, and the suspicion that they are inconsistent with the present scientific picture of the world are probably all factors contributing to the unwillingness of natural scientists to take psychic phenomena seriously.

In this book, a number of investigators of psychic phenomena present some results of their studies. Evaluation of their conclusions must now be undertaken by the scientific community at large. For the purpose of discussion, however, let us assume that some phenomena of the types described in the book truly occur and consider the possible role of such phenomena in the wider contexts of science.

Natural science takes as its purview everything that occurs at any place or time and tries to relate these occurrences to one another and to understand them. Therefore, if psychic phenomena do occur, natural scientists have the problem of understanding them and, eventually, of integrating them into our general description of nature. This might happen either by explaining psychic phenomena as unexpected consequences of known scientific principles or by modifying and extending these principles to include the new phenomena. These procedures have occurred with other new phenomena time and again in the evolution of contemporary science, and there is every reason to expect them to occur in the future, with or without psychic phenomena.

Physicists in particular have always searched for laws, such as that of the conservation of energy, that are universally applicable. Consequently, when new phenomena are discovered, it is of major concern to physicists to learn whether the previously known laws are applicable to them and, if not, how these laws must be modified to fit the new phenomena. For example, certain aspects of radioactive decay, when first discovered, seemed to involve a breakdown of energy conservation but eventually were found to obey an extended form of this law.

21

These considerations suggest that if psychic phenomena are eventually analyzed by physicists, two distinct questions will have to be answered. The first is whether psychic phenomena contradict any of the known laws of physics. If they do not, it would become important to know whether the existence of psychic phenomena could be inferred from the present laws of physics or whether they are simply allowed by these laws. The distinction between these questions arises because present physical laws do not always determine precisely what phenomena occur but often only forbid certain things from occurring. For example, the conservation of energy forbids any change, during a process, in the sum of all the different types of energy of all the particles taking part in the process. However, this law does not specify what types of energy actually occur in the world. That must be determined independently.

Of course, the most interesting situation, both for physicists and for psychic researchers, would occur if certain aspects of psychic phenomena actually contradicted known physical laws. However, in order to convince physicists of this, a great deal of reliable data, as well as a detailed analysis of this data, would be required. I do not think existing data show that psychic phenomena contradict known physical laws. In particular, it is certainly insufficient reason for arriving at such a conclusion to say that physicists have not heretofore suspected that such phenomena exist. A little-appreciated fact is that many newly discovered physical phenomena are unexpected at the time of their discovery. This is the case even for many phenomena that are afterward found to be explicable within the existing body of physical principles. It is quite possible that some or all psychic phenomena could fall into this category. An example of this might be a proposed explanation of precognition, which has often been cited by researchers as the most "unphysical" of psychic phenomena. I refer to the suggestion that precognition may involve advanced potential solutions of the equations describing one or more of the wave phenomena already known to science. It would therefore seem prudent to reserve judgment concerning violations of physical laws until more is understood about psychic phenomena. On the other hand, if new physical laws are involved in psychic phenomena, physicists would be happy for the intellectual challenge of investigating these laws.

The influence of psychic phenomena on the developing scientific study of consciousness may be more significant than any effect they may have on physics. In particular, there are two important questions about consciousness that psychic phenomena may help to clarify. These questions can be stated as follows: What is the range of consciousness in the universe? How is consciousness related to other aspects of the world?

There is a long-standing disagreement about the answer to the first question between those approaching the study of consciousness from the perspective of natural science and those approaching it from mystical, psychic, or drug experiences. The former tend to think that the occurrence of consciousness is restricted to individual human beings and perhaps to members of a few animal species. They also usually believe that where consciousness does occur, it is relatively limited in its scope, essentially to the ordinary awareness of "normal" people. On the other hand, testimony from mystics throughout history suggests that consciousness has a much greater range in the universe. These reports suggest that human consciousness has a richer and more complex structure than does ordinary awareness and that human consciousness is only a part of a series of levels of consciousness that exist in the universe.

Some recent studies of consciousness indicate that there may be some validity to the first of these pronouncements of the mystics, in that the human mind can be induced by various means into "conscious" states with rather different characteristics than ordinary awareness. Little scientific evidence yet exists concerning the second claim, that higher forms of consciousness pervade the universe and play a dominant role in it. It has been very difficult for scientists to consider, much less to accept, this latter claim, not only because of a lack of evidence for it but also because it is not clear through what physical processes consciousness could affect most of the matter in the universe. However, if psychic phenomena do cause us to widen our notions of what occurs in the world and what natural phenomena exist, then some of the barriers to scientific consideration of the proposition that consciousness is a fundamental aspect of the universe could be removed. Of course, this would not demonstrate the proposition, which would have to be independently investigated.

The second question—the relation of consciousness to other phenomena—is not wholly independent of the first, concerning the scope of consciousness. However, the second question also involves a number of separate issues, both semantic and substantive, most of which are far too complicated to be considered here. Views on the nature of consciousness range from the idealist position that consciousness is the only reality, through the dualist view that consciousness and matter are separate but equal elements of the universe, to the materialist position that consciousness is a particular manifestation of the properties of matter. Most scientists prefer the materialist position, perhaps because it seems most amenable to scientific investigation, although not much progress has yet been made along these lines.

The precise relevance of psychic phenomena to this question is unclear to me, although it is plausible that they have some relevance. It might be thought that telepathy, in some improved form, could be used as a new tool for the study of consciousness. However, the reports of telepathy make it seem more like a kind of soundless hearing or lightless vision than a direct perception of another's consciousness, so that this use is questionable. Again, the main effect may be that if psychic phenomena do imply a significant extension of our view about what is present in the universe, it could make a dualistic notion of consciousness more acceptable.

The previous considerations lead me to suggest a strategy for psychic research. I believe it would be appropriate for researchers to emphasize detailed studies of psychic phenomena rather than to concentrate on further efforts whose primary purpose is to convince others that the phenomena exist. I have two reasons for believing this. One is that a bare statement of the existence of a phenomenon is much less useful than statements about its detailed properties and its relations to other phenomena. Also, my impression is that scientists are much more likely to believe that something is real after its properties have been studied and delimited in this way, so that the strategy I am suggesting might even be a good way of convincing others. My other reason for proposing this strategy is that only by obtaining detailed information can we hope to answer questions of the sort that I raised earlier.

Adoption of this approach would tend to make psychic research more like physics. There would be more emphasis on general aspects of the phenomena and less on fluctuations due to individual subjects. While this should not be the only side of psychic research, it is an essential ingredient if this research is to become a part of the general program of scientific investigation. Many of the contributors included here share this view and make specific suggestions for beginning such an approach. I believe that their suggestions and other ideas expressed in this book deserve serious consideration by scientists and the public.

Introduction: From Outer Space
to Inner Space . . .

EDGAR D. MITCHELL

IN FEBRUARY 1971 I had the privilege of walking on the moon as a member of the Apollo 14 lunar expedition. During the voyage I made a test in extrasensory perception (ESP), attempting to send information telepathically to four receivers on earth.

Since then, people have asked me why an astronaut would take such an intense interest in a subject as ridiculed and unacceptable in respectable scientific circles as psychic research.

It is a fair question, which I will answer in this chapter. The answer is partly implied by the title of this book: psychic research presents a challenge that science can no longer avoid. But the title is also somewhat misleading. My real interest is—and has been for many years—to understand the nature of consciousness and the relationship of body to mind. Psychic research is one facet of this larger whole. Therefore, it might be said that I have simply gone from outer space to inner space.

The study of mind and consciousness is called *noetics*. The term comes from the Greek root word *nous*, meaning "mind." As popularly used, *noetic* refers to purely intellectual apprehension. But Plato spoke of noetic knowledge as the highest form of knowing—a direct cognition or apprehension of the eternal truths that surpasses the normal discursive processes of logical, intellectual reasoning. The word *science*, of course, originally meant "knowing" but has come to mean a type of knowing derived from use of the objective, rational faculties of mind. But psychic abilities such as telepathy are another type of knowing—a subjective knowing, a nonrational, cognitive process largely overlooked by the scientific world. Consciousness appears to be the central, unifying concept behind these different aspects of mind. Thus, in the spirit of its Grecian origin, I propose to use the omega (Ω) as a symbol for consciousness and noetics.

Psychic research is one aspect of noetics but by no means all of it. Paraphysics, for example, is a new field within noetics that is extending the laws and methods of physics in an attempt to explain some paranor-

25

mal phenomena (see Chapter 18). Some of the factors that paraphysics
has found necessary to consider are the effects of geomagnetism, phases of
the moon, and solar radiation on living systems. These and other terres-
trial and celestial factors rhythmically induce changes—sometimes subtle,
sometimes striking—in our physical and mental condition. Another example is exobiology, the study of the possibility of extraterrestrial life.
The evidence of exobiology leads some scientists to wonder: If life has
existed elsewhere in the universe for periods significantly longer than has
Homo sapiens, how much more evolved in consciousness might such life
forms be? Psychic researchers would add: If mankind does contact intelligent extraterrestrial civilizations, might psychic channels prove best for
communicating?

The topic of consciousness, then, is as vast as the cosmos and as close
to us as sleep. Noetics is the discipline that is arising from this confluence
of outer- and inner-space research. It is the ultimate frontier in man's
attempt to understand himself and the nature of the universe.

If we review the history of mankind's attempt to perceive, cognize, and
interpret his environment, we find that in the last four centuries, as a
result of the growth of scientific methodology, a formalized dichotomy has
arisen between proponents of the two modes of knowing: objective observation (followed by deductive reasoning) and direct cognitive processes. These opposing modes of perception are crudely epitomized as
science versus religion, reason versus intuition, rationality versus nonra-
tionality, objective knowledge versus subjective experience, and so forth.
Only in relatively recent years have scholars of each persuasion actively
and vehemently denied the validity of the other process. In prescientific
times, scholars—whether they agreed upon their conclusions or not—at
least recognized the validity of both external and internal observation.
(We must quickly add that the truly great teachers of modern times have
always acknowledged this dual process.)

Thus, although I am identifying consciousness as the ultimate frontier
in man's attempt to gain knowledge, it is by no means a new frontier
because throughout history people have sought to resolve the differences
between their objective methods and their subjective experience—between
outer and inner. The study of mind and consciousness is the common
ground for this effort. The living system that we call man is a holistic
phenomenon which exhibits both modes of knowing.

Perhaps after 350 years of divisiveness between science and religion we
are on the threshold of a new era of knowledge and cooperation. It should
be obvious that objective observation and reason do not by themselves
produce a satisfactory ethic for living—neither for the individual nor for
social systems. Facts become divorced from values, and action from need.

On the other hand, intuition and inspiration do not by themselves produce the agreement society needs to bring about order, structure, and survival in the material world. In this case, observation frequently becomes subject to individual interpretation according to the covert biases of the individual.

The antagonism between the objective and subjective modes of knowledge can be clearly illustrated. In 1600 Giordano Bruno was burned at the stake by theologians for asserting that the earth was not the center of the solar system and that there were other solar systems with living beings in them. In 1972 the American Academy of Science asserted that science and religion are "mutually exclusive realms of thought" and therefore the Genesis theory of creation should be kept out of science textbooks. The roles of science and religion are reversed in the modern example, but the same closed-minded dogmatism is operating to limit inquiry through sanctimonious denial of other viewpoints.

Research over the last fifty years by little-known, but forward-looking, thinkers has shown there is a vast creative potential in the human mind that is as yet almost totally unrecognized by science. Nonrational cognitive processes have so far eluded scientific description. However, this potential *has* been previously known and described by a few ancient sages and enlightened religious teachers, using veiled prescientific language to express what they discovered through subjective, intuitive, experiential means. We are, in my opinion, on the threshold of rediscovering and redefining those concepts and insights through the objective, rational, experimental efforts of science—if dogmatism and outmoded belief structures do not prevent it. The proper direction of sophisticated instrumentation and laboratory techniques can be the means whereby the physical and metaphysical realms are shown to be different aspects of the same reality. If this is demonstrated, it would be ironic, but appropriate, that so-called godless technology and materialistic science should lead to the rediscovery of the essential unity of science and religion.

Noetics recognizes all this. Noetics is the research frontier where the convergence of objectivity and subjectivity, of reason and intuition, is occurring most rapidly. In the study of consciousness, the techniques and technology of science are being combined with the higher insights of mind from both East and West to provide a new methodology for scholarly inquiry. For it is quite clear that reason alone is not sufficient for total understanding of ourselves. As Michael Polanyi, the eminent philosopher of science, points out, scientific discoveries do not always follow in a sequence of perfectly logical deductions (11). Instead, many discoveries involve intuitions and hunches on the part of the scientist in a manner that cannot be completely explained.

An example of noetic research dealing with just this problem comes from the biofeedback laboratory of Dr. Elmer Green at the Menninger

Clinic in Topeka, Kansas. Green has given the name *reverie* to that state of mind in which creative insight sometimes leaps fully conceived into awareness, and he is making a psychophysiological study of it (3).

The project began, as most experiments do, when a literature search by his colleague (and wife) Alyce Green revealed that many of the great ideas in science and other disciplines came to people while they were in a dreamlike state of strong visual imagery. The state appeared similar to what is known as the hypnogogic state, that brief period between waking and sleeping in which memories and images seem to pass before the eyes and that is sometimes characterized by the production of theta brainwaves, a rhythm of four to eight cycles per second. In the reverie-imagery project, as it is now being called at Menninger, subjects learn to increase their production of theta waves so that they can explore the relationship between the theta state—reverie—and creativity. If there is a significant correlation, it may eventually prove possible to enhance creativity by teaching people to voluntarily enter the theta state. Green speculates that "an individual trained in theta reverie may be able to direct both his conscious and unconscious 'minds' to work on a problem and come up with a totally unexpected creative solution." Thus, a subjective phenomenon is being examined objectively. If the resulting expansion of awareness and self-control gained by subjects in theta reverie results in a release of creative potential, it will demonstrate a very practical benefit from theoretical and basic research.

A second example of practical gains from basic research in subjective phenomena comes from that area of noetics called meditation research. Studies of yogis, Zen masters, transcendental meditators, and people from other traditions (17, 19–21) are demonstrating that meditation produces qualitative and beneficial shifts in psychophysiological condition. Alpha and theta brain waves are two physiological correlates being found for psychological stages of meditation, along with changes in breathing, heartbeat rate, blood pressure, muscle tension, and various other metabolic correlates. The results in the meditator include release of stress and tension, increased intellectual capacity, greater self-control and self-direction, a feeling of deep rest and relaxation, improved social relations, a decrease in use of prescribed and nonprescribed drugs, and other significant changes.

Psychic research—the subject of this book—is still another area of noetics that offers an avenue to the resolution of the dilemma of outer versus inner, matter versus spirit, body versus mind, reason versus intuition, science versus religion. From the viewpoint of noetics, and especially psychic research, what appear to be opposites are really composite parts of a larger whole: consciousness. I speak from personal experience.

When I went to the moon, I was as pragmatic a test pilot, engineer, and scientist as any of my colleagues. More than a quarter of a century had been spent in learning the empirical approach to dealing with the universe. Many times my life has depended upon the validity of scientific principles and the reliability of the technology built upon those principles. I knew well that analytic and logical thought, using objective data, could produce a technology that would reveal new secrets of the universe by probing the reaches of space and, at the microscopic level, the structure of atoms. Prior to the lunar exploration, I became as familiar with the spacecraft and its vast support system of people and equipment as a man could be, with confidence in it all. Despite that familiarity and confidence, though, there were moments during the flight when I felt an amazed and profound respect for the rational abilities of the human intellect—that it could find ways to guide a tiny capsule of metal through a half million miles of space with such precision and accuracy. Yes, I was pragmatic because my experience had shown beyond all question that science works.

But there was another aspect to my experience during Apollo 14, and it contradicted the "pragmatic engineer" attitude. It began with the breathtaking experience of seeing planet Earth floating in the vastness of space.

The first thing that came to mind as I looked at Earth was its incredible beauty. Even the spectacular photographs do not do it justice. It was a majestic sight—a splendid blue and white jewel suspended against a velvet black sky. How peacefully, how harmoniously, how marvelously it seemed to fit into the evolutionary pattern by which the universe is maintained. In a peak experience, the presence of divinity became almost palpable and I *knew* that life in the universe was not just an accident based on random processes. This knowledge came to me directly—noetically. It was not a matter of discursive reasoning or logical abstraction. It was an experiential cognition. It was knowledge gained through private subjective awareness, but it was—and still is—every bit as real as the objective data upon which, say, the navigational program or the communications system were based. Clearly, the universe had meaning and direction. It was not perceptible by the sensory organs, but it was there nevertheless—an unseen dimension behind the visible creation that gives it an intelligent design and that gives life purpose.

Next I thought of our planet's life-supporting character. That little globe of water, clouds, and land no bigger than my thumb was *home*, the haven our spacecraft would seek at the end of our voyage. Buckminster Fuller's description of the planet as "Spaceship Earth" seemed eminently fitting.

Then my thoughts turned to daily life on the planet. With that, my sense of wonderment gradually turned into something close to anguish. Because I realized that at the very moment when I was so privileged to view the planet from 240,000 miles in space, people of Earth were fighting wars; committing murder and other crimes; lying, cheating, and struggling for power and status; abusing the environment by polluting the water and air, wasting natural resources, and ravaging the land, acting out of lust and greed; and hurting others through intolerance, bigotry, prejudice, and all the things that add up to man's inhumanity to man. It seemed as though man were totally unconscious of his individual role in—and individual responsibility for—the future of life on the planet.

It was also painfully apparent that the millions of people suffering in conditions of poverty, ill health, misery, fear, and near-slavery were in that condition from economic exploitation, political domination, religious and ethnic persecution, and a hundred other demons that spring from the human ego. Science, for all its technological feats, had not—more likely, could not—deal with these problems stemming from man's self-centeredness.

The magnitude of the overall problem seemed staggering. Our condition seemed to be one of deepening crises on an unprecedented scale, crises that were mounting faster than we could solve them. There appeared to be the immediate possibility that warfare might destroy vast segments of civilization with one searing burst of atomic fury. Only a little further off appeared the possibility of intolerable levels of polluted air and of undrinkable water. A more remote, but no less real, likelihood was the death of large portions of the population from starvation, abetted by improper resources management by an exploding population.

How had the world come to such a critical situation—and why? Even more important, what could be done to correct it? How could we human beings restore the necessary harmonious relationship between ourselves and the environment? How could a nuclear Armageddon be avoided? How could life be made livable? How could man's potential for a peaceful, creative, fulfilling society be realized? How could the highest development of our objective rationality, epitomized by science, be wedded to the highest development of our subjective intuition, epitomized by religion?

These thoughts and questions stayed with me through the mission, splashdown, and parades. They stayed long afterward to the point of haunting me with an overwhelming awareness of how limited a view man has of his own life and the planet's. Sometimes at night I would lie awake for hours struggling with this enigma, trying to understand it and see it in a sensible perspective. How could man, the most intelligent creature on earth, be so utterly stupid and shortsighted as to put himself in a position of possible global extinction? How had insight become divorced from instinct? Was it possible to find a workable solution?

As I pondered the matter and discussed it with concerned thinkers around the world, it became obvious that there are three major alternatives for the future—alternatives within man's control:

1. To do nothing, in which case the prevailing dominant paradigm* and resulting socioeconomic behavior will eventually result in a massive collapse of the world system. The survivors can then start to rebuild civilization.
2. To relinquish personal freedom of choice to a central world government with the expectation that a controlled and unified society, however tyrannical its leadership, is better than nonsurvival.
3. To promote the process of metanoia,† or a new awakening in which mankind can realize its self-produced dilemma and, through a change of awareness and an expansion of individual responsibility, reestablish the unity of man with man and with the environment.

I believe the last alternative to be the only satisfactory and inherently stable solution to the deepening crises facing the citizens of Spaceship Earth. It is the solution closest to the perspective of the "instant global consciousness" that I and many of my colleagues attained after our view from space.**

The process of metanoia for an entire civilization or even for a substantial segment of a large nation is not an easy task. Certainly science and technology alone cannot produce such an effect. In fact, they are partly to blame for the crises. No, it is the consciousness of people, especially those who perform scientific research, those who create new technology, and those who put it to use, that must expand. They must expand their awareness to produce a transformation of consciousness. Those who lead nations and the other institutions of civilization have a special responsibility. Only when man sees his fundamental unity with the processes of nature and the functioning of the universe—as I so vividly saw it from the Apollo spacecraft—will the old ways of thinking and behaving disappear. Only when man moves from his ego-centered self-image to a new image of universal man will the perennial problems that plague us be susceptible of resolution. Humanity must rise from man to mankind, from the personal to the transpersonal, from self-consciousness to cosmic consciousness. I see no other way to avoid the alternatives that to me are unacceptable.

This view of man's possible futures is not original with me. Others have spoken similar words and have done so at greater length with more detailed analyses and evidence. I am only offering my voice in support of

---

* The basic pattern of perceiving, thinking, valuing, and acting associated with a particular vision of reality (see Chapters 13, 19, and 23).

† *Metanoia*, coming from early Greek, is usually translated in the Bible as "repentance." However, the more precise meaning is "a change of mind" or a "a new state of consciousness." *Editor.*

** "Instant global consciousness" is the phrase Dr. Mitchell coined in a *Time* magazine interview (11 December 1972) to describe the dissatisfaction with deepening world crises and a commitment to help solve them that was expressed by many astronauts after returning from space. *Editor.*

their position. But if we are correct in this, humanity's multiple problems resolve themselves into one fundamental problem: how to change consciousness, how to achieve metanoia. How can we raise our awareness to a higher level—a level that will restore the unity of man, the planet, and the universe?

It was at this point in my thinking that the third aspect of my experience during the lunar voyage became important. I am referring to my experiment with extrasensory perception.

My interest in psychic research began in 1967. At the time I was feeling a deep dissatisfaction with the ability of philosophy and theology —at least as far as I was acquainted with them—to give answers to my questions about the meaning of life and man's place in the universe. I have always been interested in the nature of things and have read widely in the humanities and other subjects that purport to examine or explain man's purpose.

However, I found many of the concepts arising from theology and philosophy to be inadequate. Empirical knowledge from the physical sciences seemed to me to be overturning our traditional notions about man. Unfortunately, it also seemed to be doing very little about replacing those notions with stronger, more valid ones. The old answers did not apply. Where would new ones come from?

In that emotional and intellectual cul-de-sac, a friend for whom I have great respect as a thoughtful but pragmatic person suggested that perhaps psychic phenomena—*psi*, as they are collectively called—ought to be considered. It was a challenge I could not resist. As a student of science, I believe there is nothing in the universe that is unworthy of investigation. If it offers the further incentive of having possible benefit for humanity, I think it is little less than foolish to refuse to examine it. The true scientist is one who is committed to knowing, to *scientia*, which is the attempt to understand the ultimate nature of reality, without bias, prejudice, or commitment to an ideology or belief system. Otherwise, he is unworthy of the name.

I am interested in knowing. That is how I came to parapsychology and related fields. I was quite skeptical at first. I imagine anyone would be if he were unacquainted with the subject, especially in view of scientific disclaimers about the paranormal. It would seem like taking fairy tales and myths seriously.

However, those apparently fanciful stories from childhood and early history are now recognized as having important content and serious significance for man's attempt to know himself more fully. Likewise, psychic research has proved its importance. As I got deeper into the study of paranormal phenomena, I found my skepticism dissolving. In its place was a feeling of awe and excitement compounded from two elements. One was respect for the truly fine scientific experimentation done by parapsychologists and psychic researchers. The other was an inability to explain away the unusual results arising from many of those experiments. Telepathy, for example—the psychic faculty I would attempt to employ during the lunar expedition—had been extensively studied and documented for a century. The work of J. B. Rhine (12, 13), René Warcollier (18), S. G. Soal (16), and many others, including the astounding experiment between Harold Sherman and Sir Hubert Wilkins in the Arctic (15), could leave no doubt about its existence.

In view of that, my whole training in scientific endeavors compelled me to make an honest admission to myself: Psychic research was looking at phenomena that were indeed real, even if the corpus of present scientific knowledge was unable to explain them. To have concluded otherwise would have been intellectual dishonesty—something that has arisen from time to time in the history of science, always to its detriment, and that is still another manifestation of the egocentric mentality.

By 1971, when the Apollo 14 mission was scheduled, I had become an avid psychic researcher in my spare time. The opportunity that the lunar expedition offered me to experiment with telepathy in space was too good to disregard, and I think any scientist whose interests and inclinations paralleled mine would have taken it. I never intended to make the experiment public in the manner that it was—as a sensational story in newspapers and other media around the world. I had decided on the experiment only a few weeks before lift-off, and it was to have been a purely personal investigation. I did not request permission from the National Aeronautics and Space Administration (NASA) because it seemed better to do it without sanction rather than risk having permission denied. Furthermore, because of experience with "news leaks" I did not even seek the counsel of established professionals. These precautions were to no avail, however.

My colleagues in the experiment were four people on earth who tried to receive by telepathic communication the targets I attempted to send them on several days of the voyage. Three of them prefer to remain anonymous. The fourth—Olaf Jonsson of Chicago—was suggested by one of my friends at the last minute and his participation was arranged by telephone. We never met before the launch, although I have met him since. Through a news leak—the source of which is still unknown to me—and through excellent detective work by the press, Jonsson was found and revealed the story to the press, with results that brought widespread attention to us and to the whole field of psychic research.

Briefly, my experiment involved four transmission sessions during rest periods programmed into the flight. Two of the sessions were completed on the way to the moon and two were completed on the return trip. I used random numbers from 1 to 5 set up in eight columns of twenty-five numbers each. Just before transmitting, in order to minimize the possibility of precognition, I assigned each number to one of the symbols of the standard Zener cards used for some ESP tests—a cross, a square, a circle, a star, and parallel wavy lines. Circumstances during the flight made subsequent evaluation of the data difficult. We were forty minutes late during lift-off, which caused the first few rest periods to start forty minutes late as well. Thus, the arrangement I had made with the receivers meant that some of the sessions appeared to yield precognitive results, not telepathic ones.

Upon return to earth, the data was analyzed independently by Dr. J. B. Rhine of the Foundation for Research on the Nature of Man, by Dr. Karlis Osis of the American Society for Psychical Research, and by me (4, 8). The results were statistically significant, not because any of the receivers got a large number of direct hits but because the number of hits was amazingly low. The statistical probability of scoring so few hits was about 3000:1. This negative ESP effect, called *psi-missing*, is something that has frequently arisen in other psychic research work, and theorists are attempting to explain its significance. In any case, it offers good evidence for psi, because the laws of chance are bypassed to a significant degree.

But what has all this to do with the problem of changing consciousness?

For me, seeing our planet from space was an event with some of the qualities traditionally ascribed to religious experience. It triggered a deep insight into the nature of existence—the sort of insight that radically changes the inner person. My thinking—indeed, my consciousness—was altered profoundly. I came to feel a moral responsibility to pass on the transformative experience of seeing earth from the larger perspective. But further, the rational man in me had to recognize the validity of the nonrational cognitive process.

That is one reason for this book. In my opinion, the act of leaving the planet is one of the pivotal moments in human history because it represents a radical change in the course of progress and offers a new perspective of civilization. If we continue without change and without growth in our basic thinking and behavior, we will, despite spectacular technological feats, eventually end the evolutionary experiment known as man. Our planetary situation becomes more desperate daily. But basically I am optimistic because the possibility of resolving those ever-growing global crises was also made clear to me during the view from space.

Obviously we cannot send everyone to the moon in the near future. But we can provide information and experiences of another sort that will serve the same purpose and provide the same perspective. Moreover, we can do it in a way that brings objective reason closer to subjective intuition and thereby help to lessen the unfortunate gulf between these two modes of knowing. We can do this because, as I indicated earlier, inner- and outer-space research are converging. The result will be an expansion of awareness and a step toward developing higher consciousness in the race.

Throughout history prophets, sages, saints, enlightened teachers, and other illuminated men and women have pointed to the same goal as the one I seek: the further evolution of human consciousness. These people have been expert travelers of inner space. Their "reports" over the centuries contain reliable directions for contemporary psychenauts. Their "maps of inner space" provide useful guides to unfamiliar territory. They have been unanimous in declaring that selflessness and freedom from egoism are an aspect of higher consciousness and the key to direct knowledge.

There is a surprising variety of ways by which people grow into selflessness. Some are formal spiritual disciplines such as the study of yoga or Zen, the taking of holy orders, or the practice of various forms of meditation. Other paths are less systematized and more spontaneous. In fact, it may be nothing more than carrying on daily work as always—but with the intention of living a better life through prayer, study, kindness, humility, and good works.

The result of all sincerely followed paths, however, is a change of consciousness in the one who walks the path. Sometimes gradually, sometimes suddenly, the traveler perceives a previously unseen order and meaning in the universe—a recognition that gives significance to life by merging the boundaries of the self with the cosmos. He recognizes that, paradoxically, the deepest aspect of himself is one with all creation. That radical expansion of the meaning of *I* has best been termed *cosmic consciousness*. It is a state in which there is constant awareness of unity with the universe pervading all aspects of one's life. Every activity, every relationship, every thought is guided by the knowledge of oneness between the self and the world. Inner and outer space are unified, and the inhumanities that people perpetrate on one another and the stupidities that people mount against nature become impossible to commit. This internal self-regulation is the surest safeguard against the destruction of our world.

Two examples can illustrate this convergence of subjective intuition and objective reason. In the course of pursuing careers in science, Albert Einstein and Sir John Eccles both concluded that there is a transpersonal dimension to creation that is outside the space–time continuum of the three-dimensional universe and sustains it. Einstein (1, p. 413) stated it succinctly when he wrote, "I believe in [the] God who reveals Himself in the orderly harmony of what exists."

In a similar vein, Eccles (2, pp. 43–44) declared his belief that "there is a fundamental mystery in my existence, transcending any biological account of the development of my body (including my brain) with its genetic inheritance and its evolutionary origin." He concluded with this profound statement:

> I see science as a supremely religious activity but clearly incomplete in itself. I see also the absolute necessity for belief in a spiritual world which is interpenetrating with and yet transcending what we see as the material world. . . . Similarly I believe that anyone who denies the validity of the scientific approach within its sphere is denying the great revelation of God to this day and age. To my mind, then, any rational system of belief involves the conviction that the creative and sustaining spirit of God may be everywhere present and active; indeed I believe that all aspects of the universe, all kinds of experience, may be sacramental in the true meaning of the term.

I find it extraordinarily significant that Einstein, the physicist, looked at the telescopic world of outer space and Eccles, the neurophysiologist, looked at the microscopic world of inner space only to discover the same thing—the existence of God. This noetic discovery is at the heart of science and religion. It is the only thing that will counteract contemporary crises and bring meaning, direction, and fulfillment to people.

Psychic research can play an important role in helping people make that discovery. It can be a key to unlock the missing experiential component with which to expand awareness beyond the limits of objective data and logical reasoning. It can be a means of supporting the further evolution of the human race and of developing the universal man of cosmic consciousness. Quite simply, psychic experiences—like religious and mystical experiences—can, when properly developed, help a person become more aware. They can be an input to the mind that awakens curiosity, shakes the sleep from our worldly eyes, and begins to motivate us to seek paths to a different consciousness.

The primary purpose of this book is to provide a credible stimulus to the mind of the reader, but there are several others. My associates and I will demonstrate that psi are indeed real events and that psychic research is a credible, authentic, well-disciplined effort entirely compatible with the methods of science. We hope the following pages will once and for all settle the issue of whether psi exists. We hope this book will enlarge the perspective of modern science by convincing even the most skeptical critics, who have thus far rejected the evidence of psychic research. Our wish is to enlist their aid in the all-important task of studying the nature of man. Thus, science might become unified with religion, the arts, and the humanities in the common task of helping transform human life by bringing mankind to know itself and its relation to the cosmos.

I must offer a word of caution, however. As you will discern from the following chapters, the evidence indicates that psychic energy is neutral, yielding no value system. It must be used with care because *psychic development alone does not produce ethical or spiritual growth*. The history of psychic research has demonstrated this time and again, where it has exposed various sensitives with genuine gifts who nevertheless have resorted to fraud and trickery. Both scientific investigators and ordinary people seeking guidance have sometimes been deceived for a while by those psychic men and women whose main concern was not to act ethically or advance knowledge or help those in need but rather to impress others, play ego games, and increase their own status, wealth, and power over others.

Psychic energy—like atomic energy—can be applied in both creative and destructive ways. If that is so, a prayerful and cautious attitude seems proper for all concerned. It is up to each individual to find an ethical system or ethical framework within which to use psychic energy. In that regard, the injunctions in the Bible and other traditions should not be lightly dismissed. And certainly the frivolous, partylike attitude that some have with regard to séances, Ouija boards, and the like is to be discouraged.

It should be clear, then, that the psychic event must be seen in a larger perspective than usual. Both those with psychic ability and those who study them must ground themselves in a transcendent view of man and his relationship to the universe. Parapsychology must become linked with transpersonal psychology—the study of man's potential for development —as part of noetics, the general study of consciousness. Unless psychic research leads to wisdom, compassion, humility, and beneficial knowledge, it should be avoided altogether. Man is quite capable of destroying himself now. He does not need another weapon in his arsenal for perverting planetary potential.

With that perspective in mind, let us now look at what is—and is not—the subject matter of psychic research.

PSYCHIC PHENOMENA AND RESEARCH

Psychic faculties have been present in man for a long time, as anthropologists and historians are now documenting (see Chapter 11), although the emphasis on objective, rational knowing seems to have blocked it in most people. *Psychic* is defined in dictionaries as "lying outside the realm of physical processes and physical science; extrasensorimotor, nonphysical or spiritual in origin." As we shall see in the following chapters, this definition is now being questioned, especially by paraphysics, as our understanding of the "physical" increases.

Psychic research officially began nearly a century ago, in 1882, when the Society for Psychical Research was founded in London. Three years later, the American Society for Psychical Research was organized in the United States. The subject of the societies' concern can be broadly classified as extrasensory perception (ESP), psychokinesis (PK), and survival phenomena (θ). Collectively, they are referred to as *psi*, (pronounced "sigh"), the twenty-third letter of the Greek alphabet and the first letter in the Greek word Ψυχη ("psyche"), meaning "mind" or "soul."

These phenomena were obviously related to the study of the human mind and therefore came within the domain of psychologists. At least the early researchers felt that way. But professional psychologists and other scientists for the most part rejected the possibility that psi were real events. They generally dismissed them on the grounds of fraud, illusion, and delusion. Therefore, this field came to be called *parapsychology*, meaning the study of phenomena that were considered outside or beyond the main body of psychology.

However, the term *parapsychology*, although generally used by the public as synonymous with psychic research, is used by researchers in this field to designate a somewhat narrower area of investigation than what has traditionally been the domain of psychic research. It is best understood as referring to the approach developed in the 1930s by J. B. Rhine and his co-workers. This approach emphasizes controlled laboratory experiments and rigorous statistical analysis of results in ESP and PK. Although it does not explicitly forbid examination of θ, it generally avoids the subject for reasons I will state later on. Soviet researchers use the term *psychoenergetics* instead of parapsychology.

ESP is a psychic event in which information is transmitted through channels outside the known sensory channels, either in waking consciousness, trance, or dreams. It is mostly mental in character, showing few physical signs of having occurred, and even those are usually of a very subtle character. Soviet researchers prefer the term *bioinformation*. ESP includes these specific forms of psi: telepathy (which Soviets call *biocommunication*), clairvoyance, clairaudience, precognition (which is more or less synonymous with premonition, prophecy, and visions), retrocognition, psychometry, radiesthesia, and psychic diagnosis.

Rhine popularized the term *extrasensory perception*, using it as the title of his 1934 book. In recent years, however, some researchers have come to feel there is little or nothing about ESP that is "extra." They see it as a normal, but generally latent, faculty that is trainable, to some degree, in most of the population. Therefore, the term has been recast by some as *extended sensory perception* or *expanding sensory potential*.

PK is a psychic event in which objects or organisms are physically moved or affected without direct contact or use of any known force that would allow a conventional explanation. Physical signs are usually apparent during and immediately after its occurrence. The Soviets prefer the term *bioenergetics* to describe psychokinetic events in general. PK includes teleportation (also called *apportation*), materialization and dematerialization, levitation, psychic surgery and psychic healing, thoughtography, and out-of-the-body projection (popularly termed *astral projection*).

"The Theta Corridor" = Joy

θ are events due to the agency of supposed discarnate personalities. θ (spelled "theta" and pronounced "thā-tuh," from the first letter of the Greek word *thanatos*, death) include the phenomena of mediumship (or spirit communication), ghosts and hauntings, apparitions and poltergeists (although it appears that some poltergeist activity is actually caused by unconscious psychokinetic influence by living persons), spirit photography, spirit possession, and reincarnation. Mediumship has many forms. Among them are clairvoyant mediumship, in which the medium claims to have direct visual perception of spirit entities; direct-voice mediumship, in which a discarnate is alleged to speak through the medium in the discarnate's original voice and mannerisms; physical mediumship, in which the medium demonstrates so-called ectoplasmic materializations of the discarnate and other objects; and waking and trance mediumship, both of which may be combined with direct voice and/or physical mediumship), automatic writing, and, lately, automatic tape recording.

This area of psychic research has been studied since spiritualism came to wide public notice in the 1850s. For example, the renowned English scientist Sir William Crookes began investigating spirit phenomena in the late 1860s. The inventor of the Crookes tube, a device which led to the discovery of X-rays and was the forerunner of the cathode-ray tube, was eagerly watched. But when he published his experiments and observations validating many of the claims of Spiritualists, the scientific community ignored or dismissed them. Crookes is said to have replied to this treatment, "The quotation occurs to me, 'I never said it was possible—I only said it was true.' "

In America the great psychologists William James and William McDougall carried forward the efforts of the American Society for Psychical Research, which James had helped found. But it was the work of J. B. Rhine and his wife, Louisa, that defined the domain of parapsychology and made it a household word. Their work in the laboratory at Duke University, emphasizing rigorous controls, quantitative results, and statistical analysis, supported previous claims for the reality of ESP and PK. However, when the Rhines came to examine claims of spirit communication, they decided that the medium's ability to perceive beyond the senses possibly rooted in telepathy, clairvoyance, and similar sources of information, none of which need have originated with discarnate spirits but rather with living persons whose minds were being "tapped" by the medium. In their opinion, the question of postmortem existence was beyond scientific investigation at that time and hence was thereafter largely disregarded in their research.

Thus, Rhine's book *Extra-Sensory Perception* established limits for the subject that he, more than anyone else in this century, developed as a scientific discipline. But since then some others, including myself, have felt the need to expand the field of examination. My own research into the mechanism by which mediums operate has convinced me that spirit communication is a genuine possibility. Likewise, the phenomenon of primary perception in plants, rediscovered in modern times by Cleve Backster of the Backster Research Foundation in New York City, is now established beyond all doubt as genuine (see Chapter 12). Backster made his initial report in 1966, and since then some parapsychologists have rejected his conclusion that there is an undefined sensory capacity in vegetable and cellular life that is akin to, if not identical with, some forms of ESP. Another example of new phenomena is Kirlian photography (see Chapter 21) of the so-called auras of physical objects—another topic that some parapsychologists would exclude from the field.

My point in giving this account is to avoid the impression that all researchers in this area are agreed on the exact limits and subject matter of the field. There is diversity of opinion, just as there is throughout the remainder of the scientific community. And as elsewhere in the scientific community, many of the problems and controversies will not be resolved until there is more research and theorizing done and a new scientific paradigm established.

That is why I have chosen to use the term *psychic research* in this book rather than *parapsychology*. My wish is to avoid premature closure of any aspect of the field, especially as we enter a new period in which research is being aided enormously by advanced technology and sophisticated methodology. The reports published here will give numerous examples of this. In their totality, they provide a current and comprehensive survey of the field of psychic research as I am broadly defining it.

PSYCHIC RESEARCH AT A GLANCE

Psychic research is the branch of science that studies psychic (extrasensorimotor) phenomena, both in the laboratory and in the field. It dates from 1882 when the Society for Psychical Research was founded in England. Psychic phenomena are collectively designated Ψ (spelled *psi* and pronounced "sigh"), the first letter in the Greek word Ψυχη ("psyche") meaning "mind" or "soul." There are three categories of psi: extrasensory perception (ESP), psychokinesis (PK), and survival phenomena (θ, or "theta," the first letter of the Greek word $\theta\alpha\nu\alpha\tau\sigma\varsigma$, "thanatos," meaning "death").

Parapsychology is generally taken to mean the approach to ESP and PK as developed by J. B. Rhine and his co-workers from the 1930s on, emphasizing quantitative, controlled laboratory experiments subjected to rigorous statistical analysis. The Russian term for parapsychology is *psychoenergetics*; the Czech term is *psychotronics*. (However, these terms are more broadly defined.) Today the emergency of *paraphysics* is paralleling and overlapping much of psychic research and parapsychology and will probably eventually embrace them both.

Extrasensory perception (ESP) is a psychic event in which information is transmitted through channels outside the known sensory channels, either in waking consciousness, trance, or dreams. The Russian term for ESP is *bioinformation*. ESP includes:

1. telepathy (Russian term, *biocommunication*)
2. clairvoyance (Russian term, *biolocation* or *introscopy*)
3. precognition (Russian term, *proscopy*)
4. retrocognition.

When ESP occurs in situations that could be either telepathy or clairvoyance or both, it is termed *general extrasensory perception* (GESP). ESP is applied in many specific ways, including psychometry (object reading), radiesthesia (dowsing), and psychic diagnosis. The term *clairsentience* is sometimes used to include clairvoyance, clairaudience, and other expressions of ESP through sensory modalities.

Psychokinesis (PK) is a psychic event in which something is moved or physically affected without use of any known force that would allow a conventional explanation and usually without direct contact. The Russian term for PK is *bioenergetics*. PK includes:

1. teleportation
2. materialization
3. dematerialization
4. levitation (of oneself)
5. psychic surgery and psychic healing
6. thoughtography
7. out-of-the-body projection and apparitions of the living.

Survival phenomena (θ) are events possibly caused by discarnate personalities. θ include:

1. mediumship
2. hauntings
3. apparitions of the dead
4. poltergeists
5. spirit photography
6. spirit possession
7. reincarnations.

Note: This overview of psychic research is tentative and not supported by all psychic researchers and parapsychologists. Some important questions and areas of disagreement prevent unanimous agreement. For instance, some feel that all survival phenomena will eventually be shown to involve no more than ESP and PK. Others feel that certain phenomena, including most of those in the PK section, are not genuine phenomena. Still others feel that this listing is not inclusive enough and that it should include phenomena such as firewalking, UFOs (on the grounds that they may be an unconscious PK phenomenon similar to some poltergeist cases), stigmata, and other occult or esoteric subjects. Therefore, this summary is offered as a guideline—a temporary organization of the many apparently different kinds of phenomena that psychic researchers have attempted to study.

But definitions change in time, especially as new data and new insights arise. Even though all chapters of this book were written in 1973 expressly for it, this attempt to provide an encyclopedic volume on the subject of psychic research will probably be inadequate a decade from now.

Since the beginnings of psychic research, various esoteric and arcane traditions have moved in and out of its mainstream. Prophecy offers a good example. Astrology is perhaps the oldest and most enduring means of divination that man has developed. Tarot cards are a relatively new way of attempting to forecast events. Crystal gazing, the *I Ching*, the Ouija board, bone casting, animal sacrifice, the prophetic utterances of witch doctors and shamans while in trance states—the list seems endless. I am not passing judgment on the validity and accuracy of these traditions. I am only saying it is understandable that they should at one time or another be considered by researchers studying precognition, the nature of time, and other topics in psychic research. Likewise, it is understandable that such diverse subjects as witchcraft, voodoo, and yoga have been examined because they have a history in which psychic events clearly play a part.

Do all these occult practices belong in the purview of psychic research? Where do the psychic sciences end and the "occult arts" begin? If psi play some part in the religious ceremonies and training practices of primitive peoples and pagan cults, should they be studied?

There appears to be a continuum along which we may place occult, psychic, paranormal, and mystic phenomena—a continuum of consciousness. But it is not easy to draw lines of demarcation between them. Recently, for example, meditation has come into the laboratory. Studies have shown that meditation is a means of producing an altered state of consciousness in which psi are frequently manifested (see Chapter 27). Hence, meditation is being looked at, and from there it seems likely that psychic researchers will have to examine the historical background, the belief system, and the philosophical world view of various meditative traditions. After that a movement into transpersonal psychology will take place. Beyond that, it will become apparent that psi cannot be fully understood until the nature of consciousness itself is considered. That is the rationale for the organization of chapters in this book, although some psychic researchers may feel we have overstepped the bounds of our discipline.

But diversity of opinion at the level of everyday research does not mean "enemy camps" have developed. It is generally agreed by people in psychic research around the world that their work must be performed in a spirit of service to humanity. The possibility of invasion of mental privacy or of thought control is odious. My colleagues in the psychic research community, no matter what their nationality, are unanimous in their commitment to the beneficent application of psychic faculties. All indications point to the conclusion that psi may be used for good or evil. One of their finest uses can be seen in psychic healing. One of their potentially worst uses would be for "programming" people through nonconscious telepathic suggestion. This latter possibility must not be allowed.

This brings up another reason for preferring the term *psychic research*. As I noted earlier, parapsychology is becoming part of a larger whole—transpersonal psychology. In turn, transpersonal psychology is an aspect of the general convergence of science and religion in noetics. Only as we study consciousness and the nature of man and other living systems will we really begin to understand psi and how they relate to human potential and fulfillment. Without that perspective, psi and psychic research will probably go the way of most other scientific work. Either by design or ignorance, they will be turned against humanity in physically and psychologically destructive ways because man's morally imperfect desires are generally uncontrolled by his rational intelligence.

WHY PSYCHIC RESEARCH?

The question "Why psychic research?" has already been briefly answered by saying it can be an important element in the long-sought formula for enriching human awareness, reconstructing society, and generally aiding nature in the great work of evolution. But let us consider the question in greater detail and see specifically why psychic research is a challenge for science.

In the course of our psychosocial progress through the study of consciousness, some fundamental assumptions of the current scientific world view will be questioned. This is inevitable, as Thomas S. Kuhn points out in *The Structure of Scientific Revolutions* (7). Psychic research is perhaps the primary area from which the revolution will come and from which a new paradigm of science will be constructed (see Chapter 29).

Fundamental to science is objectivism, a view of nature as a collection of discrete parts that scientists can observe and manipulate in a detached, impartial manner. Natural events occur as natural forces work through natural laws, while the scientist stands aside, neutral and emotionally uninvolved. He simply lets things happen as they may. There can be cause-and-effect relationships; there can be interactions. But they all happen outside the observer. The principle of separate identity remains in effect.

Another principle of science is materialism, the notion that reality is thoroughly explainable by the existence of matter alone. Operating on that basis, science has been eminently successful in exploring the physical world and learning to control it. Dramatic accomplishments over the past hundred years leave no room for doubt about that.

At the same time, however, science has been responsible for putting in man's hands knowledge that he has sadly used for unprecedented killing, destruction, and harm of his own kind and his environment. Why? Why has our sophisticated knowledge of the physical universe not led to wisdom? Why can we not live in harmony with each other and with the planet?

Part of the answer, I believe, can be found in the two fundamental assumptions of contemporary science: objectivism and materialism. Although they are valid in a limited domain, they have been unwisely viewed as universally applicable. Studies in such diverse fields as logic, metalinguistics, and quantum mechanics have demonstrated that the concepts of subjective versus objective, matter versus energy, and perhaps even causality itself are arbitrary constructions that man imposes on nature. The universe is holistic—a *uni*verse. But most people, including scientists, seem unaware of this, and therefore, these assumptions combine to form a nonconscious philosophy of life—a paradigm. The scientific emphasis on matter has led to an overemphasis on the material things necessary for living. Likewise, the scientific emphasis on objectivity has led to a loss of unity and empathy among people. In its place are aloofness, impersonality, and apathy.

The unfortunate results are apparent everywhere. On the individual level, our awareness of personhood is lost to the view that personality is a commodity to be packaged and sold over cosmetic counters, in clothing stores, and through self-development courses. Objects are seen as having more value than persons themselves, and there is a widespread tendency to treat people as things to be manipulated like machines.

On the social level, we are only a step away from enshrining the objective, rational mode of thought as the source of all goodness and wisdom. Reinforcing this is the objectification—rather, the reification—of abstract ideas such as nation and state. From this viewpoint it is only logical to make war on other countries and on the countryside.

This denial of the nonmaterial aspect of life—its sacred participation in the miracle of existence—leaves people with no source of meaning and direction. The resulting view may be stated thus: I am simply a prisoner of my flesh, fighting for survival in a hostile and competitive world, and death is the end of me because life is only physical. I am just a skin-encapsulated ego, locked in a soulless body that will someday perish and decay.

Psychic research presents a direct challenge to this shortsighted view of reality by calling into question the assumed primacy of objectivism and materialism. Telepathy demonstrates that there is an informational linkage between people that goes beyond the laws of science as they are presently understood—a linkage we are normally unaware of—and the discovery of primary perception in cell life apparently extends that linkage downward in the ladder of molecular organization. Clairvoyance challenges our understanding of sensory perception. Precognition and retrocognition challenge our concept of time. PK challenges our concepts of energy and energy transfer. So too does psychic healing, which also brings into question our concepts of physiology and medicine.

Studies in all these areas seem to indicate that mind and consciousness can operate at a distance from the body, interacting with the outside world in ways that cannot be explained in terms of known laws. Beyond that, survival research is pointing to the possibility that mind and consciousness may operate *independently* on the body. In short, psychic research is leading to an extraordinarily challenging conclusion: Science's basic image of man and the universe must be revised. Because of this new light on the nature of humanity and our position in the cosmos, science will have to divest itself not only of some deeply cherished "facts" but also of its philosophic foundations—the whole intellectual outlook upon which our present civilization is based. That outlook, says Arthur Koestler in *The Roots of Coincidence* (5), is "the greatest superstition of our age—the materialistic clockwork universe of early nineteenth-century physics."

We are living, in William Irwin Thompson's words, "at the edge of history." A linear extrapolation of current conditions shows that mankind has, conservatively speaking, less than a century before it goes the way of the dinosaur. Many scientists and planetary planners think the remaining time could be only a few decades. Granted, some unforeseen circumstance such as the "green revolution" or a breakthrough in pollution control may favorably alter that prognosis and thereby lend support to the dictum that civilization totters but it totters steadily onward. Nevertheless, survival seems to depend more than anything on a transformation of conscious-ness, an evolution of the mind. That includes our philosophy of science—the physicalistic way in which we conceive and behave.

For some scientists, that will mean a tremendous shift in thinking. It will mean relinquishing some long-held views that are no longer correct and that threaten our very existence. This need for disillusioning has arisen before in the history of science. The theory of phlogiston and the concept of the role of the neutral observer in quantum mechanics are examples. But never before has the need for jettisoning false beliefs had such global importance. If science maintains its old attitude toward psy-chic research, it will merely prove that Max Planck was correct when he said, "A new scientific truth does not triumph by convincing its opponents and making them see the light, but rather because its opponents eventually die and a new generation grows up that is familiar with it."

The only possible basis for rejecting the evidence of psychic research is prejudice and diehard stubbornness born of insecurity. Psychologist Donald O. Hebb admitted this plainly as far back as 1951. "Why do we not accept ESP as psychological fact?" he asked. "Rhine has offered enough evidence to convince us on almost any other issue where one could make some guess as to the mechanics of the disputed process. Personally, I do not accept ESP for a moment because it does not make any sense. I cannot see what other base my colleagues have for rejecting it, but my own rejection of Rhine's views is, in the literal sense, prejudiced."

That is a candid admission. I do not know if Hebb has since discovered the "sense" of psychic research, but in any case, Aldous Huxley's reply to his statement is worthy of consideration by those inclined to reject the findings and implications of this subject. Huxley said, "That a man of science should allow a prejudice to outweigh evidence seems strange enough. It is even stranger to find a psychologist rejecting a psychological discovery simply because it cannot be explained. Psi . . . is intrinsically no more inexplicable than, say, perception or memory."

One of the major objections to the authenticity of psychic research is the credibility of its evidence. Some critics, such as Dr. C. E. M. Hansel in England and Dr. George R. Price in America, have raised the questions of incompetence, self-deception, and even outright fraud. The first two mat-ters are adequately dealt with, I think, by the very contents of this book. The third can best be rebutted in the words of psychic researchers themselves who have been forced to answer such accusations.

S. G. Soal of London University writes: "It would be interesting to meet the psychiatrist or psychologist who has perused every page of the

49 volumes of the *Proceedings of the Society for Psychical Research,* and who remains a skeptic. It is no coincidence that those most skeptical of ESP research are almost invariably those who are least acquainted with the facts."

H. J. Eysenck, head of the Department of Psychology at Maudsley Hospital in London, answers the charge of fraud like this: "Unless there is a gigantic conspiracy involving 30 university departments all over the world, and several hundred highly respected scientists in various fields, many of them originally hostile to the claims of the psychic researchers, the only conclusion the unbiased observer can come to must be that there are people who obtain knowledge existing either in other people's minds, or in the outer world, by means yet unknown to science."

One of my associates, Dr. Montague Ullman of Maimonides Medical Center in Brooklyn, New York, levels this criticism at the detractors of psychic research: "If the only answer to the vast amount of solid experimental evidence is incompetence or fraud on a global scale by men with credentials equal to those of their scientific peers, working in academic surroundings, and whose work extends historically in time over at least three generations, then the adherents of this position would seem to have adopted a stance that is even more difficult to defend than the psi hypothesis. In fact, it would seem to represent a last ditch stand—in short, the bankruptcy of the critical effort."

It is the epitome of intellectual honesty to admit that one has been wrong or made a mistake. Such honesty is what Dr. Price displayed in a letter to *Science* in January 1972: "During the past year I have had some correspondence with J. B. Rhine which has convinced me that I was highly unfair to him in what I said in an article entitled 'Science and the Supernatural,' published in *Science* in 1955. The article discussed possible fraud in extrasensory perception experiments. I suspect that I was similarly unfair in what I said about S. G. Soal in that paper." Price's recantation brought what might be called "a psi of relief" to psychic researchers. Its primary significance, however, is not that it reestablishes the integrity of their efforts but rather that it demonstrates Price's own integrity as a man of science dedicated to supporting the search for truth, even at the expense of his own public image and pronouncements.

This commitment to science is what must motivate all scientists. Until recently there has been a notable lack of this attitude toward psychic research. However, the admission of the Parapsychological Association to the American Association for the Advancement of Science in 1969 is a credit to the scientific establishment and an indication that the tide of opinion is turning.

More recently, a questionnaire on parapsychology was distributed by *New Scientist* magazine. The results (10, p. 209) were most heartening to the psychic research community. The first conclusion, *New Scientist* reported, is that "parapsychology is clearly counted as being exceedingly interesting and relevant by a very large number of today's working scientists." A full 25% of the respondents held ESP to be an established fact, with another 42% declaring it to be a likely possibility. This positive attitude was based, in about 40% of the sample, on reading reports in scientific books and journals. More surprising, however, was the answer of the majority, whose conviction arose as the result of some definite personal experience: "This could be either in the form of a convincing experiment they had conducted," the article stated, "or, more commonly, as the result of a striking telepathic experience." There was a strong undercurrent among respondents that too much time was being spent proving the existence of ESP, when the real need was to "get on with finding out how it works."

Clearly, the tide is turning. When the turn is completed, the unity of all knowledge and experience will become apparent. The complementary nature of the objective and subjective modes of knowing reality and investigating the nature of the universe will be demonstrated.

The result, I think, can only be a new appreciation by both science and religion for each other's mode of operation. Thus far, science has dealt only with the rational and the irrational. It has not recognized the nonrational. Nonrational forms of knowledge transcend the categories of ordinary logic and perception that the discursive intellect works with. These areas of mind can, when properly used, be just as meaningful in providing knowledge about ourselves and the universe. Nonrational forms of knowing are our most ancient sources of wisdom. As yogi-philosopher Gopi Krishna points out in *The Secret of Yoga* (6), from them spring religious truths, artistic creativity, the insights of genius, psychic abilities, and those related forms of ESP that we call intuition, hunches, and gut feelings. Collectively, they have been called *the unconscious*—a somewhat misleading term, incidentally, because the unconscious is supremely intelligent. It is at the deepest level of our personal unconscious that the boundary between the subjective and objective modes disappears and that our limited sense of self merges with its universal source of being.

We must get in touch again with the unconscious. If we honestly and courageously let that aspect of mind speak to us, if we make the unconscious conscious, there will be a fundamental alteration in present attitudes, values, and beliefs, followed by a fundamental change in our behavior. Our objective and subjective experiences will fuse synergistically in a quantum leap of understanding, a higher level of awareness. *This could be the transformation of human consciousness that is necessary for solving our critical dilemma.*

Such a change would ensure that any course of action planned would be sane, practical, and sufficient in scope to meet planetary problems in a holistic manner. It would restore health to our divided psyches, unity to our fractured society, and harmony to the unbalanced environment. Thus far, science has mostly produced fragmentation. But health is wholeness. To "cure" science, we must, as philosopher Dane Rudhyar (14) says, "build greater wholes."

Psychic research is an avenue to the unconscious, a means for building greater wholes (10). Now is the time for us to begin building a single whole of humanity. Now is the time to develop our nonrational abilities into a "subjective technology," which will begin the wedding of science and religion, reason and intuition, the physical and the spiritual. This union of head and heart, insight and instinct, will ensure that as science comes to comprehend the nonmaterial aspect of reality as well as it knows the material—that is, as science approaches omniscience—our knowledge will become wisdom, our love of power will become the power of love, and the universal man of cosmic consciousness can then emerge.

[handwritten annotation: " Brain - Bridging to Love" - Greeting the OTHER Half of Reality as "Authentic" JPS]

REFERENCES

1. Clark, Ronald. *Einstein: The Life and Times.* World: New York, 1971.
2. Eccles, John. *The Brain and the Unity of Conscious Experience.* Cambridge University Press: New York, 1965.
3. Green, Alyce M.; Green, Elmer E.; and Walters, E. Dale. "Psychophysiological Training for Creativity." Paper presented at the 1971 meeting of the American Psychological Association, Washington, D.C.
4. "Interview: Captain Edgar D. Mitchell." *Psychic*, September–October 1971.
5. Koestler, Arthur. *The Roots of Coincidence.* Random House: New York, 1972.
6. Krishna, Gopi. *The Secret of Yoga.* Harper and Row: New York, 1972.
7. Kuhn, Thomas S. *The Structure of Scientific Revolutions.* University of Chicago Press: Chicago, 1962.
8. Mitchell, Edgar D. "An ESP Test from Apollo 14." *Journal of Parapsychology*, 35, no. 2 (1971).
9. Ornstein, Robert, ed. *The Nature of Human Consciousness.* Freeman: San Francisco, 1973.
10. "Parapsychology—What the Questionnaire Revealed." *New Scientist*, 25 January 1973.
11. Polanyi, Michael. *Personal Knowledge.* Routledge and Kegan Paul: London, 1958.
12. Rhine, J. B. *The Reach of the Mind.* Apollo: New York, 1960.
13. Rhine, J. B. *Extra-Sensory Perception.* Rev. ed. Humphries: Boston, 1964.
14. Rudhyar, Dane. *The Planetarization of Consciousness.* Harper and Row: New York, 1972.
15. Sherman, Harold. *Thoughts Through Space.* Fawcett: New York, 1973.

16. Soal, S. G., and Bateman, F. *Modern Experiments in Telepathy*. Yale University Press: New Haven, Conn., 1954.
17. Tart, Charles, ed. *Altered States of Consciousness*. Anchor: New York, 1972.
18. Warcollier, René. *Mind to Mind*. Collier-Macmillan: New York, 1964.
19. White, John, ed. *The Highest State of Consciousness*. Anchor: New York, 1972.
20. White, John, ed. *Frontiers of Consciousness*. Julian: New York, 1974.
21. White, John, ed. *What Is Meditation?* Anchor: New York, 1974.

I   Parapsychology:

Foundations of a New Science

This section surveys the traditional areas of parapsychology. A chapter on the history of parapsychology traces its beginnings to the present. Another chronicles events in the lives of famous sensitives. The last chapter describes the state of parapsychology today, including research facilities, libraries, educational opportunities, periodicals, and organizations that are related to the field in some aspect of their work.

Martin Ebon

MARTIN EBON *served as administrative secretary of the Parapsychology Foundation from 1953 to 1962. He was managing editor of* Tomorrow *magazine (1953–1965) and of the* International Journal of Parapsychology *(1959–1962), as well as editor of* Spiritual Frontiers *(1969–1970).*

Mr. Ebon conducted a lecture series at the New School for Social Research in New York City, entitled "Parapsychology: From Magic to Science," from 1966 to 1968, and has lectured widely throughout the United States. His articles and reviews have appeared in a number of general and scholarly publications, including Contemporary Psychology, The Psychoanalytic Review, Saturday Review, the New York Times Book Review, Psychic, Journal of Parapsychology, Journal of the American Society for Psychical Research, *and* Journal of the Society for Psychical Research. *A biographer, anthologist, and editor, Mr. Ebon is also the author of several volumes on current affairs. Among his recent books are* Prophecy in Our Time *(New American Library, 1968),* Beyond Space and Time *(New American Library, 1969),* The Psychic Reader *(World, 1970)* They Knew the Unknown *(World, 1971) and* The Devil's Bride: Exorcism, Past and Present *(Harper, 1974).*

1 A History of Parapsychology

MARTIN EBON

SUMMARY

Although the word parapsychology *suggests a field of research that exists "beside psychology," its studies are not only related to psychology but to religion, anthropology, physics, and other areas as well. Parapsychology's history may be divided into three periods: from prehistory to the latter part of the nineteenth century; the last three decades of the nineteenth century and the first decades of the twentieth; and the present period.*

Such concepts as mind over matter, the power of thought, life after death, and clairvoyance antedate the earliest recorded history of Babylonian and Assyrian civilizations. Ancient China, with its religiophilosophical speculations related to ancestor worship, provides parallels to prehistoric Near Eastern practices. The emergence of modern science and the attendant questioning of religious traditions (Darwin) created efforts to find a link between scientific research and religion (Society for Psychical Research, London). Beginning with mediumistic sittings, this research arrived at points suggesting that clairvoyance and/or telepathy might be at work rather than communication with discarnate entities.

In the late 1920s and early 1930s, this trend was sharpened and laboratory tests of ESP extended to precognition and PK. The laboratory work undertaken during this period (Rhine) established a foundation for the current efforts to widen research scope and link parapsychology with studies and concepts now being advanced in other scientific disciplines.

Parapsychology is a microcosm of modern science. Its history parallels that of human civilization, particularly that of the West; it also has strong roots in the prehistory of other societies, notably that of ancient China. Just as the natural sciences are indebted to the hopes, methods, delusions, and ambitions of the alchemists and just as modern medicine and psychology are indebted to the skills and ideas of herbalists and shamans, so modern parapsychology builds upon religiocultural foundations created by

53

earlier civilizations, which, to a degree, continue to exist in contemporary nonindustrial "primitive" societies.

To define parapsychology, to delineate it, to trace its borders, is like kicking an anthill that is covering up a hornets' nest. In today's climate of fashionable trends, there is a temptation to turn parapsychology into an alphabet soup, containing everything from astrology to Zen. And while it would be shortsighted to exclude some of the less respectable tenets, practices, and practitioners simply because they lack prestige, specific lines must nevertheless be drawn and limits established.

The word *parapsychology* was introduced in Germany (4) in the nineteenth century. According to the *Brockhaus Enzyklopädie*, the philosopher–psychologist Max Dessoir (1867–1947) was "critically concerned with occult phenomena and originated the term *parapsychology*, which today is in international use." But as *parapsychology* literally means "beside psychology," it does not accurately reflect the field of research to which it now applies. Is parapsychology really closer to psychology than, for example, to biology (7) or anthropology? Psychology, conscious of its own inner ferment, is certainly not uniformly hospitable to the concepts and methods of parapsychology. Anthropology, theology, physics—these are disciplines that may be counted among the friends and neighbors of parapsychology today.

Similarly, ESP somehow assumes that the perceptions involved are necessarily nonsensory. This prejudges the limits or even the exact number and categories of our senses. If we admit to the limits of our knowledge, we cannot rule out that certain unexplained phenomena may, in one way or another, be nevertheless sensory in nature. But ESP it is called, and that is what we must call it, unless and until a more exact knowledge or terminology is developed. Among terms that come and go are *parapsychical, metapsychical,* and *parasensory.* In the Soviet Union, the word biocommunication is now frequently used.

One word that parapsychologists totally disdain, regardless of geography or nationality, is *occult.* It is too closely linked with the field's not-quite-respectable antecedents. After all, no shipping tycoon likes to be reminded that his great-grandfather was a pirate. Next to *occult*, the word *superstition* is anathema to modern parapsychologists. Still, much of today's fascination with psychic experiences belongs to a world of wonder and magic that has been with us since mankind's infancy; it reflects, to use a once-fashionable Freudian phrase, the individual's "infantile magical thinking." With full awareness of these historic and all-too-human connotations, a visible dividing line must nevertheless be drawn between modern research in parapsychology and some of its antecedents.

Delusions, religious or otherwise; legends of miraculous happenings; and supernatural powers abound through recorded history. Certainly, judging by oral traditions and myths preserved by such means as clay tablets, unrecorded history included practices that later mixed, as well as collided, with Christian concepts. Psi phenomena were recorded in the lives of saints; but while sinners and all other folk presumably experienced them, too, records are scant.

The flow and counterflow of traditions, rituals, practices, and experiences make it impossible to establish specific historic dates for the conscious acknowledgment, study, and exploration of the psychical. Yet as a matter of convenience, such a division should be attempted. The history of parapsychology may be roughly divided into three periods: first, the early period, both prehistoric and historical, a wide and sweeping panorama of phenomena recorded up to the nineteenth century; second, the last decades of the nineteenth century and the first half of the twentieth century; and, third, recent decades.

Of course, these periods overlap. We can find, in both the recent and the fairly distant past, hypotheses, developed and discarded, that anticipated much current thinking. Early studies of psi often followed prevailing fashions in thought and method; but they did not, in many cases, lack sophistication. Attitudes of passionate interest, even in antiquity, did not rule out detachment and skepticism, examination of independent witnesses, allowance for faulty observation, and recognition of the need for repetition. Such objectivity existed, then and now, side by side with the passion of True Believers.

The past, like the present, is often thought of in terms of categories, be they prophecy, incantation, ritual, dialogues with the dead, ancestor worship, visions, miraculous or spiritual healing, sorcery, or any other of an immense variety of religious, pseudoreligious, or profane practices and claims. But, categories aside, much of human history must be viewed in terms of the men and women who either dramatized or explored its events, including psi. No matter how glibly one may speak of historical "periods" and "trends" or how modest some pioneers may wish to be, the decisive role played by individuals in the history of parapsychology must be recognized.

Among the respectably distant names in the history of parapsychology are the Witch of Endor, King Croesus of Lydia, and, interestingly, Aristotle. Linguistics plays havoc with historical certainty, and this has happened to the Endor story in the Old Testament (I Sam. 28:3–25). King Saul was upset and confused when he went to Endor. There, the "witch" was instrumental in bringing back the spirit of Samuel, who denounced Saul's wickedness and prophesied his end. According to Tiemeyer (33), the original Hebrew word for the practices of the woman of Endor "can be translated as necromancy, divination, sorcery, prophetic power, magic or fortune telling" because the ancient language "groups all of these in one word." The Witch of Endor, in other words, was a "medium" who apparently was able to permit spirits of the dead to manifest themselves to the living. In modern parlance, she might be called a *psychic*, a *sensitive*, a *psychic sensitive*, or a *medium*. The reader is free to make his own choice.

King Croesus was unsure whether he should fight the Persians. With a researcher's skepticism, he first wanted to test the powers of the competing oracles whom he might consult for advice. He devised a test that would be complex enough to rule out pure guesswork or mediumistic gobbledygook, which was as rampant then as in more recent days. The Oracle of Delphi alone replied correctly: "Croesus is boiling a lamb and a tortoise together, in a copper vessel with a copper lid." When Croesus checked with the Delphic oracle on his planned war against Persia, she said that if he crossed the river Halys, which meant war with the Persians, he would "destroy a great empire." Croesus interpreted this to mean destruction of the Persian Empire; in fact, it led to the destruction of his own. But then, his tortoise experiment had tested the oracle on clairvoyance or telepathy, not on precognition.

Aristotle spoke about precognition with a detachment that has remained standard among objective researchers. He wrote:

> As to divination which takes place in sleep, and is said to be based on dreams, we cannot lightly either dismiss it with contempt or give it implicit confidence. The fact that all persons, or many, suppose dreams to possess a special significance, tends to inspire us with belief, based on the testimony of experience; and indeed that divination in dreams should, as regards some subjects, be genuine, is not incredible, for it has a show of reason; from this one might form a like opinion also respecting all other dreams. Yet the fact of our seeing no probable cause to account for such divination tends to inspire us with distrust.

At any rate, cultural patterns in precognition have not changed; to this day, most spontaneous cases of premonition are connected with a subject's dreams.

THE EARLY PERIOD

The impact of Emanuel Swedenborg (1688–1772) was remarkably strong and lasting. This man defies categorization. He was a highly respected authority on metallurgy, he claimed to have spoken with God, and he outlined a detailed concept of universal law, as well as a structure of life beyond death. On June 19, 1759, a fire broke out in the Södermalm section of Stockholm. Swedenborg is reported to have arrived in the city of Göteborg, 300 miles away, that afternoon. At dinner with a party of friends, he reported to them a vision of the burning town. By 8:00 P.M. he is reputed to have told them that the fire had halted three doors from his own home. The next day, a Sunday, the mayor of Göteborg, who had heard of Swedenborg's clairvoyant impressions, discussed the fire with him. The next night, a messenger from Stockholm confirmed that the fire had stopped.

No one can now sort out the various reports dealing with this event. What is beyond doubt is the impact that Swedenborg's visions had on his contemporaries and later writers and thinkers. Broad, in a critical essay on the Stockholm fire (5), noted that "none of these accounts has the least evidential value." He was, of course, viewing the case in retrospect and from the validation standards of the nineteenth and twentieth centuries.

Research scientists, particularly in an area of rich public interest and strong emotional involvement, are peculiarly at the mercy of legend makers. The power of fiction writers should not be underestimated. In our own time, the motion picture has been added to the novel and short story, and these have taken the place of the epics of the past. Thus, while Swedenborg's major work, *Arcana Coelestia*, at first interested such philosophers as Kant and, later, artists of the caliber of William Blake and poets of the distinction of William Butler Yeats, such imaginative approaches created certain difficulties to contemporary researchers.

This can be illustrated by reference to a phenomenon that was for a time closely linked with psychic research, then fell into the background, and has now found a new role within it: hypnosis. Try as they may, specialists in the field have found it difficult to overcome the Svengali label. George Du Maurier, in his novel *Trilby* (1894), introduced Svengali as a "tall and bony character between 30 and 45, well featured but sinister," who managed to put young and innocent Trilby O'Ferrall under his hypnotic spell.

I am introducing this piece of literary trivia because fiction, legend, fear, desire, and wish fulfillment played a strong role in the early history of the psychic. Du Maurier, like Charles Dickens, reflected the interests of his times. The ebb and flow of general, as well as scientific, interest in psi—real or imagined—reflect the cultural and psychological profile of each historical period. And while we may view accounts of stigmata or reports on levitations of St. Theresa of Avila (1515–1582) or of St. Joseph de Copertino (1603–1663) with a retrospective smile, we must keep in mind that religious mysticism has been a decisive part of psychic traditions (11).

Whether the miraculous was regarded as white or black, benign or malign, it nevertheless reflected the role of Christianity in the history of Europe and the United States through the centuries. The concept of testing the accuracy and validity of reported phenomena emerged gradually over a long period of time. Henri More, in his *Antidote Against Atheism* (1653, 1655), related a number of events that included apparitions, poltergeist phenomena and possession which he categorized as free "from all suspicion of either Fraud or Melancholy." The word *fraud* has not changed meaning in 300 years; he used *melancholy* in the sense of a hallucination induced by emotional imbalance. He was, in other words, quite aware that objective phenomena needed to be separated from fakes and delusions.

More's disciple, Joseph Glanvill (1636–1680) has been mentioned by Parsons (10, p. vii) as a forerunner of psychic research. In particular, he developed a questionnaire on case histories designed to document events that were "near and modern" and "sufficiently fresh" to permit reliable testimony. Glanvill, according to Parsons, sent out questionnaires "about time, place, deed, and doer" and "character testimony was collected to establish the disinterestedness of witnesses"—a method that foreshadowed international verification standards defined in 1955 at the Conference on Spontaneous Phenomena in Cambridge, England (20). Glanvill had to resist the temptation to be a teller of popular stories. The seventeenth century, still fascinated by witchcraft, moved from more or less objective treatment of alleged events to out-and-out storytelling for the thrill and diversion of the reading public; it is a situation that persists. Glanvill helped to mold the evolving technique of the short story, no matter what his preferences or protestations: "I Know it is Matter of very little Credit to be a Relator of Stories, and I of all Men living, have the least Reason to be fond of the Employment; for I never had any Faculty in telling of a Story, and have always had a particular indisposition and backwardness to the Writing any such."

Much like a circus bareback rider who has one foot on each horse, galloping side by side, Glanvill was at once a collector and verifier of psychic case histories and an early master of the brief and dramatic narrative. Daniel Defoe (1660–1731) and Edgar Allan Poe (1809–1849) were among the prominent writers in this tradition. The early writers told their stories of supernatural events or encounters in order to instruct, to provide contemporary documentation of religious ideas. However, much depended on the mixed motives of the readers, who might well wish to be educated but also to be thrilled, amused, horrified, or entertained. Nineteenth-century materialism, the age of Charles Darwin and Karl Marx, brought about the assertion of objective fact over the subjective and religiomystical. Darwin's *Origin of Species* (1858) symbolized and strengthened the scientific–materialistic concepts of the period, and reaction to it indirectly caused the development of modern psychic research, which began as an effort to synthesize scientific and religious tradition.

THE MIDDLE PERIOD

In 1848, two sisters, Margaretta and Catherine Fox, experienced rapping phenomena in their parents' house in Hydesville, New York (5, 31). Attributed to spirits, these rappings soon echoed throughout the United States. Spiritualism became a fad, a pseudoreligion, the focus of sincere belief, as well as after-dinner entertainment. It reached the White House, where Mary Todd Lincoln, the President's wife, held séances at various times. Nelson (17, p. 3) writes that before this there had been "no Spiritualism in the modern sense of that term." He notes,

There were indeed many instances of the occurrence of the phenomena that later became distinctive of Spiritualism before 1848, for such phenomena . . . are a universal element in all human societies, and many groups and individuals throughout history have claimed the ability to communicate with the "dead" or other spirits as part of their religious practices, but there had been no movement in civilized societies entirely based on a belief, and the practice of, regular communication with the dead.

Mesmerism (later known as *hypnosis*) was another precursor of Spiritualism. Franz Anton Mesmer's (1734–1815) concept of "animal magnetism" and his experiments were the rage of the Continent. Reports that entranced persons could practice such esoteric tasks as receiving thought-borne instructions at a distance were numerous. The mesmeric, or hypnotic, trance bears a close resemblance to the mediumistic trance. Alleged "supernatural" phenomena were shared by mesmerism and Spiritualism, while the Christian traditions of mysticism, often as structured by Swedenborg (5), provided a variety of patterns for mediumistic phenomena. Nelson maintains that the outbreak of the Civil War in the United States cut short the rise of Spiritualism. The war diverted attention, disrupted home life, and destroyed Spiritualist organizations. Nelson notes that the established churches developed national organizations during the war, while Spiritualism failed to maintain its early promise because of its failure to develop either organization, ritual, or doctrine.

Great Britain, which had earlier imported American mediums and séance-room methods, now adopted the new Spiritualist rationale. In France (2), a Spiritualist structure was developed by Allan Kardec

(1804–1869), whose books *Le Livre des Esprits* and *Le Livre des Médiums* remain popular to this day, notably in Brazil (where African influence has given Spiritualism an impetus rivaling that of Roman Catholicism). The post-Darwinian dilemma of the British can be personalized in the life and thought of Henry Sidgwick (1838–1900). He belonged to the local ghost society while still an undergraduate at Cambridge University. He attended séances, but his reaction was ambivalent. Still, his concern with human ethics, conduct of behavior, and their roots in Christianity provided him with a strong motivation for extensive thought and research. He later became professor of moral philosophy, but only after a period of personal evolution, which included a slowly developing collaboration with Frederic W. H. Myers (1843–1901). Both were deeply concerned with their own, and man's ambiguous position in a post-Darwinian world. Gauld, in his history of the personalities in British psychic research (9), notes that Myers, after a near-fatal illness in 1869, "realised he was no longer a Christian" and then "vacillated between complete agnosticism and a troubled half-belief." To Myers, "the thought of personal extinction was dreadful." He was a brilliant, vain, emotional, ambitious, handsome, and hard-driving man who invited the disdain, as well as the admiration, of his contemporaries and biographers.

Myers and Sidgwick had a deep-delving talk during "a star-light walk [probably on November 13, 1871] which I shall not forget," as Myers put it. The two men began a consistent study of mediumistic phenomena, mainly among their common friends. Gauld notes that until then

Sidgwick's investigations of Spiritualism and related phenomena had been fitful, waxing and waning as his opinions vacillated; but for much of the rest of his life he was to be constantly prodded into action by the eager and relentless Myers. . . . During the next quarter of a century the Sidgwick group investigated many physical mediums (mediums who seem to act as instruments for the physical manifestations of "spirits"); and the same pattern of events was repeated a number of times. Myers would become enthusiastic about such-and-such a medium; Sidgwick and his wife Eleanor would acquiesce far enough to support or participate in an investigation; and everyone would in the end be more or less disappointed.

There was a high-level social touch to these collaborations. Sidgwick married Eleanor Balfour in 1876. Gauld observes (p. 116) that this made him the "brother-in-law to a future Prime Minister (Arthur James Balfour, First Earl of Balfour, British Prime Minister, 1902–1905); and through his sister's marriage to E. W. Benson he was already brother-in-law to a future Archbishop of Canterbury. To say that the Sidgwicks had friends in high places would be an understatement." Social prominence can, of course, be a drawback. It may discourage criticism and self-criticism. Moreover, distinction in one field, such as literature or public affairs, does not necessarily make a researcher immune to fraud or self-delusion in another, such as psychic research.

The Society for Psychical Research (SPR) was officially constituted in London on February 20, 1882. Henry Sidgwick became its first president. Seven years later, in his presidential address on "The Canons of Evidence in Psychical Research" (31, 6:1–6), Sidgwick referred to the dilemma faced by Christians in reevaluating the "marvellous narratives of the Gospels." He noted that the society's research into "the possible action of intelligences other than those of living human beings in the world of our experience" had made it the target of attacks "with equal vigor by Materialists and Spiritualists." He called the physical phenomena of Spiritualism "the strangest of the marvels we are investigating." Sidgwick said that anyone who "is convinced himself of the reality of any alleged marvel" should first try to "diminish the improbability of the marvel by offering an explanation which harmonizes it with other parts of our experience; and second, to increase the improbability on the side of the testimony, by accumulating experiences and varying conditions and witnesses."

These sentiments were echoed in a characteristically more poetic manner by Myers in his obituary of Sidgwick (31, 15:459–460). He wrote that the society's basis for existence was "the extension of scientific method, of intellectual virtues—of curiosity, candour, care—into regions where many a current of old tradition, of heated emotion, even of pseudo-scientific prejudice" prevails. He added: "We must recognize that we have more in common with those who may criticise or attack our work with competent diligence than with those who may acclaim and exaggerate it without adding thereto any careful work of their own. We must experiment unweariedly, we must continue to demolish fiction as well as to accumulate truth; we must make no terms with hollow mysticism, any half-conscious deceit."

Myers's psychological insights, his deep motivations and his own considerable diligence contributed to the makings of his monumental work *Human Personality and Its Survival of Bodily Death* (16). The book, published after Myers's death, remains one of the seminal works in this field. It not only provides a comprehensive survey of the society's work over a period of two decades, but it places psychic research within a wider framework of scientific inquiry that reflects Myers's own wide-ranging interests and perceptions. Its sections on psychology reflect his respect for the ideas of William James (1842–1910), notably his *Principles of Psychology* (1890). It was Myers's alertness to Sigmund Freud's developing concepts of psychoanalysis that prompted Freud to become a member of the society and to publish in its periodicals. Myers once prompted Henry James, the novelist, to read one of his brother William's reports before the Society.

William James, a commanding figure in the history of twentieth-century psychology (12, 15), assumed the intellectual leadership of the American Society for Psychical Research (ASPR) more or less reluctantly (16). The American Society had been established in 1885 during a visit to the United States by Sir William Barrett. In 1887, Richard Hodgson came from England to become the society's executive secretary; it was a branch of the London organization until Hodgson's death in 1905. It was then reestablished, with James H. Hyslop as its secretary and director. Hyslop had resigned his position as professor of logic and ethics at Columbia University in 1902 in order to devote himself fully to psychic research. Lydia W. Allison (1880–1959) said (1, p. 3) that long and intensive investigation convinced Hyslop that "survival of personality and the possibility of communication was a more reasonable interpretation of the facts he obtained than the alternative telepathic explanation."

This point goes to the heart of a question that is central to the history of psychic studies: Are the data forthcoming from a medium in trance the manifestation of a discarnate personality, a spirit (13), or merely the dramatic presentation of information gathered telepathically or clairvoyantly from persons present or from other living sources? Much of today's emphasis on research in telepathy, clairvoyance, precognition, and other forms of ESP assumes that known scientific methods cannot be applied to research into life after death, mainly because the ESP alternative cannot be eliminated. Still, some projects have been designed specifically to screen out ESP (see Chapter 17).

At any rate, Hyslop undertook a series of experiments with mediums, notably Mrs. Leonore Piper (1859–1950), that provided the basis for his conclusions concerning postmortem survival and telepathy. Mrs. Piper's mediumship was, for nearly a generation, central to psychic research in the United States. (But I must certainly mention, in this connection, the prestige of at least one other medium, Mrs. Gladys Osborne Leonard, whom one researcher, W. Whately Carington, once called "the British Mrs. Piper"). I have noted elsewhere (8) that the investigatory approach of William James was artistic, intuitive, and subjective, that "striking examples of mediumship provoked him into reports, analysis and conclusions that combined daring with caution: the scientist and the artist were struggling for his soul, but neither, we can now say, won the final victory." From his father, the elder Henry James, William had inherited an interest in Swedenborg's concepts; to this he added professional psychophysiological knowledge. He found the Sidgwick circle in London, in late 1882 and early 1883, to his liking. His report to the SPR dealing with Mrs. Piper was presented in 1890. James summarized the Piper phenomena with circumspection. She knew, he said, "things in her trances which she cannot possibly have heard in her waking state, and the definitive nature of her trances is yet to be found." He concluded: "The limits of her trance information, its discontinuity and fitfulness, and its apparent inability to develop beyond a certain point, although they end by rousing one's moral and human impatience with the phenomenon, yet are, from a scientific point of view, amongst its most interesting peculiarities, since where there are limits there are conditions, and the discovery of these is always the beginning of explanation."

Another strong personality in the history of psychic studies is Dr. Walter Franklin Prince (1863–1934), who served as research officer of the two societies for psychic research in the United States. He joined the ASPR at Hyslop's behest in 1917, having already contributed his monumental study on "The Doris Case of Multiple Personality" (IX and X, pp. 1–1420). The manifestations might easily have been interpreted as successive "possession" of "Doris" by various spirit entities. Prince, however, insightful and cautious, allowed for psychological alternatives, as well as for unknown factors. Prince's writings were precise, and occasionally acerbic; he did not suffer fools or frauds gladly.

Hyslop's death in 1920 brought Dr. William McDougall (1871–1938) to the presidency of the ASPR. Three years later, the Reverend Dean Frederick Edwards became president and replaced Prince as editor of the society's journal. According to Lydia Allison (1), "Within three years the policy of the Society deviated vastly from the standard established by Professor Hyslop. It was desired to spread the influence of psychical research by popularizing the subject. The Boston members of the Society who had loyally supported Professor Hyslop, and had met for a number of years as a local group, felt they could work to greater advantage as an independent organization." Prince went to Boston and continued his high-quality research.

The ASPR passed through a difficult period, dominated by the fascination of several of its most prominent members with the apparent phenomena displayed by Mrs. Mina Stinson ("Margery") Crandon of Boston. The Crandon case gained international notoriety, as researchers and laymen in the United States and Great Britain and on the Continent took positions for or against the "Margery mediumship." Colorful personalities, including master magician Harry Houdini, used the controversy as a springboard for personal publicity. Charges of fraud were made, rebuffed, renewed, and rebuffed once more.

The ASPR was reorganized in 1941, with Dr. George H. Hyslop, son of James Hyslop, as president. At the same meeting, Dr. Gardner Murphy, who had been on the council of the Boston society since it was established in 1925, was elected an ASPR trustee and chairman of its research com-mittee. The presence of Murphy, a leading psychologist, dramatized yet another element of continuity. He had joined the SPR when he was in London in 1917, as a U.S. soldier on leave; he held a Richard Hodgson Fellowship at Harvard; in the footsteps of William James, he studied the mediumship of Mrs. Piper. He edited, with Robert O. Ballou, a collection of essays, entitled *William James on Psychical Research* (15).

Characteristically, Murphy's book *The Challenge of Psychical Research* (14), written with Laura A. Dale, is dedicated to Myers, Sidgwick, and Prince. The cases presented in this volume show the shifting in em-phasis in psychic subject matters, dealing with spontaneous cases (those that occur outside the laboratory or mediumist circles); experimental tele-pathy, experimental clairvoyance, precognition, PK, and, finally, survival after death. Murphy, who served as president of the ASPR from 1966 to 1970, is perhaps best known for his work as director of research at the Menninger Foundation in Topeka, Kansas, but he was also president of the American Psychological Association in 1944. Contact between psychic research societies in Britain and the United States remained close; Murphy was the third American to be president of the SPR (1949), following James (1894–1895) and Prince (1930–1931).

THE RECENT PERIOD

I said at the outset that the history of parapsychology, like much of history in other fields, is the outgrowth of individual initiatives, motiva-tions, skills, and, one should add, often of personal charisma. Sidgwick's serious involvement needed Myers's egocentric charm to get psychic research off to a running start. In the United States, two other men were responsible for the evolution of research in the 1920s, the 1930s, and beyond. They were William McDougall (1871–1938) and Joseph Banks Rhine. McDougall had been a professor of psychology at Oxford; his ideas, expressed in the book *Social Psychology* (1912), were so novel that, in the words of Gardner Murphy (14), they "swept everything before it."

McDougall left Oxford in 1920 to fill, most appropriately, the chair in psychology that had previously been held by William James; at the same time, he became president of the ASPR. But the Harvard work paled, the ASPR went through its internal crisis, and McDougall transferred to Duke University in Durham, North Carolina, where he became head of the Department of Psychology. Rhine has recorded the genesis of parapsy-chological research at Duke (26), stating that McDougall took over the Duke psychology department in 1927. Rhine and his wife, Louisa, then two young biologists, came to Duke in September of that year for postdoctoral study under McDougall "of the claims to scientific value of the field known as psychical research." Rhine recalls that they saw McDougall as "the man best prepared at that time to serve as a mentor in the difficult appraisals they had come to make."

The events in Durham during the decades that followed were certainly as crucial to the history of parapsychology as had been the two closing decades of the nineteenth century to the history of psychic research. Rhine and his associates gave an account of this period that calls for relatively extensive quotation (26, p. 6):

> The special mission which brought the Rhines to Duke, although it did not measure the entire range of their interest in psychical measures, had to do with the claims of mediumistic communication with discarnate personalities, the question of spirit survival. Even more specifically, they had come laden with a large collection of records of stenographic notes taken at sittings with mediums, with the aim of evaluating this material under the guidance of Professor McDougall. This material belonged to the Assistant Superintendent of Schools of the city of Detroit, Mr. John F. Thomas and it was with his financial support that their visit to Duke was made.
>
> It is of some importance to note that parapsychology came to Duke because of an interest in the problem of postmortem survival, not only on the part of the sponsor, Mr. Thomas, but on the part of the Rhines and Dr. McDougall as well.

This history of the Duke laboratory notes that

> the emphasis given to the studies of mediumship and possible communication with incorporeal [spirit] personalities [may seem] more unusual today to the student of parapsychology than it appeared in 1927. It is important, however, that it was this same "survival" problem that brought parapsychology to scientific attention everywhere. There had, of course, been scattered instances of attention given to other parapsychological claims (for example, in connection with mesmerism or hypnotism), but it was the Spiritualist movement more than anything else that drew scientific interest to the associated claims. As always in the vanguard of scientific progress, here was a strong and widespread human need—in this case, the need to know whether any continuation of personality beyond the grave could be demonstrated.

Rhine, after his first year at Duke, was on the staff of the Department of Psychology, specializing in experiments with telepathy and clairvoyance. The results "were barely encouraging enough to warrant continuing," but there were various encouraging elements. Test cards, now standard equipment in ESP experiments, were first developed there. The high point in these tests was reached in 1933, when Rhine undertook distance-telepathy tests that brought in startling results. These were later to be known as the Pearce–Pratt experiments, as the two participants were Herbert Pearce and J. G. Pratt, who subsequently worked for some three decades within the Duke laboratory. Over a period of 300 trials, Pearce achieved a total score of about twice the number of hits, or correct guesses, than could be expected by pure chance. Rhine published these and other results in a monograph, *Extra-Sensory Perception* (23), that created widespread interest, a good deal of controversy, and some hostility toward the ESP experiments within the psychology department of the university.

The Parapsychology Laboratory became a separate unit in 1935. It broadened its range of experiments from telepathy and clairvoyance to precognition and psychokinesis. The laboratory began publication of the *Journal of Parapsychology* in 1937. McDougall, introducing the first issue of this journal, wrote that future research should concentrate on "strictly laboratory studies which most need the atmosphere and conditions to be found only in the universities, and it is these which the universities can most properly promote, leaving the extra-academic groups the still important task of collecting and recording all such reports of phenomena apparently expressive of unusual mental powers as occur spontaneously, obscure warnings and premonitions, veridical phantasms of the living and the dead and other sporadic manifestations of mysterious origins."

The Duke laboratory results at first occasioned chagrin, disbelief, and hostility among psychologists and within other segments of the scientific community. Some sought to duplicate the Duke work and were unsuccessful; others, although skeptical, found, at times to their annoyance, that they achieved positive results. One early critic of the Rhine work had been Prof. S. G. Soal of London University. As noted by Pratt (21), Soal's interest in the field was aroused during the years that followed World War I; he had "experiences with a medium that convinced him of the genuineness of telepathy, but for a long time all his efforts to obtain results in quantitative tests had been unsuccessful." Soal criticized the Rhine work and engaged in a long series of experiments that, at first, seemed to bear out his anticipation of negative results; these experiments, with Gloria Stewart and Basil Shackleton, lasted more than four years and yielded startlingly significant results.

The Rhine work was summarized in 1940 in a collaborative volume, *Extra-Sensory Perception After Sixty Years* (29), that placed the activity of the Duke laboratory within the framework of historical relationships. As a matter of fact, attempts to harness psi in experiments of the laboratory type had been made throughout the history of organized psychic research. According to *Introduction to Parapsychology* (19), the Sidgwicks engaged in telepathy experiments whereby Alice Johnson visualized two-digit numbers and "sent" them to the entranced subjects in another room. The experiments were so constructed that the results could be contrasted with chance expectations. The account also recalls the pioneer experiment undertaken at the psychology laboratory of the University of Groningen in the Netherlands in 1921. Drs. H. I. F. W. Heymans and G. Brugmans worked in two rooms, one above the other in the same building, as follows:

In the lower room sat a blindfolded student inside a black cloth cage with a slit in it. Above were the experimenters, looking down and observing him through a large hole covered with glass. Upstairs, they selected slips of paper from a bag which corresponded to squares on a checkerboard outside the subject's cage. The subject reached out of his cage and knocked on the particular square on the board which, he felt, had been selected. In 187 trials, he was right 60 times; chance would have made him right only 4 times.

The Duke experiments in telepathy, clairvoyance, and precognition were carried out with the help of specially designed cards, approximately the size of playing cards, using a deck of 5 circles, 5 crosses, 5 wavy lines, 5 squares, and 5 stars. Chance would enable a test subject to guess 5 out of these 25 cards correctly. Following the Pearce–Pratt experiments, the Duke laboratory developed a large variety of methods designed to define and explore the apparent faculties at work in the ESP process. Refinement led to additional precautions. The Pratt–Woodruff screened touch matching experiments, conducted in 1939, assured that two experimenters were present at all times, that duplicate records were kept in locked boxes, and that sheets were serially numbered and stamped with the laboratory's seal. Rao (22) observes that this experiment was "one of the most successful experiments performed with several unselected subjects." He comments, "The interesting point in the experiment is that none of the participants by himself could consciously or unconsciously commit an error that would produce an artifact. [Joseph] Woodruff did not know the order of the key cards, and Pratt, who knew their order, had nothing to do with the target cards. Pratt and Woodruff kept independent records of key cards and targets respectively." Thirty-two subjects participated in the test. Out of a total of 2400 runs, a positive deviation of 489 hits was obtained. Rao notes that these results are equivalent to odds of 1,000,000:1 and thus "cannot reasonably be attributed to chance." He adds, "No one could attribute such a result to normal causes unless he were willing to accuse the experimenters of deliberate fraud on the ground that a similar result could not have been obtained otherwise."

Accusations of fraud or of the "doctoring" of experimental results have, in fact, been directed at parapsychologists from time to time. Aside from the cruder charges that the experimenters and subjects must have engaged in a conspiracy, criticisms have been directed at such aspects of experimentation as the statistical evaluations, the gap between original data and published material, the selection of significant results from a much wider body of tests that did not yield such results, or the possibility of unconscious distortion of data during recording, tabulation, evaluation, and summarizing. On the whole, parapsychological experimenters, some of whom remember the earlier disillusionment of researchers with certain mediumistic subjects, are eminently alert to such dangers (24, 27, 28).

The Pearce–Pratt and Pratt–Woodruff experiments in the United States, as well as the British experiments with Stewart and Shackleton undertaken by Soal with the cooperation of Mrs. K. M. Goldney, are now, in a sense, classical. Retrospective analyses of these and related tests have led to further refinement of procedures, aimed at more elaborate randomization and control conditions on all experimental levels. These efforts, of course, continue; the need for continuous alertness is being passed on to younger researchers.

Elsewhere, the recent history of parapsychology is also linked with names of leaders in the field. Thus, in Germany, Prof. Hans Bender of Freiburg University directs the Institute for Border Areas of Psychology and Mental Hygiene. In the Netherlands, Prof. W. H. C. Tenhaeff has for many years directed the Parapsychology Institute of the University of Utrecht. In the Soviet Union, Prof. Leonid L. Vasiliev (1891–1966), who had been close to the Western European experimenters in the 1920s, was instrumental in reviving research in the Soviet Union through the physiology department of Leningrad University in the 1960s. In France, the Institute Métapsychique in Paris has long been the center of psychic research activities. Parapsychology centers have also been active in Italy, various Latin American nations, and Japan. On the initiative of Rao, who spent several years at the Duke laboratory, a parapsychology laboratory was established at Andhra University, Andhra State, India.

While it is often assumed that there has been a substantial increase in university studies in the field of parapsychology, the pattern has actually been more of work done by individual researchers within universities or by groups or institutions affiliated in various ways with a university. The University of Virginia established a Division of Parapsychology in 1967 under the direction of Dr. Ian Stevenson, whose research in cases suggestive of reincarnation is illustrative of specializations associated with individual scholars. Thus, Dr. Gertrude Schmeidler of the psychology department at

the College of the City of New York has for several decades explored correlations between attitudes and ESP scoring. Dr. Charles Tart of University
of California at Davis has done a series of experiments with apparent out-of-
the-body phenomena. These and others whose work is described elsewhere
in this volume illustrate the diversity that characterizes past and present research avenues and methods.

Diversity, while in many ways adding to fermentation in the field of
parapsychology, has not been without its problems. Historically, a great
deal of naïveté and charlatanism could be observed, at times involving
researchers with claims to considerable distinction in other areas of work.
To this day, claims and counterclaims concerning the Margery mediumship may still be heard. And the relationship between Sir William Crookes
and the young medium Florrie Cook is one of those Victorian tales that
mix science with titillating gossip that makes for a certain type of history.
Myers, too, was subject to similar retroactive evaluation of his many-sided
endeavors. But beyond sheer anecdote, it certainly cannot be denied that
parapsychology—as Myers said in his obituary of Sidgwick—at times may
need more defense from its so-called friends than from objective critics.
Above all, public interest has been a two-edged sword. While Rhine's
work in the early 1930s probably gained from the favorable publicity it
received, it also focused a strong spotlight on what was still a relatively
young investigative technique, and it also aroused the jealousy of others.

Today, we find Rhine concerned about the need to redefine parapsychology and guard against intrusions or scattered attention. He wrote
(25, p. 174):

> Perhaps mesmerism and spiritualism could be said to have done for
> the 19th-century beginnings of parapsychology what might be held up
> as a possible danger today. These and a number of related movements
> such as Theosophy and Christian Science were founded on assump-
> tions that since have come to be regarded as basic elements in para-
> psychology. There was a long period of struggle over whether science
> could extract and liberate these principles from the institutions to
> which they had become so essential. Gradually, however, the para-
> psychical elements were pulled away from mesmerism and hypnosis,
> and later psychical research achieved its independence of the spiritu-
> alist movement.

Speaking, as it were, from the position of an elder statesman of parapsychology, Rhine noted that most workers in the field "would consider it
unthinkable that parapsychology could be completely captured now by
any alien ideology or discipline," but he suggests that present trends might
retard progress in parapsychology, throw it off course, or set it back if it

should lose, even temporarily, "the guiding concepts and standards that have given it so promising a start." Specifically, Rhine cited "Kirlian photography" as one of the developments that "as of now is nothing on which to get side-tracked." He warned of "confusion over astrology" and spoke of claims that plants respond to human thoughts and "can react intelligently on a polygraph" as still lacking in "scientific findings to justify the claim." Rhine felt that the Parapsychological Association and some of its leading members failed to screen such claims adequately. The association, established in 1957 and admitted to membership in the American Asscciation for the Advancement of Science (AAAS) in 1969, functions as the professional organization of parapsychologists in the United States and abroad. It holds annual meetings at which papers are presented and discussions held, it publishes its proceedings, and it coordinates other activities.

Rhine stated that parapsychologists "need to decide whether we really do know where we belong and just what our territory is." He added, "When and as we know on what we can effectively concur and can sufficiently share this remapping of our area of investigation, it should give needed assurance that we have a branch of science that is both well identified and logically outlined." The key literature of the field is not easily selected (35). The pull of popular and dramatic fields of study on psi research is certainly strong, and the cordiality with which parapsychologists have been received in such circles as the humanistic psychology movement may certainly have been seductive and gratifying. At the same time, such fields as meditation and biofeedback have offered seemingly fruitful areas for the development and exploration of ESP faculties, often providing new settings and conditions in the promising area of consciousness expansion.

The research undertaken by Dr. Karlis Osis illuminates the current trend. Osis began work at the Duke laboratory in 1952, took the post of director of research at the Parapsychology Foundation (established by Mrs. Eileen J. Garrett in 1952) in 1957 and has since 1962 served as director of research of the ASPR. His work during this period of some 20 years has included studies on psi in animals, research with mediums in the survival field, deathbed observations by doctors and nurses, and out-of-the-body phenomena. The hypothesis that altered states of consciousness might facilitate the function of ESP has provided links between parapsychological experimentation and studies in biofeedback, "mind-expansion," and related practices. In their private lives, a number of experimental parapsychologists have shown an interest in the implications of practices of current interest, including various forms of meditation and even such physiological practices as acupuncture.

When we said at the outset that the history of parapsychology is a microcosm of modern science (30), we viewed this aspect as a reflection of the field's sensitivity to the evolution, ideas, and even controversies of science (and, for that matter, religion and philosophy) as a whole. Religion, as much in crisis today as it was when the British psychic researchers began their quest, cannot even now be separated from parapsychology, if only as a motivating force to research activity. The growth of Spiritual Frontiers Fellowship in the United States and the Churches' Fellowship for Spiritual and Psychic Studies in Great Britain illustrates an undercurrent of interest among clergy and laymen of virtually all denominations. The raison d'être for parapsychological studies in the Soviet Union, on the other hand, has been that discoveries of material, physiological bases of psychic phenomena would tend to remove them from the religiomystical. Vasiliev (34) stated that telepathy research might well prove "a strong and sharp weapon [in] the hands of materialistic-analytical science, capable of combating certain difficult-to-eradicate mystical views and assumptions."

The material presented in this volume is indicative of the variety of distinctly scientific inquiries that are going on today, evolving from the foundations of psychic research as it emerged from man's history, by way of the Sidgwick–Myers "star-light walk" of nearly a century ago (18). Caution and optimism have been key attitudes among serious searchers and researchers in this field. This was true of Aristotle's hesitancy, mixed with open-mindedness, concerning claims for premonitory dreams. It was equally true of William James (15), who could speak of "one's moral and human impatience with the phenomena" but who also expressed in patient optimism that "we must expect to mark progress not by quarter-centuries, but by half-centuries or whole centuries." As is often the case, we can do no better than to let James have the last word.

REFERENCES

1. Allison, Lydia W. "Fifty Years of American Psychic Research." *Newsletter of the Parapsychology Foundation, Inc.*, March–April 1956.
2. Amadou, Robert. *La Parapsychologie*. Editions Denoël: Paris, 1954.
3. American Society for Psychical Research, *Proceedings of the American Society for Psychical Research.*
4. Bender, Hans, ed. *Parapsychologie: Entwicklung, Ergebnisse, Probleme.* Wissenschaftliche Buchgesellschaft: Darmstadt, 1966.
5. Broad, C. D. *Religion, Philosophy and Psychical Research.* Humanities: New York, 1969.
6. Brown, Salter. *The Heyday of Spiritualism.* Hawthorn: New York, 1970.
7. Driesch, Hans. *Lebenserinnerungen.* Reinhardt Verlag: Munich, 1951.
8. Ebon, Martin. *They Knew the Unknown.* World: New York, 1971.
9. Gauld, Alan. *The Founders of Psychical Research.* Schocken: New York, 1968.

10. Glanvill, Joseph. *Saducismus Triumphatus*, with an introduction by Coleman O. Parsons. Facs. ed. Scholars' Facsimiles and Reprints: Gainesville, Fla., 1966.
11. Haynes, Renée. *The Hidden Springs*. Hollis and Carter: London, 1961.
12. Le Clair, Robert C., ed. *The Letters of William James and Théodore Flournoy*. University of Wisconsin Press: Madison, 1966.
13. Litvag, Irving. *Singer in the Shadows*. Doubleday: New York, 1972.
14. Murphy, Gardner. *The Challenge of Psychical Research*. Harper and Row: New York, 1961.
15. Murphy, Gardner, and Ballou, Robert O. *William James on Psychical Research*. Viking: New York, 1960.
16. Myers, F. W. H. *Human Personality and Its Survival of Bodily Death*. Longmans Green: London, 1903.
17. Nelson, G. K. *Spiritualism and Society*. Schocken: New York, 1969.
18. Nicol, J. Fraser. "Lo, the Poor Researcher." *Tomorrow*, III, 4, Summer 1954.
19. Parapsychology Foundation, Inc. *Introduction to Parapsychology*. New York, 1965.
20. Parapsychology Foundation, Inc. *Proceedings of Four International Conferences of Parapsychological Studies*. New York, 1957.
21. Pratt, J. Gaither. *Parapsychology: An Insider's View of ESP*. Doubleday: New York, 1964.
22. Rao, K. Ramakrishna. *Experimental Parapsychology: A Review and Interpretation*. Thomas: Springfield, Ill., 1966.
23. Rhine, J. B. *Extra-Sensory Perception*. With a foreword by William McDougall and an introduction by Walter Franklin Prince. Humphries: Boston, 1934; repr. 1964.
24. Rhine, J. B. *The Reach of the Mind*. Sloan: New York, 1947.
25. Rhine, J. B. "News and Comments." *Journal of Parapsychology* (1972): 170–176.
26. Rhine, J. B., and Associates. *Parapsychology: From Duke to FRNM*. Parapsychology Press: Durham, N.C., 1965.
27. Rhine, J. B., and Brier, Bob. *Parapsychology Today*. Citadel: New York, 1968.
28. Rhine, J. B., and Pratt, J. G. *Parapsychology: Frontier Science of the Mind*. Thomas: Springfield, Ill., 1957.
29. Rhine, J. B.; Pratt, J. G.; Smith, Burke M.; Stuart, Charles E.; and Greenwood, Joseph A. *Extra-Sensory Perception After Sixty Years*. Holt: New York, 1940; Humphries: Boston, 1966.
30. Smythies, J. G., ed. *Science and ESP*. Humanities: New York, 1967.
31. Society for Psychical Research, *Proceedings of the Society for Psychical Research*.
32. Somerlott, Robert. *Here, Mr. Splitfoot*. Viking: New York, 1971.
33. Tiemeyer, T. N. "In Defense of the Witch of Endor," *Spiritual Frontiers*, III, 1, Winter 1971.
34. Vasiliev, L. L. *Mysterious Phenomena of the Human Psyche*. University Press, 1965.
35. White, Rhea A. "Parapsychology: The Psychic World." *Wilson Library Bulletin*, November 1972.

Alan Vaughan

ALAN VAUGHAN *is co-editor of* Psychic *magazine in San Francisco and an instructor in parapsychology and psychic development at Sonoma State College's Humanistic Psychology Institute in Rohnert Park, California. In 1967–1968, on a grant from the Parapsychology Foundation, he made a special study of European mediums and psychic sensitives. His formal education includes a bachelor's degree in classics from the University of Akron in 1958 and graduate study in librarianship at Rutgers University.*

Mr. Vaughan has published more than two dozen interviews and articles on parapsychology for Psychic. *He was co-editor of the book* Psychics (*Harper and Row, 1972*) *and, in collaboration with Dr. Montague Ullman and Dr. Stanley Krippner of the Maimonides Dream Laboratory in Brooklyn, wrote the recent book* Dream Telepathy (*Macmillan, 1973*). *His recently completed book on his European researches,* Patterns of Prophecy, *was published by Hawthorn.*

Developing his own psychic ability at the College of Psychic Studies in London, he has since participated in research programs as a psychic sensitive at a number of laboratories and has lectured extensively on psychic perception and on prophecy. He is an associate member of the Parapsychological Association and a member of both British and American Societies for Psychical Research.

Mr. Vaughan can be reached at Psychic Magazine, 680 Beach Street, San Francisco, Calif. 94109.

2 Famous Western Sensitives

ALAN VAUGHAN

SUMMARY

Since the advent of Spiritualism over a century ago in America, certain individuals with unusual psychic abilities have dominated the scene of psychic research. At first these psychic sensitives were mainly mediums, persons who allegedly act as an intermediary between the living and the dead. Some of them expressed their psychic ability in physical phenomena, including even levitation. Twentieth-century investigations of trance mediums shed light on the puzzling nature of their trance personalities. Other types of sensitives include trance diagnosticians, readers of past lives, and even mediums who produce voices directly on recording tape, an electronic equivalent of automatic writing. Sensitives often combine a number of psychic skills, including psychometry (telling an object's past by touching it), PK, precognition (foreknowledge of events), clairvoyance (direct perception of a distant or concealed object), telepathy (direct perception of information in a person's mind), and clairaudience (hearing words of a paranormal nature). Recent work in parapsychological laboratories by a number of sensitives is bringing increased interest in parapsychology to scientists and laymen. The latest trend is to develop methods for training sensitives.

THE GOLDEN AGE

The beginning of psychic research in the late nineteenth century was inextricably rooted in the phenomena displayed by Spiritualist mediums who began to appear in America in the mid-nineteenth century. The famous Fox sisters of Hydesville, New York, specialized in raps from alleged spirits who answered questions by code. In something of a stage-show atmosphere, they toured the country, producing raps (fraudulently, some said, but it was never proved) to the spoken and mental questions of their paying customers. Hundreds of imitators sprang up across America, giving rise to millions of followers who called themselves Spiritualists.

74

The prince of mediumship's golden age was a Scot named Daniel Dunglas Home, who developed his mediumship in New York State. Home extended his extraordinary career of physical phenomena to impress the nobility of all Europe and even Russia. Among his specialties were levitation, of which over a hundred instances were recorded; elongation (seeming to grow in height); and handling live coals and even inducing others to handle them without harm. Home's physical phenomena attracted the attention of the illustrious physicist Sir William Crookes, who tested Home's ability to move objects at a distance and pronounced it genuine. Most spectacular was Home's ability to play an accordion without touching it when the instrument was locked in a caged box.

While Home has the distinction of never being implicated in any attempts at fraudulent mediumship, Sir William Crookes's reports of his physical phenomena were not received with approval by his colleagues at the Royal Society. Home's phenomena did not comply with Newton's laws, nor did Home's reliance on an alleged spirit "control" who aided him in his feats impress the advocates of scientific materialism.

Nevertheless, the materialistic era of the Victorians produced more physical mediums than any other era. Mediums began also to flourish on the European continent. In Poland, Kluski materialized phantom humans and animals and conjured up phantom hands to make wax gloves. In Germany, Rudi Schneider produced phantom arms to play musical instruments. In Italy, famous scholars of science converged to study an ignorant peasant named Eusapia Palladino.

Palladino became an international cause célèbre. She levitated tables without touching them, played two-handed musical instruments at a distance and often conjured up "spirit" hands to accomplish this as well as to touch her sitters. She also, she confessed, would attempt to do it with her own hands if someone did not hold them. When she came to the United States, she was offered ample opportunity to cheat and did so, which proved that she was indeed right about her moral weakness while in trance. Her control, she claimed, was a robust pirate named John King, a traditional séance-room figure from England, whose unlikely collaboration with an Italian peasant did little to impress her dignified investigators.

Some modern commentators such as British psychologist H. J. Eysenck (13) find the séance-room phenomena of the Victorian era difficult to take seriously:

However odd the behaviour of the furniture may have been, the behaviour of the three Victorian gentlemen investigating the case must have seemed even odder to the observer; indeed it reads like a mixture of Henry Miller at his pornographic best, and *Punch*. One investigator would hold the poor woman down on her chair pinning her arms from behind, while the others would lift her skirts and feel her legs to make sure that there was nothing linking her to the pieces of furniture in question. These shinnanigans undoubtedly detract from the odd facts which do emerge . . . and which raise many serious questions because they are very difficult to explain in scientific terms.

But facts—however risible the conditions under which they are gathered —remain just as solid.

More dignified were the investigations of the nineteenth-century American medium Mrs. Leonore Piper of Boston. While in a trance state, Mrs. Piper was controlled by a supposed French doctor named Phinuit, who produced astonishing facts about deceased persons. The distinguished psychologist William James investigated her intensively and reported to the American Society for Psychical Research in 1886 that "I now believe her to be in the possession of a power as yet unexplained." Later, James dubbed her the "white crow" who proved the existence of a class of persons as illogical as white crows—trance mediums who were able to provide detailed information about the dead. Mrs. Piper's communications in a trance state began with vocal statements but later changed to automatic writing. Her controls changed also. The mysterious and not very French Phinuit was supplanted by a group of controls named after their leader, Imperator. This unlikely group had been communicating earlier through the English medium and cleric Stainton Moses, founder in 1884 of the London Spiritualist Alliance (now the College of Psychic Studies).

TRANCE CONTROLS

Twentieth-century investigations of trance mediums tried to solve the puzzle of "controls," or "trance personalities." Were these controls actually "split-offs" from the medium's own personality or were they what they claimed to be—discarnate entities with their own personalities and individual memories? The Swiss psychologist Carl Jung devised a word-association test by which to compare the medium's responses with those of the control. Highly emotional words would evoke a delay in response, whereas less emotionally charged words would require a shorter association time. Using this method, the British researcher Whately Carington tested the control of Mrs. Gladys Osborne Leonard, a prominent British medium whose control was a little girl named Feda. Carington found that the medium and her control responded in almost a mirrorlike way: highly charged words for the medium had little effect on the control, and vice versa. Perhaps, Carington reasoned, the two personalities were complementary to each other. This seemed to be evidence that the control was indeed split off from the medium's personality. Yet, somehow, the control had access to paranormal information that the medium in a normal state did not.

Probably the most thoroughly investigated medium of modern times was Mrs. Eileen Garrett, an Irish woman who worked as a trance medium for many years in London and who came to the United States to work with parapsychologists and later founded the Parapsychology Foundation in New York. In the early years of her mediumship, Mrs. Garrett had two trance controls. The first to come was Uvani, who claimed to be a soldier from India of centuries before. Then Abduhl Latif arrived. He claimed to be a physician from the twelfth-century court of Saladin, and his primary interest was in healing. Since he had been known to come through a number of mediums, Mrs. Garrett sometimes humorously referred to him as "the traveling salesman of the spirit world." Mrs. Garrett herself was ambiguous about her controls; sometimes she felt they must be split-offs from her own personality, inspired by her early training with the Scottish Spiritualist Hewatt MacKenzie at the British College of Psychic Science (now defunct). At other times, she seemed to accept them for what they claimed to be.

Mrs. Garrett's own curiosity about the nature of her controls led her into many investigations of them. In the 1930s she went to Duke University's Parapsychology Laboratory for experiments in ESP-card guessing. Both she and her control Uvani scored above chance and at about the same level. This suggested to her investigators, J. B. Rhine and J. G. Pratt, that Uvani was probably a split-off personality. The same conclusion was reached by Whately Carington from his intensive quantitative investigations, whereas the American researcher Hereward Carrington concluded that the two were independent personalities. When Hereward Carrington asked Uvani about it, the control said that the medium split off a portion of her unconscious, which he then manipulated.

But the question of mediumistic controls became even more puzzling with the advent of two additional controls to Mrs. Garrett's trance state. Tehotah claimed to be an entity which personified the Logos. He said he had never been a person as such. Rama claimed to be the personification of life and also said he had never been incarnated as an individual. In his book *Image of an Oracle*, psychiatrist Ira Progoff presents us with fascinating interviews with the four controls of Eileen Garrett. Tehotah and Rama seemed to come from a deeper level of the unconscious, and indeed, Rama came rarely, since his presence caused Mrs. Garrett considerable strain in her trance state. In some ways, these latter controls resemble Jungian archetypes of the collective unconscious.

Although her early hypnotic training had been in walling off from the conscious mind any contact with her controls, Mrs. Garrett later developed her own extrasensory abilities in a waking state. And gradually, over the years, more and more mediums have come to work in a conscious state—what they call *waking clairvoyance*. This is in contrast to what was believed two generations ago: that contact with discarnates could come only while in a trance state.

DIRECT VOICE

Midway between physical mediumship and mental mediumship is *direct voice mediumship*, in which the voice of an ostensible communicator comes from a point in space, generally a few feet away from the medium. Some Spiritualists claim that a voice box is materialized for such productions, although that would not seem to account for the other aspects of vocalization, such as movements of the tongue and breathing. Mrs. Blanche Cooper was one such direct voice medium who is known to us mainly because of an extraordinary sitting given to the British psychic researcher S. G. Soal, in which a living person named Gordon Davis communicated. Soal had thought that Davis had been killed in World War I, so he accepted as probable fact the Davis personality's claim to be a spirit, since Davis's voice and mannerisms were the way Soal had remembered them. Davis communicated a number of evidential facts to prove his identity. Yet some years later Soal found that Davis was very much alive. Just as extraordinary, some of the facts given by Davis turned out to be precognitive, such as a description of a house where Soal was to live later. The medium's control seemed to have difficulty with that session —the voice started coming in too loudly.

An intriguing interpretation of that sitting has been offered by Gracia-Fay Ellwood: that a communal consciousness—incorporating Soal's memories of Davis, Mrs. Cooper's Spiritualistic beliefs and Davis's own consciousness—formed the communicating voice. Surprisingly, the challenging problem of the production of a voice in the air—no mean psychic talent in itself—has received little attention from parapsychologists.

Today direct voice mediumship is extremely rare, although a British medium, Leslie Flint, is well known. His cockney control, Mickey, brings through a number of communicators to make an entertaining (if not always evidential) séance.

ELECTRONIC MEDIUMSHIP

The newest twist in mediumship (whether or not it *is* mediumship is contested) is the production of voices directly onto magnetic tape or through the microphone of a tape recorder. Prof. Hans Bender of Freiburg University in Germany has investigated the Swede Friedrich Jürgenson and has obtained under controlled conditions "extra voices" on magnetic tape. The experimental setup is to run two tape recorders, with microphones placed well enough apart to obtain a stereo effect, and carry on a conversation. Although no voices are heard by the people in the room, sometimes when the tape is played back extra voices appear in the pauses of the ordinary conversation. Bender obtained voiceprints of one such voice and was convinced that it was indeed a true paranormal vocalization and not a trick of hearing. The voice appeared on only one of the tape recorders.

Great interest is now being shown in the voice phenomena of Konstantin Raudive, a Latvian living in Germany. Raudive's voices, obtained in a number of ways, speak in the languages Raudive knows (as do the voices of the polylingual Jürgenson), and often combine words from different languages in a single sentence. The voices sometimes claim to be those of the dead. When I visited Raudive to listen to his tape-recorded voices, I found some of them extremely clear, although most others require a trained ear for listening. Some parapsychologists who have heard Raudive's voices agree that some of the voices are a paranormal phenomenon, although other researchers, notably David Ellis, find only misrepresentations of natural sounds. Whether or not they are voices of the dead, as Raudive claims, is debated. Raudive also says that he is not a medium, and that the voices can be captured by anyone's tape recorder. As more and more people try this experiment, we may begin to get some answers about a most puzzling phenomenon.

TRAVELING CLAIRVOYANCE

Yet another style of psychic sensitivity sprang from the experiences of the early French and American mesmerists. Subjects were hypnotized (generally by making mesmeric passes) and put into an altered state of consciousness that allowed them access to knowledge they did not have in their conscious state. Such mesmerized subjects would often also display *traveling clairvoyance*, an ability to describe events taking place at a distance as if they were able to project their consciousness to those far places.

A young cobbler named Andrew Jackson Davis became an American celebrity on the nineteenth-century lecture circuit with his profound trance lectures, which sparked the sale of his many books, dictated while in trance. Davis's weighty tomes seem a remarkable production for a young man in his twenties, yet there is some evidence that he was picking up this information by ESP from the scholars of his day. Davis's descriptions of the planets, for instance, tallied well with expert thought of his day but now strike us as ludicrous.

Of greater impact today is the trance work of Edgar Cayce, whose influence in the 1970s is greater than it was in his lifetime. While in a trance state (achieved first by hypnosis and later by autohypnosis), Cayce was able to describe medical infirmities of people miles away whom he had never seen and to prescribe remedies for their conditions. The records kept by the Association for Research and Enlightenment, founded by Cayce and maintained today at Virginia Beach, Virginia, show ample evidence of Cayce's extraordinary extrasensory abilities while in trance. In his normal waking state, Cayce claimed no such abilities, although a few anecdotes related by his son Hugh Lynn Cayce suggest that the elder Cayce did indeed have some unusual abilities while awake—for instance, being able to will someone to visit him.

READINGS OF PAST LIVES

In his later years, Cayce began doing a different type of psychic work while in trance. He claimed access to a collective unconscious (sometimes called the *akashic record*) in which were recorded past lives of persons living now. Reportedly Cayce found this difficult to accept rationally, since his upbringing had never included the concept of reincarnation. Many of Cayce's readings of past lives seem romantically at odds with known facts about past civilizations. In ancient Egypt, for instance, Cayce said he had been a priest named Ra-Ta, who had a relationship with a girl named Isris. Later, their memories were deified as Ra and Isis. Historically, however, the cults of Ra and Isis came into being centuries apart. Many of Cayce's readings were about former lives in Atlantis, which historically still remains problematical. Very few of the readings are sufficient for any sort of verification, yet those few that are have captured the imagination and support of several writers, such as Dr. Gina Cerminara. In one reading Cayce predicted for an infant, on the basis of presumed past lives, that the child would become a great doctor of the mind. Although the child's father wanted him to go into business, the boy instead took a degree from Harvard Medical School to become a psychiatrist.

As with most psychic sensitives, Cayce's trance utterances have to be weighed carefully against known fact. Because he is right about one thing does not automatically ensure correctness on another, nor is the reverse true. If indeed he were tapping the collective unconscious, then it would seem to be as fallible as the rest of humanity.

Today there are many psychic sensitives who specialize in giving readings about past lives. Separating the wheat from the chaff is nearly impossible, since so few of these readings are capable of being verified, nor are most of the sensitives' clients interested in the scientific approach. So far, parapsychologists have not published any investigations of these past-life readings in the journals, although a number of popular writers have written books about their researches. In my own experience of getting readings from many sensitives, many past lives have been mentioned, but never did two sensitives agree on any one of them. The whole question is tremendously complex and difficult but of such potential importance that it deserves serious investigation.

The British sensitive Joan Grant, who first gained fame for her novels about her presumed past lives, is now working in collaboration with her psychiatrist husband, Dr. Denys Kelsey, in an effort to apply reincarnational concepts to psychiatry. If a patient's situation seems to warrant an investigation into a past life for the cause of a psychiatric problem, Kelsey hypnotizes the patient to try to locate the problem through regression to the past life. Joan Grant then tries to get an independent reading of the past-life conflict with which to compare her husband's findings. They have reported a number of psychiatric successes with this method. So even if the parapsychological concept of reincarnation remains in the balance, it would at least seem to have validity as a concept of healing.

A similar approach was used by another British psychiatrist whose sister was the famed Irish automatic-writing medium Geraldine Cummins. Miss Cummins, whose mediumship developed through the use of a Ouija board and later to automatic writing, had many illustrious sitters. The poet William Butler Yeats, for instance, was astonished when the text for a play he was working on came through her Ouija. Prime Minister Mackenzie King of Canada consulted the late Franklin Delano Roosevelt through Miss Cummins's mediumship. Yet some of her most intriguing psychic work was done when the sitter was not present; her psychiatrist brother would hand her an envelope containing something from one of his patients whom she had never met. Then, in trance (controlled by a personality named Astor), she would describe by automatic writing the patient's condition and often point out as the cause for a neurosis an incident that took place before the patient was born—from the so-called racial unconscious of the patient's forebears. On a few occasions, the patients seemed to be cured by merely reading Miss Cummins's statement of the origin of their disorder.

MEDIUMS TODAY

If the British have achieved preeminence in producing good mediums, it is probably because of the Spiritualistic organizations that have nurtured them. In London the British College of Psychic Science (now defunct), the College of Psychic Studies, and the Spiritualist Association of Great Britain are representative of organizations through which inquirers into survival and other psychic questions can book a sitting with a medium. Many also free-lance from their homes. And, of course, Spiritualist churches across Britain always have their resident medium.

Among the best known of today's mediums who still use trance are Ena Twigg and Douglas Johnson. Most of their sittings, however, are given in waking clairvoyance. Johnson has worked extensively with parapsychologists in England, the United States, and Israel, but little of this experimental work has yet been published. In experiments for W. G. Roll at the Psychical Research Foundation in Durham, North Carolina, Johnson scored more "hits" about people when they were present than when doing absent psychometric readings. In investigating a "haunted house," Johnson was able to describe accurately the entities that the occupants of the house had reported earlier. And in experiments at the Maimonides Dream Laboratory in Brooklyn, Johnson was able to dream telepathically about a distant art-print target. In my own experiments with Johnson, in which he tried to predict events in my future, a number of detailed predictions were fulfilled. As with many psychic sensitives, Johnson frequently receives visual symbolic images, which he must interpret, although at other times he receives impressions in words (so-called clairaudience). Some readers may recall a filmed trance sitting in the 1966 ABC-TV production "The Baffling World of ESP," in which a woman sitter was so overcome by the information Johnson's trance control, Chiang, related about her deceased father that she broke into tears. The sitter, a London psychiatrist, told me she had never met Johnson before.

Providing survival evidence is the chief work of Mrs. Ena Twigg, about whom Bishop James Pike wrote in his book *The Other Side*. Typically, Mrs. Twigg receives impressions in words (clairaudience), which she then relays to the sitter. Her control is her deceased father. Mrs. Twigg has also done a great deal of experimental work, including absent sittings. In one such sitting, when she was holding an object belonging to someone in South Africa, she told the note-taker that the communicator was alarmed at the prospect of a lion confronting the absent sitter. It was later learned that the absent sitter was, at that time, driving along a jungle road when she was startled by a lion leaping in front of the car's path.

In Mrs. Twigg's autobiography, a number of sitters offer written testimony of some quite remarkable survival evidence. For instance, a British theatrical producer wrote of the evidence from her deceased brother (30, p. 287):

In order to convince me of his identity, my brother reminded me of a scarf I had given him for a birthday present. He was very fond of that scarf, and he told me he had hidden it in the back of a certain drawer, and there I would find the scarf. It was there—exactly as he said—and since I did not know of this, and no one else in the world did, I was convinced that I had been talking with my brother.

Few mediums of modern times can equal the impact of the late Arthur Ford, whose televised séance with Bishop James Pike received press coverage the world over. A later sitting for Pike convinced him that his son James, who had committed suicide, was in contact with him through Ford. The evidentiality of the televised séance, arranged in Toronto by Allen Spraggett, came under question when Spraggett and William V. Rauscher revealed in their book *Arthur Ford: The Man Who Talked with the Dead* that a clipped newspaper obituary found in Ford's effects could have provided the striking "hits" about Pike's deceased friend, Bishop Block.

A generation before, Arthur Ford had made headlines with the secret code of Houdini, which he revealed to Houdini's wife in a series of sittings. The explanation of the code had been known to no one else except the late Houdini and his wife, who used it years before in a mentalist act. Charges, countercharges, and heated newspaper headlines have kept the controversy alive. A signed note from Houdini's widow that Ford had produced the message she and Houdini had agreed on before his death as a sign of his continued existence seems to outweigh the other evidence.

In his early years of "platform clairvoyance" Arthur Ford made some startling hits with complete strangers. Visiting London to give a demonstration in 1928, Ford told a woman (known to me) the names of her deceased husband's servants in India, the complete name of a friend of her husband's, and how her husband had died. Ford was practically unique in his ability to get such detailed information as full names. In later years Ford abandoned platform demonstrations for trance sittings in which his control, Fletcher, took over.

Perhaps Ford's greatest impact was in helping found the Spiritual Frontiers Fellowship, a religiously oriented psychic-interest group that flourishes today. An ordained minister of the Disciples of Christ Church, the Reverend Arthur Ford presented both a spiritual message and a mystery to those who knew him.

PSYCHOMETRY

Although psychic sensitives vary tremendously in their specialties, nearly all of them have in common the practice of psychometry—getting psychic impressions about a person by holding an object belonging to him. If the person is dead, then the impressions will likely be interpreted as survival evidence. If the person is alive, then the impressions about the person's past, present, or future will likely be interpreted as evidence of ESP. (Of course, some researchers interpret *all* impressions, including those about the dead, as ESP.) In spite of the prevalence of this psychic talent, it has received relatively little attention from modern parapsychologists, although the work of W. G. Roll in investigating his psi-field theory may be a promising development.

Among the best known of psychometrists today is the Dutch sensitive Peter Hurkos, now living in Los Angeles. Although his frequent television appearances are basically for entertainment, there seems little doubt that he can sometimes very accurately describe a person by touching an object belonging to him. Dr. Barbara Brown of the Veterans Administration Hospital in Sepulveda, California, informally commented on some pilot experiments with Hurkos in which she was investigating possible brain-wave differences between the times he was "hot" and less successful times. She found a distinct difference in the brain-wave patterns; when he was "hot" there appeared an abnormal double spike in his EEG record. Experiments with Hurkos conducted by Dr. Andrija Puharich in the 1950s indicated that under a special laboratory setup in a double Faraday cage, in which the outer cage was electrified with a resonating current, Hurkos's ability at telepathy became greatly enhanced. Better known are Hurkos's adventures in "crime-busting," in which he has helped police (sometimes successfully, sometimes not) solve murder cases.

Another Dutch sensitive who has worked with parapsychologists is Gerard Croiset, who lives in Utrecht. Since the 1940s he has cooperated with the parapsychologist W. H. C. Tenhaeff of the State University of Utrecht in documenting and investigating the many police cases he is called upon to help solve psychically. Croiset specializes in finding missing persons, often children who have fallen into Holland's many canals. Croiset himself nearly drowned in a canal as a child, which may have made him especially sensitive to that situation. Like other sensitives, Croiset often relies on psychometry, yet he can on occasion get impressions by talking to someone on the telephone. His impressions are mostly visual, often sufficiently detailed to provide police with a sketched map.

A case he helped solve when I was in Utrecht to interview him makes an interesting example. Croiset received a telephone call (all calls are tape-recorded) from a man in a town some miles away. "A man has disappeared," he said. "Can you help me find him?" Croiset told him that the man had committed suicide by jumping into a canal from a bridge. He described the locale with such accuracy that the police were able to find the drowned man that afternoon. It turned out that he had murdered his family that morning. The next day, a newspaper item from that town told the whole story, including Croiset's involvement in the case.

Unlike Peter Hurkos (who charges $5000 a case), Croiset does not charge for his clairvoyant services, although he tends to work mainly on cases that he finds exciting. Scotland Yard, for instance, flew him to Britain to investigate the notorious Moors murders a few years ago. When Croiset was handed a piece of clothing from a murder victim, he described (as it turned out, in vain) the circumstances of the next murder. As Tenhaeff has pointed out, a number of Croiset's psychic statements have been failures by police standards but most illuminating for the parapsychological study of such phenomena.

In Holland, Croiset is well known for his healing abilities, by which he makes his living (he charges about a dollar for a few minutes' treatment). Yet little investigation of his healing ability has been made by parapsychologists. Films taken of Croiset in his youth (shown in an unreleased BBC-TV program) indicate that he has PK ability: he was shown knocking a figurine off a mantel by making a pass at it some feet away. These highly provocative "home movies" show a dachshund dragging along its paralyzed hind legs. Croiset made a few passes over the animal, and it ran out of the room.

PRECOGNITION

In many controlled experiments in precognition (so-called *chair tests*), Croiset has had stunning success in describing people who will later be chosen by chance to sit in a certain seat in a hall. In one such experiment, filmed and reported by parapsychologist Jule Eisenbud, Croiset made statements in Utrecht to describe in detail two persons who were chosen by chance weeks later in Denver, Colorado. Especially intriguing were some correct details of those persons' lives that happened *after* Croiset's reading. In a chair test I witnessed—both the recording of impressions in Freiburg, Germany, and the actual selection of persons a few days later in Zürich, Switzerland—Croiset's accurate impressions of a target woman included the odd (and embarrassing) fact that she had taken a plant from someone's garden for her own house and that someone had thrown a brick through her window. The incident had happened in the days between the recording of impressions and the actual chair test. These chair tests have been quantified by several researchers to give extremely high odds against chance.

America's most famous sensitive is, of course, Jeane Dixon, the seeress of Washington who became world famous for her prediction of President John Kennedy's assassination. Her prediction had been published in the May 13, 1956, issue of *Parade* magazine: "As for the 1960 election, Mrs. Dixon thinks it will be dominated by labor and won by a Democrat. But he will be assassinated or die in office 'though not necessarily in his first term.' " Ruth Montgomery's book about Mrs. Dixon, *The Gift of Proph-ecy*, misquoted the prediction as well as its date and did not mention that the prophecy was based on the 20-year presidential death cycle, in which presidents elected in 20-year intervals since Harrison have been assassi-nated or died in office, although not necessarily in the first term.

Mrs. Dixon has so far declined invitations to parapsychological labora-tories, so no scientific assessment can be placed on her abilities as a precognitive sensitive. This has had little effect on her admirers and friends, who are quoted in her books with testimony of some startlingly accurate personal prophecies. Mrs. Dixon fares less well with her pub-lished predictions of world events, although this is a general pattern with precognitive sensitives. They may be able to get detailed impressions of a person's future but flounder with more abstract prophecies of world events, especially those about which they hold firm opinions. Yet enough anecdotal evidence accumulated over the years from responsible persons suggests that Mrs. Dixon's reputation is not without foundation. Certainly, she is unique in the amount of publicity accorded her predictions.

Mrs. Dixon's nearest competitor in fame is the seeress of Chicago, Mrs. Irene Hughes. Mrs. Hughes has had a number of hits in her published prophecies and, in a particularly convincing way, predicted on Canadian radio the outcome of political kidnappings that shook that nation. Mrs. Hughes is also a psychometrist and, like a number of other sensitives, has helped solve police cases. She has also done work as a trance medium with the aid of her Japanese trance personality. In laboratory work at the Psychical Research Foundation in Durham, North Carolina, Mrs. Hughes was tested in a number of ways, including her ability to assemble police "Identikit" facsimiles of faces of target persons by using psychometry.

A similar mixture of psychic abilities is exhibited by Mrs. Shirley Harri-son, of Maine. She has worked her Ouija board to get clues for the police to find the body of a missing person or to locate a missing plane. She has done experiments in ESP for Dr. Stanley Krippner in which she success-fully described concealed target pictures. And she even predicted in the presence of Krippner the target locale for the next murder by the Boston Strangler some years ago. Oddly, her impression that the next victim would be a nurse living near the police station turned out to be somewhat incorrect. The next victim was a teacher. She *did* live near the police station and in an apartment recently vacated by a nurse.

LABORATORY SUBJECTS

A sensitive who became famous overnight is Olof Jonsson, a Swede living in Chicago, when *Life* magazine told of his involvement with Edgar

Mitchell's Apollo 14 ESP test. Actually, though, both Jonsson and an anonymous subject in another city scored equally well at guessing ESP symbols. Jonsson is unusual among sensitives in that he enjoys doing ESP-card tests, at which he has gotten some astonishingly high scores. Especially convincing evidence came from W. E. Cox of the Foundation for Research on the Nature of Man in Durham, since Cox, an amateur magician, took precautions to eliminate any chance of the magician's art being employed. Other experimenters who did not take such precautions were less confident of their results. And it is, of course, the experimenter's responsibility—not the sensitive's—to insure that all alternatives to ESP be eliminated in their tests. In the case of the Apollo 14 test, there had been no chance of manipulating anything, since the symbols (numbers, actually) were on a piece of paper 200,000 miles away.

Few sensitives have the determination to do the thousands of quantitative ESP guessing tests necessary for extended experimental programs. That is what makes Lalsingh ("Sean") Harribance unique among sensitives today. A native of Trinidad, Harribance has been working for several years in quantitative experiments at the Psychical Research Foundation in Durham. In the foundation's EEG investigations of Harribance's ESP performance—for instance, guessing the sex of persons whose photos are concealed—a cumulative record has been established that independently demonstrates by astronomical odds the existence of ESP. The primary focus in these experiments had been to discover possible relationships between alpha brain-wave patterns and ESP performance.

Harribance has given "psychic readings" for thousands of persons, often for charity fund-raising efforts in Trinidad. Now living in Washington, D. C., Harribance is working as a professional psychic consultant.

Increasingly, the scientific establishment is showing interest in the talents of psychic sensitives, giving rise to investigations in laboratories that are not primarily parapsychological. At Stanford Research Institute in California (not to be confused with Stanford University), physicists Harold Puthoff and Russell Targ (see Chapter 22) have been investigating the paranormal abilities of an Israeli sensitive, Uri Geller. Experiments in telepathy and clairvoyance gave astonishing odds against chance —a trillion to one in one instance. But it is Geller's reported PK ability to break rings and bend sturdy metal that aroused more interest. *Time* (27, p. 110) suggested that Geller's physical effects could be duplicated by a magician, but I became certain that it was no trick when Geller was able to bend a sturdy metal key that I was holding. Geller did not touch the key at all, but it bent about 30° while his hands were laid on mine.

A provocative report by researcher Dr. Henry (Andrija) Puharich indicates that Geller has even more fantastic PK abilities, such as dematerializing objects (20 attempts, 75% successful) and rematerializing them (20 attempts, 60% successful). If these materialization phenomena can be replicated under controlled conditions, then we may well begin to wonder what happens to those three vanished objects. Researchers complain that it is difficult to film such productions, since sometimes vital parts of the cameras dematerialize. If physics can solve this problem, then it may open up a whole new dimension (literally) of science.

As always, people react more strongly to things that they can actually *see* that defy their common-sense world, although PK is no more a threat to current scientific theory than, say, precognition. If Geller is able to maintain his PK ability (physical mediums are notorious for losing their talents or dying young from overuse of their gift), then he may be able to make a unique contribution to paraphysics. At last report he was attempting to teleport to earth a camera left on the moon by Apollo 14 astronaut Edgar Mitchell.

The combination of ESP and PK in one person happens so frequently that one is startled at the lack of research effort to find out possible relationships between them. Could it be that some persons can tune a psychic-energy field either to receive (telepathy) or to focus for beamed transmission (PK)? Recent Soviet research with the PK sensitive Nina Kulagina (who also had demonstrated "eyeless vision") hints that this may well be a fruitful research hypothesis.

For those who wonder why it is that only persons in distant history or other countries can display such gifts, the arrival on the parapsychological scene of Ingo Swann proves of great interest. A New York artist whose specialty is "cosmic art," Swann came into his paranormal abilities only comparatively recently. Provocatively, he maintains that these abilities were "rehabilitated" by work with Scientologist L. Ron Hubbard in exploring past lives. I interviewed the people who first tried an informal experiment with Swann. He said he could produce lights from his hands and above his head by leaving his body. They took photographs of him, using a highly sensitive new film from Kodak, while he was attempting to do this in a dark room. The photos showed the lights coming from his hands, and above his head in another photo was a self-portrait in faint light. In tightly controlled experiments in "out-of-body vision" at the ASPR, Swann was able to sketch distant unknown targets with sufficient accuracy to get all of them right, according to an independent judge. His brain-wave recordings showed a consistent effect—decreased voltage in the occipital area—when he was supposedly out of the body.

In an experimental program at New York's City College, as reported by Dr. Gertrude Schmeidler, attempts by Swann to influence the temperature of distant graphite thermisters were also statistically significant. By demonstrating physical and mental paranormal abilities—such as going out of the body to view the inside of a magnetometer and penetrating the superconducting shield to perturb the magnetic field inside—Swann was the inspiration for a research program at Stanford Research Institute that is attempting to discover relationships between extraordinary human functioning and presently known physical laws.

TRAINING SENSITIVES

Parapsychologists have often complained of a dearth of subjects who could perform well in their quantitative ESP tests. In the past, such ESP-card-guessing stars as Hubert Pearce in America and Basil Shackleton in England eventually lost their ability. But a Czech professor, Dr. Milan Ryzl, was able to train subjects by hypnosis to obtain above-chance scores in simple ESP tests, such as distinguishing a white card from a green card. His most famous subject is Pavel Stepanek, who continues to work with American experimenters (notably J. G. Pratt of the University of Virginia Division of Parapsychology) in replicating these results in search of meaningful psychological patterns of ESP responses. Now living in San Jose, California, Ryzl is marketing an ESP training course complete with recorded instructions.

In London, at the College of Psychic Studies, psychic development classes have been taught for several generations. Under the guidance of medium Douglas Johnson, a young Englishman named Malcolm Bessent was able to develop his psychic abilities sufficiently well to come to the United States for an experimental research program at the Maimonides Dream Laboratory in Brooklyn. Bessent's first task was to give the staff absent readings by psychometry. All but one of the eight staff members were able to judge which reading had been given for them. In two series of precognitive dream experiments in which targets were chosen randomly after his dreams had been recorded, Bessent performed at a level on the order of 1000:1 against chance, and he was able to do as well even with an electronic apparatus set for a precognition experiment. A long-distance (45 miles) dream telepathy experiment in which the agents were 2000 young people at a rock concert also gave statistically significant results when Bessent's dreams were independently judged.

My own psychic abilities were also developed in training begun with Douglas Johnson at the College of Psychic Studies. The basic methods were meditation and practice at psychometry. At the Maimonides Dream Laboratory, I have had success at being a dream telepathy subject and also using other altered states of consciousness in receiving information about art-print targets. In psychometry experiments for researchers at New York's City College, I was able to get a number of hits in describing written material and giving information about the writers. I hasten to add that many other subjects are able to do as well in many of these experiments, suggesting that ESP abilities may be far more widespread than is generally believed. Since my own particular research interest is precognition, I have registered a number of prophecies (including some interesting hits) with the Central Premonitions Registry in New York (see Chapter 6). And again, many other people have registered precognitive hits at a level that exceeds chance expectation. Using methods developed in workshops over the past few years, I am now attempting to teach young people ways of exploring their own psychic potential. I hear of others attempting the same with somewhat different methods. In the long run, the more who try, the more likely we are to find reliable methods of psychic development.

What might this lead to? The veteran medium Arthur Ford sized up the situation in an interview (34, pp. 23–24) we had shortly before his death: "The day of the professional medium is about over. We've been useful as guinea pigs. Through us, scientists have learned something about the conditions necessary for it to happen. I have taught a great many groups, and find they all have some spiritual gift. Any group of seven to eight people who take time to listen and read, to understand the techniques involved, and practice faithfully will generally have some psychic experience within a few months. One or two of them may become very good psychics. . . ."

THE FUTURE

Today's young sensitives who are drawn to work with scientists seem increasingly interested in probing their own psychic talents in an effort to understand more profoundly the basis for their gift and the possible humanitarian benefits that might accrue through disciplined application of psi. As public interest (a fad perhaps) in the paranormal increases, there is an increasing acceptance of psychic gifts. The old question "Does ESP exist?" is yielding to "How does it work?" and even, "Can I make it work for me?" If the sensitive is losing a bit of his mystery, he is at least gaining a place in society. As Anne Armstrong, a California sensitive who specializes in psychological counseling, remarked recently at a lecture seminar at the University of California at Berkeley, "I used to be afraid to talk about these things. But now I'm *in*!"

Utimately the psychic sensitive flourishes when society approves. The very nature of his psychic development is determined in part by what society wants from him and what dovetails with the ideals, beliefs, and direction of his time. Perhaps, at last, we may be on the verge of a time when society will try to utilize its psychic sensitives to further its higher goals. This has never been done before, so it could indeed be a leap toward a utopian society. Before that could happen in even a small way, science must invest the human being with at least as much meaning as it accords its computers—for basically, psychic sensitives are human beings who can do things that no machine can. Yet sensitives are neither omniscient nor omnipotent, and they probably would be as bad as philosophers at being kings. A sensitive may be able to foretell possible futures, but the choice of them is up to society.

REFERENCES

1. Bender, H. "The Phenomena of Friedrich Jürgenson. *Journal of Paraphysics* (Paraphysics Laboratory, Downton, Wiltshire, England), 6, no. 2 (1972): 65–75.
2. Bolen, J. G. "Eileen Garrett in Interview." *Psychic*, June 1970; repr., in *Psychics*, by the Editors of *Psychic*. Harper & Row: New York, 1972.
3. Brown, S. *The Heyday of Spiritualism*. Hawthorn: New York, 1970.
4. Carington, W. W. "The Quantitative Study of Trance Personalities." *Proceedings of the Society for Psychical Research* (London), Vols. XLII, 173–240; XLIII, 319–361; XLIV, 189–222; LXV, 223–251.
5. Carrington, H. *The Case for Psychic Survival*. Citadel: New York, 1957.
6. Cayce, H. L. *Venture Inward*. Harper & Row: New York, 1966.
7. Connell, R. (pseud.). *Healing the Mind*. Psychic Book Club: London, 1957.
8. Crookes, W. "Phenomena," T. R. Tietze, ed. *Psychic*, February 1973.
9. Ebon, M. *Reincarnation in the Twentieth Century*. World: New York, 1969.
10. Eisenbud, H. J. "A Transatlantic Experiment in Precognition with Gerard Croiset." *Journal of the American Society for Psychical Research*, 67, no. 1 (1973): 1–25.
11. Ellis, D. "Tape Recordings from the Dead?" *Psychic*, February 1974.
12. Ellwood, G.-F. "The Soal-Davis-Cooper Communal 'I.'" *International Journal of Parapsychology*, 10, no. 4 (1968): 393–409.
13. Eysenck, H. J. "Levitating with the Alpha Rhythm." *Science Journal*, December 1967.
14. Fodor, N. *Encyclopedia of Psychic Science*. University Books: New Hyde Park, N.Y., 1966.
15. Kelsey, D., and Grant, J. *Many Lifetimes*. Doubleday: New York, 1967.
16. Mitchell, J. "Experiments in Out-of-Body Vision." *Psychic*, April 1973.
17. Pike, J. A. *The Other Side*. Doubleday: New York, 1966.
18. Podmore, F. *Mediums of the 19th Century*. University Books: New Hyde Park, N.Y., 1963.
19. Progoff, I. *Image of an Oracle*. Garrett: New York, 1964.
20. *Psychic* Editors. *Psychics*. Harper and Row: New York, 1972.
21. *Psychic* Editors. "Ingo Swann in Interview." *Psychic*, April 1973.
22. Raudive, K. *Breakthrough*. Taplinger: New York, 1971.
23. Ryzl, M. *How to Develop ESP in Yourself and Others*. Milan Ryzl, Box 9459, Westgate Station, San Jose, California, 1973.

24. Smith, S. *The Mediumship of Mrs. Leonard*. University Books: New Hyde Park, N.Y., 1964.
25. Spraggett, A., with W. V. Rauscher. *Arthur Ford: The Man who Talked with the Dead*. New American Library: New York, 1973.
26. Steiger, B. *The Psychic Feats of Olof Jonsson*. Prentice-Hall: Englewood Cliffs, N.J., 1972.
27. "The Magician and the Think Tank." *Time*, 12 March 1973.
28. Tietze, T. R. "Psychical Research in America: The Early Years." *Psychic*, December 1970.
29. Tietze, T. R. "Eusapia Palladino." *Psychic*, February 1972.
30. Twigg, E., with Ruth H. Brod. *Ena Twigg: Medium*. Hawthorn: New York, 1972.
31. Ullman, M., Krippner, S., and Vaughan, A. *Dream Telepathy*. Macmillan: New York, 1973.
32. Vaughan, A. "Mediumship in England Today." *Psychic*, November 1969.
33. Vaughan, A. "Development of the Psychic." *Psychic*, August 1970.
34. Vaughan, A. "Arthur Ford in Interview." *Psychic*, October 1970; repr., in *Psychics*, by the editors of *Psychic*, Harper & Row: New York, 1972.
35. Vaughan, A. "ESP Comes to Maine, and as Maine Goes . . ." *Psychic*, February 1971.
36. Vaughan, A. "The Psychical Research Foundation." *Psychic*, August 1971.
37. Vaughan, A. "Irene Hughes in Interview." *Psychic*, December 1971; repr. in *Psychics*, by the Editors of *Psychic*. Harper & Row: New York, 1972.
38. Vaughan, A. "2001: A Psychic Odyssey." *Psychic*, September 1972.
39. Vaughan, A. "The Phenomena of Uri Geller." *Psychic*, June 1973.
40. Vaughan, A. *Patterns of Prophecy*. Hawthorn: New York, 1973.

Gertrude Schmeidler

GERTRUDE SCHMEIDLER, *Ph.D., is a professor in the psychology department at City College of the City University of New York, where she has been teaching since 1946. Prior to that she held a variety of teaching and research positions at Worcester State Hospital in Massachusetts, Monmouth College, Harvard University, and the American Society for Psychical Research.*

Dr. Schmeidler earned a bachelor's degree from Smith College, a master's degree from Clark University and a doctor's degree from Radcliffe College (Harvard University). In 1964 she was awarded the William McDougall Award for distinguished work in parapsychology.

She is author of more than a hundred scientific articles and two books: ESP *(Yale University Press, 1958), which she co-authored with Robert A. McConnell, and* Extrasensory Perception *(Aldine-Atherton, 1969).*

Dr. Schmeidler can be reached at the Department of Psychology, City College of New York, 138 Street and Convent Avenue, New York, N.Y. 10031.

3   The Psychic Personality

GERTRUDE SCHMEIDLER

SUMMARY

Descriptions of the lives of some great psychics show that they share no single obvious common factor like sex, intellectual brilliance, asceticism, or spiritual devotion. This raises the problem of whether there are psychological concomitants of the psychic personality.

Research in the laboratory and observations of psychics suggest that there are. A "stilling of the mind," as in meditation, seems conducive to psychic success; the social surroundings, methods, or tasks that a person finds congenial and that relate favorably to his needs give him more success than those that make him defensive or withdrawn; and so on. As would be expected, personality traits associated with readiness to enter these favorable states also relate to psychic success. This gives solid grounds for hope that as research continues, it can predict with increasing exactitude both the conditions when a particular person will have more or less psychic success and also what particular individuals will have most success under the conditions best for them.

INTRODUCTION

What sort of people are psychics?

It's a fair question but hard to answer. The obvious ways of dividing people are no help. Psychics come male and female; young and old; rich and poor; black, yellow, brown, red, and white; bright and dull; active and passive; fat and thin; leaders and followers.

But if the obvious categories do not identify them, what about others? Perhaps they have distinctive brain areas that are structured in a certain way, special endocrine or other chemical functioning, or distinctive personality traits? To these questions all we can honestly say is, "Perhaps they do." We know nothing of psychics' brain structure or body chemistry, and about personality traits we know a little but not nearly enough. This chapter will explore the hints we have from their life histories and

94

from scattered observations that they or others have made and then try to tie that fragmentary material in with the sizable body of data on unselected subjects who tried to achieve psychic successes. The conclusions that seem most plausible can in a few cases be stated firmly, but most will be presented as hypotheses that need further research.

Let us turn to life histories first—thumbnail sketches of half a dozen of the greatest psychics.

SAMPLE LIFE HISTORIES OF PSYCHICS

St. John Bosco has been described as "the most amazing dreamer of all time" (13, p. 121). He had many prophetic or precognitive dreams and should also be classed as a medium because he reported conversations with the spirits of the dead. One small episode from his early life can show the level of his psychic ability. When he was a student, he dreamed that he was reading his next day's Latin dictation. He woke and wrote out the passage that he had dreamed. Because an earlier similar dream had been correct, he took what seemed to him the practical course of handing it in (without comment) as his Latin dictation at the end of the next day's class. The passage was entirely correct but startled his teacher, who had run out of class time and dictated only half the passage that the boy had written in its entirety.

St. John's life was passed in poverty, begging, charitable works, administration, and spiritual contemplation. It is tempting to take him as a paradigm for the psychic personality, because he fits so well the model that has come to us from Eastern mystics, that of an ascetic and meditative life, associated with great psi ability. But this will not do. It is not that easy—as the rest of the histories will show.

Emanuel Swedenborg, like St. John Bosco, was a mystic who reported many other-worldly visions (although Swedenborg's other world was so different that St. John would have classed it as heresy). The two best-known and best-authenticated of Swedenborg's many psychic experiences are extraordinarily different from each other. One came to him unbidden, and the other was a response to a direct request. The spontaneous one interrupted him while he was visiting a friend in Göteborg immediately after his return to Sweden from England. He had a vision of a great fire raging in his home city of Stockholm, more than 200 miles away. He described the progress of the fire while his vision continued, giving such circumstantial detail as the time that it was contained and the particular houses burned or spared. His report became the talk of the town. The mayor sent a special courier to Stockholm to find out if it was true, and (we are told) every detail was confirmed.

The second of these famous anecdotes concerns a widow who was being dunned for an expensive silver service. She was sure her husband had paid the bill but could not find the receipt. In desperation she turned to Swedenborg because of his psychic reputation and asked him to locate it. After three days he visited her to say that her husband's spirit had told him where the receipt was: pulling out the left drawer of an upstairs bureau would uncover a board that in turn could be pulled out to reveal a secret drawer holding correspondence containing the receipt. The widow declared that she knew nothing of any such drawer, but she and her guests naturally went upstairs with Swedenborg, went through the prescribed operations, and found the drawer, the receipt, and other correspondence within it.

Swedenborg, then, was a psychic and a mystic like St. John. But Swedenborg was also a man of the world, a busy scientist, assessor for the Swedish bureau of mines, sometimes a lobbyist for a favorite political cause, a research worker and lecturer on economics and science, dedicated to the intellectual and political, as well as the spiritual, life.

D. D. Home stands in contrast to both of the above. If he lived in our time, we would call him a member of the jet set: he was interested in women, was married, was a bon vivant who frequented the courts of kings. He was sometimes unscrupulous. He laid claim to being a medium in contact with the spirits of the dead, and there are indications that the claims were occasionally supported by veridical evidence. However, on one occasion they were so outrageously calculated to obtain money from a credulous widow that he was required to return the money by a court of law. As a physical medium, in contrast, his feats are well authenticated. William Crookes, the distinguished physicist (later Sir William), found under laboratory conditions that Home could make a lever move by merely stretching an arm in its direction, under conditions where air currents and vibration could not have made the lever move. Home was repeatedly observed to levitate, in good light and good viewing conditions; to carry burning embers without having them scorch him; to wrap them in a handkerchief and prevent their scorching the handkerchief; to be able to transfer these abilities, temporarily, to others; and to show various bizarre controls over physical objects (for example, holding a glass of fluid over his head and in some mysterious way making it empty, then having the liquid descend back into the glass and wet the fingers of an onlooker who held his hand over the glass).

Next let us look briefly at some women who were psychics. Mrs. Leonore Piper was in her time acclaimed as the greatest psychic who had ever lived. She was a blameless woman, exhaustively investigated by William James, Richard Hodgson, and many of the luminaries of the SPR and never found to have given any hint of deliberate fraud. A Boston housewife, she led the simple, secluded life expected of the virtuous Victorian matron—except for the interruptions caused by her psychic gifts. When in trance, and especially in the moments of coming out of trance, she gave extraordinarily accurate information about details of the past life of the dead and of their physical and personality characteristics and turns of speech. She also gave technical information that would have been known by them as specialists in a variety of fields but could not conceivably have been known by her. All accounts agree that she was a quiet, docile person. The kindest comment made about her intellect by those most friendly to her was that it was normal.

Mrs. Gladys Osborne Leonard was later called the greatest of all psychics. Like Mrs. Piper, she was intensively studied by the most qualified members of the SPR and by Americans and others. Detectives were sometimes employed to check on the possibility of her having used normal means to acquire her remarkable information, but no grounds for suspicion of fraud were ever uncovered. She had begun a stage career but in her middle and later years lived a quiet, contented life as an English housewife. The phenomena she produced were in general like Mrs. Piper's and also included, on occasion, the production of a voice timbre identified as that of the dead.

Her most extraordinary results included many produced under tightly controlled conditions—what we would now call "blind" conditions because the sitter (note-taker) was ignorant of facts. These facts could be about the dead who were described or about the existence of some book or notebook that Mrs. Leonard described with accurate details of location, appearance, and wording on specified pages. She seems to have been a livelier and more demanding person than Mrs. Piper but fit into a similar picture of contentment with domestic routine and cooperation with the visitors who came to her.

From these cases we might be tempted to infer an active personality for male psychics but a quiet one for females, corresponding perhaps to some sex-related hormonal differences—but we would quickly have to discard the inference because of counterexamples for both sexes. One case can illustrate this.

Mrs. Eileen Garrett was an active businesswoman and effective executive. She was also a novelist and had a richly varied social life, being charming, sophisticated, lively, capricious, and highly intelligent. Her long career as an outstanding psychic was signalized not only by mediumistic successes but also by high scores in a variety of laboratory researches (although again and again her initial extrachance scores dropped as the procedure was repeated until it lost its challenge and bored her). She could apparently work equally well in trance or out of it, and she characterized her life as a search for the meaning of mediumship. Only one incident in her long series of remarkable sittings will be cited here—one that may seem the more interesting because, in contrast to St. John Bosco's dream as a boy, it occurred when she was in her seventies and in poor health but with indomitable zest. L. L. LeShan (11), a New York psychologist, learned indirectly of a man who had vanished from a midwestern city, leaving no trace of what had become of him. Mrs. Garrett, also in New York, was given a square of cloth from one of the man's shirts. She identified him as being in La Jolla, California. It was later learned that he had indeed gone there. She also added such other details, unknown to LeShan, as that he was in his middle forties and was about 5'10" and that he had had a loss in his family between the ages of 13 and 15. Investigation showed that he was 42, 5'9", and that when he was 14 his father had deserted the family and not been heard from for 25 years. Here then was another of the great psychics, but one whose active life and sparkling personality were in marked contrast to Mrs. Piper's quiet style, whose successful long-term business career contrasted markedly with D. D. Home's drifting, and whose skepticism about the meaning of the phenomena that occurred to her was in diametric contrast to the religious certainty of St. John Bosco and Swedenborg.

What have we learned from these studies? Only that no simple description of outstanding psychics will show a common factor to explain their remarkable abilities.

RESEARCH SURVEYS OF POSSIBLE PSYCHICS

What of larger, better organized surveys than this arbitrary selection of a few individuals? Three deserve detailed attention because they were aimed at studying personality. Two that used similar samples of subjects confirm each other; the third uses a different sample and contradicts them. The contrast is especially interesting because all were conducted in the same period and the same general area: the 1950s and early 1960s in Germany and Holland.

Sannwald (21), working at Bender's laboratory in Freiburg, and Tenhaeff (28), at the University of Utrecht, report on a large number of professional psychics. Presumably all gave prima facie evidence of psychic ability, and some were tested with good success. All volunteered for the psychological investigations. Findings were based on interviews and especially on data from a long battery of such tests as the Rorschach. Both Sannwald and Tenhaeff report that these psychics showed so much commonality as to justify general conclusions about their personality. The psychics were strongly extrovert, imaginative, and sensitive to external stimuli. They tended to be hysterical as opposed to neurasthenic (i. e., dissociated rather than obsessive-compulsive), to identify too readily with the persons around them, to be inadequate in will, and to have "disintegrative personalities."

What have we here? These indecisive, disintegrative persons sound most unlike St. John Bosco (who was for many years the successful administrator of a large grammar and technical school that he had founded). They are certainly unlike Swedenborg, whose laboratory studies of such wide-ranging problems as characteristics of metals and brain activity in relation to blood circulation were scientific landmarks. Neither do they resemble Mrs. Garrett, with her long continued executive success nor the sedate and self-contained lives of Mrs. Piper and Mrs. Leonard. Many other counterexamples come quickly to mind, such as Mrs. Willett, who was not only a carefully investigated and highly gifted sensitive but also a magistrate and Great Britain's representative to the League of Nations at the height of its prestige.

On the other hand, the Sannwald and Tenhaeff descriptions are based on careful testing, are statistically sound, and offer independent replication of earlier research conducted in Bender's laboratory with similar population and procedure. With so many strong counterexamples, we cannot accept any one of them as a general description of the psychic personality, but neither can we brush them aside.

A clue to the discrepancy comes from psychological research. If two projects give unlike findings when they are expected to confirm each other, the reason is often that they sampled different populations of subjects. For example, college sophomores in New York City, on the one hand, and, on the other, sophomores at the University of Texas, whose achievement goals and social responses are not in general alike. We can look at the special population sample of Sannwald and Tenhaeff and try to characterize it. Common factors immediately appear: the period; the area; the fact that these were self-proclaimed psychics not rigorously screened for ability in all cases; their being volunteers for psychological testing; and especially their being professionals who gave psychic sittings.

The earlier items on the list seem uninteresting. We may disregard the lack of rigorous screening on the assumption that Bender, Tenhaeff, and their professional associates had such wide prior experience that they were likely to spot and then exclude the frauds. We can presume that the greater part of their groups, if not necessarily every individual, had more marked psychic ability than is common. The place and time similarly seem unimportant (although the social climate may have been more favorable to psychic claims in central Europe during the post–World War II period than is usual in the West). The fact that they volunteered for psychological testing? Perhaps; other research indicates that volunteers are more open and usually more neurotic or more troubled about themselves than nonvolunteers. The fact that they gave sittings professionally? This seems to be a clue.

A key observation comes from a psychiatrist, O. L. Trick, who studied two American professional psychics, using psychological tests and interviews (29). He found both to be competent and well adjusted but markedly "field-dependent"—perceiving in a global rather than a differentiated way, oriented toward context and social settings, and especially responsive to other persons. He suggests that among all those with psychic gifts, the career choice of becoming a professional psychic might be decided by the field-dependence–independence factor. Someone who was field-dependent would find great satisfaction in the warm, emotional response that sitters can give.

This seems insightful. We can take it to say that, among all possible psychics, Sannwald and Tenhaeff were testing the more field-dependent ones. The traits they found fall neatly in line with other data on field-dependent individuals who in many independent studies are shown to be more responsive to social warmth, more extrovert, more likely to hallucinate under conditions of sensory deprivation, more hysterical (as opposed to neurasthenic), and so on than the field-independent. We should infer, I think, that the Sannwald and Tenhaeff conclusions apply only to one special subclass of psychics—as biased a sample as if they had tested only the most dominant or the most submissive.

The third large-scale survey is consistent with this interpretation. A questionnaire about psychic experiences was distributed in Amsterdam to a very large number of respondents, and Greiner (7) selected for testing 21 who reported strong, frequent experiences; 21 who reported none; and another random sample of 21. The extensive test battery overlapped with that of the previous workers and included the major test of field-dependence–independence. No difference between groups was found.

THE DEFINITION OF "PSYCHICS"

Greiner's work forcibly raises the problem of definition of terms. Do we restrict the word *psychic* to individuals who have been critically studied and authenticated as having frequently given clear evidence of ESP or PK? (If so, how often is "frequent"? What are our criteria for "clear evidence"?) Or should we also include those who have had one or two extraordinary and authenticated experiences? Or those who have had very frequent but minor ones? Or those who seem to have had such experiences if we trust their reports and those of their associates but who have not been critically examined?

We might say that the dimension of psychic ability is anchored at both ends. One anchor is the authenticated psychics, like Mrs. Leonard or Basil Shackleton, who have been studied for long periods under well-controlled conditions and have shown great success. The other anchor is the class of individuals that can be defined in theory but has never been reported to exist, those who both say they have had no psychic experiences and show only chance results in extensive laboratory testing. Should we try to study only those two clear extremes and look for differences between them? Or should we infer (from dozens of experiments with unselected subjects that have given affirmative ESP results) that most of the world lies between the two—then set up criteria that permit us to study large numbers of subjects?

Consider the theoretical implications of the two choices. One possibility is that the true psychic is qualitatively different. There is precedent in psychology for this possibility. Some few adults have such extremely strong imagery that their "eidetic" images give them new, accurate information about what they have seen or heard. There seems a sharp break between them and the rest of the population, whose imagery may be rather good or rather poor but in either case tells nothing except what is already known. People who are lightning calculators may be another example of such a two-category division into those who can and those who cannot. If this is true, we should look for one set of descriptors for the true psychic and then (if it interests us) also look for other factors that correlate with stronger or weaker psychic ability in the general population.

The other possibility is that there is a continuous range in psychic ability. This is the finding for most characteristics. In creativity, for example, one end of the spectrum would be represented by the greatest geniuses and the other by those with some tendency toward creativity, or perhaps none. If there is a spectrum of psychic ability, we can look for some personality factors that correlate with it along its entire length. This would parallel the findings in creativity research, where the personality traits of the more creative among unselected high school students are remarkably similar to the personality traits of carefully selected groups of creative adults.

The only good way to resolve the theoretical issue and to hammer out an adequate definition of a psychic is to do more research. We need two strategies: full personality studies of the best, authenticated psychics to see what commonality they show and comparable studies of others for whom we have ESP or PK scores. If the two sets of findings mesh, we accept the second possibility above, a continuous range in psychic ability. If they are discrepant, we accept the first (a qualitative difference). We may find the sharp break between psychics and others that lets us conclude we are studying two kinds of people; but if we do not, we may end by concluding that it is as odd to call someone "a psychic" as to call him "a creative." In that case, we should distinguish only degrees or subtypes of an ability common to all or nearly all. Because most psychological traits seem to show a continuous distribution, let us tentatively take as a working hypothesis that psychic ability is also continuously distributed.

CORRELATES OF PSYCHIC ABILITY: PERSONALITY TRAITS

An excellent start has been made on studying personality correlates of ESP scores in the general population; in fact, there are so many research reports that it is impossible to cite even a fair sample of the best. Early studies showed significant association between good ESP scores and spontaneity (22), extroversion (8), and good social adjustment (24). Other studies show a relation between low ESP scores and such traits as being withdrawn (26) or defensive (9). One recent report (10) offers a good summary listing of most of the traits proposed in prior studies (Table 1)—although we need to bear in mind as we read it that it applies to the special demands of laboratory or classroom testing.

TABLE 1

LIST OF PERSONALITY TENDENCIES ASSOCIATED WITH ESP SCORES
IN INDIAN HIGH SCHOOL STUDENTS

Positive ESP Scores (psi-hitting)	Negative ESP Scores (psi-missing)
warm, sociable	tense
good-natured, easygoing	excitable
assertive, self-assured	frustrated
tough	demanding
enthusiastic	impatient
talkative	dependent
cheerful	sensitive
quick, alert	timid
adventuresome, impulsive	threat-sensitive
emotional	shy
carefree	withdrawn
realistic, practical	submissive
relaxed	suspicious
composed	depression-prone

Source. Adapted from Kanthamani and Rao (10).

Eysenck, a distinguished psychologist, has put forth the simplest generalization about the psychic personality (4). He surveyed a large number of experiments, then proposed the hypothesis that extroversion was the major determinant of psychic success. Extroversion, as he thinks of it, is measured by questionnaires or certain perception and learning tests. It represents a pervasive tendency toward a high ratio of neural inhibition to excitation and affects not only social behavior, learning, and perception but also is associated with hysterical, as opposed to neurasthenic, tendencies. His clear statement has naturally prompted others to include extroversion tests in their batteries, with mixed results. No experimenter found a 1:1 relation between ESP scores and questionnaire scores for extroversion; some found no relation. Typical results show a small positive association, indicating that it is only a minor predictor of ESP success.

Some fragmentary data of my own look more promising but are too scanty to depend on. Instead of a questionnaire, I used a short perceptual measure that had previously been shown to tie in with extroversion and gave this behavioral test to the three authenticated psychics available to me. All three gave such extreme scores in the extrovert direction that they almost lie outside the normal distribution. This and the mildly encouraging questionnaire data make me think that Eysenck's hypothesis deserves further study.

Another factor seems basically important in psychic personality traits, one that Eysenck might consider only a variant of extroversion but that most of us would describe in other words. It has not been identified as a psychological test score, although perhaps it is the opposite of rigidity. I think of it as lability (adaptability) or as labile openness. Various tests like the Rorschach or the sensation-seeking scales give scores that could contribute to it. Let me describe it at more length.

Some people seem in their thinking or in the way they look at things to give a clear response and then stay with it. Others shift readily: they let some concept or point of view merge with another or give way to another, and—at that moment—are unconcerned about discrepancies. This latter tendency, the readiness to accept incoming impressions without critical censorship, is what I am proposing as an important component of psychic ability. It is probably very close to hypnotizability or to what Murphy has called a tendency to dissociation (14). My guess is that many of the people who are very high in this factor later integrate their various impressions, so that they end up with a single firm, clear result. This means that examining only the end result—the simplicity and decisiveness of final action, for example—will not tell us whether a labile openness to new impressions was present before the decision.

TRAITS VERSUS STATES

Has this discussion given the impression that psychic ability was constant in a person from time to time and that a single score could represent it? Or that personality traits were consistent over time and that each trait could be represented by a single score? If so, consider it only an attempt to write straightforwardly in a complicated area, which led to oversimplifying, for in my opinion neither is true. Test–retest data bear out my skepticism because personality measures are notorious for their low reliability and even the best psychic is not successful in every session.

But does this imply that neither the personality nor the ESP (or PK) measures can be meaningful? Many of us think just the opposite. One example may serve to make the point. Suppose we develop a test to measure the tendency toward cheerfulness. We administer the test twice to see if it is self-consistent. The first time that we give it to a particular high school girl, she happens to be at ovulation in her menstrual cycle; her parents have just approved of her buying a new dress because yesterday the young man she likes best invited her to the most important dance of the year; and immediately before our test she received an A for an examination in her hardest course. The time of the second test happens to come just before her menstruation and on a day when she has had a series of snubs and rebuffs. Surely the cheerfulness test will yield different scores even if she is an outstandingly cheerful person, and tests of adventuresomeness, aggression, or need for achievement could be expected to vary too. Low self-consistency or reliability may mean high validity.

To put the point another way, a single personality-test score or ESP score gives a sample of the range within which a person varies. The state a person is in, as well as the general strength of his traits or abilities, helps determine the single score. Both trait and state need to be specified.

Sometimes the lack of reliability may make research results turn out better than they "should," and this is especially true of personality data. If scores on both a personality measure and ESP are raised (or lowered) by a certain mood, then *when both tests are given in the same session*, the two scores will vary together. A natural inference is that the trait itself is related to ESP scoring. But this would be disconfirmed by research that administers the tests at widely separated times. Moods need study too, and such procedural details as the timing of tests need specification.

CORRELATES OF PSYCHIC ABILITY:
MOODS AND STATES OF CONSCIOUSNESS

Little space will be given here to the important topic of altered states of consciousness, because it is treated elsewhere in this book (see Chapter 27). Briefly, many psychics find it necessary or helpful to go into trance for their psychic impressions; and hypnotic trance, with appropriate suggestions, seems to facilitate ESP success. Other psychics use such forms of dissociation as automatic writing or use a perceptual prop to absorb their attention, such as a crystal ball or its currently more fashionable equivalent, the Tarot cards. Many do not, and few or no systematic comparisons have been made. Perhaps the best summary comes from White (30), who suggests after studying many psychics that there are four major steps in the psychic process: relaxation; engaging the conscious mind (i. e., "stilling" the mind); waiting and tension; and release when the desired impression enters consciousness. Another hint of what is involved comes from the psychics, who tell us that they first found going into trance helped them but that later trance was unnecessary. This implies that the shift from a normal to a paranormal mode of perception can with practice come more readily and require fewer preliminaries.

Trance shows many resemblances to meditation, and recent studies indicate that subjects who meditate in order to enhance their ESP tend to make high ESP scores immediately after meditation (1, 2). Since it has been established that meditation is accompanied by physiological changes, this offers interesting openings for new research on physiological and mood changes in relation to ESP.

Moods vary, and everyone from psychics to experimenters says that ESP success tends to vary correspondingly. Little systematic work has been done under the appropriate double blind conditions to study them. (It is no aid to research to have a person learn he failed and *then* announce that the mood was wrong!)

An early careful study to investigate moods and ESP (6) found pleasurable moods associated with higher ESP scores than unpleasurable moods. But before we agree with that, let us consider the data of another study, which found ESP scores higher with intensely pleasant or unpleasant moods than with everyday, reasonably contented ones (15). If, as before, we look to see who the subjects were in these two projects, which apparently contradict each other, we find that the many subjects in the first one were randomly selected but that the few subjects in the second one were deeply involved in parapsychology. The data no longer seem contradictory. How a task relates to one's interests and values will determine whether unhappiness mobilizes or dissipates attention to that task. In our worst moods, working at something we care about may be a refuge and solace; something we care less about is likely to be a nuisance and thus be rejected.

Osis and Bokert in a meditation experiment (16) found self-transcendence and openness related in complex ways to ESP scores. In a somewhat different experiment, Osis, Turner, and Carlson found relaxation related to scoring (17). Recently some co-workers and I found evidence that the favorable moods for ESP success depend upon the situation one is in (25). We were able to predict the favorable moods for ESP only by using a pretest to hand-tailor a hypothesis for a particular group and then a retest. Rogers (20) and others have found in an impressive series of experiments that as moods become livelier the ESP score variance seems to increase (high variance represents high scores or low scores or both, in contrast to middling scores). There are complex relationships here worth studying.

Perhaps the most incisive research on moods is still waiting to be done: identifying the factors that make moods change and then studying the effect of those factors on performance.

CORRELATES OF PSYCHIC ABILITY: NEEDS AND ATTITUDES

Needs and attitudes affect psi performance in both global and specific ways. Neureiter's Ilga K., a feeble-minded child unable to read normally, showed in careful tests conducted first by Neureiter and then by Bender that she could read telepathically when her excitable mother, placed in a sound-shielded room, sent urgent "messages" about the correct words (3). Instance after instance demonstrates that high motivation relates to more ESP or PK activation than does low motivation. The point is well made in other chapters and will not be further elaborated here.

When we ask which specific needs make motivation high, the answer will surely vary with the situation, the individual, and the society in which he was reared. Suppose that a child's parents and all others important to him discourage his reports of ESP. Strong needs for conformity will then work against psychic performance. In a social setting where ESP is taken for granted, needs for conformity and affiliation will work for it. Specifics are likely to be found only when there is careful attention to the individual case.

An example of such attention comes from Gerard Croiset, a psychic studied by Tenhaeff for many years. Tenhaeff (27) reports that Croiset was most likely to locate a missing person or help solve a crime when there was some involvement with a grocery or with a maltreated child, because Croiset had worked in a grocery and had been bereft and beaten when he was a boy. Many psychics fail with impersonal material like ESP cards but show success with material that involves human beings. Mrs. Chapman, whose normal perception showed brilliant analysis of small detail but weak integration of broad generalities, expressed the same tendencies in absent sittings (23) with significant success on small details related to the absent sitters but only chance scores in general comments about them. Some psychics respond to light, fire, radiance; some to money; some to anguish; some to events in the future that concern them.

Data from unselected subjects show the same pattern strongly. Fisk and West (5) describe a unique case of a man whose ESP scores were near chance with ESP cards, except for the circle and cross, on which his scores were high. When questioned, he said that he saw them as erotic symbols, with the circle representing the female and the cross, the male (the classic Freudian pattern). In a check-up series the other targets were left unchanged, but the circle and cross were redrawn to have clearer sexual denotation. The man again scored near chance on each of the other symbols but above chance on the erotic ones (with odds of more than 100,000:1 for the female symbol and about 100:1 for the male). Rao (19) summarizes a long series of experiments on the issue of systematic score patterns and shows that when subjects respond to two types of concealed targets or have two modes of responding (e.g., speaking or writing), the ESP scores are different for the two types.

Usually, as would be expected, scores are significantly higher with the preferred targets (although there is some provocative evidence that if the whole setting is unpleasant, the result reverses—a sort of double negative effect).

By now, of course, we are discussing both needs and attitudes. The relation is a complex one, but we have made a beginning toward teasing out the strands. In general, for example, a person whose attitude toward ESP is unfavorable and who thinks he has no possibility of success at his task will score lower than someone who considers success to be possible (18). However, some subjects who strongly need to avoid failure seem to make low scores if they state success is possible and then higher ones when they state that no one can succeed. It is perhaps some such combination of patterns that makes the "tough" and self-assertive subjects in Table 1 score better than the timid and sensitive. In a setting where different needs are elicited, we might expect different traits associated with psi-hitting.

The general finding that has emerged again and again is that it is the subject's feeling about the method and the materials, not the objective condition, that determines ESP success. Some people work better with male and others with female experimenters; some when they feel the personal warmth of a telepathic agent and others with the safe detachment of clairvoyance or precognition; some with the challenge of a new procedure and others with the reassurance of what is familiar.

The acid test of such generalizations is whether we can use them to predict behavior, and recently an increasing number of successful experiments have shown that we can. A neat example comes from McBain et al. (12), who selected subjects interested in ESP and high in hypnotic suggestibility, and before each session gave posthypnotic suggestions for good scoring. A key part of the procedure, the relevant part in this context, is that they pretested each subject for emotional reactions toward over 20 concepts like sex, money, peace, friendship, and death and then matched as sender and receiver those with similar reactions, using as ESP targets for each pair the concepts toward which the subjects had similar feelings. Results showed overall ESP success, especially marked for like-sex pairs and for those who were stronger in hypnotic suggestibility. This indicates, as do many other recent researches, that we are on the right track. If we set up conditions based on prior findings, the results are likely to fall into line.

OVERVIEW

Personality factors, from traits and states to needs and preferences, seem to tie in closely with psychic performance. Enough has been done to give us a few clear findings and many plausible hypotheses. We have made a beginning. But we need more research, more testing out of hypotheses, to trace the interactions of the separate factors.

Perhaps our best working hypothesis is that psychic ability, like color vision or intelligence or muscular coordination, varies from high to low in the population and is released or inhibited or misdirected by personality factors. This gives us two directives: to find the concomitants of psychic ability per se and to identify for each person the factors that release or inhibit it for him.

REFERENCES

1. Braud, W. G. "Preliminary Exploration of Psi-Conducive States: Progressive Muscular Relaxation." *Journal of the American Society for Psychical Research*, 67 (1973): 26–46.
2. Breitstein, H. "Meditation and ESP." M. A. thesis, City College of New York, 1972.
3. Ehrenwald, J. "Telepathy and the Child-Parent Relationship." *Journal of the American Society for Psychical Research*, 48 (1954): 43–55.

4. Eysenck, H. J. "Personality and Extra-Sensory Perception." *Journal of the Society for Psychical Research*, 44 (1969).

5. Fisk, G. W., and West, D. J. "ESP Tests with Erotic Symbols." *Journal of the Society for Psychical Research*, 38 (1955): 1–7.

6. Fisk, G. W., and West, D. J. "ESP and Mood: Report of a 'Mass' Experiment." *Journal of the Society for Psychical Research*, 38 (1956): 320–329.

7. Greiner, R. P. "An Investigation into the Personality Traits of People with So-called Spontaneous Paranormal Phenomena." *Journal of Parapsychology*, 28 (1964): 284 (abstract).

8. Humphrey, B. M. "Introversion-Extroversion Ratings in Relation to Scores in ESP Tests." *Journal of Parapsychology*, 15 (1951): 252–262.

9. Johnson, M. "The Psi Research Project at Lund University." *Journal of Parapsychology*, 28 (1964): 296 (abstract).

10. Kanthamani, B. K., and Rao, K. R. "Personality Characteristics of ESP Subjects: II. The Combined Personality Measure (CPM) and ESP." *Journal of Parapsychology*, 36 (1972): 56–70.

11. LeShan, L. L. "The Vanished Man: A Psychometry Experiment with Mrs. Garrett." *Journal of the American Society for Psychical Research*, 62 (1968): 46–62.

12. McBain, W. N.; Fox, W.; Kimura, S.; Nakanishi, M.; and Tirado, J. "Quasi-Sensory Communication: An Investigation Using Semantic Matching and Accentuated Affect." *Journal of Personality and Social Psychology*, 14 (1970): 281–291.

13. Meseguer, P. *The Secret of Dreams.* Newman: Westminster, Md., 1961.

14. Murphy, G. "Research in Creativeness: What Can It Tell Us about Extra-sensory Perception?" *Journal of the American Society for Psychical Research*, 60 (1966): 8–22.

15. Nielsen, W. "Mental States Associated with Success in Precognition." *Journal of Parapsychology*, 20 (1956): 96–109.

16. Osis, K., and Bokert, E. "ESP and Changed States of Consciousness Induced by Meditation." *Journal of the American Society for Psychical Research*, 65 (1971): 17–65.

17. Osis, K.; Turner, Jr., M. E.; and Carlson, M. L. "ESP Over Distance: Research on the ESP Channel." *Journal of the American Society for Psychical Research*, 65 (1971): 245–289.

18. Palmer, J. "Scoring in ESP Tests as a Function of Belief in ESP. Part I. The Sheep-Goat Effect." *Journal of the American Society for Psychical Research*, 65 (1971): 373–408.

19. Rao, K. R. "The Bidirectionality of Psi." *Journal of Parapsychology*, 29 (1965): 230–250.

20. Rogers, D. P. "Negative and Positive Effect and ESP Run-Score Variance. Study II." *Journal of Parapsychology*, 31 (1967): 290–296.

21. Sannwald, G. "Beziehungen zwischen parapsychischen Erlebnissen und Persönlichkeitsmerkmalen." *Zeitschrift für Parapsychologie und Grenzgebiete der Psychologie*, 5 (1962): 81–119.

22. Scherer, W. B. "Spontaneity as a Factor in ESP." *Journal of Parapsychology*, 12 (1948): 126–147.

23. Schmeidler, G. R. "Analysis and Evaluation of Proxy Sessions with Mrs. Caroline Chapman." *Journal of Parapsychology*, 22 (1958): 137–155.

24. Schmeidler, G. R. *ESP in Relation to Rorschach Test Evaluation.* Para-psychological Monographs, Parapsychology Foundation: New York, 1960.

25. Schmeidler, G. R., and Craig, J. G. "Moods and ESP Scores in Group

Testing." *Journal of the American Society for Psychical Research*, 66 (1972): 280–287.
26. Shields, E. "Comparison of Children's Guessing Ability (ESP) with Personality Characteristics." *Journal of Parapsychology*, 26 (1962): 200–210.
27. Tenhaeff, W. H. C. "Aid to the Police." *Tomorrow*, 2 (1953): 10–18.
28. Tenhaeff, W. H. C. "Summary of the Results of a Psychodiagnostic Investigation of Forty Paragnosts." *Proceedings of the Parapsychological Institute of the State University of Utrecht*, No. 2 (1962).
29. Trick, O. L. "Psychological Studies of Two 'Mediums.'" *Journal of Parapsychology*, 30 (1966): 301–302 (abstract).
30. White, R. A. "A Comparison of Old and New Methods of Response to Targets in ESP Experiments." *Journal of the American Society for Psychical Research*, 58 (1964): 21–56.

Stanley Krippner

STANLEY KRIPPNER, Ph.D., is senior research associate for education and training in the Division of Parapsychology and Psychophysics at Maimonides Medical Center in Brooklyn, New York. From 1964 he was director of the Dream Laboratory there. He is also director of research for the New York Institute of Child Development, a position he has held since 1968. Additionally, he holds adjunct and visiting professorships at Humanistic Psychology Institute, California State College at Sonoma, and the University of Puerto Rico. From 1966 to 1972 he was lecturer in the graduate school of Wagner College, Staten Island, New York. Prior to that he was director of the Child Study Center at Kent State University in Kent, Ohio.

Dr. Krippner obtained his doctorate in 1961 at Northwestern University. He is a fellow of the American Society of Clinical Hypnosis, and has chaired the first three International Conferences on Humanistic Psychology, beginning in 1970. In 1972 he chaired the first western hemisphere conference on acupuncture, Kirlian photography, and the human aura. Subsequently he co-edited the proceedings as Galaxies of Life (Gordon and Breach, 1972) and The Kirlian Aura (Anchor, 1974).

With his colleagues at the Dream Laboratory, Dr. Montague Ullman and Mr. Charles Honorton, Dr. Krippner pioneered the study of telepathic dreaming. In 1972 the National Institute of Mental Health awarded the laboratory a two-year grant to continue the research. Dr. Krippner and Dr. Ullman reported the work at length in Telepathy and Dreams (Parapsychology Foundation, 1970) and more recently in Dream Telepathy (Macmillan, 1973), co-authored with Montague Ullman and Alan Vaughan. Dr. Krippner's 200 articles have appeared in psychological, psychiatric, and educational journals.

Dr. Krippner can be reached at Maimonides Medical Center, Division of Parapsychology and Psychophysics, 4802 Tenth Avenue, Brooklyn, N.Y. 11219.

4 Telepathy

STANLEY KRIPPNER

The authenticity of this phenomenon can no longer be disputed today. I have found by experience that telepathy does, in fact, influence dreams, as has been asserted since ancient times. . . . I would not, of course, assert that the law behind them is anything 'supernatural,' but merely something which we cannot get at with our present knowledge.

C. G. JUNG, 1960

SUMMARY

Telepathy is one manifestation of the collective phenomena that parapsychologists refer to as ESP. It involves information received by a subject (percipient, recipient, or receiver) from an agent (transmitter or sender), apparently through some type of "mind-to-mind" contact. It is differentiated from "clairvoyance," in which objects rather than thoughts are perceived extrasensorially; however, some parapsychologists suggest that telepathy is basically clairvoyant perception of another person's neural processes. When the investigation of telepathy moved from the anecdotal and clinical level to the experimental level, such phenomena as the "decline effect," "the sheep–goat effect," and the "differential effect" were noted. These effects, as well as variables involving subjects, agents, targets, and setting, have led to a number of theoretical positions on the nature of telepathy. Some writers postulate wave transmission; others speak of interpersonal "resonance" or "psychic fields." In any event, the role of telepathy in affecting human behavior needs further exploration, as it may be more influential than is commonly suspected.

INTRODUCTION

In 1879, Sir John Drummond Hay, who was for many years Queen Victoria's minister to Morocco, awakened upon hearing his daughter-in-law's anguished voice crying, "Oh, I wish papa only knew that Robert is ill." A few minutes later, Sir John heard the same remark. He recorded the event in his diary, although he did not believe in telepathic dreams. Furthermore, his son, who lived 300 miles away, had been in good health at the time of their last communication. Later, Sir John discovered that his son had been stricken with typhoid fever and that his daughter-in-law had repeated the phrase, "Oh, I wish papa only knew that Robert is ill." This happened the very night that Sir John was awakened by the voice (48).

This type of report can be found in all societies and at any point in history. These experiences are described in Taoist writings, the Hindu Vedas, Buddhist sutras, Judeo-Christian scripture, Greek and Roman records, and folk tales from American Indian and African cultures. The word most commonly applied to this phenomenon is *telepathy* (from the Greek roots *tēle*, or "distant," and *pathe*, or "feeling," "occurrence"). Another current term, used primarily by Soviet researchers, is *biocommunication*. In both instances, reference is being made to one of several manifestations of ESP (the others being precognition, retrocognition, and clairvoyance). In telepathy, a person is apparently aware of the mental imagery, thoughts, or feelings of another person, even though the distance between them is so great that ordinary sensory communication is not possible. These experiences have gradually woven their way into the fabric of scientific investigation as well as the tapestry of mythology, folk literature, and legend.

EARLY INVESTIGATIONS

In the middle of the eighteenth century, Mesmer used steel magnets to treat illness. His "magnetotherapy" was based on an elaborate theory of "animal magnetism," involving a "universal fluid" felt to join all living things. Telepathy and other forms of psi purportedly occurred during "mesmeric sleep" and were thought to be inseparable from it. Later, Mesmer found that he could induce this type of sleep (later called "hypnosis," or "great sleep") without magnets.

Still later, Charles Richet, a Nobel Prize–winning French physiologist, demonstrated that telepathy could occur apart from hypnosis. Richet (58) was the first scientist to apply statistics to telepathy data. Another French investigator, Pierre Janet, induced hypnosis at a distance, presumably through a telepathic signal. Janet feared to publish a report, knowing that his colleagues would disapprove and that his professional reputation would suffer.

Similar telepathy–hypnosis experiments were carried out in England by Gilbert Murray and by Henry Sidgwick, who also introduced statistical analysis to these types of data. In these tests, the hypnotist visualized randomly selected two-digit numbers and telepathically "sent" them to a hypnotized subject in another room. The results were better than could have been expected by chance (42), and Sidgwick (70) presented a historic report on the experiment. Another researcher, Sir William Barrett, read a paper on telepathy to the British Association for the Advancement of Science in 1876, describing how the experimenter induced a hypnotized subject to have tastes and smells that the experimenter was experiencing at a distance. The association refused to publish the paper (3).

One of the SPR's founders, Frederic W. H. Myers, coined the word *telepathy* to describe the extrasensory perception of another person's mental activities. Another SPR member, Sir Oliver Lodge, had become interested in telepathy as a young man and initiated a series of studies in which he attempted to communicate with friends or relatives who were deceased.

During the last part of the nineteenth century and the first quarter of the twentieth century, both the SPR and the ASPR stressed the study of mediumistic phenomena, postmortem survival, and spontaneous cases (e.g., 19). However, there were occasional analyses of telepathic reports (e.g., 3).

René Warcollier (76) initiated a series of attempts to transmit a pictorial impression from one person (the agent, transmitter, or sender) to another person (the subject, receiver, recipient, or percipient). Although no statistical evaluation was attempted, some provocative results were obtained, one of which follows (76, pp. 25–28):

> In one experiment, the object was presented to the agent. . . . The object was the lower jawbone of a woman found in the crypts of St. Etienne du Mont. . . . She felt the object and said, "Horns of a little deer. . . . It is a stag's horn." . . . In a room at a distance . . . , R. W. . . . drew a tined *pitchfork*, a *claw*, and antlers. . . . The thought provoked by mistaken interpretation . . . was transmitted, while the actual object, and what the experimenter knew about it, were not transmitted.

In this example, one can notice the possible role played by the percipient's intent. Had clairvoyance been operating, perhaps the object would have been perceived as a jawbone instead of as a pair of antlers. If the percipient had been concentrating on the experimenter (who knew the identity of the bone), perhaps the jawbone would have been directly perceived. Instead, the percipient apparently focused upon the agent; in so doing, the agent's mistaken interpretation of the jawbone was perceived rather than the jawbone itself.

A similar series of tests was carried out by Upton Sinclair (64), whose wife served as percipient for telepathy experiments. The transmitter, in these studies, would draw a design, which Mrs. Sinclair would attempt to receive. Of the 290 attempts by his wife, Sinclair rated 23% hits, 53% partial hits, and 24% failures. The sessions were not always carefully controlled, and the subjective judging did not utilize a statistical analysis. Nevertheless, the correspondences between the pictures sent and the pictures received are often remarkable, as when Mrs. Sinclair drew a knight's helmet in exactly the same format as it was transmitted.

An experiment conducted by H. I. F. W. Brugmans (6) attempted to incorporate statistical controls into a telepathy test. The target material involved a checkerboard with 48 squares in which the horizontal direction gave the letters $A–H$, and the vertical direction the numbers 1–6. A square (e.g., B_2, D_5) was selected by randomly pulling a letter from one bag and a number from another; three agents (in a room that was directly above the percipient and that contained a double-glazed aperture) took turns attempting to influence the percipient to select the designated square. The percipient was blindfolded and seated in a shielded cubicle; a slit permitted his hand to move on the board and select the square he thought had been designated. The results were highly significant; in a total of 187 trials, the subject correctly indicated the square 60 times, while coincidence would have enabled him to succeed 5 times.

Whatley Carington (7) also applied statistical techniques to a telepathy test. Carington's usual procedure was to open a large dictionary at random, select the first word that could be embodied in a drawing, and make the drawing. By prearrangement with his subjects (who were generally scattered throughout England), he would receive the perceived impressions within a certain time period. He evaluated the results by looking over all the guesses made by all the percipients, giving a certain amount of "credit" for each item. The rarer items received more credit than the common items; thus, if an albatross was transmitted and received, more credit would accrue to the matching than if a more common item (e.g., cat) had been reported. Although this procedure was an important contribution to telepathy research, it lacked precision; the subjects did not always concentrate at a prearranged time, and the judging was not done blind," with the evaluator being unaware of the target word used to elicit particular responses.

PARAPSYCHOLOGY AT DUKE UNIVERSITY

The experimental investigation of psi changed dramatically when J. B. Rhine and Louisa E. Rhine were encouraged to study telepathy, clairvoyance, and related areas at Duke University by William McDougall in 1930. The Rhines decided to use 5 symbols in a deck of 25 cards, each deck containing 5 of these symbols (circles, squares, stars, crosses, wavy lines). Thus, each experiment involves one chance in five of getting a given trial right if nothing but guessing is involved (52). Controls were eventually built into the experiment to avoid sensory cues (e.g., placing the cards in opaque envelopes, putting the agent and the subject in separate rooms).

A series of 25 trials in an ESP test was referred to as a *run*, while a successful trial was a *hit*. Five hits per run was the *mean chance expectation* per run. When the expected number of hits in a given series of trials is subtracted from the actually observed number of hits, the deviation is obtained. Statistical methods were then used to determine the probability that a deviation would occur by chance (44, pp. 22–48; 52).

Using these techniques, J. B. Rhine (50) found eight subjects who fairly consistently made hits that exceeded the mean chance expectation. In the total of 85,724 ESP trials he conducted with them, they obtained 24,364 hits—that is, 7219 more hits than expected by chance.

An admitted skeptic, S. G. Soal obtained nonsignificant results when he tested 160 subjects at London University in an attempt to disprove Rhine's experiments. At this point, Soal was informed by Whatley Carington of the displacement effect—the tendency of some subjects to respond to a target for either the forthcoming or the previous call. On rechecking his data, Soal discovered that two of his percipients were remarkably successful in guessing the next card to be looked at by the agent. Soal then attempted to learn whether one of these subjects, Basil Shackleton, would continue to respond successfully to the card next to the target card.

Soal's experiments were similar to Rhine's except that his cards were printed with animal figures: elephants, giraffes, lions, pelicans, and zebras (65). Shackleton was in one room, the agent was in another room; there was an experimenter with both of them. The trials were carefully synchronized; various outside observers were invited to oversee the experiments to insure that no errors of recording or falsification of the records took place. The experiments demonstrated Shackleton's ability to identify the card immediately following the target card, a skill sometimes referred to as *precognitive telepathy*. In one of the experiments, Shackleton obtained 1101 hits in 3789 trials on the next card; the expected number of hits was 776.

The Soal experiments were hailed by G. Evelyn Hutchinson (23) as the most carefully conducted investigations of their kind ever to have been made. J. B. Rhine (51, p. 59) spoke of the experiment with approval, comparing it favorably with the best of the Duke experiments. C. E. M. Hansel (20, pp. 111–124), however, suggested a number of ways in which the percipient, agent, and experimenters could have altered the results through fraud.

Hansel (20, pp. 63–64) also criticized a telepathy study carried out by B. F. Riess (59). Riess exposed ESP cards at an appointed hour, noting their order. The subject, one-quarter of a mile distant, recorded her guesses on a record sheet. Through a series of 74 runs, the recipient averaged 18 hits per 25 guesses instead of the 5 hits one would expect through chance. Hansel's criticism was that Riess kept his records in an unlocked drawer and did not receive the subject's records until the following day; thus, the records were easily accessible to anyone in the house. It should be noted that Riess (59) himself wrote, "In view of the many uncontrolled factors, the data as presented are to be thought of as suggestive only."

Hansel (20, pp. 129–152) made his most serious charges in the case of Glyn and Ievan Jones, two boys tested by Soal and Bowden (66). Using several varieties of ESP cards, both telepathy and clairvoyance tests were attempted, with the overall results surpassing chance levels. Hansel noted, however, that the boys' best scores were made when they could see each other and that their scores were less impressive when all sensory cues were eliminated. Describing one experiment, Hansel (20, p. 133) writes:

At the first sitting, Glyn made high scores in the first 3 runs of 25 guesses and scored at the chance level during the next 3 runs after he was moved just out of alignment with Ievan through the open doorway. During subsequent tests, it was found that on occasions when the boys were out of alignment with one another or when the door was shut, scores were always at the chance level.

Other criticisms of telepathy experiments have come from Joseph Jastrow (24), who explained the phenomenon on the basis of "muscle-reading," "involuntary whispering," and outright deception. Another writer, Martin Gardner (17, pp. 299–314), accused Rhine of selecting for publication only a small portion of the total number of telepathy experiments made. He added that this selection "is not a deliberate process, but something which operates subtly and unconsciously."

The most highly publicized attack on psychic research was an article by G. R. Price (46) that appeared in the prestigious journal *Science*. Price took the position that significant ESP data were often "dependent on clerical and statistical errors and unintentional use of sensory cues." Price added that the other significant data resulted from a system of collusion between experimenters, such as Rhine and Soal, and their subjects. This article was widely quoted throughout the 1960s by skeptics. However, Price (47) eventually withdrew his original charges and apologized to Rhine and Soal, stating he had been "highly unfair."

The constant criticisms faced by parapsychologists have led to an increased sophistication in the designing of ESP experiments. Indeed, investigators have not always been vigilant in their attempts to reduce the possibility of fraud in telepathy experiments. Precautions that should be taken include the following:

1. Isolating the telepathic transmitter from the percipient so that no sensory cuing can occur.
2. Taking precautions to insure that the person who records the responses is "blind" as to the identity of the target material.
3. Using a randomization method to select target material.
4. Deciding how many trials will be attempted before an experiment begins.
5. Testing high-scoring subjects in different laboratories in an attempt to replicate earlier findings.
6. Imposing proper security measures that will prevent the alteration of experimental data.

A number of observers (e.g., 16, pp. 131–132; 33; 34, pp. 25–27; 58; 62) have noted that many of the attacks on parapsychology have been irresponsible and inaccurate. Yet the net effect has been to improve the quality of experimentation, making additional criticism a difficult matter.

COMPLEXITIES OF TELEPATHIC PHENOMENA

Questions in other areas began to concern Rhine, Soal, and their associates as the exploration of ESP continued. It became apparent that a target in a telepathy test could also have been perceived through clairvoyance (53, pp. 554–556). As the agent always has an object that theoretically could have served as the target just as easily as the agent's thought about that object, the term *general extrasensory perception* (GESP) was coined to cover both possibilities. A few studies (35; 65, pp. 255–258) attempted to surmount this problem by using a veiled method of recording that depended for its meaning upon common memories of the agent (who is sending the symbol on the ESP card) and the experimenter (who is recording the ESP symbols as they are transmitted). No one else, even if he heard them, would have known what the two meant in their conversation, which transferred the code, unless telepathically he knew what the two persons were thinking and what their common memories had been. Although these tests yielded significant data, the possibility still remains that the receiver had some clairvoyant impression of the agent's nervous system, vocal cords or other physiological concomitants of the thoughts being transmitted. For this reason, experiments in telepathy may be conceptualized as GESP tests, leaving the possibility of clairvoyance an open one.

Various effects have been reported in telepathy, clairvoyance, and GESP experiments. The "decline effect" was first noted by G. H. Estabrooks (14, 15) in a 1926 study. It proved to be characteristic of many long series that a subject's score would decline as the experiment proceeded. For this reason, it is important to specify in advance how many trials will be included in a series so that the experimenter will not be tempted to stop testing when the decline effect is first noted.

The *differential effect* refers to ESP experiments in which subjects tend to respond differentially to a dual situation, without meaning to do so. For example, a percipient sometimes responds to two different sets of targets in two different ways, scoring above chance on one set of targets and below chance on another set. C. E. Stuart (68) found that his receivers obtained significantly positive scores when their senders were relatives and significantly negative scores when the senders were unrelated. G. W. Casper (9) reported a significant difference in the rate of his subjects' scoring when they were working with the agents they liked most and with those they liked least. The differential effect was also noted in telepathy experiments by G. E. Rice and Joyce Townsend (57) and in a school classroom experiment by Rhea A. White and Jean A. Angstadt (79).

Another observed phenomenon became known as the *sheep–goat effect* (e.g., 61). The subjects' attitude toward ESP was registered in advance of card-guessing tests; it was found that those with the more negative attitude ("goats") tended to score at a lower rate than those taking a more positive attitude ("sheep"). The sheep–goat effect was found in many experiments by various investigators (e.g., 74). This effect is not obtained in every experiment (e.g., 1), indicating that other variables may supersede attitude. These other variables include the telepathic agent, the experimental setting, and the critically important matter of the telepathic target.

TARGET MATERIALS

The target in ESP tests is the object of a percipient's response (49, p. 55). In spontaneous cases, the target is typically a real-life situation, such as a close friend's involvement in a disaster. For example, a Soviet sailor, E. M. Kamintze, submitted the following report (21):

While serving on a submarine, I became ill and the ship had to leave without me. During an afternoon nap I had the following dream: I was right back on the submarine, standing on the deck. The

boat began to descend into the water, but I was unable to reach the
conning tower and make my way down into the safety of the ship; I
was overwhelmed by the water, began to swallow it and felt that I was
drowning. At this point I awoke, sweating and with my pulse racing. I
remembered the dream quite vividly afterward. When the submarine
returned to its base and I rejoined the crew, I heard that one of my
comrades had drowned. He had accidentally remained on deck while
the boat submerged. When I checked the ship's log, I discovered that
the accident had happened at the very moment I experienced the
nightmare of my own drowning.

Several analyses of spontaneous cases have produced valuable results.
Best known are the cases collected by L. E. Rhine (54–56). She notes
that most of her respondents are women (54, p. 132) and that most of the
events involved are crises and disasters (54, pp. 115–130; 55).

L. E. Rhine has compared telepathic phenomena in intuitions, in "realistic" dreams, in "unrealistic" dreams, and in hallucinatory experiences (56, p. 218), concluding that telepathic messages in hallucinations
"are really secondary effects arising in the formation of intuitive experience" and that the key difference between the telepathic imagery of "realistic" and "unrealistic" dreams is the fact that "in the latter it is based on
an idea suggested by the news, rather than on direct meaning of the
news" (56, p. 209).

Gardner Murphy (41), following a survey of spontaneous cases, cited
several ways in which telepathy can manifest itself:

1. Fragmentation. A picture or event will rarely be transmitted as
    intended. Rather, portions and pieces will be transmitted, some-
    times removed from the original context.
2. Duplication. The material is often repeated in various forms as
    if to say, "Ah, I got through. I'll do it again!"
3. Accretion. Having given some details, there is often an attempt
    to put them together in a meaningful way. Often a dream con-
    tains telepathic material which is combined with one's day residue.

Murphy goes on to point out how these manifestations characterize
anecdotal material as well as the pioneer telepathy experiments of Sinclair (64) and Warcollier (76), concluding that

all these things have long been known in the study of so-called spontaneous telepathy, in the impressions that are received of people
dying, or suffering accidents, or of movements of great excitement or
joy. . . . It is not only because the experience is unpleasant that it is

fragmented or hidden from us. There seems to be something about the very nature of the process which involves a breaking up and a repetitiousness. It may be due to the fact that, after all, we have to live our lives in terms of the Darwinian principle of the struggle for existence, and it may be that there is much about the telepathic process which would interfere with everyday living. . . . One often gets the impression that . . . there is something deep within us that is reaching out and does want to make the contact, but really cannot bear the full impact of it, and so fragments it; then, in a moving tide, it tries to duplicate it and support it. Not able to do this, it finally flounders in the accretion of detail which can never assume the meaningful form of the totality.

An intensive analysis of 35 telepathic impressions by Ian Stevenson (67) reflected many of the points made by Rhine and Murphy. For example, Stevenson found that the impressions had to do with death in 6 instances, with illness or accidents in 20 instances, and with joyous or neutral events only 9 times. Of the 25 percipients involved in the 35 cases, 6 were male and 16 were female. In those cases involving a discernible agent, 14 were male and 11 were female. The impression could occur while the receiver was ordinarily awake or in an altered conscious state; however, the hallucinatory and dream varieties were more impressive to the percipient.

In clinical cases, the target is often some aspect of a psychotherapist's personal life that comes to a patient in a dream, in a reverie state, or during the psychotherapeutic session. For example, W. H. Gillespie (18) reports that

on the last evening of my holiday I read Elizabeth Bowen's short story "The Inherited Clock." Next day a patient in the second month of his analysis began his session by relating a dream from that night which contained an essential part of the story—not only a similar clock, but a similar sinister significance attached to it. He did not know Elizabeth Bowen's story. Relevant facts are that the story had made a strong, eerie and psychopathological impression on me.

Many other possible instances of telepathy during psychotherapy have been reported (e.g., 12, 72). The evidential nature of these accounts has been criticized by Albert Ellis (13), who once selected one of a patient's dreams at random and found that it corresponded in many ways to the daily events of his own life.

Although spontaneous material is provocative, the gathering of spontaneous, anecdotal material and the analysis of clinical material never satisfies an experimental scientist. Typically, he attempts to find a way to take something apart, scrutinize something closely, or cause something to happen repeatedly (40, p. 51). Parapsychology has followed this path as regards telepathy, attempting to create, in a laboratory, phenomena that are generally less dramatic but that lend themselves more easily to scrutiny and analysis. What is gained from an experimental point of view, therefore, is often obtained at the expense of the richness and intensity that characterizes real-life telepathy.

In a laboratory situation, the target can be a geometric form on an ESP card, a drawing, or a randomly selected object. The extensive work done by J. B. Rhine (e.g., 50) almost invariably utilized ESP cards; Soal and Bateman (65), however, used animal cards. Drawings were used by Sinclair (64) and Warcollier (77). Randomly selected squares on a checkerboard were used by Brugmans (6), while Carington (8) used drawings of randomly selected words.

Responses to these various types of target material can be categorized as "free" or "restricted." If the telepathic receiver knows that the range of materials is limited to five cards bearing geometric designs, his responses will be restricted. However, if he is told that a picture will be transmitted to him, his responses will be free, as the target could be anything at all.

Among the more unusual examples of restricted-telepathy targets are those of L. L. Vasiliev (75, p. 178). In Vasiliev's experiments, the subject responded either by going into deeper hypnosis or by waking up, once hypnotized. E. D. Dean (10) used a plethysmograph to record blood flow in his subjects' fingers during a telepathy experiment. The agent looked at randomly arranged target cards consisting of names known to the subject and other, randomly chosen names, such as those selected from a telephone directory. Dean found significant changes in finger pulse volume to occur while the agent was looking at names known to the subject but not while unknown names were being observed. T. Tart took electroencephalograph (EEG) recordings and galvanic skin responses of his percipients as well as plethysmographic records. When an agent in another room was given electrical shocks, a faster EEG pattern emerged as well as more frequent galvanic skin responses and changes in the percipient's finger pulse volume.

In his 1966 review of the ESP literature, Rao (49, p. 58) noted that "free-response material seems to have gradually lost most of its adherents. Hardly any parapsychologist now is doing any serious research with such materials." About this time, however, there was a revival of interest in the association between altered states of consciousness and psi. Because a sleeping percipient could hardly be expected to dream about geometric forms, free target material was utilized.

Thelma Moss and J. A. Gengerelli (38), surmising that experiments with cards might not be the best way to test telepathy, experimented with the transmission of emotionally charged material. Senders viewed slides and listened to tapes on various subjects that were likely to arouse emotion of some sort. One slide–tape presentation concerned the assassination of President John F. Kennedy, including excerpts from his speeches and pictures from his years in office. The receiver responded.

I seem to have the feeling of sadness or sorrow . . . as if I were crying . . . or something tragic has happened, and that I was grieving over something . . . much the same as one might feel attending a funeral of a dear friend . . . or a well-known figure in whom one had faith. . . .

When Moss and Gengerelli asked a group of judges to match the responses of 30 senders and 30 receivers to the various slide–tape presentations, 7 out of 12 judges were able to do so significantly more accurately than they would have by chance.

In another series of telepathic experiments using free-response techniques, Ullman and I (31) found that emotionally toned materials shown to agents in one room can affect the dreams of sleeping subjects in a distant room. For example, on one night, the agent randomly selected a print of Hiroshige's painting *Downpour at Shono*. In the envelope accompanying the picture was a Japanese umbrella and instructions to "take a shower," which would enable the agent to recreate the scene depicted in the painting. On that night, the subject dreamed the following:

Something about an Oriental man. . . . A fountain. . . . Two images and a water spray that would shoot up. . . . Walking with someone on the street. . . . It seemed it was raining a little bit and . . . we had to walk out into the street. . . . It was raining, and it was night.

Three judges were able to match the agent's materials and the subject's dreams at high levels of significance. Thus, the use of free-response approaches may enable experimenters to involve emotion in telepathy experiments by making the situation more lifelike.

UNANSWERED QUESTIONS

There are many areas in telepathy research that have gone virtually unexplored and that need to be considered by researchers in the future. Rhea A. White (78) notes, "In present-day experimental reports, mention is rarely made of the subject's subjective, introspective reactions during the test." The value of experiential reports was demonstrated in a study by Charles Honorton, Sally Ann Drucker, and H. Hermon (22). The subjects were placed in sensory isolation, while an agent attempted to transmit an art print. Statistically significant results were obtained; those subjects who reported drastic alterations in consciousness did better than those who reported little change from their ordinary state of awareness.

Developmental studies of telepathic ability have never been attempted. L. E. Rhine (54, pp. 148–165) has presented a survey of her anecdotal material, noting that "some of the children who give evidence of it while very young no longer do so as they grow older. The fact that this change comes about at the time their family relationships, particularly parental, widen may be significant." A psychoanalytic interpretation of similar case material has been presented by B. E. Schwarz (63).

Another unexplored area regards the telepathic agent. Murphy (41) suggests that experimenters work out a target and a set of conditions meaningful to the agent and that they use the network of associations in the agent's mind as part of the target. This would help psychic researchers to discern more carefully the importance of the telepathic transmitter. A few studies indicate that subjects are able to receive from some agents but not from others (e.g., 73). Sex differences in agent–subject combinations were found in our telepathy studies at the Maimonides Dream Laboratory (29). Both of these provocative leads deserve more attention. In addition, the biological rhythms of agent and subject deserve to be studied, and the question raised by V. M. Bekhterev (4) regarding possible telepathic communication with animals needs resolution (see Chapter 9).

Finally, the effect of the geophysical environment upon telepathy deserves closer scrutiny. A post hoc analysis of 80 sessions at the Maimonides Dream Laboratory produced data indicating that telepathy functioned best on the nights of the full moon (30). Weather conditions, sunspot cycles, atmospheric oxygen levels, and geomagnetic storms are only a few of the other variables that may affect telepathic communication.

THEORETICAL SPECULATIONS

The scientific approach to new phenomena ultimately requires theory as well as observation (34, p. 48). Over the years, a variety of theoretical speculation has centered on the question of how telepathy may function despite the time and space barriers that prevent other forms of communication from taking place.

One theory postulates the transmission of energy from one brain to another in a manner resembling the radio. EEG research demonstrated that rhythmic electrical currents emanate from the brain; it is suggested, therefore, that the brain of a transmitter may emit to the receiver a series of waves corresponding to his thought patterns. B. B. Kazhinsky (26) hypothesized a process of *electroduction*, in which electromagnetic waves carry the message from agent to subject. This explanation could be applied to long-distance telepathy experiments such as a Moscow–Leningrad series (28).

One of the objections offered to this theory is that any transmission of energy between two brains would have to be subject to the inverse-square law, which governs this type of physical phenomenon. This objection has been answered in two ways. Karlis Osis (e.g., 43) has conducted a series of ESP experiments involving distances of several thousands of miles. His data can be interpreted to suggest that ESP diminishes as the distance expands—a finding consistent with the inverse-square law. In the meantime, other writers (e.g., 21) have pointed out that although the intensity of an energetic transmission decreases with the square of the distance, if the transmission is merely a signaling device the question of distance is not as critical.*

L. L. Vasiliev (75) investigated the electromagnetic theory of telepathy by inducing hypnosis at a distance while the subjects were in metal chambers. Vasiliev claimed that telepathic hypnosis succeeded even when the subjects were in chambers that shielded off any possible electromagnetic waves within the range of ultrashort, short, and medium wavelengths. Thus, Vasiliev concluded that electromagnetic wave transmission from the brain is not associated with telepathy.

Another attempt to explain telepathy has been made by Ninian Marshall (36). Assuming that new physical laws may be needed to explain the behavior of complex structures (such as the brain), Marshall postulates that two human brains have a sufficient degree of similarity to act on one another by some kind of direct resonance without the obstructions of space and time. He proposes that "any two structures exert an influence on each other which tends to make them become more alike. The strength of this influence increases with the product of their complexities, and decreases with the difference between their patterns." Resonance, therefore, of a pattern in one brain with another brain leads to telepathy. Although this position is appealing to many people, Rao (49, p. 143) notes that telepathy and clairvoyance are "the same phenomenon mani-

---

* For a positive space–time propagation model, if the information is in the form of a wave packet or bursts of wave packets that are being emitted by the brain, then, although the intensity of wave packets must fall off inversely as the square of the distance, the information content does not. The recipient need only be intersected by one (or a critical burst) of these information bullets to be in telepathic communication with the sender. The distance effect then becomes a time effect needed for such an impingement event. If the velocity of this wave packet is much larger than the velocity of light, then the time delay might become negligibly small.

festing under two conditions" and does not see how Marshall's theory would explain clairvoyance. He notes, "A card is not complex enough to resonate, nor does it possess consciousness to produce psychic energy."

W. G. Roll (60) has advanced a theory that utilizes the concept of a psychic (or psi) field. This field is analogous to electromagnetic or gravitational fields; further, every object, living or nonliving, has a psychic field. In the case of ESP, a psychic or mental event at the target, or source, is copied in the target's psychic field; this copy, or "psychic trace," is then communicated to the psychic field of the percipient. It interacts with his brain and the brain's memory bank to produce ESP. In telepathy, a person's memory produces information that resembles the psychic trace of the target; it is this information that emerges into consciousness and that serves as evidence for telepathy.

Other theoretical observations about telepathy that deserve attention have been made by H. H. Price (45), who spoke of a "collective unconscious"; by Whatley Carington (8, p. 257), who postulated an "associative bond" between agent and subject; and by J. B. Rhine (50, p. 169), who wrote about an agency of mind that has the ability to "go out" to meet a target object. R. H. Thouless and B. P. Wiesner (71) coined the term *Shin* to denote an information-processing quality of the personality that operates in ESP as well as in sensory perception; thus, telepathy is described as Shin "acting on, or being acted on by, a nervous system other than its own." Arthur Koestler (27) brought insights from theoretical physics to bear upon possible explanations for ESP phenomena. For example, some physicists hypothesize the existence of "psitrons," which could convey information to subjects from dimensions of the universe that subjects do not ordinarily utilize (27, p. 69).

Murphy (41) stresses the interpersonal relationships between sender and receiver in his articles on telepathy. Altered states of consciousness often reduce self-awareness, bringing people together at a deeper level than usual; this may be the best level in which telepathy may occur. Murphy (39, p. 198) states that "from this point of view, a subject and an experimenter in a telepathy experiment represent phases of an organic whole both at the ordinary normal level of interaction and also, more profoundly, at the deeper level at which paranormal processes occur." When an individual acts as an "interpersonal entity," according to Murphy (40, p. 192), he may possess an "extraordinary capacity to make contact with phases of reality which transcend time and space." The notion of two levels of reality is also developed by Lawrence LeShan (32), who has hypothesized that each individual has his own reality in which he operates. Mystics and psychic sensitives have similar individual realities, which permit them access to information denied to those who operate within other reality systems. LeShan also noted that the descriptions of the universe presented by some theoretical physicists resemble the individual realities of mystics and psychics.*

IMPLICATIONS

Some scientists deal with psi by agreeing that ESP may occur but insisting that the effect is too small to be of any importance to society or to individual behavior. However, Ian Stevenson (67, p. 187) holds that telepathic impressions occur much more than most persons now realize; furthermore, he proposes that they influence our conduct to a greater degree than we suspect: "It is altogether possible that important unrecognized exchanges of feelings through extrasensory processes are occurring all the time to most of us and perhaps significantly influencing our emotions and behavior."

Mystics from both Eastern and Western cultures have contended that we are linked to each other in subtle ways that are, from time to time, powerfully influential. Many of the early pioneers in telepathy research took the same position. For example, Warcollier (76) stressed the importance of unconscious telepathic communication between people working closely together, citing it as one factor in the attainment of high levels of motivation and creativity.

Warcollier (77, p. 104) also used telepathy as an example of a phenomenon that would alter the practice of psychotherapy and the field of psychology. He stated, "The entire problem of transference and counter-transference in a psychoanalytic sense is involved with the question of telepathy." The importance of telepathy in the psychotherapist–patient relationship has been repeatedly pointed out by parapsychologists who are also psychoanalysts (e.g., 11, 37, 62).

Duncan Blewett (5, p. 268) predicts that the eventual result of studies in hypnosis, fantasy, and meditation will be to open "to ready observation and controlled study by psychologists [such phenomena] as telepathy, now considered to lie in the realm of parapsychology."

To acknowledge a universal force that binds us all is not, of course, to assert that telepathy is a daily event manifested consciously. Yet even if we can only observe it occasionally, as in the case of persons united by love and during times of crisis, this should arouse the curiosity of psychologists and other scientists who purport to be interested in the nature of human beings. Our notions of human personality are still poorly formulated. The human animal's physical and intellectual limitations in the face of the complexity of the universe may, in the words of Arthur Koest-

---

* An excellent presentation and critique of parapsychological theories has been prepared by Rao (49, pp. 140–171).

ler (27, p. 140) "condemn us to the role of Peeping Toms at the keyhole of eternity." Yet Koestler's advice is worth heeding: "But at least let us take the stuffing out of the keyhole, which blocks even our limited view."

REFERENCES

1.   Adock, C. J., and Quartermain, D. "Some Problems in Group Testing of ESP." *Journal of Parapsychology*, 23, no. 4 (1959): 251–256.
2.   Ballantine, M. "Against the 'Supernatural.'" In M. Ebon, ed., *Psychic Discoveries by the Russians.* New American Library: New York, 1971.
3.   Barrett, W. F.; Gurney, E.; and Myers, F. W. H. "First Report on Thought Reading." *Proceedings of the Society for Psychical Research*, 1, pt. 1 (1882).
4.   Bekhterev, V. M. "Telepathy with Dogs." In M. Ebon, ed., *Psychic Discoveries by the Russians.* New American Library: New York, 1971.
5.   Blewett, D. *The Frontiers of Being.* Award: New York, 1969.
6.   Brugmans, H. I. F. W. "A Communication Regarding the Telepathy Experiments in the Psychology Laboratory at Groningen Carried Out by M. Heymans, Dr. Weinberg and Dr. H. I. F. W. Brugmans." *Proceedings*, First International Congress of Psychical Research: Copenhagen, 1922.
7.   Carington, W. *Thought Transference: An Outline of Facts, Theory and Implications of Telepathy.* Creative Age: New York, 1946.
8.   Carington, W. *Matter, Mind, and Meaning.* Yale University Press: New Haven, Conn., 1949.
9.   Casper, G. W. "Effect of Receiver's Attitude Toward Sender in ESP Tests." *Journal of Parapsychology*, 16, no. 3 (1952): 212–218.
10.   Dean, E. D. "The Plethysmograph as an Indicator of ESP." *Journal of the American Society of Psychical Research*, 41, no. 4 (1962): 351–353.
11.   Ehrenwald, J. *Telepathy and Medical Psychology.* Norton: New York, 1948.
12.   Eisenbud, J. "The Dreams of Two Patients in Analysis Interpreted as a Telepathic *Rêve à Deux." Psychoanalytic Quarterly*, 16, no. 1 (1947): 39–60.
13.   Ellis, A. "Telepathy and Psychoanalysis: A Critique of Recent Findings." *Psychiatric Quarterly*, 21, no. 4 (1947): 607–659.
14.   Estabrooks, G. H. "A Contribution to Experimental Telepathy." *Bulletin of the Boston Society of Psychical Research*, 5 (1927).
15.   Estabrooks, G. H. "A Contribution to Experimental Telepathy." *Journal of Parapsychology*, 25, no. 3 (1961): 190–213.
16.   Eysenck, H. J. *Sense and Nonsense in Psychology.* Penguin: Bungay, England, 1957.
17.   Gardner, M. *In the Name of Science.* McGraw-Hill: New York, 1952.
18.   Gillespie, W. H. "Experiences Suggestive of Paranormal Cognition in the Psycho-Analytic Situation." In G. E. W. Westenholme and E. C. P. Miller, eds. *Extrasensory Perception: A Ciba Foundation Symposium.* Citadel: New York, 1966.
19.   Gurney, E.; Myers, F. W. H.; and Podmore, F. *Phantasms of the Living.* Trubner: London, 1886.

20. Hansel, C. E. M. *ESP: A Scientific Evaluation*. Scribner's: New York, 1966.

21. Hoffman, B. "ESP and the Inverse Square Law." *Journal of Parapsychology*, 4, no. 1 (1940): 149–152.

22. Honorton, C.; Drucker, S. A.; and Hermon, H. C. "Shifts in Subjective State and ESP Under Conditions of Partial Sensory Deprivation: A Preliminary Study." *Journal of the American Society of Psychical Research*, 67, no. 2 (1973): 191–196.

23. Hutchinson, G. E. "Is an Electron Smaller than a Dream?" *Journal of Parapsychology*, 27, no. 4 (1963): 301–306.

24. Jastrow, J. *Fact and Fable in Psychology*. Houghton Mifflin: Boston, 1900.

25. Jung, C. G. *The Structure and Dynamics of the Psyche*. Pantheon: New York, 1960.

26. Kazhinsky, B. B. *Biological Radio*. Ukranian Academy of Sciences: Kiev, 1962.

27. Koestler, A. *The Roots of Coincidence*. Random House: New York, 1972.

28. Kolodny, L. "Telepathy Proven? The Moscow–Leningrad Tests." In M. Ebon, ed., *Psychic Discoveries by the Russians*. New American Library: New York, 1971.

29. Krippner, S., "Electrophysiological Studies of ESP in Dreams: Sex Differences in Seventy-four Telepathy Sessions." *Journal of the American Society for Psychical Research*, 64, no. 3 (1970): 277–285.

30. Krippner, S.; Becker, A.; Cavallo, M.; and Washburn, B. "Electrophysiological Studies of ESP in Dreams: Lunar Cycle Differences in 80 Telepathy Sessions." *Human Dimensions*, 1, no. 1 (1972): 14–19.

31. Krippner, S., and Ullman, M. "Telepathic Perception in the Dream State: Confirmatory Study Using EEG–EOG Monitoring Techniques." *Perceptual and Motor Skills*, 29, no. 2 (1969): 915–918.

32. LeShan, L. *Toward a General Theory of the Paranormal*. Parapsychological Monographs, Parapsychology Foundation: New York, 1969.

33. McConnell, R. A. "The ESP Scholar." *Contemporary Psychology*, 13, no. 1 (1968): 41.

34. McConnell, R. A. *ESP Curriculum Guide*. Simon and Schuster: New York, 1972.

35. McMahan, E. A. "An Experiment in Pure Telepathy." *Journal of Parapsychology*, 10, no. 2 (1946): 224–242.

36. Marshall, N. "ESP and Memory." *British Journal of Philosophical Science*, 10, no. 2 (1960): 265–286.

37. Meerloo, J. A. M. *Hidden Communion*. Garrett: New York, 1964.

38. Moss, T., and Gengerelli, J. A. "Telepathy and Emotional Stimuli: A Controlled Experiment." *Journal of Abnormal Psychology*, 72, no. 4 (1967): 341–348.

39. Murphy, G. "Field Theory and Survival." *Journal of the American Society for Psychical Research*, 39, no. 2 (1945): 181–209.

40. Murphy, G., with L. A. Dale. *Challenge of Psychical Research: A Primer of Parapsychology*. Harper: New York, 1961.

41. Murphy, G. "A Qualitative Study of Telepathic Phenomena." *Journal of the American Society for Psychical Research*, 56, no. 2 (1962): 63–79.

42. Murray, G. "Presidential Address." *Proceedings of the Society for Psychical Research*, 49, pt. 181 (1952).

43. Osis, K.; Turner, Jr., M. E.; and Carlson, M. L. "ESP Over Distance: Re-

search on the ESP Channel." *Journal of the American Society for Psychical Research*, 65, no. 3 (1971): 245–287.

44. Pratt, J. G.; Rhine, J. B.; Smith, B. W.; Stuart, C. F.; and Greenwood, J. A. *Extra-Sensory Perception After Sixty Years*. Humphries: Boston, 1940.

45. Price, H. H. "Some Philosophical Questions About Telepathy and Clairvoyance." *Philosophy*, 15, no. 3 (1940): 363–374.

46. Price, G. R. "Science and the Supernatural." *Science*, 122, no. 3165 (1955): 359–367.

47. Price, G. R. "Apology to Rhine and Soal." *Science*, 175, no. 4020 (1972): 359.

48. Prince, W. F. *Noted Witnesses for Psychic Occurrences*. University Books: New Hyde Park, N.Y., 1963.

49. Rao, K. R. *Experimental Parapsychology: A Review and Interpretation*. Thomas: Springfield, Ill., 1966.

50. Rhine, J. B. *Extrasensory Perception*. Humphries: Boston, 1934; repr. 1964.

51. Rhine, J. B., *New World of the Mind*. Sloane: New York, 1953.

52. Rhine, J. B., and Pratt, J. G. "A Review of the Pearce–Pratt Distance Series of ESP Tests." *Journal of Parapsychology*, 18, no. 3 (1954): 165–177.

53. Rhine, J. B., and Pratt, J. G. *Parapsychology: Frontier Science of the Mind*. Thomas: Springfield, Ill., 1957.

54. Rhine, L. E. *Hidden Channels of the Mind*. Sloane: New York, 1961.

55. Rhine, L. E. "Psychological Processes in ESP Experiences, I. Waking Experiences. II. Dreams." *Journal of Parapsychology*, 26, nos. 1 and 2 (1962): 88–111; 171–199.

56. Rhine, L. E. *ESP in Life and Lab: Tracing Hidden Channels*. Macmillan: New York, 1967.

57. Rice, G. E., and Townsend, J. "Agent Percipient Relationship and GESP Performance." *Journal of Parapsychology*, 26, no. 3 (1962): 211–217.

58. Richet, C. *Thirty Years of Psychical Research*. Macmillan: New York, 1923.

59. Riess, B. F. "A Case of High Scores in Card Guessing at a Distance." *Journal of Parapsychology*, 1, no. 4 (1937): 440–463.

60. Roll, W. G. "ESP and Memory." *International Journal of Neuropsychiatry*, 2, no. 4 (1966): 505–521.

61. Schmeidler, G. R., and Murphy, G. "The Influence of Belief and Disbelief in ESP Upon ESP Scoring Level." *Journal of Experimental Psychology*, 36, no. 2 (1946): 271–276.

62. Schwarz, B. E. "Built-in Controls and Postulates for the Telepathic Event." *Corrective Psychiatry and Journal of Social Therapy*, 12, no. 2 (1966): 64–82.

63. Schwarz, B. E. *Parent–Child Telepathy*. Garrett: New York, 1971.

64. Sinclair, U. *Mental Radio*. Thomas: Springfield, Ill., 1930.

65. Soal, S. G., and Bateman, F. *Modern Experiments in Telepathy*. Yale University Press: New Haven, Conn., 1954.

66. Soal, S. G., and Bowden, H. T. *The Mind Readers*. Faber: London, 1959.

67. Stevenson, I. *Telepathic Impressions: A Review and Report of Thirty-Five New Cases*. University of Virginia Press: Charlottesville, Va., 1970.

68. Stuart, C. E. "GESP Experiments with the Free Response Method." *Journal of Parapsychology*, 10, no. 1 (1946): 21–35.

69. Tart, C. T. "Possible Physiological Correlates of Psi Cognition." *International Journal of Parapsychology*, 5, no. 4 (1963): 375–386.

70. Sidgwick, H. "Presidential Address." *Proceedings of the Society for Psychical Research*, 1, p. 1 (1882).

71. Thouless, R. H., and Wiesner, B. P. "On the Nature of Psi Phenomena." *Journal of Parapsychology*, 10, no. 2 (1946): 107–119.

72. Ullman, M. "On the Occurrence of Telepathic Dreams." *Journal of the American Society for Psychical Research*, 53, no. 1 (1959): 50–61.

73. Van Busschbach, J. G. "A Further Report on an Investigation of ESP in School Children." *Journal of Parapsychology*, 19, no. 1 (1955): 69–81.

74. Van de Castle, R. L., and White, R. A. "A Report on a Sentence Completion Form of Sheep-Goat Attitude Scale." *Journal of Parapsychology*, 19, no. 3 (1955): 171–179.

75. Vasiliev, L. L. *Experiments in Mental Suggestion*. Institute for the Study of Mental Images: Church Crookham, England, 1963.

76. Warcollier, R. *Experimental Telepathy*. Boston Society for Psychic Research: Boston, 1938.

77. Warcollier, R. *Mind to Mind*, 2nd ed. Collier: New York, 1963.

78. White, R. A. "A Comparison of Old and New Methods of Response to Targets in ESP Experiments." *Journal of the American Society for Psychical Research*, 58, no. 1 (1964): 21–56.

79. White, R. A., and Angstadt, J. A. "Student Preferences in a Two-Classroom GESP Experiment with Two Student Agents Acting Simultaneously." *Journal of the American Society for Psychical Research*, 57, no. 1 (1963): 32–42.

Rex G. Stanford

REX G. STANFORD, *Ph.D., is assistant professor of psychology at St. John's University. Prior to joining the university in 1973, he was research associate in the Division of Parapsychology, Department of Psychiatry, University of Virginia School of Medicine. Earlier, he was on the graduate faculty of Western Carolina University and a staff member of the Institute for Parapsychology in Durham, North Carolina.*

Dr. Stanford majored in psychology at University of Texas at Austin, where he received a B.A. in 1963 and a Ph.D. in 1967.

He is a member of the Parapsychological Association and a trustee of the Gardner Murphy Research Institute. He was vice president of the Parapsychological Association in 1970 and 1971 and president in 1973. He has published a score of articles in Journal of Parapsychology *and* Journal of the American Society for Psychical Research. *Two of his articles appear in* Parapsychology Today, *edited by J. B. Rhine and Robert Brier (Citadel, 1968), and two in* Progress in Parapsychology, *edited by J. B. Rhine (Parapsychology Press, 1971).*

Dr. Stanford can be reached at the Department of Psychology, St. John's University, Jamaica, N.Y. 11439.

5   Clairvoyance

REX G. STANFORD

SUMMARY

Clairvoyance is regarded as having occurred when an organism behaves as though it has extrasensory knowledge of some object or physical event unknown to any other organism.

Two classes of evidence for clairvoyance are examined: (a) studies showing satistically significant correspondences between subject responses and target (concealed) objects, and (b) studies showing a functional relationship between level of performance on clairvoyance tests and certain independent variables, such as whether or not subjects are hypnotized and whether or not they believe ESP can occur in the test at hand. The latter class of evidence is regarded as superior because it does more than pose an anomaly: it provides knowledge that makes the events in question less anomalous. It indicates what factors facilitate, inhibit, or block the appearance of those events and thus establishes that we are concerned with scientifically meaningful events rather than "empty correlations."

The historical significance of clairvoyance for parapsychology is that it has simplified and made more efficient the study of extrasensory response (as contrasted with what would have been the case for telepathy studies). Thus, it has encouraged a large body of process-oriented research.

Evidence is considered that clairvoyance most commonly functions to subserve the needs of the organism in ways that are nonintentional, unconscious, and nonperceptual or noncognitive. The possibility is examined that the influence of clairvoyance in life experience may be more common than has previously been suspected but that it may usually go unrecognized because of the subtlety of its function.

INTRODUCTION

Perhaps no term in the parapsychological jargon is as confusing to the newcomer to parapsychology as the term *clairvoyance*. The word itself is of French origin and literally means "clear seeing." If that fact alone were not enough to hopelessly confuse matters, historically the word has often had meanings quite different from its current scientific usage. At places and times in the past, *clairvoyance* was used to denote the operation of any form of ESP, and in the popular mind and in some journalistic quarters a person called a "psychic" could equally well be labeled a "clairvoyant." In a few instances the concept of a clairvoyant has been very narrow: a person having extrasensory visions when gazing into a crystal ball (or a similar device).

Wisdom dictates, then, that this chapter, which is an overview of clairvoyance, begin by considering the current scientific use of the term. If a person or animal behaves as though it has extrasensory knowledge of some currently existing object or current physical event that is unknown to any other organism, we term this clairvoyance. For example, if a person is able to guess accurately the order of a concealed deck of conventional playing cards (to a degree that reasonably well rules out chance as an explanation) and if the order of that deck of cards was, at the time of the subject's guessing, unknown to anyone through sensory means, we say that clairvoyance has occurred.

Some parapsychologists have quarreled for decades about whether clairvoyance has been established or whether telepathy ("thought transference") may explain all the "clairvoyance" results or vice versa. But if we adopt the definition of clairvoyance given above, we shall have to admit, as will be clear below, that there is good evidence for clairvoyance.

One should not read more into the definition of *clairvoyance* than what is strictly involved in the definition. These remarks can be extended to the definitions of the supposed extrasensory phenomena in general: clairvoyance, telepathy, and precognition. If we use strictly operational (i.e., situation-oriented, theoretically unbiased) definitions of each of these phenomena, we have no problem, but if we begin to think that the use of separate terms for these phenomena necessarily implies that we are concerned with separate forms of ESP, then we may have problems. Nor should this be construed to mean that a single process underlies the three classes of observations that we term clairvoyance, telepathy, and precognition. We are very ignorant of the basic nature of psi, and just because we can make certain classes of observations using various experimental designs does not, strictly speaking, imply anything about the nature of our phenomena. Further, to say that clairvoyance involves "physical objects or events" and telepathy involves "mental events" does not help at all. It only confuses science with metaphysical assumptions.

Therefore, in this chapter we shall ignore the decades of fruitless discussion (e.g., 26, 30, 34) of whether supposed telepathy (and even "precognitive telepathy") explains clairvoyance results and vice versa. We have very good evidence that persons can meaningfully respond to physical events when these events are unknown to any other person. Therefore, we will call this clairvoyance and recognize it as a *class of observation* rather than an explanation of observations.

It is at least remotely conceivable that the single class of observation we term clairvoyance will ultimately have to be subdivided for theoretical reasons; events that fit the definition of clairvoyance may not all have the same underlying cause. At this stage of our research, we cannot realistically guess what the future may reveal about the underlying nature of the phenomena we study. The reader of this review should not, however, be deceived in his thinking about clairvoyance by the host of names sometimes used to describe events that can sometimes be classified as clairvoyance: psychometry, dowsing, radiesthesia, or automatic writing. From an objective standpoint, these differing names only serve to distinguish different ways or contexts in which the events we call ESP (including clairvoyance) sometimes occur. The person giving a psychic reading (which may involve clairvoyance or other classes of extrasensory events) may hold an object belonging to, or associated with, the target person whom he is reading. Then we say he is doing *psychometry*, or—to use a more scientific and perhaps more appropriate term—a *token-object reading*. If the ESP subject uses a bent wire or a forked stick to indicate the presence of a target object, we call this *dowsing* and recognize it as a form of motor automatism used as a potential mediating vehicle for the expression of psi. If the subject gives his responses using a swinging pendulum, this may be termed *radiesthesia*, but a more scientific and less theoretically biased term would be *motor automatism*. Similarly, automatic writing, if it is used to convey veridical information unknown to the writer by sensory means, is termed a motor automatism used as a mediating vehicle for extrasensory response. In short, names like *psychometry, dowsing, radiesthesia*, and *automatic writing* should not at present be construed to designate separate forms of ESP. Psychometry represents a special experimental setting for the study of ESP; the other terms simply represent specific mediating vehicles for the expression of information that may (or may not) be of a psychic nature. The term *clairvoyance*, like the general term *ESP*, cuts across such distinctions. If by any means a person or other organism behaves as though it has extrasensory information about some currently existing physical object or current event that is unknown to any other organism, we by definition term this clairvoyance.

The next section will briefly discuss the major studies of whether the class of observation termed clairvoyance in fact occurs. Although such experiments have provided evidence of the occurrence of clairvoyance, it would be misleading to think of these as "conclusive experiments" establishing the occurrence of clairvoyance. Contrary to a popularized conception of science, no experiment is ever conclusive in the sense that the proof of a mathematical theorem (e.g., a geometrical theorem) is conclusive.

Further, only to the degree that we can produce evidence of clairvoyance on demand or at least predict ahead of time when an experiment will or will not be successful can we say that we have compelling evidence for clairvoyance. To the degree that we cannot do this, the skeptic can always find a way around accepting our evidence, even if his stated reasons are unorthodox and generally scientifically unacceptable. C. E. M. Hansel (7) provides a notable example.

Therefore, I begin this review of the evidence for clairvoyance, by discussing the experiments aimed strictly at providing a demonstration of the occurrence of clairvoyance, but I will later move on to the classes of evidence—mostly more recent—that do not merely raise questions but that help to answer questions about the conditions under which such events do and do not occur. The latter are surely the best evidence for the reality of clairvoyance as a scientifically interesting and meaningful event.

THE MAJOR STUDIES AND EVIDENCE

Demonstration Experiments

Probably the earliest quantitatively assessed successful clairvoyance experiment is one reported in 1889 by Charles Richet (28). He worked with the outstanding subject Léonie B., who under hypnosis seemed capable of paranormal feats. Richet studied her for evidence of clairvoyance. In some earlier work, she had shown no success with playing cards, but in the study we will now consider, her results were outstanding.

The card that she was trying to identify was concealed in an envelope in part of the work and in double envelopes in another part. Success was essentially the same in both cases. She held the envelope while making her responses. The card had been randomly selected from 10 packs consisting of 52 cards each. She would talk casually with the experimenter while she attempted to get impressions of the card. She would often take hours to identify a single card and would never make a definite commitment identifying the card until she felt quite certain of her response. Unfortunately she was allowed to finger the envelope without restrictions and even to write on it freely during the period when she was attempting to get impressions.

Sometimes she was able to get an impression that she felt could identify the card completely, sometimes not. Of the 15 responses she produced that could (potentially) completely identify a card, 12 were correct. The odds against this happening by chance are immense.

The drawback to this work was the loose conditions under which it was conducted. Sensory cues cannot be ruled out as an explanation of the results, although Richet felt they were very unlikely. (In my own opinion, sensory cues should be considered a probable explanation of the outcome in this case.) A later block of work with the same subject under conditions designed to eliminate any chance of trickery failed to produce striking results.

In 1928, Ina Jephson (9) published work on clairvoyance that proved very important in a historical sense as well as being of value in its own right. Jephson's work did much to stimulate J. B. Rhine to a strong interest in clairvoyance (25, p. 34). As we shall see later, the work from Rhine's laboratory on clairvoyance is the most extensive, and possibly the most important, that we have.

Jephson used playing cards as the targets in her study. Subjects not previously known to have ESP ability tested themselves at home under Jephson's instructions. Each person was to complete 25 trials, but was not to attempt to guess more than 5 of those on a given day. The procedure was to shuffle the deck thoroughly, draw out a card face downward, guess the card, record the guess, record also the identity of the card, replace the card, reshuffle, and repeat the operation until 5 guesses and targets were recorded.

Thus, Jephson collected 1200 sets of 5 guesses and of these 245 were completely correct as against 115 expected by chance. As concerns color, 3307 were correct (3000 were expected by chance) and 1832 suit guesses were correct (1500 were expected by chance). The odds against such outcomes occurring by chance are very great.

Additionally, Jephson noted very striking "position effects" within the set of five calls—for example, a sharp drop from the first guess of the set to the second in certain groups of the test data. Such effects, including the decline effect, have been noted in many subsequent experiments in various contexts. Unfortunately, the psychology of "internal effects" (such as boredom, distraction, etc.) has not been adequately explored, although such effects, properly studied, may someday provide important clues to the function of ESP in forced-choice situations (i.e., where the subject must make a guess on each trial from among a known group of possibilities). Jephson's careful attention to such effects in her early study gives her work additional historical importance.

A paragraph from Jephson's paper (9, p. 225) illustrates the degree to which her conclusions were indications of things to come in parapsychology:

These records which I shall show do confirm in my view the possibility of this direct divination of objective facts without the use of our normal senses. They also confirm the natural expectation, which I have already expressed, that first, if such a faculty exists at all it would be widespread, and that we can experiment with it as we can with other senses; and secondly, that it is bound at least by some of the known and recognized psychological habits and laws.

These words run counter to the English tradition of thinking of the person possessing psi as "a rare bird indeed," but they served as a timely prelude to the major thrust of American parapsychology, with its emphasis on volunteer or "unselected" subjects and the focus on the psychology of ESP performance. We could fairly say that Jephson's clairvoyance work and Estabrooks's (4) work on telepathy in persons not known as "psychic" set the stage for the democratization of parapsychology and for the highly productive work of later decades.

In spite of its historical importance, Jephson's work did suffer the methodological difficulties one can expect when a person tests himself with what may be a much used and familiar deck of cards. It is unfortunate that a later SPR clairvoyance series done to tighten up the conditions of the original experiment (1) failed to confirm the earlier work. In my opinion, such a failure of confirmation should not be taken as devastating the value of the original work. However, it must be admitted that the conditions of the original work left much to be desired from the standpoint of assuring that the results were best described as clairvoyance, and the value of the work must remain largely the impact of its innovative character upon the research of subsequent decades.

It was the publication in 1934 of J. B. Rhine's *Extra-Sensory Perception* (25) that did the most to bring to the attention of the scientific community the claim that clairvoyance exists as a human ability and can be studied in the laboratory. It would be highly impractical to try to review all the studies of clairvoyance reported in Rhine's volume. The serious student should read for himself this very important work. I do wish, though, to introduce the reader to some of the best evidence for clairvoyance in Rhine's early monograph. This is the work with Hubert E. Pearce, Jr., as subject.

Rhine (25, p. 97) describes this outstanding subject as follows:

Pearce is a young Methodist ministerial student in the Duke School of Religion, very much devoted to his work though fairly liberal in his theology. He is very sociable and approachable, and is much interested in people. There is also a pretty general artistic trend to his personality, expressing itself mainly in musical interest and production, but extending into other fields of art as well.

Pearce has not, himself, had any striking parapsychological experiences other than numerous "hunches" and "intuitions," but he reports that his mother and others of her family have had certain clairvoyant experiences.

Pearce was tested under a considerable variety of conditions, ranging from tests in which sensory cues seem a possibility to those in which they were certainly excluded. This included very successful work with the down-through-the-deck (DT) clairvoyance technique. One could summarize his performance by saying that in general when a new test condition was introduced (including the presence of a stranger in the testing room), Pearce's normally above-chance performance tended to drop dramatically for at least one run through the deck, and usually more, and then returned to a fairly stable above-chance level.

Conditions of working with Pearce were gradually tightened up, culminating in the well-known Pearce-Pratt series (24, 25, 27). Before each session, Pratt and Pearce synchronized their watches. Then Pearce went to a cubicle in the Duke Library, and Pratt to the Physics Building (now the Social Sciences Building). Percipient and experimenter were thus about 100 yards apart. Pratt shuffled a deck of standard ESP cards and, at a specified time, removed the top card and, without looking at it, placed it face down on a book at the center of the table. Thirty seconds later, by prearrangement, Pearce wrote down his guess. A minute after he had removed the first card, Pratt removed the next card, and Pearce made his guess thirty seconds later. This continued through the deck. Thus, Pratt removed the top card from the deck and put it on the book once each minute. The cards removed were kept in order for later recording. Two runs (50 trials) were made per day. Before leaving their respective buildings, both Pratt and Pearce made duplicate records of their respective cards or calls, each sealing one copy in an envelope to be delivered directly to Rhine and keeping the other to check the results when the two met following the session.

At the 100-yard distance, 750 trials (Series A, C, and D combined) were made, yielding 261 hits (150 were expected by chance). The associated critical ratio, a statistical measure of deviation from chance expectation (see Glossary), is 10.1. The probability of a result this extreme or more extreme happening by chance is very small. The average number of hits per run was 8.7, compared with chance average of 5.0.

In a longer series of trials (Series B), Pearce and Pratt were about 250 yards apart and used the same test arrangement. Pratt, with the cards, was in the medical building; Pearce was in the library. This series of 1075 trials yielded 288 hits, or an average score per run of 6.7. The associated critical ratio is 5.6, corresponding to a probability of a chance result of less than 3.8×10^{-8}.

In 1937, Pratt reported statistically significant clairvoyance results in a

blind-matching study done at Columbia University with a subject identified as Mrs. M. This study (22) employed the conventional ESP-card
deck. The subject was sitting before a screen with a slit at the bottom.
Before her, next to the screen, was a row of cards, 1 for each of the 5
symbols involved in the standard ESP-card deck. Each symbol was concealed beneath a blank card. The subject was to indicate which of the
cards in front of her matched the one on top of the desk held by the
experimenter. She had no normal way of knowing either the card on top
of the deck or the nature of the symbol against which she was matching it.
Neither Pratt nor the subject knew the order of the 5 concealed symbols
on the subject's side of the screen. By pointing in the slit beneath the
screen, the subject indicated to Pratt the position of a concealed card that
she believed matched the card on top of the deck. Pratt then lifted that
card from the top of the deck and placed it face down opposite the
position indicated by Mrs. M. For each run of trials (the number of cards
per run varied, being 50 or 100), a new arrangement of the 5 key cards
(and, of course, the ESP target cards) was established, with precautions
to insure that neither Pratt nor Mrs. M. knew the order.

In an initial series of 7800 trials using this technique, Mrs. M. obtained
188 hits more than chance expectation, producing a critical ratio of 5.3,
which is highly significant ($p = 1.2 \times 10^{-7}$).

Near the end of this series, the subject's performance declined. She was
then tested on a less rigorous procedure in the hope of helping her to
recover her initial level of performance, but this was to no avail. She was
then tested again for 13,700 trials with the blind-matching technique
described above. This produced only chance results. Nevertheless, if the
results of these two blocks of testing are pooled, the results are still
highly significant.

In 1938 and in 1940 extensive work in clairvoyance at the University
of Colorado was reported by Dorothy R. Martin and Frances P. Stribic
(16–18). The most important part of this work was with thirteen subjects
who were tested individually using the DT clairvoyance technique with
the standard ESP deck. The cards were shuffled and placed face down on the
opposite side of the screen from the subject. After twenty-five calls, the
checkup was made. The reader is referred to the original reports for
details of the procedure and checkup; the latter varied somewhat in differing parts of the testing. Most of the time a student did the testing instead
of the chief investigators, but because scoring rate did not differ with
respect to the experimenter, there is no reason to think that the student
assistant might have been either incompetent or dishonest.

The most outstanding of the thirteen subjects, C. J., was tested for
25,000 trials (1000 runs) and produced an average (mean) score per run
of 6.89. This produces a critical ratio of 29.35. The latter is one of the

larger critical ratios in the history of parapsychology and thus provides some of our most striking evidence for the occurrence of clairvoyance.

A number of the other 13 subjects also produced results of extraordinary statistical significance.

In a most interesting variation, C. J. was tested with 10 decks of cards on the table (behind the screen) at one time and was asked to guess down through one of the decks pushed forward toward the bottom center of the screen and to ignore the other decks. C. J. called 110 decks in this selective way. His mean score per run was 8.17, associated with a critical ratio of 16. For comparison, his guesses for the deck pushed forward were matched against the cards in each of the other 9 decks. In this control comparison the mean score per run was 5.02, which is about as near to mean chance expectation of 5.00 as one could ever expect, given sampling error. This series shows a remarkable selectivity for the extrasensory process. It also provides strong refutation of the arguments of people who, like G. Spencer Brown (3), claim that ESP results are caused by slight aberrations from "ideal" randomness in the target arrangements and, correspondingly, in subject calls.

C. J. was also tested (17) for 25,000 trials with the same experimental arrangement as before except that he was to guess up through the deck of cards rather than down through it as he had done earlier. In this instance his performance was still better: a mean run score of 7.39, associated with a critical ratio of 37.

All the clairvoyance series done at the University of Colorado during 1937–1939, a series of 12,470 runs (or 311,750 trials) using 322 subjects, yield cumulatively high significance. The mean run score was 5.83, associated with an immensely significant critical ratio of 45.70. Non-ESP control comparisons were made, and these produced a mean run score of 4.98 and a critical ratio of 1.00.

In 1939, J. G. Pratt and J. L. Woodruff at Duke University reported extensive work using a matching test of clairvoyance (23). They tested 66 unselected subjects. In two experimental series that differed methodologically, a total of 3868 runs (96,700 trials) were completed with a mean run score of 5.25 and an associated critical ratio of 7.80, which is very highly significant ($p < 2.6 \times 10^{-12}$). Each of the two series showed independent statistical significance, although Series B was better safeguarded against various possible sources of error. In Series B there were 2400 runs (60,000 trials) contributed by 24 undergraduate women from Duke and 8 other adults. The mean run score was 5.20, contributing a critical ratio of 4.99, which is highly significant ($p < 7.42 \times 10^{-7}$).

Process-Oriented Research

Much of the evidence for clairvoyance summarized above is often regarded as the strongest available evidence of the existence of clairvoyance. It is certainly strong evidence, but there is another class of evidence that must be given equal, if not greater, weight than the demonstration (or "proof-of-existence") -oriented evidence just cited. This is the evidence from studies that vary test conditions or measure subject differences and observe the effect on scoring; that is, the results are treated as a dependent variable. All such work can be termed *process-oriented research*, because it is aimed at providing understanding, prediction, and control of psi.

A few parapsychologists have talked of process-oriented research as though it were opposed in aim to so-called proof-oriented work, or what I have termed demonstration-oriented work. This is a false dichotomy. Both classes of research can be interpreted as providing evidence for the occurrence of psi or, in our special case, clairvoyance. As concerns process-oriented work, some of the best evidence for the existence of clairvoyance comes from work that helps us to understand the conditions under which clairvoyant observations will occur. Such process-oriented studies not only provide understanding of what would otherwise be considered anomalous events; they also give some assurance that the events in question are scientifically meaningful events. The latter statement deserves further explanation.

E. G. Boring (2), who was a well-known critic of parapsychology, complained that parapsychologists know nothing of the boundary conditions of their supposed phenomena—the conditions under which these events do and do not occur. His argument was that in the typical ESP test, we simply have correlations between events (e.g., calls and target cards) but that such observations are completely anomalous in that we cannot predict when they will or will not occur (i.e., we have no positive knowledge about them). Thus, he called the results of ESP tests "empty correlations" —observations without scientific meaning. Why should scientists take an interest in supposed phenomena that are thought to be rare to the point of appearing miraculous and that are unpredictable in their occurrence? In short, events that cannot be predicted and (in the case of experimental observations) controlled are considered random events, and scientists are not inclined to get interested in random events.

Such a line of argument is in one sense reasonable and justifiable. It is simply a statement of the kinds of events with which science is basically concerned. However, the argument is unfair because it assumes that parapsychologists have no knowledge of the factors that influence the manifestation of ESP. It is true that at the moment we have no definite knowledge of physical factors (e.g., distance or type of target material) that inhibit the function of ESP (including clairvoyance), but we do have considerable knowledge of the way psychological factors influence ESP performance. Some instances of this knowledge will be given below. Thus, Boring's argument contains a false assumption.

In my own opinion, further efforts to do experiments to prove the occurrence of clairvoyance (or other forms of ESP) are misguided. The evidence in parapsychology that best answers the criticism of Boring is from the process-oriented research. All such work aims at obtaining knowledge of specific functional relationships between measurable and/or controllable non-ESP factors and the level of ESP performance. To the degree that such research is successful, it leads to prediction of and control over psi. Thus, the results of successful and replicable process-oriented parapsychological research constitute the most scientifically meaningful and satisfactory evidence for occurrence of the particular form of psi under investigation.

We can easily imagine that the phenomena we study will remain scientifically controversial until process-oriented research, presently becoming predominant in parapsychology, removes the events we study from the realm of the anomaly and the miraculous. The fact of growing scientific interest in psi is probably related, at least in part, to the feeling that scientists studying such events are finally beginning to gain some understanding of those events. Understanding means the ability to predict and/or to control the events in question.

It is neither accidental nor surprising that the bulk of the process-oriented ESP research has been clairvoyance work. I earlier noted that this work is much less cumbersome than telepathy or general-ESP studies and that it is easier to control against sensory communication.

Below I will briefly discuss what I believe to be some of the main types of process-oriented work concerned with clairvoyance. The examples I will give are not intended to be exhaustive, but are only illustrative. It would require a volume at least the size of this one to begin to adequately describe the rather massive amount of process-oriented clairvoyance work.

Belief and Performance on Clairvoyance Tests

An old Protestant hymn says, "All things are possible, only believe!" Parapsychologists have long been asking whether belief influences performance on ESP tasks.

In an extremely useful review of the experimental evidence about the effects of belief upon ESP-test performance, Palmer (20, 21) points out that four rather different definitions of *belief* have been used by experimenters studying this problem area:

1. Belief in the possibility of ESP occurring under the specific test conditions employed in the experiment. This was the definition originated by Schmeidler (29) in her extensive work in this area—the work that started the major interest in the belief variable. (Note that affirming this kind of belief is not equivalent to saying that one feels it is possible for oneself to show ESP in this given circumstance.)
2. Belief in the existence of ESP in an abstract or theoretical sense.
3. Belief that one may oneself have psychic ability or may have had one or more psychic experiences.
4. Belief that one can demonstrate or has demonstrated ESP in the experiment by scoring above chance on the ESP test.

There is a tradition in parapsychology, originated by Schmeidler, that when a given criterion of belief about ESP is considered, a subject who definitely affirms the belief in question is called a "sheep" and one who disavows the belief is called a "goat." If a subject is undecided about a given belief statement, there is a problem of whether to classify him as a sheep or a goat or in a third category. Different experimenters studying belief and ESP have made different decisions about how to classify undecided subjects (20).

Palmer, in his review of the sheep-goat literature (20), concludes that there is good cumulative evidence that persons classified as sheep according to either criterion 1 or 2 above are apt to produce higher scores on ESP tasks (especially forced-choice tasks) than are persons classified as goats according to the same criterion. Considerable studies now exist regarding the sheep–goat problem, and there would be no place in this paper for a thorough review of that problem. Suffice it to say that the largest block of the sheep–goat work has involved clairvoyance testing and thus is relevant to the topic at hand. Further details of this work are available in the Schmeidler–McConnell book on personality patterns and ESP performance (29), the Palmer review (20), and the original literature cited in those sources.

In short, belief either that ESP is possible in the test at hand or belief in ESP in the abstract is associated with a better chance of positive scoring in an ESP test than is disavowal of such belief. Here is a weak, but somewhat reliable, functional relationship, and this relationship has been established largely in clairvoyance testing, particularly in forced-choice (e.g., card-calling) clairvoyance tasks. This provides an important base of evidence for the reality of clairvoyance. It is worth adding that a number of independent experimenters, using rather varied experimental situations, have contributed evidence for the sheep–goat effect. The sheep–goat effect certainly suggests that there may be some validity to the folk belief that psychic things may not function as well for skeptics as for believers.

Precisely why sheep should perform better than goats is not, however, really understood and deserves much further study.

Hypnosis and Clairvoyance

Hypnosis has long had a popular association with ESP. The idea that "trance," hypnotic or otherwise, might somehow facilitate extrasensory performance comes to us not only from Spiritualism and the early days of psychic research but from many cultures wherein shamans enter trance-like states and sometimes perhaps receive extrasensory information. Also, there is a popular, if rather naive, notion that extrasensory information is somehow unconscious and that being in hypnosis puts one in an unconscious state, which allows one to use the unconscious extrasensory information. It is not, therefore, surprising that there has been considerable work on hypnosis and ESP performance.

This work has recently been carefully reviewed by Honorton and Krippner (8) and by Van de Castle (35). Both reviewers conclude that at least under certain conditions, hypnosis can be used to facilitate ESP performance. It is also apparent from these reviews that the very great majority of the quantitative studies in this area have involved clairvoyance testing. Honorton and Krippner conclude that hypnosis definitely influences ESP performance. Moreover, although it would appear that the effects of hypnosis can facilitate a negative deviation (psi-missing) if factors in the experiment (e.g., subject variables) militate in favor of a negative deviation (8), the great majority of the studies report that the hypnosis condition favors positive scoring (8, 35).

In this hypnosis work, then, we have not only useful knowledge about the function of ESP, but also another kind of evidence for the reality of clairvoyance. I wish to repeat that the great bulk of the quantitative-experimental work with hypnosis has involved clairvoyance testing. Indeed, all but one of the classifiable studies at least permitted the possibility of clairvoyance (35).

Personality—ESP Studies

Much work has been done to discover personality correlates of success in typical laboratory experiments. Such studies have been reviewed elsewhere (15, 29) and are discussed in Chapter 3. A considerable proportion of this work—including some of the work that seems most replicable—has involved clairvoyance testing. As an outstanding example of this work, I will focus here on the recent extensive work done at Andhra University in Waltair, India, by Kanthamani and Rao (11–14) with young students (16–18 years) in English-language schools in Waltair.

This clairvoyance work indicates that (at least in India under the circumstances of the testing) better ESP performance is turned in by subjects showing warmth and sociability, dominance, happy-go-lucky dispositions, toughness and realism, extroversion and freedom from neuroticism than by subjects with opposite dispositions. The personality test used was the Cattell High School Personality Questionnaire.

In the Kanthamani–Rao work it was evident that when a broad dimension of personality (e.g., extraversion or neuroticism) consists of a group of component factors (or traits) separately measurable by the personality test, the combination of these factors when used to predict clairvoyance scores makes for more successful prediction than does any one of the factors used singly. It would appear that the individual traits measured by the component factors may affect ESP performance more because of their relation to the broader personality dimension (e.g., extroversion) than in their own right. Kanthamani and Rao suggest in the case of extroversion (13, p. 210) that "the greater the relationship between these traits and extraversion, probably the more reliable is their prediction of ESP scoring direction."

The Kanthamani–Rao clairvoyance–personality findings help in some degree to understand apparent inconsistencies sometimes reported in the personality–ESP work. Usually in such work only individual trait measures have been used to predict ESP performance. As indicated above, such work may be much more successful when a broad dimension of personality is studied (with prediction based upon a combination of factors) than when factors or traits are studied individually as predictors.

Of special interest is the Kanthamani–Rao work in relation to extroversion. As these authors' own survey of the literature shows (13), measures of extraversion have shown a considerable consistency in their relation to ESP performance, both between experiments and between experimenters. They further have shown that measures conceptually related to extroversion, but not designed directly to measure it, very often have shown the same relation with ESP scores that one might expect from the positive correlation of extroversion and ESP performance.

Considering the quality of the Kanthamani-Rao work, the consistency of the outcomes of their work, and the convergence of several of their major findings with earlier work, the block of studies cited above must be considered one of the important pieces of evidence for clairvoyance. The reader is referred to the materials cited earlier, and especially to Chapter 3, for further evidence on the relations of personality factors to ESP performance. The amount of work in this area, much of it consisting of clairvoyance studies, is perhaps the greatest in any area of parapsychology.

General Comments on Process-Oriented Work as Evidence of Clairvoyance

It seems clear from the above information that it is possible to experimentally manipulate the level of performance on a clairvoyance task through the use of hypnosis and to predict probability of success on a clairvoyance task by measuring subjects' beliefs regarding ESP or by measuring their personality characteristics. Other examples could be cited of promising work relating clairvoyance-task performance to psychological variables. Clairvoyance studies really form the backbone of process-oriented research in parapsychology during the past few decades. (A smaller but substantial amount of process-oriented work has been done with precognition—see Chapter 6.) The use of clairvoyance testing rather than the much more cumbersome and less easily controlled telepathy (or "general ESP") testing has made possible, rather economically, a great mass of work with groups of unselected or volunteer subjects, and this work has provided a considerable basis for understanding the psychology of ESP as it functions in the typical ESP test.

Thus, the early Duke emphasis on clairvoyance studies appears to have been a wise one and has its fulfillment in a growing body of knowledge of the psychology of extrasensory response.

POSSIBLE SIGNIFICANCE OF CLAIRVOYANCE IN THE BIOPSYCHOLOGICAL SPHERE

At the beginning of this chapter I suggested that the term *clairvoyance*, with its literal translation "clear seeing," confuses the issue of the nature of this psychic capacity.

The term *clairvoyance* more or less implies a perceptual model. Indeed, the term *extrasensory perception* suggests an analogue with sensory perception. As it happens, this perceptual analogue is faulty in being far too limited to encompass even the sphere of activity that we shall have to call clairvoyant—even if we confine clairvoyance to events that have been experimentally studied. Recently I reviewed some of the evidence indicating that extrasensory information gains expression in nonperceptual ways (e.g., through memory or through associative processes), but there is not space here to discuss the full extent of the evidence (32). I will mention just as an example that studies of PK with hidden targets (in this case dice) provide evidence that subjects can use ESP without the development of conscious perceptions about the target (5, 6, 19, 33). In these studies the subject (and usually the experimenter also) is unaware, on a given trial, of which die face is the target—that is, which face of the die the subject is supposed to make come up—that information being written on a hidden sheet. Yet subjects have shown success on such tasks.

The importance of the proposition that clairvoyance (or ESP in general) can function nonperceptually is this: the range of potential extrasensory influence upon behavior—everyday behavior included—is vastly expanded. We do not have to develop a conscious awareness, cognition, or perception of something apprehended extrasensorially in order to respond to that information. To put it in somewhat popular parlance: it may very well be that clairvoyance (and other ESP) can occur entirely unconsciously. Further, this basically unconscious extrasensory response may function in the service of personal needs, and there is now experimental evidence for this supposition (32). This is what I have termed *psi-mediated instrumental response* (PMIR), the use of psi (including extrasensory knowledge) by the organism to enable it to make responses that are *instrumental* in fulfilling its needs.

In the review just cited (32) I have described a conceptual model for PMIR. That model, among other things, implies that PMIR can occur (*a*) without a conscious effort to use psi, (*b*) without a conscious effort to fulfill the need subserved by PMIR, (*c*) without prior sensory knowledge that the need-relevant circumstance even exists, and (4) without the development of conscious perceptions (e.g., mental images) or ideas concerning this circumstance. PMIR can thus occur without the person's being aware that anything extraordinary is happening.

All this is not to deny that clairvoyance can and does function, at times, to produce a perception or cognition of the ESP object (or target); it is, rather, to correct the unfortunate historical overemphasis on the possible perceptual function of clairvoyance. Clairvoyant "visions" (hallucinations or dreams) or cognitions (ideas) sometimes happen, but they are only two of many mediating vehicles by which extrasensory knowledge can have its impact upon the organism and by which such knowledge can influence behavior. The full description of the PMIR model (32) contains detailed and testable assumptions about a variety of ways in which PMIR can accomplish its ends without the development of conscious perceptions or cognitions of the kind just discussed.

The relevance of such a model to psychology and biology should be obvious. The specific assumptions of the model are amenable to experimental test, but the kinds of studies that will best test the model are a radically different type of ESP experiment: studies in which an individual has an opportunity to use psi unconsciously in an instrumental fashion but in which he never knows psi is being studied. This kind of study is optimally relevant to understand psi in life situations because in typical life situations we are generally not making a conscious effort to use psi and we are often not consciously aware of the objects or events in our environment to which it would be useful to respond via psi. The earliest published study of this type was my work on extrasensory effects upon memory (31). Martin Johnson of the University of Utrecht has also been working on these problems (10), apparently from a similar perspective.

One of the fundamental assumptions of the PMIR model is that the organism actively uses clairvoyance to scan its environment for need-relevant objects or events and that when extrasensory information is thus obtained, there arises a disposition toward PMIR.

The PMIR model attempts to place extrasensory response in a natural-istic, functional context. The model has considerable experimental evi-dence behind some of its assumptions; but much more work is needed to test the full model, and the model will certainly be modified through future experimentation.

The reality of clairvoyance now seems well established—perhaps better established than any other form of psi (if, indeed, there are as many separate forms as is sometimes supposed). What we must recognize as a result of decades of research is that clairvoyance is very likely a general ability among humans and probably—I should say almost certainly—extends into lower animals. There is now good evidence at least for one or another form of ESP in certain nonhuman species (see Chapter 9). Thus, we must begin to ask questions about how this form of psi fits into the psychological and biological scheme of things. Surely clairvoyance does not exist purely to call cards in the laboratory.

Thus, it may be appropriate to close this overview with a bold sugges-tion: Far from being something rare, supernatural, or paranormal, clair-voyance (like, perhaps, other forms of psi) may be an important, if often subtle and unrecognized, factor in some of the interactions that make up the everyday experience of organisms, human and otherwise.

REFERENCES

1. Besterman, T.; Soal, S. G.; and Jephson, I. "Report of a Series of Experi-ments in Clairvoyance Conducted at a Distance Under Approximately Fraud-Proof Conditions." *Proceedings of the Society for Psychical Re-search*, 39 (1930): 375–414.
2. Boring, E. G. "The Present Status of Parapsychology." *American Scientist*, 43 (1955): 108–117.
3. Brown, G. S. "Statistical Significance in Psychical Research." *Nature*, 172 (1953): 154–156.
4. Estabrooks, G. H. "A Contribution to Experimental Telepathy." *Bulletin of the Boston Society for Psychic Research*, 5 (1927): 1–30.
5. Fisk, G. W., and West, D. J. "Dice-Casting Experiments with a Single Subject." *Journal of the Society for Psychical Research*, 39 (1958): 277–287.

6. Forwald, H. "An Experiment in Guessing Cards by Throwing a Die." *Journal of Parapsychology*, 27 (1963): 16–22.
7. Hansel, C. E. M. *ESP: A Scientific Evaluation.* Scribner's: New York, 1966.
8. Honorton, C., and Krippner, S. "Hypnosis and ESP: A Review of the Experimental Literature." *Journal of the American Society for Psychical Research*, 63 (1969): 214–252.
9. Jephson, I. "Evidence for Clairvoyance in Card-Guessing." *Proceedings of the Society for Psychical Research*, 38 (1928): 223–271.
10. Johnson, M. "A Written Academic Exam as a Disguised Test of Clairvoyance." Paper presented at the Fifteenth Annual Convention of the Parapsychological Association, Edinburgh, Scotland, September 2–5, 1972.
11. Kanthamani, B. K., and Rao, K. R. "Personality Characteristics of ESP Subjects: I. Primary Personality Characteristics and ESP." *Journal of Parapsychology*, 35 (1971): 189–207.
12. Kanthamani, B. K., and Rao, K. R. "Personality Characteristics of ESP Subjects: II. The Combined Personality Measure (CPM) and ESP." *Journal of Parapsychology*, 36 (1972): 56–70.
13. Kanthamani, B. K., and Rao, K. R. "Personality Characteristics of ESP Subjects: III. Extraversion and ESP." *Journal of Parapsychology*, 36 (1972): 198–212.
14. Kanthamani, B. K., and Rao, K. R. "Personality Characteristics of ESP Subjects: IV. Neuroticism and ESP." *Journal of Parapsychology*, 37 (1973): 37–50.
15. Mangan, G. L. *A Review of Published Research on the Relationship of Some Personality Variables to ESP Scoring Level.* Parapsychological Monographs, No. 1, Parapsychology Foundation: New York, 1958.
16. Martin, D. R., and Stribic, F. P. "Studies in Extra-Sensory Perception: I. An Analysis of 25,000 Trials." *Journal of Parapsychology*, 2 (1938): 23–30.
17. Martin, D. R., and Stribic, F. P. "Studies in Extra-Sensory Perception: II. An Analysis of a Second Series of 25,000 Trials." *Journal of Parapsychology*, 2 (1938): 287–295.
18. Martin, D. R., and Stribic, F. P. "Studies in Extra-Sensory Perception. III. A Review of All University of Colorado Experiments." *Journal of Parapsychology*, 4 (1940): 159–248.
19. Osis, K. "A Test of the Relationship Between ESP and PK." *Journal of Parapsychology*, 17 (1953): 298–309.
20. Palmer, J. "Scoring in ESP Tests as a Function of Belief in ESP: Part I. The Sheep–Goat Effect." *Journal of the American Society for Psychical Research*, 65 (1971): 373–408.
21. Palmer, J. "Scoring in ESP Tests as a Function of Belief in ESP: Part II. Beyond the Sheep–Goat Effect." *Journal of the American Society for Psychical Research*, 66 (1972): 1–26.
22. Pratt, J. G. "Clairvoyant Blind Matching." *Journal of Parapsychology*, 1 (1937): 10–17.
23. .Pratt, J. G., and Woodruff, J. L. "Size of Stimulus Symbols in Extra-Sensory Perception." *Journal of Parapsychology*, 3 (1939): 121–158.
24. Rhine, J. B. "Some Selected Experiments in Extra-Sensory Perception." *Journal of Abnormal and Social Psychology*, 31 (1936): 216–228. (See also Rhine, J. B. "Some Basic Experiments in Extra-Sensory Perception: A Background," *Journal of Parapsychology*, 1 [1937]: 70–80.)

25. Rhine, J. B. *Extra-Sensory Perception*. Humphries: Boston, 1934; repr. 1964.
26. Rhine, J. B. "Comments: Fruitless Research on Unsolvable Problems." *Journal of Parapsychology*, 35 (1971): 306–307.
27. Rhine, J. B., and Pratt, J. G. "A Review of the Pearce-Pratt Distance Series of ESP Tests." *Journal of Parapsychology*, 18 (1954): 165–177.
28. Richet, C. "Further Experiments in Hypnotic Lucidity or Clairvoyance." *Proceedings of the Society for Psychical Research*, 6 (1889): 66–83.
29. Schmeidler, G. R., and McConnell, R. A. *ESP and Personality Patterns*. Yale University Press: New Haven, Conn., 1958.
30. Soal, S. G., and Bateman, F. *Modern Experiments in Telepathy*. Faber: London, 1954.
31. Stanford, R. G. "Extrasensory Effects upon 'Memory.'" *Journal of the American Society for Psychical Research*, 64 (1970): 161–186.
32. Stanford, R. G. "The Integration of Cognitive Processing Factors: ESP in Life Situations." Paper presented at the AAAS Annual Meeting, Washington, D.C., December, 1972, as part of the symposium "Understanding Parapsychological Phenomena: A Survey of Four Possible Areas of Integration," sponsored by the Parapsychological Association.
33. Thouless, R. H. "A Report on an Experiment in Psycho-Kinesis with Dice, and a Discussion on Psychological Factors Favouring Success." *Proceedings of the Society for Psychical Research*, 49 (1951): 107–130.
34. Thouless, R. H., and Rhine, J. B. "Comments: Dialogue on Bad-Risk Problems." *Journal of Parapsychology*, 36 (1972): 242–244.
35. Van de Castle, R. L. "The Facilitation of ESP Through Hypnosis." *American Journal of Clinical Hypnosis*, 12, no. 1 (1969): 37–56.

E. Douglas Dean

E. Douglas Dean, *M.S., has been research director of the Psi Communications Project at Newark (New Jersey) College of Engineering since 1962. He has also taught computer programming and statistics at the college and lectured on parapsychology to many professional groups in the United States and abroad.*

After earning a bachelor's degree, a bachelor with honors degree, and a master's degree in electrochemistry at Liverpool University in England, doing postgraduate research at Cambridge and Princeton, he held a variety of positions in industry, research, and College Board testing. From 1959 to 1962 he was assistant director of research at the Parapsychology Foundation in New York, developing electroencephalographic and plethysmographic methods of measuring telepathy.

As president of the Parapsychological Association in 1967, he began the effort to obtain membership for his organization in the American Association for the Advancement of Science. He successfully completed this in 1969 when the Parapsychological Association was granted full affiliation with the AAAS. Since 1970 he has been president of the Jersey Society of Parapsychology, where he introduced Kirlian high-voltage photography methods of testing psychic healing.

He is author of numerous articles in the scientific and popular press and co-author of Executive ESP *(Prentice-Hall, 1974), which details 10 years of work at Newark College of Engineering with presidents and managers of business companies. His 1966 report "Plethysmograph Recordings as ESP Responses" in the* International Journal of Neuropsychiatry *(2, no. 5) is considered a classic experiment in parapsychology.*

Mr. Dean can be reached at Newark College of Engineering, Department of Industrial and Management Engineering, 323 High Street, Newark, N.J. 07102.

6 Precognition and Retrocognition

E. DOUGLAS DEAN

SUMMARY

Precognition is the hardest aspect of parapsychology for us to understand yet the easiest to experience and to test scientifically in the laboratory. Retrocognition occurs but is reported much more rarely.

The Greek civilization accepted precognition and made decisions based on what the oracles said. In Biblical times also there was strong belief in it. Then it died in the Middle Ages and now it is slowly beginning to come back.

Hundreds of studies have been made of spontaneous precognition experiences and of controlled experiments in the laboratory. The use of modern electronic instruments has confirmed this. Even dreams have been shown to come true in the laboratory.

Theoretically, electromagnetic theory now requires "effects before causes," as does precognition. Thus, electromagnetic theory may help precognition take its place in the larger understanding of consciousness that is beginning and may come to be regarded as normal similar to ancient times.

INTRODUCTION

This aspect of parapsychology—namely, precognition and retrocognition—in which the results suggest getting accurate information directly from the future and from the past, is the hardest part for us to understand. Yet surveys (28) show that precognitions occur more often than any of the other kinds of ESP, particularly in dreams. And then if we go into the laboratory to try to evoke psychic experiences under controlled scientific conditions, precognition experiments are the easiest to do. (Here *easiest* means accomplishing precognition while preventing such information being obtained by means of the five senses.) The information barrier arises because the information is about a future event, such that it cannot be known or inferred from what is known. Precognition experiments are

153

so easy and safe that they have even been used in a mass test of 100,000 school children (see below).

The definition of *precognition* makes a distinction between (a) future events that can be predicted (e.g., "There will be a total eclipse of the sun starting at 8:25 A.M., six months hence") and (b) future events that can only be precognized (e.g., Jeane Dixon stated in *Parade* magazine in 1956 that "in the 1960 election it will be won by a Democrat, but he will be assassinated or die in office"). The assassination of President Kennedy occurred on November 22, 1963. There is implied in Jeane Dixon's precognition that neither President Eisenhower before nor President Johnson after would be assassinated in office, and that also came true. In a similar manner, the definition of *retrocognition* distinguishes between (a) past events that can be recalled using memory when the person took part in the event (e.g., if he remembers voting on a Tuesday last November) and (b) past events that can only be retrocognized. An example of the latter is Gardner Murphy's case of Mrs. Buterbaugh (20, p. 5), who saw open fields and a few trees on a summer afternoon 50 years ago through an open office window, instead of the Nebraska Wesleyan campus, Madison Street, and Willard Sorority House as it is now. In contrast to precognitions, which occur more often, retrocognitions seem to be rarely reported.

The difficulty of understanding how a person can know the future when the future has not yet happened makes some people think that the future must be determined; they have a fatalistic attitude. This is easily shown to be wrong. Suppose, for instance, that you drive home in your car and run over somebody. When the police officer comes to arrest you, you cannot say to him, "I am sorry, officer. It is not my fault. The future is determined, and I could not do anything about it." This is *not* so. Of course it is your fault. You could have driven more slowly or carefully; you could have gone a less traveled route; you could have taken a bus. There is no question—the future is not determined. Yet people precognize the future. Can the future then be both not determined and precognizable? Yes—just as physicists discovered that light is both a wave and a particle and that matter is both a particle and a wave. Our brains are not yet evolved enough to understand the logical paradox of reality. The logic so helpful to us in living our normal, everyday lives reaches its limit in these paradoxes. A higher order of logic becomes necessary for understanding precognition and retrocognition.

The difficulty of comprehending how one can know the future is made worse when the information contains a warning of disaster, injury, or death. In perhaps one-third to one-half of these cases it seems one can make use of the warning to prevent the disaster. An example is given by Louisa E. Rhine (28, p. 199):

It concerns a mother who dreamed that two hours later a violent storm would loosen a heavy chandelier to fall directly on her baby's head lying in a crib below it; in the dream she saw her baby killed dead. She awoke her husband who said it was a silly dream and that she should go back to sleep as he then did. The weather was so calm the dream did appear ridiculous and she could have gone back to sleep. But she did not. She went and brought the baby back to her own bed. Two hours later just at the time she specified, a storm caused the heavy light fixture to fall right on where the baby's head had been—but the baby was not there to be killed by it.

The warning information in the mother's apparently precognitive dream, plus her decision to act on the warning, seems to have saved the baby's life. Here logic is really overwhelmed when, first, information is obtained from the future and, then, by an act of will the future is changed. Yet this is the real world we live in, whether or not we like it.

There are some people who cannot abide such a breakdown of logic. They prefer an alternative interpretation that is perfectly legitimate but that brings its own disturbing logic. In the above example, the dream carrying the warning ahead of time is the incredible event, and the storm making the fixture fall is a normal event, which is what is understood by precognition. From the other viewpoint, the dream beforehand is a normal event and the storm that made the light fixture fall is the incredible event. The latter, disturbing alternative is that the dream contained enormous energy that forced the calm weather to change into a storm to crack the ceiling holding the light fixture. Often such immense energy, particularly in dreams, is linked with Jung's archetypal energy, which can supposedly create events in the future.

This alternative, then, is not precognitive but of the mind-over-matter, or PK, variety. Many attempts have been made to decide between these two interpretations, without success. The precognitive one seems less distasteful to the majority and also more in accord with the facts. This is the view that will be followed in this chapter.

Thus, with this preamble we arrive at a definition of *precognition*: the prediction of future events, the occurrence of which cannot be inferred from present knowledge. Premonitions are similar but have the extra meaning of forewarning.

Retrocognition, then, is the experiencing of past events directly that are not in the memory of the person undergoing the experience (*directly* means other than by the senses or by inference based on the senses). Retrocognition is sometimes called *postcognition*, and it is possible that clairvoyance may have been responsible, but it has yet to be verified.

Prophecy is the same as precognition, but not all precognition is prophecy. Prophecy involves contact with what have been described as the eternal principles in man or the larger dimensions of experience.

Forecasting, trend analysis, and other forms of futuristics are not precognition. They are extrapolations into the future of present-day trends. They come under the heading of prediction, when by definition precognition has to be unpredictable.

Déjà vu—French for "already seen"— is used for the feeling of "having been there before" and the consequent ability to predict. For example, you meet a person for the first time, yet on shaking hands, you know all about him. You go to a new city never visited before, yet you find you know it well and can find an address without the aid of maps or asking the way. In a conversation you know what everyone will say next. The best explanation may be that it is a dream coming true, a dream one had forgotten. If so, it is precognition and is very common. Murphy (19, p. 8) notes that in questioning college classes, 60–70% of the students claim to have had déjà vu.

A BRIEF HISTORY OF PRECOGNITION

The historical records for precognition go back to Greek civilization of about 700 B.C. Although most historians tend to debunk or ignore facts such as this, there is no doubt that Greek behavior was based on precognitions made by the priestesses in the oracle temples. The most famous was the Oracle of Apollo, at Delphi, a village clinging to the slopes of Mt. Parnassus, about 100 miles from Athens. Hundreds of correct Delphic precognitions have come down to us (24). Apparently sulfurous fumes that came out of a hole in the ground affected the priestess's brain, inducing a trance state and perhaps aiding in precognition. Critics have gleefully jumped on this as evidence of the oracle's fairy-tale character, claiming no volcanic fumes could have come from this mountainside location of the temple, which I visited in 1969. However, the critics forget that there is a cavern beneath the temple floor where tree branches, leaves, or foliage could be burned to provide the fumes. In addition, the priestess is said to have chewed laurel leaves as a further aid. Greek laurel is not the same as the American laurel; it is equivalent to West Indian bay-rum herbs.

The best-known oracular precognition was that vouched King Croesus of Lydia. He tested many of the oracles, and the Delphic oracle won by stating that Croesus himself was cooking a lamb and a tortoise in a brazen pot, a most unusual job for a king. Then, when Croesus asked about a military campaign he was considering, the reply was that it would result in the destruction of a great army. The king took this to refer to the enemy, but it turned out to be his own. Thus, we get introduced early in history to the fact that ESP is not always explicit and must be carefully and rationally interpreted.

The precognition of greatest importance in ancient history occurred around 480 B.C. The Persians, under Xerxes, decided to attack Athens and built 1400 lumbering ships to carry the vast Persian army across the Aegean Sea. Athenians learned of it and sent to the Delphic oracle to ask for guidance. The precognition was pessimistic. "Everybody has to leave Athens as the city will be sacked; put your trust in walls of wood." Half the Athenians refused to leave their homes and, instead, just put up token wooden structures. The other half, under the naval chief Themistocles, left to go to the port of Piraeus, where they built 300 wooden ships with strong bows. The Persians came and burned Athens, as foretold by the oracle. Then the Persian fleet attacked the Greek ships, but Themistocles lured 200 Persian vessels into the Straits of Salamis, where his small boats rammed and sank the larger Persian ships. Then the rest of the Persian fleet fled home, leaving the Persian soldiers to get back across the mountains in winter as best they could; the majority died on the way. This, one of the greatest victories recorded in ancient history, the Battle of Salamis, was a result of Themistocles' believing and carrying out the prophecy of the Delphic oracle. Later, General Pericles of Athens, to celebrate the victory of Salamis, built the Parthenon, the greatest architectural wonder of the Seven Wonders of the Ancient World (25). We owe its existence to the Delphic oracle.

The Old Testament has many examples of precognition. Of the Old Testament's 39 books, 18 are headed "The Book of the Prophet." In Gen. 41: 15–36 is found the best known, Joseph's precognitive interpretation of the pharaoh's dreams. In that instance, the pharaoh dreamed he saw seven fat cows coming out of a river. Then seven lean cows came out and ate up the seven fat ones. Then seven thin ears of corn devoured seven good ears. Joseph predicted there would be seven years of good harvest, during which part of the crop must be stored in preparation for seven terrible years of famine that would follow. Gen. 41: 46–57 records that this came true.

Even more precognitive dream interpretations are found in the Book of Daniel. In Dan. 2: 1–45, Daniel not only had to interpret King Nebuchadnezzar's dream but also find what the dream was, since the king had forgotten it. During sleep Daniel found that the dream was of a great image—head, gold; arms, silver; body, brass; legs, iron; feet, part iron and clay and broken by a stone. Another dream was of a tree that was hewn down. These meant that the king's own kingdom and self were to be destroyed, as did occur. The son, King Belshazzar, saw a hand writing at a feast the famous words *Mene, mene, TEKEL, UPHARSIN.* Daniel interpreted it to mean that God had finished with his kingdom, had weighed

Belshazzar in the balance, had found him wanting, and had given the kingdom to the Medes and Persians. That night Belshazzar was slain and the kingdom given over as Daniel predicted.

In the New Testament, the day after the birth of Jesus, Joseph was warned in a dream to flee with his family to Egypt. Shortly afterward, King Herod fulfilled the warning with the terrible slaughter of male children in Bethlehem. Mark 14: 17 records Christ saying at the Last Supper, "One of you which eateth with me shall betray me." Then later Judas Iscariot did so (Mark 14: 43–46). Again, in Mark 14: 30, Christ predicts that on the same night, before the cock crows twice, Peter will deny Him three times. Mark 14: 66–72 states that this prediction came true. There are many such examples.

The Middle Ages were sad times for psychic events. Witch burnings went on in Europe from about 1250 to 1770, when the rise of science began to provide alternative explanations for paranormal events. Nevertheless, Nostradamus in France is celebrated for his sixteenth-century poetic quatrains that foretold the future. It is easy to criticize the quatrains, but to an unprejudiced mind it seems that many of them were exact hits.

Under the eyes of the SPR and the ASPR, a number of mediums—Mrs. Piper of Boston, Mrs. Verrall, Mrs. Leonard of London, and Mrs. Fleming (sister of the poet Rudyard Kipling) of India—became famous for obtaining psychic information, even with detectives watching Mrs. Piper 24 hours a day to make sure she did not get it by normal means.

In the 1920s Edgar Cayce of Virginia Beach began giving "life readings" of people's futures, some of which were very accurate. In the 1930s Mrs. Eileen Garrett became famous for precognition with her forecast of the R-101 airship disaster and others. Arthur Ford earned widespread public notice as the medium who got lists of those killed in action during World War II before the deaths occurred. More recently, Mrs. Jeane Dixon of Washington forecast presidential elections in print and was correct from 1928 to 1968. She also predicted February 20, 1947, as the date of the partition of India and Pakistan months before it happened. Gerard Croiset of Utrecht is a famous psychic well known for his precognitive "chair tests," predicting who and what kind of person will sit in a particular seat at a forthcoming meeting.

Such experiences, happening to people naturally, do not prove to the satisfaction of scientists that precognition truly exists. Presumably, that can only be done in the laboratory under strict conditions. But if such experiences did not happen, no one would go into the laboratory to try to evoke such experiences. The best combination of naturally occurring precognitions and strict scientific control is from Dr. Hans Bender at the Institute for Border Areas of Psychology at Freiburg University in West

Germany and from Mrs. Chrystine Mylius, a film actress, who noted her dreams were coming true (3). In 1954 she offered to send her dreams every two weeks for filing at Bender's institute. This has continued to date for nineteen years and now totals 2000 dreams. Very many of them proved precognitive. The best known occurred in 1958. She dreamed of a film story in which she seemed invited to take part. She dreamed also of other events happening at the same time and also of another film story, which was not connected with her. This went on for weeks and was filed meticulously in Bender's files at Freiburg. Then a writer whom she did not know in the winter of 1958 wrote a book that was published in the spring of 1959. The film company decided to film the book, a tragedy called *Night Fell upon Gotenhafen*, and asked Mrs. Mylius to be in the film, starting production in the autumn of 1959. Sure enough, her dreams of this story had already been in Bender's files for more than a year. In addition, another film story, a comedy called *Triplets on Board*, which the same film company was shooting but which she was not in, was already in the files. The film company directors were so astonished that they decided to make another film about the precognitions. This film was shown by Bender in New York at the Parapsychological Association Convention in September 1960.

J. B. Rhine and his co-workers at Duke University were the first to attempt large-scale evoked-precognition experiments in the laboratory with ESP cards in 1933. The tests worked, and precognition was found; but Rhine was so concerned about the implications (perhaps meaning that effects precede causes) that he delayed publication until 1938 (27).

Meanwhile S. G. Soal, a mathematician at London University, heard of Rhine's other experiments in telepathy and clairvoyance, which had started in 1930, and set out to try to confirm them with English people. From 1934 to 1939 he tested 162 persons with five animal cards and got zero ESP results with everyone (31), so much so that he doubted whether Rhine had really got any positive ESP results either.

However, Whately Carington (5) had been doing drawing experiments at Cambridge early in 1939 with about 300 people guessing the random drawings each day for 30 days. There were no significant matches on the evening of Carington sending a random drawing, but there were on $+1$, $+2$, -1, and -2 days, symmetrically with regard to time into the future and into the past, although not at all on earlier and later days. This was pretty fair evidence in itself for precognition and retrocognition. Also, it provided Carington with the first evidence for displacement away from the target drawing for the day on to 1 or 2 days into the future and the past. So, when Carington heard of Soal's failure, he suggested Soal look through his data to see if the displacement effect was present. Soal refused. Either the ESP occurs on the target card, he said, or it does not occur. Carington continued to try to persuade Soal, and Soal persistently refused. At last Carington broke through Soal's resistance, and Soal rechecked "in no very hopeful spirit" (3, p. 124). He found two persons, Basil Shackleton, a creative photographer, and Mrs. Gloria Stewart, a housewife, who displaced on to the +1 animal card, which had not yet been randomly chosen, suggesting precognition. For the next ten years Soal continued testing them (although Shackleton left after 3 years), and he obtained results statistically significant with odds of 10^{35}: 1 against the results being caused by coincidence. Basil Shackleton normally guessed at a rate of one card every 2.5 seconds, and he got hits on the card one ahead (+1) that had not yet been chosen. When Soal speeded him up to one card every 1.25 seconds, he failed on the card one ahead (+1) but then hit the card two ahead (+2).

For the skeptical scientist who yet retained an open mind, this event in 1939 was historically the point of no return. This evidence for precognition could not be argued with, although many tried. This even overcame the critics' charge of fraud. Twenty-three professors had been witnesses at Soal's experiments over the years. At first Soal reported he had no ESP results from 162 persons and queried Rhine's results. Yet the positive precognition results were in his data all the time, and 10 more years of results only confirmed it. From then on, because of the work of Rhine and Soal, the honest scientist had to accept that precognition was real. One famous attempt was made in 1955 by G. R. Price (26) to show that Soal's and Rhine's results were the product of fraud. Yet 16 years later (26) Price felt obliged to retract his charge.

Since then, positive laboratory results have continued. Edgar Mitchell's 1971 ESP experiment on the way to and from the moon (17) appears to be in part a precognition one, owing to timing beyond anyone's control. The experiment had to be kept secret to avoid the risk of its being banned; indeed, Mitchell might conceivably have lost his place on the mission if his interest had been too widely publicized. Thus, secrecy might have been the factor that made the results psi-missing (instead of hitting). Rhine, Soal, and others encountered similar problems: a person uses his ESP to know what the target card is and, influenced by anxiety and secrecy, displaces on to a wrong card consistently. The moon results were 3000:1 against chance, whereas 100:1 is commonly obtained in ESP experiments.

Bringing history right up to date, there are the other important series of precognition experiments by W. J. Levy (15) at Rhine's laboratory, based on original work by Duval and Mentredon in France. In these a mouse jumped from one half of a cage to the other half to avoid a random electric shock to either half. Its good luck in jumping *away from* the side due for a shock and its bad luck in jumping *into* the side due for a shock should be equal with no ESP because each side was being electrified randomly. But the nonshocking jumps occurred more often in both the French work and Levy's, suggesting that the mouse was using precognition. The method is now automated with computer checking, and since mice are active at night, the human experimenter removes himself to bed. This may be why these precognition experiments are perhaps the first repeatable experiments that satisfactorily answer the critics. The human being with his possible skepticism and fear of ESP, which block the results, has removed himself to bed and has let the mouse exhibit precognition without interference.

SPONTANEOUS PRECOGNITIVE EXPERIENCES

Evidence of precognition may be classified under two headings: spontaneous experiences and laboratory studies. The latter have rigorous controls against sensory leakage, since the event has not happened. But the former also have criteria for assuring their validity. H. F. Saltmarsh (29) in 1934 conducted a study of 349 cases published by the SPR. He accepted as genuine only those reports that fully satisfied the following criteria:

1. It was recorded in writing, or told to a witness, or acted upon in a significant manner, before the subsequent event verified it.
2. It contained sufficient amount of detail verified by the event to make chance coincidence unlikely.
3. The conditions were such that one could rule out telepathy and contemporary clairvoyance, autosuggestion, inference from subliminally acquired knowledge and hyperesthesia.

Applying these criteria to the 349 cases, Saltmarsh whittled them down to a resistant genuine core of 183.

L. E. Rhine (28) relaxed the rigid criteria of Saltmarsh to study precognitive ESP in comparison with other types of ESP. She maintained year by year comparisons of percentages of the relaxed criteria as a check on validity. They remained relatively constant, a result hardly expected to occur if the cases had been invented or sent in as a joke. If there were sufficient correct details normally not inferable and if the experience occurred prior to the actual event, it was considered precognition. Of 3290 reported cases, 1324 were of precognition type—about 40%. In Germany, Sannwald found precognition accounting for 52% of 1000 cases. In England recently, Green found precognition accounting for 34% of 300 cases. Older studies were reported by Mrs. Sidgwick, Rayleigh, Lyttleton, Lodge, Richet, and Besterman.

Dr. Ian Stevenson (35) gives a good example from Mark Twain's biography:

> One night when Mark Twain was at his sister's house in St. Louis, he dreamed that Henry, his brother, was a corpse lying in a metallic burial case in their sister's sitting room supported on two chairs with a bouquet of flowers and a single crimson bloom in the center on his chest. Next morning he told his sister the dream. A few weeks later Henry's ship's boilers blew up and he later died exactly as in the dream.

This is typical precognition, as it occurred in a dream and contained verified details that no one could have rationally foreseen at the time of the dream. It contained also a common discrepancy: the dream placed the funeral proceedings in St. Louis, whereas it actually occurred in Memphis, Tennessee.

Prasad and Stevenson report a survey in Northern India of 2494 school children: 36% claimed ESP experiences, and of these, 40% had precognitive ESP. The American, European, and Indian surveys suggest precognition is a natural and widespread human experience.

Most precognitions seem to occur during dreaming. Of ESP in dreams, 66–70% are precognitive in American and British surveys. Also people frequently comment that the precognitive dreams differ from normal as being more vivid; Stevenson states that 45% of the 125 precognitive dreams he analyzed were reported as being more vivid. Many precognitive dreams are recurrent. Stevenson reports 14% being recurrent. He reports also that 27% of the persons tried to avert fulfillment of the precognition. For comparison, L. E. Rhine found 162 out of 433 (37%) dreams were ones the dreamers wished to avoid or tried to avert fulfillment. Symbols were reported only in 13.5% of Stevenson's 125 dreams and 5–6% of those of Saltmarsh. Thus, the manifest content of the dream usually comes true.

L. E. Rhine (28) also analyzed 3290 spontaneous cases to compare precognitive with here-and-now ESP. There were 1324 precognition cases reviewed and 1966 not involving time. For precognition, 68% occurred in dreams and 32% when awake. The here-and-now ESP percentages were reversed—35% in dreams and 65% waking. She analyzed the content of the perceptions against four classifications:

1. Intuitive (thought or idea)—Only 10% of the precognitions seemed intuitive compared with 35% for the others.
2. Hallucinatory (sensory impression)—Only 6% of the precognitions seemed hallucinatory compared with 25% for the rest.

3. Unrealistic (fantasy or daydream—imaginative or symbolic)—15% of the precognitions fell in this category and 21% fell in the others.

4. Realistic (true detail—no embroidery)—60% of the precognitions were realistic compared with 19% for contemporaneous.

She then compared the subjects' conviction of meaningfulness across all four classes, using as a criterion whether the subject took relevant action or else expressed certainty. Of the precognition cases, 36% carried conviction, compared to 62% for the others. Breaking it down further, precognition when the subjects were awake was convincing in 71% of the cases, with 75% for the "now" ESP events. Precognition when dreaming was convincing in only 19% compared with 37% for the "now" ESP events. The low 19% conviction in precognitive dreams contrasts sharply with the 71% for precognitions when awake.

Mrs. Rhine checked also on intervention. Of 1427 precognitive cases, only 574 showed conviction, and of these, 141 did not want to avoid the outcome. Two-thirds did not attempt intervening, so that she had 191 who attempted it. Sixty failed and 131 were successful. She whittled these down to 9 because of alternative explanations, nonspecific warnings, and outside persons not mentioned who intervened in avoiding the calamity. Of the 9 cases, 6 were open to counterhypothesis, and so, she was left with 3 who intervened successfully.

Regarding the themes of precognition, serious and shocking events predominate. One survey gives a ratio of 4 unhappy to 1 happy. Births and marriages do get precognized, although in the minority. Stevenson gives a table showing death as the commonest theme and illness less often than accidents. He suggests that accidents, being almost by definition unexpected, are likely to generate more shock than illness. Emotional shock is a factor tending to generate precognition experiences (and other types of ESP). Also, persons rarely seem to precognize some hostile attack on themselves by other persons, although President Lincoln (14) had the well-known dream of his own assassination a few weeks before it happened.

One wonders why, when a person gets a precognition, it is of a particular event and not others. Stevenson gives a partial answer: a close personal relationship. However, 15–20% occur with strangers. Here it seems that events of particular significance get precognized. For example, one was of a distant airplane crash. The person had had a lifelong interest in airplanes and wished to be a pilot himself. This is not surprising because we tend to dream of past events of special significance to us. So the dream of the future may be similarly influenced.

With regard to the time interval, Stevenson (35) states that it is usually short, within a few hours or days of the event. In precognition of major disasters, the number of precognitions increases with the approach of the time of the event. Consider the Welsh mining disaster in Aberfan on October 21, 1966. A massive slag tip slid down a mountainside and killed 128 children in the local school. Of the 35 recorded predictions, 18 were made within four days of the event, 8 between 4 and 14 days, 8 others scattered over months before. This decline of number of precognitions with greater time into the future agrees with Soomere's (32) data; he noted a relation between the number of precognitions of an event and the time proximity of the event. Dunne (9) also shows this time-proximity decline in his data for precognition and retrocognition.

In precognizing disasters with multiple deaths, Cox (7) investigated 28 serious U.S. railroad accidents. The number of passengers was significantly smaller on days of the accidents compared with that day in previous weeks. The effect was greater for coach than for Pullman cars. Cox suggested people precognized the disaster and decided not to travel. Pullman passengers made reservations much further ahead and were more "locked in." Stevenson analyzed 19 apparent precognitions related to the sinking of the *Titanic*, 10 being precognitive. The *Titanic* was thought to be unsinkable and so perhaps produced more emotional shock than, for example, the *Lusitania*, the sinking of which was not unexpected in wartime. Again J. C. Barker (2), a psychiatrist, investigated the Aberfan mining disaster. He appealed in the London *Evening Standard* for premonitions, and 35 were published with confirmation before the disaster occurred. Many mentioned the black slimy substance and the school. One man even gave the name Aberfan. As a result of this, the newspaper went on to run a Central Premonitions Registry and recorded 487 correct during the next two years. Then a similar registry was started in New York by Robert Nelson (22) and his wife.* This has also been very successful, recording disasters, unexpected events in trips to the moon, and the like before they happen.

LABORATORY STUDIES

No investigator has yet completely precluded the alternative hypotheses to precognition, such as PK or clairvoyance, from being possible explanations of his results, but some experiments that I will now discuss do approach it.

In 1933, J. B. Rhine and his associates reasoned that just as ESP results transcended space limitations, so they might transcend time also. And so, subjects proven at clairvoyance by guessing "down through" 25 ESP

* Located at Box 48, Times Square Station, New York City 10036. *Editor.*

cards placed out of sight in a box, attempted their guessing ahead of the time when the deck was hand- (or later machine-) shuffled. Forty-five hundred runs of 25 trials gave odds of 3,000,000:1 against coincidence. In some of these runs, the deck was cut using a scheme based on future temperature records (27).

G. L. Mangen devised an extremely complicated mathematical method using dice, a calculator, and random number tables, which it had been thought for 16 years that PK could not overcome, yet he and others got very significant precognition results.

Helmut Schmidt (see Chapter 7) developed a precognition random-number generator that has found wide use. A subject guesses which of four lamps will be lighted by a process using random strontium-90 radio-activity emissions, a tenth of a second after the guess. Schmidt checked the randomness on 100 different days before, during and after testing people. Of 100 people, 3—a housewife, a medium, and a truckdriver—gave in-creasingly diverging scores from chance. Repeated testing of these 3 in 60,000 trials gave 1 billion to 1 results against chance. On confirmation, one person successfully tried to miss the light that lit, thus proving the randomness, although the possibility of PK is allowed. Schmidt and L. Pantas tried separating precognition from its PK equivalent and suggested that it is not merely a combination of clairvoyance and PK.

E. Harraldsson (11) replicated Schmidt's experiment with 11 subjects, but used full immediate feedback of seeing the lamp light. This technique yielded better results than when using total hit counts as feedback.

Russell Targ independently developed his own machine based on a radio oscillator (see Chapter 22). A subject guesses which of four slides will light and presses the button under it, which triggers selection of the next correct answer, one-fifth of a second later. Targ's great advance was to add a "pass" button so that the person tries to learn his feelings when he gets a hit or to pass if he does not feel it, thus eliminating the pressure of being forced to guess. The majority could not, but one woman was able to increase her scoring rate clairvoyantly, and later precognitively, with 19 hits in the first 96 tries contrasting with 38 in the last 96.

C. McCreery (16, p. 119) in 1967 deduced that the attention required for ESP would be associated with an accelerated alpha EEG frequency, from, say, 9.5 cycles per second up to 10.5. Stanford (33) in 1969 found this result for precognition, not knowing about McCreery. Then Stanford in 1970 confirmed his own data, discovering a straight-line relationship between the quartile division of alpha-frequency shift and precognition score.

In one of my own experiments, 301 high school students were tested to see if they could separate clairvoyance from precognition without knowing which I was giving them. Clairvoyance often gives a sequence of high scores, low scores, and then high scores again, when checking from the start, through the middle, to the end of the test. By contrast, precognition gives high, low, high, and very low, respectively. Results were significantly positive. In another experiment I reported on the ability of a psychic, C. Liaros, to precognize to a very significant extent ($p = 10^{-15}$) future events in the lives of my ESP class members.

R. Morris tried pitting the clairvoyant faculty of one person against the precognitive faculty of another, using temperature values for randomness. Clairvoyance won slightly over precognition.

R. Brier and J. Freeman (4) conducted a mass test of precognition with 100,000 junior high school students through the educational magazine *Read*. Not all were scored, but for two groups totaling 20,000, girls showed precognition ($p = 0.001$) and boys did not. V. M. Cashen and G. C. Mamseyer found 32 college students could predict forthcoming exam questions ($p = 0.001$) (6).

Osis and Fahler (23) reported subjects, hypnotized by Fahler, scored very significantly higher on trials where they felt they were correct than on others ($p = 2 \times 10^{-8}$).

Gertrude Schmeidler (30) used a standard psychological test to separate 75 undergraduates into three groups: dynamic–hasty, naturalistic–passive, and humanistic. These subjects made three sets of 50 precognition guesses. Persons with a dynamic, highly competitive set of drives were found to do well at precognition when they were provided feedback of their results.

John Mihalasky and I confirmed Schmeidler's results by testing 107 top executives of business companies. In our precognition tests the presidents punched 100 guesses of the digits 0–9 into three IBM Port-a-Punch cards. The cards went directly from their hands into a computer that generated a separate 100-digit target for each executive an hour after his guess. This simulated their jobs, since by hunch, "sixth sense," or business acumen, they claimed precognition. We tested 5000 more people in management, engineering, scientific, and women's groups and confirmed Schmeidler's findings very significantly (8). We also tested the top executives for belief in ESP. I tested 67 of them, and by a ratio of more than 3:1, we found they believed in ESP. Mihalasky tested 40, and the ratio of believers to skeptics was 5:1. For chief decision-makers of five years standing, high precognition scores correlated with profit doubling over a five-year period.

Thus, the laboratory evidence suggests that the factors involved in precognition are both conscious, or stable, and unconscious, or labile.

Last of all, Ullman, Krippner, and Honorton (37) showed that dreams can come true in strict laboratory conditions using REM methods to detect dreams. They tested Malcolm Bessent over an eight-night period for ability to dream of events that would take place the next morning. The events to take place were planned by investigators *after* Bessent's dreams were recorded, using a random word in *The Content Analysis of Dreams* book. The team members selecting the events did not know the content of the dreams. One example of a random word was *leaves*. They chose as the events a painting of a bird on a branch with leaves, played a recording of "Autumn Leaves," took him to a wooded area of Long Island across the Verrazzano Bridge in a car, gave him a basket to pick up leaves, and then had him describe leaves back in the laboratory. Although they did not know it, he had dreamed of "heavy traffic," "being in the country," "bridge," "trees," "a bird," "basket." Three independent judges rated the matching of dream content to circumstance of the events from "little" to "very great." If the mean score of the judges for the correct target–transcript pair was higher than the mean of all others matching, it was considered a hit. He got five hits out of eight ($p = 0.002$). In the second series, targets were prepared in advance to prevent PK or telepathy. On eight nights he again got five right ($p = 0.001$). On eight alternate nights he was shown the target *before* going to bed, and he did less well. Thus, precognition produced a stronger effect on Bessent's dreams than the experience itself.

R. Johnson, a physicist, states that "the experimental work shows its (precognition's) existence beyond any shadow of a doubt" (12, p. 149).

THE SITUATION TODAY

General

The precognition experience, hard as it is for our brains to understand it and try as the critics do to avoid giving it credence, seems to be valid. Even though behaviorists accept only what is a concrete object (that means not accepting atoms and certainly not consciousness), precognition is as proven as it ever will be. The lesser problem of retrocognition, relating to the past and not producing effects before causes, seems also to occur but does not draw the critics' fire, as precognition does. But not only is precognition proven, but in perhaps up to 50% of precognition cases, if a warning is received with the precognition, it seems use can be made of the information to save lives. The work of the Central Premonitions registries in New York and London is still very little known, and they are working on very low budgets. Further, people are somewhat inhibited or embarrassed to send in their premonitions because the events have not happened yet, even when they know full well about the registries. However, the New York registry presently receives 60 letters per week because of publicity, although many premonitions have to be discarded as invalid or unconfirmed in the news event. Such events as the tragedy at Chappaquiddick, the sinking of an Onassis tanker, space-program failures, accurate descriptions of the Jablonski killers before their identities were known, Robert Kennedy and Martin Luther King's assassinations, Nasser's fatal heart attack, the crash that killed Rocky Marciano, and the deaths of Khrushchev and Stravinsky were all hits in registry files before they occurred. Nelson hopes that a group of highly successful "hitters" from among his regular correspondents will prove accurate enough to prevent disasters before they happen (22).

One of the problems is predicting the date accurately. This is a well-known problem of psychic people, although some are learning how to overcome it. One way Liaros does it is to imagine a bar in her mind's eye representing, say, six months; then she sees how far the event goes down the bar before disappearing. She precognized the death of Chester Carlson, the inventor of the Xerox process, three months before in this way. With the registries, the Aberfan experience suggests that more predictions are received as the date of the disaster approaches, so that a date range of a few days might be set when an acceleration of the number of letters coming in occurs. If this were possible, then the registries could change over to disaster early-warning services. At this time two more registries have started—one at Toronto, Canada, run by the Toronto Society of Psychical Research, and the other at Monterey, California, run by the Parapsychological Sciences Institute.

Illustrative Cases

L. E. Rhine (28, p. 45) quotes one unconfirmed case illustrating that numbers can be obtained in dreams that seem to come true:

> The district manager of a sheet and tin plate company went for a fishing trip in the deep woods of Canada, cut off from all news sources. On the night before returning, he dreamed of an accident at his plant where a crane carrying a heavy load of scrap iron toppled over railroad cars and came to rest near the riverbank. In his dream he noted the damage done, but also the numbers of the crane and the railroad cars. When he returned to the mill the next day, the master mechanic showed him the damage which corresponded even to the numbers he had dreamed about. On checking the time of his dream it was about two hours before the accident happened.

Sir Winston Churchill had several such experiences, which are recorded in his wife's biography (10, p. 136).

One has to do with his habit of going out to boost the morale of London's civil defense forces at night in a car during air raids in World War II. This night the driver held the near-side door open for him as he always sat on the near side. But when he got to the open door, he stopped, went round to the off-side, opened the off-side door, got in and sat on the off-side. He had never done this before. He told the driver to start, so the driver closed the near-side door and they proceeded to drive along the Kingston by-pass at 60 miles per hour. Suddenly a bomb fell near the off-side of the car and the force of the explosion lifted it up on to the two near-side wheels. However before somersaulting right over, the car righted itself and sped on. At 60 mph it is very probable that if it had gone over both Churchill and the driver would have been killed. "That was a near one," joked Winston. "It must have been my beef on this off-side that brought the car back down."

He did not tell his wife so as not to scare her, but she heard about it from the driver, and decided to challenge him about the incident. "Winston, why did you get in on the off-side of the car?" "I don't know, I don't know," Winston answered at first, but his wife pierced him with her gaze and he realized he could not get away with that answer, so he said, "Yes I do know. When I got to the near-side door held open for me, something in me said 'Stop, go round to the other side and get in there,' and that is what I did."

This is a report of a man getting information about a half-hour into the future. The information was not conscious but gave him instructions to do something he had never done before. He obeyed and seemingly saved his own life and his driver's.

Mrs. Rhine (28) was given a two-year precognition where intervention seemed to work. This is one of the three that withstood her elimination tests:

A mother had a waking picture of her eldest son, Herbert, *dead* in the bath tub. It haunted her so that she made a special point of listening that nothing went wrong, but she did not tell him her impression although she told her younger son, Peter. After a couple of years Herbert went away and when he came home for a holiday she still remembered it. One evening on this visit she heard him whistling and singing in the bath tub. She was dressed to go out, but could not leave. After a while she heard the water running out but did not hear him singing so she opened the door, and there he lay, exactly as she had seen him two years before. There was gas heat and the window was closed and he had apparently been overcome by fumes. She immediately opened the door and windows, and called the doctor and he was revived. If she had not been there, he doubtless would have died.

The classic case of retrocognition is that of the two English ladies, Anne Moberly, principal of St. Hugh's College, Oxford, and Eleanor Jourdain, the vice-principal (18):

> They visited Versailles in August, 1901, and went to the Petit Trianon, a small columned building in the palace gardens, as tourists do. While there they seemed to be not in their time but back in the time of Marie Antoinette. They saw persons dressed in the period and apparently living as persons living a century or more ago did.

The women each wrote separate accounts with enough information for the book *An Adventure*. Although some details vary, their accounts are substantially the same but stress the depth of the experience. As would be expected, critics have tried to explain it all away.

A good illustration of the Central Premonitions Registry cases came from Alan Vaughan, editor of *Psychic* magazine, who was in Germany doing research in precognition there. He registered by mail his thought that Robert Kennedy would be assassinated. It reached CPR director Robert Nelson two days before it happened (22).

HOW DOES PRECOGNITION OCCUR?

J. W. Dunne (9) first proposed a hypothesis in 1938 based on his book *An Experiment with Time* (1927). He recorded his dreams and found a beautiful symmetrical matching of some dreams with events in his precognition and with events in his retrocognition. Dunne's hypothesis involves an infinite series of time dimensions with an observer or self that recognizes the self that is observing, in each dimension. This parallels the infinite series of metalanguages that are put forward to overcome logical paradoxes, of which precognition is one. However, most people shy away from infinite regressions, including physicists, who have met this problem many times. They have learned to live with light being *both* waves and particles, and they developed quantum theory to predict experimental results.

In 1929 Dirac had the problem that his relativistic equation for the electron gave both a positive energy solution of a negatively charged particle of unit mass—that is, the electron—and also a negative energy solution of a positively charged particle of unit mass (not to be confused with the proton of 1837 unit masses). This latter particle is now known to be the antiparticle of the electron, with negative energy. It is to Dirac's credit that he did not flinch from proposing this particle, called the positron, despite there being no known meaning to negative energy. He had to find meaning. Then in 1932, Anderson found the positron in cloud-chamber tracks of cosmic rays. Dirac was rewarded with the Nobel Prize in physics in 1933, and Anderson won it in 1936. Feynman later developed the Feynman diagrams, with time on one axis, and suggested that electrons went forward in time, not in space, and that positrons went backward. He also got the Nobel Prize in 1965 for his idea.

Another example of there seemingly being no meaning in a concept is the square root of -1 ($\sqrt{-1}$). When first proposed, it was ridiculed and ignored. Heron of Alexandria (c. A.D. 100) and G. Cardan (1545) tried, but the square roots of negative numbers were considered meaningless, so the term *imaginary* was applied to them. They have since become indispensable in mathematics, mechanics, and electricity and are called complex numbers. This was because of the discovery of the graphical interpretation, first by J. Wallis (1685) and then by C. Wessel (1799), both ignored. Then J. R. Argand (1806) rediscovered it, as did Gauss (1831), although it was incontrovertibly introduced by Hamilton (1835). Now we have the introduction of the square root of $+1$ ($\sqrt{+1}$) with a new, totally unexpected nontrivial meaning (21). The square root of -1 is named i, and the square root of $+1$ is named ϵ. All electrical engineering students routinely use i to calculate AC currents for generation, transmission, electric motors, lasers, holograms, and the like. Real numbers represent points on a line, complex numbers (with i) represent points on a plane, and hypercomplex numbers (with ϵ) represent points in space. Thus, if there is no logical meaning to a theoretical result, it should not bother us. Perhaps it might lead to an understanding of how precognition works.

However, in the precognition case, there is involved a further test of logic—where logic breaks down completely. This occurs in the fact that someone gets information from the future. Thus, instead of a cause preceding the effect, it seems that the effect precedes the cause. Logic has broken down—even worse than the "no logical meaning" cases above. We need not worry about it, though, as there are ways through mathematics to get around it, as in $\sqrt{-1}$. Physics even has a rule: If something is not forbidden in nature, it occurs. Effects coming before causes are not forbidden in nature; they are only forbidden in our brains, which work with logic circuits composed of neurons like computer logic circuits. Thus, we should not flinch, as Dirac did not in his case, to use breakdowns of logic if they explain precognition.

There is at least one point in electrical engineering where the mathematics suggests that logic breaks down—that is, effects precede causes—

as posited by Targ and Puthoff (see Chapter 22). This has to do with advanced potentials. Stratton's 1941 book *Electromagnetic Theory* (36, p. 424) states that the field equation (of Kirchhoff derived from Maxwell's equations) admits of *both* solutions $(t + r/v)$ and $(t - r/v)$, where t is time, r is the distance of the field from a moving charge, and v is the phase velocity. $(t + r/v)$ leads to retarded potentials, but

> $(t - r/v)$ leads to an advanced time, implying that the field can be observed before it has been generated by the source. The familiar chain of cause and effect is thus reversed and this alternative solution might be discarded as logically inconceivable. However, the application of "logical" causality principles offers very insecure footing in matters such as these, and we will do better to restrict the theory to retarded action, solely on the grounds that this solution alone conforms to the present physical data.

Already by 1941, J. B. Rhine (27) had sure data for precognition that needed advanced time or advanced potential solution. Dirac himself used the advanced potential without flinching again in his theoretical quantum theory, but it was ignored. Harrington stated that $f(t - r/v)$ is a wave traveling outward from the origin event and $(t + r/v)$ inward to the origin. Anderson (1, p. 25) updated this in 1968 by stating that in electrical engineering, despite effects preceding causes,

> advanced potentials are now receiving a great deal of attention since they seem to be a means of avoiding some of the difficulties which beset electromagnetic theory. Advanced potentials were first invoked to try to solve the problem of obtaining an equation of motion for an electron moving in an electromagnetic field, which would take into consideration the radiation reaction, which is the force which acts on an electron due to its own electromagnetic field. Attempts using retarded potentials only are unsuccessful. Other problems of this type are concerned with structure and stability of charged particles where advanced potentials give hope of success.

Thus, if required in electromagnetic theory, advanced potentials may also apply to precognition perception. Perception is the information transfer from waves to the brain. If the advanced potential wave can interact with the person's brain before the event occurs, as seems to be correct in electromagnetic theory, then the precognition problem is solved and need only be worked out in detail.

The secondary problem of how information transfers from waves to the brain seems to be solved best as follows: Again following Targ and

Puthoff, consider that information is carried as a time-varying hologram. (A hologram is a three-dimensional nonphotographic picture produced with coherent—single-frequency—light.) Each point in space contains some information about the whole of the space, perhaps similarly with a time-varying hologram. Each point of time contains some information about time future and time past. Interaction of the information from the advanced potential waves may be through the skin cells, bone, or DNA, as with the people who can transduce radio waves without a receiver. Retrocognition would be explained similarly.

The Soviet physicist Kozyrev (13) has developed experiments suggesting that cause and effect cannot be infinitely close in space or time. Some of his ideas, coupled with the concepts of advanced potential, may lead to direct physical experiments to demonstrate the relation of ESP effect and time.

Musès (21) also has shown how precognition can be developed from another electrical effect. L. Brillouin in 1930 showed that if an electric current is severely perturbed (as in a cutoff), two precursor waves go ahead of the cutoff event. One goes at the speed of light, but the other is slowed down by the dielectric constant of the medium. The event arrives later yet at a relatively slower speed. Thus, one can get information from the first precursor wave, even if the event does not occur, because it gets deflected. An example is an arrow shot from a bow, expected to go to the target but deflected from the target, so that the event of arrow-in-target does not take place. But the electrical precursor wave does take place, so information goes ahead of the event that does not take place. Here would be an explanation, deriving directly from electromagnetic theory, of precognizing an event with a warning and then changing some part of the precognition to save someone's life. All we have to do is give up the dogma that effects cannot precede causes. In reality, effects can precede causes and are not forbidden in physics, so they can occur. With appropriate mathematics, there is relatively little difficulty. Retrocognition here would have to be different, as the past does not seem as amenable to change.

Puthoff and Targ in their model (see Chapter 22) have suggested that the accuracy of the precognition predicted from their model will (1) increase with the magnitude of the event for the perceiver and (2) fall off with increasing temporal distance from the event. Regarding their first point, accuracy increasing with the magnitude would fit in with the emotional-shock idea of Stevenson, where unhappy events—accidents and disasters—have more shock value than happy ones and are precognized more often (as we find). Physiological stress (measured by EEG coefficient of amplitude variation) could perhaps be used to measure shock value.

Accuracy falling off with increasing time to the future event—Puthoff and Targ's second point—also finds some, but not total, agreement with experiment. Dunne (9) in his own dreams recorded a drop-off. He gives data only for a few days into the future and past, since it is harder to pinpoint a dream coming true a year ahead. Conversely, Carington (5) got a sudden *increase* of matching drawings at +2 and −2 days, less on +1 and −1 days, and still less on day 0. There were about 300 people involved. This, however, may be a space-displacement effect due to the circumstances of the test rather than a measure of time to the future event. Osis found about equally high scoring for precognition over days 1–7 as for days 8–33. However, he mentions that conditions could not be kept the same for the range of days. Anderson even got considerably larger scores for calls checked after one year than calls checked immediately.

However, Soomere (32, p. 199) gives the number of direct precognition cases he found in Estonia from 1900 to 1971. He classifies 18 for one minute up to one hour, 82 for one hour to one day, 23 for one day to one week, 19 for one week to one month, 18 for one month to one year, and 10 for over one year. This works out on average (making all on a one-day basis) to 927 for the category hour, 265 for the day, 22 for the week, 7 for the month, 0.3 for the year, and $0.1/n$ for over a year as the number of years (n) is not given. This decline *cannot* be accounted for by difficulty of remembering a dream and its coming-true-event a month or a year ahead as Dunne suggested. Soomere also gives precognition cases totaling 45.6%, the highest of all his psychic classes.

CONCLUSION

Today precognition and retrocognition occur in ordinary experience, if not for everybody, and they also occur in the laboratory. However, we do not have an explanation, even a partial one as we have for electricity, although one may be on the way. Also, a warning is needed about the danger of excessive reliance on precognitive statements.

What does this mean for science? It seems there is a range of experiences and experiments that could extend our knowledge of the universe. There are many possibilities for further research. Examining the negative domains in physicists' formulas seems to offer the strongest avenue of approach. If successful, physicists and electrical engineers would come over to the psychic research side. If using advanced potentials could give us quantitatively exact results, then Stent's (34) comment would be applicable: "No other set of hypotheses in psychology has resisted the amount of critical scrutiny that psychic research has, but until it is shown in simple logical steps how psi results connect with generally accepted scien-

tific knowledge, no demonstration of ESP's existence could be appreciated." Hence, this approach has the highest priority for theoretical
research. Continuing Stanford's (33) relation of precognition with alpha
frequency shift would also connect it with physiology. Retrocognition
studies need to be started also.

There is much to be done by way of applying the research, too. Support
and development of the premonitions registries to try saving lives would
have widespread and positive effects on society. If the registries can become well enough known and used so that they can change over to
disaster-warning agencies, modern social science will have caught up with
quantum physics. Such is essentially what the Greeks had and made use of
in their oracles.

Thus, there is a part of life and the universe that defies categorization
and explanation in terms of the prevailing materialistic Western philosophy. Psi in general and precognition–retrocognition in particular defy the
generally accepted world view based on linear, sequential, either-or thinking. Of course, some philosophies (e.g., pantheism, panpsychism, various
oriental philosophies) already agree with the conclusion that precognition
is real and a part of ordinary life. Western philosophy and science need to
integrate precognition also and recognize that there is a part of life and the
universe that is beyond the logic we use in discursive reasoning.

When this happens, the place of materialism in our lives will be seen for
what it is, and it will take its place in a larger perspective of the nature of
man and the universe. Then the perceptions of sages and mystics, which
many have found to be quite logical but on a higher level of consciousness, can be incorporated. Instead of our present logical positivist philosophy, denying precognition and retrocognition, we can reach for a higher
consciousness and a philosophy that will accept precognition as normal
and allow its beneficial use for the improvement of human living.

REFERENCES

1. Anderson, N. *The Electromagnetic Field*. Plenum: New York, 1968.
2. Barker, J. C. "Premonitions of the Aberfan Disaster." *Journal of the
    Society for Psychical Research*, 44 (1967).
3. Bender, H. "The Gotenhafen Case of Correspondence Between Dreams
    and Future Events: A Study of Motivation." *International Journal of
    Neuropsychiatry*, 2, no. 5 (1966).
4. Brier, R. "A Mass School Test of Precognition." *Journal of Parapsychol-
    ogy*, 33, 2 (1969).
5. Carington, W. "Experiments on the Paranormal Cognition of Drawings."
    Proceedings of the Society for Psychical Research, 46 (1940–1941).

6. Cashen, V. M., and Mamseyer, G. C. "ESP and the Prediction of Test Items in Psychology Examinations." *Journal of Parapsychology*, 34, 2 (1970).
7. Cox, W. E. "Precognition: An Analysis I and II." *Journal of the American Society for Psychical Research*, 50 (1956).
8. Dean, E. D., and Mihalasky, J. *Executive ESP*. Prentice-Hall: Englewood Cliffs, N.J., 1974.
9. Dunne, J. W. *An Experiment with Time*, 3rd ed. Faber: London, 1926.
10. Fishman, Jack, and Allen, W. H. *My Darling Clementine*. Pan: London, 1964.
11. Harraldsson, E. "Subject Selection in a Machine Precognition Test." *Journal of Parapsychology*, 34, 3 (1970).
12. Johnson, R. *The Imprisoned Splendour*. Harper & Row: New York, 1953.
13. Kozyrev, N. A. *Possibility of Experimental Study of the Properties of Time*. Joint Publications Research Service, Department of Commerce: Washington, D.C., 1968.
14. Lamon, W. H. *Recollections of Abraham Lincoln, 1847–1865*. McClurg: Chicago, 1937.
15. Levy, W. J. "The Effect of the Test Situation on Precognition in Mice and Birds: A Confirmation Study." *Journal of Parapsychology*, 36, no. 1 (1972).
16. McCreey, C. *Science, Philosophy and ESP*. Faber: London, 1967.
17. Mitchell, E. D. "An ESP Test from Apollo 14." *Journal of Parapsychology*, 35 (1971).
18. Moberly, A., and Jourdain, E. *An Adventure*. Faber: London, 1904.
19. Murphy, G. "Direct Contacts with Past and Future: Retrocognition and Precognition." *Journal of the American Society for Psychical Research*, 61 (1967).
20. Murphy, G., and Klemme, H. L. "Unfinished Business." *Journal of the American Society for Psychical Research*, 60, no. 4 (1966).
21. Musès, C. "Trance States, Precognition, and the Nature of Time." *Journal for the Study of Consciousness*, 5, no. 1 (1972).
22. Nelson, R. "The Central Premonitions Registry." *Psychic*, 1, no. 5 (1970).
23. Osis, K., and Fahler, J. "Space and Time Variables in ESP." *Journal of the American Society for Psychical Research*, 58 (1964).
24. Parke, H. W., and Wormell, D. E. W. *The Delphic Oracle*, 2 vols. Blackwell: London, 1956.
25. "Parthenon: Greco-Persian Wars," *Encyclopedia Britannica*, Vol. X. Benton: Chicago, 1966. See also Hammond, N. G. L., "The Battle of Salamis," *Journal of Hellenistic Studies*, 76 (1956).
26. Price, G. R. "Science and the Supernatural," *Science*, August 26, 1966; and "Letter to the Editor," *Science*, January 28, 1972.
27. Rhine, J. B. "Experiments Bearing upon the Precognition Hypothesis: III. Mechanically Selected Cards." *Journal of Parapsychology*, 5, no. 1 (1941): (See also "Precognition Reconsidered." 9 [1945]).
28. Rhine, L. E. "Frequency of Types of Experience in Spontaneous Precognition." *Journal of Parapsychology*, 18, no. 2 (1954): (See also "Precognition and Intervention." 19 [1955]; and *Hidden Channels of the Mind*. Sloane: New York, 1961.)
29. Saltmarsh, S. F. *Foreknowledge*. G. Bell & Sons: London, 1938.
30. Schmeidler, G. "An Experiment on Precognitive Clairvoyance." *Journal of Parapsychology*, 28, 2 (1964).

31. Soal, S. G., and Bateman, F. *Modern Experiments in Telepathy*. Yale University Press: New Haven, Conn., 1956.
32. Soomere, I. "Report No. 4." *Journal of Paraphysics*, 6, no. 5 (1972).
33. Stanford, R. "EEG Alpha Activity and ESP Performance: A Replicative Study." *Journal of the American Society for Psychical Research*, 65, no. 2 (1971).
34. Stent, G. S. "Prematurity and Uniqueness in Scientific Discovery." *Scientific American*, December 1972.
35. Stevenson, I. "Precognition of Disasters." *Journal of the American Society for Psychical Research*, 64, no. 2 (1970).
36. Stratton, J. A. *Electromagnetic Theory*. McGraw-Hill: New York, 1941.
37. Ullman, M.; Krippner, S.; and Honorton, C. "A Precognitive Dream Study with a Single Subject." *Journal of the American Society for Psychical Research*, 65, no. 2 (1971): (See also "A Second Precognitive Dream Study with Malcolm Bessent." 66, no. 3 [1972]).

Helmut Schmidt

HELMUT SCHMIDT, *Ph.D., is former director of the Institute for Parapsychology in Durham, North Carolina, where he still continues in research. He has been at the Institute for Parapsychology since 1970.*

In 1954 Dr. Schmidt received a Ph.D. in physics from the University of Cologne in Germany. Thereafter, he held various research and teaching positions. Among them are Dozent *for theoretical physics at University of Cologne from 1960 to 1963; NATO exchange professor in 1962 at Southern Methodist University in Dallas, Texas; visiting lecturer at the University of British Columbia in Vancouver, Canada, from 1964 to 1965; and senior research scientist for Boeing Company in Seattle, Washington, from 1965 to 1969.*

Dr. Schmidt is the author of more than two dozen articles on physics and parapsychology. His publications on physics deal with solid-state physics, plasma physics, cosmology, and the foundations of quantum theory. His parapsychological writings are concerned with precognition and psychokinesis tests using electronic equipment, much of it invented by himself.

Dr. Schmidt can be reached at 2404 Perkins Road, Durham, N.C. 27706

7 Psychokinesis

HELMUT SCHMIDT

SUMMARY

During the last four decades, careful laboratory work has shown that man can, to a certain degree, influence the outside world by pure thought. This process is called psychokinesis (PK). It appears in the laboratory as a mental influence on random events like the outcome of die throws or the operation of electronic random devices. Like ESP, to which it seems closely related, PK cannot be explained within the framework of present physics, and we are still far from a satisfactory understanding of the underlying "mechanism" through which it operates. Furthermore, we do not yet know whether ESP and PK are basically distinct processes or whether they are just different manifestations of one universal psi principle. However, experimental parapsychology has already illuminated many of the strange properties of PK that set it apart from the usual physical forces and that could serve as a basis for future theoretical models.

INTRODUCTION

Can the human mind affect the outside world directly by pure thought? This question has captured human imagination throughout the ages. Experimental parapsychology has shown that there exists some interaction between man and the outside world in which the mind influences external events without muscular action or any other link within the known range of physics. Serious attempts to study this possibility scientifically were begun toward the end of the last century in Europe, at a time when spiritistic mediums and other psychic performers had aroused public interest and were willing to subject themselves to scientific study. Some of these investigations, reported by highly reputable scientists, suggested the occasional occurrence of quite spectacular PK effects, like the mental movement of heavy objects well outside the reach of the test subject. This early work in PK was not continued into the present as vigorously as one might have expected, in part because the number of gifted subjects seemed to decline and in part because a large number of exposures of fraudulent mediums raised doubts about whether the researchers had sufficiently guarded against fraud.

A different approach to PK was suggested by the claims of some gamblers that they could mentally influence the fall of dice. Following this lead, J. B. Rhine (12–14) reported in the 1940s that not just a few gamblers but a large fraction of the population can mentally influence the fall of dice. Rhine's statistical method for the study of PK did not produce results as spectacular as reported in some of the earlier studies. However, since no spectacular performers seemed to be available, the highly sensitive statistical approach, which permitted experimentation with rather ordinary subjects, dominated PK research for the following decades, and only quite recently have serious efforts toward stronger PK effects been resumed.

THE EARLY STATISTICAL TESTS

The feeling that the outcome of a die throw may be partly determined by our mental attitude, rather than by blind chance alone, appears rather widespread. To most scientists such a possibility would have seemed too absurd to be worthy of serious consideration. The researchers in parapsychology, however, could see such a PK effect as a rather natural complement to ESP. Both phenomena suggest an interaction between the human mind and the physical world outside. In the ESP case, external events (not accessible to our physical senses) become apparent to the subject, and in the PK case, the subject's mind seems to act on the external world.

Systematic tests of a possible mental influence on dice was begun in 1934 by J. B. Rhine and his research group at Duke University (12–14), and somewhat later the idea of using dice for PK tests was independently developed by C. B. Nash (10). The dice were thrown at first by hand and in later tests from a cup, while the subject tried mentally to enforce the appearance of a specified die face. By using all six sides equally often as target, one could compensate for a possible bias due to dice imperfections.

After eight years of experimentation with dice, Rhine considered the existence of PK as sufficiently established to publish the results obtained by several researchers. The strongest evidence for PK appeared in these early data as a decline effect. The subjects showed a general tendency for scoring slightly higher at the beginning of a test run than toward the end. Furthermore, if several test runs (usually of 24 die falls) were held in one session, the scores also tended to decline from the first to the last test run. This decline seems psychologically plausible insofar as it could just reflect the decline in the subject's interest in the test.

In order to eliminate a possible simulation of PK effects by manual skill completely, Rhine introduced in 1936 an automatic mechanical die-tumbler with a motor-driven wire-mesh cage that stopped automatically at regular intervals. One or more dice bounced in the cage, and the subject tried to enforce the appearance of many sixes (or some other predetermined target number) at the next stop. With this machine a complete separation between subject and dice seemed achieved, but the PK effect still persisted.

A typical example for the magnitude of the effect is given by an experiment reported by Rhine in 1943 (11). In the course of this experiment the tumbler with two dice inside was operated a total of approximately 900 times during a two-day period. Three adult subjects participated. The target face appeared in 19.2% of the die falls, whereas the chance expectancy was only 1 in 6, or 16.7%. The size of this effect may not seem very impressive, and one might wonder whether the score could just have been the result of a statistical fluctuation. Such fluctuations do occur, both in the presence and in the absence of psi. Fortunately, mathematics gives us information about what size fluctuation we may reasonably expect in the absence of psi. In the case of the 1800 trials that produced 45 more hits than expected by chance, pure chance would give such a high, or a higher, score only once in every 400 such experiments. If, therefore, the result was caused by pure luck (without psi), the subjects were very lucky indeed, since the odds against chance being responsible for the high score were 400:1. Most experimenters express the statistical significance of their results in terms of the probability p for obtaining by chance such a high, or a higher, result. In this case, then, $p = 1/400$, or $p = 0.0025$. A number of further PK experiments with dice have confirmed the existence of an effect, sometimes with much higher statistical significance.

At the early stages of research it seemed natural to consider PK as some force similar to electric, magnetic, or gravitational forces. An interesting attempt to measure the "PK force" in physical units was made by the Swedish engineer Haakon Forwald (6, 7). A new type of PK test, the "placement test," designed by W. E. Cox (4) was used for this purpose. The dice were made to roll down an incline onto a tabletop divided by a center line, and the subject tried to deflect the dice to the right or the left side. Forwald, acting (as in most of his numerous experiments) simultaneously as subject and experimenter, observed a significant deflection of the dice in the desired direction. Then he calculated how much physical force, acting sideways on the dice, would have been required to produce the same average side deflection. His result suggested the existence of PK forces up to 10% of the gravitational forces acting on the dice. The concept of a PK force of this magnitude, however, is not consistent since the force should also be able to deflect a die suspended by a string, but no such effect could be observed. Forwald continued attempts to interpret PK in terms of familiar physical forces and energies. Since electric and magnetic forces could be ruled out rather easily, Forwald directed his speculations toward the somewhat less known gravitational forces. A critique of Forwald's theoretical concepts is given by J. H. Rush (15).

Much of Forwald's work was concerned with the question of whether the size of the PK effect depends on the physical nature of the dice. Experiments with precision-made dice of different compositions and with wooden dice with metal coats of different thicknesses seemed to indicate some lawful relationships between the material of the dice and the PK effect. These results have to be considered with caution, however, since PK has been found to depend to a large degree on subtle psychological factors. It is thus quite possible that the subject's (Forwald's) conscious or subconscious expectations on the outcome determined the results rather than the physical nature of the dice per se.

For a quantitative study of PK, dice may not be the ideal tool, since the physical and mathematical analysis of rolling dice, even in the absence of PK, presents a mathematically very complex problem. Qualitatively one can say that the outcome of a die fall is determined in part in a causal manner by the die's initial position and the physical structure of the tumbler and in part by pure chance. The effect of pure chance becomes the stronger (and can practically reach 100%) the more thoroughly the die is shaken. Consider as an example a die that is automatically released at the top of an incline and rolls down to the tabletop. If the incline is very short we may find that the die face appearing on top is completely determined by the initial die position (0% chance). As the incline becomes longer and the die can bounce more and more actively, the outcome becomes more and more unpredictable. This unpredictability is not caused solely by our lack of a good computer to calculate the die fall in full detail. Rather, it is connected with the basic "uncertainty principle" of modern physics.

This principle implies that the relevant starting conditions—such as the internal oscillations of the die, the atomic vibrations in the incline surface, and the motion of the air molecules that collide with the die—cannot be observed with sufficient accuracy to permit an accurate prediction of the die fall. E. H. Walker (20) has given some numerical estimates for the degree of randomness to be expected in Forwald's experiments. The calculations, which are very complicated in spite of some simplifying assumptions, show that the degree of randomness depends, under otherwise equal test conditions, on the size, the weight, and the moment of inertia of the dice. Furthermore, the calculations suggest that some of the differences observed by Forwald, when comparing different dice, might be caused by differences in the degrees of randomness provided by the different test situations. Forwald did better in the tests that provided a good randomization than in the tests in which the dice did not bounce enough, so that the outcome was already largely determined by the die's starting position.

While most of the earlier PK work was done with dice, other tools for observing PK were gradually introduced. A large variety of everyday occurrences that depend on chance processes—the formation of smoke rings, the emergence of water from a shower nozzle, the next rainfall, the fluctuations of the stock market, the outcome of a roulette game—might perhaps respond to PK efforts, but most of these occurrences are ill suited to quantitative laboratory tests. An example of early studies of PK without dice is an experiment by Cox. There the random element came in through some randomness in the time required by a relay to make an electric contact. A sequence of relays was activated, each relay triggering the next one, and the time required for the last relay to close was measured by a clock accurate to one-hundredth of a second. Considerable statistical fluctuations in the closing times were observable, indicating the random nature of the processes. The subject tried once to speed up, and once to slow down, the closing of the last relay. In tests with six groups, one group obtained in 726 trials a success rate of 56.7% where chance was 50%. Such a high score would be expected by chance approximately once in a thousand test groups, so that the result can be considered as statistically significant (5).

STATISTICAL PK TESTS WITH
MODERN ELECTRONIC EQUIPMENT

For a better understanding of the basic nature of PK, it might be most helpful to study its action on very simple systems and in particular its possible action on nature's most elementary source of randomness provided by "quantum jumps." A typical case of quantum jumps is found in radioactive decay. Consider, for example, the atoms in a sample of the radioactive element strontium 90. The nuclei of these atoms are so unstable that they decay spontaneously after an average life of 30 years. This does not mean that the atoms go through some aging process. Rather, they appear unchanged until the very moment of decay. What "causes" the atom to decay at a particular instant? The answer given to this question by modern physics is that there need not be any specific cause, that the decay is a pure chance effect typical of events at the atomic level. If this interpretation is correct, radioactive decays (and other quantum jumps) should form an interesting target for PK efforts, since we have a basically simple and (unlike the case of dice) purely random process. The basic randomness of radioactive decays makes them also interesting for precognition tests (see Chapter 6).

Radioactive decays are, furthermore, particularly challenging for PK tests insofar as it is extremely difficult to affect the decays by physical means. Since the atomic nucleus is such a small, tightly bound and sheltered system, the decay process is highly insensitive to electric and magnetic fields, to temperature fluctuations, and to other external effects. This aspect has been emphasized by Beloff and Evans (2), who tried for the first time to influence radioactive decays through PK. These researchers mounted a radioactive sample inside a counter that registered each decay process and displayed the total number of decays in one-minute intervals to the subject. The random variable to be influenced by PK was the number of decays recorded in a one-minute interval. The subject, looking at the display, tried for the first minute to obtain a high count and then for another minute to obtain a low count. This experiment, performed with 30 students, did not show a PK effect—that is, the number of decay processes registered during the one-minute intervals seemed to be independent of the subjects' mental effort. The authors note, however, that perhaps the experimental setup might not have provided sufficient challenge for the subjects to activate potential PK abilities.

Very promising results with a similar arrangement were reported by Chauvin and Genthon (3), but unfortunately this work was discontinued.

A certain practical disadvantage of the described setup is that the counter for the radioactive decays has to be carefully shielded so that the radiation from, say, the subject's watch dial (or from some other perhaps fraudulently introduced radioactive source) cannot affect the counting rates. Furthermore, the physical conditions, like the supply voltage for the counter, have to be kept constant with high accuracy. In order to avoid these difficulties, I utilized in my own later PK tests the random nature of radioactive decays in a slightly different manner (16).

In these tests the radioactive decays served as the basic source of randomness in a binary random generator, an "electronic coin-flipper," which could produce a random sequence of heads and tails. The basic parts of the electronic coin-flipper are a Geiger tube which registers the randomly occurring decay processes in a sample of strontium 90, and an electronic high-frequency switch, which oscillates very fast (1 million times per second) between two possible positions, a head position and a tail position. Whenever the device is activated, the switch continues oscillating only until the next decay is recorded by the Geiger tube. The average waiting time for the next decay is in the specific setup one-tenth of a second, but otherwise, the waiting time is random, so that there is an equal chance for the switch to be caught in the head position or the tail position. Thus, we have a nearly ideal electronic coin-flipper, and even if the strength of the radioactive source or the sensitivity of the Geiger tube should change, the randomness in the sequence of generated heads and tails would not be impaired.

In a PK test, the subject tries to enforce the generation of, say, more heads than tails. In order to make this task psychologically challenging, a display panel with nine lamps in a circle is connected to the coin-flipper. One lamp at a time is lit, and whenever a head or tail is produced, the light jumps one step in a clockwise or counterclockwise direction, respectively. Thus, the light, moving at a rate of one step per second, performs a random walk among the nine lamps. In a standard test run, the coin-flipper is set to produce 128 decisions, which takes approximately two minutes. The subject sits in front of the panel and tries to force the light to move more steps in a clockwise direction than counterclockwise—that is, to enforce an overall clockwise motion of the light. This task is equivalent to enforcing the generation of more heads than tails in the coin-flipper, but the subjects were instructed to direct their exclusive attention to the light on the display panel. None of the subjects had a precise knowledge of the internal structure of the coin-flipper.

The first experiment with this arrangement gave a somewhat surprising result. Most of the (nonselected) subjects who happened to be available showed a negative scoring tendency. Whenever they wanted to enforce an overall clockwise motion of the light, the light displayed a tendency for counterclockwise motion. And next, when I asked the subjects to try for counterclockwise motion, the light moved more in the clockwise direction. Such a tendency of PK missing had been reported in earlier experiments, particularly when the subjects felt uneasy with the test situation. (The subject sat alone with the display panel in a dark closet.) Since at that stage I was mainly interested in observing any PK effect, no matter in which direction, I tried in a following confirmatory test to reinforce the subjects' negative feelings. Thus, I either asked the subjects to associate feelings of failure with the test ("Imagine very vividly some situation where you failed or got very embarrassed") or tried to discourage them otherwise. Under these conditions, we obtained a significantly negative PK effect, with odds against chance of more than 1000:1 ($p < 0.001$).

For prolonged tests it is certainly not very pleasant to keep the subject in a state of frustration. Thus, in most of the later tests, I tried, through encouragement and through proper subject selection, to obtain PK effects in the desired direction. The first outstandingly positive subject was an outgoing girl who had come to me because she felt herself to be very "psychic" in everyday situations, mainly in the way of receiving psychic impressions about other people. This girl obtained in a first experiment, comprising 50 two-minute test runs of 128 trials each, a scoring rate of 52.2% on the desired heads, instead of the 50% expected by chance, and an even higher scoring rate (53.5% hits in 25 test runs) in a later, follow-up test. These results are far outside the range of possible chance fluctuations. The odds against chance are more than a billion to one ($p < 10^{-9}$). Even with this very gifted subject, however, PK results did not come easily or in a routine manner. Each session required a new, special effort, and on many days, we did not hold tests because the subject did not feel up to the task.

Experiments with the same or similar equipment were resumed also by other researchers. Thus, Eve André (1) reported an intensive study with three subjects who were highly motivated and seriously interested in psi research. The general question to be investigated was whether one could identify certain moods, mental attitudes, or external conditions (such as the time of day or the weather) that would be particularly conducive to PK performance. The results gave evidence for PK and showed that these subjects scored significantly higher in the early mornings than in the mid-afternoons, in agreement with the subjects' general feeling of b ng more alert and cheerful in the early mornings.

The same type of target generator (but a different display) was used in later experiments by Honorton and Barksdale (9). There the subject saw just two lamps that lit up whenever a head or tail was generated, respectively, and the subject tried to make one lamp light more frequently. The specific question studied was whether PK could operate better when the subject was in a state of muscular tension or in a state of relaxation. This question was raised by reports, partly on the anecdotal level, that some spectacular PK subjects used to work in states of high body activity and probably high muscular tension. Out of the 17 subjects studied, at least 1 produced a highly significant result: positive scoring in the runs with muscle tensions and nearly as strong a negative scoring (PK-missing) in the runs with muscle relaxation. This suggests that PK worked in the tense and the relaxed states but that the subject's attitude was differently oriented in the two conditions.

TOWARD HIGHER EFFICIENCY IN PK TESTING

In the reported experiments PK appeared as a small effect on random events. One might try to increase the efficiency of PK testing by operating with a large number of individual random events. This could be done either by working with a very fast succession of random events or with many simultaneously occurring random events.

Following the first approach, I built an electronic coin-flipper that could produce a sequence of heads and tails at rates of 30 and of 300 decisions per second (18). The numbers of heads and tails were cumulated by read-out tubes, but during a run the readings changed so fast that the subject could not keep track of his performance and saw only his final score.

For a more direct feedback of the subject's momentary performance, I used two types of display. The more simple, but very useful, display was provided by a pair of headphones that presented each generated head or tail as a click in the right or left ear, respectively. For obtaining more heads than tails, the subject was instructed to concentrate on the right ear, trying to receive there an increased number of clicks. The volume of the clicks was usually kept rather low, and the most successful subjects would often close their eyes and listen to the clicks in the target ear as one would listen to a distant voice, in a relaxed but alert state. The other display was given by the needle of a pen chart recorder, which was connected so that each generated head or tail moved the needle by a small step to the right or left, respectively. The subject concentrated on the statistically fluctuating needle and tried to move it to the right.

This test situation is reminiscent of the case in which a subject tries to influence the motion of a feather suspended by a thin thread. But whereas PK might be able to affect the suspended feather as well as the instrument needle, a good experiment with a suspended feather would require extreme precautions (shielding against thermal air currents, heat radiation from the subject, etc.) and a high-precision device for recording the feather movement. In the described setup, where the needle acts only as a psychologically favorable display for the activity of the binary generator, we need no such precautions and no other device to record the needle movement, since the generator already displays the numbers of heads and tails that cause the needle movement.

It might be worth mentioning that this display is analogous to some displays used in biofeedback training, where the subject learns to control body functions that are normally not subject to the conscious will. Take as an example Elmer Green's experiments (8) in which subjects learned to increase their skin surface temperature (for the purpose of enhancing relaxation). A thermistor attached to the person's skin was connected to a display so that an increase in skin temperature would be indicated by movement of a needle to the right. Thus, the subject could see immediately which of his efforts favored a temperature increase, until he was finally able to control the temperature at will. While this was certainly not a PK test, one might wonder whether some PK faculty could be brought under conscious control in a similar manner.

One objective of the tests with the high-speed generator was to explore whether the scoring rate would decline with increased generation speed, in which case the subject would have less time to spend on each individual random event. Comparing the speeds of 30 and 300 events per second, a considerable decline was found under both feedback conditions. In order to equalize the test situations as well as possible, the single test runs at the lower and higher speed contained 100 and 1000 events, respectively, so that each test run lasted approximately 3 seconds. In a typical session, between 10 and 40 such short test runs were made. The whole experiment comprised 400 runs at the lower speed (total = 40,000 events) and 400 runs at the higher speed (total = 400,000 events). Since each run lasted only 3 seconds the total actual test time in the whole experiment was only 40 minutes, but much more time was spent between the runs (typically 10 seconds) and at the beginning of a session. Instead of the 50% expected by chance, the slower runs produced an average of 51.6% heads and the faster runs an average of only 50.37% heads. Both results are statistically highly significant ($p < 10^{-9}$ and $p < 10^{-4}$, respectively).

Compared with the earlier tests with the circular light display, where the targets were produced at the rate of 1 per second, the fast generator demonstrated PK much more efficiently insofar as a higher statistical significance could be obtained in a given time. On the other hand, the increase of the generation rate from 30 to 300 per second did not lead to a further increase in this efficiency, because of the decline in the scoring rate on the individual events. Thus, a further increase in the generation speed, which is technically quite feasible, might not be profitable.

The other approach to higher efficiency was begun by the simultaneous throwing of many dice. But one could go much farther in this direction and try, for example, to influence chemical reactions, which result from the statistical interaction of many billions of particles. An example of this kind might be found in studies on the action of PK on living organisms or on a photographic emulsion (see Chapter 13).

PK AND THE LAWS OF PHYSICS

The results of experimental parapsychology indicate that the current concepts of physics are not quite adequate, at least for the complete description of animate nature. One can appreciate the significance of this finding only if one realizes the fantastic success of modern physics in describing nature at the microscopic and the macroscopic level.

Soon after quantum theory was developed, the theory could be used to bring a quantitative understanding of a tremendously large variety of phenomena. This theoretical understanding led to spectacular new inventions ranging from the atom bomb to the laser. The success of quantum theory, combined with its mathematical elegance and internal simplicity and consistency, suggested that perhaps this theory would be sufficient to account, in principle, for all observable phenomena, including the processes of living nature.

This trust in the omnipotence of quantum theory was not shared by all physicists. Thus, for example, Niels Bohr, who became in his later years very interested in molecular biology and the origin of life, was convinced that some basically new principle besides quantum theory had to enter where life begins. But it was the experimental result of parapsychology that showed for the first time explicitly that quantum theory is not a complete description of nature and that some experimental results are definitely inconsistent with the present formulation and interpretation of this theory.

This raises a large number of intriguing questions. What is wrong with current physics? Which of the generally accepted laws of physics are inconsistent with the results of psi research? Is physics seriously wrong or does it just require minor modifications? Should psi effects have a bearing on experiments with inanimate systems in the physics laboratory or should psi appear only in living nature? If so, at which level of complexity should psi first appear—in a virus, in a single cell, in a cockroach, in a mouse, or only in man?

Quantum theory describes nature in terms of two types of laws—the conservation laws and the statistical laws. Well-known conservation laws are those for energy and momentum of a freely moving particle. These laws are familiar to us already from the older classical physics, but they are equally valid in the microscopic world of quantum mechanics. The statistical laws, on the other hand, play a much more fundamental role in quantum theory than in classical physics because quantum theory assumes randomness as one of the basic features of nature. Considering an atom of radioactive strontium 90, for example, quantum theory implies that the occasional decay of such an atom is a basically random process and need not have any specific "cause." Physicists were certainly very hesitant to abandon the concept of strict causality, which was one of the pillars of classical physics. Some physicists have considered the possibility of a hidden mechanism—say, inside the atomic nucleus—that would determine the exact decay time. So far, however, none of these theories has been generally accepted, because they are too complicated and too implausible and because physicists have become accustomed to the concept of a purely random elementary process.

The statistical nature of the reported PK experiments may suggest that PK perhaps affects only the statistical laws of physics, while the conservation laws (for energy, momentum, etc.) remain intact. This possibility seems particularly attractive to the physicist who wants to incorporate psi as smoothly as possible into the existing framework of physics. By affecting statistical events "only," PK might still achieve rather spectacular results, since statistical laws play a dominant role in our daily lives. If, for example, you run hot and cold water into your bathtub, the statistical laws provide for an even temperature distribution after some time. A PK subject who could invert the process and make one side of an evenly warm bath hot and the other half cold, therefore, would "only" have to affect the statistical laws (like the second law of thermodynamics) but not the conservation laws (like the energy-conservation law).

THE GOAL-ORIENTED NATURE OF PK

In most of the reported tests with complex electronic equipment, the subjects did not know the internal structure of the test machine. They succeeded just by concentrating on the final outcome as indicated by the display device. This suggests that PK may not be properly understood in terms of some mechanism by which the mind interferes with the machine in some cleverly calculated way but that it may be more appropriate to see PK as a goal-oriented principle, one that aims successfully at a final event, no matter how intricate the intermediate steps.

This viewpoint is supported by tests that compared the action of PK on binary random generators of different complexity. For example, when I replaced the usual coin-flipper mentioned in the PK test with the circular lamp display with a device twice as complex (obtained by mixing the outputs of two of the usual binary generators), I did not obtain any decline in the PK scores. Again, in a more recent test with two still more drastically differing random generators, no difference in the scoring rates on the two generators was observed (19). In each of these experiments, the generators to be compared were connected to the same display device and the subjects were kept unaware of the difference between the generators in order to eliminate the possible effect of some conscious or subconscious preference that a subject might have for one or the other test situation.

The concept of a goal-oriented process goes against our conventional understanding of nature in terms of cause and effect. But the conventional cause–effect structure is also overturned in precognition tests where the subject predicts successfully the outcome of a later random event. There the later event somehow acts on the subject's present state of mind.

The relationship between PK and precognition seems to be generally rather close, to the extent that a rigorous separation between PK and precognition might in the statistical laboratory tests not be possible. Consider as an example the hypothetical case where a coin is flipped and the subject is instructed to try to predict (precognition) the upcoming side in one experiment and then to mentally enforce the appearance of, say, a head in the next. In the first experiment we cannot really distinguish whether the subject passively predicts the event or unknowingly uses PK to make the outcome conform to his prediction. Thus, this is no way to demonstrate the presence of "pure precognition." The observation of "pure PK" in the second case seems a bit clearer. But even there apparent "PK results" might be obtained from a subject who could predict the outcome of the next coin-flips and would "feel like doing" a test only if the conditions for success seemed right. This example should remind us that the distinction between PK and precognition is at present primarily a practical matter, which need not imply that basically different mechanisms are at work.

SEARCH FOR PK IN INANIMATE NATURE AND IN PRIMITIVE ORGANISMS

The usual definition of PK as a mental influence on random events (or other physical processes) may be too narrow to encompass the whole phenomenon. In particular, this definition presupposes the presence of some "mind" as origin of the PK effect and thus excludes possible PK-like effects in inanimate nature or in primitive organisms. Let us try to formulate a more general definition of PK so that, in a wider framework, we can discuss the question of the existence of PK in inanimate nature.

In an experiment where, say, a coin is flipped (mechanically or electronically) the outcome depends on the subject, who, after the event has happened, sees the result. Emphasizing the goal-oriented nature of PK, we might interpret a successful experiment in the sense that more heads were generated because the appearance of a head made the subject (or the experimenter who later checks the result) "happy." Then the outcome of a coin-flip depends on the effect that this particular outcome causes later. From this viewpoint we can try to define PK generally as a principle that makes the outcome of a random event depend on the effects produced by this outcome.

This new definition suggests an experiment in which a binary generator is set up so that the produced heads and tails trigger different physical processes (other than happiness or unhappiness in human subjects).

In a first experiment of this kind, a 200-watt lamp was connected to the generator so that each generated head lit the lamp for a moment and each tail left the lamp dark. In a total of 700,000 binary numbers generated at the rate of one per second, while the lamp was positioned under a clear night sky, no deviation from randomness was observed—that is, this particular difference in the effects of heads and tails did not unbalance the generation rates.

Such an unbalancing appeared, however, in tests with animals linked to the generator so that they received with each generated head a certain stimulus. Tests with cockroaches which received electric shocks as stimuli gave the first statistically significant results (17) and further tests along these lines have been done or are in progress (see Chapter 9). It would be at present still premature to conclude that really the animals in these tests are the "source of PK," since, even in a fully automated experiment, the human experimenter may still play a vital role.

OUTLOOK

This chapter has emphasized the statistical PK work, because so far it is there that the most reliable and—to some extent—reproducible results have been obtained. These experiments not only have shown the existence of PK but also have indicated its strange properties, such as its goal-oriented feature and its relationship to precognition.

This solid evidence for PK has made experimenters more open-minded toward occasional reports of seemingly more spectacular PK phenomena. One of the most frequent of these, poltergeists, is discussed in Chapter 16.

Another source of particularly strong PK effects may be available in a few highly selected subjects, some of whom are already active as "psychic performers." One such person is Uri Geller, a native of Israel now living in the United States. Geller can well match the feats of the spectacular performers studied by the early workers in the field. Critical researchers as well as TV audiences have seen Geller bend heavy metal objects "mentally," just by touching them slightly or even without any touch.

Such demonstrations would seem to lend themselves naturally to detailed studies of the associated "mechanism" in the physics laboratory. A first beginning in this direction has already been made by Puthoff, Targ and Mitchell (see Chapter 22 and Appendix), who studied Geller for more than a month at the Stanford Research Institute and confirmed some of Geller's unusual psychic abilities.

REFERENCES

1. André, E. "Confirmation of PK Action on Electronic Equipment." *Journal of Parapsychology*, 36 (1972).
2. Beloff, J., and Evans, L. "A Radioactivity Test of PK." *Journal of the Society for Psychical Research*, 41 (1961).
3. Chauvin, R., and Genthon, J. "Eine Untersuchung über die Möglichkeit psychokinetischer Experimente mit Uranium und Geigerzähler." *Zeitschrift für Parapsychologie und Grenzgebiete der Psychologie*, 8 (1965).
4. Cox, W. "The Effect of PK on the Placement of Falling Objects." *Journal of Parapsychology*, 15 (1951).
5. Cox, W. "The Effect of PK on Electromechanical Systems." *Journal of Parapsychology*, 29 (1965).
6. Forwald, H. "An Approach to Instrumental Investigation of PK." *Journal of Parapsychology*, 18 (1954).
7. Forwald, H. *Mind, Matter, and Gravitation.* Psychological Monographs, Parapsychology Foundation: New York, 1969.
8. Green, E.; Green, A.; and Walters, E. "Voluntary Control of Internal States." *Journal of Transpersonal Psychology*, 2 (1970).

9. Honorton, C., and Barksdale, W. "PK Performance with Waking Suggestions for Muscle Tension Versus Relaxation." *Journal of the American Society for Psychical Research*, 66 (1972).

10. Nash, C. "PK Tests of a Large Population." *Journal of Parapsychology*, 8 (1944).

11. Rhine, J. B. "Dice Thrown by Cup and by Machine in PK Tests." *Journal of Parapsychology*, 7 (1943).

12. Rhine, J. B. *The Reach of the Mind*. Sloane: New York, 1947.

13. Rhine, J. B. *New World of the Mind*. Sloane: New York, 1953.

14. Rhine, L. E. *Mind Over Matter*. Macmillan: New York, 1970.

15. Rush, J. "Review of Forwald's *Mind, Matter, and Gravitation*." *Journal of the American Society for Psychical Research*, 65 (1971).

16. Schmidt, H. "A PK Test with Electronic Equipment." *Journal of Parapsychology*, 34 (1970).

17. Schmidt, H. "PK Experiments with Animals as Subjects." *Journal of Parapsychology*, 34 (1970).

18. Schmidt, H. "PK Tests with a High Speed Random Number Generator." *Journal of Parapsychology*, 37 (1973).

19. Schmidt, H. "Comparison of PK Action on Two Different Random Number Generators," *Journal of Parapsychology*, 38 (1974).

20. Walker, E. H. "Foundations of Paraphysical and Parapsychological Phenomena" (in press).

Rhea A. White

RHEA WHITE, *M.L.S., has been assistant reference librarian at East Meadow Public Library and director of information for the American Society for Psychical Research since 1965. She is a charter member of the Parapsychological Association and was its first secretary.*

After graduating from Pennsylvania State University in 1953, Ms. White became a research fellow in the Parapsychology Laboratory at Duke University. She remained there until 1958 when she took the position of research and editorial associate in the American Society for Psychical Research. In 1962 she became a research fellow of the Menninger Foundation and three years later assumed her present post.

Ms. White is the author of numerous articles in the Journal of Parapsychology *and the* Journal of the American Society for Psychical Research. *With Laura Dale, she is co-author of* Parapsychology in Print, 1971–72 *(ASPR, 1971) and* Parapsychology: Sources of Information *(Scarecrow Press, 1973).*

Ms. White can be reached at 2 Plane Tree Lane, Dix Hills, N.Y. 11746.

8 Parapsychology Today

RHEA A. WHITE

SUMMARY

This chapter surveys the area of research and resources in parapsychology today. It is hoped that by this review of the primary centers of parapsychological activity, educational opportunities, information facilities, and publications, interested persons may find answers to their questions about parapsychology today. Keeping in mind that any foothold in parapsychology is going to be tenuous, this survey is aimed at opening the way for those who are brave, adventurous, and willing to persist until they find what they are looking for.

INTRODUCTION

Parapsychology today is more active and far-ranging than it has ever been in its century-long history. There has been an expansion of research and related activities in the past few years. This growth is evident in the number of people engaged in parapsychological activities; in the spectrum of topics being investigated; in the large increase of books, periodicals, and articles appearing in scientific and popular literature; and in the emergence of new educational opportunities for directed and individual study.

This growth seems to be the result of several converging factors. First, within the field itself the research being carried out is growing in sophistication. Moreover, it is not only more intensive than much of the research of the past, but it is also more extensive. As for the former, compare the early attempt to study telepathy in dreams by Ermacora with the sophisticated research of the Maimonides Dream Laboratory (recently changed to the Division of Parapsychology and Psychophysics of Maimonides Medical Center). As for the latter, compare the secondhand literary method primarily used to investigate cases of apparent reincarnation by Shirley and other early writers with Stevenson's firsthand worldwide field studies.

Second, there is a definite interdisciplinary trend, pioneered two decades ago by the Parapsychology Foundation. Parapsychologists are incorporating the findings, techniques, and theories of other disciplines in their research, while scholars in many other fields are either investigating some aspect of psi from their particular points of view (as did G. K. Nelson, who got both an M.Sc. and a Ph.D. for sociological studies of spiritualism) or are considering the relevance of the psi hypothesis to their own specialties (as a number of psychiatrists such as Ehrenwald, Eisenbud, and Ullman have been doing for many years). An encouraging aspect of this interdisciplinary trend is that it is so widespread. In hopeful moments it makes one feel that now, in the 1970s, pieces of the psi puzzle are being collected from myriad directions and at a tremendous rate. This may be one of the preconditions for a scientific breakthrough in the understanding of psi. The behavioral sciences are involved, along with physics, biology, engineering, medicine, sociology, and even religion, philosophy, literature, and education. All are finding points of reference in common, as well as mutual stimulation and cross-fertilization.

Third, there is the increased acceptance of parapsychology within the larger scientific community, typified by the fact that the AAAS has finally granted affiliation to the Parapsychological Association (PA) and that the response by other scientists to the symposia sponsored by the PA at AAAS annual meetings has been gratifying.

Finally, the much touted "occult revolution" is having an effect, not entirely deleterious, although certainly it can be embarrassing to a field trying to establish a reputable scientific position.

Throw all these active ingredients into the pot, let them steam in the high-pressured activities of our times, and after they have blended and cooked for awhile, what may emerge before this century ends could be not just a parapsychological brew, or an anomalous island in the vast academic sea, by definition "beyond" psychology and therefore mankind, but a discipline that is connected to the mainstream of science integrated with and accepted as part of our culture and our thought.

Parapsychology today is a volcanic island, sometimes erupting above the waves, and sometimes disappearing beneath them. It is often inaccessible to the newcomer. This survey is offered as a map to guide those who wish to enter the maze. It is in three major sections: institutions and organizations; educational opportunities and information facilities; and publications.

In order to facilitate the cross-referencing of descriptions of the organizations, institutions, lectures, and publications described, each item has been given a number. It should be noted that if an organization is referred to in more than one section, the address of that organization will be given only the first time it is described, but later entries are followed by the item's reference number.

I. INSTITUTIONS AND ORGANIZATIONS

The centers in this section have been listed according to their primary function: research or membership. However, many parapsychological organizations engage in several types of activity, thus qualifying them for inclusion in several categories in the chapter. For example, the Foundation for Research on the Nature of Man (FRNM) is described in Section I as a research organization and in Section II as a center for parapsychological training. Its library is also described in Section II, and its publication, the *Journal of Parapsychology*, is listed in Section III.

On the other hand, an organization such as the Human Dimensions Institute, which is not a center devoted specifically to parapsychology, is only described in Section II (under Lectures) even though it is a membership organization, sponsors courses, has a library, and publishes a periodical. This is because for purposes of this chapter the lectures are the most important aspect of the work of the Institute, and its other activities are too broadly conceived to be described here in detail. When this is the case, information on an organization will be provided in that section in which it appears.

Research-Oriented Organizations and Institutions

These organizations and institutions, listed in alphabetical order, represent the major research centers of parapsychology today. The most productive centers, judged both by number of associated research workers and number of publications, undoubtedly are the FRNM, the Division of Parapsychology at the University of Virginia, the Division of Parapsychology and Psychophysics at Maimonides Medical Center, the Psychical Research Foundation, and the Institut für Grenzgebiete der Psychologie in Freiburg. Considered from the viewpoint of the number of research projects undertaken, the most diverse organizations are again FRNM, the Division of Parapsychology, and the Freiburg institute. Other research organizations worthy of note described elsewhere are the Research Department of the American Society for Psychical Research (13), the SPR (16), the Department of Psychology and Parapsychology, Andhra University (17), the Parapsychology Unit, University of Edinburgh (20), and the Department of Psychology, City College of the City University of New York (19).

1. Center for the Study of Psychic Phenomena, Research Center, Rockland State Hospital, Orangeburg, N.Y. 10962

Headed by Aristide H. Esser, M.D., the center was established in 1969.

It is part of the Social Biology Laboratories at Rockland State Hospital, which Dr. Esser also heads. Other staff members include T. Etter and R. Frank. The work of the center stresses the study of the biological factors in psi communication. The electronic and computer facilities available for parapsychological research are highly sophisticated, and most of the ESP experiments of the staff involve the use of an on-line computer. In addition to research, Esser says the center was "created as a forum for the exchange of information and a meeting place for investigators."

2. Division of Parapsychology, Department of Psychiatry, School of Medicine, University of Virginia, Charlottesville, Va. 22901

Under the direction of Ian Stevenson, M.D., the Division of Parapsychology was established in 1968 as an integral part of the Department of Psychiatry. A parapsychology research endowment fund supports a research professorship in psychiatry with the stipulation that the recipient devote at least half his time to research on the survival problem. In addition to survival, psi research in a variety of areas is carried out, along the lines of the special interests of individual staff members: spontaneous psi experiences; high-scoring ESP subjects; and quantitative investigations of psi and physiological variables, and various altered states of consciousness. In addition to Stevenson, there are three full-time staff members: Dr. J. G. Pratt, Dr. Rex Stanford, and Dr. John Palmer. Visiting research fellowships and student fellowships on a summer or yearly basis are sometimes available.

3. Division of Parapsychology and Psychophysics, Department of Psychiatry, Maimonides Medical Center, 4802 Tenth Avenue, Brooklyn, N.Y. 11219

The Division of Parapsychology and Psychophysics was established in 1962 by Montague Ullman, M.D., head of the Department of Psychiatry, in order to investigate dreams and telepathy by means of the rapid-eye-movement (REM) monitoring technique. It was then known as the Dream Laboratory. In 1973, however, the name was changed to the present one in order to reflect the expanded goals of the staff: the investigation of the influence of other altered states of consciousness on psi; work with psychedelic drugs as means of inducing altered states; studies of psychopathology and psi; use of feedback techniques; the conduct of PK experiments; and the expansion of the division's informal educational training programs in parapsychology. Three more rooms and specialized PK and biofeedback equipment are now available to the division. The enlarged staff includes Ullman, as director, and a number of senior research associates for various subject areas: Charles Honorton for parapsychological research; Dr. Stanley Krippner for education and training; Dr. Harry Hermon, for clinical and pharmacological studies; and Dr.

Gary Gruber for physical science. There also are a number of consultants in specific subject areas on the staff.

4. Foundation for Research on the Nature of Man, Box 6847, College Station, Durham, N.C. 27708

Established in 1962, with Dr. J. B. Rhine as executive director, the FRNM is the successor to the Duke University Parapsychology Laboratory. It has, however, a more universal aim: the creation of an international world center to forward parapsychology and to integrate its findings with those of other sciences. The Parapsychology Press is owned by FRNM and publishes the *Journal of Parapsychology* (59) and a few book titles.

FRNM has a research unit, the Institute for Parapsychology. Recent research has emphasized the investigation of ESP and PK by means of electronic equipment and the investigation of psi in animals. The institute houses the huge Duke collection of spontaneous cases and serves as an international clearinghouse for parapsychological information and as a meeting place for research workers. At present the acting director of the institute is Walter J. Levy, Jr.

5. Institut für Grenzgebiete der Psychologie (Institute for Border Areas of Psychology), 78 Freiburg im Bresgau, Eichhalde 12, West Germany

The institute, under the direction of Dr. Hans Bender, comprises two institutions: the Institut für Grenzgebiete der Psychologie und Psychohygiene (Institute for Border Areas of Psychology and Mental Hygiene) and the Abteilung Grenzgebiete der Psychologie des Psychologischen Instituts der Universität Freiburg (Department for Border Areas of Psychology of the Psychological Institute of Freiburg University). The latter is described in the next section (21).

The institute is the main center for parapsychological research in Germany, and it was set up in 1950. Bender and four collaborators engage in all kinds of parapsychological research. It has a 6000-volume library and publishes the semiannual *Zeitschrift für Parapsychologie und Grenzgebiete der Psychologie* and some monographs.

6. Institute of Psychological Research, 118 Banbury Road, Oxford, OX2 6JU, England

Some graduates of Oxford who were also members of the SPR organized the institute in 1962. Its purpose is the scientific investigation of psi, with emphasis on a physiological approach. Since its inception, its director has been Celia E. Green. There are three full-time staff members and three assistants. The results of the institute's research are published in parapsychological periodicals and in its own *Proceedings* (published irregularly, in book form, by Hamish Hamilton in London). There have been four to date.

7. Paraphysical Laboratory, Downton, Wilshire, England

Organized in 1966, the Paraphysical Laboratory has as its director Benson Herbert and Manfred Cassirer is its research officer. Its aim is to study the physical aspects of psi. It publishes the *Journal of Paraphysics* (58).

8. Parapsychological Division of the Psychological Laboratory, Varkenmarkt 2, Utrecht, The Netherlands

Originally the Parapsychology Institute of the State University of Utrecht, this organization was founded by Dr. W. H. C. Tenhaeff, who was made Privaatdozent in parapsychology when he received his doctorate for work in parapsychology from Utrecht University in 1933. In 1953 he was appointed full professor and made director of the institute. The institute is entirely supported by state funds, a first in the history of parapsychology. When Tenhaeff retired, the institute became part of the Psychological Laboratory and Tenhaeff's successor is now appointed on an annual basis. The current incumbent is Dr. Martin Johnson, who, in addition to doing research, gives lectures and seminars. The division maintains a library on parapsychological subjects and publishes intermittently a *Research Letter* of about 50 pages, in which the research of the division is described and contributions from other parapsychologists are published.

9. Parapsychology Laboratory, St. Joseph's College, Philadelphia, Pa. 19131

St. Joseph's College was one of the first institutions of higher learning in this country to have a parapsychology laboratory. It was founded in 1956, largely through the efforts of its director, Dr. Carroll B. Nash. Located in the Department of Biology (where both Dr. Nash and his wife teach), its purpose is twofold: (1) the conduct of psi research by both Nashes and their students, and (2) teaching parapsychology, which Dr. Nash has done for many semesters, primarily in the evening division. A small library is maintained, consisting of about 300 books and complete runs of most of the major parapsychological journals.

10. PSI Communications Project, Suite 501W, Newark College of Engineering, 323 High Street, Newark, N.J. 07102

The purpose of the PSI Communications Project, which was founded in 1962, was originally "to develop the engineering techniques and systems required to obtain reliable information via telepathic processes as a means to gaining a better understanding of the nature of man." Current emphasis is on the entire psi process, including precognition and clairvoyance, as well as telepathy. The project is housed at Newark College of Engineering in two rooms plus the office of the project director, Prof. John Mihalasky. E. Douglas Dean is a research associate. The project is primarily research-oriented, and computer applications to psi research are emphasized.

11. Psychical Research Foundation, Duke Station, Durham, N.C. 27706

The Psychical Research Foundation, which is housed in two buildings near the Duke University campus, was established in 1960 to investigate problems bearing on the survival of bodily death. The project director is William G. Roll, with Dr. Robert L. Morris as research associate. The research program, which draws on a number of interdisciplinary consultants within the university, has emphasized the investigation of gifted sensitives, field studies of poltergeists and haunting cases, and out-of-the-body experiences. Information on the foundation's activities and on survival research in general is published in its newsletter, *Theta* (68). Visiting research assistantships are available for summer work or longer periods.

12. Religious Experience Research Unit, Manchester College, Oxford, OX2 6JU, England

The unit, which was established in 1969, is under the directorship of Prof. Alister Hardy. It was initiated in order to collect and study experiences of ordinary people who have felt themselves "upheld or given new strength by some kind of power which seems to come from beyond themselves." The unit is also interested in investigating telepathy, particularly regarding its relation to prayer.

Membership-Oriented Organizations and Institutions

Although only four major parapsychological membership organizations are described below, there are numerous smaller groups throughout the world. Many can be located by means of the "International Directory of Parapsychological Associations" (63). There are many scattered throughout the United States alone—for example, the Southern California Society for Psychical Research (an affiliate of the ASPR), the Illinois Society for Psychical Research, and the Psychical Research Society of Kansas City (Missouri). A sampling of membership societies in other countries includes Sällskapet för Psykisk Forskning i Finland (The Society for Psychical Research in Finland), the Israel Parapsychology Society, the Societá Italiana di Parapsicologia, the South African Society for Psychical Research, the Turkish Society for Parapsychological Research, and the Japanese Society for Parapsychology (the last is described below).

There are also a number of student parapsychological organizations. Two of the oldest and most active in the United States are the MIT Parapsychological Research Group and the Minnesota Society for Parapsychological Research.

Finally, there are a number of membership organizations (whose scope includes more than just parapsychology) described in other sections of this chapter: Association for Research and Enlightenment (28), College of Psychic Studies (30), Human Dimensions Institute (39), and Spiritual Frontiers Fellowship (35).

13. American Society for Psychical Research, 5 West 73rd Street, New York, N.Y. 10023

First organized under the leadership of William James in 1885, the ASPR later became a branch of the SPR (16) and then once more was independently organized in 1905 by James H. Hyslop. Its purpose is to investigate claims of all kinds of psi and to disseminate information on the findings. The ASPR has an active research department under the direction of Dr. Karlis Osis and a newly organized education department headed by Marian Nester. It publishes a quarterly *Journal* (60), an irregular *Proceedings* (64), and the *ASPR Newsletter*, which is aimed at informing members of the society's activities. It also holds lectures, forums, and workshops and has a library (27). The president is Montague Ullman. There are no membership requirements. In 1972, there were 2300 members. Dues are $15.00 (regular) and $5.00 (students) per year. Members receive the society's publications and may borrow books from the library and attend lectures sponsored by the society.

14. Japanese Society for Parapsychology, 26-14, Chou 4, Nakamo, Tokyo 164, Japan

The society was founded in 1963 with the purpose of promoting parapsychological research by improving communication between investigators. One of the co-founders and its president is Dr. Soji Otani, a Japanese psychologist and leading parapsychologist. Its membership is composed of specialists, some of them being Japan's foremost psychologists. Monthly meetings are held at which experimental plans and results are discussed. From the beginning an effort was made to foster relations with psychology; for example, since 1967 it has held an annual meeting in conjunction with the convention of the Japanese Psychological Association, which in 1970 granted affiliation to the Japanese Society for Parapsychology. The society publishes a bulletin, *Parapsychology News* (in Japanese).

15. Parapsychological Association. No permanent address. Inquiries should be addressed to the secretary, if known. Otherwise contact FRNM (4) or ASPR (13).

This is the professional organization of parapsychology. It was founded in 1957 and is international in scope. Its stated purpose is "to advance parapsychology as a science, to disseminate knowledge of the field, and to integrate the findings with those of other branches of science." It holds an annual convention (41) and publishes an account of it in its yearly *Proceedings* (65). In 1969 it was granted affiliation with the American Association for the Advancement of Science (38). It is governed by a seven-man council, with the president elected annually. The membership for 1973 was 221 members, of which 99 are full members, 117 are associate members, and 5 are honorary members. Announcements of the Parapsychological Association are carried in its affiliated journals: *Journal of the ASPR* (60), *Journal of Parapsychology* (59), and *Journal of the SPR* (61).

16. Society for Psychical Research, 1, Adam and Eve Mews, London, W8 6 UQ, England

Organized in 1882, the SPR states that its purpose is "to examine without prejudice or prepossession and in a scientific spirit those faculties of man, real or supposed, which appear to be inexplicable on any generally recognized hypothesis." Most of the SPR's research activity is currently carried out by six committees of members. It publishes a quarterly *Journal* (61) and an irregular *Proceedings* (66). The society sponsors lectures, provides speakers upon request, and has a fund to support graduate work in parapsychology in British universities (23). It also has a library (34). Membership is international. Qualifications include sponsorship by two members and payment of $15.00 per year ($10.00 for students). In 1971 there were 1180 members.

II. EDUCATION OPPORTUNITIES AND INFORMATION FACILITIES

This section describes how and where to find information on parapsychology. The first part deals with training, formal and informal. Details on scholarships for research and training in parapsychology are given next. The major psychic research libraries are described in a third category, followed by a review of the more important conferences and lecture series.

Training for Work in Parapsychology

The prospects for work in parapsychology and the best means of obtaining the required training for such a career was outlined in the *Bulletin of the Parapsychological Association*, no. 3 (1970): 1–2 as follows:

It is important to emphasize that there are still very few opportunities for a full-time career in parapsychology. There are not more than a dozen really full-time scientific workers in the field of parapsychology in the world. Yet there are well over a hundred other scientists who contribute actively to the field by working part-time in it. So long as opportunities for full-time investigation remain limited, it is important for the aspirant to a career in parapsychology to qualify himself for work in a conventional branch of science. From such a base he can begin to work in parapsychology. More and more institutions are permitting, and some are encouraging, young scientists to work in parapsychology provided they perform satisfactorily their other responsibilities of teaching or service.

If a student is interested in a career in parapsychology, his best course, therefore, is to graduate from a good college or university and then continue into graduate school for a doctorate or equivalent degree in some branch of science. Since parapsychology involves some research with people or animals, training in the behavioral sciences, such as experimental psychology, psychophysiology or animal behavior, is likely to be particularly valuable. The student should also keep in mind that parapsychological occurrences take place within the known physical world and that a background in the biological and physical sciences is likely to be helpful. Courses in the history and philosophy of science will enable the student to see parapsychology within the general context of science and scientific discovery. After completing training in his selected area, a year or two of supervised research as a postdoctoral fellow in a parapsychological research center may be appropriate before undertaking completely independent investigations.

Although opportunities for graduate work in parapsychology are almost as rare as full-time jobs, at the undergraduate level with increasing frequency institutions of higher learning are allowing students majoring in a variety of subjects to take courses, do independent research, or study in parapsychology on the side, often for credit. For a listing of specific schools and opportunities, see items (43) and (56).

Graduate Training

Listed below are some of the institutions where higher degrees may be obtained for work in parapsychology. Emphasis is on academic institutions where parapsychologists have set up facilities for parapsychological research and study. It should be pointed out, however, that this list is only partial. For example, graduate work in parapsychology may be undertaken at Duke University, Wesleyan University, West Florida University, and West Georgia College, to name just a few. For more detailed information, see items (43) and (56).

17. Department of Psychology and Parapsychology, Andhra University, Waltair, Visakhapatam-3, India.

Established in 1967, the department is under the direction of Dr. K.

Ramakrishna Rao. Both M.A. and Ph.D. degrees may be obtained for work in parapsychology. In 1972 there were seven staff members and four doctoral candidates, all of whom were involved in parapsychological research. See item (56) for further details.

18. Department of Psychology, University of California, Davis, Calif. 95616

Dr. Charles T. Tart will accept thesis topics on parapsychology for the Ph.D. in psychology.

19. Department of Psychology, City College of the City University of New York, New York, N.Y. 10031

This has long been a center of parapsychological activity primarily because of the presence of Dr. Gertrude R. Schmeidler. Not only has she conducted and published much of her own research while teaching at City College, but over the years she has supervised work in parapsychology at the undergraduate, master's, and doctoral levels for degrees in psychology. Some fellowship aid is available.

20. Department of Psychology, University of Edinburgh, 60 Pleasance, Edinburgh EH8 9TJ, Scotland

One room in the Department of Psychology at the University of Edinburgh has been set aside as a parapsychology unit. Dr. John Beloff is the director, and a postgraduate student, Adrian Parker, is currently working under Beloff's supervision toward a Ph.D. degree in psychology on a parapsychological topic.

21. Abteilung Grenzgebiete der Psychologie des Psychologischen Instituts der Universität Freiburg (5)

This department of the Psychological Institute of Freiburg University was established in 1966. It is the center of academic parapsychology in Germany. Also in 1966 the Chair for Border Areas of Psychology, held by Prof. Hans Bender since 1954, was changed to the Chair for Psychology and Border Areas of Psychology, thus integrating parapsychology within the framework of academic psychology at Freiburg University. Courses are offered in parapsychology, and higher degrees in psychology may be obtained for work in parapsychology under the direction of Bender.

22. Humanistic Psychology Institute (Association for Humanistic Psychology), 325 Ninth Street, San Francisco, Calif. 94109

Beginning in the fall of 1973 a program leading to a Ph.D. in parapsychology will be offered by the Humanistic Psychology Institute at California State College, Sonoma. Dr. Stanley Krippner, who is associated with the program, reports that emphasis will be in three areas: (1) the history of psychic research, (2) laboratory experience and experimental methodology, and (3) experiential work and travel.

Informal Research Training

One of the best methods of receiving training in parapsychology is to serve as an apprentice at a reputable parapsychological research center. Several of these organizations permit both graduate and undergraduate students to gain research experience, especially in the summer, and sometimes for an entire year. Although no credit is given for this experience, it is invaluable as a means of learning how to conduct parapsychological research, becoming familiar with the parapsychological literature, and meeting and discussing parapsychology with some of the current workers in the field. The following parapsychological research centers, already described in Section I, offer informal educational training, sometimes with stipends: Division of Parapsychology, University of Virginia (2), Division of Parapsychology and Psychophysics, Maimonides Medical Center (3), Foundation for Research on the Nature of Man (4), and the Psychical Research Foundation (11).

Scholarships and Grants for Work in Parapsychology

In addition to money obtained from regular granting institutions for partial or full support for education and/or research in parapsychology, there is available a very limited amount of money earmarked for parapsychology. The sources are described below.

23. Cutten Parapsychology Studentship Fund, Society for Psychical Research (16)

This fund was established in 1970 at the initiative of John Cutten and has been officially recognized by the Society for Psychical Research (16). Its purpose is to give assistance to graduate students doing work on parapsychology at British universities. Graduates from anywhere in the world are eligible, however. Selected students will receive a grant of up to £750 ($1800) per year for a maximum of three years. The first grantee is Adrian Parker, who is working on a doctorate at Edinburgh University (20). Funds are available for a second applicant. For more details, see *Parapsychology Review*, 3, no. 8 (1972).

24. Oliver Lodge Grant, College of Psychic Studies, 16 Queensberry Place, London SW7 2 EB, England

In 1972 the college announced this new grant "intended to finance the successful candidate in the production of a thesis based on qualitative research" on (1) "mental phenomena which *prima facie* suggest" survival and/or (2) "extended modes of perception or levels of consciousness seldom used in ordinary daily existence." The Oliver Lodge Grant is for a one-year period and is to be from £600 to £1000.

25. Parapsychology Foundation, Inc., 29 West 57th Street, New York, N.Y. 10019

This nonprofit organization was founded in 1951 by Eileen Garrett for the purpose of supporting "impartial scientific inquiry into the total nature and working of the mind and to make available the results of such inquiry." The foundation encourages an interdisciplinary approach to psi. It is one of the major sources of financial support for both individuals and institutions as regards both research and education. An idea of the type of activities for which funds have been granted in recent years can be obtained by reading the foundation's annual report, published in the January –February issue of *Parapsychology Review* (63).

26. Perrott-Warrick Studentship in Psychical Research, Council of Trinity College, Cambridge University, Cambridge, England

This fund was established in 1940 as a bequest to Trinity College as a memorial to F. W. H. Myers. The first holder of the studentship was Whately Carington. Others have been G. Spencer Brown, Anita Gregory, Trevor H. Hall, S. G. Soal, and George Zorab. The award for academic year 1972–1973 went to Adrian Parker, a graduate research student at Edinburgh University (20). Research grants were also given to Dr. Alan Gauld of Nottingham University and James Webb of Cambridge. The studentship is granted for one year at a time and is open to anyone 21 or older. A student may be reelected for one time only. The amount of the studentship is "of such value, not exceeding £300, as the Electors may award."

Libraries with Large Parapsychology Collections

The libraries listed below are only the major collections in the United States and Great Britain. There are valuable collections in several other countries, but there was not enough information available on them to warrant inclusion here.

27. American Society for Psychical Research Library (13)

Housed in two rooms, one is the circulating library, containing books that may be borrowed by members, and the other the reference library, containing materials that must be used on the premises: books, periodicals, special indexes (including a card index to the society's publications), and the pamphlet and clipping file. There are approximately 4000 book titles; complete runs of most parapsychological periodicals, English and foreign; and a clipping and pamphlet file of 2000 cataloged items. Books and pamphlets are indexed in the card catalog by author, title, and subject. Open 9:00–5:00 on weekdays, anyone may use the library, but only members may borrow books. Inquiries should be addressed to the director of information, Rhea A. White.

28. Association for Research and Enlightenment (ARE) Library, Box 595, Virginia Beach, Va. 23451

This library is primarily for the use of ARE members. The book collection consists of over 6000 volumes, plus 150 bound periodicals, and the readings of its founder, Edgar Cayce. Members may borrow books by mail. An annual *ARE Library Book List* contains a selection of 1500 titles most likely to be of interest to members. They are listed under 16 subject headings, those most relevant to parapsychology being dreams, prophecy and earth changes, psychic phenomena, and reincarnation and survival. An impressive new library building, which will serve as a research and study center, is due to be completed early in 1974. The library is open weekdays from 9:00 to 5:00.

29. Brown University Library, Brown University, Providence, R.I. 02912

In 1955 the Brown University Library acquired about 700 items from the John William Graham Collection of Literature of Psychic Science in the Swarthmore College library. A catalog of the collection was published by the Library of Swarthmore College in 1950, which covers 312 titles. It is an author listing, with brief annotations, and with title and subject indexes. The addition of these books to what the Brown University Library already possessed on the subjects of parapsychology and Spiritualism brings the library's resources in this and closely related fields to nearly 2000 titles. The library also has complete sets of the *Proceedings* and *Journals* of the British and of the American SPR and of several European psychic research societies.

30. College of Psychic Studies Library, 16 Queensberry Place, South Kensington, London SW7 2 EB, England

This group has a long history. Under the name of the London Spiritualist Alliance, it was founded in 1884 as the successor to the British National Association of Spiritualists. It changed its name to the College of Psychic Science in 1955, with the stated aim "to seek, collect and obtain information respecting and generally to study and investigate, phenomena commonly known as psychic . . . and in particular to study their application to the subject of survival and communication with the discarnate." *Science* was changed to *Studies* in 1970, as the former seemed premature at that time. The president of the college is Paul Beard. It maintains a library of 11,000 volumes, especially strong in Spiritualism. A 209-page catalog of the collection was published in 1931 by the London Spiritualist

Alliance. Printed supplements were published in 1939 and 1950. Since then, 11 typed duplicate supplements have appeared, the most recent being dated July 1971. The library is open from 10:00 to 9:00 Monday through Thursday and from 10:00 to 6:00 Fridays. Miss M. Lee, a professional librarian, is in charge. Only members of the college may borrow books, but nonmembers may use the library.

31. Eileen J. Garrett Library, Parapsychology Foundation (25)
This is strictly a research library; no materials may be borrowed. It is housed in three rooms with a professional librarian, Grazina Babusis, in charge. Holdings consist of 7500 volumes, 106 periodical titles, a vertical file, and a limited number of tapes, filmstrips, and recordings. The collection is cataloged by author, title, and subject. In 1967, Mrs. Babusis began an index to literature in periodicals of special interest to parapsychologists, as yet unpublished. The library is open to the public for study and research weekdays from 9:30 to 4:30.

32. Institute for Parapsychology Library, 402 N. Buchanan Boulevard, Durham, N.C. 27708
This is strictly a research collection, located at the Institute for Parapsychology, which is part of FRNM (4). Pamela J. Hilligoss, who is in charge, reports that the library contains approximately 1700 books and currently receives 65 periodicals (dealing with philosophy and psychology as well as parapsychology). It also has a file of unpublished manuscripts, theses, and parapsychological reprints. The library is open to the public for use on the premises weekdays from 8:00 to 5:00.

33. Harry Price Collection, Senate House Library, University of London, London, England.
This historical collection put together by bibliophile and psychic researcher Harry Price is now at the University of London, having been located originally in the National Laboratory of Psychical Research, which became the University of London Council for Psychical Investigation, both under Price's direction. Price published a 6000-item author-and-subject catalog of his library, entitled *Short-title Catalogue of Works on Psychical Research, Spiritualism, Magic, Psychology, Legerdemain and Other Methods of Deception, Charlatanism, Witchcraft and Technical Works for the Scientific Investigation of Alleged Abnormal Phenomena from circa 1450 A.D. to 1929 A.D.* (*Proceedings of the National Laboratory of Psychical Research*, Vol. I, pp. 67–422, April, 1929) and a 2500-item *Supplement* through 1935 (*Bulletin I*, University of London Council for Psychical Investigation, 1935).

34. Society for Psychical Research Library (16)
Mrs. B. Fortier is in charge of the SPR's library and reports that in 1973 it had approximately 10,000 books and receives 26 periodicals. The

book collection is arranged in 20-odd subject categories. The card catalog contains author and title cards with a colored tab on each that indicates the subject area where each may be located. Anyone may use the library, but only members may borrow books. The library is open 10:00–5:00 on weekdays.

35. Spiritual Frontiers Fellowship (SFF) Library, Spiritual Frontiers Fellowship, 800 Custer Avenue, Suite No. 1, Evanston, Ill. 60202

The Spiritual Frontiers Fellowship was founded in 1956 "to sponsor, explore and interpret the growing interest in psychic phenomena and mystical experience within the church, wherever these experiences relate to effective prayer, spiritual healing and personal survival." The membership of 7000 consists primarily of ministers and laymen. The fellowship has a lending library of about 3500 book titles, plus about 300 tapes of lectures, seminars, retreats, and conferences sponsored by SFF. Books and tapes may be borrowed by members by mail. Occasionally SFF publishes its lending-library catalog. The library has 85 periodical titles (but by no means complete runs in many cases) and a vertical file arranged by the same subject headings as the lending-library catalog. Mrs. Vivian Finklestein is in charge of the lending library, which lends an average of 1000 books a month. Anyone may use the library on the premises.

36. William Perry Bentley Collection on Psychical Research, Parapsychology and Cognate Subjects, Bridwell Library, Southern Methodist University, Dallas, Tex. 75222

This collection consists of over 500 volumes, including scholarly books and bound periodical runs. It was established in 1971 by William Perry Bentley "to underwrite the application of all the canons of scholarship and scientific research to the fuller understanding of psychic phenomena." Fully cataloged, the cards for the collection may be found in the appropriate card catalogs of the university library. The collection is available for use only within the Bridwell Library.

Lectures Stressing Parapsychology Topics

Many people prefer to learn about a subject through hearing about it. Opportunities for hearing single lectures or symposia on parapsychological subjects presented by leaders in the field are increasing. Some organizations that can usually be depended upon to present lectures or symposia at least once a year are described below. Although not specifically mentioned here, it should be kept in mind that both the ASPR (13) and the SPR (16) hold several lectures throughout the year. The ASPR lectures are open to the public at a nominal cost, but most SPR lectures are open only to members and their guests. However, occasionally public meetings are held, including the Myers Memorial Lectures (usually biennial), delivered by those who have "made notable contributions to thought or knowledge in psychical research."

37. Academy of Parapsychology and Medicine, 314 Second Street, Los Altos, Calif. 94022

This nonprofit educational organization, headed by Robert A. Bradley, M.D., was founded in 1970 "to provide a catalyst for the study of all forms of paranormal and unorthodox healing. It was formed by a group of scientists and physicians who believe that a common but as yet little understood rationale lies behind all healing experience." However, its interests, thus far, have tended to stress the "unorthodox" (De la Warr box, acupuncture, Kirlian effects) rather than the "paranormal" factors in healing. Although the academy's functions include research and publication, thus far its primary activity has been to hold symposia and workshops. In 1971 the academy and Lockheed Management Association sponsored an interdisciplinary symposium, "The Varieties of Healing Experience" (which has since been published by the academy). An acupuncture symposium was sponsored in cooperation with Stanford University in 1972 and a five-day symposium, "The Dimensions of Healing," was held at both Stanford and at UCLA. There are no restrictions on membership in the academy, and the symposia are open to the public.

38. American Association for the Advancement of Science Annual Meeting (held in a different location each year at the end of December). 1515 Massachusetts Ave. NW, Washington, D.C. 20005.

Each year since 1970 the Parapsychological Association (15) has sponsored a symposium on parapsychology at the annual convention of the AAAS. In 1970 it was a three-hour symposium entitled "Techniques and Status of Modern Parapsychology" (see 50). In 1971 it was a day-long symposium called "Data from EEG and Other Areas of Parapsychology." And in 1972 the symposium stressed the interdisciplinary nature of psi research and was called "Undergraduate Parapsychological Phenomena: A Survey of Four Possible Areas of Integration."

39. Human Dimensions Institute, 4380 Main Street, Buffalo, N.Y. 14226

This nonprofit educational organization, headed by Ms. Jeanne P. Rindge, espouses a holistic view of man and seeks to expand human awareness on all levels. It is located at Rosary Hill College and often uses its facilities for its programs but is independent of the college. It conducts research on paranormal healing, holds several noncredit courses in aspects of parapsychology, meditation, transpersonal psychology, and related subjects. It also sponsors several weekend symposia and individual lectures throughout the year, many of which have been by parapsychologists on aspects of psychic phenomena. These activities are open to the public at a minimal charge.

40. Institute of Noetic Sciences, 575 Middlefield Road, Palo Alto, Calif. 94301

The Institute of Noetic Sciences is a nonprofit, tax-exempt public corporation established in 1973 by Dr. Edgar D. Mitchell to sponsor and perform basic research and education in the nature of consciousness and the mind–body relationship. It communicates with society at large through various information channels, and it advises and consults with government, industry, science, education, and other areas of society on application of knowledge in the noetic sciences to planetary problems and their solution. Public lectures on consciousness research and its implications for science and society are given around the country. A graduate internship program was begun during the summer of 1973 and will be expanded in subsequent years. The institute publishes a newsletter and will soon add a magazine and scientific journal to its publications. Various categories of membership are available.

41. Parapsychological Association Convention (15)

The Parapsychological Association holds an annual convention, usually in New York, but of the 15 conventions held thus far, two were in Durham, North Carolina, one at Oxford University, one at Freiburg University, one at the University of Edinburgh, and, in 1973, at Charlottesville, Virginia. It is usually held on the Thursday through Saturday following Labor Day. The convention of the Parapsychological Association is probably the best opportunity to learn what is going on inside parapsychology today. However, the meetings of the association are restricted. The rules governing attendance are as follows: "Attendance at the convention . . . is restricted to Members and Associates and to guests who hold professional positions in academic institutions, or who are professional scientists or medical doctors, or college students actively engaged in research, or persons whose maturely scientific interest in the work of the Association has been clearly established." Approved convention guests must register and pay the convention fee but may not participate in the discussions.

42. University of California Extension Lectures and Symposia

The University of California Extension in a number of centers has been actively engaged in presenting parapsychological topics. In 1965 the extension at Los Angeles held a symposium entitled "Extrasensory Perception: Fact or Fantasy" and another in 1969 called "A New Look at Extrasensory Perception," both lasting two days. The extension at Berkeley conducted a weekend symposium in 1970 entitled "ESP and Psychic Phenomena: The Invisible Forces of the Mind." In 1971, the extension at Davis held a weekend symposium called "Extrasensory Perception in Laboratory and Life."

III. PUBLICATIONS

Described below are some of the major parapsychological publications. Periodicals are stressed because they publish most of the original experimental and theoretical articles, as well as field studies and investigations of spontaneous cases. The books were selected primarily because they will lead the reader to further sources of information—bibliographies, abstracts, indexes, surveys, and reviews.

Reference Works, Reviews, and Bibliographies

The titles in this selected list were chosen because they are either reviews of modern parapsychology; provide information on where specific material may be found; or are sources of additional information on parapsychological organizations, educational institutions, and information on what is happening in parapsychology today. In addition to the bibliographies described below, it should be kept in mind that printed library catalogs are a form of bibliography; for these, see (28), (29), (30), (33), and (35).

43. American Society for Psychical Research. Education "Courses and Other Study Opportunities in Parapsychology." Rev. ed. New York, 1973. 10 pp.
This is a chart of educational institutions offering courses or other research and study opportunities. Where available the information provided in each case is the name of the institution; the department(s) involved; name of the instructor or person to contact; brief information on the course, seminar, or tutorial; and number of credits.

44. Angoff, Allan, and Shapin Betty, eds. *Parapsychology Today: A Geographic View. Proceedings of an International Conference.* Parapsychology Foundation: New York, 1973, 258 pp.
This book provides an extensive view of the historical development and current state of parapsychology in a number of geographic areas: the United Kingdom, California, Japan, India, Turkey, Israel, Eastern Europe, South Africa, Scandinavia, Switzerland, Argentina, Holland, Italy, France, Canada, and the United States. The work of each area is described by someone from that area or closely involved with it. (Articles

based on some of the chapters have already appeared in *Parapsychology Review.*).

45. Ashby, Robert H. *The Guidebook for the Study of Psychical Research.* Weiser: New York, 1972, 190 pp.

Following an introductory chapter on the nature of psychic research is a bibliography "for the beginning student." It is a listing of books by subject, of which 40 are annotated and 69 not. Chapter 3 is similarly arranged but aimed at advanced students. Chapter 4 provides instructions for sitting with a medium. Chapter 5 briefly describes organizations, periodicals, libraries, and bookstores specializing in parapsychology. The sixth chapter provides paragraph-length biographies of 85 important figures in psychic research, and the final one is a glossary of 104 terms (38 from the *Journal of Parapsychology*).

46. *Biographical Dictionary of Parapsychology with Directory and Glossary 1964–1966.* Helene Pleasants, ed. Garrett–Helix: New York, 1964, 371 pp.

There are 467 entries in this biographical dictionary, arranged alphabetically. It includes persons associated with parapsychology, living and dead. In addition to biographical information, bibliographies for each entry are included. Entries are not only for parapsychologists but for mediums and sensitives and famous people in other fields who were interested in parapsychology.

47. Fodor, Nandor. *Encyclopaedia of Psychic Science.* University Books: New Hyde Park, N.Y., 1966, 416 pp.

This reprint of the 1933 edition is still very useful, although mainly for historical, nonquantitative materials. It describes persons, phenomena, terms, places, events, and publications relating to Spiritualism, mediumship, and psychic research. Some entries contain bibliographic information.

48. McConnell, Robert A. *ESP Curriculum Guide.* Simon and Schuster: New York, 1971, 128 pp.

This educator's guide, available in hardcover or paperback, is aimed at "secondary-school and college teachers of psychology, biology, and general science who may wish to teach extrasensory perception and related topics, either briefly or as a formal course unit, or who may have occasion to recommend the purchase of library materials for student projects on this subject" (p. 9). It contains a syllabus for teaching parapsychology and instructions for carrying out experiments. The application of scientific method to the data of parapsychology is stressed.

49. Naumov, E. K., and Vilenskaya, L. V. *Bibliographies on Parapsychol-*

ogy (Psychoenergetics) and Related Subjects. Joint Publications Service: Arlington, Va., 1972, 101 pp.

This dual bibliography lists the "more important" books and articles published on Soviet parapsychology in the last 70 years. Both parapsychological and nonparapsychological sources are included. The main arrangement is by subject. For some subjects the technical and popular literature is listed separately. The longer bibliography is of Russian materials, with English titles, and the other deals with foreign literature (primarily in English).

50. Parapsychological Association. *Techniques and Status of Modern Parapsychology.* PSI Communications Project: Newark, N.J., 1971, 106 pp.

This is the text of the Parapsychological Association's first symposium presented at the one hundred thirty-seventh annual meeting of the AAAS held in Chicago in December 1970. Not only does it contain survey articles on current research and theory in parapsychology, but the research being conducted at several major parapsychological research centers is described.

51. Rao, K. Ramakrishna. *Experimental Parapsychology: A Review and Interpretation, with a Comprehensive Bibliography.* Thomas: Springfield, Ill., 1966, 255 pp.

This is a review of experimental parapsychology aimed, among other things, at updating *Extrasensory Perception After Sixty Years* (52). Rao summarizes and discusses work on the major experimental variables such as the evidence for psi, the subject, the target stimuli, experimenter, testing conditions, experimental methods, psychology of psi, theories of psi, and the implications of psi regarding the nature of man. There is a 1251-item bibliography of books and articles.

52. Rhine, J. B., and others. *Extrasensory Perception After Sixty Years: A Critical Appraisal of the Research in Extrasensory Perception.* Humphries: Boston, 1966, 463 pp.

This is a reprint of the major review of experimental parapsychology to 1940, the year of its first publication. It is based primarily on the research carried out at the Duke University Parapsychology Laboratory. It not only describes the experiments, their conditions, and results but also criticisms and replies to them. It is also a useful handbook on the methodology of ESP research. A number of statistical tests are described in an appendix and tables presenting the conditions and results of all ESP experiments published between 1882 and 1939 and of published criticisms presented in terms of the alternative hypotheses. There is a bibliography of 361 items.

53. Rhine, J. B., and Pratt, J. G. *Parapsychology: Frontier Science of the Mind.* Rev. ed. Thomas: Springfield, Ill., 1962, 224 pp.

This is the first book conceived as a textbook of parapsychology. Part I reviews present knowledge (circa 1960) including the basic facts revealed by experimental psi research. There is a chapter on the psychology of psi, and psi is related to other sciences and humanities. Part II is on basic testing methods. There are eight useful tables on evaluating test results.

54. Techter, David. *Bibliography and Index of Psychic Research and Related Topics for the Year 1962*. Illinois Society for Psychical Research: Chicago, 1963, 81 pp. (also issued separately for 1963 and 1964).

These three bibliographies attempt to list everything published in English on psychic research for the respective years involved. Books, articles, book reviews, and correspondence are included. The popular as well as the scientific literature is covered. The main arrangement is by author, but there is a subject index.

55. Thouless, Robert H. *From Anecdote to Experiment in Psychical Research*. Routledge and Kegan Paul: London and Boston, 1972, 198 pp.

This is one of the most general surveys of parapsychology, covering all aspects of research but stressing quantitative investigations. There are chapters reviewing not only the major subject areas but also criticisms, problems of experimental design and evaluation, and patterns thus far known about the nature of psi and how it operates. Although it is aimed at scientists in other fields, it is indispensable reading for newcomers to experimental parapsychology.

56. White, Rhea A., and Dale, Laura A. *Parapsychology: Sources of Information*. Scarecrow: Metuchen, N.J., 1973.

This is a guide to sources of information on parapsychology. In eight parts, the first and largest is an annotated list of 282 books arranged under 24 subject headings. The content and special features of each book are described. Reading level ratings, type of library indicators and book review citations are provided. Part II is on parapsychology in 31 general and specialized encyclopedias. The third part describes 15 major parapsychological research organizations and the fourth 14 English-language parapsychological periodicals. Part V is on academic and scientific acceptance of parapsychology. There is a glossary of 116 terms. There is an index to illustrations and to books with bibliographies of 100 or more items.

57. Zorab, George. *Bibliography of Parapsychology*. Garrett–Helix: New York, 1957, 127 pp.

This is a multilingual bibliography of selected books and periodical articles from earliest times through 1954. It was updated through 1959 in a supplement published in *Les Cahiers de la Tour Saint-Jacques*, no. 9

(1960). The primary arrangement in each is by subject and within that the listing is chronological. There are author and finer subject headings.

Periodicals

The major English-language periodicals are described below. For a general survey the annual *Proceedings of the Parapsychological Association* is very useful. The best sources of experimental articles are the *Journal of Parapsychology* and the *Journal of the ASPR*, while the latter and the *Proceedings of the SPR* are the primary vehicles for theoretical papers and field studies. *Parapsychology Review* is strong on current events in the field, and *Psychic* provides popular coverage.

58. *Journal of Paraphysics*, Paraphysical Laboratory (7)
Edited by Benson Herbert, the primary aim of this bimonthly, first published in 1967, is to present material on the paranormal that provides evidence of *phi*, as opposed to psi, referring to "physical (or alternatively objective) effects which do not appear to be attributable to the operations of living humans." It carries experimental and theoretical papers and spontaneous case reports. It contains translations of articles in East European languages and considerable space is given to accounts of Soviet work. One issue per year is a "Classified Directory of [British] Spontaneous Phenomena." It is illustrated, averages 40 pages in length, and costs $6 per year.

59. *Journal of Parapsychology*, Parapsychology Press, FRNM (4)
This quarterly, first published in 1937 by the Duke Parapsychology Laboratory, is now published by FRNM (4). Edited by Louisa E. Rhine and Dorothy H. Pope, it is "devoted primarily to the original publication of experimental results and other research findings in extrasensory perception and psychokinesis." Review articles, criticisms, methodological papers, and some theoretical discussions are published. There are also book reviews, correspondence, and "Parapsychological Abstracts" (71). As an affiliated organ of the Parapsychological Association (15), it carries that association's announcements. Each issue has a glossary. It costs $8 per year and averages 88 pages.

60. *Journal of the American Society for Psychical Research*, ASPR (13)
First published in 1907, the *Journal of the ASPR* has been a quarterly since 1942. Edited by Laura A. Dale, it averages about 100 pages per issue. It carries experimental reports of work carried out at the ASPR (13) and other research centers, case reports, theoretical and methodological papers, and book reviews. It is an affiliated organ of the Parapsychological Association (15) and carries its announcements. It is free to members and $3 per issue to others.

61. Journal of the Society for Psychical Research, SPR (16)

First published in 1884, the *Journal of the SPR* became a quarterly in 1955. It contains experimental reports, mediumistic studies, spontaneous case reports, book and periodical reviews, news items, and a lively correspondence section. The current editor is Renée Haynes. It averages 52 pages and is free to members and $6 per year to others.

62. *Parapsychological Monographs*, Parapsychology Foundation (15)

Although not a periodical, this series is included because of the importance of several titles. Published irregularly beginning in 1958, each one usually consists of a single work, averaging 94 pages. Twelve have been published, and all are in print at varying prices averaging $2.

63. *Parapsychology Review*, Parapsychology Foundation (15)

Edited by Betty Shapin, this bimonthly is the successor to the *Newsletter of the Parapsychology Foundation* and has a magazine-type format. It has an average of 24 pages, is illustrated, and serves primarily as a vehicle for news items of the foundation and parapsychology the world over. It stresses personnel, grants, courses, lectures, conferences, seminars, degrees, and news of parapsychological centers. It also has articles, book reviews, profiles of leading parapsychologists, obituaries, and a list of books received by the foundation's library (31). A special feature, published every few years, is the "International Directory of Parapsychological Associations." (The last one was in 1 (1970):5–9. It is a geographic listing of 150 parapsychological organizations and fringe groups interested in psi.) *Parapsychology Review* costs $4 per year.

64. *Proceedings of the American Society for Psychical Research*, ASPR (13)

Published irregularly since 1905, the *Proceedings* is edited by Laura A. Dale. It ranges in size from 32 to 500 pages. Experimental reports, methodological and theoretical papers or field studies too long to be published in the *Journal of the ASPR* are published in the *Proceedings*, usually one per issue. It is free to members, and the price to nonmembers varies according to size of the volume.

65. *Proceedings of the Parapsychological Association*, Psychical Research Foundation (11)

The purpose of this annual publication, which is put out by the Parapsychological Association(15), is to provide a record of the annual convention of the association. The first one, published in 1966, summarized the conventions held from 1958 to 1964. Beginning with the second one, each one covers the convention of one year, containing the complete texts of the presidential and invited dinner addresses and long abstracts or summaries of the papers delivered, arranged by subject. It is edited by

W. G. Roll, R. L. Morris, and J. D. Morris. Beginning with No. 9, it was published by Scarecrow Press under the title *Research in Parapsychology*, Vol. 1 (1972) and will be an annual hardcover edition only.

66. *Proceedings of the Society for Psychical Research*, SPR (16)

Since 1882 this irregular publication of the Society for Psychical Research(16) has been one of the major publication vehicles for substantial and lengthy experimental, theoretical, and critical papers. It also carries the addresses of the SPR presidents. It is free to members. Cost to nonmembers varies according to size, which ranges from 30 to 600 pages.

67. *Psychic*, 680 Beach Street, San Francisco, Calif. 94109

Edited and published by James Bolen, with co-editor Alan Vaughan, *Psychic* was first published in 1969 to provide forthright, popular coverage of "the extended nature of man and the universe." Published bimonthly, each issue averages 48 pages. There are three or four feature articles accompanied by illustrations (many in color), interviews with prominent persons associated with parapsychology, case reports, news items, a reader's column, and book reviews. It costs $5.50 per year.

68. *Theta*, Psychical Research Foundation (11)

Edited by W. G. Roll, *Theta*, named after the first letter of the Greek word for death, is the organ of the Psychical Research Foundation (11). It was initiated "in order that the work of the Foundation, as well as other research and educational efforts concerned with the survival problem, might become more widely known." Each issue is about forty pages long and contains a lead article describing current research and activities relevant to survival research, plus book reviews or abstracts of published works of relevance to the survival problem. It is published quarterly for $3.50 per year.

Abstracts and Indexes

Although a complete index by subject, author, and title to materials relevant to parapsychology is not available on a regular basis, there are some useful tools. The major parapsychological periodicals usually publish their own annual indexes and table of contents, and a makeshift kind of index can be made by putting these together, by photocopying, if necessary. Also, Techter (54) has an index to his annual bibliography.

69. *Journal of Parapsychology*, Table of Contents (59)

A table of contents for Volumes 1–16 (1947–1953) was published in 17 (1953):231–246. This can be a useful tool, especially when searching topics dealing with the literature of experimental parapsychology, book reviews, and the evolution of the Duke Parapsychology Laboratory.

70. National Institute of Mental Health, National Clearinghouse for Mental Health Information, 5600 Fishers Lane, Rockville, Md. 20852.

The clearinghouse provides annotated bibliographies in the form of a computer print-out on specific subjects. In 1972 a bibliography was provided of 505 items published 1968–1971, under the search headings of Psychic Phenomena, Parapsychology, Extrasensory Perception, and Telepathy. The abstracts provided are an average of 220 words long. The indexing for this service is done automatically, with an average of 60 search terms selected per abstract. The file was started in 1968, half of it consisting of abstracts of journal articles and the remainder of books, chapters, technical reports, and the like. In addition to the terms mentioned above the search vocabulary contains Psi, Psychokinesis, Precognition, Medium, Survival, and Trance. This service is provided free of charge to mental-health workers and researchers.

71. "Parapsychological Abstracts," *Journal of Parapsychology* (59)

This is not a separate publication but a feature of the *Journal of Parapsychology* (59) initiated in 1958. It includes abstracts of papers on parapsychology published in both parapsychological and nonparapsychological periodicals, mainly in English but also in other languages. All abstracts are in English regardless of original language of publication and are about half a page long. Unpublished manuscripts are also abstracted. Xerox copies of the full reports may be ordered from the *Journal* at 10¢ per page.

72. *Psychological Abstracts.* American Psychological Association, 1200 Seventeenth Street, N.W., Washington, D.C. 20036

There are four approaches to the material in *Psychological Abstracts*: by author's last name; by broad subject category (i.e., table of contents classification); by the brief subject index in each issue; and by the semi-annual subject index. Of these, since 1961 the second has been the most important for locating parapsychological material, as then *Psychological Abstracts* began to use "Parapsychology" in its contents classification. (Before that, articles on psi were listed under many scattered headings.) The brief subject index was introduced in 1963, the two main parapsychological headings being "Extrasensory Perception" and "Parapsychology." These are also the terms to look under in the more complete semi-annual indexes. The parapsychological periodicals regularly indexed in *Psychological Abstracts* are *Journal of the ASPR* (60), *Journal of Parapsychology* (59), *Journal of the SPR* (61), *Parapsychology Review* (63), and *Proceedings SPR* (66). It is a very useful tool for locating articles on parapsychology appearing in nonparapsychological behavioral science journals.

73. Society for Psychical Research. *Proceedings and Journal. Combined Index.* Washington, D.C., Carrollton Press, 1972, 600 pp.

This reprint is based on a number of indexes already published separately by the SPR (some of which are still available, if not all). It consists of author and subject indexes to *Proceedings of the SPR*, Volumes 1–26 (1882–1913); *Journal of the SPR*, Volumes 1–15 (1884–1912); and *Proceedings of the First ASPR*, Volume 1 (1885–1889). It also contains a table of contents of *Proceedings* and a classified list of the contents of the *Proceedings* and *Journal* from Volume 1 of each to June 1932, compiled by Theodore Besterman. Finally, it contains an index to *Phantasms of the Living*, by Gurney, Myers, and Podmore (a classic that recently was reprinted in two volumes by Scholars' Facsimiles, Gainesville, Florida), which is more detailed than that published with the book.

A table of contents of both *Proceedings of the SPR* and *Journal of the SPR* is available from the SPR (16).

II The Expanding Range of

Psychic Research

As parapsychology matured, some border areas began to merge with other disciplines of science. Anthropology, psychiatry, medicine, and electroencephalography are four examples of nonparapsychological fields that now have distinct, strong relations with psychic research. This section shows their commingling with the mainstream of psi investigation.

Robert L. Morris

ROBERT L. MORRIS, *Ph.D., is research coordinator for the Psychical Research Foundation and a research associate of the Gardner Murphy Research Institute in Chapel Hill, North Carolina.*

After earning his doctorate from Duke University in 1969, Dr. Morris became a postdoctoral research fellow at the Center for the Study of Aging and Human Development at Duke until he obtained his present post at PRF in 1971. From 1970 to 1972 he was an editor of the Proceedings *of the Parapsychological Association. During his academic training, he spent three years as a U.S. Public Health Service research trainee. He also held a three-year summer research fellowship in parapsychology at the Foundation for Research on the Nature of Man, and a two-year research assistantship at Duke University. His articles and reviews have appeared in parapsychological and zoological journals.*

Dr. Morris can be reached at The Tutorial Program, University of California, Santa Barbara, Calif.

9 The Psychobiology of Psi

ROBERT L. MORRIS

SUMMARY

This chapter concerns itself with the processing of psi information once it is within the organism, from a psychobiological perspective. Little is known about higher-level biological processing of information, such as memories and thoughts. A survey of animal research reveals that psi may be present throughout much of the animal kingdom and that it bears some resemblance in its manifestation to psi in humans. Psychophysiological studies of psi performance in humans have produced conflicting results but suggest in general that optimal processing of psi information does not involve active cognitive processing—that is, does not require rational thought. Although embryonic in their development, these areas of research hold great promise for our understanding of how psi information is processed and how that processing can be improved. (As this book went to press, it was found that W. J. Levy had used improper experimental procedures in a recent unpublished study. This raises doubt about conclusions drawn from his published work. Therefore the reader should regard those sections of this chapter dealing with Levy's work as tentative unless confirmed by independent research. *The Editor*)

INTRODUCTION

Psi can be construed as an information flow between an organism and its environment that lies outside of the bounds of the information channels we presently understand. In ESP, information appears to flow from the environment to the organism; in PK, the information appears to flow from the organism to the environment.

Developing theories about how psi works can be done at two levels. We can theorize about how the information crosses those barriers—how it gets from environment to organism and vice versa, the kind of energy involved, and so on. This aspect of psi is often considered the most important because it involves either extensive elaboration of the present constructs of physics or the development of a new set of concepts, perhaps as part of a totally new discipline. The beginnings of such theory development can be seen in some of the other chapters in this book.

We can also develop theories about how the information is handled or processed while it is within the organism. This area is also important to understand because it represents the translation of raw psi information into information usable by the organism. For known means of information reception, such as the visual or the auditory, processing within the organism modifies that information extensively, so that it can be used most effectively. Some information is filtered out peripherally (such as daily background sounds); some is amplified (such as a child's cry of distress); some is combined with other information (like the feel, taste, or smell of food); some is distorted ("I know you think you heard what I said . . ."). Such processing can be done to the original message or it can be done to representations in memory of that message. Processing of the original message involves mechanisms within the nervous system (22, 27). Processing of memory representations appears to involve central nervous system mechanisms (23, 54) as well as psychological mechanisms (60). Behavior (including thought) is thus dependent upon biological as well as psychological factors. Since psi manifests itself in overt behavior as well as covert thought, it also must be affected by biological and psychological factors.

At this point we encounter a dilemma common to all behavioral sciences: Are the psychological aspects of the organism dependent exclusively upon biological aspects or is there some additional, nonbiological aspect of behavior—that is, is there more to life than tissue? If exclusively dependent, we must expect psi-mediated behavior to have biological dependence also. Thus, an understanding of neurophysiological bases of behavior becomes of paramount importance for the understanding of psi. If there is some additional aspect, we must obviously understand that aspect as well as the biological if we are to understand psi. This dilemma is generally referred to as the mind–body problem, a topic debated by philosophers long before behavioral scientists had to face the question. The next section presents a brief overview of the present state of the art of our empirical attempts to understand the relationship of psyche and biology, or psychobiology.

THE PSYCHOBIOLOGY OF MENTAL ACTIVITY

For present purposes, description of the inadequacies of contemporary psychobiology will be more appropriate (and feasible) than an extensive chronicling of its many successes.

The main failure of psychobiology is in the area of information storage and retrieval—in other words, memory. A common psychobiological approach is to look for the location within the central nervous system of each mental phenomenon. The hypothalamus has been found to regulate most autonomic nervous system functions; the cerebellum is responsible for coordination of motor activites; and so on.

The main evidence suggesting localization of thought-related mental functions is the discovery of the speech center under the left temporal lobe of the cortex (designated Broca's area) in right-handed people. (Speech localization for left-handers is more variable.) Injury to Broca's area invariably results in a decrease in verbal performance. This localization of function shows up in *split-brain studies*. When information is taught to a right hemisphere that has been surgically separated from the left hemisphere (by cutting the connecting neural fibers), the person cannot describe the information verbally but can show knowledge via hand signals. If information is presented only to the left hemisphere of such a person, verbal response occurs readily (71). Such studies are done with people who have had these fibers cut to control epilepsy.

No specific location for storage of memory has been found, however. One of the first strong indications of this occurred in Lashley's investigations of learning and memory in rats (26). He and others found that surgical destruction of large portions of the cerebral cortex in lower mammals did not disrupt specific memories. Removal of various brain parts failed to show that a specific memory was stored in a specific part of the brain. Instead, performance seemed to decrease in proportion to the overall amount of the brain tissue destroyed. Lashley referred to this as the law of mass action.

A similar finding emerged from the studies of the neurosurgeon W. Penfield (49). Working with people having portions of their cortex removed to control epilepsy, Penfield found that specific memories could be evoked by electrical stimulation of certain areas of the cortex, yet surgical removal of these areas produced no detectable loss of memory. Such findings have led to speculation that the site of memory may be in subcortical structures. Many tentative explanations have been offered, but good evidence is lacking.

If memory (and thought) is bound to biological tissue, why has it not been localized? One possibility that has not received much attention in formal discussions of the topic is the redundancy of experience. We know that we are capable of remembering past original thoughts (e.g., dream recall); thus, each time we recall a memory, the thought involved may be creating a new memory. Also, each time we reexperience something, we may be creating a new memory. How many objects in your living room have you experienced only once? If you look at an object for 30 seconds, how many memories of that object will you have at the end? Only one? In short, there is no reason to assume that experiencing or remembering an experience is unitary and must thus be localized or represented in any one place in the brain. In fact, if memories are stored in discrete places in brain tissue, they are likely to be stored in a great many places, not just one.

Also, as Pribram (53) has emphasized, memory for many (if not all) experiences and concepts probably involves a real reconstruction, a re-

remembering, whereby the individual members or components of an experience are reassembled to generate anew the original experience. Only 26 letters of the alphabet are needed to construct (or reconstruct) millions of words; perhaps there are many experiential "letters," each located in many different places in our cortex, with which we reconstruct memories.

Regardless of whether one views memories as stored discretely or in some more diffuse fashion, memory still implies information stored as permanent modifications to something within the central nervous system. The four general kinds of modification that have been hypothesized are discussed here.

Modification of Electrical Activity in Neural Circuits

Hebb (17) postulated "cell assemblies," or reverberating neural circuits. A simple reverberating circuit would be as follows: neuron A activates neuron B, which activates neuron C, which activates neuron A again, and so on. Thus, activation of neurons A, B, or C would result in activation of the whole circuit in the sequence A, B, C. The main idea was that a series of neurons could "learn" to become activated in a certain pattern so that a specific pattern would be more likely to occur again upon general stimulation of its parts. The retention of information (memory) would be contained in the increased likelihood that that pattern would be reactivated in toto upon stimulation of its component neurons. Complex information would be retained in series of such cell assemblies known as *phase sequences*.

How might such circuits be formed? One possibility is that electrical impulses traveling from one neuron to another may lead to growth or degeneration of neural activity in such a way as to modify the likelihood that firing of neuron A would lead to firing of neuron B (that is, changing the proximity of neurons or their contact areas changes their ability to stimulate one another). Rosenzweig et al. (68) review recent electron-microscope studies and show that differential experience in lower mammals can produce increases or decreases in the number of synapses (neuron-to-neuron junctions) as well as increases or decreases in the size (contact area) of the synapses. Pribram (53) has hypothesized that such neural growth may even be guided by glial cells (see below) in the same way that peripheral nerve regeneration is guided by Schwann cells (cells closely related to glial cells). Thus, both neurons and the surrounding glial tissue are responsible for information storage, in Pribram's view. (Glial cells are small cells found in the spaces between neurons in the higher levels of the central nervous system. They outnumber neurons 9:1 in the cerebral cortex. Originally they were regarded solely as supportive cells, serving only to hold the neurons they surrounded in place. It is now known that they are capable of slow bioelectric activity and that they are capable of ephaptic [nonsynaptic] communication with neighboring neural and glial cells. Some of them are mobile, like white blood cells.)

Such mechanisms, if validated by further research, would provide a basis for the formation of coordinated cellular activities, be they reverberating circuits or other cellular patterns. There is some preliminary neurophysiological evidence that reverberating circuits do exist (78), but much further research is needed before their actual role in information storage can be made clear.

Macromolecular Storage of Information

Recent advances in our understanding of the storage of enormous amounts of genetic information in giant molecules have raised the possibility that such macromolecules may be involved in memory storage. Speculation that such molecules may actually contain the information of memory has been spurred by several recent studies on the apparent transfer of information from one animal to another through injected brain extract. McConnell (37) found that planaria (a kind of worm) that ate other planaria would develop certain of the behavior patterns of the planaria they had eaten. Later several others found that if one rodent were injected with homogenized brain extract from another rodent taught a certain behavior, the recipient would show the learned behavior. Rosenblatt (67), in a recent survey of such studies, has pointed out that the results have been inconsistent, occasionally even producing significant reversals (injected animals show less of the learned behavior than control animals). He suggests that these inconsistencies may disappear as more factors are taken into account. This optimism is not shared by all writers on the topic (15), and the exact role played by these molecules in memory storage must be considered in doubt.

Macromolecular Modification of Neural Activity

There is little doubt that large molecules in neural and glial cells are extensively involved in the functioning of these cells. Many researchers are developing hypotheses about how the information-storing capabilities of these molecules may interact with neuron–neuron and neuron–glia interfaces to produce permanent central nervous system changes. Three recent books (5, 14, 77) summarize the extensive research and attempts at theory development at the macromolecular level.

Overall Firing Patterns Involving Large Numbers of Cells

Certain authors have hypothesized that memory storage and retrieval involve large masses of cortical cells firing in complex patterns, such that the overall pattern recreates the memory. Perhaps Pribram's attempts to draw analogies between memory storage and retrieval and holograms are the best known (52, 53). These hypotheses are too complex to be described in detail here and are all in a very preliminary stage of formulation.

In general, despite certain promising beginnings, none of the major memory researchers will claim to have done anything more than develop an intelligent model around which further research can be based. A major difficulty for all models is the retrieval problem. Even if we do develop a comprehensive theory to explain information encoding and storage, how is this information retrieved and used in conjunction with other memories to produce new information (i.e., creative ideas)? What level of organization is necessary? How is retrieval initiated? The great complexity of these problems and the inaccessibility and delicacy of the brain will undoubtedly prevent conclusive research on the nature of memory for some time.

All of the above hypotheses have related memory and thought to activation or reactivation of some complex biochemical subsystem. Three kinds of relationships can be suggested: (a) thought is activation; (b) thought has a 1:1 correspondence with specific activation; (c) thought is interfaced with the physical body through activation of components of the central nervous system but not necessarily on a one-to-one basis and not necessarily through a principle involving reactivation of specific structures. There is no resolution of this problem at present; it remains a philosopher's delight and will do so for some time unless new lines of research should develop and bear fruit far more rapidly than is presently expected.

Parapsychological findings have quite often been interpreted as providing evidence for a nonphysical aspect of mind because of their purported independence of physical variables (63). Whether such independence is apparent or real remains to be seen, as stated earlier. Whether psi indicates an aspect to mental processes beyond the realm of present-day physics, as seems likely, will become gradually, but directly, evident as we unravel the exact relationships between psi and psychobiological findings. At present, two major lines of relevant research are emerging: psi in animals and psychophysiological studies of humans.

PSI IN ANIMALS

There have always been a great many anecdotes suggestive of psi in animals (62, 65), and their number grows daily. Recently, experimental studies have been published that embellish and support these anecdotes. (For a recent, but already obsolete, review, see Ref. 42.)

Why study psi in animals? Such studies will eventually tell us the effect of central nervous system complexity upon psi performance, as well as the effect of specific central nervous system components present in some species but not in others. We will also learn about the evolutionary and ecological aspects of psi, including the genetics of factors relevant to psi performance. Such information will be long in coming, but it will be invaluable in our attempts to examine the interface between psi behavior and psychobiology. Additionally, many behavioral scientists are attracted by the fact that studies with animals are methodologically much more straightforward than those with humans, with fewer factors to control, greater ability to manipulate the organism's environment, greater ease of systematic follow-up studies (including fewer restrictions upon studies involving active interference with the nervous system), and so on.

Several kinds of animal behavior often considered to be indicative of psi have now been studied extensively. One of these is the ability of certain animals to "home"—that is, to return to a place of origin after having been removed from it and released at a distance great enough to eliminate the possibility that the animal is using recognition of familiar landmarks. The problem of homing has produced extensive research, especially with pigeons and certain migratory birds. Matthews (40) provides the best recent summary of these studies.

Homing involves two components: (*a*) selecting the correct initial direction and (*b*) maintaining that direction long enough to bring the animal within the range of familiar landmarks. Celestial cues, such as the position of the sun, moon, and certain star configurations, are involved in direction maintenance. No adequate theory has yet been developed to explain how the proper direction is initially chosen. Pratt (51) has provided a summary of research that attempted to find an experimental design with pigeons that would provide a clear-cut test of the "psi hypothesis." He concluded that an adequate study would require extensive funds and time, and for these reasons it has not yet been carried out. Thus, there is at present no experimental evidence bearing directly on the question of the involvement of psi in animal homing ability.

A related phenomenon is *psi-trailing*. A typical case might go as follows: A family moves away, leaving behind a favorite pet. Some time after the family has left, the pet disappears. A few days or even weeks later, an animal very closely resembling the pet arrives at the new home of the family and shows definite signs of recognizing them as its old owners.

Rhine and Feather (65) have presented the only serious attempt to assess the validity of the psi-trailing phenomenon. For their analysis they drew upon their laboratory's collection of spontaneous animal cases.

Fifty-four cases were judged by the authors to meet their criteria (e.g., adequate details in reporting and unusual identifying characteristics of the pet). Long-range trailing cases (over 30 miles) involved 10 dogs, 12 cats, and 3 birds. As the authors point out, however, these cases do not conclusively demonstrate the involvement of psi. We do not know how many pets were left behind that tried to find their owners and failed. It is hard to evaluate the likelihood of psi-trailing occurring by chance, other than that it would decrease with distance. Some have argued that a heightened sensory capacity could have been used, such as smell. If this is to be seriously considered for cases involving several weeks of elapsed time and over a hundred miles in distance covering well-traveled major highways, then we are dealing with a phenomenon of sensory acuity just as unknown as any other possibilities involving psi.

As in the case of homing, an adequate experimental examination of the role of psi in psi-trailing has not yet been done. One possibility is to see whether or not pets left at a boarding kennel by owners on vacation tend to orient toward the direction of the new location of the owners.

Several early naturalists were impressed by the unusual precision in the activities of social insects, especially those living in hives. Maeterlinck, following up on the work of Eugene Marais, felt that the simultaneous performance of complex behavior patterns by so many simple insects could not be adequately explained in terms of inherited traits or learned behavior patterns. His term for the communication mechanism was "spirit of the hive" (39). Selous (quoted in Ref. 16) felt that thought transference was involved in the coordination of the sudden turns of large flocks of birds. Reik (61) discussed psi communication in groups of caterpillars. He also called attention to Freud's notion that the original presence of a "group will" in hive societies has been replaced in evolution by the apparently superior method of communication through processing of external sign-stimuli.

These theories were formulated during the early stages of the science of animal behavior. Recent developments in our understanding of the roles of high-frequency sounds and external chemical information transmitters (e.g., pheromones), as well as advances in our understanding of the evolution of social behavior, have made psi-related theories less necessary.

Occasionally one hears of an animal that can talk, do arithmetic, or read the future. Such an animal generally turns out to be a horse or dog that has been taught to respond to verbal questions by barking, tapping, pawing an appropriate number of times, or selecting an appropriate lettered block from a tray. Several extensive reports of such cases exist, the most famous of which are the horse Clever Hans (50) and the famous dogs of Durov (2).

Genuine intelligence has been ruled out by the consistent failure of such animals to succeed when no one present knows the correct answer, together with our present knowledge of the limitations of animal intelligence. For most of these cases some sort of subtle cue from the handler or from someone else present who knew the answer was found to be responsible. People watching Clever Hans tap his hoof would lean forward slightly. Just as he completed the correct number of hoof taps everyone who knew this would relax and lean back slightly. This slight change in posture was apparently all that was necessary to cue Clever Hans as to when to stop (thus exhibiting a perception sensitivity almost as remarkable as a psi hypothesis, although it does not offend our classical theories).

Some of the clever animal cases appeared to overcome these difficulties (38, 84, 85). The last of these was especially interesting. Chris, a "clever" dog, was taught by his owner, George Wood, to guess down through a stack of ESP cards enclosed in opaque envelopes by pawing once for circle, twice for square, and so on. Wood, who did not know what cards were in what envelopes, presented them one by one to Chris and recorded the dog's responses. This procedure produced very strong positive results when Wood and Chris worked together; when an outside investigator was called in to witness the results, Chris's scores became negative to a statistically meaningful degree. Unfortunately, further studies were not done to find out if this shift was similar to the often reported negative scoring of humans in the face of stress.

Rhine and Feather (65) have described three additional categories of animal behavior suggestive of psi interactions between human and animal: (a) reaction to impending danger for the animal itself or its owner; (b) reaction to the death of a distant owner; and (c) anticipation of a positive event such as the return home of the owner after a long absence. In one instance, a dog was left at a veterinarian's while the owners went to Florida. One morning the dog started howling at 10:00 and continued for a full hour. This behavior prompted the veterinarian to mention this unusual event to the family upon their return. They were astonished, since on that morning they had been marooned in a flash flood from 10:00 to 11:00. Such coincidences, although striking, are difficult to deal with in other than a descriptive manner.

Rhine (64) investigated experimentally a trainer–dog interaction in the location of hidden dummy underwater mines. The dog, guided by the trainer, would "guess" at the location by sitting in one of five possible target areas. Results were very strong, but interpretation is difficult because of the possibility that the trainer may have located the targets by psi and communicated them nonverbally to the dogs or that sensory cues were inadvertently provided when the study was set up.

Several studies have been done in laboratories using animals tested in artificial environments. Osis and Foster (47) did several experiments with cats run in a two-choice T-maze. The cats were required to choose which of the two arms of the maze led to concealed food. Olfactory cues were minimized by a fan blowing air toward the food cup positions. The cats scored positively under "good" conditions, such as affectionate handling, and negatively under "poor" conditions, in which distractions were deliberately introduced, such as rubbing the cats' fur the wrong way or altering the lighting of the room. This difference in scoring is similar to that obtained by Honorton (21) with humans run under experimenter-induced positive and negative conditions. An additional finding was that the evidence for psi was weakest when the animals were showing rigid or stereotyped choices (such as always going to the left).

A similar study, but testing precognition, done in South Africa by Bestall (3) involved male mice run in a two-choice maze. Each mouse made one choice. Some time after all the mice had made their choice, a randomizing procedure was used to designate for each mouse which side was correct and which side incorrect. Correct choosers were given access to a female six hours later; incorrect choosers were put to death. Bestall obtained positive results with this precognition procedure and even found suggestive evidence for cyclic variations in scoring from day to day.

Craig (7) used a similar precognition procedure with rats in a two-choice maze. The rats showed no tendency to choose the correct side. However, those rats that chose the right side took longer to run the maze. This was found in two successive studies.

The strongest and most consistent set of animal studies of which we are presently aware involves mice, gerbils, and hamsters in a two-choice precognition procedure. Several variations have been tried; the basic procedure is as follows: The animal is placed in a small cage divided in two by a low partition over which the animal can easily jump. At periodic intervals a mild shock is administered to the floor on one side or the other. The animal presumably is motivated to avoid the shock by anticipating which side will be shocked so that it can be on the nonshocked side. A logic circuit constantly records the animal's position. At periodic intervals a random-number generator designates one side or the other as the side to be shocked, and shock is administered for five seconds if the animal is on that side. A print-out of the animal's position plus the side designated as shock each time provides automated recording of the data. At present over 20 successful experimental series have been run using variations on this general procedure, encompassing work in both France and America (11, 29–34).

Several findings of interest have emerged. The most important are as follows: (a) rigid or stereotyped behavior does not show evidence of psi; (b) a very mild shock is more effective than no shock or an extremely high shock, suggesting that low stress or activation levels may be most conducive to psi; (c) extensive running of the same animal decreases the results, suggesting habituation; (d) complete automation by computer to eliminate handling by an experimenter and to provide tallying of results does not decrease the effect, and even appears to enhance it; (e) variable versus fixed intertrial interval appears not to affect the results, nor does duration of interval; (f) highest results consistently occur on the trials following trials when the animal was correct and on which he showed relatively little jumping activity (interpretation of this finding is uncertain at present, but it is consistent with the notion of low stress as efficacious for psi); and (g) use of a running wheel divided in half by two barriers opposite each other is just as effective as a stationary chamber.

Schouten (70) did a somewhat similar experiment in Holland, using drops of water as a reward for thirsty rats rather than shock as a punishment. He found that his animals also scored best when they were not showing rigid or stereotyped behavior. He also found suggestive evidence that having another animal aware of the correct choice helped the subject animal to make that choice. Two follow-up studies use similar, but not identical, procedure; Schouten has not confirmed these results, however.

Several preliminary studies have been done in which behavior related to emotional state, such as activity level, has been used to assess an animal's response to impending (precognition) or distant (clairvoyance) events, with some success (42). No procedure has been repeated often enough to enable real evaluation of the results, however.

An additional set of studies has involved experiments in which the psi abilities of animals have been tested through PK procedures (28, 69, 80). Cockroaches, lizards, chickens (including about-to-hatch eggs), and cats are placed in mildly unpleasant environments. Factors affecting the pleasantness of the environment, such as periodic shock or stimulation from a heat lamp (in a cold environment), are controlled by a random-number generator. The hypothesis is that the animals will influence the generator in such a way as to make the environment less unpleasant. The results are mixed. Schmidt's cockroaches (see Chapter 7) were shocked more often than one would expect by chance rather than less often; Watkins's lizards in cool environments showed different tendencies to receive heat from a heat lamp, depending on barometric pressure and humidity of the surrounding environment; Levy's chickens and eggs received heat from the lamp more often than chance when in a cool environment. For Schmidt's study there exists the possibility that Schmidt himself, who does not like cockroaches, might have been the real PK agent. The mixed results of the Watkins study are interpretable as consistent with the differing heat needs of the lizards as they found themselves in slightly different environments from day to day. Levy's eggs received more heat when their surrounding temperature was below their optimal temperature range and less heat when the temperature rose above the optimal temperature range. Also, the random generator produced random results when no organism was present. These findings are regarded as very tentative by all authors concerned and await further repetition and refinement before conclusions can be reached about just where in the procedure the information flow is occurring.

A final set of studies involves examination of human–animal interactions, in which a human attempts to influence the behavior of an animal. Several preliminary studies have been done by a variety of people (42, 58). Graham Watkins's research group has reported several successful studies in which humans, especially "healers," attempted to revive target anesthetized mice earlier than control mice anesthetized at the same time (81, 82). Although the procedure does involve an influence on behavior, this influence can be construed as affecting behavior through affecting the biochemical components of that behavior. Thus, this set of studies straddles the subject matter of this chapter and the topic of psychic healing.

Several other studies involve attempted human influence over an animal. Metta (41) found some evidence that a human could influence butterfly larvae to crawl into specified sectors of a petri dish. Extra (12) did two studies which found some evidence that a human could influence rat running behavior in a shuttle box. Interestingly, Metta thought of his own study as employing a PK procedure, whereas Extra thought of his own study as employing a telepathy procedure. They agreed on the direction of information flow across the barrier but disagreed on which species was the subject.

Richmond (66) found evidence that he could influence the direction of locomotion of paramecia viewed through a microscope. Randall (55) used a better experimental design but was unable to repeat his results, as was Knowles (58). Later, Randall (56) found some evidence that wood lice could be influenced to enter one of five sectors of a circular board and evidence (57) that gerbils could be influenced to jump on certain blocks of wood as opposed to others. He does not regard his results as conclusive, however. Osis (46) attempted to influence cats in a two-choice maze. As in his cat ESP work (47), there were predicted high runs and predicted low runs, depending upon running conditions and treatment of the cats. Predicted low runs produced statistically significant psi-missing, whereas the predicted high runs produced only slightly positive results. In none of these studies has the evidence for the ability of humans to influence overt choice behavior of a lower species been based on overall statistically significant positive results. The Watkins data (reviving anesthetized mice) are exceptions, but any PK influence exerted in these studies would have been over physiological processes rather than choice behavior.

What have we learned from these animal studies? Very little so far, mainly because few of the procedures described have been thoroughly explored or followed up in any systematic way. Some points may be tentatively offered, however.

Studies involving animals as subjects appear to be more consistent than studies involving humans, both in proportion of overall studies that yield results and in proportion of follow-up studies yielding results similar to the initial study. The latter point is dramatically emphasized by the success of the shock-avoidance procedure with mice, gerbils, and hamsters. Perhaps animals do better in laboratory testing, because there is less distraction, less "noise" in their psychobiological systems. One might expect response to the laboratory situation to be more stable than for humans—no exams, no personality clash with the experimenter, no culturally mediated expectations, no fears about success and failure at the psi task, and so on. The maintenance of results despite increased instrumentation and automation may be pertinent here: animals probably are less concerned about the "dehumanizing effect" of machinery and computers than are humans.

Evidence for psi seems obtainable from a wide range of species and central nervous system complexity levels. Does complexity level have an effect? The several studies involving human interaction with lower animals suggest that the human nervous system (and/or associated psyche, if any) may be capable of dominating, or directing, a less complex nervous system (and/or associated psyche, if any). Of course, we have not designed any studies so far to see if the reverse is also true (perhaps because of the distasteful implications of positive results). The only study so far done in which two levels of nervous system complexity may have been directly competing is the Schmidt cockroach study, in which the human appeared to be the winner. This problem is easy to approach with systematic research, especially using the PK procedure. For instance, one could pair off a day-old egg with an egg about to hatch, so that when one gets heat, the other does not (controlling, of course, for differential optimal temperature ranges).

A moderate level of arousal or activation seems optimal for psi performance. Excessive arousal, in terms of negative running conditions, strong shock, and the like, seems to produce chance or negative results. This finding, if valid, indicates an interaction between structures affecting level of arousal and the processing of psi information.

In many ways, animals appear to respond to psi tasks in the same ways that humans do—psi-missing under negative conditions, habituation, response bias effects, and so on.

One last point about animal research should be made: until we understand more about psi in humans and its limits, we will have difficulty in most studies (if not all) in being certain that human psi is not somehow involved in production of the results, either totally or partly.

PSYCHOPHYSIOLOGICAL STUDIES OF HUMANS

Psychophysiology is the study of relationships between measurable physiological signals coming from the body of an organism and the mental activity within that organism. It is well established that such relationships exist.

The best known have been those relating autonomic nervous system activity and emotional states. General arousal or excitement makes the heart beat faster; fear or sudden shock is accompanied by a pale face, caused by constriction of the peripheral blood vessels (vasoconstriction); embarrassment or anger is accompanied by a red face, caused by expansion of these vessels (vasodilation). When we see something we like, the pupils of our eyes expand; when we see something we do not like, they contract. All of these reactions are controlled by the sympathetic and parasympathetic branches of the autonomic nervous system. There are many more examples, but the above will suffice. Such reactions are generally considered to be the adaptive response of the body—the "fight or flight" response as it has been called—to strong stimulation from the environment.

Of more recent interest is the burgeoning literature on relationships between the electrical activity of various parts of the cerebral cortex and cognitive processes. Of central importance are the alpha rhythms as obtained from EEG recordings from the scalp surface. The power source and pacing mechanism for these rhythms are still not understood, but a frequent guess is that they represent bioelectric activity in cortical cell dendrites, paced or regulated by centers in the thalamus that communicate with various areas of the cortex by a network of neural fibers (the thalamocortical projection system). Most of the evidence comes from animal research. For a far more complete discussion, see Andersen and Anderson (1) and Kooi (25).

Presence of an occipital alpha rhythm is, for most people, associated with a feeling of "relaxed awareness" when one is not actively imaging or processing visual information (24, 36). Some people, however, do not have a recordable alpha rhythm at all. Mulholland (45) has called attention to the fact that the absence of an alpha rhythm during the process of paying specific attention to aspects of the visual environment may be caused by the kinds of eye movements that we make at those times (and that we do not make during a state of "relaxed awareness"). Also, the alpha rhythm can be produced by extreme elevation of the eyeballs (13) and can be increased by behavior leading to cerebral vasoconstriction, such as hyperventilation (8).

Several writers, especially White (83), have noted that a general state of relaxed awareness with mind free of extraneous thoughts has been reported by many sensitives to be conducive to strong psi experiences. As a result several attempts have been made to relate aspects of the occipital alpha rhythm to ESP scoring success. Some of these have found no meaningful relationship (43, 79). Some have found a negative relationship between amount of alpha and ESP score, for unselected subjects (19, 73). Others have found a positive relationship (6, 18, 44, 20). Of these, the first three studied people preselected for ESP ability. The fourth used people preselected for their ability to show alpha and included several who were familiar with the experimenters. Lewis and Schmeidler (35), using unselected subjects, found a positive relationship when their subjects were unaware that they were performing an ESP task and a negative relationship when they were aware. Stanford (72, 74) found no relationship between ESP scoring success and amount of alpha but did find a positive relationship between ESP scoring success and an increase in the frequency (in cycles per second) of the alpha rhythm from just prior to the ESP test to the test itself. The other studies reported above have not looked at alpha frequency shifts. Stanford tentatively interprets this increase in alpha frequency as a "coping" effect in which the subject continues to be in a state of relaxed awareness but is at some level becoming mobilized for what he may view as a difficult ESP task ahead. Stanford suggests that his finding may therefore not be generalizable to ESP tasks in which the subjects are more comfortable and feel more confident (he used a precognition procedure, whereas most of the other studies cited involved a clairvoyance procedure).

White's (83) article, suggesting a positive relationship between ESP success and a relaxed, but aware, state free of extraneous mental imagery, was based on extensive reports by people doing free-response tests. They were not doing ESP tests that resembled those used in the studies reported above (where the target possibilities were limited). Two EEG studies involving free-response ESP tests have been done. Stanford and Stevenson (75) asked the subject (Stanford himself) to clear his mind and then to allow an image to form of the target—in this case, a line drawing. During mind-clearing, the alpha frequency was negatively related to ESP success. An increase in frequency from mind-clearing to image-formation was positively related to ESP success. Amount of alpha was not related to ESP success. Rao and Feola (59) used a subject who had been trained by alpha feedback techniques and had practiced meditation for 25 years. He was asked to produce either high or low alpha during periods of concentration upon target pictures from magazines. His success was higher during the times he was asked to produce high alpha than during the times of low alpha.

Each of these free-response studies produced results compatible with certain of the results of limited-choice studies. In each case, however, the subject may have had specific expectations about the internal state most conducive to psi, and this could have affected the outcome.

Two of the earlier-mentioned studies warrant further comment because of the methods they employed. Honorton, Davidson, and Bindler (20) employed the "convergent operation" technique (76); see also Chapter 27), in that description of internal state by the subject was combined with external psychophysiological measures in defining the optimal state for occurrence of psi. They found positive psi results associated with high amounts of alpha plus a strongly altered state but not with either alone. Some of the disparities in the psychophysiology and ESP results might well drop away if the psychophysiological measure were used more in conjunction with the internal report.

The Morris et al. (44) study is of interest because we used Lalsingh ("Sean") Harribance, who had previously scored very highly on the particular ESP task he tried in the EEG experiment. His results were once again outstanding, so that we were able to compare directly very high-scoring runs with completely chance runs and to obtain a fairly clear-cut result linking high alpha with strong ESP scores.

The EEG results, considered as a whole, are somewhat confusing. Differences in procedure, nature of the test, experimenter hypotheses, subject characteristics, and so on have undoubtedly contributed somewhat to the inconsistency. Since the EEG measures taken seem to reflect general aspects of internal state, they may simply serve as indicators of what kind of internal state is most conducive to the kind of ESP called for under the given circumstances. Perhaps a positive relationship between amount of alpha and ESP success is only to be expected in situations highly conducive to the production of both ESP (in terms of relaxed surroundings and subjects who have previously done well) and the sort of relaxed, but aware, state generally associated with alpha. Both Honorton's subjects (20) and Harribance had shown in advance that they could produce alpha in a psychophysiological laboratory. Such laboratories often are not the easiest places in which to relax. At any rate, it is of interest that so many studies have implicated the alpha rhythm as related to ESP. Further attention to the specific aspects of the alpha and other rhythms, including adequately done biofeedback research, should shed further light on the complexities of the relationship.

Other psychophysiological variables have not been extensively assessed. Otani (48) found that psi performance was higher when the galvanic skin-response measure indicated the person was relatively relaxed. Other preliminary findings have suggested that a general state of relaxation is conducive to psi. Braud and Braud (4) found this to be the case, employing a standard relaxation technique to facilitate psi.

One additional point of interest concerns the use of psychophysiological measures as the ESP response itself. Dean (9) has done the most extensive research along these lines, using peripheral vasoconstriction and vasodilation (in particular blood volume in the finger as measured by a plethysmograph) as an indicator of emotional response to "telepathic" messages. The procedure has produced a fair amount of success and deserves further attention. Its major theoretical interest is that it offers an opportunity to bypass higher processing centers and the noise they contribute, in that the subject need not be aware of the target to respond to it (see Chapter 5 for a further description of psi information processing below our level of awareness). Along somewhat similar lines, Duane and Behrendt (10) found some evidence that inducing alpha in one identical twin led to alpha in the other twin when they were located at some distance from each other. This was found for one pair of twins particularly, but not in others they tested.

OVERVIEW

Understanding the psychobiology of psi can be said to have two interlocking goals: (a) further understanding of the nature of thought and memory and the extent to which they are dependent upon the biological organism, and (b) learning how to control and amplify psi through applied understanding of the psychobiological processing of psi information within the organism itself.

It now appears that these goals can be pursued through research with animals as well as humans. Some evidence for psi has been found at several levels of central nervous system complexity, possibly including systems not yet beyond the embryonic stage. Psi as it has been manifested at these levels has shown characteristics similar in several respects to characteristics of human psi, suggesting that common underlying processing mechanisms may be involved. A crucial difference is that psi in animals has seemed more consistent than in humans. Whether this is an artifact of differences in testing procedures or is caused by a difference in processing (e.g., less interference by cognitive elaboration and distortion from higher centers of the brain) remains to be seen.

There is also evidence that in humans certain internal states (such as relaxation) having specifiable physiological concomitants may be more favorable to psi. At present the most promising line of research deals with brain-wave correlates of internal state such as the alpha rhythm. These findings, together with the suggestion that psi can be elicited through autonomic nervous system responses, suggest that the optimal processing of psi information does not involve extensive higher cognitive processing and that such filtering or restricting of information as need be done can be accomplished at lower levels.

Both general lines of research are very much in their developmental stages and need a great deal of refinement, even at the level of basic methodology, before we can do the systematic research that will lead to the solid information we so badly need. We do have our beginnings, however, and they should be sufficient to intrigue and challenge the ingenuity of the psychobiologist as never before.

REFERENCES

1. Andersen, P., and Anderson, S. A. *Physiological Basis of the Alpha Rhythm.* Appleton: New York, 1968.
2. Bechterev, W. " 'Direct Influence' of a Person Upon the Behavior of Animals." *Journal of Parapsychology,* 13 (1949).
3. Bestall, C. M. "An Experiment in Precognition in the Laboratory Mouse." *Journal of Parapsychology,* 26 (1962) (abstract).
4. Braud, W. G., and Braud, L. W. "Preliminary Explorations of Psi-Conducive States: Progressive Muscular Relaxation." *Journal of the American Society for Psychical Research,* 67 (1973).
5. Byrne, W. *Molecular Approaches to Learning and Memory.* Academic: New York, 1970.
6. Cadoret, R. J. "An Exploratory Experiment: Continuous EEG Recording During Clairvoyant Card Tests." *Journal of Parapsychology,* 28 (1964) (abstract).
7. Craig, J. G. "The Effect of Contingency on Precognition in the Rat." In W. G. Roll et al., eds., *Research in Parapsychology 1972.* Scarecrow: Metuchen, N.J., 1973.
8. Darrow, C. W., and Pathman, J. H. "The Role of Blood Pressure in Electroencephalographic Changes During Hyperventilation." *Federation Proceedings,* 2 (1943): (abstract).
9. Dean, E. D. "The Plethysmograph as an Indicator of ESP." *Journal of the Society for Psychical Research,* 41 (1962).
10. Duane, T., and Behrendt, T. "Extrasensory Electroencephalographic Induction Between Identical Twins." *Science,* 9 September 1965.
11. Duval, P., and Montredon, E. "ESP Experiments with Mice." *Journal of Parapsychology,* 32 (1968).
12. Extra, J. "GESP in the Rat." *Journal of Parapsychology,* 36 (1972).
13. Fenwick, P., and Walker, S. "The Effect of Eye Position on the Alpha Rhythm." In C. R. Evans and T. B. Mulholland, eds., *Attention in Neurophysiology.* Appleton: New York, 1969.
14. Gaito, J., ed. *Macromolecules and Behavior,* 2nd ed. Appleton: New York, 1972.
15. Grossman, S. "Some Psychological Considerations." In G. Ungar, ed., *Molecular Mechanisms in Memory and Learning.* Plenum: New York, 1970.
16. Hardy, A. "Biology and ESP." In J. Smythies, ed., *Science and ESP.* Humanities: New York, 1967.
17. Hebb, D. O. *The Organization of Behavior.* Wiley: New York, 1949.
18. Honorton, C. "Relationship Between EEG Alpha Activity and ESP Card-

Guessing Performance." *Journal of the American Society for Psychical Research*, 63 (1969).

19. Honorton, C., and Carbone, M. "A Preliminary Study of Feedback-Augmented EEG Alpha Activity and ESP Card-Guessing Performance." *Journal of the American Society for Psychical Research*, 65 (1971).

20. Honorton, C.; Davidson, R.; and Bindler, P. "Feedback-Augmented EEG Alpha, Shifts in Subjective State, and ESP Card-Guessing Performance." *Journal of the American Society for Psychical Research*, 65 (1971).

21. Honorton, C.; Ramsey, M.; and Cabibbo, C. "Experimenter Effects in ESP Research." In W. G. Roll et al., eds., *Research in Parapsychology 1972*. Scarecrow: Metuchen, N.J. 1973 (abstract).

22. Hubel, D. H., and Wiesel, F. N. "Receptive Fields and Functional Architecture of Monkey Striate Cortex." *Journal of Physiology*, 195 (1968).

23. John, E. R. *Mechanisms of Memory*. Academic: New York, 1967.

24. Kamiya. J. "Operant Control of the EEG Alpha Rhythm and Some of Its Reported Effects on Consciousness." In C. Tart, ed., *Altered States of Consciousness*. Wiley: New York, 1969; repr. Anchor: New York, 1972.

25. Kooi, K. *Fundamentals of Electroencephalography*. Harper and Row: New York, 1971.

26. Lashley, K. S. "In Search of the Engram." *Symposium of the Society of Experimental Biology*, 4 (1931).

27. Lettvin, J. Y.; Maturana H. R.; McCulloch, W. S.; and Pitts, W. H. "What the Frog's Eye Tells the Frog's Brain." *Proceedings of the IRE*, 47 (1959).

28. Levy, W. J. "Possible PK by Chicken Embryos to Obtain Warmth." *Proceedings of the Parapsychological Association*, 8 (1971) (abstract).

29. Levy, W. J. "The Effect of the Test Situation on Precognition in Mice and Birds: A Confirmation Study." *Journal of Parapsychology*, 36 (1792).

30. Levy, W. J. Personal communication, 1973.

31. Levy, W. J.; Artley, B.; Williams, C.; and Owens, B. "Effects of Factors Interpretable as High and Low Stress States on Precognition in Small Rodents." In W. G. Roll, ed., *Research in Parapsychology 1972*. Scarecrow: Metuchen, N.J.. 1973 (abstract).

32. Levy, W. J.; Davis, J. W.; and Mayo, L. A. "An Improved Method in a Precognition Test with Birds." *Journal of Parapsychology*, 37 (1973).

33. Levy, W. J., and McRae, A. "Precognition in Mice and Birds." *Journal of Parapsychology*, 35 (1971).

34. Levy, W. J.; Terry, J. C.; and Davis, J. W. "A Precognition Text with Hamsters." *Journal of Parapsychology*, 37 (1973).

35. Lewis, L., and Schmeidler, G. R. "Alpha Relations with Non-Intentional and Purposeful ESP after Feedback." *Journal of the American Society for Psychical Research*, 65 (1971).

36. Lindsley, D. B. "Attention, Consciousness, Sleep and Wakefulness." In J. Field, H. W. Magoun and V. E. Hall, eds., *Handbook of Physiology, Section II: Neurophysiology III*. American Physiological Society: Washington, D.C., 1960.

37. McConnell, J. V. "Cannibalism and Memory in Flatworms." *New Scientist*, 21 (1964).

38. Mackenzie, W. "Rolf of Mannheim: A Great Psychological Problem" (with notes by J. H. Hyslop). *Proceedings of the American Society for Psychical Research*, 13 (1919).

39. Maeterlinck, M. *The Life of the White Ant*, A. Sutro, trans. Allen and Unwin: London, 1928.

40. Matthews, G. V. T. *Bird Navigation*. Cambridge University Press: Cambridge, 1968.
41. Metta, L., "Psychokinesis on Lepidopterous Larvae." *Journal of Parapsychology*, 36 (1972).
42. Morris, R. L. "Psi and Animal Behavior: A Survey." *Journal of the American Society for Psychical Research*, 64 (1970).
43. Morris, R. L., and Cohen, D., "A Preliminary Experiment on the Relationship Among ESP, Alpha Rhythm and Calling Patterns." *Proceedings of the Parapsychological Association*, 6 (1969).
44. Morris, R. L.; Roll, W. G.; Klein, J.; and Wheeler, G. "EEG Patterns and ESP Results in Forced-Choice Experiments with Lalsingh Harribance." *Journal of the American Society for Psychical Research*, 66 (1972).
45. Mulholland, T. B., and Peper, E. "Occipital Alpha and Accommodative Vergence, Pursuit Tracking, and Fast Eye Movements." *Psychophysiology*, 8 (1971).
46. Osis, K. "A Test of the Occurrence of a Psi Effect Between Man and the Cat." *Journal of Parapsychology*, 16 (1952).
47. Osis, K., and Foster, E. B. "A Test of ESP in Cats." *Journal of Parapsychology*, 17 (1953).
48. Otani, S. "Relations of Mental Set and Change of Skin Resistance to ESP Score." *Journal of Parapsychology*, 19 (1955).
49. Penfield, W., and Jasper, H. *Epilepsy and the Functional Anatomy of the Brain*. Little, Brown: Boston, 1954.
50. Pfungst, O. *Clever Hans*. C. L. Rahn, trans. Holt, Rinehart: New York, 1911.
51. Pratt, J. G. *Parapsychology: An Insider's View of ESP*. Doubleday: New York, 1964.
52. Pribram, K. H. "The Neurophysiology of Remembering." *Scientific American*, January 1969.
53. Pribram, K. H. "Some Dimensions of Remembering: Steps Toward a Neuropsychological Model of Memory." In J. Gaito, ed., *Macromolecules and Behavior*. Appleton: New York, 1972.
54. Pribram, K. H., and Broadbent, D., eds. *Biology of Memory*. Academic: New York, 1970.
55. Randall, J. L. "An Attempt to Detect Psi Effects with Protozoa." *Journal of the Society for Psychical Research*, 45 (1970).
56. Randall, J. L. "Experiments to Detect a Psi Effect with Small Animals." *Journal of the Society for Psychical Research*, 46 (1971).
57. Randall, J. E. "Two Psi Experiments with Gerbils." *Journal of the Society for Psychical Research*, 46 (1972).
58. Randall, J. L. "Recent Experiments in Animal Parapsychology." *Journal of the Society for Psychical Research*, 46 (1972).
59. Rao, K. R., and Feola, J. "Alpha Rhythm and ESP in a Free Response Situation." In W. G. Roll et al., eds., *Research in Parapsychology 1972*. Scarecrow: Metuchen, N.J., 1973 (abstract).
60. Rapaport, D. *Emotions and Memory*. Science: New York, 1961.
61. Reik, T. *Listening with the Third Ear*. Farrar, Straus: New York, 1949.
62. Rhine, J. B. "The Present Outlook on the Question of Psi in Animals." *Journal of Parapsychology*, 15 (1951).
63. Rhine, J. B. *New World of the Mind*. Sloane: New York, 1953.
64. Rhine, J. B. "Location of Hidden Objects by a Man-Dog Team." *Journal of Parapsychology*, 35 (1971).

65. Rhine, J. B., and Feather, S. R. "The Study of Cases of 'Psi-Trailing' in Animals." *Journal of Parapsychology*, 26 (1962).
66. Richmond, N. "Two Series of PK Tests on Paramecia." *Journal of the Society for Psychical Research*, 36 (1952).
67. Rosenblatt, F. "Induction of Behavior by Mammalian Brain Extracts." In G. Ungar, ed., *Molecular Mechanisms in Memory and Learning*. Plenum: New York, 1970.
68. Rosenzweig, M. R.; Møllgaard, K.; Diamond, M. C.; and Bennett, E. L. "Negative as Well as Positive Synaptic Changes May Store Memory." *Psychological Review*, 79 (1972).
69. Schmidt, H. "PK Experiments with Animals as Subjects." *Journal of Parapsychology*, 34 (1970).
70. Schouten, S. "Psi in Mice: Positive Reinforcement." *Journal of Parapsychology*, 36 (1972).
71. Sperry, R. W. "Hemisphere Disconnection and Unity in Conscious Awareness." *American Psychologist*, 23 (1968).
72. Stanford, R. G. "EEG Alpha Activity and ESP Performance: A Replicative Study." *Journal of the American Society for Psychical Research*, 65 (1971).
73. Stanford, R. G., and Lovin, C. "EEG Alpha Activity and ESP Performance." *Journal of the American Society for Psychical Research*, 64 (1970).
74. Stanford, R. G., and Stanford, B. E. "Shifts in EEG Alpha Rhythm as Related to Calling Patterns and ESP Run-Score Variance." *Journal of Parapsychology*, 33 (1969).
75. Stanford, R. G., and Stevenson, I. "EEG Correlates of Free-Response GESP in an Individual Subject." *Journal of the American Society for Psychical Research*, 66 (1973).
76. Stoyva, J., and Kamiya, J. "Electrophysiological Studies of Dreaming as the Prototype of a New Strategy in the Study of Consciousness." *Psychological Review*, 75 (1968).
77. Ungar, G., ed. *Molecular Mechanisms in Memory and Learning*. Plenum: New York, 1970.
78. Verzeano, M.; Laufer, M.; Spear, P.; and McDonald, S. "The Activity of Neuronal Networks in the Thalamus of the Monkey." In K. H. Pribram and D. Broadbent, eds., *Biology of Memory*. Academic: New York, 1970.
79. Wallwork, S. C. "ESP Experiments with Simultaneous Electroencephalographic Recordings." *Journal of the Society for Psychical Research*, 36 (1952).
80. Watkins, G. K. "Possible PK in the Lizard *Anolis sagrei*." *Proceedings of the Parapsychological Association*, 8 (1971): (abstract).
81. Watkins, G. K., and Watkins, A. M. "Possible PK Influence on the Resuscitation of Anesthetized Mice." *Journal of Parapsychology*, 35 (1971).
82. Wells, R., and Klein, J. "A Replication of a 'Psychic Healing' Paradigm." *Journal of Parapsychology*, 36 (1972).
83. White, R. A. "A Comparison of Old and New Methods of Response to Targets in ESP Experiments." *Journal of the American Society for Psychical Research*, 58 (1964).
84. White, R. A. "The Investigation of Behavior Suggestive of ESP in Dogs." *Journal of the American Society for Psychical Research*, 58 (1964).
85. Wood, G. H., and Cadoret, R. J. "Tests of Clairvoyance in a Man-Dog Relationship." *Journal of Parapsychology*, 22 (1958).

Montague Ullman

MONTAGUE ULLMAN, M.D., *is director of the Division of Parapsychology and Psychophysics at Maimonides Medical Center in Brooklyn, New York. He is also president of the Gardner Murphy Research Institute in Chapel Hill, North Carolina, and professor of psychiatry at the State University of New York, Downstate Medical Center. Dr. Ullman is a graduate of New York University College of Medicine and of the psychoanalytic program at the New York Medical College.*

Prior to his present position, Dr. Ullman was in psychoanalytic practice and engaged in psychosomatic research in the Department of Psychiatry at New York University College of Medicine and at the Cornell Division of the Bellevue Medical Center. In 1962 he initiated the Dream Laboratory at the Maimonides Medical Center, where pioneering work has been carried out on the experimental study of telepathic dreams in conjunction with his colleagues, Dr. Stanley Krippner and Mr. Charles Honorton. The laboratory was the recipient in 1972 of a grant from the National Institute of Mental Health to carry on this research.

Dr. Ullman is a fellow of the American Association for the Advancement of Science, past president (1961) of the Parapsychological Association, and, since 1971, president of the American Society for Psychical Research. His current writing deals with the experimental studies on telepathy and dreams. He has edited (with R. Cavanna) the Proceedings of the International Conference on Hypnosis, Drugs, Dreams and Psi (*Garrett Press, 1968*), *in which his paper "Dreams and Psi: The Experimental Dimension" appeared. Earlier books include* Behavioral Changes in Patients Following Strokes (*Chas. Thomas, 1962*) *and with G. Stokes et al.,* The Giant Step (*Faculty Press, 1969*). *His most recent is* Dream Telepathy (*Macmillan, 1973*) *co-authored with Stanley Krippner and Alan Vaughan.*

Dr. Ullman can be reached at Maimonides Medical Center, Division of Parapsychology and Psychophysics, 4802 Tenth Avenue, Brooklyn, N.Y. 11219.

10 Psi and Psychiatry

MONTAGUE ULLMAN

SUMMARY

This chapter traces the close connection that has always existed between medical psychology and psychic research. Beginning with the interest of some of the pioneers of both the SPR and the ASPR in the exciting discoveries of the unconscious dimensions of human personality and the possible relevance of the study of abnormal mental states to their pursuits, the theme of this interconnection was examined by the founders of the psychoanalytic movement and their followers down to the contemporary scene. The contributions from the clinical setting have provided a rich store of information concerning the emotional atmosphere in which psi occurs, the personality dynamics at play, the relative roles of patient and therapist, and the clinical criteria for the recognition of the telepathic dream. An example of one such dream is included.

EARLY HISTORY

Psychiatry is the branch of medicine that deals with disturbances in thought, feeling, and behavior. Such disturbances may be mild and reversible or severe and irreversible. They may be functional or organic, depending on whether there are identifiable changes in brain structure or physiology. Psychiatry as such may be viewed as an applied science coming under the broader heading of the behavioral sciences. The latter designation is multidisciplinary and includes both theoretical and applied sciences having to do with behavior; it addresses itself to the full range of human behavior, both normal and pathological. Several common threads bind the behavioral scientists of today with their precursors of the last century. These include an interest in the unconscious determinants of behavior, the range of human potential, and the roots of eccentric, deviant or unusual behavior.

All of these interests are prominently revealed in the writings of the early group of scholars and scientists who struggled to initiate and develop psychic research on a scientific basis. Thus, major themes filling the

247

publications of the SPR and the ASPR during their formative years were the problems of subliminal consciousness, the nature of suggestion and hypnosis, the nature of trance states, possession, and multiple personality. All of these concerns are very much with us today, in more modern dress, in the attention we pay to the unconscious dimension of human personality and in our various investigations into the broad range of phenomena associated with altered states of consciousness (reverie, trance, hypnosis, dreams, hypnogogic states, psychotic states, etc.). Then, as now, psychic researchers were intrigued with the possible relevance of these states to psychic or paranormal phenomena.

A number of distinguished psychologists and medical men specializing in "nervous disorders" were associated with the early work of the SPR. Their efforts were both exploratory and reactive—exploratory in terms of their dogged efforts to study, evaluate, and record instances of paranormal phenomena and reactive in the sense of taking issue with what they felt were the limiting aspects of the materialism and determinism that characterized the science of their day and the outlook of scientists generally. They were perhaps the humanistic psychologists of their time, open to all that could shed new light on human nature and its potential. Holding that the danger of mechanistically boxing man in was far greater than the almost inevitable social stigma and the frustration of false leads that one encounters in tracking down the paranormal, they nevertheless chose the latter course. They set themselves the task of examining occult claims, including the evidence for survival, designing experiments in thought transference and clairvoyance and exploring the emerging field of hypnosis for its possible relevance to the phenomena they were studying. They took a second look at various psychopathological syndromes with the same end in mind. Hysteria (45, 46) was studied not only in relation to unconscious mental functioning but also for the light it could shed on such well-known effects as the sensory and motor automatisms that often occurred in trance states. Cases of multiple personality (45, 47) were assiduously observed for their bearing on a theory of consciousness and the role of the subliminal or subconscious. Cases of paranoia and obsession (53) were studied from the standpoint of possible spirit possession and the question of the continued existence of discarnate entities.

The contributions of two men in particular stand out. F. W. H. Myers and William James both played critical roles during this early phase. Myers's lifework is embodied in an encyclopedic two-volume study (47). Over 20 years in the making, this work covers what we would now classify as almost the entire spectrum of altered states of consciousness in relation to normal, pathological, and paranormal manifestations. Myers skillfully and persuasively engaged in theory-building leading toward the elaboration of his concept of the subliminal self and his conviction concerning the survival of this self following death. Slowly and methodically he derived supporting evidence for this from the realm of sleep and dreams, insanity, hysteria,* genius, hypnotism, automatism, and the evidence for thought transference and clairvoyance. It was Myers who coined the term *telepathy*. His mapping of this psychic underworld led him to what James (35) referred to as an "evolutive" concept of the unconscious realm. The subliminal self, according to Myers, served a higher, regenerative, inspirational function in contrast to the prevailing "dissolutive" point of view of neurologists that these unconscious manifestations were regressive and degenerative in nature.

Myers concluded that the various states alluded to above could be best linked together and explained in terms of a subliminal self that constituted an unconscious, but organized, agency, one that was active at all times but that only under special circumstances could break through into consciousness. Hypnotic phenomena, for example, occurred as a consequence of a successful appeal to the subliminal self through suggestion. More esoteric phenomena such as phantasms of the living and dead, bilocation, or traveling clairvoyance suggested that the subliminal self could establish independent relations with space as well as with other minds. Mediumistic trances, hypnosis, and reverie were all states favorable for the breakthrough of sensory (hallucinatory experiences) and motor automatisms (automatic writing, etc.). Viewed from the waking state these various properties of the subliminal self appeared discontinuous. Myers sought to establish them in their unity and continuity, suggesting that each merged imperceptibly into the next. Thus, hyperesthesia or increased sensory acuity merged into telepathy. This in turn merged into phantasmogenetic telepathy in which the phantasm of a living person might appear to a percipient and, finally, the phantasmogenetic space invasion by a dead person, or—in more common parlance—a ghost.

William James maintained a strong and even passionate interest in psychic research in the last 30 years of his life and was active in both the SPR and ASPR, lending his prestige to both organizations. His open empirical approach to the psychological realities of man did not stop short in the face of those difficult or seemingly impossible to explain. He discovered the well-known medium Mrs. Piper and engaged in many sittings with her.* A keen admirer of Myers, he took issue with his particular formulation of survival, preferring his own transmission theory (36), namely, that individual consciousness flowed from, and back to, a universal stream.

---

* His view of hysteria as a "disease of the hypnotic spectrum" was remarkably similar, although independently derived, to the view of Breuer and Freud.

* Mrs. Piper was for James his one white crow. He set himself the task of doing what he could to make room in the universe for this anomaly.

Another leading figure who engaged with the challenge of psychical research from a psychological point of view was the neurologist and medical psychologist T. Weir Mitchell. In his writings on multiple personality (43, 44) and hysteria (45), he conjectured on the possible relevance of psychic research to these syndromes. Early investigators, including Mitchell, were intrigued by the possibility that supernormal powers (44) might occasionally be manifest in the more dramatic instances of dissociated states, particularly under circumstances where seemingly distinct and separate personalities seemed to emerge (41, 45).

Mitchell, like James, acknowledged the importance of psychic research, James in relation to psychology in general and Mitchell in relation to psychopathology. Streams of thought had been coming together in the work of a number of various investigators (30, 31, 35, 41, 45, 47, 52, 53) linking dissociated states and hysteria to the diverse and supernormal properties of what was variously called the subconscious (65, 66), the subliminal (47), and the coconscious (52), as well as to speculative theories concerning the human soul (35, 41, 47). With the establishment of Freudian psychoanalysis, this richly speculative period seemed to go out of fashion (as indeed did the syndrome itself of multiple personality). The streams that had been coming together now separated, psychic research going in one direction and psychoanalytic psychiatry in another. This was the general trend, although there were people in both camps, Freud included, who tried to bridge the gap and people who, like Mitchell, felt it could be bridged. With the advent of psychoanalysis, however, a narrower instinctual and biological view replaced the more broadly philosophical and more richly speculative and imaginative view of the hidden dimensions of personality that so characterized the thinking of the early pioneers in psychic research. Interestingly enough, it is precisely this more expansive view of human potential that is coming back into focus in reaction to the mechanistic framework of much of modern psychiatry. And, as was the case a century ago, the link to the paranormal is also becoming more apparent.

Edmund Gurney, a scholar with a medical background, made many notable contributions to the early history of hypnosis and to the careful recording of cases of phantasms of the living. He elucidated the various stages of hypnosis and the range of memory under hypnosis and felt that hypnotic phenomena suggested the persistence of an hypnotic self as an agency in its own right, a remembering and reasoning entity persisting into the waking state (30, 31).

The idea of an agency with special powers derived further support from the French investigators studying hypnosis at a distance. Gibert, a French physician working with a middle-aged peasant woman, was able, among other things, to induce hypnotic trance by mental commands when he himself was situated at a considerable distance from the subject—for example, in another part of the town. The distinguished psychiatrist Pierre Janet and the Nobel laureate physiologist Charles Richet both witnessed and reported these experiments (37, 54). Richet conducted experiments on his own suggesting that the woman had telepathic abilities while in a hypnotic trance.

FREUD AND JUNG

Sigmund Freud devoted several papers (26–29) to a consideration of the occult and, more specifically, to the questions of the relationship of psychoanalysis to telepathy and of dreams to telepathy. In his public statements there is no question that he seriously entertained the telepathy hypothesis, although he consistently stopped short of any indication that he himself had any firm conviction about the matter. Despite this equivocation, he offered practical and theoretical suggestions from a psychoanalytic perspective as to how to make the prognostications of fortune-tellers and others claiming occult powers dynamically understandable. He suggested that information is picked up via thought transference from the unconscious of the person seeking the reading and the logical inferences are then fed back as seemingly accurate prognostications.

For the most part the material Freud worked with was secondhand. He did, however, come to certain conclusions on the basis of the facts called to his attention. One was that someday claims concerning thought transference might have to be taken seriously. Another was that telepathic information reaching the unconscious is subject to the same laws of transformation as other material rising into consciousness. He accordingly emphasized that telepathy, were it to be established, would have no bearing on the theory of dream formation. Whereas his discovery of the dynamic transformation of unconsciously perceived telepathy content was in fact an important step forward, his point about dream theory seems gratuitous and unwarranted in the face of how ignorant we still are concerning the nature of the relationship between the paranormal and the various states of consciousness.

The most complete account of Freud's encounter with the occult appears in Ernest Jones's biography (38). Here the disparity between Freud's public position of interested, but neutral, openness and his private statements concerning his growing conviction that thought transference may represent the pure and important distillate from the morass of the occult comes most sharply into focus. Jones exerted a powerful negative influence on Freud with regard to occult matters, stressing the harmful impact that any dabbling in this field by the founder of psychoanalysis would have on the then controversial public image that newborn specialty was itself experiencing at that point in its history. A countervailing pull came from another disciple, Ferenczi, who matched Jones's closed-mindedness with an opposite measure of belief. Jones's caveats were the stronger, and Freud's most explicit public statement (29) did not appear until after his death in 1939.

On the private side, Freud maintained membership in both the British and American societies (38), published an article in the *Proceedings* of the British society (25) and engaged in a lively correspondence with some of the leading psychic researchers of the day. In a letter to Hereward Carrington, Freud acknowledges that if he had his life to live over, he would devote it to psychic research (38). Although Freud later denied the contents of this letter, Jones himself, on the basis of an exact copy provided by Fodor, came to the conclusion that it was true.

Perhaps the most dramatic confrontations around occult issues occurred between Freud and Jung. The background of Jung's interest in the occult and in the emerging discipline of parapsychology is given in Jung's autobiographical volume (39). The development and exposition of the theoretical system he evolved to account for the range of inexplicable phenomena noted by psychic researchers appears in a book written in collaboration with the physicist Wolfgang Pauli (40).

Jung's interest early in his own life may have stemmed from the stories his mother told of her encounters with "ghostly phenomena" and "presentiments." At any rate, he had his own share of clairvoyant and precognitive dreams and on rare occasions witnessed what he felt to be genuine PK effects. He devoted his doctoral thesis to work based on experiments he had conducted with a 15-year-old cousin whom he considered a medium. He himself participated in mediumistic experiments conducted by the then-prominent German psychiatrist and psychic researcher Albert von Schrenck-Notzing (58). These séances involved one of the most famous mediums of the time, Rudi Schneider, and the results were impressive to Jung. Eugen Bleuler, the distinguished Swiss psychiatrist, also attended these sittings.

Jung became more and more convinced that paranormal phenomena could not be accounted for within the accepted scientific doctrine of causality. One had to look elsewhere for an explanatory system. He postulated the theory of acausal meaningful coincidences or synchronicity (40), whereby events that appear to be intrinsically meaningful and that cannot be accounted for on the basis of any chain of causal events are nevertheless linked together on the basis of meaning and come into being as a consequence of the realization, or "constellation," of an archetypal upsurge precipitated by the context in which the coincidental events occur. Jung thus postulates a coming together in a meaningful way of an event in the outside world synchronously with a subjective state and where the meaning can be understood in relation to the specific archetype energized at that moment in time.

Jung regarded the work of Rhine and his co-workers as establishing the existence of this acausal order, an order that could not be accounted for in terms of space, time, causality, or energy relations. He felt that the further elaboration and experimental verification of this principle of acausal synchronicity would require a fresh look at both Eastern philosophy and the mantric and divinatory practices that characterized ancient Chinese and other oriental cultures. This led Jung into active explorations of astrology and observations using the *I Ching*, seeking further corroboration of the dovetailing of outer and inner events that were psychologically meaningful to the individual involved. Jung's investment in the occult was too much for Freud and was one of the issues leading to the break between them.

EARLY PSYCHOANALYTIC INTEREST

Some interest in the subject of telepathy was manifest among the early disciples of Freud and the early practitioners of psychoanalysis. Stekel's report (67) in support of the telepathy hypothesis appeared two years before Freud's first published account. As might be expected, the controversial nature of the subject exerted a polarizing influence on those enthusiasts of the psychoanalytic method who themselves were engaged in a struggle to establish a scientific beachhead of their own. As already noted, the strongest negative voice was that of Ernest Jones, who strongly cautioned Freud against the danger to psychoanalysis that would be posed should the founder himself publicly and favorably acknowledge his interest in the subject. That this influence was effective is apparent in the discrepancies that exist between Freud's public utterances and his more private admissions as noted in recorded comments and in his correspondence.

The psychoanalytic and psychiatric writings on the subject served to clarify the interpersonal context in which telepathic events were reported in the clinical setting, either in the form of exchanges between therapist and patient during the analytic hour or in the form of a telepathic dream reported by the patient. It failed, as even its most avid proponents knew it would, to bring about any substantial increase in scientific respectability and, more important, responsibility toward the field of psychic research. Attacks from within the psychiatric arena were based on the ease with which alternative dynamic explanations based on the wish-fulfilling propensities of the unconscious could account for much of the evidence offered in support of the telepathy hypothesis. Critics from the outside took very little heed of the clinical data, lacking as it did any quantitative dimensions as well as any controlled or experimental base.

Despite the generally negative atmosphere that prevailed toward this subject during the first half of this century (an atmosphere that in any final reckoning would be hard to account for in the face of the evidence, clinical and experimental, that had accumulated by that time), a number of noteworthy contributions were made. Many of these early contributions have been compiled in a work by Devereux (4).

Although Freud foresaw much that was later written about telepathy and psychoanalysis—that is, the distortion that unconsciously perceived telepathic content was subjected to, and the significance of countertransferential factors*—it remained the task of later analysts to explicate more fully these relationships based directly on their own clinical case material. Hollós (34) noted a number of characteristics of the telepathic dream, emphasizing the importance of libidinal and affective aspects of the message, the role of repression (the connection of the message with a wish in the process of being repressed), and the vulnerability of the analyst as the source of the message as a consequence of the operation of countertransference. Hann-Kende (32) and Servadio (62) linked the occurrence of telepathic events to transferential factors, positive transference favoring the occurrence. Ehrenwald (6) arrived at a more specific formulation based both on investigations he carried out with a gifted subject and on clinical observations. He referred to telepathy as a minus function, one that developed in a compensatory way to offset a preexisting lack or handicap. He also reexamined the psychopathology of the psychoses in the light of the telepathy hypothesis and suggested that in schizophrenia, the individual is deluged by, and fails to cope with, heteropsychic (telepathically perceived external content) as contrasted to autopsychic content (derived from within). Burlingham's observations (1) led her to speculate concerning the possible role of telepathy in the early mother–child situation.

It is of interest to see how writers, often dealing with very similar material, come to different conclusions when what is at issue is the serious consideration of the telepathy hypothesis. Some, like Hitschmann (33), Zulliger (77), and Schilder (56), prefer an explanation based on a rather extended view of coincidence acting in combination with unconscious dynamisms. Some, like Deutsch (3) and Saul (56), stress the existence of a heightened sensitivity of normal powers occurring under certain circumstances—that is, intuitive empathy in the case of the former and heightened sensitivity in the case of the latter. Hann-Kende (32), Deutsch (3), and

* Attitudes and feelings in the analyst inappropriately directed toward the patient but having their origin in the analyst's own past. Analogously, transference is the reverse of this.

Hollós (34) each stress the emergence of these special sensitivities under conditions where the therapist, because of his own preoccupations, turns away from the patient. This decathexis or withdrawal of attention (and libido) from the plight of the patient creates a condition of stress for the patient and provides a favorable setting for a telepathic event to occur. This is interpreted by Hann-Kende as a maneuver within the framework of a positive transference aimed at regaining the analyst's attention. Róheim (55) linked the telepathic event to the same unconscious voyeuristic needs initially related to the primal scene.

There was agreement among a number of these writers that psychoanalytic theory could be used to expose and reveal a telepathic event. By the same token psychoanalytic theory could unmask a case of presumptive telepathy, establishing it instead as a case of pseudotelepathy.

THE CURRENT SCENE

Two articles by Eisenbud (13, 14) resulted in a resurgence of interest in the subject of telepathy and dreams. He has perhaps been bolder than most others in ferreting out and working through possible telepathic linkages not only between his patients and himself but also among his patients. Agreeing with earlier writers (34, 62) concerning the connection of telepathy to repression, he emphasized that this was true for both patient and analyst. He stressed the ubiquitousness of telepathy and that if properly recognized and dealt with it could augment, extend and validate psychoanalytic theory. Eisenbud made active and explicit use of the telepathy hypothesis in his work with patients. His book (18) provides many fascinating accounts of telepathic interplay between his patients, including the occasional occurrence of a *rêve à deux*, as well as telepathic events and dreams touching on intimate and highly charged aspects of his own life.

In 1948 a medical section of the ASPR was established to further interest and study of psi in the psychotherapeutic setting. Prominent among the founders and participants were Eisenbud, Ehrenwald, Meerloo, Booth, Pedersen-Krag, Laidlaw, and Ullman. During the eight years of its existence, it served the useful purpose of allowing a small, but enthusiastic, group of psychiatrists to share and evaluate the telepathic incidents that came to their attention, to discuss dynamics from a variety of points of view and to work out criteria for the recognition and identification of a dream or other report as telepathic (9, 72). Much of the material presented at these meetings later appeared in the literature, and many of the participants maintained an active interest long after the section itself was disbanded.

Pedersen-Krag (49), influenced by Eisenbud, noted presumptively telepathic events in a number of her patients. This kind of receptivity and openness to the phenomenon seems to be a factor in its occurrence, much as more favorable attitudes among percipients in experimental studies yield more positive results.

Fodor (21) noted the occurrence of shared dreams between several of his patients as well as between his patients and himself. He regarded telepathy as a cognitive faculty of the unconscious. Love prepared the unconscious for telepathic communication.

The strongest critical voice to be raised in response to the clinical evidence offered in support of telepathy was that of Ellis (20). He felt that the factor of coincidence was underplayed in a kind of unconsciously motivated self-serving search for correspondences. In this way a forced fit was established between the events reported by the patient and the so-called telepathically perceived events in the life of the therapist. Although somewhat polemical exchanges ensued in the wake of Ellis's critique (4), an exchange critical of both his knowledge of the literature of parapsychology and psychoanalytic theory, the fact remains that the evidence from clinical sources simply was not compelling enough to turn a skeptic into a supporter.

Early clinical observations and speculations developed along two lines. In the one instance, emphasis remained on the intactness and integrity of the psychoanalytic method with psi effects noted as occasional, but meaningful, eruptions from an archaic residue from our phylogenetic heritage. Freud set the tone for this point of view, and it was basically the one adhered to by a number of writers down to the present day, with each in his own way contributing either new observations or important points of emphasis. Thus, Stekel (67) underscored the importance of a charged significant relationship between patient and therapist as a condition for the appearance of telepathy. In addition to Freud (28), Ehrenwald (9), Fodor (22, 23), Perrbolte (50, 51), Meerloo (42), and Servadio (64) all regarded these effects as linked to an archaic communicative system gradually submerged in the course of man's evolution because of its dysfunctional adaptive features. In a monograph devoted to the theme of telepathy as an archaic mode of communication, Meerloo (42) accounts for sudden mass reactions and panics and for the occasional eruption of telepathic happenings in the clinical situation on the basis of the reemergence of this information-gathering and communication system when other forms of communication are "congested or frustrated," Fodor (23) and Peerbolte (50) described psi as an archaic mode originating in the symbiotic relationship of the mother and child at the prenatal stage of development. Ehrenwald (12), more in keeping with observable facts, suggested that the early parent–child symbiosis formed the nexus for future paranormal abilities. Schwarz (61), eschewing theoretical controversy, documented a great many instances of telepathic interplay involving him, his wife, and their children throughout the entire course of their childhood. His book contains a total of 505 such pointed vignettes, in which the effects sometimes extended to patients and others as well. As therapists took a closer look at psi in the clinical setting and as their initial hesitations, defensiveness, and inhibitions were ignored, were rationalized, or simply faded away, the implications of the telepathy hypothesis inevitably extended the range of operations beyond that of the dyadic patient–therapist relationship. Fodor (21) spoke of "telepathy à trois" and also cited telepathic exchanges between pairs of patients. Eisenbud (18) also wrote about telepathic networks involving a number of his patients and himself. Coleman (2) called attention to the telepathic sensing by patients of the intrusion of a third force in the person of the supervising analyst. She referred to this as the paranormal triangle and, along with Eisenbud and Peerbolte, emphasized its origin in the oedipal conflict.

The existence of an altered state of consciousness on the part of one or both participants in a telepathic occurrence has been noted by Ehrenwald (5) (he uses the term *minus function* to refer to a deficit state of any kind, including sleep and dreams as well as the passive quiescent state structured by the analytic situation itself), Schwartz (61) (the occurrence of "mental diplopia" or minor dissociated states—momentary reverie or distraction), Servadio (62) (state of impaired awareness), and Ullman and Krippner (75) (the facilitating influence of dreaming).

Specific characterological features seen in patients who appear to be star telepathic performers (withdrawn, borderline, schizoid, narcissistic character structures) were noted by Ehrenwald (6), Ullman (70), and Coleman (2). It should be noted that this is only in apparent contradiction to the fact that under experimental circumstances, healthier and more outgoing types do better. The goals in the two situations are quite different. In the clinical situation the patient may be compelled to employ telepathy for immediate and vital self-protective reasons, because characterological handicaps limit more direct kinds of exchanges. Under natural circumstances or under experimental conditions, the healthier person may have a greater ability to deploy his psi abilities under circumstances where the limitations are objective and imposed from without instead of being subjective and characterologically imposed.

The problem of precognition, which in the anecdotal literature is more frequently linked to dreams than is telepathy, has come under scrutiny in the clinical context and has been reported on by Fodor (24), Ehrenwald (7), Meerloo (42), Servadio (64), Eisenbud (17), and Nelson (48). The last notes two kinds of functional relationships linked to the precognitive experience. One is referred to as *paranormal preening* and comes about in the interest of self-praise or ego enhancement. The other is revelatory in nature and involves the transformation from a closed, or self-contained, context into a more open, interpersonal one where an event in the outside world is precognized in the interest of extending beyond the confines of the self. Ehrenwald and Servadio stress the influence of the operation of unconscious dynamic configurations evolving in the two parties concerned and surfacing in what then appears as a precognized event. Eisenbud simply notes such "chronologically extraordinary correspondences" as facts of our psychic life, dynamically significant and therefore meaningful to the psychoanalyst.

Telepathy between husband and wife has been noted by Fodor (21), Schwarz (61), and Nelson (48).

Telepathy and possible psychosomatic complications is referred to in passing by Eisenbud (13) and is again raised as a possibility by Stevenson (69) in his discussion of telepathic impressions and by Schwarz (59), who refers to them as *telesomatic effects*. Stevenson cites cases suggestive of the paranormal transmission of pain and other physical symptoms and calls attention to the possible implication of such transmission in obscuring physical symptoms and psychosomatic syndromes in general.

A second trend evolved as psychiatrists attempted to come to terms with the challenge of psi. Here the concern was not with how to fit psi into the existing order but how to reshape the existing order so as to accommodate psi as an intrinsic and necessary feature. Two qualitatively divergent approaches evolved. Ehrenwald (8) felt that this accommodation could come about if personality theory were to undergo the same transformation that took place in modern physics as discoveries in quantum physics and relativity theory expanded and enriched our understanding of the physical world. He likened current personality theory to Euclidean geometry and Newtonian physics in its rigid adherence to outworn Aristotelian and Cartesian traditions. An open model based on field theory interconnecting the world of the living and the world of the nonliving would accommodate psi on its own terms. Buttressing this point of view, Ehrenwald developed a model based on the operation of psi in the early mother–child symbiotic relationship, followed by the gradual submergence of psi potential as the evolving human organism learned to adapt to the external forces about it, this in turn followed by its occasional emergence in later life under special circumstances. Linking the mystery of psi to the more familiar, but still mysterious, operation of mind on the body, Ehrenwald formulated the concept of the symbiotic gradient to depict the decline, but not total loss, of ego control over the events to be influenced as these events begin to extend beyond the physical and neurological limits of the body proper. Paranormal abilities first cradled in the early mother–child relationship later impinge as a manifestation of the symbolic gradient upon the extended family and finally society at large.

Ehrenwald (12) defines the conditions under which these later manifestations occur as an "existential shift," meaning by this any major change in state (i.e., from waking to sleeping).

The thread that runs through Ehrenwald's writings over the three decades spanned by his writings in the field is his search for a neurobiological model to account for psi. From the time his attention was drawn to the paranormal abilities of a retarded dyslexic girl (6), to his most recent reports, he has drawn attention to certain similarities between psi effects and deficit states, the so-called minus function. More specifically, he has noted the resemblance between the fragmentation and displacement effects apparent as percipients attempt to reproduce the target picture to the productions of brain-damaged patients. He has evolved a theoretical model based on these considerations, containing four major premises: (a) the extension hypothesis, whereby psi effects are seen as compensatory extensions of normal sensory and motor abilities; (b) the hypothesis of a symbiotic gradient (11), whereby the range of abilities, normal and functional in early childhood, are in time both extended in range but become more sporadic in their manifestation; (c) to account for precognitive and PK effects he links these phenomena to ESP, noting that they are simply different aspects of the same psi syndrome; and (d) he identifies the existential shift as the circumstance that facilitates a psi event.

Ehrenwald has had a knack of coining rather felicitous terms to designate one or another aspect of telepathy as he has observed its operation clinically. The terms *minus function, existential shift,* and *symbiotic gradient* have already been mentioned. He spoke of manifest correspondences, particularly in dreams, between an element in the dream of the percipient and the actual occurrence as tracer effects, drawing an analogy to bodily substances that, when radioactively tagged, become more readily identifiable. He spoke of telepathic leakage as psi induction in connection with the spread of telepathic effects from one patient to another. He noted that patients under analysis by analysts of different schools often tended to employ dream symbols characteristic and supportive of the particular theoretical orientation of the analyst. He referred to this as *doctrinal compliance* (10) and felt that unconscious telepathic exchanges between analyst and patient may play a role in bringing it about.

He spoke of the *scatter effect* (6) to denote the fact that telepathic communications often tend to be approximate, fragmented, and scattered both spatially and temporally. To account for the fact that occasionally the percipient has an accurate and detailed vision of the distant target or scene, he regarded telepathy as "biphasic" involving at first a "catapsychic," or fragmentation, effect, followed in some cases, presumably when the affective changes are great enough, by an "anapsychic" phase, where the picture comes together in an accurate presentation.

A second and different line of theoretical speculation has been taken by Eisenbud (15, 19). In his view, psi, far from being an archaic voice from our distant past, is a significant, meaningful, and ever present aspect of our current reality. It is in fact the cement that operates in an underground or unconscious fashion to link our otherwise disparate lives together. In trying to account for the obdurate, intransigent resistance of science to the existence and importance of parapsychology despite the enormous accumulation of evidence over long periods of time and from diverse sources, he in effect turns the table and interprets the scientific endeavor as originating and still maintaining itself as a defense against the reality of psi and the powerful role it could conceivably play were it ever to become legitimated as a fact of life, all life. Eisenbud sees psi effects as not only at the root of primitive concerns with magic and the omnipotence of thought but as currently playing a hidden but meaningful role in all the affairs of men and more broadly still in maintaining—often in strange and inexplicable ways—the subtle and complex exchanges that maintain an ecological balance.

A number of contemporary psychiatrists have extended their interest in psi beyond the consulting room. Eisenbud (16) has investigated thought photography, Stevenson (68) the problem posed by claims of reincarnation, Servadio (63) the investigation of a clairvoyant, Schwarz (60) the investigation of well-known mentalists, and Ullman (73–76) the study of telepathic dreams in a laboratory setting.

Any patient undergoing analysis may, like anyone else, on occasion have a telepathic dream. In my experience, however, there have been only a very few who have appeared to be consistent "telepathic dreamers." The conditions outlined as favoring the occurrence of telepathic dreaming may in each instance be experienced as prejudicial by the patient. In one way or another, the patient may sense the interest, need, and tension of the analyst as in some way adversely influencing the relationship or as interfering with the maintenance of the analyst's clear focus solely on the therapeutic situation. The occurrence of a telepathic dream under these circumstances constitutes a safe way of "needling" the therapist insofar as it both exposes the patient's awareness of the therapist's dereliction and at the same time does so in a way that leaves the therapist impotent to do anything about it unless he owns up to the manner in which his own preoccupations and concerns may at the moment obstruct the progress of the analysis. Telepathic rapport seems to occur in the clinical setting under conditions in which there is a temporary loss of effective symbolic contact between therapist and patient at those times when the patient considers such contact to be vital. Anxiety or other deflecting negative emotions in the therapist act as predisposing influences. By means of the telepathic maneuver the patient does succeed in exposing the countertransferential block and releases a contradictory message to the therapist. He makes his own awareness of the therapist's secret known to the therapist and at the same time remains in a position to disclaim any responsibility for so doing. The inhibited, obsessively organized individual who tends to use language in the service of distance mechanisms rather than to facilitate contact is in my experience the kind of patient most likely to fall back on this maneuver. Telepathic contact appears as one way of establishing contact at critical points in the management of the contradictory needs for distance and inviolability, on the one hand, and the inextinguishable needs for closeness and contact, on the other hand.

The following example drawn from my own practice illustrates the difficulties involved in the management of one's own private domain when telepathic sensitivity is abroad during therapy.

CASE HISTORY

The patient was a 40-year-old male, married and with one child, who had been under therapy for a period of a year prior to the occurrence of the dream to be presented. He worked as a sales promoter for children's wear. The impression he created in therapy was that of someone who avoided any direct or spontaneous interchange in treatment and who seemed to wrap himself up in an unending series of speculations about the nature and cause of his difficulties. His dreams revealed attitudes of distrust and belligerence in relation to the therapist (myself). His approach to people was essentially defensive and evasive. In the face of any criticism by his wife, his withdrawal and hostility deepened. Outside relationships carried little depth of feeling or real interest in others.

On Monday, December 24, 1951, the patient presented the following dream, which had been recalled upon awakening the previous Saturday morning:

> I'm in a hotel room (the same one where the last exhibit I attended was held). I was there with a man I represent. He is from Texas. I was wrapping up a few of the samples that had been on exhibit and was preparing to leave. Someone gave me, or I took, a chromium soap dish. I held it in my hand and I offered it to him. He took it. I was surprised. I asked him, "Are you a collector, too?" Then I sort of smirked and said knowingly, "Well, you're building a house." He blushed. He smirked and kept on smoking his cigar. . . .
>
> I was preparing his new spring line. We disagreed as to how to go about it, but I became convinced he was right. It was his decision to make something for girls. He implied I was weak in this field. He is

262   THE EXPANDING RANGE OF PSYCHIC RESEARCH

now the mainstay of my income. I always feel the relationship will be broken off and he is capable of doing it. He wants me to expand and would pay my rent to do so, but it means putting all my eggs in one basket. I've been wary and unsure, yet he seems to be sound. . . .

I have no associations. It was a glittery, shiny thing. When I was at the hotel for the exhibit we did swipe a few towels but later threw them out. I used to swipe books from the library. I once swiped 15¢ from my aunt for the movies and got a terrific thrashing.

The pertinent data in my own (the therapists's) life in regard to the dream are as follows: My new home had been completed a year and a half before. It was built cooperatively as one of 13 homes in the community. At the time of the original building operations, an extra chromium soap dish had been shipped to my house by mistake. In a spirit of belligerent dishonesty (resenting the ever-increasing costs of the house), I had made no mention of it to anyone. About six months prior to the dream report, it had been noted that owing to uneven settling, a large picture window had gotten very much out of line, requiring attention of the builders. On Sunday, December 16, a week before the dream, the men who were involved in the original building operations came over to see what had to be done. One of them spied the chromium soap dish lying about unused in the cellar and embarrassed me by calling attention to it and making a wisecrack about my having gotten away with it. On Saturday, the day of the patient's dream, one of my neighbors, whose home had been built at the same time as mine, drove me to my office in the city. On the way in I told him the story of the trouble with the picture window and the plan to fix it. The incident of the soap dish occurred to me, but I said nothing about it to him.

The dream occurred a week after the original incident and on the same morning as the day I had recalled the soap dish incident in discussing home-building problems with the neighbor. The most striking correspondence centered around the unusual occurrence in the dream of a chromium soap dish and my experience with just such a dish the week before, an experience disturbing enough to have it come to my mind a week later. The patient indicated his knowledge of the house that the other man was building. (The patient had no normal knowledge of any of the facts connected with my home.) Furthermore, the patient, aware of the other's vulnerability, teased him about it, as in reality the therapist was the butt of a joke based on his own collecting tendencies.

Again including the telepathic elements in the interpretation of the dream, we see a situation in which the patient, protesting the inroads of therapy, concerns himself with vulnerable areas in the therapist's own structure. The chromium soap dish lying about unused and unconnected with the rest of the house is a borrowed experience that serves admirably for the purpose. The dish is a potential container for a cleansing or healing substance. In its isolation and lack of connection with an appropriate setting and in its characterization as "stolen goods," the symbol expresses the patient's profound distrust of the therapist and his unwillingness to put his eggs in the therapist's basket. This dream illustrates the problem of potential anxiety in relation to the vulnerability of the analyst (71).

THEORETICAL CONSIDERATIONS

Anecdotal and clinical experience suggest two generalizations concerning psi. The first is that situations of impending loss or threat favor the occurrence of such events. The second is that the character of the loss may be twofold: it can take the form of the threatened dissolution of a significant affective bond or it may reflect a more personal threat to one's sense of physical or psychological intactness. If paranormal abilities are mobilized under extreme conditions, as anecdotal accounts of spontaneous psi appear to suggest, then the first kind of loss would occur when the precipitating event poses a threat to the continuation of the species—that is, a threat to the continued operation of affectionate and unifying dynamisms. The second kind of loss would occur in response to events threatening the preservation of the individual. Anecdotally, the first is illustrated by the telepathic perception of tragic events involving loved ones, and the second, by the telepathic or precognitive awareness of events posing a personal danger to the percipient.

This formulation suggests that the paranormal event is part of an emergency response system evoked under conditions of threat to sustaining affective bonds or threat to the physical integrity of the organism.

I have elsewhere (72) developed a theory of dreaming based on the vigilance hypothesis. This view suggests that dream consciousness is an elaborate form of orienting activity designed to attend to, process, and respond to certain aspects of our residual experience, with an endpoint being reached in either the continuation of the sleeping state or its interruption and consequent transformation to awakening. While dreaming, conscious experience is organized along lines of emotional contiguity rather than temporal and spatial contiguity. The affective or feeling residue that makes its presence felt in the dream operates reflexively or automatically as a scanning mechanism. Ranging over the entire longitudinal history of the person, it exerts a polarizing influence, drawing to itself aspects of past experiences that are related to it in emotionally meaningful ways. This enables the sleeping organism to assess fully the meaning and implications of the novel or disturbing stimulus and, through the development of the ensuing dream, either allows sleep to continue or helps bring about awakening.

The affective scanning that takes place while dreaming can, on occasion, bridge a spatial gap and provide us with information independent of any known communication channel. Emotional contiguity, under conditions we know very little about, appears capable of integrating transpersonal, as well as personal, content into the dream. Anecdotal accounts have for a long time pointed in this direction, and the circumstances under which they occur strongly suggest that in matters of life and death the vigilant scanning of one's emotional environment reaches out across spatial boundaries in a manner that has yet to be explained.

At a practical level there are clear-cut technical and instrumental gains when there is explicit recognition of the telepathy hypothesis and its possible application to the therapeutic situation. Eisenbud (18) is the foremost exponent of this point of view. As he notes, anyone sensitive to the occurrence of such effects would be in a position to recognize and handle countertransferential difficulties more promptly and more honestly.

There is one perhaps somewhat tangential, but nevertheless relevant, aspect to the work on telepathy. Those of us who have taken a public position espousing the reality of psi are aware of a lost battalion of people who are in distress and wish to seek psychiatric help but who hold back out of fear of rebuff. They are people who have had paranormal experiences that they consider to be both genuine and either central to their problem or related to it. They fear exposing themselves to an entrenched bias but at the same time recognize their need for objective assessment and help. Many of them know from the kind of past experience they have had along the straight psychiatric route that no credence is to be expected and that what they have experienced as valid is received as if it could not be anything but pathological. Caught in this bind, many such individuals ultimately gravitate toward mystical, spiritual, or occult fringe groups in search of the support they need. One hopes that greater knowledge and a deeper understanding on the part of the therapist of the nature and reality of psi will someday save these individuals from the pain and distress of a frustrated search for help and at the same time broaden the horizon of the helping profession itself (75).

REFERENCES

1. Burlingham, D. T. "Child Analysis and the Mother." *Psychoanalytic Quarterly*, 4 (1935): 69–92.
2. Coleman, M. L. "The Paranormal Triangle in Analytical Supervision."

Psychoanalysis and the Psychoanalytic Review, 45, no. 3 (1958): 73–84.

3. Deutsch, H. "Occult Processes Occurring During Psychoanalysis." *Imago*, 12 (1926): 418–433.
4. Devereux, G., ed. *Psychoanalysis and the Occult*. International Universities: New York, 1953.
5. Ehrenwald, J. "Telepathy in Dreams." *British Journal of Medical Psychololology*, 19, pt. 2 (1942): 313–323.
6. Ehrenwald, J. *Telepathy and Medical Psychology*. Norton: New York, 1948.
7. Ehrenwald, J. "Precognition in Dreams." *Psychoanalytic Review*, 38, no. 1 (1951): 17–38.
8. Ehrenwald, J. *New Dimensions of Deep Analysis*. Allen and Unwin: London, 1954.
9. Ehrenwald, J. "Telepathy: Concepts, Criteria and Consequences." *Psychiatric Quarterly*, 30, no. 3 (1956): 425–445.
10. Ehrenwald, J. "The Telepathy Hypothesis and Doctrinal Compliance in Psychotherapy." *American Journal of Psychotherapy*, 11, no. 2 (1957): 359–379.
11. Ehrenwald, J. "A Neurophysiological Model of Psi Phenomena." *Journal of Nervous and Mental Disorders*, 54:6 (1972): 406–418.
12. Ehrenwald, J. "Psi Phenomena and the Existential Shift." *Journal of the American Society for Psychical Research*, 65, no. 2 (1971): 162–172.
13. Eisenbud, J. "Telepathy and Problems of Psychoanalysis." *Psychoanalytic Quarterly*, 15, no. 1 (1946): 32–87.
14. Eisenbud, J. "The Dreams of Two Patients in Analysis Interpreted as a Telepathic *Rêve à deux*." *Psychoanalytic Quarterly*, 16, no. 1 (1947): 39–60.
15. Eisenbud, J. "Why Psi?" *Psychoanalytic Review*, 33, no. 4 (1966–1967): 147–163.
16. Eisenbud, J. *The World of Ted Serios*. Morrow: New York, 1967.
17. Eisenbud, J. "Chronologically Extraordinary Psi Correspondences in the Psychoanalytic Setting." *Psychoanalytic Review*, 56, no. 1 (1969): 9–27.
18. Eisenbud, J. *Psi and Psychoanalysis*. Grune and Stratton: New York, 1970.
19. Eisenbud, J. "Some Notes on the Psychology of the Paranormal." *Journal of the American Society for Psychical Research*, 66, no. 1 (1972): 27–41.
20. Ellis, A. "Telepathy and Psychoanalysis: A Critique of Recent Findings." *Psychiatric Quarterly*, 21, no. 4 (1947): 607–659.
21. Fodor, N. "Telepathic Dreams." *American Imago*, 3, no. 3 (1942): 61–87.
22. Fodor, N. "Telepathy in Analysis." *Psychiatric Quarterly*, 21, no. 2 (1947): 171–189.
23. Fodor, N. *The Search for the Beloved*. Hermitage: New York, 1949.
24. Fodor, N. "Through the Gate of Horn." *American Journal of Psychotherapy*, 9, no. 2 (1955): 283–294.
25. Freud, S. "A Note on the Unconscious in Psychoanalysis." *Proceedings of the Society for Psychical Research*, 26, pt. 66 (1912): 312–318.
26. Freud, S. "Dreams and Telepathy." *Imago*, 8 (1922): 1–22.
27. Freud, S. "The Occult Significance of Dreams." *Imago*, 9 (1925): 234–238.
28. Freud, S. "Dreams and the Occult." In *New Introductory Lectures on Psychoanalysis*. Hogarth: London, 1934.
29. Freud, S. "Psychoanalysis and Telepathy." In *Gesammelte Werke*, Vol. XVII. Imago: London, 1941, pp. 25–40.

30. Gurney, E. "The Stages of Hypnotism." *Proceedings of the Society for Psychical Research*, pt. 5, vol. 2 (1884): 61–72.
31. Gurney, E. "The Problems of Hypnotism." *Proceedings of the Society for Psychical Research*, pt. 7, vol. 2 (1884): 265–292.
32. Hann-Kende, F. "On the Role of Transference and Countertransference in Psychoanalysis." In G. Devereux, ed., *Psychoanalysis and the Occult*. International Universities: New York, 1953.
33. Hitschmann, E. "Telepathy and Psychoanalysis." *International Journal of Psycho-analysis*, 5 (1924): 423–438.
34. Hollós, I. "Psychopathologie alltäglicher telepathischer Erscheinungen." *Imago*, 19 (1933): 529–546.
35. James, W. Review: Myers, F. W. H., "Human Personality and Its Survival of Bodily Death." *Proceedings of the Society for Psychical Research*, 18, pt. 46 (1903): 22–33.
36. James, W. *The Will to Believe and Other Essays*. Dover: New York, 1956.
37. Janet, P. "Deuxième note sur le sommeil provoqué à distance et la suggestion mentale pendant l'état somnambulique." *Revue Philosophique de la France et de l'Étranger*, 21 August (1886): 212–223.
38. Jones, E. *The Life and Work of Sigmund Freud*. Basic Books: New York, 1957.
39. Jung, C. G. *Memories, Dreams, Reflections*. Collins: London, 1963.
40. Jung, C. G., and Pauli, W. *The Interpretation of Nature and the Psyche*. Pantheon: New York, 1955.
41. McDougall, W. Presidential address. *Proceedings of the Society for Psychical Research*, 31, pt. 80 (1920): 105–124.
42. Meerloo, J. *Hidden Communion*. Helix: New York, 1964.
43. Mitchell, T. W. "Some Types of Multiple Personality." *Proceedings of the Society for Psychical Research*, 26, pt. 66 (1912): 257–285.
44. Mitchell, T. W. "The Doris Fischer Case of Multiple Personality." *Proceedings of the Society for Psychical Research*, 31, pt. 69 (1920): 30–74.
45. Mitchell, T. W. *Medical Psychology and Psychical Research*. Dutton: New York, 1922.
46. Mitchell, T. W. Presidential address. *Proceedings of the Society for Psychical Research*, 33, pt. 85 (1923): 1–22.
47. Myers, F. W. H. *Human Personality and Its Survival of Bodily Death*, Vols. I and II. Longmans, Green: London, 1903.
48. Nelson, M. C. "Paranormal Patterns and the Life Style." *International Journal of Parapsychology*, 6, no. 4 (1964): 408–417.
49. Pedersen-Krag, G. "Telepathy and Repression." *Psychoanalytic Quarterly*, 16, no. 1 (1947): 61–68.
50. Peerbolte, M. L. "Telepathy and Psychoanalysis." *Psychics International*, 1, no. 1 (1964): 55–60.
51. Peerbolte, M. L. "Extra-Sensory Perception and Psychoanalysis." *Psychics International*, 1, no. 4 (1965): 70–75.
52. Prince, M. *The Unconscious, the Fundamentals of Human Personality, Normal and Abnormal*. Macmillan: New York, 1914.
53. Prince, W. F. "Two Cures of 'Paranoia' by Experimental Appeals to Purported Obsessing Spirits." *Bulletin 6*, Boston Society for Psychic Research, Dec. 1927: 36–72.
54. Richet, C. "Somnambulisme à Distance." *Revue Philosophique de la Pays et de l'Étranger*, 21 (1886): 199–200.

55. Róheim, G. "Telepathy in a Dream." *Psychoanalytic Quarterly*, 1, no. 2 (1932): 277–291.
56. Saul, L. "Telepathic Sensitiveness as a Neurotic Symptom." *Psychoanalytic Quarterly*, 7 (1938): 329–335.
57. Schilder, P. "Psychopathology of Everyday Telepathic Phenomena." *Imago*, 20 (1934): 219–224.
58. Schrenck-Notzing, A. von. *Phenomena of Materialisation*. Kegan Paul, Trench, Trubner: London, 1920.
59. Schwarz, B. E. "Possible Telesomatic Reactions." *Journal of the Medical Society of New Jersey*, 64, no. 11 (1967): 600–603.
60. Schwartz, B. E. *The Jacques Romano Story*. University Books: New York, 1968.
61. Schwarz, B. E. *Parent–Child Telepathy*. Garrett: New York, 1971.
62. Servadio, E. "Psychoanalysis and Telepathy." *Imago*, 21 (1935): 489–497.
63. Servadio, E. "Processes of Identification and Conversion Phenomena in a Mediumistic Clairvoyante." *International Journal of Psychoanalysis*, pt. 1, 18 (1937): 89–90 (abstract).
64. Servadio, E. "A Presumptively Telepathic-Precognitive Dream During Analysis." *International Journal of Psycho-analysis*, 37, pts. 4–5 (1956): 1–4.
65. Sidis, B. "The Theory of the Subconscious." *Proceedings of the Society for Psychical Research*, 26, pt. 66 (1912): 319–344.
66. Sidis, B. *The Psychology of Suggestion*. Appleton: New York, 1921.
67. Stekel, W. *Der telepathische Traum*. Baum Verlag: Berlin, 1921.
68. Stevenson, I. "Twenty Cases Suggestive of Reincarnation." *Proceedings of the American Society for Psychical Research*, 26 (1966).
69. Stevenson, I. "Telepathic Impressions: A Review and Report of Thirty-Five New Cases." *Proceedings of the American Society for Psychical Research*, 29 (1970).
70. Ullman, M. "On the Nature of Psi Processes." *Journal of Parapsychology*, 13, no. 1 (1949): 59–62.
71. Ullman, M. "On the Occurrence of Telepathic Dreams." *Journal of the American Society for Psychical Research*, 53:2 (1959).
72. Ullman, M. "Dreaming, Altered States of Consciousness and the Problem of Vigilance." *Journal of Nervous and Mental Disease*, 133, no. 6 (1961).
73. Ullman, M. "An Experimental Approach to Dreams and Telepathy." *Archives of General Psychiatry*, 14 (1966): 605–613.
74. Ullman, M., and Krippner, S. *Dream Studies and Telepathy*. Parapsychological Monographs, Parapsychology Foundation: New York, 1970.
75. Ullman, M. "The Telepathic Dream: Experimental Findings and Clinical Implications." *Science and Psychoanalysis*, Vol. 21. In J. H. Marma, ed., Grune and Stratton: New York, 1972.
76. Ullman, M.; Krippner, S.; and Vaughan, A. *Dream Telepathy*. Macmillan: New York, 1973.
77. Zulliger, H. "Prophetic Dreams." *International Journal of Psycho-analysis*, 15, pts. 2–3 (1934): 191–208.

Robert L. Van de Castle

ROBERT L. VAN DE CASTLE, *Ph.D., is professor of clinical psychology in the Department of Psychiatry at the University of Virginia Medical School, where he directs the Sleep and Dream Laboratory.*

Dr. Van de Castle earned his Ph.D. at the University of North Carolina in 1959. Following that he taught at Idaho State College and the University of Denver. He has engaged in research activities at the Institute of Dream Research in Miami and in clinical activities in the Department of Psychiatry at the University of North Carolina Medical School.

Dr. Van de Castle has served on the Council of the Parapsychological Association since 1969 and was elected president of the association in 1970. He is also a trustee of the Gardner Murphy Research Institute. He co-authored the book The Content Analysis of Dreams *(Appleton-Century-Crofts, 1966) and a college textbook module* The Psychology of Dreaming *(General Learning Press, 1971). In addition, he is the author of 5 book chapters and nearly 40 articles on psychology, parapsychology, and dream research. He also serves as an editorial consultant on dream manuscripts for several professional journals.*

Dr. Van de Castle can be reached at the Department of Psychiatry, University of Virginia Medical School, Charlottesville, Va. 22901.

11 Anthropology and Psychic Research

ROBERT L. VAN DE CASTLE

SUMMARY

Very little cross-fertilization of ideas, concepts, or techniques has developed between the fields of anthropology and psychic research. Anthropologists have cataloged various forms of magical practices and attempted to account for their persistent presence in all societies as arising from efforts to explain misfortunes and to provide socially approved channels for expressing intragroup tensions and deprivations. Cultural variations in the nature of religious activities and the characteristics of supernatural figures are considered to originate from learned responses to early authority figures. The vast majority of anthropologists have been unwilling to entertain the hypothesis that genuine parapsychological events may be occurring in some magical or religious ceremonies. This chapter reviews several firsthand reports of field observations that offer encouraging anecdotal support for the existence of psi. Also reviewed are the statistically significant card testing experiments by Foster with American Indians, by the Roses with Australian aborigines, and by the author with Panamanian Indians. A proposal is advanced that non-Western societies will display more frequent examples of psi because of their strong belief in such phenomena and because greater cultural sanction exists for participation in altered states of consciousness. Techniques for investigating psi during anthropological expeditions are suggested.

INTRODUCTION

A book entitled *The Making of Religion*, published in 1900 by Andrew Lang (36), provides a large number of anecdotes describing anthropological observations that might be of relevance for the field of psychic research. In referring to them, Lang says:

I do not give anecdotes of such savage successes as evidence to *facts*; they are only illustrations, and evidence to *beliefs* and *methods* . . .

which, among the savages, correspond to the supposed facts examined by *Psychical Research* among the civilized. I can only point out, as Bastian had already pointed out, the existence of a field that deserves closer study by anthropologists who can observe savages in their homes (p. ix).

My purpose is to do, by way only of *ébauche*, what neither anthropology nor psychic research or psychology has done: to put the savage and modern phenomenon side by side. Such evidence as we can give for the actuality of the modern experiences will, so far as it goes, raise a presumption that the savage beliefs, however erroneous, however darkened by fraud and fancy, repose on a basis of real observation of actual phenomena (p. 45).

Anthropology must remain incomplete while it neglects this field, whether among wild or civilized men. In the course of time this will come to be acknowledged (p. ix).

Acknowledgment has seemed to come quite slowly, and the field of anthropology continues to remain incomplete and to neglect the field of psychic research. Anthropologists still view savage beliefs as erroneous and darkened by fraud and fancy. Typical of the view held by most contemporary anthropologists would be the following statement found in a standard reference book on magical practice (44, p. 3). In discussing witchcraft and sorcery, the authors state:

They are termed magical from the point of view of the anthropologist because there are no grounds in terms of Western science for believing them able to accomplish the ends claimed for them.

TYPES OF MAGICAL PRACTICES

Before proceeding to examine the types of research that anthropologists have initiated in attempting to understand the magical practices of non-Western societies, it may be helpful to differentiate between the various types of magical practitioners. For the purposes of this chapter we will use some working definitions, recognizing that a particular individual may possess capabilities that fall into several categories. A *witch* is a person who possesses innate capabilities for carrying out extraordinary activities beyond the range of ordinary human beings. A witch may deliberately direct his supernormal power toward another individual, but it is also possible that his powers may be released unconsciously because he is often considered to possess an unstable personality. The power of witchcraft thus resides within the witch himself, and catastrophic events can be triggered off by his mere presence in a village. A *sorcerer* is a person who uses certain techniques such as incantations or effigies to deliberately harm another individual. The power of sorcery lies within the technique, and any ordinary villager could theoretically employ the methods of sorcery. A *shaman* is a person who enters a trance and who allows various spirits to speak through him. The term *shaman* is more frequently reserved for practitioners in Siberia and North America. A *seer* is a person who is able to perceive the presence of spirits, although he does not become possessed by these spirits himself. A *diviner* is a person who can describe events taking place at a distance or that will happen in the future. A person who attempts to cure various native ailments may be referred to as a *medicine man*. The label *witch doctor* is most often employed by laymen rather than anthropologists and carries no specific connotation as to the type of magic practice involved. Since a practitioner may engage in all of the above roles at different times or combine them on a particular occasion, it is extremely difficult to categorize a given practitioner. It has been suggested that the term *wizard* be assigned to an individual who engages in any form of magic. Anthropologists, however, are far from having reached any consensus on nomenclature and so the term *magical practitioner* will be generally used throughout this chapter.

Magic is sometimes popularly divided into two classes that are distinguished by their intended purposes. *White magic* is practiced to effect some beneficial aim such as healing, while *black magic* is carried out to cause some harmful consequence for another. Sir James Frazer (21) distinguishes between two types of magic that play a role in sorcery. *Imitative magic* involves the principle that like produces like; a familiar example would be the attempt to injure a person by inserting pins into a doll that possesses a resemblance to the intended victim. *Contagious magic* is based upon the assumption that things that were once joined together possess a permanent linkage; consequently, an act rendered to one unit will affect the other unit even though they are physically separated. Thus, a sorcerer could cause a victim to suffer some misfortune if the sorcerer were to obtain some hair or fingernail clippings from that person and subject these body products to some painful or harmful manipulation.

EXPLANATIONS OF MAGICAL PRACTICES

Anthropologists have been interested in the personality of magical practitioners and several case histories are available (6, 24, 58). Some writers (13, 32, 60) maintain that mental illness is characteristic for shamans but a more recent review of the issue by Lewis (39) seems to indicate that such an extreme view is not held by most modern anthropologists. The situation seems well summed up in an evaluation by Handelman (25, p. 354): "Stated bluntly, data do not yet exist for properly evaluating the personality developments and personality dynamics of shamans."

In dealing with magic, anthropologists have focused their attention upon understanding the functional role that magic plays in sustaining social institutions. Magic may be viewed as binding members of a community together in a cooperative fashion, as when Trobriand islanders jointly participate in mandatory rituals at various stages of canoe-building. It may also provide institutional recognition for intragroup jealousy and hostility and provide methods for expressing them. Persons who possess wealth are often considered to have gained it through illicit means, and those who are economically deprived can vent their jealousy and envy through accusations of witchcraft. Thus, Nadel (45) explains that it is only women who are accused of being witches among the Nupe tribe in Africa because women maintain economic dominance in that culture. Kluckhohn (31) notes that among the Navaho there is a correlation between their general state of tension and the amount of fear and talk about witches. Witchcraft can also provide a sanction against antisocial behavior, as is illustrated among the Azande in the Southern Sudan (17), where a tribal member must be careful not to antagonize others lest he become bewitched by someone he has offended or lest he be accused of being a witch himself.

According to Middleton and Winter (44), witchcraft tends to be emphasized in societies in which unilineal kinship principles are employed in the formation of local residential groups larger than the domestic household, whereas sorcery is emphasized when such unilineal lines are not employed. Whiting and Child (66) found that societies that had high levels of anxiety about being aggressive displayed more fear of sorcerers and animal spirits, while societies with low levels of anxiety about aggression possessed a greater fear of ghosts. The specific nature of the beliefs about witches' activities is accounted for in terms of the types of deprivation that may be experienced within a particular society. In comparing the belief system of two African groups, Wilson (68) observed that in a society in which sex partners are relatively limited, tribal members believe that witches engage in relationships with a secret sex partner, while in a society in which the rules of inheritance limit the possibility of a villager participating in the acquisition of cattle, the witches are considered to lust after meat and milk.

The nature of interpersonal relationships is also considered to exert an important influence upon the nature of religious practices. Margaret Mead (43) found that societies characterized by the cooperation of its members conceive of a supernatural system that has its own pattern of rules and that man may propitiate in an orderly way, while in competitive societies the relationship to the supernatural is antagonistic and lacking in trust or submission to a higher power. A study by Lambert et al. (35) found that supernatural beings were considered to be mainly benevolent in societies in which indulgent treatment and lack of pain from the nurturing agent was found during the first 18 months of life; societies with beliefs in aggressive supernaturals were more likely to punish children if they did not display self-reliance and independence. It is interesting to note that these latter authors reported that there was no apparent relationship between the properties of deities and the amount of subsistence insecurity.

The preceding review is intended to sketch in broad outline form the stance that has been taken by most anthropologists studying magical and religious practices of non-Western societies. They have cataloged the forms of magical and religious practices and theorized about their societal function in terms of the contributions of demographic, economic, and psychological variables. They believe that these forms of magical and religious behavior have persisted only because such forms have proved effective in diminishing or controlling intragroup tensions. These practices are viewed as offering a culturally acceptable explanation for misfortune and a means for attempting to alleviate the resultant anxiety when members are confronted with what would otherwise be inexplicable phenomena. Since anthropologists, with rare exceptions, have not been willing to consider that genuine parapsychological events may be occurring in some magical or religious ceremonies, it might be said that anthropologists also rely upon explanations that are culturally acceptable to alleviate the anxiety that results from a confrontation with phenomena that are, as yet, inexplicable to Western scientists. The approved explanation possesses elegant simplicity; all of the accounts of apparent psychic manifestations among primitive groups are greatly exaggerated, and they can be readily explained as caused by suggestion or sleight-of-hand.

A few anthropologists, however, have been impressed by some of the events they have observed. Beattie (1, p. 51), for example, has noted in referring to participation in a séance, "There is evidence, too, that 'cures' by these means of quite serious conditions are not uncommon." In reference to psychic healing, Jensen (30, p. 230) concluded, "There can be no doubt that man actually possesses such abilities." Weston La Barre (34) has attributed the ability to handle snakes among members of Appalachian cults as being some form of PK and has also hypothesized that psi may play a role in the religious ceremonies of American Indians (33). Perhaps indicative of a new stance among anthropologists is the position taken by Ralph Linton (40), who took some considerable care to distinguish between psi and delusional phenomena. In a similar vein, Long (41), commenting upon phenomena that he observed in Jamaica, cautioned that it is important for the anthropologist to distinguish between the effects of suggestion (faith or psychotherapy) and psychic energy when attempting to understand "faith-healing." A stronger stand on these matters has been expressed by Mircea Eliade (15, p. 87): "We now touch upon a problem of the greatest importance, . . . that is, the question of the *reality* of the extra-sensory capacities and paranormal powers ascribed to the shamans and medicine-men. Although research into this question is still at its beginning, a fairly large number of ethnographic documents has already put the authenticity of such phenomena beyond doubt."

REVIEW OF THE ETHNOGRAPHIC LITERATURE

One of the reasons why anthropologists have neglected to consider the possible relevance of psychic research for their field has been their unfamiliarity with the laboratory evidence for paranormal abilities that has been accumulated. There has also been a scarcity of any systematic reviews of ethnographic material containing accounts of observations that might suggest a paranormal faculty at work. The two most detailed ethnographic reviews that I have encountered appear in the books by Lang (36) and by de Vesme (14). In his *Bibliography of Parapsychology*, Zorab (69) has a section entitled "Parapsychology and Ethnology," which contains 37 titles, but most of these references are not available in English. Among them, a book by Bozzano (4) and the articles by Fischer (19) and de Martino (12) sound very relevant, but I have not been able to obtain copies of them. Eliade also refers to the work of de Martino and cites a review by him (11) in which this ethnologist, according to Eliade (15, p. 87), "subjected the testimonies of explorers concerning extra-sensory perception to a searching criticism and concluded that they were real." Accounts of psi in Australia (16), Africa (63), and Jamaica (67) are available, and there have also been some brief review articles published by parapsychologists (26, 49).

In order to provide a feeling for these ethnographic accounts, a sampling will be given of some of them that have been published. Matthews (42) has provided a report from the Bahamas of young girls accurately describing distant events while in trance. He mentions that members of this cult would go into trances at the same time, even though they were widely separated geographically and the times of entering trances were not related to any scheduled events. Hutton (27) mentions that in working with the Negas in India, on three occasions inquiries were made of him as to whether certain relatives in a regiment located in France were dead. In each instance, confirmation of the death of the person approximating the time of inquiry was obtained several months later. A West African diviner provided a specific description of Gorer's (22) home and companions in Dakar located a thousand miles away that proved to be very accurate. A Saulteux diviner made some predictions about Hallowell's (23) father and the welfare of other members of his party that was consistent with later information obtained about them.

Sometimes the incidents involve cases of apparent precognition. Firth (18) describes a Tikopia possession case in which the spirit said he arrived to announce the coming of fish. The next morning a school of fish appeared. Using animal bones, a South African diviner correctly informed Callaway (5) that he was concerned about a pregnant black goat and also accurately predicted that she would deliver a white and gray kid by the time he returned home. A West African diviner correctly predicted to Prince (51) that one of his Canadian companions would have a male child one year later.

Two detailed accounts will now be presented. If the reports were accurately recorded, they would seem to represent striking examples of psi. The first case involves apparent clairvoyance and precognition and appears in a privately printed book (38) by a South African hunter and merchant. The case was described in Lang's book (36):

> I had sent out my native elephant-hunters with instructions to meet me at a certain date at a selected spot. I arrived there at the appointed time, but none of my hunters had put in an appearance. Having nothing much to do, I went to see a native doctor who had a great reputation, just to amuse myself and see what the man would say. At first the doctor refused to tell anything, because, as he said, he had no knowledge of white men's affairs. At last he consented, and said he would "open the gates of distance and travel through it," even though it should cost him his life.
>
> He then demanded the names and number of the hunters. I demurred at first, but finally did as requested. The doctor then made eight fires, one for each hunter, and cast into them roots which burned with a sickly-smelling smoke. The man took some medicine and fell into a trance for about ten minutes, his limbs moving all the time.
>
> When he came round from the trance, he raked out the ashes of his first fire and described the appearance of the man represented by it, and said, "This man has died of fever and his gun is lost." He then said that the second hunter had killed four elephants and described the shape and size of the tusks. He said that the next had been killed by an elephant, but the gun was coming home alright. Then he described the appearance and fortunes of the next, adding that the survivors would not be home for three months, and would travel by a

road different from that agreed upon. The prediction turned out correct in every particular, and, as the hunters were scattered over country over 200 miles away, the man could hardly have obtained news of them from other natives. Nor did the diviner know that he was going to be consulted.

The second account was published by Father Trilles (62), and a brief summary of this telepathic or out-of-the-body experience is provided by de Vesme (14, pp. 115–116).

A certain Negema Nzago, who was both chief of the tribe of Yabakou and a celebrated fetish man, has extraordinary power over the natives. This has come to him because he cured sicknesses, indicated how they could make their fortunes, etc.

One day he told Father Trilles, with whom he was on friendly terms: "Tomorrow there will be a big palaver of all of the magicians of this region. We are all to meet on the plateau of Yemvi, at the old abandoned village." Now this village was four days march from that place, and, Father Trilles having shown astonishment and doubt of the possibility, the magician resumed, "You do not believe me; well, come this evening to my hut. I shall leave from there."

The missionary went to the rendezvous and found the magician at his preparations for departure. In order to verify the fact, he said: "I have a commission to give you. On your way, at the foot of the hill, you must go through the village of Nahong. You know Esaba, my catechist, who lives there. Well, as you pass before his door, would you tell him that I must see him, that he should come at once and bring me the cartridges of the shotgun which I gave him to keep?"

"Good, your commission shall be done. Esaba will get your message this evening and will set out tomorrow."

After gesticulation, words, chants, and having rubbed himself all over with a reddish liquid smelling like garlic after the intervention of a large snake, which at a certain moment descended from the roof and encircled the body of the magician, he fell into a lethargic sleep. His body was perfectly rigid. Father Trilles put a pin into his flesh; he did not wince. On his lips there was a slight white foam; there was no perceptible movement of his body. The serpent was no longer there. The missionary passed the night in the hut by the magician without leaving it for an instant, to be sure that there was no subterfuge.

During the morning of the following day the magician slowly awoke, looked around in a bewildered manner, and then, seeing the Father, he said, "I have given your message," and spoke of the reunion of magicians in which he had taken part.

On the evening of the third day after this conversation a black arrived at the mission house with a message for the Rev. Father Trilles: "Here are the cartridges which you sent for by the magician." "What! Did you see him?" "No, but I heard him during the night, and he called me from outside my hut and told me that you wanted these at once."

These anecdotes and others of a similar nature reported in de Vesme's book certainly stir one's curiosity, but they cannot be accepted as providing scientific evidence for the reality of psi. The accounts are lacking in too many details, and there are too many variables that one would like to have under some form of experimental control. De Vesme (14, pp. 208–209) mentions a story reported in the *Natal Mercury* that was reprinted in the May 4, 1906 edition of the *Two Worlds*, published in Manchester. It stated that in 1891 the English colony of Natal published the Code of Native Law and the governor, Sir Theophilus Shepstone, convoked at Pieternaritzburg all the *izangoma,* or sorcerers, of the district to explain to them the articles of the code that had reference to them. He declared that the government forbade the practice of *ukbula* (consultation of a medicine man) but if any of them would submit to an experiment and demonstrate the genuineness of their faculty, a diploma would be given to them certifying their ability. One of the tests involved asking them to identify a hidden object after they had been sent out of the room and were readmitted one by one. Two of the sorcerers were able to say immediately that the article that had been hidden was money and successfully indicated its hiding place. They were also said to succeed with other tests that were given them.

Another interesting effort to test empirically the claims of a native diviner was made by Laubscher (37), a psychiatrist at Cape Town University. One day he buried a purse wrapped in brown paper in the ground, covered it with a flat brown stone, and placed a gray stone on top of the brown one. No one witnessed his act. Laubscher immediately set off in an automobile and traveled 35 miles an hour to a Tembu diviner 60 miles away. In a séance dance, Solomon Baba, the diviner, described the purse, its location, the paper, and the color and size of the stones in accurate detail. Solomon Baba was also amazingly accurate in describing the appearance of some missing cattle from a distant region and correctly predicted the exact date that Laubscher would return to England, even though this date was several months beyond the official date that passage had already been booked for.

REVIEW OF THE EXPERIMENTAL LITERATURE

There have been a few efforts to employ the traditional ESP cards with native groups. Foster (20) trained a teacher at an Indian school in Manitoba to administer a clairvoyance test to 50 Plains Indian children enrolled at the school. Each child completed 125 trials, and the overall deviation was significantly above chance expectation. There is also a brief report (50) of a native-school headmaster using ESP cards to test a group of 9 New Guinea natives and 6 native teachers. Although their overall results were above chance expectation, the deviation was not statistically significant. A drawing task was also attempted with a target picture consisting of a concealed photograph of an American-style living room. Seven of the nine drawings were characterized as "more or less boxy-looking likenesses of the exterior of a native house."

The most extensive testing program carried out with individual members of primitive groups is that reported in several publications by Ronald Rose and his wife, Lyndon. They employed standard ESP cards; and Ronald Rose served as agent, while his wife recorded the subjects' verbal calls. Subjects were all tested individually. The agent stood out of sight and concentrated upon each ESP card until the subject made his verbal call. After each run of 25 cards was completed, the target order of the cards was recorded so that it could be compared to the record made of the subjects' guesses.

The Roses' first Australian testing expedition was carried out in August 1949 at Woodenbong, a settlement of half-castes not engaged in tribal living. A total of 23 subjects were tested, and a highly significant deviation above chance expectation was shown for the 296 runs completed (54). Their next tests were carried out several months later in Central Australia with a detribalized group and a group that was living in close tribal conditions. The latter group obtained above chance results that were statistically significant, while the detribalized natives did not (55). A third testing trip four years later was made to Woodenbong to retest the original subjects there. Once again, highly significant positive results were obtained (56). In all, a total of slightly over 50 aboriginal subjects had been tested and completed a total of 665 runs. They obtained 545 more hits than would have been expected on a chance basis.

The Roses also tested Maori subjects from New Zealand and obtained highly significant positive results for the 279 runs completed (57). A nonsignificant positive deviation was obtained for 200 runs administered in Samoa, a result attributed to the repressive efforts of missionaries since 1830 to stamp out any native beliefs in psychic matters.

Testing for PK was carried out by the Roses during each of the three

Australian trips and in Samoa. Their methodology involved placing 12 plastic dice in a shaker and throwing them on a blanket-covered table with the goal of having certain die faces appear uppermost. Only chance deviations were obtained during each of the individual trips, and neither the Australian nor Samoan results were significant. It was pointed out by the Roses that the average aborigine did not believe he could influence PK phenomena, since that was a prerogative of the "clever men" or sorcerers.

I have also been involved for several years in a testing program involving adolescent Cuna Indians residing on the San Blas Islands in Panama. A group testing procedure was involved, and 50 trials per subject were completed. All the students in a class would write on specially devised recording sheets their guesses as to what card they thought I was concentrating upon outside of the classroom. The cards displayed colored drawings of five objects that were familiar to them such as canoes, conch shells, or jaguars. The results from three years of testing revealed significant sex differences in scoring, favoring the girls, although the overall scoring level for the two sexes combined was not significant (64). A total of 344 subjects (68 girls and 276 boys) were tested on at least one occasion, and 97 subjects were tested on two or more occasions.

I also carried out individual tests for PK. The task involved an attempt to influence 12 plastic dice to fall on alternating sides of a platform after they were mechanically released from a box located above an inclined chute leading to the platform. The 108 subjects utilized for the dice testing were generally adult women or young children not attending school. It appeared to be very difficult for these subjects to comprehend the task, and they would seldom even look at the dice as they were falling. No significant results were obtained with this test.

SUGGESTIONS FOR FURTHER RESEARCH

The reports of these card-guessing experiments offer substantiation that evidence for psychic abilities can be obtained in non-Western societies under conditions that are adequately controlled and in a manner that would allow the results to be statistically evaluated. In general, however, I would discourage the investigator in the field from relying upon the standard ESP cards as his main testing vehicle. My own experience indicates that greater attention will be maintained if cards are employed that contain drawings or photographs of objects that have particular cultural relevance such as local animals, trees, or trade goods. Every effort should be made to accommodate the particular interests or preferences of a subject who might appear to possess unusual ability.

A good example of how testing conditions can be adapted to accommodate a subject's interest was shown by the staff of the Psychical Research Foundation when studying Lalsingh Harribance. Harribance is a native of Trinidad who obtained considerable local fame for his ability to give psychic readings to people on the basis of face-to-face interaction with them. His results in working with the standard ESP cards were unimpressive, but after the testing arrangements were modified so that the stimuli consisted of facial photographs of six males and six females, highly significant results were consistently maintained (53, 61). The task in this situation was to guess the sex of the person represented in the concealed photographs.

Variations of the procedures employed by Laubscher (37) might also prove fruitful. A distinctive object could be hidden in a well-concealed place, and the task for the practitioner would be to indicate the location and/or identity of the hidden object. Ideally, such an experiment should be carried out with two persons, one to conduct the inquiry with the practitioner and the other to insure that no effort was made by another person to approach the concealed object. Another procedure might involve the use of a small sturdy testing box that could be locked by the investigator. Before each testing session, an object would be placed within the box and the practitioner asked to provide a description of the concealed object. Care would need to be taken to select objects of roughly similar weight, and the box would have to be thickly lined with sponge rubber so that minimal sensory cues would be available through shaking the box.

The two-person testing arrangement could also be utilized for a situation where the practitioner would attempt to provide a description of the actions of an isolated tribal member located at a reasonable distance from the practitioner. These activities should be varied on some sort of random basis so that the activities could not be rationally inferred (eating at meal time, etc.). The distantly located associate should film or tape-record a description of the tribal member's activities at specified time intervals, and the team member conducting the inquiry should also tape-record the practitioner's statements and the time at which such statements were made. A walkie-talkie might help in coordinating the testing arrangements.

Many forms of apparent PK phenomena have been reported in field observations. Based upon my own experience and that of the Roses (57), I would not recommend dice as being the preferred method for investigating such claims. Dice tests are generally boring, and it is difficult for the native practitioner to appreciate their relevance in relation to the types of ability in which he feels he has some proficiency.

A simple type of testing apparatus might consist of a three-minute egg-timer. The task for the practitioner could be to stop or to slow down the descent of the falling sand. Control trials could be alternated with experimental trials when the practitioner uses his powers or spirits to hold the sand back. The results could be statistically evaluated by comparing the differences in elapsed time for the sand to fall under the experimental and control conditions.

Often, however, an investigator will have to be content with merely observing the practitioner while he performs his particular type of magic. One must always be careful in such situations to be on the lookout for sleight-of-hand. Chari (10) gives a useful account of some of the problems he encountered when studying cases in India. Movie recordings should be standard equipment for attempting to observe PK in the field. Careful slow motion analyses of these films should help one to decide whether to place much faith in claims such as that by Jacolliot (29), who reported that a fakir at Benares was able to move an extremely heavy bronze vase full of water in any direction that Jacolliot directed and was able to raise it seven or eight inches from the ground.

It is often extremely difficult to secure sincere cooperation from a native practitioner, because the experimenter, with his unfamiliar paraphernalia and his blunt insistence upon having some unusual phenomenon demonstrated at a time and place convenient for him, usually succeeds in "turning off" the practitioner. During my 1972 field trip to the San Blas Islands, I attempted to remedy this situation by having Malcolm Bessent, a young British sensitive, accompany me. Bessent was able to break down some of the traditional reserve of the *neles* (practitioners) by discussing some of his own psychic experiences and abilities and was willing to demonstrate to them his own rather remarkable ability at clairvoyant diagnosis and psychic healing. He was so successful at these latter skills that the whole village was eagerly requesting his services. Our visit was too short to exploit fully the possibilities of such a working arrangement between a Western sensitive and a local tribal sensitive, but the innovation was one that appears to offer very promising possibilities.

Of course, the most extreme example of an anthropologist attempting to work closely with a native practitioner is the remarkable apprenticeship described by Carlos Castenada in his three books (7, 8, 9). Castenada spent a decade learning to become a "man of knowledge" under the tutelage of Don Juan Matus, a Yaqui Indian sorcerer. As part of his training he utilized various hallucinogenic plants and went through many arduous trials and exercises in order to experience the "separate reality" of a sorcerer's world. By means of carefully recorded dialogue, Castenada has been able to provide a unique insight into the subjective experiences of a native practitioner, and many instances of apparent psi are sprinkled throughout his first-person narrative. Although I am not recommending that every anthropologist wishing to investigate psi in the field undertake the rigorous regime followed by Castenada, a willingness to become intimately immersed in the phenomena he is attempting to understand will undoubtedly repay the investigator with many research dividends.

PROPOSAL OF A HYPOTHESIS

One could make a strong argument that psychic researchers have chosen the worst of all possible cultures—namely, our own—to provide the subjects upon whom our psychic investigations are based. The excellent reviews by Palmer (47, 48) indicate that a subject's attitude of belief in ESP is an important determinant of his scoring level in an ESP task. Yet our whole Western tradition is designed to discourage such beliefs and thereby to lessen our full participation in any situation in which psychic abilities might be manifest. The difference between our own attitude and that of non-Western societies has been emphasized by Frazer (21, pp. 25–26):

> Belief in the sympathetic influence exerted on each other by persons or things at a distance is of the essence of magic. Whatever doubt science may entertain as to the possibility of action at a distance, magic has none; faith in telepathy is one of its first principles. A modern advocate of the influence of mind upon mind at a distance would have no difficulty in convincing a savage; the savage believed in it long ago, and what is more, he acted on his belief with a logical consistency such as his civilised brother in the faith has not yet, so far as I am aware, exhibited in his conduct.

Our culture also makes a determined effort to discourage those states of mind that have been referred to as "altered states of consciousness." We are frightened of hypnosis, discourage alcoholic excesses, and use law-enforcement agencies to insure that drugs are not used to seek out any forms of dissociation. This is quite different from the state of affairs in most non-Western societies. Bourguignon (3) examined the data available on 488 non-Western societies and found that there was some institutionalized form of dissociation present in 89% of these societies.

Chapter 27 of this book provides strong support for the hypothesis that psi functioning is enhanced during altered states of consciousness; our society, however, erects strict cultural prohibitions against experiencing such states. Examination of the bibliographic citations included in this chapter will reveal that almost invariably the presumptive psychic experiences or manifestations occurred either during or after a trance state on the part of the magical practitioner. Several books containing excellent photographic illustrations have been published on the topic of trances. These books deal with trances in Asia and South America (65), Bali (2), Haiti (28), and Brazil (59). It is interesting to note that these writers, all of whom have had extensive experiences with observing trance phenomena, have indicated that they witnessed many inexplicable happenings during trance states, and all of them seem receptive to the idea of the relevancy of a psychic explanation.

Most descriptions of religious ceremonies emphasize the reliance upon drinking, dancing, drumming, and the inhalation of tobacco or smoke from resinous plants. All of these activities will produce increased amounts of carbon dioxide in the blood, and it has been demonstrated (46, 52) that listening to recordings of drum music will produce alterations in brain-wave patterns similar to those produced by photic visual stimulation. These findings help to explain the physiological basis of the trance states, but we are still a long way from understanding how they facilitate the processing of psi material.

The tentative hypothesis emerging from this review is that more frequent and intensive examples of psi will be found in non-Western societies because of the greater commitment of those societies to a belief in psychic reality and because of the more frequent entrance into altered states of consciousness by members of those societies.

IMPLICATIONS FOR ANTHROPOLOGY

It is extremely unfortunate that the study of paranormal events among non-Western societies has been so sadly neglected by both anthropology and psychic research. Both fields have been diminished by this negligence.

Since anthropologists have not generally, until now, seriously considered the possible reality of psychic events, they have been reduced to explaining the persistence of magical practices primarily on the basis of sociological principles involving intragroup tensions. An equally plausible explanation would be that magical practices persevere because a learning schedule is established that is maintained through the aperiodic reinforcement provided by the occurrence of genuine psychic events. Acceptance of psi would also cause a reassessment of how the shaman or any other practitioner is perceived by anthropologists. The shaman is currently perceived as psychotic, because he keeps insisting that he is able to demonstrate phenomena that the anthropologist "knows" are nonexistent. The shaman must therefore be delusional, for there is no correspondence possible between his perceptions and beliefs and the way the "real world" of the anthropologist operates.

The ethnocentric bias, which can become instilled in our thinking and interfere with our perceptions, is nicely highlighted in the preface to *The Teachings of Don Juan* by Castenada (7):

> Anthropology has taught us that the world is differently defined in different places. . . . The very metaphysical presuppositions differ: space does not conform to Euclidean geometry, time does not form a continuous unidirectional flow, causation does not conform to Aristotelian logic, man is not differentiated from nonman or life from death, as in our world. . . . The central importance of entering into worlds other than our own . . . lies in the fact that the experience leads us to understand that our own world is also a cultural construct.

Acceptance by anthropologists that they may be prejudicing their understanding of anthropological phenomena by too closely remaining within the cultural constructs of Western science will help them to propose more creative and encompassing theoretical positions.

Psychic research must also be faulted for failing to take advantage of the rich possibilities provided by cross-cultural research into psi. It has been estimated that 4000–5000 human societies existed during the last century. Imagine the diversity that represents in terms of genetic patterns, diet, climate, child-rearing practices, forms of intrafamilial organization, styles of social interaction, emphases upon instinctual drives, uses of different hallucinogenic drugs, and types of trance states.

This listing is a highly attenuated one, and dozens of other possible relevant dimensions could be easily added. We are almost totally unfamiliar with what the contributions of any of them might be to the manifestation or enhancement of psi, yet it would be impossible to find such heterogeneous sampling strata within our own culture. Nature has provided us with a treasure trove of variables that should be assessed for their possible interactions with psychic faculties. Unless we quickly avail ourselves of this unparalleled opportunity, we may well be in the position of a modern ornithologist who would like to observe the behavior of the passenger pigeon.

REFERENCES

1. Beattie, J. "Sorcery in Bunyoro." In J. F. Middleton and E. H. Winter, eds., *Witchcraft and Sorcery in East Africa.* Routledge and Kegan Paul: London, 1963.
2. Belo, J. *Trance in Bali.* Columbia University Press: New York, 1960.
3. Bourguignon, E. "Dreams and Altered States of Consciousness in Anthropological Research." In F. L. Hsu, ed., *Psychological Anthropology.* Schenkman: Cambridge, Mass., 1972.

4.   Bozzano, E. *Populi Primitivi e Manisfestazioni Supernormali.* Verona, 1941; Zurich, 1948.
5.   Callaway, H. *The Religious System of the Amazulu.* Folk-Lore Society: London, 1884.
6.   Casagrande, J., ed. *In the Company of Man.* Torchbooks: New York, 1964.
7.   Castenada, C. *The Teachings of Don Juan.* Simon and Schuster: New York, 1968.
8.   Castenada, C. *A Separate Reality.* Simon and Schuster: New York, 1971.
9.   Castenada, C. *Journey to Ixtlan.* Simon and Schuster: New York, 1972.
10. Chari, D. T. "Parapsychological Studies and Literature in India." *International Journal of Parapsychology*, 2 (1960): 24–36.
11. de Martino, E. "Percezione Extrasensoriale e Magismo Etnologico." *Studi e Materiale di Storia delle Religione*, 18 (1942): 1–20; (1943–1946): 31–84.
12. de Martino, E. "Magismo Sciamanistico e Fenomenologia Paranormale." *Metapsichica*, 1 (1946): 164–174.
13. Devereaux, G. "Shamans as Neurotics." *American Anthropologist*, 63 (1961): 1088–1090.
14. de Vesme, C., *A History of Experimental Spiritualism*, Vol. I: *Primitive Man.* S. de Brath, trans. Rider: London, 1931.
15. Eliade, M. *Shamanism: Archaic Techniques of Ecstasy.* W. R. Trask, trans. Princeton University Press: Princeton, N.J., 1966.
16. Elkins, A. *Aboriginal Men of High Degree.* Australasion: Sydney, 1944.
17. Evans-Pritchard, E. *Witchcraft, Oracles and Magic Among the Azande.* Oxford University Press: London, 1937.
18. Firth, R. *Tikopia Ritual and Belief.* Beacon: Boston, 1967.
19. Fischer, H. T. "Ethnologie en Parapsychologie." *Tijdschrift voor Parapsychologie*, 12 (1940): 1–15.
20. Foster, A. "ESP Tests with American Indian Children." *Journal of Parapsychology*, 7 (1943): 94–103.
21. Frazer, J. G. *The Golden Bough.* Macmillan: New York, 1967 (abridged ed.).
22. Gorer, G. *Africa Dances: A Book about West African Negroes.* Knopf: New York, 1935.
23. Hallowell, A. *The Role of Conjuring in Saulteux Society.* University of Pennsylvania Press: Philadelphia, 1942.
24. Handelman, D. "The Development of a Washo Shaman." *Ethnology*, 6 (1967): 444–464.
25. Handelman, D. "Shamanizing on an Empty Stomach." *American Anthropologist*, 70 (1968): 353–356.
26. Humphrey, B. "Paranormal Occurrences Among Preliterate Peoples." *Journal of Parapsychology*, 8 (1944): 214–229.
27. Hutton, J. *The Sema Negas.* Macmillan: London, 1921.
28. Huxley, F. *The Invisibles: Voodoo Gods in Haiti.* McGraw-Hill: New York, 1969.
29. Jacolliot, L. *Occult Science in India.* Metaphysical: New York, 1901.
30. Jensen, A. *Myth and Cult Among Primitive Peoples.* University of Chicago Press: Chicago, 1963.
31. Kluckhohn, C. *Navaho Witchcraft.* Beacon: Boston, 1967.
32. Kroeber, A. L. "Psychosis or Social Sanction." In *The Nature of Culture.* University of Chicago Press: Chicago, 1952.

33. La Barre, W. *The Peyote Cult.* Schocken: New York, 1959.
34. La Barre, W. *They Shall Take Up Serpents.* Schocken: New York, 1962.
35. Lambert, W. W.; Triandis, L. M.; and Wolf, M. "Some Correlates of Beliefs in the Malevolence and Benevolence of Supernatural Beings: A Cross-Cultural Study." *Journal of Abnormal and Social Psychology,* 58 (1959): 162–169.
36. Lang, A. *The Making of Religion.* 2nd ed. Longmans Green: London, 1900.
37. Laubscher, B. *Sex Custom and Psychopathology: A Study of South African Pagan Natives.* McBride: New York, 1938.
38. Leslie, D. *Among the Zulu and the Amatongos.* 2nd ed. Privately printed: Edinburgh, 1875.
39. Lewis, I. M. *Ecstatic Religion: An Anthropological Study of Spirit Possession and Shamanism.* Pelican: London, 1971.
40. Linton, A., and Wagley, C. *Ralph Linton.* Columbia University Press: New York, 1971.
41. Long, J. "Medical Anthropology, Dance, and Trance in Jamaica." *UNESCO Bulletin of the International Committee on Urgent Anthropological and Ethnological Research,* 14 (1972).
42. Matthews, F. "An Account of an Outbreak of Religious Hallucinations in the Bahamas, West Indies, with a Brief Sketch of Some Phenomena Connected Therewith." *Journal of the Society for Psychical Research,* 2 (1886): 485–487.
43. Mead, M., ed. *Cooperation and Competition Among Primitive Peoples.* McGraw-Hill: New York, 1937.
44. Middleton, J. F., and Winter, E. H., eds. *Witchcraft and Sorcery in East Africa.* Routledge and Kegan Paul: London, 1963.
45. Nadel, S. F. "Witchcraft in Four African Societies: An Essay in Comparison." *American Anthropologist,* 54 (1952): 18–29.
46. Neher, A. "A Physiological Explanation of Unusual Behavior in Ceremonies Involving Drums." *Human Biology,* 34 (1962): 151–160.
47. Palmer, J. "Scoring in ESP Tests as a Function of Belief in ESP. Part I. The Sheep–Goat Effect." *Journal of the American Society for Psychical Research,* 65 (1971): 373–408.
48. Palmer, J. "Scoring in ESP Tests as a Function of Belief in ESP. Part II. Beyond the Sheep–Goat Effect." *Journal of the American Society for Psychical Research,* 66 (1972): 1–26.
49. Pobers, M. "Psychical Phenomena Among Primitive Peoples." In G. Wolstenholme and E. Miller, eds., *Ciba Foundation Symposium on Extrasensory Perception.* Little, Brown: Boston, 1956.
50. Pope, D. "ESP Tests with Primitive People." *Parapsychology Bulletin,* No. 30, (1953): 1–3.
51. Prince, R. "IFA: A West African Divination Technique." *International Journal of Parapsychology,* 9 (1967): 141–144.
52. Puharich, A. *Beyond Telepathy.* Doubleday: Garden City, N.Y. 1962.
53. Roll, W. G., and Klein, J. "Further Forced-Choice ESP Experiments with Lalsingh Harribance." *Journal of the American Society for Psychical Research,* 66 (1972): 103–112.
54. Rose, L., and Rose, R. "Psi Experiments with Australian Aborigines." *Journal of Parapsychology,* 15 (1951): 122–131.
55. Rose, R. "Experiments in ESP and PK with Aboriginal Subjects." *Journal of Parapsychology,* 16 (1952): 219–220.

56. Rose, R. "A Second Report on Psi Experiments with Australian Aborigines." *Journal of Parapsychology*, 19 (1955): 92–98.
57. Rose, R. *Living Magic: The Realities Underlying the Psychical Practices and Beliefs of Australian Aborigines.* Rand McNally: New York, 1956.
58. Sachs, W. *Black Hamlet.* Little, Brown: Boston, 1947.
59. St. Clair, D. *Drum and Candle.* Doubleday: New York, 1971.
60. Silverman, J. "Shamans and Acute Schizophrenia." *American Anthropologist,* 69 (1967): 21–31.
61. Stump, J. R.; Roll, W. G.; and Roll, M. "Some Exploratory Forced-Choice ESP Experiments with Lalsingh Harribance." *Journal of the American Society for Psychical Research,* 64 (1970): 421–431.
62. Trilles, H. *Fleurs Noires et Ames Blanches.* Lille: 1914.
63. Trilles, R. G. *Les Pygmées de la Forêt Equatoriale.* Paris: 1932.
64. Van de Castle, R. L. "Psi Abilities in Primitive Groups." *Proceedings of the Parapsychological Association,* 7 (1970): 97–122.
65. Wavell, S.; Butt, A.; and Epton, N. *Trances.* Allen and Unwin: London, 1966.
66. Whiting, J. W. M., and Child, I. L. *Child Training and Personality: A Cross-Cultural Study.* Yale University Press: New Haven, 1953.
67. Williams, J. *Psychic Phenomena of Jamaica.* Dial: New York, 1934.
68. Wilson, M. "Witch Beliefs and Social Structure." *American Journal of Sociology,* 56 (1951): 307–313.
69. Zorab, G. *Bibliography of Parapsychology.* Parapsychology Foundation: New York, 1957.

Marcel Vogel

MARCEL VOGEL *is a senior research chemist at the* IBM *Advanced Systems Development Division Laboratory in Los Gatos, California. He earned his bachelor's degree in chemistry at University of San Francisco in 1940, and then spent two years co-authoring a book,* Luminescence of Liquids and Solids *(Wiley Interscience, 1943). Until 1957 when he joined IBM, he was president and director of research of Vogel Luminescence Corporation.*

In addition to his book, Mr. Vogel is the author of nearly two dozen technical papers, mostly in the field of liquid crystals. He holds 30 patents, including the basic patent on the disc coating for the memory disc in digital computers.

Mr. Vogel can be reached at 819 Morse Street, San Jose, Calif. 95126.

12 Man–Plant Communication

MARCEL VOGEL

> *"As a man thinketh in his heart, so he is."*
> PROV. 23:17

SUMMARY

Modern research demonstrates that plants react to human thoughts and feelings. This chapter gives the first simple steps in showing that thoughts and emotions are energetic and that this energy can be measured by the biosystem of a plant coupled to a Wheatstone bridge amplifier.

Pioneering work on plant reactions was done by Charles Darwin, Sir Jagadis Chandra Bose, and Luther Burbank. A review of some of the work done by present-day experimenters, including Cleve Backster (discoverer of the phenomenon of primary perception in plants) and the author (whose work partly supports, but partly disagrees with, Backster) is given along with a description of the method of experimental procedures required to perform man–plant communication. The equipment, the type of plant, and the preparation of the individual to do this research is noted. Graphical results of thought and emotion in long-distance communication are given.

INTRODUCTION

no en 1906 Bose

The fact that plants are sensitive to the emotions and thoughts of people was discovered only in 1966 through the investigative work of Cleve Backster (3), especially the experiments he performed on plants and brine shrimp. Backster calls this phenomenon "primary perception" and says it is a still undefined sensory system or perception capability existing in cell life. The term is a synonym for "extrasensory perception," except in Backster's view there is nothing "extra" about it. Rather, this capability is basic or primary to the specialized senses of higher organisms. According to John White, writing in a recent issue of *Psychic* (38):

289

Backster reported his experimental results in the Winter 1968 issue of *International Journal of Parapsychology*. (That is his only published report to date.) Entitled "Evidence of a Primary Perception in Plant life," the report [brought him national] attention.

Backster's investigations began almost by chance on February 2, 1966, when he was doing some polygraph research in his New York City laboratory located near Times Square. After several hours, he felt he needed a break so he started watering a plant. When he finished, he idly wondered if he could use his testing equipment to measure the rate at which water rose from the root area into the leaves.

A polygraph measures three functions in humans: changes in breathing, changes in blood pressure and pulse activity, and changes in the skin's electrical properties. This last measurement is known as galvanic skin response (GSR) or psychogalvanic reflex (PGR) and is Backster's area of greatest expertise. Backster felt he might be able to get a PGR reading on the polygraph. So he placed an electrode on either side of a leaf of a nearby philodendron potted plant and held them in place with a rubber band. The results were indicated on the polygraph's moving paper by an ink pen which swung side to side in accordance with changes in the electrical potential measured by the polygraph.

As far as indications of moisture ascent in the plant, nothing meaningful happened. But after approximately one minute an unusual tracing appeared—a contour, Backster reported, "similar to a reaction pattern of a human subject experiencing an emotional stimulation of short duration."

Backster had never seen this before and it intrigued him. What could explain the similarity of a tracing from the plant and what he knew was a well-verified pattern of emotional arousal in humans? Earlier this year he said to me, "I still don't have any idea of what caused the initial reaction. I wasn't thinking of causing anything to happen or of harming the plant."

But it had happened and he wanted to know why. He decided that the "threat to well-being" principle, which is a clearly-recognized means for triggering emotionality in humans, might be successful in triggering a response from the plant. So he immersed a leaf in a cup of hot coffee and waited. The tracing remained steady. Nothing happened.

Then, Backster wrote in his published report, "After an approximately nine-minute interim, the author determined to make a more direct attempt by threatening the cell tissue being tested, i.e., the leaf between the electrodes. He decided to obtain a match to actually burn the plant being tested. At the instant of this decision, at thirteen minutes fifty-five seconds of chart time, there was dramatic change in the tracing pattern in the form of an abrupt and prolonged upward sweep of the recording pen. Because of his relative lack of body movement at that moment, and also his absence of physical contact with the plant and with the instrumentation, the precise timing of the pen activity suggested to the author that the tracing might have been triggered into such action by the mere thought of the harm he intended to inflict upon the plant—in fact, upon the very leaf between the electrodes. The author theorized that this occurrence, if repeatable, would tend to indicate the existence of a perception capability in plant life. . . ."

Months of testing followed this discovery. To remove the possibility of human error or unconscious interference, Backster and a [Backster Research] Foundation associate, Robert E. Henson, conducted a series of experimental runs using live brine shrimp and automated equipment. The instruments were programmed to kill the shrimp on a random basis by dumping them into boiling water. Three philodendron plants, each located in separate rooms, were wired to polygraphs. No one was present on the laboratory premises. Then, with no one able to know when the shrimp were actually dumped, the program was started by a time delay switch. Everything from the instruments was recorded automatically, and two sessions totaling seven runs were made. The result: five to seven seconds after the dumping of the shrimp the instruments registered a large burst of plant activity which, Backster says, because of the experiment's design can only have come from the shrimp. The statistics of the matter—five times greater than chance—led him to wonder: "Could it be that when cell life dies, it broadcasts a signal to other living cells?"

Since then, Backster has expanded his exploration to include fresh fruit, vegetables, mold cultures, yeasts, and forms of animal cell life (including scrapings from the roof of a human mouth, blood samples, paramecia, amoebae, and even spermatozoa). All observations supported his hypothesis of an undefined primary perception capability. The phenomenon, then, would appear to include a broad range of organisms low in the evolutionary scale, regardless of their assigned biological function. It may be, Backster hypothesizes, that an unknown kind of communication signal links all living things.

The nature of the communications channel linking cells is mysterious. "We know it is not within the different known frequencies AM, FM, or any form of signal which we can shield by ordinary means," he says, "and distance doesn't seem to impose any limitation. I've tried shielding the plants with a Faraday screen cage (which prevents electrical penetration), even lead-lined containers. It seems that the signal may not fall within any known portion of our electrodynamic spectrum." Although, he points out, somewhere in the process the signal is converted to electrical current measurable by a polygraph.

It also seems plants have an ability to discriminate signals and selectively monitor them. In his lab, Backster has been surprised to find a plant providing a tracing that matches in frequency the heart-beat of someone present in the room. For reasons unknown, the plant tuned in to that person's heartbeat alone, among all those present. This tuning-in ability is another property of the phenomenon Backster has discovered. Plants are especially attuned to their caretakers. Good thoughts and a happy mood seem to be major factors in "green thumb" gardeners. But anxiety, depression or—worst of all—hatred can almost guarantee a poor growth, especially if directed at the plants. Except for weeds, Backster jokes. They just don't seem to listen.

White further notes that Dr. Aristide H. Esser, a psychiatrist and head of the research laboratory at Rockland State Hospital in Orangeburg, New York, and Douglas Dean of Newark College of Engineering were among the first to replicate portions of Backster's work. They reported on it in *Medical World News* (17) in 1969.

The sensitivity of plants and their response to external stimuli was first investigated by Charles Darwin (12) using insectivorous plants. In his investigation of the Venus flytrap (*Dionaea muscepela*), he found that the hairy filaments responsible for triggering the leaves were insensitive to water falling on them but that a solid object of the same weight would cause a reaction, closing the leaves. Darwin found that if the material had no food value, the leaf would open shortly and be ready again. Inorganic bodies—bits of stone, glass, wood, cork—if dry could be left on the lobes and no movement was excited. But if the body was moist, leaf movement was obtained. Darwin found that both weight and moisture had to be present for the leaf to respond. A leaf exposed to sulfuric ether became insensitive in less than 3 minutes and recovered its sensitivity in 52 minutes. Experimentation also showed that the plant exhibited fatigue due to stimulation, and a period of time was required for the plant to recover.

Even more surprising, Darwin found that plants could be "domesticated" in a manner similar to cats and dogs that have been adapted to the environment of man. In his study of the power of movement in plants, Darwin (12) came to the conclusion that the root tip of a plant has the power of directing movements of the adjoining parts. The root tip, he believed, acts like the brain of a lower animal. He did not, however, believe that a plant has a nervous system, even though much of his work with insectivorous plants and plant movement implied such.

That a plant does have a nervous system was shown in the early 1900s by the Indian scientist Sir Jagadis Chandra Bose (4–9). Bose found that in the life reaction of a plant, there is a foreshadowing of many of the reactions of man and animals. In his many years of careful experimentation in India, Bose showed that plants have a nervous system capable of being stimulated by electric fields. In fact, he showed that *Mimosa pudica* can be excited by an electric shock one-tenth the intensity of that which evokes human sensation (5). Heat and cold change the rate of conduction of the impulse.

Bose temporarily arrested the conducting power in a plant by passage of an electric current in a portion of a nerve through which the impulse is being transmitted. This block is removed on stoppage of the current. In *Mimosa pudica,* Bose showed that a rise of temperature of 9° C nearly doubled the velocity of transmission of the signal (6). Potassium cyanide solution permanently blocked the conducting power in mimosa.

Bose's experimental design was to apply an electric shock to the plant and then plot the response of the plant to the shock and its recovery from the shock. Special apparatus was devised by him to plot these changes.

Bose was also able to show that the use of morphine and alcohol produced a depressant effect (8). Minute dosages of strychnine (1 part in 1000) acted as a stimulant to the plant, increasing the sap pressure. A 1% solution caused marked depressions and drooping of the plant.

From his lifetime study of plant responses to stimuli, Bose concluded that plants show many bioelectrical and physiological responses parallel to animals and humans (8).

Bose did not publish on man–plant communication. However, Luther Burbank in the 1920s showed that by a directed thought process he could modify and fit a plant into the pattern that was in his mind (10). His development of the spineless cactus was just such a modification, because he used only "love" on the original spiny ancestors to get them to breed out their sharp projections.

I tested Burbank's concept in a somewhat different fashion, using leaves removed from a saxifragia plant. I held one of the leaves in my hand for two minutes and willed it to continue living. I placed it on an 8-by-11-inch piece of white paper with a companion leaf beside it and observed both of them daily, but had no further physical contact with the leaves. At the end of one month the leaf I focused on was vital and green but the control leaf had started to turn brown. At the end of two months the control leaf was completely dehydrated and brownish black. The other leaf was still green. This experiment was repeated four times with successful results each time. My conclusion is that a directed thought has an energetic dimension that can somehow be stored by the leaf.

Baron Karl von Reichenbach (36) in his study of human sensitives and their response to fields emanating from crystals (gypsum and spar) noted that the sensitives had a feeling of an emanation coming from the crystal. In 1844, with the crystal in complete darkness, one sensitive, Angelica Sturmann, reported that the whole crystal was glowing throughout with a fine light, while a light about five inches long was streaming out of its peak in constant motion and occasionally emitting sparks. Von Reichenbach's sensitives made thousands of observations this way. A dark adaptation of at least two hours is required to observe these effects, he reported.

According to von Reichenbach, these emanations were not heat, although they are sensations similar to those of lukewarm and coolness. Nor were they electricity, since there was no excitation present to account for the eternally flowing stream. An electroscope was not affected. It was not magnetism (the crystals were not magnetic). It could not be light because there was no obvious external excitation source.

It was the opinion of von Reichenbach that the emanation fitted between electromagnetism and heat. He gave the name "od" or "odic force" to this phenomenon: "Od is a cosmic force that radiates from star to star and has the whole universe for its field, just like light and heat" (36). Our subsequent better understanding of both electromagnetic propagation in terms of Maxwell's equations and radiant energy in terms of the Stephen –Boltzman law has not been sufficient to explain von Reichenbach's observations.

Two glasses of water were placed in light, one in blue light and the other in orange light. When von Reichenbach gave these glasses to sensitives to taste, they noted that the water in the blue light was pleasant to taste but that the one in the orange light was nauseating—rather bitter and crude. A glass of water left in moonlight had a taste different from a similar glass kept in the shade. Von Reichenbach states that moonlight is an od-distributive force of great importance.

Plants also seem to show similar responses and emanations that do not behave in accordance with known light phenomena. When von Reichenbach worked with Professor Eric Licher, a botanist, Licher was able to see a *Gloxinia speciosa* in complete darkness, to recognize both its shape and color. The colyx, pistils, stamen, corolla, and stem showed a fine light. Even the leaves could be seen. This account is not particularly startling except that, again, the radiation does not seem explicable by known laws.

It is said that the flowering plant reveals in miniature, ever anew throughout the cycle of the year, the archetypal cosmic relationship of earth and sun in the root–shoot polarity that permeates the development of the whole plant. The relationship of earth and sun is a polarity in this sense. Rudolf Steiner said, "The same forces prevail in the movements of the planets as in the ordering of the leaves up the growing stem" (1).

One may hypothesize, as some esoteric traditions maintain, that living organisms—plant, animal, and man—are permeated by what may be called a "life body," which takes hold of the physical body formatively, receiving it into its sphere. It is the "etheric," or "ethereal," sphere that is the source of the forces with which the life body is imbued. This organism of formative forces is also called the "etheric body" or "ethereal body."

According to Gunther Wachsmuth (37), the ethereal forces have a quite different spatial orientation from the forces of the lifeless world (gravity, magnetism, etc.). The physical–mechanical forces are of their very nature centric. They are linked with matter and work from centers outward into space. Ethereal forces from without work inward, toward the relative center. This center is *not* their source. It is the place toward which they tend—that is, the organism with which they are concerned. Their source is not a centric but a peripheral one. It is to be found in the infinitudes of the universe. Centric forces are connected with earth (gravity); the etheric forces are connected to the universe around the earth. In living, one can become aware of the being that wrests itself from the merely physical and from the universal cosmic spaces becomes the bearer of what works down upon the earth.

Perhaps Wachsmuth's metaphysical concept becomes more understandable when Erwin Schrödinger, in *What Is Life?* (33) speaks of a living organism sucking orderliness from its environment: negative entropy. Plants have their most powerful supply of "negative entropy" in the sunlight. Everything that goes on in nature means an increase of entropy in the part of the world where it is occurring. A living organism continually increases its entropy and thus tends to approach the dangerous state of maximum entropy, which is death. Each organism can keep alive only by continually drawing from its environment negative entropy. What an organism feeds upon is negative entropy. Thus, Schrödinger is suggesting the abstract concept of entropy almost as a real "force."

The odic force—an ethereal force—can be looked on as negative entropy. We do *not* know what this force is, but it appears to be the force used in the experimentation with man and plant that will be reported below.

RESEARCH BY MODERN INVESTIGATORS

John C. Pierrakos, a medical doctor in New York City, claims to have developed his ability to see the energy field of plants (30). He says they have a radiant luminous field which pulsates rhythmically from 10 to 30 times a minute. He finds in general that there are two layers of interaction around the plant surface. The inner layer immediately surrounding the leaves and branches ($\frac{2}{16}$–$\frac{1}{8}$ inch wide) has a light blue or grayish color;

the outer layer is lighter, extending ½–1 inch with varied multicolor radial movements. From time to time, fireball emanations take place from the leaves. Pierrakos reports that leaves pulsate at different rates, depending on direction. Leaves pointing south pulsate 28 times a minute; north, 32 times a minute; west and east, 28 times a minute. This work was first noted by George and Marjorie De La Warr (14, 15). Pierrakos found that the energy field pulsates for approximately 2–4 seconds. Then there is a reversal of movement and the energy of the surrounding air streams into the plant.

In his practice as a physician, Pierrakos had a visit from a woman patient who was in a disturbed and distressed state. On his desk was a white chrysanthemum plant, which he had observed to pulsate at a rate of 14–16 times a minute. When she sat by his plant, the pulsations practically vanished, dropping to 2–3 times a minute. The brilliant field around the plant disappeared, leaving a slight gray emanation. Repeated observation showed him that plants were very responsive to the emotions of the patients at whose bedside he placed the plant.

The Reverend Franklin Loehr, in his book *The Power of Prayer on Plants* (27), tells of planting two beds of flower seeds. The conditions were identical in all respects and the plantings were cared for identically, except for one thing: one of the plantings was prayed over for a few minutes every day. The flowers that were prayed over grew faster and taller and seemed healthier.

An industrial research scientist and professor of engineering, Robert N. Miller, performed a similar experiment using instrumentation for measuring plant growth accurately (29). During a five-minute period, he reported, a blade of rye grass increased its growth 840% over the growth rate of the preceding day. The only variable during the five-minute period was that two psychic healers—the late Ambrose Worrall and his wife, Olga—"held a seedling in their thoughts" during a prayer session. Although there has been controversy surrounding Miller's results, the concept is replicable.

Dr. Jean Barry has observed the variations in mushroom growth that took place when the spores were focused on by a human. Some of the plants were retarded in their growth, apparently just by the thoughts of one person; other spores were amplified in their growth pattern, again apparently through the effect of human mental processes.

L. George Lawrence, working with a unique arrangement involving a plant coupled to a telescope, claims to have received signals from distant planets using the plant as a bioenergetic transducer (26). It is difficult to understand such results, however, until the properties of the bioenergy are more completely defined.

V. M. Pushkin, a Moscow scientist, states in his article "Flower Recall" (32) that a psyche seems to exist in living cells devoid of a nervous system. Working with V. M. Fetisov, they electroded the leaves of a garden variety geranium plant to an electroencephalograph. Another member of the group, Georgi Arrqushev, a student in psychology at the Lenin Pedagogical Institute in Moscow, was an excellent hypnotist. They had reasoned that a hypnotized person would be able to act on a plant more directly and spontaneously. The reasoning was based on the premise that if a plant is generally able to react to a person's psychological states, then it probably would respond well to strong emotional disturbances such as fear, happiness, and grief.

A good hypnotist is able to awaken in his subject the most varied strong experiences at will and on command. He is able to "plug into" a person's emotional sphere. A student, Tanya, who was of a lively temperament and emotionally spontaneous, was chosen as a subject. The geranium was electroded and placed 80 centimeters from the subject.

After being hypnotized it was suggested to her that:

1. She was very pretty. (A strong shift in the base line was registered in the plant with the visible response of the subject.)
2. She was in a sudden cold wind. (There was a physical response in the subject of shivering, and there was response again with a shift from base line.)
3. She should remain calm. (Peace and quiet were apparent in subject, and the base line remained steady.)
4. She was again in a cold wind. (There were responses similar to 2.)
5. A child approached her on a sunny day. (Plant response was similar to 1. The subject calmed down and smiled.)

These responses were repeated many times. During my visit with Pushkin in July 1973, I had the opportunity of seeing the graphs. The deviations from the base line were significant and the results are real.

Pushkin's conclusion is that our thoughts and memory all are only a specialization of the informational basis that has a place at the level of the vegetal cell. He feels that any information has a material form of existence and that delicate biophysical processes are carried out in the molecules with the cell. These processes lead to physical encoding of psychological events.

Elsewhere in the Soviet Union, cell–cell communication was recently demonstrated in a way that suggests disease is transmitted between cells by photons. Colonies of identical healthy cells were placed in petri dishes, each with one wall made either of quartz or normal glass. The cells of another colony were then infected with a virus, chemically poisoned, or toxically irradiated. Normal glass passes light throughout the spectrum except for ultraviolet (UV), while quartz passes the entire spectrum. Disease symptoms appeared in a healthy colony soon after it was placed near an affected colony if the dishes were separated by a wall of quartz glass but not if regular glass separated them. Since no chemical or biological agents could penetrate the barrier, the conclusion, according to *Science Digest*, was that "the sick cells were transmitting disease-bearing or -inducing information to the healthy side. Since this 'information' passed only through quartz glass, and quartz glass passes only ultraviolet rays, it was further concluded that the disease was somehow coded into the UV photon emission of the cells. Another conclusion: not only do cells *emit* photons, but they also can perceive and be influenced by them" (2). This report only takes into account the effect of photons. But if there is a bioenergy involved that is not of the electromagnetic spectrum, as other evidence suggests, then these results, although important, are not complete nor definitive.

Here in the United States, Cleve Backster has extended his research into primary perception down to the single-cell level. His experimental design, still unreported except for a film interview granted at the request of Edgar Mitchell,* involves yogurt bacteria (which are single-celled plants). The experiment is fully automated with humans completely removed from the microenvironment. Milk is fed into a vial containing yogurt and within a few seconds the bacteria begin to digest it. Another container of yogurt, some feet away from the first container and completely shielded by metal, is hooked up to an electroencephalograph. At the moment the first container's yogurt bacteria begin to act chemically on the milk, the EEG signal from the second container shows a significant deviation from base line. This demonstrates, Backster feels, that cells have a capability to communicate independently of the nervous system. This cellular communication capacity may be part of the process by which a body develops immunological mechanisms and immune states.

Perhaps the most incredible experiment in man–plant communication is taking place at Findhorn, a community of some 150 people living on the shore of the North Sea in Scotland. The Findhorn community claims to invoke the aid of *devas*, a Sanskrit term for angelic beings that control the elemental nature spirits responsible for the growth of plants. Moreover, following ancient Celtic tradition, the community leaves a "wild spot"— an untouched portion of the garden land—for the fairies and elves as a token of recognition and gratitude for their help. Last of all, the community meditates and talks to the plants themselves, praising their beauty and expressing love and thanks. Everything is based on a philosophy that

* Backster demonstrates this work in a film entitled *The Ultimate Mystery*, narrated by Edgar Mitchell. For information about the film, write to Hartley Productions, Cat Rock Road, Cos Cob, Conn. 06807. *Editor.*

views plants, soil, and natural forces (sun, rain, wind) as part of the community of life.

Whatever the cause of their success, the Findhorn community nevertheless has performed what might be termed a miracle in agriculture. According to Peter Tompkins and Christopher Bird (34, 35) and to the community itself (18), the barren, sandy soil at Findhorn should support practically nothing, yet there are dozens of vegetables, flowers, and trees growing in unexcelled size and beauty—many of them in a climate far less temperate than normal for them. There are, for example, reports of 30- and 40-pound cabbages. The British Soil Association has investigated Findhorn's agricultural methods and come away quite unable to explain in conventional terms how such results have been achieved.

EXPERIMENTATION BY THE AUTHOR

I began my experimentation with man—plant communication in 1969 after reading about Cleve Backster's work. Since then I have confirmed all of the effects he has reported, but I have another interpretation of the *cause* of those effects. Backster postulates the phenomenon called primary perception and believes it is an ever-present signal linkage between cellular plant life, whether or not humans are present. My own view is that human beings are the causative agency in man—plant communication by sensitizing, or "charging," the plant to be receptive of thoughts and emotions.

To establish any link between man and plant, an initial charge of thought—energy must be released to the plant by the person doing the experiment. This charging by the experimenter produces an isolation of the plant from secondary influences—that is, light, temperature, and electrical charges in the room. Charging a plant can be accomplished either in the same room or at remote locations thousands of miles away.

While the plant is being charged, the experimenter must quiet his conscious mind and body functions and work in a state as free from emotional disturbance as possible. The higher level of emotional control, the more precise the experimental results become. The experimenter may then focus his mind to get a response to (*a*) the act of damaging another plant, (*b*) the destruction of another life form, and (*c*) the release of a thought form of love and other emotions, healing, symbols, and visual imagery.

Instrumentation

The equipment used in making the following recordings is very simple. It was built from diagrams in two articles that appeared in *Popular Electronics* (16, 25). The wiring allows both a recording on a strip chart and an audible signal suitable for recording on a portable tape recorder or listening with a small speaker.

For electroding the plant, stainless-steel electrodes $1'' \times 1\frac{1}{2}''$ with rounded corners are recommended. Prior work with aluminum electrodes showed that there is continual electrical activity, which eliminates any practical consideration of their use. With stainless steel the electrode system remains stable for days and the electrodes can be left on for a week with no harmful effect on the plant leaf. Silver–silver chloride electrodes are very good provided the delicate silver chloride surface is not damaged; otherwise, severe burning and damage to the leaf takes place.

To attach the electrodes, it is recommended that a paste of agar with 1% sodium chloride be rubbed on the contact surface of the electrode. Clamping the electrodes is not recommended, although many people have used this means of support, either with tiny vises or rubber bands. A practical arrangement is shown in Figure 1.

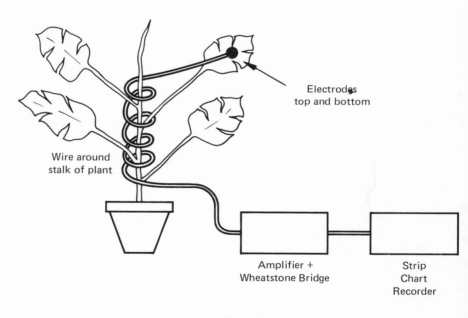

Electrodes top and bottom

Wire around stalk of plant

Amplifier + Wheatstone Bridge

Strip Chart Recorder

Figure 1

Choice of Plants and Position

The most practical plants to work with are green broad-leaved house plants. The best seem to be split-leaf philodendron, ivy philodendron, and dieffenbachia. The plant should be placed in the experimental environment for at least one week to adapt it to conditions where the research is to take place.

I have experimented for four years with various types of people—psychics and scientists, adults of mature personality and younger people still dealing with the emotional problems of being teenagers. From this work I found that the positioning of the experimenter and the subject in relation to the plant plays a part in getting the best results. Figure 2 shows the basic position still in use for my present tests.

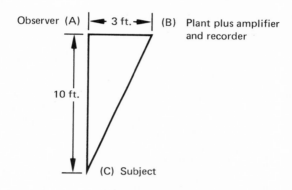

Figure 2

Preparation Necessary for the Researcher

My first attempts in man—plant experimentation were carried out along conventional lines of research and led to many problems. I found it difficult to repeat experiments. The many variables—atmospheric pressure, temperature, fatigue, intrusion of critical personalities—were found to be far more important factors than I had anticipated. In studying my data, I concluded that *there is a precise and important interaction between the researcher and the plant that is equal in importance to the equipment being used.* Once I understood and accepted this principle and incorporated it into my experimental method, repeatability was no longer a problem. The plant no longer responded to large amounts of light, heat, or external static fields—just to my thoughts and emotions.

In both the instrumentation and individual researcher, the first step is to arrive at a condition of holding a steady base line on the polygraph (or strip-chart recorder) during the course of experimentation. If deviation from the base line is present, the cause of the deviation must be determined. There are three primary responses from the bioenergetic activity of the plant: (*a*) bioenergetic responses in the plant itself due to cellular activity, (*b*) bioenergetic responses of the plant to its environment, and (*c*) bioenergetic balancing of the plant to the energetic fields of man.

Effects from the first factor will always be present, but effects from the second can be minimized through adaption to the experiment location. Thus, a stable base line can be achieved from which to discriminate signals from other causes and then proceed to identify their source.

The experimenter is a critical part of the experiment; it may be that this hitherto unaccepted component of man–plant research was the unpredictable variable that has made scientific research so difficult in the area of man–plant communication. Therefore, the research personnel—both experimenter and subject—must prepare themselves by establishing a sense of peace and relaxation. For some, listening to music may be appropriate. Others may use meditation or breathing exercises. If a person is especially tense at the beginning and finds it difficult to relax, bathing the face and hands in cool water helps to quiet the restless mind. It is also good to avoid eating for about two hours before the experiment. Finally, a sense of relaxation and cooperative participation can be gained by quiet, friendly conversation between the experimenter and the subject so that a mutual feeling of confidence and a willingness to share in the experiment will be built up.

The experimenter must be receptive enough to follow where the experiment leads. The object is to obtain a record of the emotional and mental processes of the subject. If a plan is in the mind of the experimenter, an imprint is obtained (or reflected) in the subject, thus distorting the experiment. When a thought is formed, energy is released into space, and it is this energy that we wish to transcribe and record. The experimenter's mind acts as a neutral carrier wave for both the subject and the plant. The field generated in this manner excludes all secondary interferences from either the subject or environmental (external) forces and produces very clean, simple transitions.

There should be no discussion of what the experimenter wishes to achieve with the subject. Just ask the subject to sit in any position that is comfortable to him and suggest that he feel at home with the plant. Do not have the room too brightly illuminated or allow any top or front lighting to face the subject. This lighting causes distraction and fatigue. Soft lighting should be at the side or in back of the subject. The temperature of the room should be between 65° and 70° F.

The key thought here is that when one starts, a solid base line is noted in the recorder that can be held for one minute.

Charging the Plant

Prior to experimentation and after electroding the leaf, an interplay is made by the experimenter with the plant. The experimenter should touch the leaves and watch the graphical display, noting how the plant responds to physical touch. At this time the subject is also asked to observe and touch the plant. Both experimenter and subject may have their interest become more focused by observing the rapid response to physical contact between man and plant. (With an insulated rod no such response is noted.) *

After touching the plant, the experimenter holds his left hand two or three inches from the leaf and "feels" the energy field emanating from the leaf. As this takes place, the experimenter makes a slight circular motion with his left hand, first in one direction and then in the other. Then the experimenter moves his hand in an up-and-down motion, changing his rate of breathing until he feels a strong drawing sensation between his hand and the leaf. When this takes place, the experimenter moves back two or three feet, keeping his left hand extended and serving as an antenna, thus releasing energy into the plant. There will be a strong shifting of the base line, and at this stage, the Wheatstone bridge is balanced against the shift. With a freshly electroded system using an agar paste between electrodes, this balancing process should not require more than 10–15 minutes to become established. As the deflections become weaker, mentally command the shift to "Reverse sign." When this takes place, the plant is charged and ready for the start of the experimentation.

The output from the recorder determines where the placement of the base line will be made. When the experimenter locks into the plant, there is a strong sense of peaceful awareness, devoid of stress, and a complete conviction that one is "one with the plant." The awareness seems to be a state of "knowing" rather than a sense of seeing or feeling (22).

When to Start Experimenting

Experimentation starts when a steady base line is obtained for at least one minute. Then a series of questions are asked, dealing with such topics as the person's name, vocation, feelings about one's job, feelings about a person close to the subject, aspirations in life, and sex.

From the response noted, start focusing the questions on bringing out a thought form from the individual. Five to 10 minutes is a sufficient time for any experimentation with one person. Beyond that, one's mind wanders. Exceptional people may be worked with for longer—up to an hour.

Effect of Negative Thoughts

A strong negative thought will completely stop the experimenter and the effect persists for many hours—even days. Negative thoughts are com-

* The possibility of this being due to static electricity should not be overlooked. *Editor.*

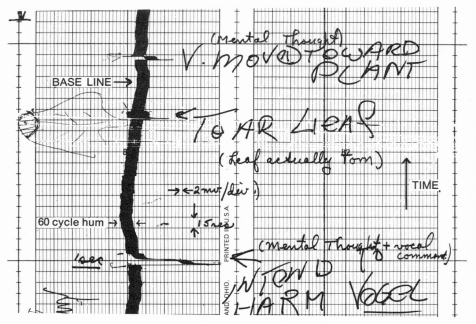

Figure 3.

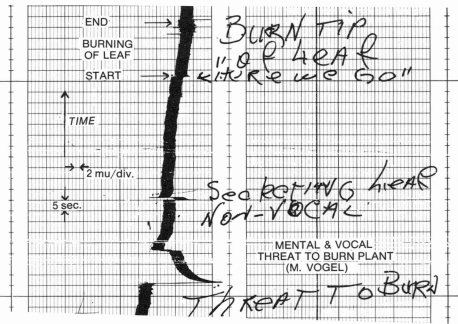

Figure 4.

plete rejection of the experimentation being done. A question then immediately sets up a defense process in the individual.

EXPERIMENTAL RESULTS

Threats to a Plant and to People

Figures 3 and 4 show the results obtained with a split-leaf philodendron
when threats to burn and harm the plant were made. In the case of Figure
3, the threat was made mentally, without words.

In another experiment a group of 13 students were used for interactive
experimentation with a plant. For more than an hour no significant results
were noted. Then one of the students asked, "What about sex?" In Figure
5 the results are shown. There was an abrupt response to the stimulus, and
it persisted throughout the evening. At this time a random signal superimposed on the 60-cycle hum appeared and built up until a constant signal
was obtained.

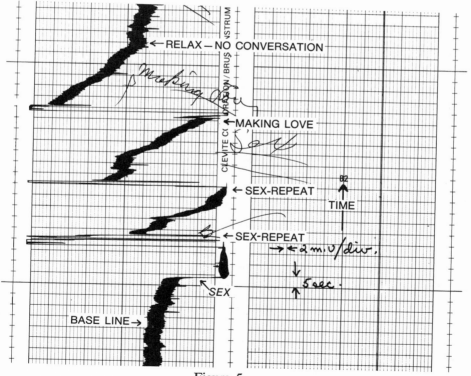

Figure 5.

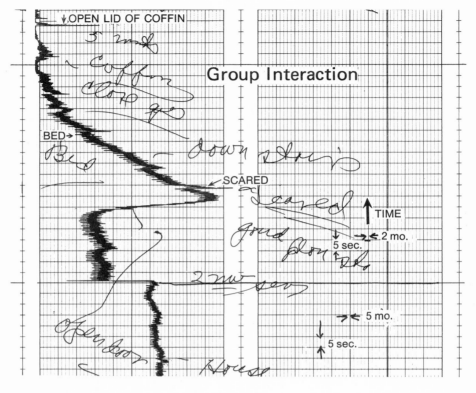

Figure 6.

In Figure 6 the group response was made to a story being told by one of the group. In the story, someone went into a forest and saw a house. Upon opening the door of the house, he saw a man with a knife. The group was scared, and the response marked "fear" in Figure 6 shows how the plant received their feeling.

Figure 7 shows response to a threat made mentally with no verbal communication. In this case the person making the threat was seated on a couch 15 feet from the plant and I was 3 feet from the plant. Two very unusual things happened. First, the subject spoke aloud a threat three times (at point 1) and, second, a mental threat was made, at which time I was pushed from the recorder to the wall with a strong feeling of pain in my solar plexus region (at point 2).

Figure 8 was made while my wife and son were picking daisies on our front lawn. I had electroded a philodendron and started the equipment half an hour before the experiment began, with no deviation from the base line during that time. Then I signaled them to begin picking daisies, and a

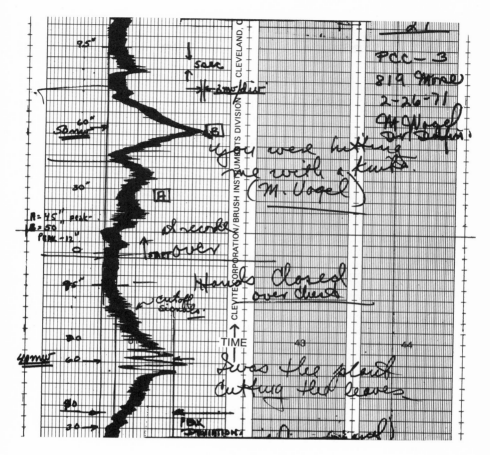

Figure 7.

marked deviation from base line occurred. This continued unabated for 25 minutes until I signaled them to stop, at which time the deviation abruptly stopped. I think this indicates that the *intention* of the experimenter is signaled to the plant.

Long-Distance Communication Utilizing a Plant

This experiment was done on June 19–20, 1973, by Dr. Ward Lamb of San Jose, California, and me. I was in Prague, Czechoslovakia; Lamb was in San Jose. Before doing this experiment, months of preliminary trials in San Jose had showed that we could communicate on a mind-to-mind basis and signals could be recorded over a distance of 12 miles. This

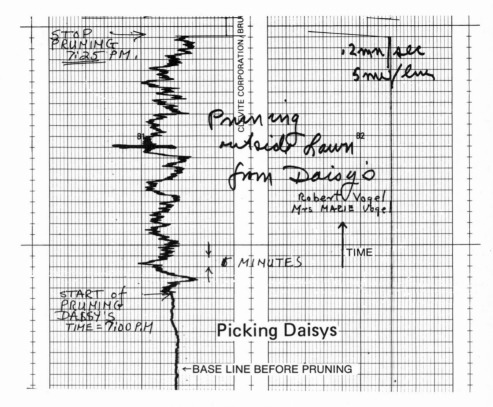

Figure 8.

was done and by focusing on the heart chakra* and willing the release of a strong pulse of energy. I have found that this can be done two or three times but not more. I must then relax for at least 15 minutes before trying again. The results are shown in Figures 9 and 10. The method of sending was to (a) agree on a time in San Jose (6:00 P.M.), (b) agree on two dates (June 19 and 20), and (c) agree on a period of not more than 15 minutes.

On June 19, I relaxed and projected three bursts of energy to Lamb. This was at 2:00 A.M. (Prague time). I then went to sleep. The next night, fatigued from the pressure of the meeting on psychotronics and parapsychology being held there, I fell asleep without sending any energetic pulses. This was not known to Lamb, of course.

There are three significant shifts in the base line on June 19 that are not present on June 20. This demonstrates long-distance communication uti-

* See glossary. Editor.

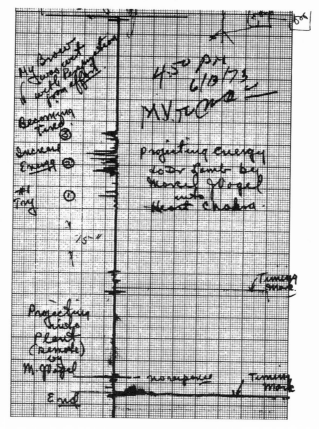

Figure 9.

lizing biological sensors as detectors and opens up real opportunities for new research.

CONCLUSIONS

In this article I have shown that the use of biological sensors coupled with a Wheatstone bridge and amplifier can act as a detector of signals produced by humans through thought and emotion and that these signals can be detected either in proximity or at a distance. The necessary conditions for doing these experiments have been given. These experiments must now be replicated by others. The most important variable found so far has been the experimenter himself and the training he must undergo for this type of work.

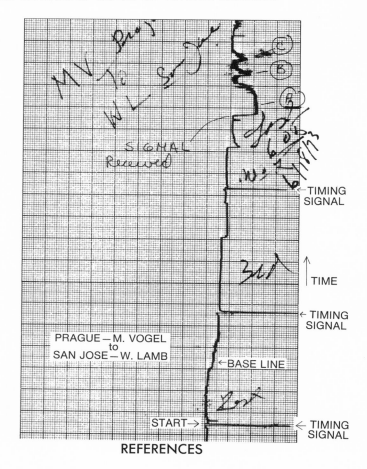

REFERENCES

1. Adams, George, and Wicher, Olive. *Plant, Sun and Earth.* Verlag Freis Geisteleben, 1952.
2. Agnew, Irene. "Disease Transmission by Light." *Science Digest*, March 1973.
3. Backster, Cleve. "Evidence of a Primary Perception in Plant Life." *International Journal of Parapsychology*, 10:6, Winter 1968.
4. Bose, Jagadis Chandra. *Response in the Living and Non-Living.* Longmans: London, 1902.
5. Bose, Jagadis Chandra. *Plant Responses as a Means of Physiological Investigation.* Longmans: London, 1906.
6. Bose, Jagadis Chandra. *The Nervous Mechanism of Plants.* Longmans: London, 1918.
7. Bose, Jagadis Chandra. *Life Movements in Plants*, Vols. I–V. Longmans: London, 1918.
8. Bose, Jagadis Chandra: *Plant Autographs and Their Revelation.* Longmans: London, 1927.

9. Bose, Jagadis Chandra. *Life Movements in Plants*, Vol. VI. Longmans: London, 1931.
10. Burbank, Luther. *His Methods and Discoveries: Their Practical Application*. Luther Burbank Press, 1914.
11. Burr, Harold S. *Blueprint for Immortality*. Spearman: London, 1972.
12. Darwin, Charles. *The Power of Movement in Plants*. Murray: London, 1880.
13. Darwin, Charles. *Animals and Plants Under Domestication*, Vols. I–II. Murray: London, 1882.
14. Day, Langston. *New Worlds Beyond the Atom*. Stuart: London, 1956.
15. Day, Langston. *Matter in the Making*. Stuart: London, 1966.
16. Devine, R. E. "Build a Psyche-Analyzer." *Popular Electronics*, February 1969.
17. "ESP: More Science, Less Mysticism." *Medical World News*, 21 March 1969.
18. *Findhorn Garden, The*. Findhorn Trust: Forres, Moray, Scotland, n.d.
19. Grad, Bernard; Cadoret, R. J.; and Paul, G. I. "A Telekinetic Effect on Plant Growth." *International Journal of Parapsychology*, 59 (1963).
20. Grad, Bernard. "A Telekinetic Effect on Plant Growth." *International Journal of Parapsychology*, 6 (1964).
21. Grad, Bernard. "Some Biological Effects of the 'Laying on of Hands' (A Review of Experiments with Animals and Plants)." *Journal of the American Society of Psychical Research*, 59 (1965).
22. Joachim, Leland. "Plants—The Key to Mental Telepathy?" *Probe the Unknown*, December 1972.
23. Lawrence, L. George. "More Experiments in Electroculture." *Popular Electronics*, June 1971.
24. Lawrence, L. George. "Do Plants Feel Emotion?" *Electro-Technology*, April 1969.
25. Lawrence, L. George. "Electronics and the Living Plant." *Popular Electronics*, October 1969.
26. Lawrence, L. George. "Interstellar Communications Signals." *Information Bulletin #72-6*. Ecola Institute: San Bernadino, Calif., 1972. (See also Goodavage, Joseph. "Contact with Extraterrestrial Life." *Saga*, January 1973.)
27. Loehr, Franklin. *The Power of Prayer on Plants*. Signet: New York, 1959.
28. Meyer, Warren. "Man–Plant Communication." *Unity*, January 1973.
29. Miller, R. N. "The Positive Effect of Prayer on Plants." *Psychic*, March–April 1972.
30. Pierrakos, John C. *The Energy Field in Man and Nature*. Institute of Bioenergetic Analysis: New York, n.d.
31. Presman, A. S. *Electromagnetic Fields and Life*. Plenum: New York, 1970.
32. Pushkin, V. N. "Flower Recall." *Knowledge Is Power* (Moscow), November 1972.
33. Schrödinger, Erwin. *What Is Life?* Cambridge University Press: Cambridge, 1967.
34. Tompkins, Peter, and Bird, Christopher. "Love Among the Cabbages." *Harper's*, November 1972.
35. Tompkins, Peter, and Bird, Christopher. *The Secret Life of Plants*. Harper and Row: New York, 1973.
36. von Reichenbach, Karl. *The Odic Force*. University: New York, 1968.

37. Wachsmuth, Gunther. *The Etheric Formative Forces in the Cosmos, Earth and Man*. Anthroposophical Press: New York, 1932.
38. White, John. "Plants, Polygraphs and Paraphysics." *Psychic*, December 1972; repr. in John White, ed., *Frontiers of Consciousness*. Julian: New York, 1974.

Jule Eisenbud

JULE EISENBUD, M.D., is an associate clinical professor of psychiatry at the University of Colorado Medical School, where he has taught since 1950. He also privately practices psychiatry and psychoanalysis. From 1938 to 1950 he was an associate in psychiatry at Columbia College of Physicians and Surgeons in New York. He has written and lectured widely on psychiatry, psychoanalysis, psychology, and parapsychology.

Dr. Eisenbud was educated at Columbia University, Columbia College, and Columbia College of Physicians and Surgeons, where he received both doctor of medicine and doctor of medical science degrees.

His publications include The World of Ted Serios (William Morrow, 1967) and Psi and Psychoanalysis (Grune and Stratton, 1970).

Dr. Eisenbud can be reached at 4634 East Sixth Avenue, Denver, Colo. 80220.

13 Psychic Photography and Thoughtography

JULE EISENBUD

There are plenty of Tycho Brahes capable of supplying details of observations, but who is to be the Kepler that will from such observations evolve a law by which they can be satisfactorily explained?

J. TRAILL TAYLOR

SUMMARY

Since 1861, more than two dozen persons in several countries have claimed to obtain on photographic plates and film a variety of types of images that could only have been produced paranormally. Although most of these claims cannot now be adequately evaluated, some of them, despite various allegations of fraud, appear difficult to refute. "Psychic photography" and "thoughtography" entered a new phase with the advent of Ted Serios and the Polaroid camera. Serios's ability to produce images and other effects at distances from the camera that would be optically impossible by any known or conceivable means and his success in getting onto film striking correspondences to selected targets about which he had no prior knowledge render normal hypotheses untenable. The significance of the findings to both psychic research and science is discussed.

INTRODUCTION

The idea that images can be produced upon light-sensitized surfaces by purely mental means is so much at variance with both scientific and commonsense notions as to be on the face of it almost impossible to accept. Nevertheless, phenomena of this sort have been reported from almost the beginnings of popularized photography in daguerreotypy—not, needless to say, without bitter controversy and allegations and counterallegations of fraud all the way.

314

The first well-defined allegedly paranormal image is said to have turned up in 1861 when William H. Mumler, the principal engraver of a leading Boston jewelry concern, was trying to get a picture of himself with a friend's camera. Mumler at first assumed the image to be the result of a previously exposed plate but later concluded that it was a "spirit-form," as which it was heralded by the Spiritualist press of New York and Boston as the first permanently visible proof of an afterlife. Mumler shortly thereafter set up a studio where, according to his own and other accounts, he was widely investigated by professional photographers, journalists, and others. When one or two of his purported spirit forms were identified as living persons, however, the inevitable allegations of trickery made it necessary for him to leave Boston. He settled in New York, where soon afterward charges of his having swindled credulous persons by means of his spirit photographs were ordered to be brought against him by no less a personage than the mayor.

In a well-publicized trial Mumler was acquitted, not only because of the lack of any concrete evidence against him but because of the number of persons who testified tellingly in his favor. It was brought out not only that in many instances he had nothing more to do with the spirit forms that turned up alongside the sitters than to lend his presence in the room but that in some cases no daguerreotypes or photographs of relatives corresponding to their inexplicable appearance on the exposed plates were known to exist (38).

From Mumler to the present, more than two dozen persons in a half-dozen countries have claimed to do spirit photography, including *scotography* (images caught directly on nonexposed film, without the mediation of a camera) and *psychography* (film messages allegedly in the handwriting of deceased persons). Many spirit photographers were said to have given independent evidence of strong psychic powers, and one, an American named Edward Wylie, was a psychometrist who allegedly obtained images of deceased persons if a lock of hair or articles belonging to them were sent to him. The supposedly paranormal images, known as *extras*, were mostly of faces or torsos but occasionally were of full figures and frequently were surrounded by shrouds or halos looking like puffs of clouds or cotton batting. This is shown in Figure 1, one of the more than 2500 pictures of extras obtained by the psychic photographer William Hope in a controversial career spanning more than two decades in the early part of this century.

It is difficult at this late date to try to assess the bewildering tangle of claims and counterclaims making up the literature of this branch of psychic photography. No less than 35 references to spirit photography can be found in the *British Journal of Photography*, mostly in the 1870s. Numerous articles and notes—more than a score on Mrs. Emma Deane alone—appear in the journals and proceedings of the SPR and the ASPR, while references to the subject in Spiritualist books and journals run into the hundreds. Unfortunately, a balanced and comprehensive treatment of the subject, free of distortion, omission, and presumptive suppression of data, has yet to be written.

One of the difficulties besetting anyone trying to get a grasp of the subject from its historians and critics is that arguments on both sides tend to be contaminated and confused by the highly charged issue of Spiritualism. The proponents of this hypothesis seemed often more eager to view every indistinct blob as the work of discarnate spirit entities than to investigate the conditions of its appearance, while antispiritualists outdid themselves in a priori hypotheses about how well-bred spirits would behave if they existed, thus laying down canons of evidence that were wholly anti-empirical (30). Disregarding the extravagances and the illogic on both sides, however, there remain a certain number of firsthand reports of spur-of-the-moment or incognito sittings (7, 8), of sittings where the photographer was not allowed to go anywhere near the camera, the specially marked plates, or the darkroom (51, 52) and of sittings where the extras that turned up were unlike any known photographs of the persons they were believed to represent, if indeed photographs of these persons were known to exist at all (7, 8, 29, 37, 54). (This last was apt to be either disregarded by skeptical critics or countered with the notion that daguerre-otypes or photographs of persons turning up as extras were to be found for the taking on every relative's doorstep.) One inexplicable extra image appeared in a sitting completely controlled by an expert photographer, conjuror, and professional "ghost-breaker" who had not long before gone to some pains to bring about the exposure of a well-known spirit photographer (32, 43, 53).

As to the "suspicious looks" of some extras (one of the a priori criteria upon which the allegation of presumptive fraud was frequently made), one investigator, the editor of the *British Journal of Photography*, testified that despite every precaution he could think of, and in the presence of multiple witnesses who were specially delegated to set a watch not only upon the photographer (the medium David Duguid) but upon himself and the camera he had supplied, extras still came out looking fake—as if "cut oval out of a photograph by a can opener" (51). Similar results were reported by others (6, 28), one stating that, so far as he was concerned, it was immaterial whether the images were produced by spirits, the devil, or Balaam's ass—it was his duty simply to make his testimony known (6) (This investigator reported that the photographer, when asked what he told his ordinary sitters when "phantasmal faces" appeared on their plates, replied that he would just say that the negative had been spoiled and that he would have to make another exposure.)

That some fraud took place seems likely. It is equally likely that attempts were made to rig tests against psychic photographers, on occasions fraudulently (8, 24, 35, 36). At all events, the dictum of one critic that "every spirit photographer who has been thoroughly and competently investigated has been proved fraudulent" (9) is simply not supported by the facts, quite apart from its questionable relevance to the one really important issue of whether images can be produced at all except through normal optical processes.

Although so-called spirit photography has by no means disappeared from the scene, interest shifted in the early part of this century to a type of paranormal photography that did not necessarily involve discarnate entities and in which a wider range of images were obtained than the usual spirit-form extra. The term *thoughtography*, which has been applied to this branch of psychic photography, originated in 1910 when a sensitive was being tested by Tomokichi Fukurai in Japan for clairvoyance of a latent photographic image of a calligraphic character that had been imprinted on a film plate but not developed. During the test it was discovered that a plate that was not part of the experiment had been accidentally imprinted by what Fukurai assumed to be the psychic concentration of the clairvoyant. This led to further trials to determine whether the sensitive could deliberately imprint film plates with characters chosen for her. Fukurai zeroed right in on the radiation hypothesis: he requested the sensitive to try to imprint only the middle plate in a triple-decker film sandwich placed inside two boxes. When the sensitive did exactly as requested, Fukurai went on to many types of experiments with this and other sensitives. The results of his work between 1910 and 1913 were published in his *Clairvoyance and Thoughtography*, which appeared in English in 1931. Figure 2, taken from that book, shows two halves of a calligraphic character that, in fulfillment of the experimental task, appeared on two plates.

Experiments somewhat similar to Fukurai's were carried out in France (28, 31, 39), England (4, 55), and America (5). For some reason, however—perhaps the publication in 1933 in the *Proceedings of the Society for Psychical Research* of a damaging exposé of spirit photography (2)—little more was heard of the subject after Warrick's extensive (and extensively neglected) studies published in 1939 until Oehler's 1962 article (40). For eight years, the article claimed, Ted Serios, a 42-year-old Chicago bellhop, had been putting images onto Polaroid film under conditions that precluded normal means of his doing so. Serios simply stared into a camera lens through a cardboard cylinder about $7/8$ inch high and $3/4$ inch wide and tripped the shutter. (The cylinder was adopted at the suggestion of one investigator, several years after the start of his work, to keep Serios's fingers away from the lens.) Although the usual result was the expected blurred close-up of his face, this would occasionally be replaced by images of people, objects, or scenes that could not be accounted for under the conditions in force.

THE THOUGHTOGRAPHY OF TED SERIOS

At the urging of several of his Chicago supporters, Serios was observed and brought to Denver by me in the spring of 1964 for what turned out to be a series of intensive investigations over several years. During this time, a number of members of the academic community—physicians, physiologists, physicists, engineers, and others—took part in experiments aimed primarily at testing the validity of the claims made for Serios's thoughtography. He was also investigated during this period by Dr. Ian Stevenson and Dr. J. G. Pratt of the University of Virginia Medical School (47, 48).

These investigations enjoyed one major advantage over all previous investigations of psychic photography: the use of the Polaroid Land Camera, which permitted 15-second development of the 3000 ASA speed black-and-white film within the camera itself. The model 95 or 95A camera mostly in use was set at an aperture of 3, which, with the fixed shutter, gave the equivalent of f 11 at $\frac{1}{30}$ second. And although variations in the distance setting seemed to make little difference, the setting of infinity was almost invariably used. When Serios pointed the camera at himself at a distance of 12–15 inches, a winklight, bouncing off his face, shirt, or torso, provided fairly constant illumination under ordinary room lighting conditions.

Observers were asked to supply their own film, initialed on the wrappers, and, if possible, cameras as well. (Several models other than the 95 series were brought and used on occasion.) All loading and developing was done by observers (or by me under their supervision), and as attested by the more than three dozen witnesses who tendered signed statements on this point, unrestricted conditions of observation of personnel, equipment, and procedures obtained at all times (11, p. 101 ff).

Prints obtained in sessions with Serios were of four main types: (a) the "normals," somewhat out-of-focus images of his face (or larger portions of him if he was some feet away from the camera being held by others); (b) the "whities," those that came out as if strongly overexposed, even when all light was prevented from hitting the film (11); (c) the "blackies," those that came out totally or almost totally black where images would have been expected (16); and (d) photographlike images of different types other than the normally expected ones. Most of these covered the full $2\frac{7}{8}$ by $3\frac{3}{4}$ inches of the Polaroid print generally in use. Over 400 images of this last type, centering around more than 100 different themes, were obtained between April 1964 and June 1967, after which mostly blackies took over. These continued to be obtained through 1969 at the rate of about 20% of all trials, after which they diminished. (They are still being obtained, however, at the time of writing, 1973. Serios is currently producing blackies through a wall of light created by an illuminated diffusing disc fitted over the camera lens.)

The task of ruling out normal means of producing those images that were not the expected ones turned out to be fairly straightforward. The possibility of preimprinting, to begin with, was eliminated by the fact that every normally exposed film is self-validating when it happens to include parts of the background (drapes, woodwork, lamps, etc.) of the home or laboratory in which a session is held. If individual prints did not happen to show this (as when Serios's face took up most of the print frame on a normal shot), control shots, done generally on the average of one per roll of film used, would certainly have revealed any departure from expected imagery. For this reason, special markings on the front and back of each film frame that one team put on the film it brought were superfluous.

With camera and film supplied and controlled at all times by people other than Serios and barring collusion (which for reasons explained below would be extremely difficult in any case), the only means whereby a full-frame image other than the expected one could be produced would be by means of something like a transparency mounted on a suitable (wide-angle) lens and either large enough itself to cover the $\frac{5}{8}$-inch diameter of the exposed camera lens (and thus prevent normal images from also coming through) or imbedded in a shield that would do so. Ordinarily, something like a built-in auxiliary light source, which would have to be in constant operation (since it could not be expected to be sychronous with shutter openings), would also be required. It has been suggested that Serios could have concealed a gimmick incorporating all this in the rolled paper cylinder, which became known as the gizmo and which in most cases he would hold in front of the camera lens (Figure 3). (After the first sessions in Denver, it became standard practice to construct these by simply folding and taping the black shielding paper which came with each package of film into cylindrical rolls approximately 1 inch wide by $1\frac{1}{4}$ inches high.) The gizmo, in fact, inevitably became the equivalent of the highly suspicious top hat and cloak of the conjuror.

On no occasion, however, was anything even faintly suspicious discovered in or about any of Serios's gizmos during all his years of using them before scores of observers, including several professional sleight-of-hand experts (11, p. 110; 23; 41). Stevenson and Pratt, who obtained both "abnormal prints" and blackies in their work with Serios, stated (48), "We have ourselves observed Ted in approximately eight hundred trials, and we have never seen him act in a suspicious way in the handling of the gizmo before or after a trial." It was always possible, moreover, for observers to maneuver themselves into position to see right through Ted's open gizmos as he got set for a shot and to ascertain that these were completely empty (Figure 3).*

The more important fact, however, is that images other than the normally expected ones were obtained with either the camera and gizmo being held at varying distances from Serios by someone else (Serios often called for the latter maneuver even though it seemed to make no sense whatever for someone other than him to hold the gizmo) or with Serios holding the gizmo at varying distances from whoever was operating the camera, or both. For the strange images obtained under these circumstances to have been normally produced would have required, in the first case, that whoever was holding the gizmo when Serios was some distance away was wittingly or unwittingly deploying a gimmick to produce these images or, in the second, a device capable of producing full-frame images through a transparency when deployed at any appreciable distance from the camera lens. But to suppose, in the first case, that a dozen more or less skeptical witnesses (other than myself) who obtained images in this way knowingly would—or unknowingly *could*—use concealed gimmicks to produce seemingly paranormal images is untenable (quite apart from instances in which transparencies for these images could not have been contrived).

As to the second case, it is optically impossible for any gimmick that could conceivably escape detection to produce full-frame images from any appreciable distance from the camera lens. Figure 4 shows what happens when a lens and transparency that was able to produce such an image when held (inside a $\frac{3}{4}$-inch-wide gizmo) flat against the camera lens, with a 200-watt light source 3 feet away, is held at a distance of about $\frac{1}{2}$ inch from the camera lens. At 1 inch the blurred image of the gimmick inside the gizmo is correspondingly smaller, again with nothing at all coming through to show what the image on the transparency might have been.

An example of an image (one of several) obtained with the camera and gizmo being held about $2\frac{1}{2}$ feet from Serios is shown in Figure 5 (11, p. 131). Figure 6 shows a control shot of an observer whipping his hand down and snapping his fingers in the same manner as Serios at the same distance from the camera. Figure 7 shows one of four images obtained on a different occasion with another investigator holding the camera and gizmo about 3 feet from Serios. Clearer images of this building appeared in a session four days earlier (11, p. 166)—the only case incidentally, in

* A team representing *Popular Photography* alleged in an article in that magazine (22, 44) that Serios, when asked to show his gizmo, drew his hand back and could conceivably have dumped a gimmick into his pocket. Not only was this account contradicted by two colleagues who were present (12), but it was pointedly not attested to by a sleight-of-hand expert (understandably not named in the article) specifically brought to catch Serios in trickery if he could.

which duplication of images occurred days apart. Still another investigator obtained the image of a far corner of a room (Figure 8) adjoining the one in which he was standing behind a partition next to an archway and with the camera pointed in a different direction. Some 15 feet away, Serios was simultaneously operating an empty dummy camera, up to which he was holding his gizmo. He had been nowhere near the camera during the previous several shots. In this case, clearly, a transparency was not in use, as Serios had never been to the house in which the session took place and the person who held the camera was not only skeptical but distressingly hostile. Several instances of this kind are described in *The World of Ted Serios* (11). I might point out here that in instances such as those shown, the problem is not only how the unexpected images got onto the film but also that of how the expected ones (of Serios or of whatever the camera was pointed at) failed to do so. This would present a formidable problem in any attempt at collusion.

Several instances in which a separation between Serios and the camera was created by an interposed physical barrier took place with Serios inside a Faraday cage (a room shielded from radio waves by wire-mesh screening), while a camera and gizmo were being deployed outside the room. Figure 9 shows one of several prints obtained in this way. James A. Hurry, a physicist who arranged and supervised these test conditions, wrote in a report of the experiment that "the cameras held either by Dr. Eisenbud or myself were at least one (1) foot or more from the subject (Ted) when [Figure 9] and others were obtained with Ted inside the shielded room and Dr. Eisenbud and myself outside." In connection with this print, Hurry wrote, "Dr. Eisenbud held the camera and I held the gizmo on the outside of the shielded lab (door closed). I looked through the 'gizmo' used by Ted in the inside of the room—there was nothing visible inside Ted's 'gizmo.' "

With preimprinting and surreptitious film-switching eliminated, instances such as the above should suffice to wrap up the case against normal means of producing nonexpected images about as conclusively as it is possible to do so.* They have done so at least for conjurors, who have unanimously shown the good sense not to come up with wildly implausible hypotheses that they are unwilling to put to the test. Not one of them, at any rate, has accepted the challenge to attempt to duplicate Serios's phenomena under close supervision (12). (Conjurors of acknowledged eminence have been directly approached on this.†) But not everybody will take the trouble to analyze a situation systematically, as

---

* For reasons of space I am omitting the evidential value of various types of anomalies and of the changes between successive versions of prints that would require elaborate gimmick arrangements or separate transparencies to produce a series of images on a given theme. See, for example, Refs. 17 and 20.

† See C. G. Fuller, "Dr. Eisenbud vs. the Amazing Randi." *Fate*, 27, no. 8 (August 1974). *Editor*

conjurors do, and a demonstration that will induce conviction in one person will fail to do so in another. For this reason, I shall cite a type of datum that, for some persons, has turned out to have as much evidential value as the foregoing.

TARGET RESPONSES

Serios customarily requested targets for him to aim at, and he preferred that these be concealed from him. Curiously, he was less concerned with the evidential than with the game aspects of this challenging procedure. Nevertheless, if he could come up with anything that might be considered a hit, the unlikelihood of his doing so through anything but outright collusion is apparent.

For my first session with him in Chicago, a week prior to his coming to Denver, I had brought photographs of the Kremlin buildings in Moscow (no specifications had been given—I was at liberty to select anything) that were sealed in heavy-grade manila envelopes with cardboard covering the images (Figures 10 and 11). One of three images that Serios got in that session was of the Chicago Water Tower (Figure 12). (The session, incidentally, had a stunning effect; I had gone to the meeting almost certain that I was about to witness some kind of shoddy hoax.) For reasons given elsewhere (11, p. 199 ff.), this struck me as a peculiar type of hit involving associations that perhaps only I could fully appreciate. The configurational aspects of the correspondence between the Kremlin buildings and the Water Tower picture were, however, on the subtle (and, some probably would hold, debatable) side. But two years later I happened to chance upon another view of the Kremlin buildings (Figure 13). In the foreground is Ivan's Bell Tower, which can just barely be glimpsed in one of the target photos. It can be seen in Figure 14a to bear an easily discernible resemblance to the Chicago Water Tower shown in Figure 14c.

Most of Serios's "successful" target responses have been on this order. In the Denver period, in fact, only one unarguable example was produced of a more or less 1:1 correspondence where someone other than Serios had selected the target (18). And I have found that target responses considered hits by some people on one ground or another are often disputed by others. The image obtained in the Faraday cage experiment, shown in Figure 9, is an example. The target selected by Serios, one of several unconcealed ones provided for him to choose from, was of stress lines in a belt section (Figure 15), which he saw as "eyes looking at a line of people." Some will readily construe the three officers reviewing troops (Figure 9) as "eyes looking at a line of people," but others will see only a parade. Figure 16 shows a concealed target, and Figure 17 Serios's response. Again, some will be impressed with the basic similarity in shape of the flatiron and the automobile, while others will be able to see only the differences between the two pictures. The upper half of the target shown in Figure 18, chosen by a colleague, was exposed, while the lower half (below the horizontal line) was concealed. My colleague was impressed (as was I) by the seeming rearrangement of elements of the target pictures in the response (Figure 19). Others will doubtlessly see a no-hit. As Pascal put it in one of his *Pensées* (in connection, I believe, with a point of theology), there is enough light for those who wish to see and enough darkness for those who are contrary minded.

That there can be any room for argument at all as to what constitutes a successful target response might seem to leave us exactly nowhere, so far as evidence for the paranormality of Serios's images goes. But for psychologists it is apt to be precisely the departures from veridicality, the rearrangements and transformations between input information and response, that intuitively send the probabilities against normal means of production of Ted's images sky high. The reason is that it is this sort of thing that is the rule when unconscious processes come into play, as in the elaboration of dream imagery and works of art. It is also a type of perceptual response seen under experimental conditions in which unconscious processes are given free rein.

An example beautifully illustrating the type of rearrangement of elements seen in the perceptual responses to tachistoscopically displayed imagery (as well as in eidetic imagery) occurred on an occasion when Serios got the Denver Hilton Hotel image shown in Figure 20, with me holding camera and gizmo about four feet from him. Figure 21, from the same session, shows a normal in which Serios, at about the same distance, has just completed whipping his right arm down and snapping (cf. Figure 6). Note the elements in the background—the planes, angles, and striations—from which the Hilton image could easily have been subconsciously derived, even though Serios had stated that he was going to try for the Chicago Hilton (cf. Figures 18 and 19).

While many will argue about whether the flatiron and auto represent a correspondence at all, psychologists, starting from the hint of similarity, will more likely speculate on why Serios rejected one idea and substituted the other. And while some of his responses—for example, those involving complex associational and symbolic connections—may leave the average reader absolutely cold, they may be most impressive to those with clinical experience in depth psychology and dream analysis. A well-known science writer, in fact, informed me that it was one of these (11, p. 209 ff.) that, on the basis of what knowledge he had of dream psychology, provided the highest degree of conviction for him. Presumably, he would no more have expected a trickster to come up with responses of this type than he would have expected one to come up with creative efforts on the order of Rembrandt's paintings or the fugues of J. S. Bach.

QUESTIONS AND PUZZLES

Granting that we know hardly less about thoughtography than we do about thought itself—thoughtography might be regarded merely as an unusual means of registration of a still-mysterious phenomenon to begin with—there are nevertheless aspects of it, and specifically of Serios's thoughtography, that add to the enigma.

One puzzling thing is that thoughtographic images have always tended to adjust themselves to the order of magnitude of the film frame used and, in the case of the older spirit photographers, of the sitters. Never has an image appeared on a microscopic scale, or as only a minute fraction of an image that might seem to have been projected to wall size on the film plane, for example. Serios sometimes got just the windows of buildings instead of whole buildings but never anything like just the eye or the finger of a person (for example, of one of the persons in Figure 9) or just a small fraction of the bark of a tree instead of a whole tree. We are told, however, that very much the same thing occurs with crystal gazers, where the images also tend to adjust themselves to the size and frame of whatever is being used for scrying (50). Apparitions, too, tend to adjust to the size of rooms, furniture, and people.

Again, Serios' images tended to conform automatically to the film size of the camera being used. If he was doing a series of images on one theme, the image adjusted itself as any normally derived one would to different cameras, exactly as would be the case if a transparency and lens gimmick were being employed with different model cameras and lenses. Swinger models and the half-size film of the model 80 Polaroid camera produced simply reduced-size versions of the images obtained on the larger print 95 or 100 series models, practically all as if within ordinary snapshot range. These images, however, would not necessarily emerge in the same position or on the same axis in relation to the print frame.

Another puzzling aspect of thoughtographic images is their essentially static nature. Indeed, critics have assumed, when spirit photographers occasionally came up with identically replicated versions of some extra, that this constituted prima facie evidence of the fraudulent use of a template of some sort. That this by no means necessarily followed, however, was emphatically pointed out by James H. Hyslop, professor of philosophy and logic at Columbia University and editor of the *Journal of the American Society for Psychical Research*, who over 50 years ago scored

Fig. 1

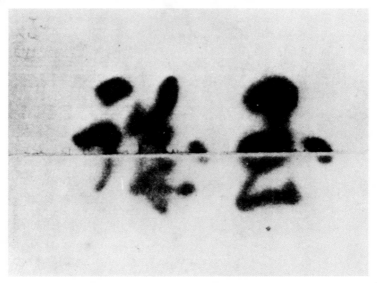

Fig. 2

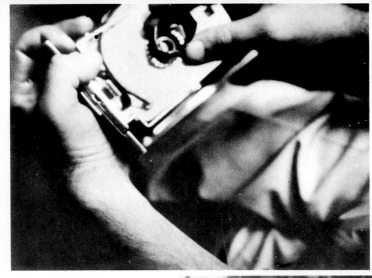

Fig. 3

Fig. 4

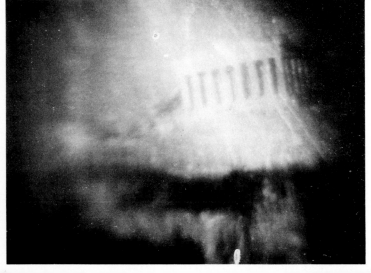

Fig. 5

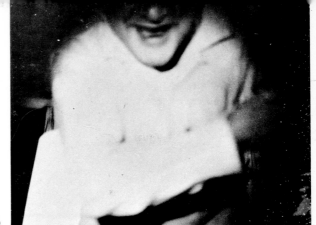

Fig. 6

Fig. 7

Fig. 8

Fig. 9

Fig. 10

Fi

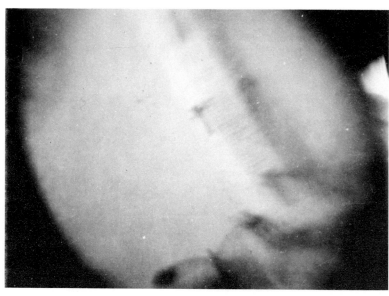

Fig. 12

Fig. 13

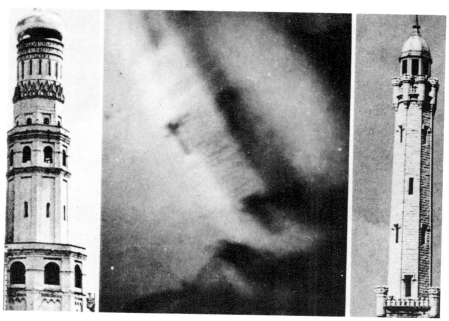

Fig. 14a   Fig. 14b   Fig. 14c

Fig. 15

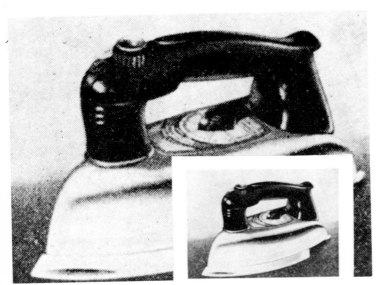

Fig. 16

Fig. 17

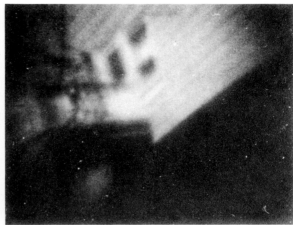

Fig. 18

Fig. 19

Fig. 20

Fig. 21

Fig. 22

Fig. 23

critics of psychic photography for their unwarranted armchair preconceptions (30).

Serios's images, at all events, have tended to be more or less static. On the numerous occasions when he has come up with more than a single print of an image (he has obtained as many as 25), there have been only few instances—and not all of these are free from doubt—of an image seeming to vary between one print and another as if really different camera angles were involved (11, Figure 94). True, there were many instances of embryonic forms of a given image making their appearance during the course of a session; but these, only adding to the puzzle, seemed to be unsuccessful or only partly "energized" attempts at the fixed primary image. (Most of these in any given case, incidentally, do not appear to be capable of having been obtained through a single transparency. They seem to emerge from the mists like incomplete ghostly forms.) And although the "camera" often seemed to swivel on different vertical or horizontal axes, this is merely as if it were panning to different portions of a single still picture, much as a TV camera sometimes moves from section to section of a painting being shown in detail. This has been the case even when the images have been of people or vehicles: they seem to have been caught in motion but in a frozen moment of time. And it has been true even on the two occasions on which Serios succeeded in putting images onto videotape, which certainly could have provided a vehicle for moving images if movement was there (21). On these occasions the images turned out to be identical to the ones he obtained on film in the same sessions, except for some panning effects. Is this the stuff of dreams? Of memory? Offhand, it would not seem so. Indeed, if transparencies and auxiliary lenses had not conclusively been eliminated as possible sources of Serios's images, this too would appear like the stuff of gimmickry.

Of the nature of the energy involved, or the process of energy transfer —if, indeed, anything at all like what we know as energy transfer is involved—our work with Serios has told us little. It has, however, given us some idea of what is not involved. Serios, unlike other psychic photographers, puts a tremendous amount of straining and concentration of the most effortful kind into the task of getting his images, even though he mostly has no specific targets consciously in mind. This is often accompanied by a rapid, pounding heartbeat, which seems nevertheless to come on independently of the physical effort he puts into his performance (or the prodigious amounts of alcohol he puts into himself). But no sign of effort showed up on his EEG tracing, which remained completely unperturbed by the paranormal pictures being produced (11, p. 254 ff.).

Equally unperturbed (or at least uninvolved) were portions of the electromagnetic spectrum tested. As mentioned earlier, the radio-wave (and to some extent, electrostatic-field) attenuation of the Faraday cage constituted no bar to good images (e.g., Figure 9), and no unusual beta or gamma radiation could be detected when images were secured in a whole radiation counting chamber (11, p. 258). The heavy shielding of a hospital X-ray laboratory was again no bar to Serios's images (19), and last of all, excellent results were obtained when the light entering the camera had to pass through magnetic fields up to 1200 gauss.

As to anything like light itself, the data have been somewhat contradictory, as inconsistent as thought on the wing. While Serios has often obtained total whities and even images with someone's hand held over the camera lens (or tightly over a small rigid gizmo held against the lens), he has never produced a sign of fogging or imagery through a rubber lens cap. Nevertheless, partial whities have eventuated on occasion when Serios has gone through the process of concentrating on producing an image but where, for one reason or another, the shutter was not triggered and no light could have entered the camera. Similarly, while heavy cardboard bars on which light sensors were mounted for certain experiments practically always constituted an effective shield against any kind of imagery, in several instances portions of one or both bars were flooded out, and in one instance (of a partial whitie), the "light" can be seen almost flowing around the bar (Figure 22). Something vaguely suggestive of light rays can even be seen proceeding from Serios's eyes in one of the prints (Figure 23) obtained in a session with Stevenson and Pratt (48). But nothing showed up on an ordinary light meter interposed between him and the camera when he was producing paranormal images, and he has, like other psychic photographers, produced imagery on opaquely wrapped film pack (16). Moreover, nothing suggestive of light was visible when Serios obtained images in total darkness (14). Finally, Serios seemed to be able to counteract or annihilate light in his blackies and when the light entering the camera impinged on sensors hooked up to an oscilloscope (16).

If there is some intuitively apprehended secret to producing paranormal images, it has escaped Serios, just as it has other thoughtographers, most of whom were gifted psychics of one sort or another to begin with. Serios obtained his last supervised full-frame thoughtograph in June 1967. As if the end of a stage performance were being announced, this was simply the image of a drapery or curtain, nothing else. Since then, Ted has not been able to produce pictures in the grand style, even though he has been supplied with camera and film for long unsupervised periods—weeks and months—with full liberty to do what he could on his own.

As to what seemed conducive to good results when Serios was at his peak, no external factor could be pinpointed—not the weather (despite his feeling that he did better in brisk or stormy weather), not the attitude of observers (friendly and encouraging ones were no more favorable to results than skeptical or hostile ones), not any experimental variation or even relaxation of conditions of control. The thing that correlated most highly with positive results was simply a feeling on Serios's part of exuberant self-confidence, which appeared on the whole to be mainly endogenous, although the appearance of images, when they did come, always seemed to prime the pump for more exuberance and more images.

When his images ceased to appear, nothing availed to bring them back. Various types of ordinary inducements and emoluments (one observer offered a $100 bill for an image), consciousness-altering drugs, hypnotic suggestions, and hypnotically induced hallucinations were all futile. A four-day closely monitored dream-deprivation experiment, undertaken in the hope that the buildup of image-need during this period might force some images to spill over onto film, resulted only in one sleep-deprived investigator. Other thoughtographers too seem to have had shorter or longer periods of total unproductivity, some lasting for several years before things started up again. They may well have felt as Serios, who, describing earlier freezes (of as long as two years), said, "It's as if a curtain comes down, *ker-boom*, and that's all, brother."

THE WORK OF OTHER LATTER-DAY PSYCHIC PHOTOGRAPHERS

Of the handful of persons currently claiming results in psychic photography, only Nina S. Kulagina of the Soviet Union and the Veilleux family of Maine have been investigated by parapsychologists to any great extent. The former is said to have caused "the appearance on sensitive photographic materials of some simple picture or letters without the use of any light source" (34), while several members of the Veilleux family, about whom a comprehensive report has not yet appeared, have been observed to produce several instances of ostensibly paranormal imagery, as well as normally inexplicable fogging (45) and other anomalies. The Veilleux work includes extras in the manner of the older spirit photographers, in some instances with the kind of "cotton wool" surround seen in many of these (e.g., Figure 1) and also in some of Mrs. Kulagina's effects (26, 33 back cover), as well as full-frame prints in the Serios style. Although the production of all but a few of their hundreds of prints has not been witnessed by trained investigators, the similarities between their pictures and the Serios prints (e.g., striated effects, 11, p. 250 ff.), as well as certain anomalous distortions, add credibility to their claims (as does the fact that they too recently went through a two-year period of nonproductivity during which no paranormal images came despite everything they could think of to do). Their work must in any case be adjudged to have a far different "antecedent probability" after the intensive investigation of Ted

Serios than it could have had before. This might also be said to be the case, by the same token, with some of the work of the early psychic photographers, as well as with other more or less current work that by itself is difficult to evaluate (1, 27).

THOUGHTS ON THOUGHTOGRAPHY

Outside of its peculiar relationship to the phenomena of light, psychic photography and thoughtography do not present anything essentially new to psychic research. It is just one more form in which information is gathered, processed, and transmitted in ways other than the generally recognized ones. Thoughtographs seem to fall somewhere between apparitional and materialization phenomena. But unlike these, which too may be thought of as at least partly originating "in the mind," they result in a more or less permanent alteration of a part of the external world. As such, thoughtographs raise questions about the external world and the mind's relationship to it in perhaps a more insistent way than many other data of psychic research.

The thoughtographic image, with all the exquisitely detailed and articulated information that goes into it, certainly lends dramatic support to the supposition, which can be derived from various other data of psychic research—from the overall cognitive picture, in fact—that potential access to existing data and states of affairs, wherever and whatever they may be, is virtually unlimited. It also lends support to the assumption that a somewhat analogous situation may obtain on the kinetic side—namely, that the ability to convey detailed information and thus pattern complex events in physical systems "outside the head" is in some measure latent in all "mind" in nature, wherever found; and, moreover, that it need not be limited to events on a molecular scale.

All this presupposes, of course, that what is so manifestly displayed in thoughtographic and other phenomena of psychic research represents only the arresting and readily observable portions of what must obtain throughout nature in more unobtrusive fashion—that thoughtographers, mediums, sensitives, and the entire host of psychics of one stripe or another, as well as all the paranormal spontaneous phenomena, represent merely the outcroppings (for reasons presumably in the realm of "need" psychology) of a deeper matrix of process in nature. It is, in fact, difficult to see how everything—or for that matter anything—could work if not for this kind of underlying machinery. If, as Bergson and others have maintained, information, thought, and action constitute a dynamic unity in nature, then something beyond the limited stock of mechanisms now accepted by science is necessary to keep things running smoothly. Indeed, something beyond this severely restricted panel of possibilities is necessary to account for the miracle of probability theory turning out to be such an apt description of the way things happen. A central intelligence and organizing principle has, of course, been widely deemed indispensable. Chance (that demon in disguise) cannot be held responsible, for paradoxically it is just as much in need of some kind of organizing principle as everything else.

Now something akin to the image has sometimes been thought of as inherent in the idea of a central organizing principle. Something of this sort has been implicit in the Platonic "form," in Aristotle's "entelechy," in Schopenhauer's "world as will and idea," and in the latter-day efforts of many kinds of scientists groping for a guiding principle behind the orderly way of the world (25, 42). Perhaps the image, so dramatically displayed in thoughtographic phenomena, is merely the visible and frozen expression of what is latent in every form, every purpose, every developing organism and species and system in nature. Perhaps God, to paraphrase those who would have him a mathematician, is the supreme thoughtographer.

But should we not take some credit ourselves, we and all living entities? The fact that we are presumably able occasionally to patternize some small segment of the universe, frozen in time though it be, would at least go far toward explaining some of the age-old notions of primitive peoples, as well as data only now coming into the field of observation (13, Chapters 14 and 15). It may also provide some support for a still only tentatively explored approach to what is one of the supreme enigmas of psychic research—precognition—in enabling us to view more tolerantly the idea of events being shaped along a time axis by the very minds that can impress form on film (10, 46, 49). There is surely more here than meets the eye but not more, probably, than can be dealt with by the inquiring mind.

REFERENCES

1. Barbanell, Maurice. *He Walks in Two Worlds.* Jenkins: London, 1964.
2. Barlow, F., and Rampling-Rose, W. "Report of an Investigation into Spirit Photography." *Proceedings of the Society for Psychical Research*, 41, pt. 129 (1933): 121–138.
3. Bergson, H. *Matter and Memory.* Allen and Unwin: London, 1950.
4. Carrington, H. "Experiences in Psychic Photography." *Journal of the American Society for Psychical Research*, 19, no. 1 (1925): 258–267.
5. Carrington, H. "We Photographed Thoughts." *Fate*, 6, no. 6 (1953): 64–72; repr. 21, no. 6 (1968): 90–98.
6. Cook, C. H. "Experiments in Photography." *Journal of the American Society for Psychical Research*, 10, no. 1 (1916): 1–56; no. 2: 57–63.
7. Cushman, A. S. "An Evidential Case of Spirit Photography." *Journal of the American Society for Psychical Research* 15 (1922): 132–151.
8. Doyle, A. C. *The Case for Spirit Photography.* Doran: New York, 1923.

9. Edmunds, S. *'Spirit' Photography.* Society for Psychical Research: London, 1965.
10. Eisenbud, J. "Compound Theories of Precognition." *Journal of the Society for Psychical Research,* 41, no. 713 (1962): 353–355.
11. Eisenbud, J. *The World of Ted Serios.* Morrow: New York, 1967.
12. Eisenbud, J. "The Cruel, Cruel World of Ted Serios." *Popular Photography,* November 1967, p. 131 ff.
13. Eisenbud, J. *Psi and Psychoanalysis.* Grune and Stratton: New York, 1970.
14. Eisenbud, J. "Light and the Serios Images." *Journal of the Society for Psychical Research,* 45, no. 746 (1970): 424–427.
15. Eisenbud, J. "Some Notes on the Psychology of the Paranormal." *Journal of the American Society for Psychical Research,* 66, no. 1 (1972): 27–41.
16. Eisenbud, J. "The Serios 'Blackies' and Related Phenomena." *Journal of the American Society for Psychical Research,* 66, no. 2 (1972): 180–192.
17. Eisenbud, J. "Gedanken zur Psychophotographie." *Zeitschrift für Parapsychologie und Grenzgebiete der Psychologie,* 14, no. 1 (1972): 1–11.
18. Eisenbud, J., and Associates. "Some Unusual Data from a Session with Ted Serios." *Journal of the American Society for Psychical Research,* 61, no. 3 (1967): 241–253.
19. Eisenbud, J., and Associates. "Two Experiments with Ted Serios." *Journal of the American Society for Psychical Research,* 62, no. 3 (1968): 309–320.
20. Eisenbud, J., and Associates. "An Archeological Tour de Force with Ted Serios." *Journal of the American Society for Psychical Research,* 64, no. 1 (1970): 40–52.
21. Eisenbud, J., and Associates. "Two Camera and Television Experiments with Ted Serios." *Journal of the American Society for Psychical Research,* 64, no. 3 (1970): 261–276.
22. Eisendrath, D. B. "An Amazing Weekend with the Amazing Ted Serios," Part 2. *Popular Photography,* October 1967, p. 85 ff.
23. Frey, H.; Lehrburger, H.; Marx, J. R.; Merrill, F. B.; Paley, A.; and Wheeler, B. W. "Correspondence." *Journal of the American Society for Psychical Research,* 62, no. 3 (1968): 330–331.
24. Fukurai, T. *Clairvoyance and Thoughtography.* Rider: London, 1931.
25. Gregory, C. C. L., and Kohsen, A. *Physical and Psychical Research.* Omega: Reigate, Surrey, 1954.
26. Herbert, B. "Report on Nina Kulagina." *Parapsychology Review,* 3, no. 6 (1972): 8–10.
27. Holzer, H. *Psychic Photography: Threshold of a New Science?* McGraw-Hill: New York, 1969.
28. Hyslop, J. H., trans. "Experiments of Dr. Ochorovicz: Report of a Commission of Naturalists." *Journal of the American Society for Psychical Research,* 5, no. 12 (1911): 678–730.
29. Hyslop, J. H. "Some Unusual Phenomena in Photography." *Proceedings of the American Society for Psychical Research,* 8, pt. 3 (1914): 395–465.
30. Hyslop, J. H. "Photographing the Invisible." *Journal of the American Society for Psychical Research,* 9, no. 3 (1915): 148–175.
31. Joire, P. *Psychical and Supernormal Phenomena.* Marlowe: Chicago, 1916.
32. *Journal of the American Society for Psychical Research,* 19, no. 8 (1925): 417–419.
33. *Journal of Paraphysics,* 5, nos. 1–2 (1971) back cover.
34. Kulagin, V. V. "Nina S. Kulagina." *Journal of Paraphysics,* 5, nos. 1–2 (1971): 54–62.

35. McKenzie, J. H. "The 'Price-Hope' Case: A Full Record." *Psychic Science*, 1, no. 4 (1923): 378–394.
36. McKenzie, J. H. "The Price-Hope Case: Conclusion." *Psychic Science*, 2, no. 1 (1923): 58–62.
37. Morse, J. J. *A Brief History of Spirit Photography.* Two Worlds: Manchester, 1909.
38. Mumler, W. H. *Personal Experiences of William H. Mumler in Spirit Photography.* Colby and Rich: Boston, 1875.
39. Ochorovicz, J. "Les Mains Fluidiques et la Photographie de la Pensée." *Annales des Sciences Psychiques*, 22, no. 4 (1912): 97–104; no. 5: 147–153; no. 6: 164–170; no. 7: 204–209.
40. Oehler, P. "The Psychic Photography of Ted Serios." *Fate*, 16, (1962): 68–82.
41. Phillips, L. W. Letter of February 15, 1968 to Professor Arlie E. Paige, Chairman of Department of Electrical Engineering, University of Denver.
42. Polanyi, M. *Personal Knowledge.* University of Chicago Press: Chicago, 1958.
43. Price, H. "Psychic Photography: Some Scientific Aids to Spurious Phenomena." *Journal of the Society for Psychical Research*, 19, no. 1 (1925): 570–587; no. 2: 617–636.
44. Reynolds, C. "An Amazing Weekend with the Amazing Ted Serios," Part I. *Popular Photography*, October 1967, p. 81 ff.
45. Rindge, J. P.; Cook, W.; and Owen, A. R. G. "An Investigation of Psychic Photography with the Veilleux Family." *New Horizons*, 1, no. 1 (1972): 28–32.
46. Roll, W. G. "The Problem of Precognition." *Journal of the Society for Psychical Research*, 41, no. 709 (1961): 115–127.
47. Stevenson, I., and Pratt, J. G. "Exploratory Investigations of the Psychic Photography of Ted Serios." *Journal of the American Society for Psychical Research*, 62, no. 2 (1968): 103–129.
48. Stevenson, I., and Pratt, J. G. "Further Investigations of the Psychic Photography of Ted Serios." *Journal of the American Society for Psychical Research*, 63, no. 4 (1969): 352–364.
49. Tanagras, A. *Psychophysical Elements in Parapsychological Traditions.* Parapsychological Monographs, Parapsychology Foundation: New York, 1967.
50. Taylor, H. D. "The Physiological Limits of Visual Hallucination." *Annals of Psychical Science*, 9, no. 54 (1910): 197–224.
51. Taylor, J. T. " 'Spirit Photography' with Remarks on Fluorescence." *British Journal of Photography*, 40, no. 1715 (1893): 167–169.
52. Taylor, J. T. In J. Coates, *Photographing the Invisible.* Fowler: London, 1911, p. 55.
53. Tubby, G. E. "Notes and Comment." *Journal of the American Society for Psychical Research*, 18, no. 4 (1924): 299–300.
54. Wallace, A. R. *Miracles and Modern Spiritualism.* Burns: London, 1874.
55. Warrick, F. W. *Experiments in Psychics.* Dutton: New York, 1939.

Henry (Andrija) K. Puharich

HENRY (ANDRIJA) K. PUHARICH, *M.D., is pursuing full-time private research into the nature of psychic phenomena.*

Dr. Puharich earned his medical degree in 1947 at Northwestern University. From 1948 to 1958 he was director of research at the Round Table Foundation in Glen Cove, Maine, where he conducted many original experiments in psychic research. He then spent 13 years in medical electronics research and holds more than 60 U.S. and foreign patents. In 1968 Dr. Puharich led a team of six doctors and eight paramedical specialists to Brazil for a study of the psychic healer Arigó.

In addition to more than three dozen professional papers, Dr. Puharich is author of The Sacred Mushroom (*Doubleday, 1959*) *and* Beyond Telepathy (*Lowe and Byrdone, 1961; paperback, Doubleday-Anchor, 1973*).

Dr. Puharich lives at 87 Hawkes Avenue, Ossining, N.Y. 10562.

14 Psychic Research and the Healing Process

HENRY K. PUHARICH

SUMMARY

The healing process is usually described within the framework of physics, chemistry, and cellular physiology. Just as the role of the observer is generally ignored in the formulations of science, so the role of the healer and the healed is ignored in modern medicine. This chapter examines the role of the healer–healed in 10 basic processes in healing: diagnosis, manual healing, self-healing, chemical agents, anesthesia, surgery, bacteriostasis, action-at-a-distance, the guide, and regeneration. Personal observations of the famed Brazilian healer Arigó illustrate the principles that emerge from this examination.

INTRODUCTION

Everyone is familiar with the process of healing. One's finger may be cut; it is then "treated" by some local custom, and in a number of days it has "healed." In the case of minor skin injuries there is some scientific knowledge of the healing process, because much of it can be observed under the microscope. We can describe this process in layman's terms.

When a foreign object cuts through tissue, many of the chemicals normally sealed inside a cell are released locally, and these chemicals are partly responsible for calling into action a complex repair process. In addition to chemical release, injury causes an established local electrical pattern to be disorganized, which serves to trigger the alarm system that calls out the repair workers. The combination of chemical and electrical alarm signals works in a way as yet unknown to bring about the following sequence of repair, or "healing," processes.

First, the injury causes blood flow, or bleeding. When such injury occurs in a hemophiliac, the process that leads to blood clotting is defective, and the person may bleed to death for lack of a chemical component of the clotting process. However, in the normal person fibrinogen is triggered to go from a particle state to fiber state. The result is that fibrin is spun out across the bleeding area very much like a spider web. This acts like a sieve, trapping the red and white blood cells, and causes the liquid-state serum to coagulate into a jell state. The entire process of blood coagulation takes about 10 minutes. Then the hole in the tissue caused by injury is filled with a jell-like blood clot. Within this blood clot the true healing process begins.

The white blood cells move about through the clot-jell scooping up tissue debris and bacteria. Antibodies are released that begin to neutralize toxic effects of other bacteria. Other large cells begin to throw out filament bridges from one wall of the injury area to the other wall, and these can be seen later as "scar tissue." The elements of the scar tissue in fact stitch together the tissue defect over a period of a week. Within this connective-tissue stitch work, blood vessels begin to tunnel, severed nerves bridge the injury gap, and so on. The skin epithelium grows out from the edge of the wound to cover the scar tissue. If all of these myriad processes carry out their assembly-line repair tasks, the healing process will be essentially complete in 9 to 10 days. This is what everyone knows about the simplest type of healing process. It is important to remember that the entire process was conceived, organized, and carried out by nature without man's knowledge or cooperation.

Now, man has had to deal with injuries since the beginning of his species' consciousness. At times, in dealing with injuries from falls, battles, fights with men or animals, and the like, "complications" arose. This means that nature's "natural healing" process could not handle the repair job. For example, the wound gap could be so great that the blood clot could not fill in the hole. Man learned that by pulling the edges of the wound together with some kind of a "stitch" process, he could in fact accelerate the healing process. When a local abscess, or pus pocket, developed, man found that by piercing the pus pocket and drawing out the pus, he could accelerate the healing process. When the local wound became full of pus and showed a severe swelling (called cellulitis), man somehow found that certain poultices reduced the swelling and infection and accelerated the healing processes. Man also found that if he ate certain substances during delayed healing of a wound, the wound-healing could be accelerated.

This simple story presents all the elements of modern medicine and surgery—namely, wound-cleaning, antisepsis, bacteriostasis, surgery, and use of chemicals as "medicines." In addition to taking care of the local wound, man learned that the poppy could relieve pain, that alcohol was a tranquilizer, that a willow-bark concoction relieved fever, and so forth through the entire medical pharmacopoeia.

But most of all man learned that the comfort given by a sympathetic person made it easier to get through all the trials of a wound-healing or a disease process. In the course of time it was learned in each tribe that some people could give more sympathy and more comfort than others. By popular demand this type of person found himself spending more and more time with wounded or diseased people. As the generations passed this kind of person became a specialist in the tribe, alongside the patriarch or matriarch, the chief hunter or warrior, and the arrow-maker. He became a "medicine man." Sometimes there were good medicine men, and sometimes there were bad medicine men. What they had in common were the arts passed on from generation to generation. These consisted of knowing the different kinds of diseases, the different kinds of spirits that were thought to be causing diseases, the kinds of herbs and offerings that were to be used to propitiate various combinations of disease–spirit entities. What was different between the medicine men was their degree of "power"—that is, their success rate. This had to do with how quickly they "divined" the nature of the disease–spirit combination and how quickly they found the right combination of medicine, surgery, and "appeasement" that would accelerate the departure of the problem.

As the aeons passed, the art of the medicine man broke up into specialties. There is evidence (3) that about 4000 years ago in Egypt there were those who practiced surgery (4), those who practiced medicine (2), and those who dealt with the spirits and the gods—i.e., priests (14). However, all three specialists paid homage to the spirits and the gods until a few hundred years ago. In fact, we can clearly state that the final split between the surgeon, the man of medicine, and the priest occurred only within this century. Since the split is so recent, there are many scars and wounds that still smart and it is a very delicate question to talk about healing as an art separate from the roles of the priest, the surgeon, the man of medicine. However, it is the purpose of this chapter to describe healing as a process separate from that of the professional priest, the surgeon, or the man of medicine.

We will begin to define the process of healing by giving an example of that process at work in a modern healer, Arigó (1918–1971). Arigó was born in Congonhas do Campo, Minas Gerais, Brazil, in 1918. Up to the age of 30 he had completed four years of primary school, worked as a farmhand, worked in iron mines as a laborer, and operated a small café for two years. From the age of 30 to 32, he suffered from depressions, nightmares, sleeptalking, and sleepwalking. The local doctor and priest could not help him. A local Spiritualist named Oliveira prayed with Arigó and told Arigó that a spirit was trying to speak and act through him.

One day in 1950 Arigó had to take a trip to the local county seat and state capital, Belo Horizonte. He stayed at a small hotel. The story is now taken up by Bittencourt, a state senator also staying at the same hotel. He states that Arigó, whom he knew, entered his room sometime after 2:00 A.M. and told him to lie down on the bed. Arigó then produced a straight razor, and proceeded to operate on his chest, removing a tumor. Arigó then left. Bittencourt states that he had been diagnosed prior to this event as having an inoperable lung tumor and subsequent to this event had another diagnosis from his doctors that the tumor had disappeared. There was some circumstantial evidence on behalf of Bittencourt's position: his pajamas were torn and an orange-sized piece of tissue was found in his room. There was blood on his pajamas and body, but no scar.

The case rested there. Arigó eventually went on to do surgery of a similar kind in public and became known as a healer. Fortunately, Arigó not only carried out his healing work for 20 years, but he was under study by doctors who were disciplined in modern medicine and surgery. I was one of these researchers and studied Arigó intermittently from 1963 to 1968.

My initial contact with Arigó was during August 1963 in the "clinic" in Congonhas do Campo. I watched Arigó doing surgery without anesthesia or antisepsis; every patient was helped, and none had postoperative complications. It was truly a mind-shattering experience to see every principle of surgery violated with impunity. Indeed, I found myself unable to accept the data of my own senses.

In order to overcome this mental blockage, I decided that I must personally experience what Arigó's patients were experiencing during surgery. If such an experience could be obtained, I felt, it might clear my shocked belief system and perceptions. Arigó agreed to operate on a lipoma (benign tumor) on my right elbow. The operation scene was a room in which some 90 people crowded around Arigó to see him operate. Arigó with a flourish requested that someone furnish him with a pocket knife, and someone in the audience produced one. Arigó took hold of my right wrist with his left hand and wielded the borrowed pocket knife with his right hand. I was told not to watch the operation on my arm, so I turned my head toward my cameraman and directed the motion-picture work. The next thing I knew was that Arigó had placed a tumor and the knife in my hand. In spite of being perfectly conscious, I had not felt any pain. In fact, I had no sensation at all at the surgical site. I was sure that I had not been hypnotized. Yet there was the incision in my arm, which was bleeding, and there was the tumor from my arm. Subsequent analysis of the film showed that the entire operation lasted five seconds. Arigó had made two strokes with the knife on the skin. The skin had split wide open, and the tumor was clearly visible. Arigó then squeezed the tumor as one might squeeze a boil, and the tumor popped out.

I felt that I had been hoodwinked, because I had experienced nothing. However, knowing that the knife was dirty, that my skin was not cleansed, and that Arigó's hands were not clean, there was a good chance of getting an infection, perhaps even blood poisoning. I felt that if this wound healed without infection, then I could believe that Arigó had an influence on the healing process. If it got infected or blood poisoning set in, I felt I could always be flown to a hospital in Rio de Janeiro and be saved by modern medicine. Therefore, I covered the wound with a band aid, which I removed every 24 hours in order to photograph the wound. The result of this experiment was that the wound healed clean (without a drop of pus) within three days, about half the time required normally.

Since I had this operation and my mind was realigned to see things as they are, I have witnessed hundreds of healing procedures by different practitioners. This has given me some understanding of what healers can do and what they cannot do. This chapter will elaborate on this statement by distinguishing between a complete healer and the modern practitioner of medicine or surgery, using 10 criteria.

DIAGNOSIS

One of the basic characteristics of the complete healer is the ability to diagnose illness. By diagnosis I do not mean the process of ordering chemical tests, blood tests, or X rays and then analyzing the data and coming to a conclusion. I refer to the ability of the healer to look at the patient for a few seconds and then to give a coherent description of the disease process that in turn can be cross-checked by the means of modern medicine. When the patient is not physically present with the healer, the healer should still be able to make an accurate diagnosis by means of an intermediary contact such as a photograph or a signature.

Arigó had two methods of making medical diagnoses. One method was to look at a patient for a few seconds and then to give the diagnosis in a form that would be clearly intelligible to a modern medical doctor. For example, he looked at a particular patient, and the patient began to talk saying he was there to see Arigó because he thought he had leprosy. Arigó replied immediately, "No you don't have leprosy. You in fact have syphilis, and you shouldn't lie to me!" Our medical research team examined this patient and found that he did indeed have syphilis. In another example, a male patient stepped up to Arigó and quite casually Arigó mentioned to us that we should check his blood pressure because at that instant it was 23 over 17 centimeters. This statement means that the man has a systolic blood pressure of 230 millimeters of mercury, and a diastolic blood pressure of 170 millimeters of mercury. When we checked this patient with a blood-pressure cuff, it was found that Arigó was correct.

The second method of making a diagnosis by Arigó can best be described as it happened and characterized later. A patient would step before Arigó. He was clearly having visual difficulties. Now Arigó would not just say, "You have eye trouble," or "You are going blind." Instead he would give a modern technical description of the cause, such as, "It is a retinoblastoma," or "It is retinitis pigmentosa." At the time I was making these observations, I was not aware—nor was anybody else—of the method whereby such crisp diagnoses were made. During a series of 1000 diagnostic statements made by Arigó, I was amazed at the incredible accuracy of Arigó and the sophistication of the diagnostic language used. I asked Arigó what his method of making such accurate diagnoses was. He replied in a surprised manner, "That's one of the simplest things for me to do because I simply listen to a voice in my right ear, and I repeat whatever it says. It is always right."

This voice, according to Arigó, was the voice of a deceased German medical student who never finished medical school, Adolphus Fritz, or Dr. Fritz. It was not possible during the course of five years of investigation to come to any conclusion as to whether this "voice" was Arigó's way of talking to himself or was as he described it. This question—and indeed the whole area—remains open as one of the great unanswered questions of human behavior. This question is intimately related to data collected by parapsychologists and psychic researchers with respect to telepathy, clairvoyance, and clairaudience. Most open-minded scientists who have examined the evidence tend to take seriously the reality of both telepathy and clairvoyance. Although I personally believe and affirm that medical diagnosis is possible by paranormal means, the scientific community still views the matter with skepticism. The basic reason for this is that medical men have yet to perform high-quality research in this area. Most of the data in this area is now pouring forth from the various "mind control" courses but has yet to reach a sufficiently sophisticated level to be received properly by scientists.

MANUAL HEALING

The second characteristic of a healer is the ability to influence the healing process by placing his hands over the afflicted area of the patient. Of all the forms of healing, this is perhaps the most common because it is so intimately related to manual manipulation of the body in the form of massage, osteopathy, chiropracty, podiatry, and the like. However, true manual healing goes beyond these formalized arts in efficacy. For example, I personally know of cases of healing by the late Ambrose Worral in which tumors (visible under the skin surface) disappeared within a few hours of his placing his hands over them (24). In my observations of Col. Oskar Estebany of Montreal, Canada, I have seen gastric ulcers clear up and disappear within 24 hours of a manual treatment by him (verification was by X ray).

There are many variations of the manual healing art. There are healers who specialize only in setting bone fractures. There are healers who can relieve pain by working on certain pressure points on the human body not too unlike acupuncture-point topography. There are healers who touch the skin and massage tissue, and there are healers who never touch the skin but pass their hands over the body without contact. There are healers who pray silently while holding their hands on the head of the patient, and there are healers who pray aloud and get others to join them (7). There is a healer I know who works only on dental problems by means of manual contact. There are healers who practice whole-body contact rather than manual contact. There are healers who treat all illnesses by manipulating the feet.

One of the elements common to all successful manual healing is that we see at work an acceleration of normal processes. For example, a skin wound may heal in one-half or one-quarter of the normal healing time with manual treatment. Nothing unique occurs—only an acceleration of a normal process. If an ulcer heals, especially one of a long duration (chronic type), we again see an acceleration of a normal process. The same holds true for bone healing, infectious processes, tumor resolution, and the like. In the case of cancer treatment by manual healing it is well known in medicine that some cancer tumors will spontaneously disappear. We do not understand what triggers the cancer process to begin, nor do we understand what signals the process to regress. It is my guess that the healer unconciously is able to trigger the cancer-regression process. I do not know of any case where a healer has triggered the cancer process to begin.

We do have some idea of what the acceleration process may be in manual healing from the research of Dr. Bernard Grad of McGill University, and from Dr. H. Justa Smith of Rosary Hill College and the Human Dimensions Institute. Grad initiated the research with Estebany in which the latter "manually treated" coded jugs of water. Then the treated and untreated water was used to water plants in a statistically controlled manner. Upon analysis it was found that the plants given the manually treated water grew much more rapidly and showed a greater net weight gain than the plants given untreated water. There was a statistically significant difference between the treated and the untreated plants.

Smith extended this study as the result of a conference between herself,

Dr. Grad, and me. What she did was to set up a standardized enzyme system whose potency was measured by the amount of amino acid hydrolysis of a polypeptide substrate. Estebany held in his hands the test tubes containing the water solution of the enzyme, and this was the treated sample; the untreated sample was identical in every way except that Estebany did not handle the test tubes. It was found that the "treated" samples showed 15% more hydrolytic or enzyme activity than the untreated or control samples. This difference is statistically significant. Another way of describing these results is to say that the manual treatment of the enzyme solution accelerated the action of the enzyme. It is well to remember that the healing process is so complex in any given organ or system of the body that hundreds, even thousands, of enzyme systems and other systems must be harmoniously accelerated in order to produce a healing effect. We have no explanation for this kind of inductive orchestration at normal rates or accelerated rates.

SELF-HEALING

In manual healing we have a two-term condition in which the healer acts inductively upon the healer. When we consider self-healing, we are talking about a person who is trying to act upon his own disease process. An example is that a person may have a toothache due to a periodontal abscess. In attempting to self-heal this condition he may do a number of things. He can try to control the pain, and up to a point people can generally achieve some degree of attenuation of the pain. He may also mentally visualize the pocket of pus surrounding the tooth root and try to cause the abscess to drain outward into the mouth or think of an acceleration of the action of the leukocyte and macrophage system that normally cleans up this kind of debris. Or the person may try to decelerate the growth rate of the bacteria that caused the abscess. In other words there are many imaginative approaches that a person may take in self-healing that attack the problem in a mechanistic way. The other approach in self-healing may be called holistic; in this approach the person relaxes and appeals to some higher power—a saint, a god, or God—to alleviate and cure the affliction. There are on record many cases of an alleviation or cure of an organic illness by just such a simple appeal. In my experience either of these methods may work for the average person in distress.

But when we consider healers of the caliber of Arigó we find a paradox with respect to self-healing. In his 20 years of public healing Arigó was never able, to the best of my knowledge, to heal himself in any way that showed an acceleration of the normal healing process. Furthermore, he was never able to do any healing for any blood relative or family relative.

For instance, during May 1968, when my medical colleagues and I were conducting research on Arigó, his wife fell and suffered a Colles fracture of the right wrist. Arigó stood by as helpless as a child and was unable to lift a finger to help his wife. We, the members of the orthodox profession of medicine, reduced the fracture and encased it in a plaster cast, and the healing process proceeded at a normal rate without any complications. I have never been able to understand this anomaly in the great healers. Arigó stated simply that since his healing powers were not resident in himself but in Dr. Fritz, he could not control who was to be healed. And specifically in the case of his family and blood relatives, he was not permitted to help them. Yet I have had testimony from his housekeeper of many years that he was able in her case to heal illness for her and her family. She was not related to Arigó in any way.

CHEMICAL AGENTS IN THE HEALING PROCESS

Many healers use various chemical agents or medicines as an adjunct to their pure healing action. These may be natural products such as mud packs, honey, greases, fats, leaves, herbs, roots, or even chemical agents such as are produced by the pharmaceutical industry as medicines. In modern times Edgar Cayce was a prime example of a healer who practiced his healing art in this manner. His castor oil packs were applied externally in a wide range of medical conditions in a way never envisaged or accepted by orthodox medicine. Yet these simple treatments proved to be highly effective and are still being used today by doctors and patients who have learned to appreciate their efficacy.

In general, the healer who uses such chemical agents in his healing practice does not use them in the manner prescribed by the manufacturer. On superficial examination it would appear that the healer uses these chemical agents in a conventional way. But my experience has shown that this is not the case. A good healer has a diagnostic ability that gives him the insight to know what is wrong in the chemistry of an illness and to fill the missing links with the appropriate additive.

In the case of Arigó, our work shows that he had this ability to an extraordinary, even superlative, degree. To begin with, his voice would dictate to him what medicines to prescribe for a given illness. In the course of this practice he has been known to prescribe every known pharmacological agent and to use these agents in a way not known to modern medicine. From a purely pharmacological point of view, those of us medical men who have studied him were quite impressed by the range of (almost nonconscious) knowledge he exhibited in manipulating molecular agents for treating both the symptoms and causes of disease.

This can be better explained with a specific example. People usually know about stomach ulcers and the problems associated with this condition. The modern physician will usually treat ulcers with diet, an antacid, a chemical that blocks vagus nerve activity, or perhaps a tranquilizer. Arigó did not treat according to this schemata. He would *not* focus his attention on the stomach as the cause of the medical problem. Instead his mind would scan the organism to seek out all the malfunctions whose summation would become expressed in the stomach. He would prescribe drugs that would treat the liver, the nervous system in general, parasites if they were present, and so on—*all the basic causes of the disease outside of the stomach area.* In this way he was able to accelerate all those processes that would lead to healing a local effect—in this case, an ulcer.

Today we are familiar with the concept of megavitamin therapy in a wide variety of mental disorders. The pioneering work of Humphrey Osmond, Abraham Hoffer, and Linus Pauling over the past 15 years has finally brought this concept and practice to fruition and into widespread use. Yet it is a matter of record that Arigó was using megavitamin therapy on mental disorders such as epilepsy and schizophrenia some 23 years ago. Since healers sometimes have this extraordinary insight into the mechanisms of molecular biology and medicine, it would behoove medical researchers to pursue these insights. Doctors generally recognize that some of their most useful and powerful drugs were found by untrained healers before the age of modern science began solely by the judicious exercise of direct knowledge of hidden processes.

ANESTHESIA

In modern medicine three methods are available for the induction of anesthesia in patients. They are the chemical, the electrical, and the hypnotic. Each of these methods has a well-prescribed ritual of application of the agent to the patient. But the fact is that modern medicine cannot explain how any of these methods work. There are healers who can perform major surgery on humans, using mechanical instruments that cut tissue, and they can do it painlessly without using any of the above three methods of anesthesia. We have solid evidence that a healer like Arigó could place a sharp steel knife into the eye of a wide awake unanesthetized patient and perform delicate eye operations without causing pain to the patient. I personally have witnessed hundreds of such operations where Arigó used a knife, scissors, and other instruments to cut into the flesh and remove tumors or perform other procedures. I have never seen a patient complain of the slightest bit of pain under these circumstances. As I stated earlier, I personally underwent an operation by Arigó that was painless, and no known anesthetic agent or method was used.

On the other hand, I have observed another healer in Mexico, Pachita, who performed major surgery of the same order of complexity and delicacy as Arigó, but she had no power to control the pain. Her patients suffered pain through surgery without anesthesia. Pachita's patients were strapped down and held down by four people during the surgery, so violent was their reaction to the pain. Thus, one cannot readily say that just because people are willing to submit to surgery at the hands of a healer with great charisma, the charisma alone automatically leads to a self-hypnotic acceptance of pain. I believe that a healer like Arigó had the power to cause a mentally induced local anesthesia that was probably the result of an acceleration of neural enzyme systems that are normally activated by chemical anesthetic agents. I feel that it should be a high-priority research aim to find out how a healer can produce such perfect anesthesia in humans without using any known agent.

INSTANT SURGERY

In preceding sections we discussed the phenomenon of surgery done by a healer. Such surgery, in fact, mimics closely all the essential *acts* of modern surgery but violates every *principle* of modern surgery. In addition the surgical procedures as carried out by Arigó are highly accelerated compared to the pace of modern surgery and, by comparison, can be properly called instant surgery. The kind of surgery that is done in modern hospitals is far from being instant, in that it takes a great deal of preparation to do an operation. One might have the impression from movies that in a modern hospital a surgeon steps to the operating table, is handed a scalpel, makes an incision, manipulates, steps away, and in a moment the operation is over. This is not the case. Each minor surgery takes a lot of preparation. The operating room had to be cleaned and sterilized, and much equipment had to be assembled by a corps of people. And, of course, the cleanup after surgery is not trivial.

Arigó's instant surgery offered a sharp contrast. He operated in a dirty combination office–waiting room. The preparation and examination of the patient took less than a minute. Arigó borrowed any available knife and did the most fantastic and skillful surgery on any part of the body in a matter of minutes. No known anesthesia was used. No hemostatic procedure was used. No gloves were worn. No draping was used. There was no suturing of the surgical wound at the end of the operation. Arigó sent the patient on his way immediately after the surgery. He usually wiped the blood off the knife on his shirt and went on to the next case of surgery. This is what I mean by instant surgery.

In the Philippines there are healers who practice surgery by simply pointing their finger, or that of a bystander, at the skin area to be incised and the flesh opens with minimal bleeding. Most good healers who practice surgery with a knife are at times capable of opening and closing surgical wounds with their bare hands—sometimes by direct contact with the tissue and at other times without contact. This type of power is, of course, extraordinary. Such wounds may heal more or less instantly, at times with normal scar-tissue formation and at other times with no observable scar-tissue formation.

BACTERIOSTASIS

Bacteriostasis is the inhibition or cessation of the growth of bacteria. It also may be manifested as a condition in which bacteria do not appear at all, especially during surgery by a healer. Although I have mentioned it before, I wish to emphasize the point that I have never seen a healer doing surgery who observes the rules of antisepsis and sterilization. They all work under what may properly be called dirty conditions. In spite of this, I have never seen a case of postoperative infection. I have never personally carried out rigid experiments in the field with bacterial culture plates to determine the range and mode of action of a healer's ability to control the growth rate of bacteria. Under the conditions in which I had to work this was not feasible from a technical point of view. However, such experiments should certainly be carried out in the future, now that the medical profession has begun to take an interest in the healing art.

HEALING AS AN ACTION-AT-A-DISTANCE EFFECT

This is an area of healing in which the healer and the patient are separated by some distance, and the healer tries to exert his healing effects across the distance. If the patient gets well, it is called a successful "absent" healing. This practice is carried on by many spiritist groups, particularly in England and South America, and by healing prayer groups in many different churches. I personally have seen successful healing at a distance effects but must confess that my observations in this area are limited. However, it is a fertile area for research that can be carried on cooperatively between religious groups and medical groups.

THE GUIDE IN HEALING

The "guide" in a healer's experience is conceived to be the spirit of some deceased person who serves to guide the work of the healer. The healer may hear the voice of his guide or feel his presence. This is one of the great mystery areas of the healing art. The main reason why I give it credence, in spite of the lack of any positive evidence for the guide's independent existence, is that the verified factual information of the healer argues powerfully for a superintelligence at work. Now it could be argued that the healer who knows all is an idiot savant in medicine and that it is not necessary to invoke an extra- or superintelligence. This is a matter that has to be decided by future research. It is one of the great frustrations of my life that I have never been able to devise an objective research technique that would clearly distinguish between Arigó's natural genius as a healer and the presence of an alter ego that he called Dr. Fritz.

REGENERATION

There are healers who have been alleged to regenerate missing tissue, such as a finger or an eyeball. I have not yet come across a healer who could regenerate organs or tissues in this fashion. Furthermore, there are cases where a healer has been alleged to restore life in a person who has been pronounced clinically dead. I have had reliable reports of three such cases in modern times, all of which occurred in India (15). However, reliable as my informants are, I suspend judgment in this area until more evidence appears.

It must be stated in all due fairness to the reader that the observations and opinions cited above are not generally shared by the medical profession in the United States. Rather we are looking at a set of phenomena that portends the shape of things to come. I suspect that each of these areas will be vigorously debated and researched in the decades ahead. What are the issues and what will be debated?

In general the issue centers around the question of paranormal powers, their existence and their nature. The paranormal powers described for the healing process fall into two categories. The first has to do with paranormal means of getting information, or what I prefer to label *direct brain perception* (DBP). The second has to do with paranormal means of inducing action in physical systems, or what I prefer to label *direct brain action* (DBA). It is admitted by all serious students of these two effects that they cannot be explained within the presently known and accepted laws of nature. Therefore, our first task as scientists is to try to propose models for DBP and DBA, and then to test these models experimentally in order to build a data base for future theoretical speculation. Arthur Koestler's *The Roots of Coincidence* is an up-to-date survey of the many competing models that have been proposed. However, each of the models and theories reviewed by Koestler presents great difficulties in terms of experimental verification.

The specific problems that biology and medicine must consider in order to understand how DBP and DBA work can be briefly outlined:

1. *The origin of life.* We must find out the shaping force that molds atoms into living forms.
2. *Replication and control in life processes.* We need a deeper understanding of "go" and "no-go" processes at the genetic level, and control processes that regulate growth states, repair, and other survival processes.
3. *Normal sensory perception.* We will surely have to understand fully normal audition, vision, taste, smell, and touch before we can begin to understand DBP processes.
4. *Artificial sense perception.* In order to understand fully normal sense perception we shall have to create at least one sensory prosthesis that can be applied to man—for example, in deafness.
5. *Memory in brain.* At the heart of any biological control process is some kind of servomechanism plus a memory. We shall have to more fully understand the workings of memory before we can understand either normal sensory perception or DBP.
6. *Memory in nature.* There are many indications that the memory function exists outside the brain and is to be found in nature. A deep understanding of this process is vital to understanding any memory or control function in both DBP and DBA.
7. *Precognition.* Inherent in any discussion of DBP and DBA is the question of time-transcendence, and this can best be studied in the phenomenon of precognition. These practical and theoretical problems have been considered by the author in some detail elsewhere (13).

Medicine lacks any coherent theory or even a philosophy of biological systems. It is quite unable to explain, say, the spontaneous remission of cancer under the healing ministrations of an Oral Roberts or Ambrose Worrall, let alone the well-documented cures at Lourdes, France, where no healers at all were involved. Such events can no longer simply be labeled anomalies by medicine and put aside. Theoreticians of medicine must now begin to consider seriously the nature of the healing process in all its aspects, including the "miraculous," as part of the larger formulation of biological theory. Fortunately, the recent advent of the theory and practice of Chinese acupuncture in the United States may help to stimulate such a quest.

REFERENCES

1. Budge, E. A. Wallis. *Syrian Medicines.* Asher: London, 1913.
2. Budge, E. A. Wallis. *The Divine Origin of the Craft of the Herbalist.* Culpeper House: London, 1928.
3. Budge, E. A. Wallis. *From Fetish to God in Ancient Egypt.* Oxford University Press: London, 1934.
4. Breasted, James Henry. *The Edwin Smith Surgical Papyrus.* University of Chicago Press: Chicago, Ill., 1930.
5. Esdaile, James. *Hypnosis in Medicine and Surgery.* Julian: New York, 1957.
6. Hammond, Sally. *We Are All Healers.* Harper and Row: New York, 1973.
7. Kuhlman, Kathryn. *I Believe in Miracles.* Prentice-Hall: Englewood Cliffs, N.J., 1962.
8. Labat, René. *Traité Akkadien de Diagnostics et Pronostics Medicaux.* Académie Internationale d'Histoire des Sciences: Paris, 1951.
9. Leake, Chauncey D. *The Old Egyptian Medical Papyri.* University of Kansas Press: Lawrence, Kans., 1952.
10. Mellaart, James. *Earliest Civilizations of the Near East.* Thames and Hudson: London, 1965.
11. Chapelain-Jaurès, Robert. *La Pathologie dans L'Egypte Ancienne.* Brodard: Coulommiers, 1920.
12. De Morant, George Soulie. *L'Acuponcture Chinoise.* La Fitte: Paris, 1957.
13. Puharich, Andrija. "Protocommunication." In *Parapsychology Today: A Geographic View.* Parapsychology Foundation: New York, 1973.
14. Sauneron, Serge. *The Priests of Ancient Egypt.* Grove: New York, 1960.
15. Schulman, Arnold. *Baba.* Viking: New York, 1971.
16. Stever, Robert O. *Aetiological Principle of Pyaemia in Ancient Egyptian Medicine.* John Hopkins Press: Baltimore, 1948.
17. Thompson, R. Campbell. *Semitic Magic.* Luzac: London, 1908.
18. Thompson, R. Campbell. *A Dictionary of Assyrian Botany.* British Academy: London, 1949.
19. Voisin, H. *Acuponture.* Maloine: Paris, 1959.
20. Wallnofer, H., and Von Rottauscher, Anna. *Chinese Folk Medicine.* Signet: New York, 1972.
21. Ware, James R., trans. and ed. *Alchemy, Medicine and Religion in the China of A.D. 320.* M.I.T. Press: Cambridge, Mass., 1966.
22. Williams, Harvey. *The Healing Touch.* Thomas: Springfield, Ill., 1951.
23. Wong, K. Chimin, and Wu Lien-Teh. *History of Chinese Medicine.* Tientsin: Tientsin, China, 1932.
24. Worrall, Ambrose, and Worrall, Olga. *The Gift of Healing.* Harper and Row: New York, 1965.

Charles T. Tart

CHARLES T. TART, *Ph.D., is associate professor of psychology at University of California at Davis.*

After studying electrical engineering at Massachusetts Institute of Technology, Dr. Tart studied psychology at University of North Carolina, where he was awarded a doctorate degree in 1963. Following that he held a postdoctoral research fellowship at Stanford University, while lecturing in psychology there. From 1965 to 1966 he was an instructor in psychiatry at the University of Virginia School of Medicine.

Dr. Tart is a fellow of the American Society for Clinical Hypnosis and of the Society for Clinical and Experimental Hypnosis. He is certified in experimental hypnosis by the American Board of Examiners in Psychological Hypnosis. He is author of more than 60 scientific articles and books, including Altered States of Consciousness *(John Wiley, 1969; paperback, Anchor, 1972) and* On Being Stoned: A Psychological Study of Marijuana Intoxication *(Science and Behavior Books, 1971). Dr. Tart's article "A Psychophysiological Study of Out-of-the-Body Experiences in a Selected Subject," in* Journal of the American Society for Psychical Research *(Vol. 62), in which he created the term "OOBE," was the first instrumental study of its kind, opening a new direction for psychic researchers. His 1972 article "States of Consciousness and State-Specific Sciences," in* Science *(Vol. 176), promises to do the same for developing a science of consciousness.*

Dr. Tart can be reached at the Department of Psychology, University of California, Davis, Calif. 95616.

15 Out-of-the-Body Experiences

CHARLES T. TART

SUMMARY

Out-of-the-body experiences (OOBE's), formerly called "astral projection" and "traveling clairvoyance," are a universal human phenomenon in the sense of having been experienced in every time and culture, although only a very small fraction of people ever experience it.

In an OOBE, a person experiences his consciousness existing outside his physical body. The effect of an OOBE on a person is almost always a conviction of survival after death, and this is probably the origin of the concept of a soul, a central doctrine in most religions.

Current physical science defines such experiences as meaningless, but solid evidence now exists that challenges that part of the belief system of modern science which denies the reality of OOBE's. This chapter reviews the evidence from anecdotal literature and recent laboratory studies of proficient OOBE subjects, and offers an interpretation of the findings.

INTRODUCTION AND HISTORY

In 1963 the following case experience was reported by L. Landau in the *Journal of the Society for Psychical Research* (6):

> I knew my wife, Eileen, for quite a number of years before we were married, and she frequently used to talk to me about her out-of-the-body experiences. These were of the usual kind, and on some occasions I was able to verify that something paranormal had, in fact, occurred. For example, she went to bed one afternoon, saying that she would see what our friend, who was on a holiday in Cornwall, was doing. When she woke up, she was able to give an accurate description of a rock plant, which our friend was photographing, the details of the surroundings, also of a gentleman who was with him. All this was subsequently confirmed, and, what was interesting, our friend was under the impression that a shadowy figure passed near him at the time.

At the beginning of September 1955, I was not very well. Much fuss was made about it, but a thorough medical examination failed to show any real trouble. Eileen, who was then living with her mother in Kent, spent several nights in my house, occupying the spare bedroom, which was opposite mine, across the landing, on the south-western corner of the house. One morning she told me that she came into my bedroom during the night (minus her physical body!) to check my pulse and respiration. I asked her to do this again the following night, this time trying to bring some object with her; I gave her my small diary, weighing 38 grammes.

That night we left the doors of both bedrooms open, as I could hardly expect a physical object to pass through solid wood. Before falling asleep, I asked myself to awake, should anything unusual occur in my room.

I woke up suddenly: it was dawn, and there was just about enough light coming in through the partly drawn curtains to enable one to read. At the point marked "A" (see Figure 1) stood the figure of

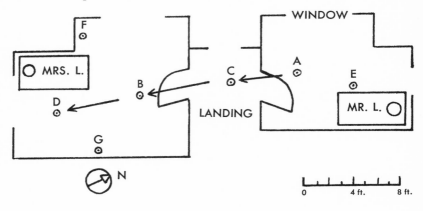

Figure 1.   Floor plan of Landau house.

Eileen, facing north-west, and looking straight ahead towards the window. The figure was wearing a night dress, its face was extremely pale, almost white. The figure was moving slowly backwards towards the door, but it was otherwise quite motionless; it was not walking. When the figure, progressing at the rate of about one foot per five seconds, reached the position "C," I got out of bed and followed. I could then clearly see the moving figure, which was quite opaque and looking like a living person, but for the extreme pallor of the face, and at the same time the head of Eileen, asleep in her bed, the bedclothes rising and falling as she breathed. I followed the figure, which moved all the time backwards, looking straight ahead, but apparently not seeing me. I kept my distance and ultimately stood in the door of the spare bedroom, when the figure, now having reached the position "D," suddenly vanished. There was no visible effect on Eileen, who did not stir, and whose rhythm of breathing remained unchanged.

I moved quietly back to my room, and at point "E," on the floor, found a rubber toy dog, which belonged to Eileen, and which stood on a small chest of drawers in position marked "F" when I last saw it. This dog weighed 107.5 grammes.

In the morning, after breakfast, I questioned Eileen about the diary. She said that she first went to the desk (position "G") on which it was, and somehow could not pick it up. She then thought that it would be easier to carry something that belonged to her, and she decided on the rubber toy, which she managed to take with her to my room. It was a pity that I woke up some thirty seconds too late.

Mrs. Landau adds the following note to her husband's report:

I remember getting out of bed (but do not recall exactly how), going over to my desk and seeing the diary. As a child, I had been told never to handle other people's letters or diaries, so probably for this reason I did not want to touch this one. Instead, I lifted my rubber toy dog, and I remember taking it through the door, across the landing, to the other room, but do not remember actually *walking*. I did not find the dog heavy, or difficult to hold. I have no recollection of what I finally did with it. I remember seeing Lucian asleep and breathing normally. I felt very tired and wanted to go back to bed. Up to this moment my consciousness appeared to me normal, and so did my ability to see my surroundings, which also appeared normal to me. I do not remember anything about going backwards to my room, or entering my bed.

What should an intelligent person, someone who has faith in the current world view of physical science, make of such a report? By our currently accepted physical view of the world and the nature of man, it cannot be taken at face value. Consciousness, as we all "know," is a by-product of the physical activity of the brain and nervous system and cannot exist independently of the brain and nervous system, or even externally to them. So Mrs. Landau's consciousness could not have left her body and gone into another room. It is simply a further impossibility to think that such a disembodied consciousness could be perceived as a figure by a sane person, and the idea that a disembodied consciousness could move a material object across space is dismissed automatically. Objects do not move except in response to known physical forces, and "disembodied souls," besides not existing, certainly do not exert known physical forces.

So, what do we make of this case? An account of a psychotic experience, even though the writer sounds sane and plausible? A gross misperception of events that are explainable in ordinary physical terms, such as Mrs. Landau sleepwalking and Mr. Landau hallucinating and/or totally misperceiving? A deliberate hoax, designed to fool the gullible?

Let us consider the Geddes case (2, pp. 72–75), this one much older than the Landau case:

> On Saturday 9th November, a few minutes after midnight, I began to feel very ill, and by two o'clock was definitely suffering from acute gastroenteritis, which kept me vomiting and purging until about eight o'clock. . . . By ten o'clock I had developed all the symptoms of acute poisoning: intense gastro-intestinal pain, diarrhoea; pulse and respirations became quite impossible to count. I wanted to ring for assistance, but found I could not, and so quite placidly gave up the attempt. I realised I was very ill and very quickly reviewed my whole financial position. Thereafter at no time did my consciousness appear to me to be in any way dimmed, but I suddenly realised that *my* consciousness was separating from another consciousness which was also me. These, for purposes of description, we could call the A- and B-consciousnesses, and throughout what follows, the ego attached itself to the A-consciousness. The B-personality I recognized as belonging to the body, and as my physical condition grew worse and the heart was fibrillating rather than beating, I realised that the B-consciousness belonging to the body was beginning to show signs of being composite—that is, built up of "consciousness" from the head, the heart, and the viscera. These components became more individual and the B-consciousness began to disintegrate, while the A-consciousness, which was now me, seemed to be altogether outside my body, which it could see. Gradually I realised that I could see not only my body and the bed in which it was, but everything in the whole house and garden, and then realised that I was seeing not only "things" at home, but in London and in Scotland, in fact wherever my attention was directed, it seemed to me; and the explanation which I received, from what source I do not know, but which I found myself calling to myself my *mentor*, was that I was free in a time-dimension of space, wherein "now" was in some way equivalent to "here" in the ordinary three-dimensional space of everyday life.

The narrator then says that his further experiences can only be described metaphorically because although he seemed to have two-eyed vision, he "appreciated" rather than "saw" things. He began to recognize people he knew, and they seemed to be characterized by colored condensations around them. He continues,

> Just as I began to grasp all these, I saw my daughter enter my bedroom; I realised she got a terrible shock, and I saw her hurry to the telephone. I saw my doctor leave his patients and come very quickly, and heard him say, or saw him think, "He is nearly gone." I heard him quite clearly speaking to me on the bed, but I was not in touch with my body and could not answer him. I was really cross when he took a syringe and rapidly injected my body with something which I afterwards learned was camphor. As the heart began to beat more strongly, I was drawn back, and I was intensely annoyed, because I was so interested and just beginning to understand where I was and what I was "seeing." I came back into the body really angry at being pulled back, and once I was back, all the clarity of vision of anything and everything disappeared, and I was just possessed of a glimmer of consciousness, which was suffused with pain.

This case does not strain our belief system as much; at least, no physical objects were moved! We can regard this as an interesting example of the disintegration of the mind as bodily functioning moves toward death, but the apparently veridical perceptions of events at a distance *must* have been illusory, since there is no known physical explanation for them.

This experience of one's consciousness existing independently of the physical body or, more accurately, of temporarily functioning at a distance from the physical body, is called an *out-of-the-body-experience* (OOBE). Older terms for it are *astral projection* and *traveling clairvoyance*. Accounts of what seem to be OOBE's can be found in very early historical records and OOBE's are a universal human phenomenon in the sense of having been experienced in every time and culture, even though only a very small fraction of people ever experience it. Although any individual case, such as the ones in this chapter, can be dismissed if one does not want to take OOBE's seriously, the temporal and cultural universality of OOBE's calls for looking at them seriously.

The effect on a person of having an OOBE is enormous. In almost all cases, his reaction is approximately, "I no longer *believe* in survival after death—I *know* my consciousness will survive death because I have *experienced* my consciousness existing outside of my physical body." The conviction gained by experiencers of OOBE's that they will survive death has undoubtedly led to the concept of a soul, a central concept in most religions.

The current physical science belief system defines such experiences as meaningless and not at all as indicating the existence of any kind of soul. This physical world view is neither psychologically satisfying nor scientifically sound. It leads to only one conclusion: death is the end for each of us.

In spite of the attempts of our culture to ignore death and to keep us too busy to think about it, this is a crucially important subject for an individual, and it is important for us psychologically and parapsychologically to understand the concept of the soul and what, if any, scientific evidence there is supporting its existence. Most of the parapsychological investigation of the concept of soul has dealt with the analysis of mediumistic communications, but there is fascinating data on OOBE's among the living that is quite important and that we shall consider in this chapter.

THE LITERATURE ON OOBE'S

Parapsychological Studies: Case-History Collections

There are three major sources of information on OOBE's. The first, which we shall consider here, involves the analysis of reports of individuals who have had the experience. The second kind, considered below, is the literature written by individuals who feel they have had the experience repeatedly and may know how to teach other people to experience it. The third and most recent source of information is the limited laboratory studies of OOBE's that has now been carried out.

A number of excellent collections of case histories of OOBE's now exist (1–3, 5, 10). Almost all of the experiences in these collections are once-in-a-lifetime experiences for the individual involved. They usually have no idea of how to make the experience deliberately come about, and their own experience happened "accidentally." From looking at large numbers of these experiences, however, certain general features of OOBE's can be discerned that tell us something about their nature.

The circumstances preceding an OOBE are varied, and we do not know to what extent they are really causal. A frequent circumstance is extreme sickness, often to the point of death. Rather jokingly, would-be experiencers are sometimes advised that the surest way to experience an OOBE is to *almost* die, but the "almost" part is rather tricky! Emotional stress also often precedes an OOBE. But in a large number of cases, we simply do not have any idea why an OOBE occurred to an individual at a given time. In a small number of cases, a person has deliberately used some technique learned from the occult or meditation literature to induce the experience.

Often one of the first features of an OOBE is the person noticing he is floating near the ceiling; apparent defiance of gravity is quite common in OOBE's. He may or may not find himself in his own bedroom, or wherever his physical body is located, and have the experience of looking at his physical body from an outside point of view. A typical reaction is seeing a body that both looks familiar and rather unhealthy, as if it were dead. Recognizing it as one's own body is something of an emotional shock.

A person frequently tells himself that he is dreaming or having some kind of "abnormal" experience during an OOBE, but upon introspective examination, he finds that he seems to be in a perfectly normal state of consciousness, possessed of all his mental abilities. So, he may *tell* himself that what is happening is totally impossible in terms of what he knows about the nature of the world, but it *is* happening. He can think about it, be critical, and use his will to try out various things. This apparent normality of consciousness during an OOBE makes it interesting to study as a state of consciousness: consciousness per se seems hardly altered, but the relationship of consciousness to the physical body is drastically altered.

Most people experiencing OOBE's find that they have a second, non-physical body. This is usually a seemingly exact replica of the ordinary physical body and is usually clothed in familiar clothing. The problem of where the clothing comes from is an interesting theoretical one and will be discussed later.

A person having an OOBE will often have some thought of seeing a loved one or some distant place, and simply thinking of it results in his being there. He may be aware of a sensation of flying there or of some kind of transition state, but often he just finds himself there. Material barriers seem to be no obstacle. It is a frequent experience for a person during an OOBE to decide to go into the next room and reach for the door to turn the knob, only to find that his arm goes right through the door and that his second body as a whole can do the same.

A person sometimes meets what seem to be other entities while he is out of his body, and these other entities may be recognizable living people or entities that he considers as spirits or other nonmaterial beings. Two-way interaction of any sort with physically embodied people is quite rare. The OOB experiencer usually feels that they do not perceive him in any way, and there is no way he can contact them.

A typical OOBE is of short duration, lasting from half a minute up to half an hour. Longer OOBE's are quite rare for ordinary experiencers.

A rather common feature is the presence of some kind of "cord" linking the physical body and the second body. Many occult writers have theorized that this cord constitutes a vital link between the two bodies and that if it were severed, death would result. The "silver cord" in the Bible (Eccles. 12:6) might be a reference to this phenomenon, although Biblical scholars generally believe it refers to the human spinal cord.

In almost all reported OOBE's, the person is totally convinced that this was a "real" experience, not some sort of dream or hallucination: he "knows" he was at some distant place and observed what was going on there. From a more critical parapsychological point of view, in most cases we cannot tell. Either the person did not recognize the place where he was, in which case we have no way of checking on the accuracy of the possible ESP involved, or the person was already familiar with the place and added no details that he did not know from his ordinary visits or added details that might have been figured out on the basis of ordinary reasoning. Nevertheless, in some OOBE cases, the descriptions of distant places are accurate and detailed and must be attributed to some kind of extrasensory knowledge.

The Landau case is quite atypical of most OOBE's. In the usual experience, people cannot affect matter, no matter how hard they try, and they are not perceived as apparitions.

If case-history collections were our only source of information on OOBE's, a number of shortcomings of this method would make us have considerable reservations about our data. For example, almost all of them are cases that have been contributed voluntarily through one or another means: we do not know how typical a person who volunteers information about an OOBE is in terms of the generality of people experiencing it. Further, many of the cases are quite old when they are reported and/or no written notes were made at the time, so we do not know how many omissions, additions, or distortions may have occurred through faults of memory. And there is always the possibility of some bias in reporting: the persons may be reporting not simply their OOBE's but their *interpretations* of their OOBE's disguised as straightforward reporting.

Nevertheless, the case-collection analysis method has been quite valuable in outlining the general features of OOBE's and will continue to be very valuable in the future. My own collection, for example, now runs to several hundred cases, and I plan to analyze features of the experiences with respect to the experiencer's individual psychological characteristics to see how they affect the experience.

Until very recently, the case-history collection was the only scientific literature on OOBE's.

THE OCCULT LITERATURE

The occult or metaphysical literature differs from the scientific in that statements are made about OOBE's on the basis of the writer's authority, not on the basis of observation, experimentation, and analyses that have been replicated by other scientists. Most parapsychologists view this literature with considerable ambivalence, finding it a useful source of ideas and hypotheses but seeing it as containing many distortions and delusions of particular writers, put forward as if they were absolute truths.

For simplicity, we can consider the occult literature as falling in two major categories. The first is the "I've got a secret that you're not spiritually developed enough to be told, but I'll hint at it" type of writing. Here we have writers who claim they can have OOBE's at will and perform all sorts of miraculous feats with them, but they are not willing to explain fully how they do this, and they do not offer to demonstrate these abilities to observers. Sometimes they hint that if you become indoctrinated with their belief system, they may tell you more. There may be a great deal of truth in what some of these writers say, but since a principal requirement of scientific investigation is that there be no secrets and all information be communicated freely and accurately, scientists cannot do much with this kind of literature.

A second major kind of occult literature on OOBE's consists of writings by people who seem quite sane and sensible and are doing their best to communicate their experiences and their conclusions about them to others. The general tenor of their writings is, "Look, I know this is a crazy experience, and you will probably think I'm crazy for writing about it, and I don't blame you. But I think it's true, and I think I know how you can learn to do it if you really try. If it works for you, then you can believe me; otherwise I understand you have a perfect right to regard me as crazy." These people, in addition to seeming sane in terms of their writing style, are willing to share all their information and let others benefit from it. The reader who would like a sensible and clear exposition of what this phenomenon seems like to someone who has had many such experiences would do well to read the writings of such people as Oliver Fox (4), Sylvan Muldoon (11), and Robert Monroe (8).

Although all three give detailed techniques for having OOBE's, we do not know whether they work generally with other people. The techniques require dedication and prolonged practice, so few people ever give them a real try.

LABORATORY STUDIES

Miss Z

In 1965, I met a young woman, whose anonymity I shall preserve by calling her Miss Z. She had had frequent OOBE's since as early in her childhood as she could remember. These experiences almost always consisted of waking up for a few seconds during the night and feeling that she was floating near the ceiling of her bedroom. If she looked down at those times, she could see her body in bed. Because this was such a common childhood experience for her, happening several times a week, she had assumed it happened to everybody. Since it was not particularly interesting, she had not mentioned it to anyone as a child. By the time she got to high school, she realized that it did *not* happen to everybody, and she had to be careful about whom she spoke to about it if she did not want to be thought crazy.

The experience was still occurring occasionally when I met her, so I raised the question with her whether it was "only" an interesting psychological experience or was extrasensory in nature (i.e., whether she was really seeing her physical body from a position near the ceiling). This particular question had never occurred to her. I suggested that she write the numbers 1–10 on 10 slips of paper and put them in a cardboard box. After she went to bed at night, she should scramble the slips in the box and pick one at random, putting it on her bedside table so that she could not see the number from her position in the bed, but so that it would be clearly visible from the ceiling. If she experienced herself near the ceiling that night, she was to memorize the number and check it for accuracy in the morning.

When I saw her a few weeks later, she said she had tried the experiment on seven different nights and found that she was correct each time. So it was quite worthwhile to try to study her experiences as parapsychological ones, although no parapsychologist would accept an experiment in which the subject reports his own data as *proof* of ESP.

Over the next few months I was able to arrange for Miss Z to sleep in a psychophysiological laboratory on four different nights. I was interested in finding out what happened in her brain and body while she was having the experience, as well as verifying the parapsychological nature of it. On each night, Miss Z slept on an ordinary, comfortable bed. Tiny electrodes were glued to her scalp and various places on her body to record her brain waves, her eye movements, her blood pressure, and the electrical resistance of her skin. The latter two measurements would tell me something about the activity of her autonomic nervous system, while the former two would tell me about her brain-wave state, particularly whether she was awake or asleep and, if asleep, whether dreaming or not. There was an observation window above her bed, so I could look through it and observe her at any time. Figure 2 shows a diagram of the laboratory setup.

After Miss Z was in bed, I retired to a separate office and, using a book of random numbers, wrote a five-digit random number on a large white card. I then placed this on a shelf, shown in Figure 2, about seven feet above the floor and well above Miss Z's head. The target number was clearly visible to any observer near the ceiling but invisible to anyone lying in bed or walking around the room. Miss Z could not get out of bed

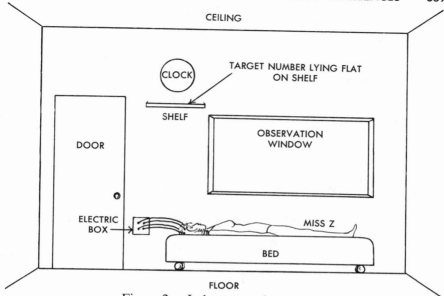

Figure 2.   Laboratory plan, Miss Z.

without disrupting the operation of the brain-wave-recording machine in the next room, so she was prevented from seeing the number by ordinary means. A clock was placed beside the target number so she could try to note the time when she had an OOBE and saw the number.

A number of interesting things were observed about Miss Z's OOBE's that have been reported in detail elsewhere (15). We will deal only with the highlights here.

She had several OOBE's over the course of the four nights; after each, she awoke within a minute or two and reported on it. In all but one, she did not feel that she had floated in her second body to a position from which she would have been able to observe the target number, and so, she did not make any guess as to what it was.

On the various occasions on which she reported an OOBE, a unique physiological pattern appeared. Figure 3 shows a diagram of her ordinary brain-wave recording, a dreaming brain-wave recording, and the pattern, which I have called an *alphoid pattern*, associated with her OOBE's. The patterns were clearly distinct in several ways. First, her ordinary waking wave pattern was quite normal and showed well-formed alpha waves at a frequency of about 10 cycles per second. Some REM (rapid eye movements), occurring under her closed eyelids, in conjunction with thought, are also seen in the waking pattern record. The stage-1 dream pattern is also quite distinct. This is the brain-wave pattern associated with ordinary dreaming. The waves from the brain are quite different, and the REM

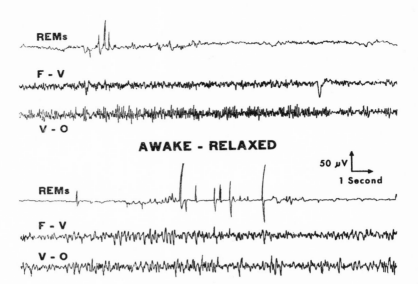

AWAKE - RELAXED

50 μV ⌐
1 Second

STAGE 1 DREAMING

Fig. 1.   A typical example of Miss Z's waking EEG pattern and an example of Stage 1 dreaming with REMs.

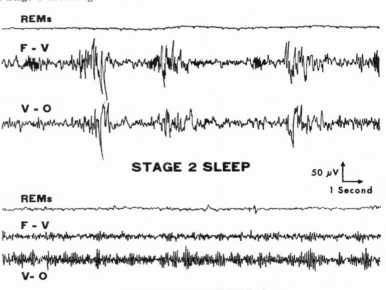

STAGE 2 SLEEP

50 μV ⌐
1 Second

ALPHOID PATTERN

Fig. 2.   A sample of Miss Z's Stage 2 sleep and an example of the alphoid pattern she showed in conjunction with her OOB experiences.

Journal of the American Society for Psychical Research, Vol. 62, 1968.

Figure 3.   EEG patterns of Miss Z.

corresponds to a scanning of the dream imagery. The alphoid pattern, on the other hand, shows alpha waves that are about $1\frac{1}{2}$ cycles per second slower than her ordinary alpha rhythm and a generally lower voltage kind of pattern. There is no REM associated with this pattern at all; the slight wiggles seen on the eye-movement channel in the figure are artifactual. The significance of the alphoid pattern is unclear, as it is not seen in ordinary people, but it seems to be associated with most or all of Miss Z's OOBE's. I say "most or all" because in a few instances the record was technically unsatisfactory and a decision could not be made as to whether the alphoid pattern was showing or not.

Although OOBE's have been associated with near-death experiences and some of the occult literature states that bodily functions must drop to a low level similar to dying for OOBE's to take place, the brain-wave measurements and the autonomic measurements contradict this with Miss Z. Her heart rate was perfectly normal—between 70 and 80 beats per minute—and her skin-resistance patterns did not show anything different than would normally be expected for sleep. Her body was in no sense in a deathlike condition during her OOBE's.

On the last night that I was able to work with her in the laboratory, she did report floating to a position in her second body from which she could see the number, and she correctly reported the number as 25132. Since the odds against correctly guessing a five-digit number when only trying once are 100,000:1, this is a highly significant result.

Psychic researchers have learned to be quite sensitive to the possibility of their subjects cheating on their experiments. I do not think that Miss Z cheated in any way, though it should be noted that the possibility of very elaborate fraud on her part is not completely ruled out. It is conceivable that she might have concealed a mirror and telescoping rod in her pajamas and used these to inspect the number at a time when she thought I might not be looking through the observation window. Again, I consider this highly unlikely, but the possibility should be mentioned.* While these results may be interpreted as showing the paranormality of OOBE's under laboratory conditions, I prefer to see them as demonstrating the feasibility of studying OOBE's under laboratory conditions, as well as giving us some clues about changes in the body during OOBE's.

Why should we care about the changes in the body? Aside from knowl-

---

* An interesting commentary on the general public's attitude toward the possibility of fraud is that when I mention the case of Miss Z in public lectures, no one ever asks about the possibility of fraud, but someone usually asks whether I, as experimenter, knew what the target number was. Since the answer is yes, the questioner then asks whether the results could be caused by telepathy rather than an OOBE. Preferring to postulate telepathy to explain this rather than accept the idea of an OOBE is certainly unusual for our culture! The results could be caused by telepathy or clairvoyance, of course, and this interpretative problem will be discussed later.

edge for its own sake, it is possible that if distinct physiological changes accompany OOBE's, we might learn to produce these physiological changes by other means, such as biofeedback or selected drugs, and thus produce a physiological state more favorable to OOBE's, even though producing the physiological state per se might not be sufficient to produce the OOBE. Thus, understanding and possibly learning to control the physiology associated with OOBE's might give us a way of producing them rather than having to wait for them to happen or hope that a lucky subject will have a technique that might work in the time we have available.

Robert Monroe

Robert Monroe is a successful American businessman in his early fifties who has recently described his more than 1000 OOBE's in a book entitled *Journeys Out of the Body* (8). I first met him in 1965, shortly after having completed my investigations of Miss Z, and was impressed with his intelligence, sincerity, and efforts to report accurately and understand his experiences. My complete reports on work with him have been published elsewhere (8, 14).

Robert Monroe had no interest in occult or mystical subjects until his OOBE's started, and they started in a way that made no sense to him. He began having a series of strange experiences that culminated in feelings of vibrations shaking his body. Medical examinations showed no ailment of any sort, and in spite of the fear arising from the lack of information, he decided to let go to this vibration feeling and see what developed. The vibrations developed into OOBE's, and over the years, he was able to develop some degree of control over inducing them. These methods are described in his book.

At the time we were able to work together, he was having about one OOBE per week, sometimes voluntarily, sometimes involuntarily. Over a course of several months, I was able to measure Monroe's brain waves and heart rate, using the Electroencephalography Laboratory at the University of Virginia Medical Center. He would lie on a cot for several hours in the evening, sometimes sleeping, sometimes deliberately attempting to produce an OOBE, while a technician monitored the recordings in the next room. A randomly selected five-digit number was placed on a shelf above the recording machine in the technician's room rather than in the room with Monroe.

On the eighth night in the laboratory, Monroe experienced two very brief OOBE's. One of them could not be checked for paranormality, because the scene was too indefinite to be identifiable. The other was a reasonably correct description of the technician's activities in another room, but still of a general enough nature that one could not feel satisfied as to whether it was paranormal or not. He did not feel himself to be in a position to view the target member. The brain-wave recordings during that time were essentially those that occur during stage-1 dreaming, although there was not very much REM. Heart rate was quite normal, and as with Miss Z, it was clear that Monroe was not in any deathlike state while experiencing these brief OOBE's.

After this study, I moved to a new position at the University of California. Sometime later, when Monroe visited me in the summer of 1968, he was able to spend a short time in a much more comfortable laboratory that I had available then, during which time he again had two brief OOBE's. The physiological pattern was similar to that seen before—namely, a stage-1-dreaming brain-wave pattern with little REM. One of his brief (about eight seconds) OOBE's was accompanied throughout by a drop of blood pressure. In neither case was the description of the distant environment specific enough to warrant discussing parapsychological aspects of the experience. Monroe did not feel he had enough control over his movements in the unfamiliar environment to see the five-digit target number.

Although the brain-wave pattern seen during Monroe's OOBE's is associated in ordinary people with dreaming, it would be questionable to conclude that his OOBE's are simply a form of dreaming. Remember, first, that OOBE's are defined in terms of their *psychological* characteristics—that is, by a person feeling himself as completely conscious and mentally functioning normally but located at a place different from where he knows his physical body to be. Second, over the years the memory of dreaming faded out for Monroe as OOBE's developed, so it looks as if OOBE's have replaced dream activity for him, even while taking over the physiological state ordinarily associated with dreaming. Whether this would hold up with more precise measurement is not known.

The differences in physiological correlates of OOBE's with Miss Z and Monroe should alert us that we may be dealing with more complex phenomena than we believe. There may be several kinds of OOBE's.

I wish to mention one other experience with Monroe that will illustrate some of the complexities of OOBE phenomena. Several months after moving to California, I decided to set up an experiment in which on one evening my wife and I would concentrate intensely for about half an hour to try to help Monroe to have an OOBE and so "travel" to our home. If he could accurately describe our home, this would be good evidence for the parapsychological component of his OOBE's.

I telephoned Monroe and told him simply that we would try to "guide" him across the country to our home at some unspecified time that night. That evening I randomly selected a time to begin concentrating, a time well after the time I thought Monroe would be asleep. It turned out to be 11:00 P.M. California time, or 2:00 A.M. East Coast time. At 11:00 my wife and I began our concentration exercise, but at 11:05 the telephone rang; we did not answer the phone but tried to continue concentration until 11:30 P.M.

The following day, I telephoned Monroe, told him only that the results had been encouraging without giving him any details and that he should write down an independent account of what he had experienced. His account was as follows:

> Evening passed uneventfully, and finally got into bed about 1:40 A.M., still very much wide awake. Cat was lying in bed with me. After long period of calming mind, sense of warmth swept over body, no break in consciousness, no pre-sleep. Almost immediately felt something (or someone) rocking my body from side to side, then tugging at my feet! (Heard cat let out complaining yell.) I recognized immediately that this had something to do with Charley's experiment, and with full trust, did not feel my usual caution (about strangers!). The tugging at my legs continued, and I finally managed to separate one second body arm and held it up, feeling around in the dark. After a moment, the tugging stopped and a hand took my wrist, first gently, then very, very firmly, and pulled me out of the physical (body) easily. Still trusting, and a little excited, I expressed willingness to go to Charley, if that was where he (it) wanted to lead me. The answer came back affirmatively (although there was no sense of personality, very businesslike). With the hand around my wrist very firmly, I could feel a part of the arm belonging to the hand (slightly hairy, muscular male). But could not "see" who belonged to the arm. Also heard my name called once. Then we started to move, with the familiar feeling of something like air rushing around my body. After a short trip (seemed around five seconds in duration), we stopped, and the hand released my wrist. There was complete silence and darkness. Then I drifted down in what seemed to be a room.

I am not reproducing all of Monroe's notes, except to add that when he finished this brief "trip" and got out of bed to telephone me, it was 2:05 A.M. his time. So the correlation with my wife and me beginning to concentrate was extremely good; he felt the tug pulling him from his body within one or two minutes from when we started to concentrate.

On the other hand, the omitted portion of his account—the description of our home and what my wife and I were doing—was quite inaccurate. He perceived too many people in the room, perceived my wife and me doing things that we did not do, and gave a rather vague description of the physical nature of the room.

This is the kind of frustrating result that happens when working with a frontier area in psychic research. It is not evidential enough to say that it was certainly a paranormal occurrence, but it is unsatisfactory to say that nothing happened. This particular event has a quality that other OOBE's have had of seeming to mix some genuinely paranormal perceptions of the physical world in with a nonreal (or certainly a nonphysically real) mixture.

Ingo Swann

Ingo Swann is an artist and writer in his thirties who has learned how to have OOBE's while maintaining a relatively normal state of consciousness (i.e., he does not go into an altered state or start from sleep). An initial series of experiments with him have been carried out by Dr. Karlis Osis and Janet Lee Mitchell at the ASPR in New York City (7).

The experiments were similar to those carried out with Miss Z and Monroe. Swann sat in a comfortable chair with electrodes attached for measuring brain waves and autonomic measures and attempted to have OOBE's and to see some target material located near the ceiling. Initially a five-digit number was used as a target, as in my study of Miss Z, but Swann was unable to identify unmistakably any five-digit number; he did not feel he could "see" that clearly during his OOBE's. So these experiments used an open-topped box near the ceiling with randomly selected objects in it, thus requiring only easier figure–ground discriminations. Swann attempted to describe verbally and to draw what the objects were. The target box was suspended high enough so that no one in a normal position in the room could see it, but it was easily open to observation from near the ceiling. This variant target procedure has some important advantages, discussed below.

Initial physiological studies of Swann's OOBE's have shown no noticeable changes in autonomic functionings (as they had with Miss Z and Monroe) but did show a decrease in the amplitude and abundance of alpha rhythm during the OOBE's. These brain-wave changes are similar in some respects to those seen in Miss Z's OOBE's but are not as large or primarily characterized by alphoid activity.

In order to evaluate the paranormality of Swann's descriptions of the target material in the suspended box, a series of eight different targets was used. Swann's verbal descriptions and drawings were randomized as to order and then an independent judge attempted to match the drawings and descriptions against the actual target objects. The judge correctly matched all eight drawings and target sets. This is a highly improbable result and would occur by chance less than 1 in 40,000 times. So there is little doubt about the extrasensory component of Swann's OOBE's.

The research with Swann is particularly focused on the implications of

OOBE's for the question of the survival of some kind of soul at death. In the studies with Miss Z, one could accept the paranormality of the results but argue that they do not prove that there is any independently existing soul—only that Miss Z used some sort of telepathy or clairvoyance to discern the five-digit number correctly and then fitted this in with her totally "hallucinatory" and "unreal" experience of floating above her body.

The research program of the ASPR will deal with this argument by using target material whose perceptual characteristics vary with respect to the point in space from which it is viewed—that is, the target in the suspended box will be chosen to present one kind of perception if "looked at" from the point of view of the physical body (even though ordinary perception is excluded) but another kind of perception if viewed from the different experiential location of consciousness during an OOBE. Optical systems, for example, will be placed between the subject and the target material in an adjacent room; this should distort the target material in known ways but should have no effect if the subject is really using some kind of ESP analogous to an X ray from the position of his physical body.

In one pilot experiment with Swann, two flickering slides of a horse were projected on to a screen in the target box in such a way that, viewed from the experiential OOBE location, an embodied observer would see the horse as running to the left, which is what Swann reported. All the initial data from studies of Swann so far seem to fit the hypothesis that he has something analogous to an eye located at the OOBE location, rather than using ESP from the position of his physical body. This is one of the most creative lines of research in modern parapsychology.*

An interesting question about the "second body" in an OOBE is whether it interacts with measurable properties of the known physical world. There are suggestive indications of this kind of interaction in some of the very old literature of psychic research, but as we have little knowledge of the conditions of these observations, modern parapsychologists give them little weight. An initial observation of the OOBE's of Ingo Swann again suggests that there can be interaction with the physical world during an OOBE, and perhaps it only requires appropriate and very sensitive modern instrumentation to detect it.

---

* Experimental investigation of OOBE's depends on finding talented and cooperative subjects who can have the experience almost at will. If you have such an ability, or know of someone who does, and would be interested in helping further our knowledge of OOBE's, please write to Dr. Karlis Osis, American Society for Psychical Research, 5 West 73rd St., New York, N.Y. 10023; to Mr. William Roll, Psychical Research Foundation, College Station, Durham, N.C. 27708; or to Dr. John Palmer, Division of Parapsychology, School of Medicine, University of Virginia, Charlottesville, Va. 22901. I will not have time for further experimentation myself for the next few years.

Swann visited a modern physics laboratory where a superconductor magnetometer was being used (see Chapter 22). This device was thoroughly covered with both aluminum and copper shields and a super-conducting cannister, to prevent external magnetic fields from affecting it. Thus, only magnetic fields from nuclear particles would ordinarily affect its output. At the time of the observation, a decaying magnetic field had been induced in the apparatus an hour previously, and its very slow decay produced a steady sine-wave output on the recording chart. Ordinarily no visible change in this smooth output would be visible over time periods of hours.

The physicist who was interested in Swann's OOBE's asked if he could affect the output by "putting his attention" (Swann's way of inducing his special OOBE's) on the inside of the magnetometer. As he did so, the frequency of the sine-wave output suddenly doubled for a couple of cycles, a period of roughly 30 seconds. Another physicist present immediately exclaimed that perhaps it was just "noise" in the apparatus, and he would really be impressed if Swann could stop the output altogether. The output immediately stopped for approximately 45 seconds, at which point Swann said he would "let go," and the output returned to normal. Similar disturbances occurred when Swann described how he performed this. Lengthy calibration runs after Swann left the laboratory showed no instabilities of any kind in the sine-wave output.

The physicists involved regard this as only a preliminary observation, not an experiment, but it strongly reinforces some suggestions I made some years ago (13) for using physical instruments (and sensitive animals or people) as "detectors" of paranormal phenomena occurring in a defined space. The research program at the ASPR will try a variety of instrumental methods for detecting the presence of the second body during OOBE's, as will a program at the Psychical Research Foundation.

SOME PROPOSED EXPLANATIONS

Many investigators have attempted to find a theory that would account for OOBE's. Such theorizing is in its infancy, since we have very little solid, factual information about the experience, but I will sketch the three major theories that have been proposed so far, suggest a new approach to OOBE's, and add one theory of my own that complements the other theories.

The Independent-Soul Explanation

The "natural" explanation that almost all people who have the experience subscribe to and that has been formally proposed by some investigators is, in effect, that there is no need to explain it: it is just what it seems to be. Man has a nonphysical soul of some sort that is capable, under certain conditions, of leaving the physical body. This soul, as manifested in what we call the second body, is the seat of consciousness. While it is like an ordinary physical body in some ways, it is not subject to most of the physical laws of space and time and so is able to travel about at will.

The main sort of objection that has been raised to this theory hinges on the observation that in many cases the OOB experiencer finds not only that he has a second body but that it is fully clothed in familiar clothing, such as the pajamas that he wore to bed. Many people are willing to believe that a human being has a soul—but his pajamas? To account for clothing and various nonphysical objects encountered in OOBE's by ascribing a soul to essentially everything makes the idea of a soul so diluted in general that it does not really "explain" anything.

There is another major disadvantage of the independent-soul explanation: *soul* is not simply a descriptive term but one that has all sorts of explicit and implicit connotations for us because of our culture's religious beliefs. Even though a person may have had no formal religious training or may have consciously rejected his early training, such an emotionally potent concept as soul can have strong effects on us on a subconscious level. Since a prime requirement of scientific investigation is precise description and clear communication, a word like *soul* is difficult to deal with scientifically because of the deep, hidden reactions it may evoke in the human practitioners of science.

The Hallucination-Plus-Psi Explanation

Those who find the idea of a nonmaterial soul unproven or unacceptable explain OOBE's as hallucinatory experiences of some sort—for example, a lucid dream, the kind in which one knows that one is dreaming (12, 17). That is, it is a (lucid) *dream* in the sense that no *thing* leaves the physical body and goes to another location. For those cases of OOBE's in which veridical information about distant events is obtained, it is postulated that ESP, which is well proven, works on a nonconscious level, and this information is used by the subconscious mind to arrange the hallucinatory or dream scene so that it corresponds to the reality scene.

The problem with this kind of explanation is that it is too general. Since we do not have any idea about what the limits of ESP are, we can use this type of explanation to explain anything in those terms. For instance, it may not be true that you are *actually* reading this book at the moment: you may be having an hallucination in an altered state of consciousness that, by the operation of subconscious clairvoyance, corresponds perfectly to the experience you would have from actually reading this book, so you will never be able to tell the difference.

Until we know some actual limits of ESP, it is difficult to know how far to extend this theory. It does have the advantage, however, of accounting for the pajamas of the second body very well. They are just as "real" or just as "unreal" as the second body itself.

The Mentally-Manipulatable-State Explanation

The problem of where the pajamas come from has led to a third class of theory, which postulates that there is indeed a second body in some real, albeit nonphysical, sense. However, the realm or space of the universe in which this second body operates is conceived of as being easily changeable or manipulatable by the conscious and nonconscious thoughts and desires of the person whose second body is in that space. Since we ordinarily think of ourselves as clothed, and this is a totally automatic and deeply ingrained habit, when having an OOBE, the stuff (sometimes called the *psychic ether*) of that space is molded into the clothing we normally picture ourselves as having. Thus, this theory can account for clothing and other nonphysical objects without attributing some kind of souls to them.

The major problem with the manipulatable-state explanation is that we have little independent evidence for the psychic ether or something similar, so we are explaining away one unknown by invoking another unknown.

Note that the independent-soul explanation and the manipulatable-state explanation of OOBE's can both include the fact that other kinds of ESP, such as telepathy, clairvoyance, or precognition, can also occur in conjunction with OOBE's.

We may not have to decide which of these theories is right in some ultimate sense but rather which theory applies to which particular case. I have emphasized what we might call "classical" OOBE's in this chapter, where the experiencer feels totally at a distant spatial location, while feeling fully conscious and totally disconnected from his or her physical body. This is the sort of case that fits the independent-soul theory well. But there are cases that have been called OOBE's in which the experiencer vividly images (or hallucinates) what it would feel like to be at the distant location but retains some awareness of his or her physical body and surroundings. This fits the hallucination-plus-psi theory much better. These latter kinds of cases might be better called *mental projections*, to use an old term, or *visualized OOBE's*. Ingo Swann's OOBE's have some qualities of the latter type of mental projection, while Miss Z's and Monroe's are classical OOBE's.

Future research will have to begin making these and similar distinctions in order to refine our understanding of OOBE phenomena: at present we do not know enough scientifically to make good distinctions.

The Altered States of Consciousness Approach

In thinking about these explanations, we approach the problem from our normal state of consciousness; that is, our biological computer, our brain or mind, is programmed with all sorts of commonplace assumptions that make the problem of explaining OOBE's take the particular form that it does. Elsewhere (16), I have argued that we need to develop what I have called *state-specific sciences*; that is, certain kinds of phenomena occurring in altered states of consciousness should be investigated *in* those states of consciousness, and explanations and theories developed in those states and tested there. This would involve an unusual extension of scientific method but still be in accord with the basic principles of science. I have not developed this idea in any detail with respect to OOBE's, but I offer it here in this very brief form just to remind us of the many hidden assumptions characteristic of our ordinary state of consciousness that bias us in even attempting to explain OOBE's. I have recently examined some of these assumptions elsewhere (18).

The Interaction Explanation

From my general knowledge of parapsychological phenomena I have no doubt that basic extrasensory phenomena (telepathy, clairvoyance, precognition) do exist, as does PK. Since these phenomena are completely inexplicable with our current knowledge of the physical universe, they indicate that our current physical picture of the universe is quite incomplete. The area that our physical, scientific world view leaves out is the whole area we might call mind. From my psychological, as well as parapsychological, knowledge—and particularly the developing science of transpersonal psychology, which deals with man's spiritual potentials—I suspect that mind does indeed constitute some kind of space or energy that exists in some sense independently of physical matter.

Applying this to classical OOBE's, the picture I have developed of man is the following: A man is composed of two sections, a physical, biological unit, and a certain quantity of mind. While each of these two domains has laws and properties of its own, we do not have a *direct* personal experience of either one alone. What we experience is mind and body forming a complete, closely linked gestalt, the whole that arises from this. This is our everyday experience of ourselves: mind intermeshes so firmly with body and body so firmly intermeshes with mind that we cannot tell the two apart. By virtue of *inter*acting, mind alters the nature of body, and body of mind.

In an OOBE, I theorize that we have a partial-to-complete separation of body and mind. Thus, we have a chance to get a temporary look at body without mind influencing it as strongly as usual and, from the person's experiences, at mind without it being as strongly influenced by body.

Both body and mind are very dynamic, active self-regulating mechanisms to a high degree—that is, each contains feedback stabilization systems to hold bodily and mental functioning within certain "normal" limits. Even though mind is part of the regulatory system for body and vice versa, we could expect each system to function in the same overall pattern for a while after the removal of the other (controlling) system because of the strength of conditioned habits.

So in the usually brief OOBE, we see consciousness functioning just as it does when ordinarily associated with the person's body, our ordinary state of consciousness. This goes to the point of continuing to treat the mental image of the body as still real. Thus, one has a second body that performs like one's ordinary physical body. The physical body, insofar as we have observed it from outside in these laboratory studies, shows no marked changes from its usual pattern of functioning. The patterns of body functioning are still highly conditioned to the imprint of mind-in-body, and the patterns of mental functioning are still highly conditioned to the imprint of body-in-mind.

In prolonged OOBE's, on the other hand, where the interactive control of one system over the other is greatly reduced, I would expect that the characteristics of mind-in-itself and body-in-itself might begin to manifest themselves, and the scant evidence we have, primarily from case reports and the occult literature, supports this idea. Monroe, for example, found that prolonged (30 minutes or more) OOBE's resulted in his body feeling cold and stiff when he "returned," and so, fear of serious malfunctioning has made him avoid prolonged OOBE's. It is as if the body by itself, without the interacting mind pattern, cannot completely regulate itself to maintain the pattern we call a living body, and small errors in control start to accumulate until the danger level is reached. I would predict that really prolonged OOBE's would lead to serious illness or death, an idea frequently met with in the occult literature.

Looking at the person's experience in prolonged OOBE's, we find that the pattern of mental functioning may indeed change away from that of ordinary consciousness in a variety of ways. The second body may change in shape or function from its physical form or disappear altogether. Mystical experiences may occur. Repeated OOBE's for a given person may have a similar effect of allowing a quite different pattern of mind functioning to emerge. Thus, our understanding of OOBE's will not progress much faster than our understanding of altered states of consciousness in this area.

The second case in this chapter, an OOBE resulting from imminent death, illustrates the kind of mental changes that can occur with prolonged OOBE or a grossly malfunctioning physical body. If the separation of mind and body is never fully complete in an OOBE, then gross malfunctions of the physical body should make alterations of consciousness more likely also, as if a regulatory connection from the physical body still exists but now, transmitting highly unusual information, it cannot hold conscious functioning within its usual limits.

The interaction theory is similar to the independent-soul theory. It differs primarily in attempting *not* to start with a philosophical or religious concept of soul, with all the cultural connotations of that term, but to be descriptive of the classical OOBE phenomenon, as we know it currently, and provide a theoretical framework that can be worked with scientifically. Classical explicit ideas about the soul, such as immateriality, immortality, and special relationships to the Creator, are too abstract to deal with by current scientific procedures. The theory of mind being capable of existing independently of the body fits well with current data, but its primary function is to stimulate us to collect more data, refine one's ways of investigating this phenomenon, and try to make predictions that can be tested. This is the function of any workable scientific theory.

The interaction theory can be seen as a supplement to the altered states of consciousness approach and the other theories.

OVERVIEW

There are several things we can be sure about with respect to OOBE's. First, some people do have the experience of feeling located at a position different from that of their physical body while nevertheless feeling that they possess all of their critical faculties and other properties of their normal state of consciousness at the time. They are convinced it is not a dream or hallucination.

Second, their perception of events from this distant location may not correspond at all to what actually goes on in physical (consensus) reality, and so the experience can be treated as a psychological phenomenon that does not demand any unusual (paranormal) explanations.

Third, the perception of events at a different location is *sometimes* accurate enough and unlikely enough that we must conclude there is a paranormal component to the experience, which immediately makes the phenomenon much more important than if it were just a psychological one: it demands a much more sophisticated explanation because it violates our physical world view.

Finally, because of the immense effect on the individual's belief system —namely, convincing him that he will survive death—the OOBE is one of the most important psychological experiences, even though it occurs rarely. I am convinced that most of our great religious traditions are based on this sort of experience. We will not be able to understand our religious heritage or our philosophies of life until we come to an adequate understanding of OOBE's. OOBE's are one of the world's most important and most neglected phenomena. Even psychic researchers generally do not pay attention to them. But their importance in understanding man cannot be overestimated.

REFERENCES

1. Crookall, R. *The Study and Practice of Astral Projection.* Aquarian: London, 1961.
2. Crookall, R. *More Astral Projections: Analyses of Case Histories.* Aquarian: London, 1964.
3. Crookall, R. *The Techniques of Astral Projection.* Aquarian: London, 1964.
4. Fox, O. *Astral Projection: A Record of Out-of-the-Body Experiences.* University: New Hyde Park, N.Y., 1962.
5. Green, C. *Out of-the-Body Experiences.* Institute of Psychophysical Research: Oxford, 1968.
6. Landau, L. "An Unusual Out-of-the-Body Experience." *Journal of the Society for Psychical Research,* 42 (1963): 126–128.
7. Mitchell, J. "Out of the Body Vision." *Psychic,* April 1973.
8. Monroe, R. *Journeys Out of the Body.* Doubleday: New York, 1971.
9. Muldoon, S., and Carrington, H. *The Phenomena of Astral Projection.* Rider: London, 1951, pp. 72–75.
10. Muldoon, S., and Carrington, H. *The Phenomena of Astral Projection.* Rider: London, 1951.
11. Muldoon, S., and Carrington, H. *The Projection of the Astral Body.* Rider: London, 1956.
12. Stewart, K. "Dream Theory in Malaya," in C. Tart, ed., *Altered States of Consciousness.* Doubleday: New York, 1972, pp. 161–170.
13. Tart, C. "Applications of Instrumentation to the Investigation of Haunting and Poltergeist Cases." *Journal of the American Society for Psychical Research,* 59 (1965): 190–201.
14. Tart, C. "A Second Psychophysiological Study of Out-of-the-Body Experiences in a Gifted Subject." *International Journal of Parapsychology,* 9 (1967): 251–258.
15. Tart, C. "A Psychophysiological Study of Out-of-the-Body Experiences in a Selected Subject." *Journal of the American Society for Psychical Research,* 62 (1968): 3–27.
16. Tart, C. "States of Consciousness and State-Specific Sciences." *Science,* 16 June 1972, pp. 1203–1210.
17. van Eeden, F. "A Study of Dreams." In C. Tart, ed., *Altered States of Consciousness.* Doubleday: New York, 1972, pp. 147–160.
18. Tart, C. "The Assumptions of Orthodox Western Science." In C. Tart, ed., *The Spiritual Psychologies.* Harper and Row: New York, 1974.

D. Scott Rogo

D. SCOTT ROGO *is a parapsychologist, educator, and writer. He graduated from California State University, Northridge, where he also carried
out graduate work in the psychology of music and its relation to altered
states of consciousness.*

*As a researcher, Mr. Rogo has published more than a dozen papers in
such publications as* International Journal of Parapsychology, Journal of
the Society for Psychical Research, Parapsychology Review, Journal of
Paraphysics, *and* Theta. *In 1973 he was a visiting research consultant at
the Psychical Research Foundation in Durham, North Carolina.*

*As an educator, Mr. Rogo coordinated an experimental course in para-
psychology under the auspices of University of California, Los Angeles,
from 1968 to 1969. He also authored a text on educational planning in
psychic research,* Methods and Models for Education in Parapsychology
(*Parapsychology Foundation, 1973*) *and has been the recipient of a grant
to study this area further.*

*Mr. Rogo is the author of three books on psychic research, including a
two-volume study of paranormal music,* NAD (*University Books, 1969
and 1972*), *and a book on survival,* The Welcoming Silence (*University
Books, 1973*). *He is a regular book reviewer for periodicals such as*
Psychic, Parapsychology Review, *and* Fate.

*Mr. Rogo can be reached at 6544 Hesperia Avenue, Reseda, Calif.
91335.*

16 Apparitions, Hauntings, and Poltergeists

D. SCOTT ROGO

SUMMARY

Apparitions represent a rich collection of phenomena. They have been seen personifying the forms of the living and of the dead, at the exact time of the agent's death and often a considerable time after. Some apparitions are seen continually and become the focal point of full-fledged hauntings. Hauntings, though, may not only include visual phenomena but auditory and tactile phenomena as well. Just as there are several hypotheses to account for apparitions, a number of theories have also been proposed to explain hauntings. While none of these theories is completely acceptable, it does seem that apparitions, as well as hauntings, represent objective or at least semiobjective phenomena. In other words, these phenomena are "physical," not hallucinatory. Poltergeists are a certain type of haunting in which objects are thrown about and other physical displays are carried out by an unseen force. In some cases apparitions have been noted. Usually such outbreaks are brief. New evidence indicates that poltergeists are engendered by psychological frustrations that are projected by a form of "mind over matter." Nonetheless, poltergeists might share a similar mechanism with haunted houses and apparitions—some sort of physical emanation from the living that may exist independent of the agent and even survive bodily death.

INTRODUCTION

Although psychic research is a relatively young science, tales of ghosts, wraiths, banshees, and haunted houses have been recorded for centuries. In fact, the chain-rattling ghost immortalized by Charles Dickens in his classic *A Christmas Carol* was actually stereotyped from an allegedly true experience recorded by the Roman scholar, Pliny the Younger. Paracelsus, the medieval alchemist and physician, wrote that spirits of the dead can

375

attract the attention of the living by creating noises, sounds of invisible footsteps, and other bizarre manifestations that we today would label hauntings.

Nonetheless, psychic research was the first science to investigate systematically tales of haunted people and haunted abodes. When the SPR was founded, one of the first committees formed by it was one to investigate claims about haunted houses. As will be seen later in this chapter, this work and interest yielded a rich harvest.

To the public's mind, no phenomenon is so linked in the imagination to parapsychology than the investigation of haunted houses. Although parapsychology today has adopted the methodology and scientific philosophy of experimental psychology, this trend is rather recent and began with J. B. Rhine's statistical ESP tests at Duke University, first published in 1934. Before that, however, the work of parapsychology was less experimental and more in line with collecting spontaneous cases of apparitions, telepathy, hauntings, and the like. This chapter will draw upon much of that work.

APPARITIONS

When one speaks of apparitions, one is talking about a group of phenomena. G. N. M. Tyrrell, a former president of the SPR, devoted his 1942 Myers Memorial Lecture to that organization to the subject of apparitions. In this lecture, later published as a book, *Apparitions* (35), Tyrrell broke down apparition cases into four categories: (*a*) apparitions of the living, (*b*) crisis apparitions, (*c*) postmortem apparitions, and (*d*) continual apparitions. These four categories represent the major "types" of phantoms. And before entering into a discussion of what apparitions are, a brief summary of each of these types will be given.

When one thinks of apparitions, one invariably imagines apparitions of either the dead or of those who died at the exact moment the apparition was seen. This is not so, however. A large portion of reported apparitions represent figures of living persons. For example, the experiments of S. H. Beard have become famous. Beard was a Victorian gentleman and a friend of Edmund Gurney, one of the founding members of the SPR and an indefatigable researcher.

Beard attempted to see if he could project an apparition of himself to his fiancée, L. S. Verity. Before retiring one night, he concentrated on appearing to Miss Verity but fell asleep. Although he did not know he had succeeded in his goal, at that very time Miss Verity saw an apparition of him, clad in full evening dress, at her bedside. She was so startled that she screamed, waking her younger sister who shared her room. The sister saw the figure also.

That the apparition was seen collectively by two percipients is a critical point. One theory of apparitions asserts that apparitions are really only hallucinations caused telepathically. The percipient receives, unconsciously, an ESP impression from the agent trying to reach him, and thereupon, the percipient's unconscious mind projects a visual hallucination to transfer this message to the conscious mind. However, in the Beard–Verity case, *two* percipients saw the form—which makes the telepathic theory rather cumbersome.

In order to verify his experiences Beard attempted his little experiment on several more occasions. Before one experiment, he notified Edmund Gurney of his forthcoming venture so that Gurney could validate the experience if it was successful. It was. Beard concentrated on Miss Verity and attempted to stroke her hair. (By this time he could transfer his "consciousness" with the apparition of himself.) His fiancée reported that while perfectly wide awake, she had seen his form and that it stroked her hair (7).

Another case of an apparition of the living is reported by Mrs. Henry Sidgwick in her paper "On the Evidence for Clairvoyance" (29). The case concerned Mrs. Wilmot, who appeared to her husband and his cabinmate aboard the ship *The City of Limerick*, which was crossing the Atlantic. Mrs. Wilmot was acutely anxious over this trip because the stormy seas had already wrecked one steamer making the same voyage. One evening, falling asleep, Mrs. Wilmot seemed "to leave her body" and travel in an apparitional body to find her husband. (This all suggests an out-of-the-body experience, a phenomenon examined in Chapter 15). She landed aboard a ship and entered a stateroom, where she saw her husband. Another man was lying in a berth above his, but nonetheless, she entered the room, kissed her husband, and departed. Her form was seen not only by Wilmot but also by the other passenger, Mr. Tait, as Wilmot's report records:

Upon the night following the eighth day of the storm . . . I dreamed I saw my wife, whom I had left in the United States, come to the door of my state-room, clad in her nightdress. At the door she seemed to discover that I was not the only occupant of the room, hesitated a little, then advanced to my side, stooped down and kissed me, and after gently caressing me for a few moments, quietly withdrew. Upon waking I was surprised to see my fellow passenger, whose berth was above mine, but not directly over it . . . looking fixedly at me. "You're a pretty fellow," said he at length, "to have a lady come and visit you in this way." I pressed him for an explanation, which he at first declined to give, but at length related what he had seen while wide awake, lying in his berth. It exactly corresponded with my dream.

Later, Mrs. Wilmot correctly described her husband's stateroom. All these reports were verified by Mr. Wilmot's sister, who was also aboard the ship.

Crisis apparitions are forms that cannot really be classified as either those of the living or of the dead. They usually appear at the exact moment, or shortly after, that the agent has undergone an accident or death. The following is a typical case.

Eldred Bowyer-Bower was a World War I pilot. On March 19, 1917, his plane was shot down over France. That same morning his apparition was seen by his half-sister, Mrs. Spearman, who was in India (37):

On March 19th, in the late part of the morning, I was sewing and talking to baby. Joan [another child] was in the sitting room and did not see anything. I had a great feeling I must turn around and did, to see Eldred; he looked so happy and had that dear mischievous look. I was so glad to see him I would just put baby in a safer place, then we could talk. "Fancy coming out here," I said, turning around again, and was just putting my hands out to give him a hug and a kiss, but Eldred had gone. I called and looked for him. I never saw him again.

In this case it would be impossible to say whether the apparition was seen at the moment of death or somewhat later.

Some important data concerning crisis apparitions were collected by the SPR in a huge survey undertaken in 1889 which was published in 1894 as "The Census of Hallucinations" (36). The project was organized to collect veridical cases of apparitions and similar phenomena and to discover what percentage of the normal population seems to have these experiences. When the "Census" was completed, it was discovered that 1684 persons out of 17,000 surveyed reported such experiences. Of these, 80 cases could be classified as crisis apparitions. When mapped out on a graph, it became obvious that these experiences showed a consistent pattern: a crisis apparition was arbitrarily defined as a form seen within 12 hours of the agent's death. When these 80 cases were analyzed to see where they would cluster, most reported cases occurred simultaneously with the crisis. Thus, a consistent sloping curve was constructed—most cases reported at the moment of death and then gradually declining as time passed.

Apparitions seen after 12 hours were classified as postmortem apparitions—that is, apparitions of the dead. Sometimes these apparitions are seen years after the agent's death. Naturally, they have often been cited as evidence that man survives death. One of the most famous of these cases is one that has been labeled the scratched-cheek case because of the peculiar evidence the apparition offered (18).

F.G.'s* sister died of cholera when only 18. Nine years later, F.G. was traveling through St. Joseph, Missouri, and was resting in his hotel room, thinking about the business matters that had brought him there. He suddenly became aware of a figure to the side of him, and glancing around, F.G. was amazed to see the apparition of his long-deceased sister. What was peculiarly noteworthy about this apparition was that it was disfigured by a long red scratch on its cheek. Just as suddenly as it appeared, it vanished. Upon returning to his home, F.G. reported this experience to his parents. When his mother heard about the scratch, she nearly collapsed. Upon recuperating, the woman admitted that when paying her last respects to the body of her daughter before burial, she had tried to "touch up" the face and had accidentally scratched the girl's cheek. However, in order to hide the accident she had carefully concealed the scratch with makeup. No one but herself knew of the incident.

The figure of F.G.'s sister was seen only once. However, some figures are seen more often, and in fact, certain apparitions appear time and time again. To use a popular term, these figures are *ghosts*. Inasmuch as continuous apparitions are usually identified with "haunted houses," discussion of these apparitions will be deferred until hauntings are considered.

I might also add, in passing, that apparitions not only represent forms of living and dead humans, but animals as well. Raymond Bayless, in his book *Animal Ghosts* (3), has collected several such accounts. Although there is little room to discuss them here, animal apparitions fall into the same topology as human apparitions—they have appeared at times of crisis and after death and have even haunted their earthly homes.

Now comes the critical question: How can we explain this range of ghostly phenomena? The reader should not be surprised when it has to be admitted that parapsychologists have no "explanation" for apparitions. We do have theories for them, but there is no general agreement on what an apparition is that can be generally subscribed to by all parapsychologists.

To begin with, a theory about apparitions must take into consideration several factors that are hard to amalgamate. For example, one prime problem in theorizing about apparitions is whether or not they are physical or nonphysical. In other words, do apparitions occupy physical space

---

* In many cases recorded in early parapsychological literature only initials were used, since years ago reporting a psychic impression was often seen as indicating some sort of abnormality. Persons reporting such experiences insisted on anonymity for obvious reasons. However, their complete names were kept in the original reports when filed with the SPR or similar organizations. *Editor*

or are they really some weird form of veridical, but subjective, hallucination? There is evidence for both. The "physical" characteristics of apparitions sum up as follows: (*a*) they are sometimes seen collectively, (*b*) they have been known to move physical objects,* and (*c*) they have been seen reflected in mirrors. On the other hand, compare these characteristics to the obvious nonphysicality of apparitions: (*a*) they are seen fully clothed, (*b*) they may *not* be seen collectively, (*c*) they often appear in conjunction with material objects (such as seen holding an object), and (*d*) they walk through walls.

Any theory of apparitions must explain these different characteristics.

One of the earliest theories offered to explain phantoms was put forward by Edmund Gurney (7). His theory states that an apparition is subjective and is caused by telepathy. The percipient receives a telepathic cue and then projects an apparition. The theory had its merits, for it did explain why apparitions are so neatly dressed. The stumbling block to Gurney's theory was that it could not explain collectively perceived apparitions. In answer to this objection he extended his theory to include the concept of contagious telepathy. This concept states that when the agent projects an apparition he might telepathically infect others in his presence to also see the same figure. Needless to say, this theory soon became unworkable when one considers that apparitions have been seen by whole groups of people as well as by animals (as will be pointed out in the section on hauntings). Gurney himself, it might be added, was not too satisfied with his own concept.

F. W. H. Myers was the second pioneer of psychic research who grappled with the problem of apparitions (18). He agreed that apparitions were not "physical" in the literal sense but felt that they might occupy physical space. Myers spoke in terms of "metetherial" space, which translated means that there may exist a fourth-dimension field (or psi field as W. G. Roll calls it [24]) that intertwines with physical space. A phenomenon, such as an apparition, occurring in this dimension might be able to affect the physical world.

If this sounds vague it is because Myers himself was unsure of his own model. As Tyrrell explains in understatement, "It will be seen that there is in Myers' theory a note of uncertainty as to what actually happens" (35). Needless to say, though, Myers's idea of another psychic dimension intertwining with our world does explain why an apparition might share both physical and nonphysical attributes.

Tyrrell also offered a theory that is more or less a revision of Gurney's hypothesis while merging it with Myers's. Tyrrell's complex and hard-to-understand concept states that an apparition is engendered telepathically.

* For example, refer to the case of Mrs. Landau reported in Chapter 15. *Editor*

This telepathic union between the agent and the percipient does not engender the apparition, however. Instead the unconscious minds of both the agent and the percipient join together and mutually build up the apparitional form (35). This union of minds builds up an "apparitional drama." An onlooker coming into contact with this drama might join in it and see the apparition himself.

It was not until 1953 that a complete reevaluation of theories for apparitions was organized. At this time Hornell Hart, a Duke University sociologist, began a lengthy project to reanalyze our whole view of apparitions. Hart and his collaborators began their project by collecting well-evidenced cases of apparitions to discern the following: (a) the relationship between apparitions of the dead and apparitions of the living, (b) whether apparitions carry motivation, awareness, and personal identity (most theories of apparitions explain them only as mindless automatons), and (c) what bearing all this had on the question of survival after death.

Hart collected several cases based on how evidential the incident was. When was the report made? Who made it? Who were the witnesses? These were some of the questions asked. He then took his apparition cases and mapped out their characteristics, classifying them into the following categories: apparitions of those who died 12 hours or more before; crisis apparitions of persons dead less than 12 hours; apparitions seen at the moment of death; apparitions of the living in which the agent knew he had been an apparition; and apparitions of the living where the agent had no such knowledge.

Hart discovered that the traits of all these apparitions were identical. In other words, they were all of the same intrinsic nature. He also discovered that apparitions do seem to have a conscious life of their own: they react to physical objects and people in their environment just as a normal person would.

From his data, Hart constructed a new theory of apparitions, which he promoted in his initial publication, "Six Theories About Apparitions," released in 1956 (9). Later he revised his concepts in light of the new research that was being carried out in the subject of OOBE's (8), and he eventually came to believe that apparitions are not only conscious entities but that they represent some form of ultraphysical vehicle that can be liberated from the human body at death or during life. Hart referred to this as a "soul body." Because this body moves about not in the physical world but in fourth-dimensional space, it partakes of both physical and nonphysical characteristics.

It is appropriate here that I offer an evaluation of these theories. I agree that apparitions are independent, spatial entities. However, the fault I find in the theories proposed by Hart, Myers, and others is that they all work from the presumption that an apparition, if independent and spatial, is seen by the physical organ of sight. I think this is a fallacy. We know that psi impressions manifest themselves *in the form of* normal sense perception (such as in clairvoyance and clairaudience), but we maintain that these experiences are really hallucinatory, although engendered psychically. I think that the same goes for seeing an apparition. We are not seeing them with our eyes. Perhaps the apparition, appearing in some sort of fourth dimension, is actually not affecting our optic nerves but rather is igniting our clairvoyance. Thus, an apparition, if a conscious aware entity, might *cause us* to see it as clothed or accompanied by a physical object. The evidence for this view comes from two factors concerning apparitions: they are seen in totally dark rooms at night in full detail, and they are often seen as glowing. Now, if these phantoms were physical objects, we would not see them as glowing or in such detail in a darkened room. So, I believe, we might resolve this paradox by postulating that an apparition, when it appears, is actually *somehow psychically causing us to see it*. Therefore, it could "drape itself" in clothing and appear to be still there *physically*.

The fact of apparitions glowing leads us right into the very controversial topic of the human aura. The aura is claimed to be some sort of psychic force field surrounding the human body. Gifted psychics claiming to see the aura say they can read character, illness, and mood by it.

The scientific evidence for the existence of the aura is rather sparse. The first scientist really to study it was W. J. Kilner, a physician who claimed that by conditioning the eyes with specially prepared colored screens, the aura could be seen. He mapped out what colors the aura might take and what they represented (14). However, Kilner's researches, published in 1912, could never be verified, although several attempts were made. Although the work of his assistant, Oscar Bagnall, did support Kilner's claims (1), later experimenters entirely failed. A. Hofmann, a German scientist, produced similar screens but only recorded visual and color distortions caused by optical fatigue (10). Gustave Geley and René Sudre, two French parapsychologists, spent hours with this type of screen but saw absolutely nothing (32).

Nevertheless, there is some anecdotal evidence that supports the existence of an aura. Dr. Gerda Walther, a German parapsychologist who was once secretary to the famous scientist and psychic researcher, the Baron A. F. von Schrenck-Notzing, was herself able to perceive auras. Such a claim by a notable scientist is not easy to dismiss. Dr. Walther saw auras on several occasions and once saw a black aura around a man who died shortly afterward. These experiences were spontaneous in nature (38).

Here we are confronted with the same problem as with apparitions. If the aura exists, why must it be physical? Or detected by the physical sense perceptors? The illusiveness of the aura, if it even exists, seems to be caused by the fact that it is probably seen psychically, not physically, as Kilner and his supporters suspected.*

A promising line of investigation into this difficult problem is presently being done by Shafica Karagulla, a psychiatrist in Los Angeles. She offers an interesting anecdotal report in her book *Breakthrough to Creativity* (13) and offers some of her ideas in a recent interview granted to *Psychic* magazine (27). Karagulla's interest in the relation of aura research to medical diagnosis, à la Kilner, may have useful medical and psychological application.

HAUNTINGS

When an apparition is seen habitually by various witnesses over a long period of time and in one specific locality, it is designated as a *haunting*. Hauntings seem to be an elaboration around an apparition. Apparitions are visual experiences, but hauntings often include visual experiences (apparitions), auditory experiences (footsteps, poundings on the wall), and even tactile experiences (cold breezes, feelings of being pushed, etc.). However, not all hauntings include the appearance of an apparition.

Several hauntings were recorded by the early psychic researchers. One such haunting was recorded by Rosina Despard, who lived in a haunted house in Cheltenham, England. Although an old case, it is noteworthy in that Miss Despard (named in the report, Rose Morton) kept a detailed diary of the experiences that befell her and her family in the house (17).

The Despard family moved into their Cheltenham home in 1882. One month later Rose first saw the apparition, which would be often seen over the next few years. Rose awoke to discover a figure patrolling the hallway outside her room. The figure was of a tall woman with a handkerchief held to her face. Rose followed the figure, but it eluded her when Rose's candle went out. During the years 1882–1884 the figure was seen several times, not only by Rose but also by her sister, brother, and a maid. On some occasions the figure could be seen by one member but not by the others (17): "On the evening of August 11 [1884], we were sitting in the drawing room, with the gas lit, but the shutters not shut . . . my eldest sister, Mrs. K. and myself both saw the figure on the balcony outside looking in at the window. She stood there some minutes, then walked to the end and back again, after which it seemed to disappear. She soon after came into the drawing room where I saw her, but my sister did not."

On another occasion Rose saw the figure, but her father in the same room did not. In fact, he *never* saw the figure.

* For an excellent summary and discussion of the problems inherent in "auras" refer to Charles Tart's paper, "Concerning the Scientific Study of the Human Aura" (32).

Attempts to experiment with the phantom were made, and strings were placed across a stairway where the wraith was often seen to ascend. Rose watched the figure glide right through the strings. Animals reacted strangely to the haunting, and on several occasions a pet dog would seem to "see" something and run away terrified when the apparition was about.

Gradually the appearances of the figure became less and less frequent. Soon the apparition was not seen at all, but ghostly footsteps could still be heard passing through the house. These, too, grew weaker and weaker and finally disappeared. On tracing the history of the house it was found that a former tenant had died there after becoming victim to chronic alcoholism. The figure reported and described by Rose seemed to resemble this deceased tenant.

Haunted houses are a rare phenomenon, and few really well-attested cases have been reported in parapsychological literature. Parapsychology today is a very different science than it was at the end of the Victorian age, when parapsychologists were mainly trying to validate "ghost stories."

How does one go about investigating a haunted house today? There are three methods that have been used recently by parapsychologists. These might be called the descriptive technique, the experimental technique, and the detection technique.

The descriptive technique is similar to what Rose Despard did. Basically, this means merely tallying up the reports of witnesses. The Psychical Research Foundation (PRF), an independent research center in Durham, North Carolina, has long been interested in investigating cases of reputed hauntings. Investigations of one such case reported by them was carried out by W. T. Joines, an associate professor of electrical engineering at Duke University. The haunting took place in Philadelphia, and Joines journeyed there to collect the evidence (11).

The Chen family had lived in the house since June 1967, but when Joines investigated the case Mrs. Chen was residing there with only three other members—a nucleus of the family that originally lived there. The family reported seeing apparitions, hearing footsteps, and witnessing the movement of objects in the house (termed *teleportation* or telekinesis). One daughter had her bed covers pulled off. She once saw an apparition, screamed, and waked a sister, who also saw the figure.

There was little for Joines to do but collect all the testimony and hope that something paranormal would manifest itself during the investigation. One peculiar incident did occur when a bowl of artificial fruit toppled over after Joines had carefully stacked it. Unfortunately, other than verifying that a haunting did seem likely to exist, this approach offers us no revelations about the nature or mechanics of hauntings.

One of the oldest methods for investigating an alleged haunting is to bring in a reliable psychic to see if his "impressions" match those of the residents. During one investigation of a haunted house, researchers from the PRF took with them the English psychic Douglas Johnson, whose impressions about the haunting matched those of the family (12).

It was Dr. Gertrude Schmeidler who refined this technique and elaborated it into a systematic experimental approach to hauntings. A friend reported to Schmeidler that her home might be haunted. Although the friend had never had any concrete visual or even auditory experiences, she did have unaccountable feelings of fear and anxiety that were associated with various parts of the house. Both her children shared these feelings.

Schmeidler had each of the family members mark off the areas of the house that seemed "infested" on floor plans. These were given back to Schmeidler. She then had a group of psychics visit the residence; they walked about the house trying to determine where the haunting, if one existed, had its focal points. Later these psychics filled out an "adjective checklist" concerning the "personality" of the infestation. The results were significant. Two of the psychics isolated the haunting at the same locales as had the family. Four of the psychics agreed among themselves and with the family about the nature of the haunting's personality (26). Again, although this approach is novel and experimentally valid, it can tell us nothing about the nature of hauntings. Further, the concordances found might only result from telepathy and clairvoyance among the participants.

A third approach to hauntings is also built upon an historical precedent: that animals react oddly in haunted houses. One experimenter who applied this detection technique was Graham Watkins* (16).

Watkins was called in to investigate a haunted room in a Kentucky house. He brought with him a dog, cat, rat, and rattlesnake to see how they would respond to the alleged haunting. The reactions were unusual and noteworthy. The dog, upon entering the room, snarled and backed out of it. It could not be induced to reenter the room. The cat reacted similarly and leaped from its owner's arms when being introduced into the room. It hissed and spit at an innocuous-looking unoccupied chair in a corner of the room. The rat did not react at all, but the rattlesnake assumed a strike position focusing on the same chair as had the cat. None of these animals reacted in any manner in a control room. A tragedy (undefined in the report) had occurred in this "target" room.

Again we come to the similar question we passed after citing several cases of apparitions: Can we possibly explain all of these different phenomena? I am afraid I have to give a stock answer so often heard in parapsychology: We have theories but no answers.

Mrs. Eleanor Sidgwick proposed one of the first scientific theories about

* In the original report the name of the investigator was not cited. However, I have the authorization from Mr. Watkins, formerly a research associate at the Foundation for Research on the Nature of Man, to reveal his capacity as investigator in this case.

hauntings. It is well known that certain individuals can touch an object and receive psi impressions about it or its owner through ESP. This phenomenon is psychometry. If somehow an object can retain memories or psychic impressions, could not also an entire house? Mrs. Sidgwick felt that this was in fact the case. She believed that somehow a house can be impregnated with the thoughts, emotions, and actions of its former tenants. A particularly psychic person introduced into the house might pick up these impressions and experience these actions and emotions directly from the house (28).

Mrs. Sidgwick's concept was elaborated further by two other parapsychologists, H. H. Price and W. G. Roll. Price postulated the existence of a psychic ether. This ether is a bridge between mind and matter and impregnates all matter and space. Under certain rare conditions, thoughts and scenes might be impressed on this ether and remain there for years. Deaths, tragedies, and the like might generate just the right psychic conditions to create these lasting impressions. Certain individuals are very sensitive to these impressions, and when they come into contact with a haunted house, they telepathically contact these thoughts and emotions, which may "replay" themselves as apparitions, ghostly sounds, and such. Price's theory might be called *deferred telepathy* (21). Unfortunately, this theory does not take into account the mysterious movements of objects reported in hauntings nor why apparitions often seem to be *conscious* beings. For example, the Despard ghost often deliberately tried to evade those viewing it.

W. G. Roll (see Chapter 17) has postulated the existence of a psi field (25). According to this theory all objects have psi fields that pervade them and extend from them. On this theory, one contacts and reads the impressions of a house from its psi field during a haunting. This theory is also subject to the same objections as Price's concept. Several hauntings have been attested to and witnessed by nonpsychic individuals, and it is hard to comprehend why these people can suddenly "read" the psi field of a house while not being able to perform psychometry, or show any other psychic talents.

When people think of ghosts, apparitions, and hauntings, they often think in terms of "spirits," the activity of the dead, and other supernatural beings. Nevertheless, the idea that haunted houses actually represent the activity of a personality of a once-living person that has survived death is one that needs considerable appraisal.

One of the foremost promoters of the spiritistic theory of hauntings was Ernesto Bozzano, an Italian parapsychologist who collected several hundred cases of hauntings and broke down their characteristics. He then applied these characteristics to the various theories of hauntings and then to the spiritistic theory and came to the following conclusions, which he felt supported his spiritistic theory: (*a*) phantoms of the dead can haunt places where they did not die and, in some cases, where they had not even lived; (*b*) hauntings consist of telekinetic movement of objects that indicates some sort of physical presence; (*c*) hauntings seem peculiarly linked with deaths, while other tragedies or emotions do not seem to engender hauntings; (*d*) hauntings are not continual but intermittent; and (*e*) when certain actions are carried out—such as exorcism, prayers for the dead and other specific acts—the hauntings often cease.

Bozzano also made a sixth point, that deserves special comment. As will be noted, all the previous theories are somewhat different from theories that have been proposed to account for apparitions. Yet most hauntings consist mainly of the appearance of an apparition or apparitions. Bozzano felt that it was a theoretical fallacy to try to explain hauntings by employing theories that differ from those employed to explain apparitions. I agree with him on this point. Somehow apparitions and hauntings are completely linked, and that linkage should help us to discover what hauntings are.

In this light, Bozzano tried to identify apparitions seen in haunted houses and found that 80% of his 304 cases were linked to a death and that usually the apparition represented the figure of the deceased. Very noteworthy from the standpoint of evidence is that often these apparitions were not recognized until old photographs or portraits were found that corresponded to the verbal description of the witnesses who had seen the phantoms (4).

In 1970 I contributed my own not-too-original theory about hauntings, which tried to unite Bozzano's views with apparitional data (23). I propose that apparitional evidence does support the view that they are conscious, aware entities that represent some form that leaves the body at death (and might be seen as an apparition) or even during life (perceived as an OOBE). This is identical to the view Hornell Hart eventually adopted. The personality that survives death may be little more than a conglomeration of personality patterns. For how long these could exist is a moot point, since the personality patterns might gradually disperse or expand into some "field consciousness" as experienced by the great mystics who describe becoming *one* with the universe. During a tragic event, these personality patterns, held together in an apparitional body, might abnormally be linked strongly together and to an associated place. This linkage thus forces them to maintain a close association with that place. In other words, they might be conscious or semiconscious personality patterns or fragments but trapped in a "psychic ether" or "psi field" of a certain house or locale. Over a long period of time, however, the psi field would rectify the "warp" and the haunting would cease. This would explain why hauntings do seem to die out over a period of time, as in the

Cheltenham haunting. As I pointed out, this theory joins together the views of Bozzano, Roll, and Price and provides a general theory of hauntings compatible with apparitional theories and data.

POLTERGEISTS

A phenomenon often linked to haunted houses is the *poltergeist* (a German word meaning "noisy spirit"). Poltergeists, like hauntings, infest a house but are more diversified in the phenomena produced. The most common phenomenon produced during poltergeist outbreaks is the mysterious movement of objects, often thrown about almost viciously. Other poltergeist phenomena include mysteriously lit fires, stones being hurled at the house, disappearance and reappearance of household objects, and apparitions.

What then constitutes the difference between a haunting and a poltergeist? There do seem to be differences between these two phenomena. Hauntings are usually visual and auditory. Poltergeists are usually motor displays. Hauntings carry on for years, while poltergeists usually are short-lived and burn themselves out rather quickly. But, most important, hauntings usually are linked with a specific house or locale, while poltergeists focus on a specific individual. This individual seems to be either the target of the poltergeist or the agent of it. It may even follow him if he changes residence.

Legends of poltergeists are as old as recorded civilization itself. Hereward Carrington did a systematic historical survey of poltergeists, ancient and contemporary, and unearthed some fascinating cases (5). It is recorded, for example, that in A.D. 530 Deacon Helpidius, physician to King Theodoric of what is now Germany, was pelted by mysterious showers of stones. This is similar to stone-throwing poltergeists recorded today. In these cases stones are thrown from an undiscernible place and attack a house; they may even appear mysteriously *within* the house of the victim. In A.D. 856, in the town of Kembden, the house of a priest was pelted by stones, and raps were sounded on the walls. One could go on and on with such anecdotal reports.

Frank Podmore, skeptical of the existence of genuine poltergeist cases, made one important observation: when a poltergeist strikes, a child around the age of puberty is the target or at least present (21). Podmore immediately seized on this pattern to argue that these children were obviously responsible for the manifestations. Of course, Podmore meant that the children were consciously faking the movements of objects and the other bizarre phenomena.

Later theorists have argued that while Podmore's observation was correct, his interpretation was not. It was maintained that somehow children of this age are undergoing certain psychological and psychosexual pressures that seem to promote poltergeist attacks. I am afraid that modern writers overplay this feature, because many historical cases can be cited that *did not* center around a child. However, several modern cases do follow this general pattern.

For many years poltergeist cases were rather ignored by mainline parapsychology. Parapsychology had adopted the rigorous methodology of experimental psychology spearheaded by Rhine's ESP research at Duke University. This type of research had little time for tales of ghosts and hauntings. However, Rhine was soon to discover that some individuals had the ability to affect physical objects. In most instances, these individuals could make dice fall with a certain side facing upward more times than could be done by chance. This mind-over-matter (PK) force seemed to indicate that poltergeist cases might be worth serious attention. This, I would like to point out, is an historical development, not a personal opinion. To my own mind, the well-documented poltergeist cases that had been recorded up to the 1930s and that parapsychologists had ignored, gave credence to Rhine's PK work as actually being some form of mind-over-matter, not vice versa.*

The first modern case that seriously interested the parapsychological community in poltergeists was a case reported by A. R. G. Owen that occurred in 1960–1961 in Sauchie, Scotland (20). Although Owen did not witness any paranormal events himself, the evidence he collected from the various witnesses was staggeringly convincing.

The poltergeist centered on an 11-year-old girl, Virginia Campbell. The girl had just moved to Sauchie from Ireland, leaving behind most of her possessions. She was desperately unhappy. Soon, odd occurrences seemed to be precipitated around her. Once, at school Virginia's teacher saw the hinged top to Virginia's desk open by itself as Virginia diligently tried to keep it closed. Later, the teacher saw another desk behind the girl levitate a few inches off the floor. A minister visited the girl's home and heard loud percussive rapping sounds. These seemed to emanate from Virginia's bed, yet she was lying perfectly still. While investigating the sounds, he saw a linen chest rock and lift into the air. Two medical doctors were the next witnesses, and they were able to tape-record a series of raps, sawing noises and other auditory phenomena. Gradually the phenomena faded out and ceased.

Our "new view" of the poltergeist derives mainly from the work of two

* There are several books recapping historical poltergeist reports that cannot be fully mentioned here. For the best of these consult Herbert Thurston, *Ghosts and Poltergeists* (34); Raymond Bayless, *Enigma of the Poltergeist* (2), and A. R. G. Owen, *Can We Explain the Poltergeist?* (20).

researchers, W. G. Roll, project director of the PRF, and Hans Bender, a German parapsychologist who heads a center for the study of psychic phenomena in Freiburg.

Roll has had the good fortune to witness poltergeist outbreaks first-hand. One such case that he witnessed occurred in Olive Hill, Kentucky (25). The Callihan home was the scene of moving objects, breaking glass, overturning furniture, and even apparitions. Roll sent a colleague, John Stump, to Olive Hill, and although by this time the Callihans had moved to another house, the poltergeist gymnastics had followed them. While visiting the family, Stump saw two bottles and a glass jar slide along a counter apparently by themselves. He also saw a chair do a somersault.

Roll himself soon arrived on the scene, and he was not disappointed.

At five minutes past midnight on Monday, December 16, 1968, I was walking behind 12-year-old Roger Callihan as he entered the kitchen of his home. When he came to the sink, he turned toward me and at that moment the kitchen table, which was on his right, jumped into the air, rotated about 45 degrees and came to rest on the backs of the chairs that stood around it, with all four legs off the floor. It happened in a twinkling of an eyelid.

Roll's investigation had to be curtailed, as the family felt that he and his colleague were aggravating, not helping, the situation.

Roll has been involved in several other poltergeist cases in which he has either seen phenomena himself or in which phenomena were produced during his own investigation. The most notable of these was the Miami poltergeist (25) investigated by Roll in conjunction with J. G. Pratt.

The Miami poltergeist occurred in a souvenir-store warehouse. During the outbreak, objects seemed continually to fall off the many rows of shelves, and most of these incidents centered around Julio, a young man employed there.

During the several days that Roll investigated the outbreak, objects did indeed fall or hurl themselves off the shelves, but no one could ever be found faking the incidents. Finally, he took Julio back with him to Durham where Julio could be examined psychologically and tested for ESP and PK. The poltergeist followed Roll and Julio to Durham, or so it seems. While in a laboratory room at the Foundation for Research on the Nature of Man, a vase fell off a table when no one was near it. During PK tests, the apparatus used in the experiment inexplicably malfunctioned, which seemed to indicate that it was being affected by Julio's PK.

What is of interest here is that in this case, Roll was able to get a complete psychological profile of Julio. He also had been able to do this with a few other poltergeist agents. Thus, Roll has assembled a mass of details on the psychology of poltergeist agents. We will get back to this shortly. Roll has also constructed detailed graphs of the movement of objects to see if any physical laws seem to govern poltergeist movements.

Bender has made a similar profile of poltergeist agents in his researches in Germany. He has been involved in a number of active poltergeist cases and has found a psychological setting similar to that Roll had found with his agents.

In the early years of psychic research it was felt that poltergeists were either spirits of the dead or fakes. Later, John Layard suggested that poltergeists were psychological projections from the living (15) taking the form of PK. Still later, Nandor Fodor offered psychoanalytical evaluations of the poltergeist that seemed to support Layard's theory (5). But these evaluations were highly speculative and in Fodor's case excessively so. However, Roll and Bender have discovered very convincing data that a poltergeist is a means of nonverbal communication representing the expression of repressed hostility.

In those agents that Roll has examined, a consistent pattern has emerged. Poltergeist agents usually have a low ability at verbal expression. This is coupled with built-up hostility that is being repressed from consciousness. These agents seem to be persons who have a deep feeling of hostility and frustration, and a crippling inability to express this hostility. Normally when such a situation arises, a person will allow psychological mechanisms to help him release his frustration as in "displaced agression," in which a child, angry at his sister, will kick a door or a pet. Another such mechanism is "acting out," as when a child, perturbed at his parents, will rip pictures of adults out of a magazine. The poltergeist does just this. But instead of the individual carrying out his hostilities physically, his PK does it for him.

Poltergeist agents also seem to show "suppression" and "denial." These are attempts by the child or adult to deny feelings of hostility or suppress them into the hidden regions of the unconscious. Because of this, it is not odd that poltergeist agents are often unaware that they actually are causing the outbreak (25).

Roll has found that the movements of objects do seem to follow certain principles. These principles are enormously complicated, but they point to the effect that objects around the agent will tend to be moved more often than objects at a farther distance. The trajectories of these objects seem to indicate that some moving force field or vortex is responsible for the actions (25).

Does all this explain the poltergeist? Certainly not. While Roll has made significant breakthroughs in the psychological study of the poltergeist, he has not *explained* the poltergeist nor has he explored the actual mechanisms of the poltergeist. But the door that will eventually lead to an understanding of these mysteries has certainly been opened.

Roll *has* outlined the type of psychological setting and family milieu that might prompt the poltergeist. Nevertheless, all this does not explain certain phenomena of the poltergeist. For example, how can some sort of PK force explain apparitions seen during these cases? An apparition was seen on two occasions during the Olive Hill incidents by the Callihan family. Roll cites a poltergeist case in Iceland (25), in which a table was often seen to move inexplicably, and on one occasion an apparition was seen standing by it. In short, the "psychologically induced PK" explanation cannot fully explain *all* the manifestations of the poltergeist.

Ian Stevenson has recently reevaluated the characteristics of poltergeists and comes to a similar conclusion (31). His main point is that the trajectories of objects during some outbreaks seem not caused by PK from the living in any form so far recorded in experimental parapsychology. Stevenson writes:

> Sometimes there occur physical phenomena during poltergeist disturbances which we can only with difficulty ascribe to living human agency, even when equipped with important paranormal powers. I refer to those cases in which an object is observed flying through the air and suddenly changes its speed or trajectory. Sometimes the objects turn at a sharp angle to continue flight in a new direction. On other occasions they are reported to show abrupt variation in the speed of flight. . . . If it can be granted that the observers have not all hallucinated, then I think such cases suggest some discarnate agency actually carrying the objects transported or somehow otherwise controlling their flight. I have not myself been able to imagine how such effects could be produced solely by the unconscious mind of the living agent.

From this position, Stevenson feels that the old spiritistic explanation is still a working hypothesis.

I think a resolution can be made between Roll's and Stevenson's views. And at this point I would like to offer my own suggestion as to what a poltergeist *might* be and bring it into relief along with apparitions and hauntings.

Apparitions have been seen during poltergeist cases and these seem to link poltergeists to hauntings. Earlier in this chapter I tried to explain hauntings along the lines of apparitions and with theories to account for them. Altogether, the evidence, as I see it, indicates that man possesses some sort of apparitional body that projects as an apparition and during OOBE's. Now there is considerable evidence that persons undergoing the OOBE can move physical objects.* Furthermore, there is evidence that

---

* Again refer to the Landau case quoted by Tart. *Editor*

people even while awake and conscious may project this apparitional body unconsciously (18). Thus, it appears that poltergeist phenomena might actually be caused by this projected "double," or parasomatic body. For example, an early French researcher, H. Durville, succeeded in inducing OOBE's in gifted subjects. During these experiments the agent, in the OOB state, was able to move a chair and create other physical manifestations, though the apparitional form itself was invisible to the experimenters. Later, after much diligence, the human "double" was successfully photographed (6).

It seems feasible to me that a poltergeist represents a similar phenomenon. A poltergeist would be engendered by a tense psychology setting, but the actual agency would not exactly be PK from the living. Instead, the agent would project some element of his own personality into the same ultraphysical body which is seen as an apparition and during OOB experiences. This form, usually invisible, might become somewhat autonomous from the physical body and create the disturbances. It would explain why apparitions *are* seen during poltergeist outbreaks and how odd and complicated trajectories, such as the ones Stevenson has cited, might be explained.

There is one bit of direct evidence in favor of this theory. This is found in the poltergeist of Brookhouse in Great Britain (30). The report, although recorded in a popular publication, nevertheless comes from the principal witness, Ralph Hastings. Twice during the outbreak, Hastings saw an apparition that seemed identical with the figure of his fiancée, a young woman who lived in the house. Once Hastings and his fiancée jointly saw the figure, so we can be sure that it was not actually the real woman that he saw.

This supports my theory of what a poltergeist *might* be—some sort of independent apparition created or projected by the principal agent. Another attraction of this theory is that it pulls into line and offers a similar mechanism for apparitions, hauntings, and poltergeists.

A WARNING

In this chapter I have cited examples of apparitions, hauntings, and poltergeists. I have also outlined various theories put forward to account for them. Since I have offered a few of my own ideas about the nature of these phenomena, I will end not with any conclusions but rather with a warning. We tend to be very simplistic in our approach to psi. We consider a theory and then often throw it out and construct a new one. I think that we should realize that psi, especially the types of phenomena I have considered here, may not have one single mechanism. There may be different types of apparitions with different mechanisms. For example, the existence of a spatially present apparition does not rule out the possibility that some apparitions might be telepathic hallucinations. The same goes for hauntings and poltergeists. Because of our unfamiliarity with these strange phenomena, it may well be that we are classifying various different phenomena under general headings only because they share common characteristics. This is a problem inherent in any young science trying to create a taxonomy of its subject matter.

Apparitions, hauntings, and poltergeists represent various forms of psi. Understanding them may help us to comprehend *all* psi—from telepathy to the possibility that man survives death.

REFERENCES

1. Bagnall, Oscar. *The Origin and Properties of the Human Aura.* University Books: New Hyde Park, N.Y., 1972.
2. Bayless, Raymond. *The Enigma of the Poltergeist.* Parker: West Nyack, N.Y., 1967.
3. Bayless, Raymond. *Animal Ghosts.* University Books: New Hyde Park, N.Y., 1970.
4. Bozzano, Ernesto. *Les Phénomenes de Hantise.* Alcan: Paris, 1920.
5. Carrington, H., and Fodor, N. *Haunted People.* Dutton: New York, 1951.
6. Durville, H. *Le Fântome des Vivants.* Paris, 1890.
7. Gurney, E.; Podmore, F.; and Myers, F. W. H. *Phantasms of the Living.* Trubner: London, 1886.
8. Hart, Hornell. "Scientific Survival Research." *International Journal of Parapsychology*, 9 (1967).
9. Hart, Hornell and Associates. "Six Theories about Apparitions." *Proceedings of the Society for Psychical Research*, 50 (1956).
10. Hofmann, A. *Die odische Lohe.* Baum: Plüffingen, 1920.
11. Joines, W. T. "Philadelphia Haunting." *Theta*, No. 23 (1968).
12. Joines, W. T., and Artley, J. L. "Study of a Haunted House." *Theta*, 27 (1969).
13. Karagulla, Shafico. *Breakthrough to Creativity.* De Vorss: Los Angeles, 1967.
14. Kilner, W. J. *The Human Atmosphere.* Rehman: London, 1912.
15. Layard, John. "Psi Phenomena and Poltergeists." *Proceedings of the Society for Psychical Research*, July 1944.
16. Morris, Robert L. "An Experimental Approach to the Survival Problem." *Theta*, Nos. 33–34 (1971–1972).
17. Morton, Rose. "A Record of a Haunted House." *Proceedings of the Society for Psychical Research*, 27.
18. Myers, F. W. H. *The Human Personality and Its Survival of Bodily Death.* Longmans: London, 1903.
19. Osborne, Arthur. *The Meaning of Personal Existence.* Sidgwick and Jackson: London, 1966.
20. Owen, A. R. G. *Can We Explain the Poltergeist?* Garrett: New York, 1964.

21. Podmore, Frank. "Poltergeists." *Proceedings of the Society for Psychical Research.* 12.
22. Price, H. H. Presidential address to the SPR, 1939.
23. Rogo, D. Scott. *NAD, A Study of Some Unusual Other-World Experiences.* University Books: New Hyde Park, 1970.
24. Roll, W. G. "The Psi Field." *Proceedings of the Parapsychological Association,* No. 1, 1957–1964.
25. Roll, W. G. *The Poltergeist.* Doubleday: New York, 1972.
26. Schmeidler, Gertrude. "Quantitative Investigation of a Haunted House." *Journal of the American Society for Psychical Research,* 60 (1966).
27. "Shafica Karagulla in Interview." *Psychic,* August 1973.
28. Sidgwick, Eleanor. "Phantasms of the Dead." *Proceedings of the Society for Psychical Research,* 3.
29. Sidgwick, Eleanor. "On the Evidence for Clairvoyance." *Proceedings of the Society for Psychical Research,* 12.
30. Stead, W. T. "More Ghost Stories." *Review of Reviews,* 1892.
31. Stevenson, Ian. "Are Poltergeists Living or Are They Dead?" *Journal of the American Society for Psychical Research,* 66 (1972).
32. Sudre, René. *Treatise on Parapsychology.* Citadel: New York, 1960.
33. Tart, Charles. "Concerning the Scientific Study of the Human Aura." *Journal of the Society for Psychical Research,* 46 (1972).
34. Thurston, Herbert. *Ghosts and Poltergeists.* Regnery: Chicago, 1954.
35. Tyrrell, G. N. M. *Apparitions.* Ducksworth: London, 1953.
36. "Report on the Census of Hallucinations." *Proceedings of the Society for Psychical Research,* 10.
37. *Proceedings of the Society for Psychical Research,* 33.
38. Walther, Gerda. *Zum anderen Ufer,* Germany, 1960.

William G. Roll

WILLIAM G. ROLL *is project director of the Psychical Research Foundation, in Durham, North Carolina. Prior to taking the post in 1961, he was on the staff of the Parapsychology Laboratory at Duke University.*

After earning a bachelor of arts degree from the University of California at Berkeley in 1949, he entered psychic research and held a series of research grants from Oxford University, the Society for Psychical Research, and the Parapsychology Foundation. He became a research fellow of the Parapsychology Laboratory in 1957, a research associate the next year, and project director in 1960. Also in 1960 he received the B.Litt. from Oxford University on the basis of his work in parapsychology.

Mr. Roll is editor of Theta, *published by the Psychical Research Foundation. He was co-editor of the* Journal of Parapsychology *from 1958 to 1960 and co-editor of the* Proceedings of the Parapsychological Association *in 1964. Since 1965 he has been the chief editor of the* Proceedings. *Mr. Roll has published many articles and reviews in American and British parapsychological and scientific journals and is author of* The Poltergeist *(Doubleday, 1972; Signet Paperback, 1974).*

Mr. Roll can be reached at the Psychical Research Foundation, Inc., Duke Station, Durham, N.C. 27706.

17 Survival Research: Problems and Possibilities

WILLIAM G. ROLL

SUMMARY

When we ask whether consciousness continues after death, we usually assume that a surviving self will exist in some kind of body and will include the personality familiar from waking experience. In the course of their work, however, psychic researchers have encountered mediumistic communicators and apparitions that were apparently created by the living but not inhabited by their consciousness. These communicators and apparitions are indistinguishable from those representing the dead. It does not seem possible, therefore, to discover whether there is a continuation of experience after death by the study of communicators, apparitions and other surviving residues of the living. We must look elsewhere for evidence of the survival of consciousness.

Since the consciousness that may continue after death presumably exists before, we may explore it in the living. An examination of parapsychological research with living subjects suggests that consciousness is not private to any individual but can be shared by others. If a person's consciousness does not "belong" to him, it is unlikely that it will disappear at his death. This kind of consciousness, however, is different from ordinary states of consciousness, which are experienced as private to each individual. The consciousness that may survive death will be an altered state of consciousness with the following characteristics: (a) there must be an experience that the self has extended beyond the body, (b) this extension must be real in the sense that the person must be able to interact with events at the location to which he has extended, and (c) the extended self must be able to function independently of his central nervous system.

In some altered states of consciousness, people have the impression that their self extends beyond the body. The experience ranges from OOB travels, where the self is felt to occupy a distinct location in space, to experiences of field consciousness, in which the self may be identified with all there is. Anecdotal stories and laboratory testing suggest that the feel-

ing of extension may be real in the sense that the person is sometimes able to observe events at the location occupied by his consciousness or can be detected by others in that area. There is not sufficient evidence so far to indicate whether or not such experiences depend on the central nervous system.

INTRODUCTION

Private Frank Soal, Sixth Leicester Regiment, died in France at the age of 19 from wounds received in action on September 5, 1918. He was the youngest brother of Dr. Samuel G. Soal, the British parapsychologist. When Dr. Soal later began experimenting with the British medium Mrs. Blanche Cooper, Frank was one of the communicators. In the course of the sessions, he correctly described many events from his and Soal's childhood in Rochford, which Mrs. Cooper could not have known about. But it was as an intermediary in reaching another communicator that Frank caused a shock that still reverberates in parapsychology.

Frank began the session, which Dr. Soal (34) recorded with his own comments:

> *F.*   Sam, I've brought someone who knows you.
> *S.*   All right, let him speak.
> *Voice.*   (Pause.) Well, Soal, I never expected to speak to you in this fashion. (. . . This sentence was delivered with an extraordinary variety of tone, and also with great energy.)
> *S.*   Who are you then?
> *Voice.*   Remember Davis—Gordon from R—R—Roch—Roch— (. . . This word was not completed, but I easily understood it was an attempt to say "Rochford.")
> *S.*   By Jove, and it's like Gordon Davis, too.
> *Voice.*   The dead to the living. Queer world, what? My poor wife is my only worry now—and kiddie.
> *S.*   Can you really be Gordon Davis? I had heard you were killed.
> *Voice.*   The same—what's left of me.

Soal now asked for proof that this was indeed Gordon Davis. The voice continued.

> *Voice.*   Remember the old school? How I always argued with H—H—Hs—oh, confound these names—for brighter geog—brighter geography—harpoons and things.
> *S.*   I remember about your arguing with Histed but nothing about harpoons. Try to tell me where you lived. That's something I don't know.

Voice.   At Roch—you mean?

    S.   That will do.

Voice.   (Not so strong) Near the M—Ma—Malt . . . Remember our last little talk?

    S.   Yes, I do quite well. Where was it?

Voice.   In the train—about guards—not trains guards though. A little confab on the work of guards. That help you?

    S.   I can recall it excellently.

Voice.   Seems ages since to me—remember Playle and O—Over—Over—

    S.   I think I know who you mean, but tell me where your wife lives.

Voice.   Old chap, I can't hold on—not a second longer.

Before completely losing control, Davis showed the medium two capital letter E's, which she thought had to do with the address of his wife. "He's very anxious to send news to her, poor thing. It was a great shock to her."

Soal had last met Davis in a train in 1916 a short while before Davis was sent to the front in France. Soal later heard that he had been killed. During this train ride, Davis had spoken about a lecture he was to give on guard duties.

Soal and Davis went to the same school in Rochford but were not close friends, Soal being younger and in a lower grade. However, they had attended the same class in geography, and Soal remembered Davis arguing with the teacher, Mr. Histed. Davis had a collection of spears, boomerangs, and the like and sometimes brought these to class. Two of his friends were Playle and Overell. Davis's home was called The Malting, a fact either unknown to Soal or forgotten.

Five days later Soal had another sitting with Mrs. Cooper, during which Davis gave additional information about the home of his wife and child. Davis was not married when Soal met him. Unknown to Soal, he had married afterward and had had a child. Their home was on Eastern Esplanade in Southend-on-Sea—an address with two capital E's. The house was "joined up to others," and the medium thought the street was "like half a street." She also spoke about the house having "a funny dark tunnel." As Soal later discovered, the house was part of a block of houses and there were houses on only one side of the street, the other being open to the sea. What most struck Soal was a long dark passageway from the front of the house to its back. Several other details of the exterior and interior were also accurately described, including the pictures and other decorative items.

But the most convincing aspect of the communication was the manner of speech and general personality style so characteristic of Davis. The word *confab* (for discussion) and his frequent insertions of *old man* and *old chap* were typical.

It is sometimes argued that mediumistic communications are actually initiated by the medium and the person seeking the communication—in this case, Soal. According to this theory, the medium responds to the sitter's desire to reach someone on the other side and then unconsciously uses her ESP to cull facts from such sources as the memories of the living, diaries, obituaries, and so forth to simulate the communicator. But Soal made no attempt to reach Gordon Davis. The initiative appeared to be entirely Davis's. His compelling motive seemed to be concern for the wife and child he had left behind. Perhaps he hoped that Soal would look them up and give them some reassuring words. Of course, Soal did pay a visit to the house on Eastern Esplanade.

So far this looks like the kind of mediumistic communication familiar to the psychic researcher. It was unusually successful compared to the common run of sittings, and the fact that they were conducted by Soal gives them special credence. The case has one flaw, but it is a serious one. Gordon Davis was not dead. At the time of Soal's sittings, Davis was planning to move with his family to Southend, where he had a real estate business.

WHO IS THE COMMUNICATOR?

If Gordon Davis was not dead, who or what was the communicator? An answer to this question is important to the understanding of the evidence attributed to survival in general and not just to our understanding of the Gordon Davis case.

William James (11), in his study of one of the communicators who came through Mrs. Leonore Piper, thought there was "an external will to communicate." The messages, he thought, could not just be accounted for by the ESP ability of the medium. But James was not certain that the communicator was the discarnate personality he claimed to be.

In the Gordon Davis case, there seemed to be a particularly strong will to communicate. During the first session Nada, Mrs. Cooper's spirit control (the entity that manages the communications), commented that "he's a very strong spirit—may hurt the medium." At the end of the session, when Soal asked to speak to Davis again, Nada replied, "Not this time— the medium could not stand it. She went right out of her body."

Perhaps after all it was Gordon Davis who came through. Perhaps he was having an OOBE and, believing he had died, visited Mrs. Cooper and Soal. But this hypothesis, attractive though it may seem, does not fit the facts. Davis was not having an OOBE, nor was he in any other state of altered consciousness: during both of Soal's sittings, he was consulting with people on business matters. Interestingly enough, the Davis family had not moved into the house on Eastern Esplanade at the time of Soal's sittings. It was only two days after the first sitting that Davis inspected his future home for the first time. (The descriptions at least of the paintings seemed to be precognitive, since Davis did not possess them at the time. This information came at Soal's second sitting, after Davis had visited the house.)

It is common in telepathy for thoughts and ideas to be transmitted without the agent being aware that he is sending. To explain telepathy (and PK), H. H. Price (25) the Oxford philosopher, suggests that once an idea has been formed in a mind it has,

> so to speak, an independent life of its own [and] . . . is no longer wholly under the control of the consciousness which gave it birth. Though it began its career in consciousness, it persists outside of consciousness ("in the unconscious" as we say). It may return into consciousness from time to time or it may not. Moreover, we will also suppose that every idea is endowed with *causal efficacy*; and that it not only exists but also operates independently, apart from the consciousness in which it originates.

Psychologists have discovered a great deal about the causal efficacy of ideas. For instance, we know that emotionally intense and vivid ideas are more likely to return to consciousness than emotionally neutral ones. The same is true for frequent and recent ideas. These tendencies are described in the laws of association. But what gives strength to ideas in the mind where they originated also seems to work when they appear somewhere else as in ESP. This is illustrated by the Gordon Davis case. At the time of the sittings, one of Davis's main preoccupations undoubtedly was the move to Eastern Esplanade. The information about his future home may be accounted for by the laws of recency and vividness. At the time, Davis may also have been thinking about Playle, one of his childhood friends, since he was to have an interview with him two days later. Davis's interest in weapons was one of long standing. The reference to harpoons may have illustrated the law of frequency. When Davis saw this passage he said, "All my life since I was a small boy, I have collected weapons of various kinds—especially spears, boomerangs, etc." Soal noticed, in the hall of the Davis house, "a large collection of spears and other savage weapons."

Another point about ideas that is important to remember is that they do not exist in isolation but are part of large associative clusters. To say that an idea can operate independently of the consciousness in which it was formed is tantamount to saying that the whole associative system of which it is part may have such a life. Hornell Hart (8) suggests something like this in his persona theory. A deceased personality provides the impetus for a communication, and the expectations of medium and sitter add other pieces to create a communicator. Afterward, this persona may go on existing more or less independently. Usually the stimulus comes from a deceased personality, according to Hart, but sometimes from a living one, as in the Gordon Davis case.

From what we know about ESP and psychology, the Gordon Davis case makes good sense. It is not the only one of its class. There are others like it. It is also easy to find cases in which the communicator does not exist at all. In my work with mediums, I have often been presented with a full-fledged personality giving a name, supposed times and places of birth and death, a nonexisting address, and other spurious information. Such material does not come as a surprise, since persons in dissociated states, such as mediums, are often highly suggestible and will try to accommodate themselves to the wishes of the inquirer. The fact that a person has died and that "he" can supply information about his earthly existence, attitudes, and so forth does not enable us to infer that he exists as a conscious, experiencing self. There can be mediumistic communications without anyone communicating.

APPARITIONS OF WHAT?

We have the first-hand account of Lieutenant S____, one of the two percipients, which is as follows. He says that Herr _____n had come to spend the night at his lodgings. "After supper," he continues, "and when we were both undressed, I was sitting on my bed and Herr _____n was standing by the door of the next room on the point also of going to bed. This was about half-past ten. . . . Suddenly the door out of the kitchen opened without a sound, and a lady entered, very pale, taller than Herr _____n, about five foot four inches in height, strong and broad in figure, dressed in white, but with a large black kerchief which reached to below the waist. She entered with bare head, greeted me with the hand three times in complimentary fashion, turned round to the left towards Herr _____n, and waved her hand to him three times; after which the figure quietly, and again without any creaking of the door, went out. We followed at once in order to discover whether there were any deception, but found nothing (41).

The lady seen by the two officers had been dead for five years. But she and the two men were not the only participants in the ghostly performance. A fourth, Herr H. M. Wesermann, government assessor and chief inspector of roads at Düsseldorf, played an important role.

In a book published in 1822 Wesermann described several experiments in which he caused apparitions of himself to be seen by others. Phenomena of this type are not unusual. G. N. M. Tyrrell (41), who quotes the Wesermann case in his classical work on apparitions, cites several cases in which someone succeeded in making his apparition be seen by someone else. But here Wesermann produced an apparition of someone else. Wesermann had expected Lieutenant _____n to be asleep and tried to project an image of the lady to him at 10:30 P.M., when he supposedly would be in the bedroom. At that time, however, the officer had not gone to bed but was with his friend in the anteroom. As Tyrrell says, "If an apparition represents a dead person . . . this is not sufficient proof that the dead person is the agent."

The Wesermann ghost also supports Tyrrell's theory that an apparition is usually the product not only of its creator but also of the perceiver. The lady ghost would have performed in an empty room had something not brought her to the anteroom—that something presumably being the unconscious minds of the officers reacting to Wesermann's attempts. In Hart's terminology, the three men had together produced a persona. This all sounds rather strange, but in fact, it is typical of ESP. Even in card tests, the result is rarely an exact copy of the target but an interaction between the target, the mind of the subject, and often of the experimenter's mind too.

There are very few reliable reports of the kind of third-person ghost Wesermann produced. It is more common to see an apparition of the agent himself. In addition to the experimental cases, Tyrrell gives several examples of people "whose apparitions seem to stray about while they know nothing about it." He suggests that such apparitions may be caused by an unconscious wish by the person to be somewhere else.

Sometimes the apparition of a person is seen by the person himself. About a year ago my 11-year-old son, William, said he saw himself seated cross-legged at the foot of his bed. We sometimes discuss psi at home, but I believe we have never spoken about seeing an apparition of oneself. In Norway, there is a special word, vardøgler, for precognitive experiences such as footsteps and apparitions that herald the arrival of the person in question.

At times a person who has an OOBE is perceived as an apparition in the area in which he finds himself in the OOB state. But it is only by questioning him afterward that we can know that this apparition was conscious. The occurrence of an apparition of the living, as of the dead, is not by itself proof of the existence of a conscious entity.

What about apparitions of people who have been dead for a long time, such as haunting apparitions, when it seems unlikely that a Herr Wesermann was conducting a ghostly experiment in the background? Edmund

Gurney (7) reports a case that involved an apparition of an old woman who repeatedly was seen on a bed in a kitchen, fully dressed and with her face to the wall. The description matched a previous occupant as she was found after a beating by her husband from which she did not recover. Gurney thought it unlikely that the spirit of the woman had remained on her bed and suggested instead that the apparition was "the survival of a mere image, impressed, we cannot guess how on we cannot guess what."

The possibility that mental processes may leave residues or traces on physical objects has often come up in connection with so-called psychometry tests. In such tests, the ESP subject seems to obtain information about events by holding an object that has been associated with these events. Many mediums and psychics use this procedure when they try to obtain information about the past lives of people. It is possible that haunting apparitions result from the same process.

I mentioned Price's theory about ideas. He has a similar theory about images. Mental images, according to Price (24), are "persistent and dynamic entities which, when once formed, may have a kind of independent life of their own, and may escape more or less completely from the control of their author." Apparitional hauntings result from the tendency of images to get themselves localized in physical space. "Once localized there, they might continue to be so localized for a considerable period, retaining the telepathic charge which they had at first, though this might gradually diminish in intensity." In other words, an image of a person may survive his death without being inhabited by his consciousness. This has been called a *thought form* in some oriental traditions.

Because the "telepathic charge" of a haunted house or a psychometric object is similar to the magnetic, gravitational, and other fields that surround physical objects, I have used the concept of psi field to describe psi phenomena that seem to depend on such objects (29). For the present purpose, we can think of the psi field of an object, whether animate or inanimate, as a pattern of associations. In the same way as a magnet may magnetize another piece of metal and then be destroyed without affecting the new magnet, so may the images, ideas, and so on of a person continue to exist as part of the psi fields of objects with which he was once in contact long after he has gone. The image of a person seen in an apparition, whether this image was produced by him or someone else, may survive his death without being inhabited by his consciousness.

SURVIVAL OF PERSONALITY

If the origin of mediumistic communications and apparitions is so uncertain, why have survival researchers placed so much emphasis on them in the search for evidence of survival?

Before we go into this question, let us consider the more basic one—whether the material we are discussing includes genuine psi or whether it can be explained away as fraud, sensory cues, and chance guessing. I find it difficult to suppose that all the cases admit of such easy explanations, in view of the precautions often taken. However, this area of parapsychology is in need of a more systematic approach than it has received so far. Some progress has been made. Gertrude Schmeidler (33) has devised an ingenious statistical test of haunting apparitions. At the PRF we are building instruments with which to register physical energies that may be involved with such cases—a costly and difficult enterprise.

Mediumistic research is faced with two tasks: (*a*) the development of experimental techniques that stimulate, rather than impede, the phenomena and (*b*) reliable methods of statistical analysis. It may seem surprising that statistics are needed for mediumistic studies. In the Gordon Davis case, the correspondences between the statements of the medium and Davis's circumstances may be too striking to dismiss as chance, but generally the results are less clear-cut. Soal (34) himself realized this and helped to lay the groundwork for a statistical assessment of mediumistic statements. The method was improved by J. G. Pratt (23) in a series of experiments with Mrs. Eileen Garrett at Duke University. Pratt (22) later helped to devise a new method, which we have further improved at the PRF with the aid of Donald S. Burdick (30), a statistician at Duke. We have used the new method successfully in an experiment with the Trinidad sensitive, Lalsingh Harribance (31). Robert L. Morris (15), a member of our group, has also developed a method for the evaluation of mediumistic data and similar material.

For most of the material reported in the literature, the methods of observation and assessment were not highly developed. The reports, however, show that the investigators were often cautious and aware of the many pitfalls. It is unlikely that the data can all be explained away. Take the cross-correspondences. In these experiments, which were apparently initiated by the deceased communicators themselves, two or more mediums produced disjointed and apparently meaningless statements that, however, turned out to refer to common themes, such as a Greek play or a poem known to the deceased. It is not difficult to suppose that there might be chance correspondences as a result of the sheer mass of writings produced by the several mediums. However, some of the cases, such as the "Hope, Star, and Browning" case (21) could hardly be the result of chance, considering the obvious relations between many of the items produced by the mediums.

The information was often beyond the educational background of the mediums, but it was familiar to the supposed communicators. Moreover, it was flavored by their attitudes and personality styles. The same was also true of the "book tests" developed by Drayton Thomas (40). In these experiments, the ostensible communicators found a book passage that was unknown to the medium and others taking part in the experiments but that expressed the interests or memories of the communicator.

In the previous section, I pointed out that some apparitions are localized in space. This relation between a surviving entity and physical space or matter also comes up in the mediumistic material. In most of these, there is a physical connection between the medium and the ostensible communicator. Sometimes this link is a person who is present at the experiment and who knew the deceased when he was still living. Alternatively, a psychometric object is used. (*Psychometric* is also used in the sense of mental measurement, so parapsychologists prefer other terms; I use the phrase *associated object*.) In these types of ESP tests, the medium appears to obtain information about some person or event by holding an object that belonged to the person or that he had been in physical contact with, such as a scarf or a pipe. Such objects are also used in tests in which the subject tries to obtain information about the living. Because of the similarity to the mediumistic experiments involving a deceased agent, it is natural to suppose that these experiments too are in fact ordinary object-association tests and that the discarnate communicators are only creations by the mind of the medium.

There is a special type of mediumistic communication that apparently does not rely on such connections. These are the drop-ins. A drop-in communicator, as the term suggests, is unknown to either medium or investigator and appears spontaneously at a mediumistic sitting. No psychometric objects are used. Alan Gauld (6), a British psychologist and parapsychologist, has published a study of several drop-ins, and Ian Stevenson (37), head of the Division of Parapsychology at the University of Virginia, has also from time to time reported such cases. However, drop-ins show a geographical clustering effect: they usually come from the same area as the medium or others connected with the experiment or from areas that these persons have visited. In other words, there seems to be the same linkage or association with physical space that we find with mediumistic communicators.

Because of the efforts of Stevenson (36) in recent years reincarnation cases have figured prominently in survival research. The cases usually involve young children who spontaneously appear to recall persons and episodes from a previous life. Because of their youth and general circumstances, it appears unlikely that the material has been obtained by normal means; and since the children do not generally show evidence of other psychic abilities, there is nothing to suggest that they have picked up the information by a more common form of ESP. In addition to memories of the past, the children often show the emotional reactions and interests of their previous incarnations. As with many mediumistic communicators, they are realistic. These cases also show the geographical focusing effect. A person is likely to reincarnate in the same general area in which he spent his previous life. This "attachment" to familiar objects and locations runs through most of the data suggestive of the survival of personality.

We generally suppose that our memories, thoughts, and emotions belong to only one physical object, our own brain. When this brain disappears, we suppose that our memories, ideas, and so on also disappear. But if we think of these as field phenomena, it is easier to accept the possibility that they may persist in other physical systems than the brain in which they were formed and that they may be available to others, as in ESP. After the disintegration of the brain, our thoughts, images, and ideas remain part of the psi fields of the other objects with which they have been associated, retaining their "telepathic charge" and thereby the capacity to reproduce a more or less full picture of the deceased.

One of the laws describing the connections in the psi field is the law of contiguity, one of the primary laws of association (the other is the law of similarity). In its psychological form, this law says that two ideas or percepts that have been experienced together by a person thereby become associated. The strength of this association depends on the secondary laws (of vividness, frequency, and so on), which I have referred to before. Generally we do not extend these laws to relations between a person and inanimate objects in his environment, but this is an exclusion that does not seem to be justified by the facts of parapsychology.

The relation between a surviving personality and material objects is sometimes discussed by the communicators themselves. In a session with Mrs. Leonard Piper by W. R. Newbold (17), the communicator said:

> Objects carry with them a light as distinct to us as the sunlight is to you. The instant you hand us an object, that instant we get an impression of its owner, whether the present or the past owner and often both. In some cases the impression is as clear as possible, in others it is vague, and I find upon examination that almost invariably the object presented to us for information has been of long standing, or otherwise unhandled—untouched by its owner for a period of long duration, or sometimes it may have been handled often and by a great number of persons. This often causes confusion.

Another communicator once requested, "Don't give me anything belonging to George because if you do, it will call him back and I don't want to disturb him" (17).

It is premature to state any conclusions with respect to the survival of personality, either in its full-fledged form or as partial systems of memories, emotions, ideas, and feelings. The indications are, however, that what we call personality continues to exist after the death of the body as a kind of field or system of associations around the objects with which the person was in physical contact when he was alive. It seems that a living person's brain functions as the primary source of information about the person available to another through ESP. But when the body and brain have dissolved, the physical objects associated with him become the main source of ESP information about him.

The indications that personality survives as a causally efficient and more or less integrated whole do not, however, allow us to infer that it is animated by a consciousness and—even if it is so animated—that this is the consciousness "belonging to" the person when he was living.

The possibility that a replica or image of the physical body and the cluster of memories, emotions, and the like that constitute human personality may survive death is interesting in the same way as it is interesting that a person may "survive" in photographs and tape recordings. This possibility, however, is not nearly as interesting as the possibility that consciousness may survive. For the survival of consciousness provides a continuation of actual experiences, while the survival of an image of the body, memories, and so forth do not necessarily imply such continuation.

SOME BASIC ASSUMPTIONS

Research on the survival question has been guided by certain implicit assumptions about what it is that may survive death and by certain assumptions about the nature of ESP.

In any discussion of evidence for survival, ESP plays a central role. ESP is presumably used in supposed communications with the dead, and people who see apparitions apparently do so by ESP. When we try to explain away the evidence for communicators, we often say that they were created by the medium who obtained the necessary facts by ESP from existing sources, such as the minds of living people who knew the deceased, obituaries, and so on. We use similar explanations for people who see apparitions and for other survival evidence. It is therefore important to have some notion of ESP when we discuss the survival issue.

Most of us believe that ESP information originates in one mind or place and is then transmitted over space (and/or time) to another mind. Furthermore, we restrict the meaning of ESP to the acquisition of veridical information about the distant mind or place. We generally assume that if the ESP response does not in some way correspond to verifiable mental or physical events, we are not dealing with ESP.

These beliefs about ESP are not the results of empirical observations. They derive from our ordinary state of consciousness in which we experience ourselves as separate from others and from the physical environment. Being separate, we suppose that all communication is a stimulus–response process, either sensory or extrasensory. But the stimulus–response model, which works reasonably well for sensory perception, does not work well for ESP. For instance, the size of the ESP target, its distance from the subject, physical barriers, and so on do not affect results in the manner we should expect if ESP followed this model.

In our ordinary state of awareness we experience an outside world that consists of objects and people separate from ourselves. Obtaining information about that world seems very different from obtaining information about our own mental states. Since we limit ESP to the acquisition of veridical information about the outside world, we suppose that the ESP process is quite different from the process whereby we become aware of our own psychological states. As a rule, when responses appear in ESP tests that do not correspond to anything in the familiar world, we dismiss them as ESP failures. But the veridical responses are usually indistinguishable from the responses that originate in the unconscious mind of the subject, except that the former match objective events in other minds or places and the latter do not. The implication is clear: What is called ESP is a process whereby the individual gains awareness of his unconscious. This way of explaining ESP is more satisfactory than the stimulus–response theory. As with other unconscious material, access to ESP information seems to be increased during relaxation, hypnosis, meditation, dreams, and other states that encourage material such as forgotten memories and repressed emotions to emerge into awareness. On the other hand, such states are impediments, not aids, to known responses by the body to outside stimuli. It seems that the aspects of the physical and social world that lie outside a person's direct sensory awareness should be regarded as part of his unconscious. In ESP a person apparently becomes aware of those aspects of his unconscious to the extent that he can dissociate himself from the narrower world of ordinary sense perception. This collective unconscious, as it is sometimes called, is the same as the psi field mentioned earlier, and the same laws apply to both.

When parapsychologists discuss the aspect of man that may survive his death, they make further assumptions. Since we usually conceive of the human self as restricted to a physical body and to the kind of consciousness in which most of us spend our waking hours, we expect survival to be in terms of the same kind of body and consciousness. Since our consciousness is generally tied up with the external and internal stimuli of the physical body, we look for survival evidence in the form of apparitional phenomena, dreams of the deceased, and other experiences that provide a replica of this body. Our ordinary state of consciousness is intimately associated with memories of the past, plans for the future, our special skills—in short, with the associative cluster we call human personality. When we seek evidence for survival after death, we look for the continuation of this cluster as in mediumistic experiences, reincarnation phenomena, and the like.

This assumption has guided survival research until the present time. As a rule we have taken for granted that if we can demonstrate the independent existence of apparitions, mediumistic communicators, and the like, then we shall have demonstrated the continuation of consciousness. Conversely, we have supposed that in their absence there is no continuation of consciousness (or at least there can be no evidence for such continuation). It has therefore been the basic concern of survival researchers to try to determine whether apparitions and mediumistic communicators exist independently or whether they are products of the psychic abilities of the living. In addition to mediumistic, apparitional, and reincarnation cases, there is the evidence from dreams in which the dead appear and from cases in which the dead seem to make their presence known by some kind of physical action, such as stopping a clock belonging to them or causing their pictures to fall. Whatever the evidence, it generally involves the reproduction of an image of the body of the deceased or of his memories and other personal characteristics. But we cannot infer the survival of consciousness after death from the survival of a body image, as seen in an apparition, or even from the survival of a full-fledged "personality" in a mediumistic communication. An apparition or a mediumistic communicator may be the sole product of the "telepathic charge," psi field, or whatever name we give the energy associated with the thoughts, ideas, and images formed by man.

DOES CONSCIOUSNESS CONTINUE?

Consciousness includes awareness of an experiencing I, or self. When we are unconscious, we are not aware of the self or not aware of parts of it. In the sense in which I use the term, the unconscious can become conscious, and the conscious can become unconscious.

The Gordon Davis communicator was not inhabited by Davis's consciousness, and the ghost projected by Wesermann was not inhabited by his consciousness. We cannot conclude from this, however, that the communicator and ghost were not conscious. But if we ask the further question as to who might have animated them, we make an assumption based on our ordinary waking consciousness that is not justified by the findings of parapsychology. This assumption is that consciousness is private to each human self.

A person's experience of his self may be confined to his physical body.

But it appears that in ESP others may directly apprehend the contents of his consciousness and may even identify with it to the extent of experiencing it to be part of their own consciousness. This suggests that consciousness is not private to anyone but is public. In the same way as the gravitational field of a material object is part of the gravitational field of the earth, the consciousness of a person seems to be part of wider consciousness of which he may or may not be aware.

If consciousness and the feeling of selfhood is in fact not private to the individual but is something that can be shared by others, it would be illogical to expect consciousness to disappear with the death of the individual. And, of course, myriads have died without diminishing the consciousness of the survivors. Moreover, if consciousness is public and continues beyond the death of the person, it is difficult to suppose that his ability to share in this consciousness ceases or even diminishes when he dies.

On the contrary, we should expect that the range of consciousness would increase when the body ceases to function. The sense organs and central nervous system seem to contribute to the impression that the self is restricted to the body; their disintegration should therefore permit easier access to further reaches of consciousness.

There is good reason for taking seriously the hypothesis that consciousness continues after bodily death. Let us now consider the evidence needed to support this hypothesis.

SURVIVAL RESEARCH WITH THE LIVING

Studies of mediumistic communicators, apparitions, and other post-mortem residues of the living have not established that they are conscious entities. A different approach is needed to determine if consciousness persists after death.

If there is survival after death, then that which survives must exist beforehand in the living. In other words, it should be possible to approach the survival question by a study of consciousness in the living.

There are many kinds of consciousness in addition to the waking state most of us experience most of the time. There is dream consciousness, of which, in turn, there are several types. There are states of consciousness that result from being hypnotized, taking drugs, engaging in meditation, and so on. In other words, a person is potentially able to experience himself and the world in many different ways. In the search for the kinds of consciousness that may survive death, we need something similar to the testing situation explorers of outer space have created in their simulated space laboratories. In these laboratories conditions that they expect to encounter in outer space are reproduced as closely as possible on earth. Parapsychologists need simulated survival laboratories in which they can explore the nature of a possible life after death by studies of the characteristics of the consciousness in living people that may continue after their death.

Several centers are developing laboratory techniques which meet this purpose. They include the ASPR; the Division of Parapsychology at the University of Virginia, Charlottesville; the Maimonides dream laboratory; and the PRF in Durham, North Carolina. The research falls into three main categories, deriving from three characteristics of the kind of consciousness that may survive death: (a) there must be actual awareness that the self extends beyond the body; (b) it must be possible to verify that this self extends beyond the body; and (c) this self must be capable of existing independent of the physical organism.

These three hypothetical characteristics can be explored (a) by state reports of the experience, (b) by parapsychological tests, and (c) by physiological studies.

State Reports

People occasionally report that their consciousness, what they regard as their self or I, moves or extends beyond the boundaries of the body. The experience ranges from the feeling in OOBE's that something like ordinary waking consciousness leaves the physical body and moves to another distinct location in space and time to the feeling that the self simultaneously occupies or becomes identified with all space and time. The latter has been called the "peak experience" by Abraham Maslow (14). I shall use the term *field consciousness* (FC) for experiences that seem to take in part or all of the environment outside what is usually considered a person or individual.

At the PRF we have done most of our OOBE research with Blue Harary, a Duke student and PRF research assistant. He had the following experience before we began work with him. One evening he went to bed at his home in New York City thinking about an elderly lady friend in Maine with whom he had lost touch. After he fell asleep, he reported,

> I found myself floating out of my body which lay below me on the bed. I had this experience many times in the past and so was not surprised. I now could travel to find my old friend. I decided to bring my close friend George, who was living elsewhere in New York, with me. I concentrated on George and soon was floating above him where he lay asleep on his bed. I awoke George's out of the body self and grasped his hands and pulled him up out of his body. George readily

decided to accompany me. None of this seemed the least bit unusual to either of us. We passed a barrier and then had only a short distance to travel. On the way to Maine, George and I walked through wooded areas, and up and down green, rolling hills. At one point when we stopped to rest on a hillside, George began to wander too close to a pool of pink, hot, bubbling liquid. I warned George not to wander too close because it was dangerous, even in an OOBE state.

We reached an area near where we thought the woman would be, and were surprised to find that the woman had been waiting for us. I recognized her reddish blond hair and high cheekbones. We sat for a long while and discussed many of the things that had been disturbing all of us in our Earth lives. We seemed to find calm and reassurance in existence in that other-worldly level and in each other's warm company.

We said our goodbyes and George and I went back, and I helped him into his body which still lay asleep on his bed. I went back and found my own body safe and sound where I had left it. I floated in the air for a moment and then climbed back into my body. The next morning I awoke with complete recollection of the experience.

I didn't see George again until later the next day. He said that when he awoke in the morning, he had the strangest sensation of having forgotten something.

Later in the evening when George and I were discussing dreams a sudden strange look came across his face. He held his hands over his eyes and then pointed a finger at me and looking up with a shocked expression, said "Last night!" He then proceeded to ask me if we had been out of our bodies together and if what seemed so real to him at the time actually was a real experience. I told him very little at first and asked him to tell me all of the details that he could remember. "A lady," he said; "there was this fantastic lady." "Was she an elderly lady?" I asked him. "Yes, but not with gray hair like most old ladies," he answered, "but with reddish blond hair and with high cheekbones." He also remembered that there had been a danger and "something about a pool."

In this experience, Harary's consciousness was quite similar to his waking consciousness, and his own OOBE "body" and that of George were near duplicates of their physical ones.

Harary has also experienced field consciousness:

I had been lying on my bed trying to keep myself awake long enough to study effectively for my college midterms. It was becoming increasingly difficult for me to keep my eyes open. Finally, I fell back upon the bed and when I did so almost immediately found myself out of my body and flying through space at an enormous speed. When I slowed down, I found myself floating somewhere in space. I cannot hope to describe the experience as vividly as it occurred to me but I will try.

All around me I could see planets and smaller particles in rhythmic motion. My vision seemed to at once focus in front of me and at the same time cover a three hundred and sixty degree radius. All of my "senses" were perceiving in similar intense fashion. I could hear a wonderful harmony which seemed to accompany every particle. I felt a chord was playing from within my total being. When I moved, the sounds and the movements of the particles around me moved in a balance to my movements. I felt not only that I was experiencing nature; I *was* nature. Always there was the incredibly balanced, harmonious movement of the universe.

Then I remember thinking of myself lying on the bed in my room back at college. It seemed that it was time to be back there. In a few moments I felt a jolt in my physical body and opened my eyes to find myself lying on the bed. I felt a complete love flowing through me. I looked at my books lying where I had dropped them and almost laughed at the seeming stupidity of studying earthly knowledge from books. I felt energetic and almost jumped up out of bed to run outside. It had seemed that several hours had passed but actually only about five minutes had.

Let us now turn to the question of whether experiences like these are only private fantasies or whether in some sense they involve extensions into or awareness of the objective world.

Parapsychological Tests

Only a few parapsychological experiments have been done with OOBE subjects. Since Charles Tart reviews this material elsewhere in this volume (see Chapter 15), I shall not report it here. I shall also not discuss the rich anecdotal literature, which has been explored by Hornell Hart (8) and Robert Crookall (5).

At the PRF we conduct two types of psi tests to explore OOBE and FC states. The first focuses on the question of whether persons in such states can be detected in areas apparently occupied by their consciousness. The other type of test concerns the question of whether they can obtain verifiable information there.

DETECTION STUDIES

Anecdotal evidence, including some from our own preliminary studies, suggests that a friend of a person who has an OOBE or a member of his family occasionally has a feeling of "presence" about this person at the same time as he has the experience of visiting his friend. In six experiments with Harary in which people functioned as detectors, they felt he was present more often than they should by chance when he believed he was visiting the detection room in the OOB state.

Upon occasion we hear anecdotes in which pets respond to the presence of a person in the OOB state. A young woman we tested said that her cats followed her around when she was "out" in her apartment. In our detection work with Harary, the best results have been with a kitten. Laboratory gerbils and hamsters have not responded, but the kitten calms down when Harary visits it in the OOB state. We measure the kitten's level of activity in terms of the number of meows during a given period and the number of squares it crosses in the observation chamber. The results were more significant than with the human detectors and quite striking. The cat meowed 37 times during the control periods and not at all during the OOBE periods. Another kitten from the same litter did not react. In one of the tests where both kittens were supposed to have been used, Harary claimed he saw only one. It turned out that the experimenter had decided to remove the other.

Sometimes the presence of a person in the OOB state is said to result in physical changes in the area. We have built devices that measure electromagnetic fields and magnetic permeability, but the results are indefinite. We are planning to measure slight temperature changes and other physical conditions as our resources allow.

In designing detection studies of FC states we are mainly guided by anecdotal stories as to what changes may take place in the target area and by the state reports of the person having the FC experience. If he experiences a joining with a plant or an inanimate object, the plant or object can be monitored by physiological or physical devices. If he reports having expanded throughout his environment, we would expect that all detectors oriented to him would respond. If he reports a joining with one specific person but not with others, that person might respond more strongly than the rest. Behavioral observations of the detector by the experimenter, periodic verbal reports, and physiological data that may help to identify the psychophysiological state of the detector will provide the detection data in the FC studies.

Some practicers, such as advanced yogis, are said to be in constant expansion, and people near them often claim to be affected by their physical presence. These claims can readily be explored by our detection procedures.

ESP BY SUBJECT

In our first OOBE experiments with Harary, the ESP targets were large colored letters of the alphabet located in another house. On five of nine occasions Harary's description of the color of the target was close to the actual one. In three cases, he gave evidence of homing in on the general shape of the letters: In one case, he named three or four possible shapes, then said he also saw an *S* "as if you stood an *N* on its side." The target was a *Z*. In another, he said the target was round or circular. It was a *Q*. In a third, he said the target was a *V* or something with a long diagonal: it was a *W*. The results, however, were not statistically significant.

The detection studies suggested that Harary might interact more closely with people than with inanimate objects. We therefore changed his task to that of discovering the locations of people in the target room in the other house. There were three possible locations, each to be occupied by one of two or three persons. Harary was highly successful at first, and then his performance declined.

It is interesting that in several cases the animal or human detectors responded during OOBE periods when Harary's impressions about the physical targets were wrong. According to one criterion, Harary was at the target location, and according to another criterion, he may have been aware only of his "own" mental constructs. We are reminded of the "pool of pink, hot, bubbling liquid" Harary saw during his OOBE visit to Maine, which probably also had no relation to anything in the known physical world. In OOBE's, as in other forms of ESP, there are no sharp distinctions between mental and physical and between objective and subjective facts.

It is sometimes argued that OOB and FC experiences involve only an imaginary extension into the environment and that ESP information comes to the physical body of the person and is not acquired at the place he experiences himself to be. According to this theory, people and animals who seem to detect the presence of a person in an OOB or FC state would become aware only by ESP of his intention or belief that he has extended. Arguments of this type, however, rest on the assumptions about ESP that I discussed earlier and that seem to be mistaken. ESP, it seems, is awareness of what already is part of the self. OOBE's verify what we already know about ESP: the person is not going anywhere or seeing anything other than where and what he already is. It is only from the restricted perspective of ordinary states of consciousness that he may appear to observe the familiar physical world (and that he is not having a "real" OOB or ESP experience when he reports something different). The relationship between ESP, on the one hand, and OOB and FC states, on the other, is apparently this: in OOB and FC states, the person is aware of what is going on, while ESP as such may or may not be associated with a conscious experience.

As Lawrence LeShan (13) has shown, FC experiences are often strikingly similar to the descriptions of the universe by modern physicists (see Chapter 22). But FC experiences are rarely of the type that allow one to determine if consciousness actually occupies known physical space. This is not surprising, since FC sometimes seems to be everything and everywhere. There are, however, anecdotal accounts that suggest that on entering or leaving this state, the person's perspective narrows sufficiently to detect discrete events. It also appears that people who often have FC experiences may have more ESP awareness than others.

Richard Alpert (26), formerly a professor of psychology at Harvard who is known as Baba Ram Dass since his initiation by an Indian teacher of meditation, says that when he was "being a Holy Man" at Esalen in Big Sur, California, somebody asked if he had any psychic powers. Alpert replied,

> "No, I'm happy I don't, . . . I have a big ego, and I'd misuse them." And then I looked at this man—he had just arrived and . . . I said, "Could you imagine . . . if I could look at you, sir, and I could say, 'You were walking up the hill to get here and you looked down on the ground and you saw what you thought was a jewel and you picked it up and you threw it away.' " . . . He stood up and turned ashen white . . . and he says, "I was walking up the hill," and he said, "I saw this . . . and I picked it up and I thought it was jade and it turned out to be a piece of ginger ale bottle and I threw it away."

Ram Dass (27) has similar stories about his teacher. They will be found in most other accounts of persons seeking transpersonal experiences, whether they be Hasidic Jews (3), Sufi Moslems (18), or possessors of any other religious or cultural backgrounds.

Just as we find many ESP stories around persons who seek transcending experiences, there are many accounts of transcending experiences from persons who seem to be endowed with unusual ESP abilities. Mrs. Coombe-Tennant (1), the British medium known as Mrs. Willett, once described her experience of communicating with a deceased person: "I can only describe it by saying I felt myself so blending with him as almost to seem to be becoming him." Another time, when she returned from the trance state, she said, "There isn't any time or place, and either you're loosed or they're entered, and you all of a sudden know everything that ever was. You understand everything. It's like every single thing and time and thought and everything brought down to one point."

W. H. C. Tenhaeff (39) quotes from Alexis Didier, a French psychic of the mid-1800s, who mainly used object association: "With the help of a simple lock of hair or a letter, I come into contact with them [the owner of the hair or letter], irrespective of the distance separating us. . . . I see them, I hear them, they live their lives in me. I feel myself suffer their pains, having part in their joys. My soul . . . comes into touch with them and between them and me arises a community of consciousness."

In his own studies of 47 Dutch psychics, Tenhaeff found a "great 'sensitivity' for everything coming from the outside world. . . . Also, they endeavor to identify with persons and objects near them. There is an attempt to attain what . . . Lucien Levy-Bruhl has called 'participation mystique.'" In an ESP experiment with a group of meditators at the ASPR Karlis Osis and Edwin Bokert (20) stated that the people who did best in ESP had a "feeling of merging with the others . . . and a feeling of oneness as if the boundaries between 'what is me and what is not me' were dissolving."

In exploring the relationship between meditation and ESP abilities, it is interesting that persons who have such abilities to a marked degree often use procedures to activate them that are similar to the procedures advocated by many meditation systems. In most forms of meditation, the meditator seeks a deep state of relaxation yet remains fully awake. Usually, the mind is either kept a blank or is engaged in some simple task, such as repeating a word mentally or visualizing an object, with the hope that this will reduce discursive thinking and allow the meditator to experience the unity between himself and the rest of the world. ESP receptivity seems to be facilitated by similar procedures (see Chapter 27).

In a survey of 18 particularly successful ESP subjects, Rhea White found that they would first relax and clear their minds of extraneous thoughts either by keeping them blank or focusing attention on something such as a mental image. After a period of waiting, this image would be released and an ESP impression might enter consciousness (43).

William G. and Lendell W. Braud (2) obtained high ESP results from students at the University of Houston in tests preceded by muscular and mental relaxation. The studies of Charles Honorton (10) at Maimonides Medical Center involving hypnosis, EEG biofeedback, and sensory deprivation suggested that ESP performance is improved to the extent that the methods provide "attenuation of external stimuli and shifts from externally directed to internally directed attentive activity."

FC experiences sometimes result from taking hallucinogenic drugs such as LSD. In a report on the use of LSD for psychotherapy, R. Holzinger (9) said that some of his patients described apparent ESP experiences while in a state of expanded awareness. He checked some of the statements and found them to be correct. On the other hand, Roberto Cavanna and Emilio Servadio were not particularly successful in attempts to elicit ESP in tests with persons who had taken LSD (4).

At the PRF, we are preparing a project to explore FC. Our pilot work includes a one-year study conducted at Andhra University, India, by Hamlyn Dukhan in collaboration with Dr. K. Ramakrishna Rao (28). Dukhan tested students and disciples at two Indian yogi ashrams with ESP cards. He found that newcomers to the ashrams tended to score negatively, while persons who had been in training for some time had positive ESP scores.

Physiological Studies

One of the few physiological studies of OOB states was done by Charles Tart (see Chapter 15), who found considerable alpha activity in the two subjects he tested. In our OOBE work with Harary, he first enters a state of deep relaxation, which he calls his "cool down" period. This is characterized by a great deal of alpha in both hemispheres of the brain that persists into the OOB state. In the OOB state there is a reduction in eye movements and a decrease in skin potential. The latter suggests a relaxed condition. Surprisingly, there is also an increase in respiration and heart rate, which suggests increased activity or arousal. The interpretation of these data must wait for further research. So far the evidence suggests that Harary's body functions at a near normal rate during his OOB states, while his central nervous system may be less active.

Several studies have been made of persons during meditation. Unfortunately, the reports do not always indicate whether or not the persons were having transcending experiences at the time. R. Keith Wallace and Herbert Benson (42) tested meditators at Harvard University and found sharp drops in the body's use of oxygen and in heart rate and respiration. There were increases in the electrical resistance of the skin and decreases in the amount of lactic acid in the blood, both showing reduced arousal. There were also increases of alpha waves. T. Hirai and A. Kasamatsu (12) found an increase of alpha during Zen meditation and, sometimes, emergence of the still slower theta waves.

The alpha wave may also be associated with ESP, suggesting that meditation, ESP, and the "alpha state" are related. For instance, in an experiment with Lalsingh Harribance at the PRF, we found his ESP to be best when the production (percent-time amount) of alpha was highest (16). Harribance usually prefaces his tests with a period of quiet and prayer. In a study by Rex Stanford and Ian Stevenson (35) at the University of Virginia, the subject used a meditation procedure before each ESP trial to clear his mind and then tried to develop a mental image of the ESP target. His ESP scores were highest when the alpha frequency was low during the mind-clearing period, perhaps indicating that the more tranquil his state, the better was he prepared for the ESP task. Scoring was also good when there was an increase in frequency between the mind-clearing and image-development phases, which may suggest that the development of the ESP response involves an increase in mental activity.

If brain functions are related to OOB and FC states, we might find different characteristics for the two types of experiences. In OOBE's there is often the same experience of temporal succession and sequential progression through space that we experience in ordinary states of consciousness and that is characteristic of left-hemisphere mentation. Conversely, the global experiences in FC suggest right-hemisphere involvement.

On the other hand, if the brain is largely dormant during OOB and FC experiences, then we may suppose that such experiences are independent of the brain and will continue when the brain has ceased operating altogether. Reports of OOBE and FC during heart stoppage, near drowning, anesthesia, or reduction by voluntary control of brain and body functions (as reportedly done by yogis and meditators) raise the possibility that the central nervous system is not responsible for these experiences. Karlis Osis (19) has found that people near death sometimes seem to experience another world and other entities, including deceased friends and relatives.

CONCLUSION

A distinction must be made between the survival of consciousness and the survival of personality or of an image of the body. There is suggestive evidence from mediumistic communications, reincarnation studies, apparitional sightings, and so on that images of the body and more or less full-fledged personalities may persist after death at least for a time.

But such survival does not imply the survival of the consciousness that animated the people in question when they were alive. There is, however, evidence from the findings of parapsychology that human consciousness is not private to any person but can be shared by others. If this is the case, consciousness will continue beyond the death of any one individual.

Since we do not know whether mediumistic communicators, apparitions, and the like are conscious but do know that the consciousness that may continue beyond death exists in the living, it seems that the best place to look for this consciousness is in living beings.

A survey of persons who have had the experience that their consciousness extended beyond the body suggests that consciousness exists along a spectrum ranging from very constricted to very expanded. Close to the constricted end of the scale, but probably not at its extreme end, is the kind of consciousness that we identify with the physical body. This type of consciousness may be involved in most OOBE's; after death it may be involved in apparitional sightings. At the other end of the scale, the person experiences an identification with the whole universe, so that everything in it is felt as "his" and no distinctions are recognized. Some individuals may be limited to a particular place on the scale, while others may be able to move up and down its length.

The findings also suggest that experiences of extending into the environment are sometimes real in the sense that persons who have such experiences may be able to interact with people and things at the distant locations in question. On the other hand, it is still uncertain whether or not such experiences require a living body.

When we have discovered the characteristics of the consciousness that may survive—whether this be the type experienced during OOB travels or the FC type—we may look for these characteristics in apparent survival phenomena. Parapsychology has discovered one such characteristic: the consciousness that may survive is public. It should then be possible for the living to experience the world of the dead. Charles Tart (38) suggests that scientists who study altered states of consciousness develop the ability to enter such states themselves. In parapsychology we have insisted on a sharp separation between the scientist and the people he studies. But the assumption that there is a real distinction is another of the dubious ideas born of the limited perspective of ordinary consciousness. It is clear from the research findings that the experimenter often affects the results of his subjects. Perhaps we should encourage the subjects to share in the role of the experimenter and participate in the planning and interpretation of research. And perhaps the experimenter should learn to enter altered states such as OOB and FC experiences. Personal familiarity with the states of consciousness in which psi seems to originate might reduce the number of false assumptions about them. Such familiarity might also lead to better maps of states of consciousness that may exist after death. Until now we have tried to trace the characteristics of these states from afar, mainly on the basis of the stories that OOBE subjects, mediums, and others bring back. But the most interesting stories about any land are told by people who have been there themselves, and the most credible stories are told by those who are trained observers and who bring the necessary tools along for reliable recording.

In the past it has sometimes seemed that the question of survival after death was a minor issue in a field of research that was itself at the fringe of science. If the main focus for survival research is extended states of consciousness, this research becomes relevant to any discipline concerned with the human mind. In turn, any science—from physics to transpersonal psychology—that has something important to say about consciousness may contribute to our understanding of a possible next world.

Expanded states of consciousness or FC are of special interest because they may reveal potentials in man for wider interactions than are generally thought to be possible. FC appears to be an experiential demonstration of the connections that parapsychology, physics, and other sciences have shown to exist between man and his environment. The exploration of FC could be particularly important in today's society, which adopts the premise that people are separate. If more people could actually experience the whole of which all may be part, they might encroach less on each other and on their physical environment. By exploring such states of consciousness, we may contribute to man's survival and well-being in this world at the same time as we point to what may come in the next.

REFERENCES

1. Balfour, Gerald William. "A Study of the Psychological Aspects of Mrs. Willett's Mediumship, and of the Statements of the Communicators Concerning Process." *Proceedings of the Society for Psychical Research*, 43 (1935).

2. Braud, W. G., and Braud, L. W. "Preliminary Exploration of Psi Conducive States: Progressive Muscular Relaxation." *Journal of the American Society for Psychical Research*, 67 (1973).

3. Buber, Martin. *Tales of the Hasidim Early Masters*. Schocken: New York, 1947.

4. Cavanna, Roberto, and Servadio, Emilio. *ESP Experiments with LSD 25 and Psilocybin. A Methodological Approach*. Parapsychological Monographs, Parapsychology Foundation: New York, 1964.

5. Crookall, Robert. *The Supreme Adventure*. James Clarke: London, 1961.

6. Gauld, Alan. "A Series of 'Drop-In' Communicators." *Proceedings of the Society for Psychical Research*, 55 (1972).

7. Gurney, Edmund. "On Apparitions Occurring Soon After Death." *Proceedings of the Society for Psychical Research*, 5 (1888–1889).

8. Hart, Hornell. *The Enigma of Survival*. Thomas: Springfield, Ill., 1959.

9. Holzinger, R. "LSD 25, a Tool in Psychotherapy." *Journal of General Psychology*, 71 (1964).

10. Honorton, Charles; Drucker, Sally; and Hermone, Harry. "Shifts in Subjective State and GESP: A Preliminary Study Under Conditions of Partial Sensory Deprivation." In W. G. Roll, R. L. Morris, and J. D. Morris, eds., *Research in Parapsychology, 1972*. Scarecrow: Metuchen, N.J., 1973.

11. James, William. "Report on Mrs. Piper's Hodgson-Control." *Proceedings of the Society for Psychical Research*, 23 (1909).

12. Kasamatsu, Akira, and Hirai, Tomio. "An Electroencephalographic Study on the Zen Meditation (Zazen)." In Charles T. Tart, ed., *Altered States of Consciousness*. Wiley: New York, 1969.

13. LeShan, Lawrence. "Physicists and Mystics: Similarities in World View." *Journal of Transpersonal Psychology*, No. 1 (1969).

14. Maslow, Abraham, *Religions, Values and Peak Experiences*. Ohio State University Press: Columbus, 1964.

15. Morris, R. L. "An Exact Method for Evaluating Preferentially Matched Free-Response Material." *Journal of the American Society for Psychical Research*, 66 (1972).

16. Morris, R. L.; Roll, W. G.; Klein, J.; and Wheeler, G. "EEG Patterns

and ESP Results in Forced-Choice Experiments with Lalsingh Harribance."
Journal of the American Society for Psychical Research, 66 (1972).

17. Newbold, Wm. Romaine. "A Further Record of Observations of Certain Phenomena of Trance. Part II.A." *Proceedings of the Society for Psychical Research*, 14 (1898).

18. Nicholson, R. A. *The Mystics of Islam*. Routledge and Kegan Paul: London, 1966.

19. Osis, Karlis. *Deathbed Observations by Physicians and Nurses. Parapsychological Monographs*. Parapsychology Foundation: New York, 1961.

20. Osis, Karlis, and Bokert, Edwin. "ESP and Changed States of Consciousness Induced by Meditation." *Journal of the American Society for Psychical Research*, 65 (1971).

21. Piddington, J. G. "A Series of Concordant Automatisms." *Proceedings of the Society for Psychical Research*, 22 (1908).

22. Pratt, J. G. *On the Evaluation of Verbal Material in Parapsychology. Parapsychological Monographs*. Parapsychology Foundation: New York, 1969.

23. Pratt, J. G., and Birge, W. R. "Appraising Verbal Test Material in Parapsychology." *Journal of Parapsychology*, 12 (1948).

24. Price, H. H. "Haunting and the 'Psychic Ether' Hypothesis: With Some Preliminary Reflections on the Present Condition and Possible Future of Psychical Research." *Proceedings of the Society for Psychical Research*, 45 (1939).

25. Price, H. H. "Mind over Mind and Mind over Matter." *Enquiry*, 2 (1949).

26. Ram Dass, Baba. "Baba Ram Dass Lecture at the Menninger Foundation: Part II." *Journal of Transpersonal Psychology*, No. 1 (1971).

27. Ram Dass, Baba. *Be Here Now*. Lama Foundation: San Cristobal, N.M., 1971.

28. Rao, K. Ramakrishna, and Dukhan, Hamlyn. "Meditation and ESP Scoring." In W. G. Roll, R. L. Morris, and J. D. Morris, eds., *Research in Parapsychology, 1972*. Scarecrow: Metuchen, N.J., Inc., 1973.

29. Roll, W. G. "The Psi Field." *Proceedings of the Parapsychological Association*, 1 (1964).

30. Roll, W. G., and Burdick, D. S. "Statistical Models for the Assessment of Verbal and Other ESP Responses." *Journal of the American Society for Psychical Research*, 63 (1969).

31. Roll, W. G.; Morris, R. L.; Damgaard, J. A.; Klein, J.; and Roll, M. "Free Verbal Response Experiments with Lalsingh Harribance." *Journal of the American Society for Psychical Research*, 67 (1973).

32. Saltmarsh, H. F., and Soal, S. G. "A Method of Estimating the Supernormal Content of Mediumistic Communications." *Proceedings of the Society for Psychical Research*, 39 (1930–1931).

33. Schmeidler, Gertrude. "Quantitative Investigation of a 'Haunted House.'" *Journal of the American Society for Psychical Research*, 60 (1966).

34. Soal, S. G. "A Report on Some Communications Received Through Mrs. Blanche Cooper. Section 4. The Case of Gordon Davis. A 'Communication' from a Living Person." *Proceedings of the Society for Psychical Research*, 35 (1926).

35. Stanford, Rex G., and Stevenson, Ian. "EEG Correlates of Free-Response GESP in an Individual Subject." *Journal of the American Society for Psychical Research*, 66 (1972).

36. Stevenson, Ian. *Twenty Cases Suggestive of Reincarnation*. American Society for Psychical Research: New York, 1966.

37. Stevenson, Ian. "A Communicator of the 'Drop In' Type in France: The Case of Robert Marie." *Journal of the American Society for Psychical Research*, 67 (1973).
38. Tart, Charles T. "States of Consciousness and State-Specific Sciences." *Science*, 16 June 1972, 176 (1972).
39. Tenhaeff, W. H. C. "Some Aspects of Parapsychological Research in the Netherlands." *International Journal of Neuropsychiatry*, 2 (1966).
40. Thomas, C. Drayton. *Some New Evidence for Human Survival*, with Introduction by W. F. Barrett. Collins: London, 1922.
41. Tyrrell, G. N. M. *Apparitions*. University Books: New York, 1961.
42. Wallace, Robert Keith, and Benson, Herbert. "The Physiology of Meditation." *Scientific American*, February 1972.
43. White, Rhea. "A Comparison of Old and New Methods of Response to Targets in ESP Experiments." *Journal of the American Society for Psychical Research*, 58 (1964).

III The Emergence of a
New Natural Science

No longer a stepchild of science, psychic research is now thoroughly grounded in both technology and theory. This section describes the emergence of paraphysics through the marriage of sophisticated research methodology and hardware with general systems concepts and an expanded view of the nature of man. Other chapters describe the latest physical research into the nature of the psyche. Probing insights into the theoretical basis of mind and consciousness are offered.

JAMES D. BEAL

JAMES B. BEAL *is an aerospace engineer in the Quality and Reliability Assurance Laboratory at the National Aeronautics and Space Administration's Marshall Space Flight Center near Huntsville, Alabama.*

In 1956 Mr. Beal earned a bachelor of science degree in mechanical engineering from the University of Colorado and then took a position as quality control engineer for the Boeing Company. He has been with NASA in the area of nondestructive testing of aerospace structures since 1964.

Mr. Beal has published many articles on nondestructive testing in technical journals. He is also the author of "Paraphysics and Parapsychology" in the April 1973 issue of Analog; *"The Methodology of Pattern in Awareness" in* Fields Within Fields . . . Within Fields, *Vol. 5, No. 1;* "The New Biotechnology" in Frontiers of Consciousness *(Julian Press, 1974), John White, ed.; and "Electrostatic Fields, Electromagnetic Fields and Ions," in the proceedings of the Neuroelectric Society's 1973 symposium on the effects of low-frequency magnetic and electric fields on biological communication processes.*

Mr. Beal can be reached at 4209 Fortson Lane, N.W., Huntsville, Ala. 35810.

18 The Emergence of Paraphysics: Research and Applications

JAMES B. BEAL

SUMMARY

Paraphysics is a blending of physics, electronics, biology, biofeedback, and the new science of subjective awareness with the methodology already established in some areas of psychic research and systems engineering. Research is underway and applications are being made that will bring increased awareness and understanding of the universe and its complex actions. The implications for science, medicine, technology, psychology, philosophy, and culture in general are vast.

This chapter outlines some of the areas in which outer-space research, in a synergistic blending of many disciplines, has produced benefits to inner-space research. Potential spin-off applications of paraphysical research into medical, psychological, and environmental areas are pointed out.

INTRODUCTION

Physics. That branch of knowledge treating of the material world and its phenomena; natural philosophy, the science of matter and motion.
Paraphysics. The study of the physics of paranormal processes—i.e., phenomena that resemble physical phenomena but are without recognizable physical cause.
Metaphysics. A division of philosophy that includes ontology, or the science of being, and cosmology, or the science of the fundamental causes and processes in things.

Paraphysics (a term invented by the nineteenth-century German scientist Baron von Schrenck-Notzing) emerged concurrently with improved electronic equipment for the complex task of monitoring internal, external, and emotional effects associated with living systems. It is a rapidly evolving discipline—a blending of physics, electronics, biology, biofeed-back, and the new science of subjective experience with the methodology already established in some areas of psychic research and systems engin-eering. Involved with living-systems phenomena that are beyond, or ab-normal to, currently accepted scientific beliefs, it is concerned primarily with objective manifestations of energy associated with the nature of mind.

Paraphysics has risen in response to the multitude of ecological, sociol-ogical, psychological, and physiological interactions (primarily unplanned) of humanity. The broadest possible overview of human effects on the environment, environmental effects on human beings, and their mental–physical results is thus needed as a basis for the self-insight and self-control necessary to realize optimum self-potential. The total effect of the interacting systems on, and within, a person is greater than (or different from) the sum of the effects of the individual systems. The end effect is synergistic. It cannot be ascertained by a study of the discrete compon-ents. Thus, there is needed a synergistic, or total-systems, approach to the study of the nature of the human being.

A new age is rapidly emerging based on noetics, the general study of consciousness, which will supply knowledge of the imperfectly understood subjective, psychic, and spiritual side of "self." This area of discovery will bring about far-reaching and rapid changes in our way of life. Newfound knowledge is affecting us in ways far different from, and more rapid than, anything we have witnessed in the past. The degree of change being caused by emergence into a postatomic, computerized, solid-state elec-tronic, interplanetary age can only be remotely compared to that of the Industrial Revolution of the nineteenth century. Science and technology are inundating society with inventions and knowledge about the universe that not only influence our way of living but also challenge the founda-tions of the social order.

It appears we went "out" objectively and materialistically before we went "in" subjectively and spiritually to handle our new knowledge with wisdom and insight. We must find a positive way to cope with future shock and the knowledge explosion. With all our scientific knowledge of the physical universe, we still know virtually nothing about our subjective nature and how to live in harmony with our environment, technology, and each other. Indeed, the information available on the subjective nature of mind is usually highly speculative, misleading, contradictory, inconclusive, and mostly qualitative. Despite heroic efforts by early psychic researchers, only within the past decade has technology advanced to the point where both environment and individual can be monitored (with a minimum of disturbance) as a symbiotic interrelated system and the mind–body inter-actions studied quantitatively. The extension of scientific method to the essential phenomena of altered states of consciousness is now underway. The results will prove—to use an apt expression—to be mind-blowing.

Life in the future can be and must be favorably affected by the study and understanding of subjective experiences, altered states of consciousness and pantheistic or intuitive (psychic) awareness. Without this understanding, our knowledge of the physical world will continue to grow, but our ability to utilize it intelligently and humanely will decrease. The lack of knowledge about our inner nature and capabilities is a gaping hole in our concept of the universe.

It would seem that the realization that all knowledge is basically experiential knowledge (the objective world is a "special case" of the subjective world and is limited) would have stimulated the "open-minded, unprejudiced seekers after truth" to apply the scientific method to subjective experiences long before now. Not so! It was easier in the past to engage in reducing all external reality to basic physical entities that could be "black boxed," observed, cataloged, and tested according to theory. As scientists became more specialized, the bias against the influence of subtle external factors tended to be built in as "a sense of security." Important higher patterns of information were overlooked because of cultural conditioning of the "condemnation before investigation" attitude. It was easier to deal with inanimate systems.

The evolution of awareness has depended upon a complex combination of initial sensory inputs detected by specialized biosystems. Phenomena associated with the human being will not be completely understood by studying the individual sensing systems alone or in isolation. It is how the inputs are combined that counts, and how the combinations act temporally and in symbiosis with the environment.

The advent of computers and solid-state electronics has made the study of complex systems more accessible. Thus, the interdisciplinary evolvement of the "hyphenated sciences" and "scientific generalists" has occurred to apply the systems-engineering concepts basic to aerospace developments. Interdisciplinary efforts can now be applied to the questioning of basic life processes and the electrochemical, rhythmical patterns that can be combined in a hierarchy of systems toward increasing stages of complexity, awareness, and higher-order effects.

A BRIEF HISTORY OF PARAPHYSICS

Many persons find confusing the distinctions between parapsychology, paraphysics, psychoenergetics, and psychotronics. Parapsychology places the accent on certain unusual aspects of psychology. Paraphysics accents the physical aspects; thus, poltergeist phenomena and PK should appropriately be included under this heading. *Psychoenergetics* is the Russian term for parapsychology. *Psychotronics*, a brilliant expression popularized by the efforts of Dr. Zdenek Rejdak of Czechoslovakia, illustrates well the Eastern European attitude that psychic research is an empirical science, a technological extension of electronics and biochemistry that includes such developments as bioplasmic energy and Kirlian photography (18, p. 104).

There is not space here to include all those who deserve mention for their part in the emergence of a scientific methodology and theory of paraphysics prior to 1965. However, some of the pioneers in the study of mind–body–environment relations must be mentioned.

Baron von Reichenbach was a nineteenth-century German scientist and occultist who studied ill psychic individuals and their hypersensitivity to magnetic fields. He was the inventor of asphalt and coined the term odic force to describe psychic energy.

Sir William Crookes, an English chemist and physicist of the nineteenth century, was a keen student of psi and the correlation between them and ordinary physical laws. He made an extensive investigation of the famous psychic D. D. Home, utilizing a crude but effective chart recorder to record deflections during PK tests on weight increase or decrease of objects on a cantilever beam. He also noted a feeling of cold temperature around objects affected by PK.

F. Cazzamalli was the Italian scientist who around 1923 developed an ultrahigh-frequency (UHF) apparatus for testing human telepathy. Cazzamalli saw the need for machine systems capable of testing for psychic ability in an unbiased, impartial manner. He placed his subjects inside a Faraday cage and claimed that some of those individuals could produce radio-frequency beat pulses when undergoing emotional stimulation of the brain. Since VHF–UHF techniques were rather crude, it is open to conjecture whether this purported "brain radiation" was heterodyning with fundamental frequencies between 60 and 400 megahertz of the local oscillator or interacting with more or less high harmonics. Unfortunately, Cazzamalli's experiments have never been repeated in depth (28, p. 27). However, there may be some tie-ins with the more definitive recent work on emission of electromagnetic radiation from the human body in the microwave region, discussed later in this chapter.

S. W. Tromp, director of the Biometeorological Research Centre in Leiden, Netherlands, produced a notable book in 1949 entitled *Psychical Physics*, which contained comprehensive chapters on electromagnetic fields in and around living organisms, the influence of external electromagnetic fields on living organisms and their relation to dowsing, hypnotism, and animal navigation.

Henry K. Puharich, neurologist and former president of Intelectron Corporation, now involved in full-time psychic research, published

Beyond Telepathy in 1962 (recently reissued in paperback; 34) in an attempt to relate the phenomena of psychic research to the physical side of man. Puharich has tried to rationalize the anatomy and dynamics of the mind and to relate the facts of mind to the facts of biology and physics. Enhancement and supression of psychic ability using mind, body, and environmental factors in synergistic combination are described in detail and serve as feasibility studies for those who want to delve more deeply into these areas with more sensitive equipment.

Harold S. Burr, professor of anatomy at Yale University School of Medicine, and Leonard J. Ravitz, a diplomate of the American Board of Psychiatry and Neurology, developed the electrodynamic theory of life and the instrumentation to measure the electromagnetic fields that control growth and repair of living protoplasm. Burr indicated in 1936 that the field (energy matrix) both determines and is determined by the particle; it is not independent of matter but a very condition for, and causal determiner of, the behavior of matter. Thus, the electrodynamic theory of nature is more fundamental than the chemical theory, because voltage measurements of the body can be used to diagnose the condition not only of the body but also of the mind. In April 1948, hypnosis was electrometrically recorded for the first time and compared with field shifts during other state changes. Dramatic voltage shifts can be recorded on hypnotic trance termination and depth of trance measured precisely. The equipment, developed and utilized by Burr and Ravitz, was designed to measure pure field phenomena such as voltage gradients, independent of resistance and current flow, without disturbing the system under observation (7; 37, p. 120).

Benson Herbert, director of the Paraphysical Laboratory in Downton, Wiltshire, England, and editor of the *Journal of Paraphysics* (begun in 1967) and the *Paraphysical News Supplement*, has actively sought the cooperation of international scientists in order to present the journal as a global medium for the rapid advancement of research in parapsychology and paraphysics. A series of special issues reported all the proceedings of the first Symposium of Psychotronics held in Prague during September 1970, thus giving a thorough treatment of the state of psychotronic research then, and continuing to the present, as an English-language interface with the work proceeding in Eastern Europe. The Paraphysical Laboratory has performed considerable original and confirmatory research in sensory stimulation–deprivation, PK, field effects, and other factors associated with the nature of mind.

Wilhelm Reich, a neuropsychiatrist, claimed to have discovered orgone energy, a mass-free primordial energy that operates throughout the universe as the basic life energy. His scientific discoveries and publications from the 1930s until his tragic death in 1957 were numerous and in many disciplines, on subjects such as the nature of human sexuality, character analysis, cancer research, discovery of orgone energy, and development of orgone-energy accumulators and treatment methods. In 1954 the U.S. Food and Drug Administration filed an injunction against Reich to discredit Reich's discovery of orgone energy. Reich refused to be a "defendant" in matters of basic natural research, claiming that no court could decide matters of science. He was subsequently accused of criminal contempt and sentenced to two years' imprisonment, where he died in November 1957. His books were burned by the government, but not before copies were obtained by the Soviets, who today are quite familiar with, and highly interested in, Reich's work. Some books are now available again about his controversial discoveries and should be read carefully, in light of more recent information in areas of radionics, psychotronics and psychoenergetics (17, 31, 47).

The late George de la Warr, managing director of Delawarr Laboratories in Oxford, England, and his wife, Marjorie, have been researching radionics for several decades. Radionics is the application of the ESP faculty used by dowsers for the treatment and diagnosis of human, animal, and plant diseases. Original research is carried out into methods of causing changes in organic and inorganic substances using unconventional equipment and instrumentation based on certain premises about the nature of man and the universe. Research is concerned with bringing about changes using an intermediate vehicle such as a blood specimen, hair sample, or soil and seed samples (for plant life). A considerable amount of research has been performed in the area of "thoughtography." Equipment and information for the various therapies offered are readily available for ethical researchers (36, 45).

Since 1960 Russian researchers such as Vasiliev, Adamenko, Kirlian, Kogan, Naumov, and Sergeyev have been much on the scene. The study of "primary perception" in plants has emerged from the work of Sir Jagadis Bose, Cleve Backster and Marcel Vogel (see Chapter 12), providing a basic tie-in for transfer of information between living systems. Biofeedback and the voluntary control of internal states, biological-rhythm investigations and electromagnetic effects associated with living systems have all emerged from specialized studies and have accelerated amazingly within just the past decade to form new, useful combinations and tools for investigation and enhancement of the nature of mind and man.

THE SITUATION TODAY

Much of what goes on in space, especially with regard to the earth–sun relationship and cosmic rays from deep space, affect our environment, ecology, and biology. It is wise and prudent to learn the mechanism of these relationships and radiations and what trends they may be causing in the earth's evolution, climate, and ourselves (1, p. 3).

The human brain is the most complicated structure in the known universe, but since practically nothing of the universe is known, it is probably fairly low in the scale of organic computers. Nevertheless, it contains powers and potentialities still largely untapped and perhaps unguessed at. Those of us who consider ourselves cultured and educated operate for most of our time as automatic machines and rarely glimpse the profounder resources of our minds.

Until comparatively recently (the 1950s) biologists regarded a cell as a minute bag of fluid that was relatively simple in structure. But under the electron-scanning microscope, cells were seen to be exceedingly complex. What earlier seemed to be a "simple cell wall" was likely to be folded and convoluted—precisely the right kind of structure to serve as a semiconductor (14). And components of the cell are likely to include organic semiconductors such as liquid crystals—a material hypersensitive to temperature changes, magnetic and electric fields, stress, radiation, and trace contamination. To complicate matters even more, many cells have a double outer membrane. Electrically, such a membrane functions as a capacitor with the characteristics of a leaky dialectric (20, p. 33). It should be mentioned here that superconducting fluctuations have recently been observed experimentally in organic molecular crystals at transition temperatures of $60°K$ (44, p. 8). A number of investigators feel that a strong possibility exists for superconduction in special circumstances at room temperature within living systems (35).

There are many systems, natural and man-made, that are synergistic in nature and whose end effect cannot be ascertained by a study of the discrete components. The mind, as a product of (at least) the brain, the body, and environmental stimuli, may be the highest form of synergistic pattern now known to exist. The phenomenon of consciousness needs more objective study. However, this may prove a difficult research problem since consciousness or the mind has only itself to study itself with!

It may be worthwhile to start with simpler systems and work our way up. Perhaps the emerging use of "biosensors" such as plants, tissue cultures, and eggs would give us the necessary amplification and selectivity for specific quantitative data of value. Remember also the use of biosensors as environmental-hazard detectors such as the canary used by miners to detect poisonous gases. Certain animals such as cats and dogs may be sensitive to psi of specific types (see Chapter 9).

There is much work going on in Russia and Europe on the effects of electromagnetic and electrostatic fields on the central nervous system and also electromagnetic and electrostatic effects (and amplification of these effects) around the human body during certain types of paranormal phenomena. The Russian research in parapsychology and paraphysics is discussed using different terminology such as *biocommunication, psychoenergetics, information transmission, perception of space effects, meteorological feeling, generic memory,* and *bioenergotherapy.*

It seems that serendipity, hunches, and creativity are borderline cases similar to psi and are just as difficult to analyze logically. Creative processes, like psychic processes, can be stimulated by strong emotion and prolonged concentration. Creativity is also commonly accompanied by neurotic symptoms and personality, because it requires a different way of looking at things and resultant interpersonal and cultural conflicts. However, if the basis of creativity is a free flow of ideas from the subconscious to the conscious mind, it is similar to other psi. Although messages may register on the receiver's subconscious mind, there are so many stronger and more dynamic mental functions to restrict the registration of these messages on the conscious level (high noise-to-signal ratio) that more frequently than not, the message will be repressed. J. B. Rhine noted the close association of psi and creativity as early as 1934, when he indicated that the highly creative skills of the composer, the inventor, the poet, and the reflective scientist required the highest integration of the nervous system for their best creation. Not only does skepticism ("snicker effect") and low motivation preclude good test results, but so do physical fatigue and depressant drugs (38, p. 174).

The way to learn something is to try and see if it exists. When a physicist theorizes a new nuclear particle, gigavolt particle accelerators are fired up, massive hydrogen bubble chambers are activated, and 100,000 photographs are taken. Computers are programmed to search all the plates seeking the proposed behavior pattern. The physicists say, in effect, "If such a particle exists, then it should have these properties . . ." and make a test to see. It is time for the paraphysicists to do the same thing with psi, using some of the ultrasensitive testing equipment now available for application as detectors, enhancers, suppressors, and biofeedback training aids (10, p. 173).

SOME PARAPHYSICAL RESEARCH DATA

Recent brain-wave experiments indicate that electrostatic fields can influence the rate of spontaneous electrical-impulse generation by the nerves. Other recent tests have demonstrated that brightness discrimination and alertness improves under the influence of a positive electrostatic field, and the visual critical flicker frequency is affected (11, 32, 33, 43).

Overall beneficial effects of positive-electrostatic-geld applications (39) have three sources.

First, reduction of the viscosity index of blood and lymph fluid produces an antifatigue effect and acceleration of growth factors. It should be noted that the earth's potential gradient reaches a maximum during full moon and third quarter; the metabolic processes of life increase, as does O_2 consumption (6, p. 1539). Traditionally, crops are planted at this time for optimum germination. In addition, it is wise to avoid surgery at this time to prevent problems with "bleeders" (39).

Second, electrophoresis effect causes microbes, virus, and bacteria to travel to the anode of an electrostatic field because their net surface charge is negative. This produces germicidal conditions. In larger cells, the internal charges create positive surface charges. The surface charges are very important to all living processes and can be demonstrated by electrophoresis.

Third, cell renewal happens through ion exchange. Waste products are expelled partially through the skin and partially through the excretory tract. The electric field attracts these surplus ions away from the body surface, permitting rapid and unhampered renewal of all cells. This effect contributes to the general well-being of man.

The beneficial effects of electrical fields are apparently the results of the combined action of the positive field and the suspended negatively charged ions in the air. The electric field is the force of motion, and the ions are the carriers of electrical charge. This may be the explanation of why effects of positive and negative ions on living systems, without the proper electrostatic field present, have shown erratic or contradictory results. Tests have been conducted under the proper conditions with qualitative results indicating negative ions (O_2 molecules with a surplus of electrons looking for electrochemical processes to enhance) produced improved performance, disposition, equilibrium, and burn recovery and healing and relieved pain and allergic disorders; positive ions decreased performance and depressed disposition or had no effect (2). Puharich and others have noted the improved results for biological radio-communication experiments in which the receiver was exposed to a negative-ion environment inside a Faraday cage (34, p. 229).

Feasibility tests were performed by me to determine the effects of a 2000-volt electrostatic positive field, located 2.5 centimeters from the top of my head, on the "down-through" clairvoyance ability using the standard ESP-card deck. The proximity of the field generator to the head (normally placed 1.0–1.5 meters above the head) evidently caused suppression of any clairvoyance ability—that is, all results during exposure to the intense field were of zero statistical significance (100 card decks = 2500 guesses). With equipment inactive, the result for one curve obtained with 50 decks (10 decks per plotted point) was a probability of 0.007; another run of the same type produced a probability of 0.001. Based on statements made in A. S. Presman's excellent book *Electromagnetic Fields and Life*, the effects of high intensity fields on brain-wave activity are definite. When near the head, an increase in frequency is usually noted; at a distance the opposite effect is noted. It may be that a suppression of natural spontaneously occurring alpha rhythm resulted from the field exposure, thus reducing the number of "hits" when equipment was on during the test, assuming that low-frequency (7–14 hertz) alpha may be an indicator present during better ESP scores. These tests were performed in 1969 with no monitoring of mind, body, and environment; further investigations must be made under more controlled conditions (3, p. 71). There is a 1954 report available indicating a probability of 1.3×10^6 with stroboscopic red light synchronization of alpha waves between sender and receiver in telepathy tests (40). This is "bioentrainment," which will be discussed below.

So far as is known, all bodies of our universe above absolute zero are characterized by the emission of electomagnetic radiation. On theoretical grounds (corroborated extensively by experiment) a reasonable amount of energy is emitted in the X-band (9-gigahertz) microwave region, which falls within the detection capabilities of conventional microwave radiometry. Experiments were performed with an X-band microwave radiometer of the correlation type. The microwave emission shows a large increase from the body relative to the background. Other interesting features have been observed such as information about emotional, pathological, and physiological states of the system. The radiation emissivity in the microwave region changes with electrical and dielectric activity of the living system. Communication for transfer of complex information between biological systems seems plausible. More study of emission and absorption spectra in microwave regions is advised (5). There appears to be a possibility for exchange of information over long distances by temporal summation of signals until a "threshold" is attained and the message gets through; the information may be exchanged through some type of sensitive coupled-oscillator phenomena of life.

The recent advent of solid-state physics and field-effect transistors (FET) have made possible inexpensive, portable instruments, such as electrostatic-field intensity meters (or scanners), which can monitor living-system biofields as well as the local environment.* The availability of these instruments should lead to some interesting applications for mind–body–environment research in the near future. The equipment output can

---

* Sources of equipment and information are Electrofields, Inc., 1811 S.W. 98th Street, Miami, Fla. 33165; and Monroe Electronics, 100 Housel Avenue, Lyndonville, N.Y. 14098.

be fed into an X–Y recorder and area-scanning system, which with suitable electronics can produce a two-dimensional plan view of the electrostatic-field potentials around the object or person. Selective electronic "gating" can be used to produce shades of gray (or color, if color enhancement is used) on the recording to indicate field-intensity ranges of interest (2). This type of application will be slow and cumbersome with available equipment, but feasibility will be established for development of rapid imaging and recording equipment similar to present infrared medical scanner systems. Results may show that this phenomenon is an electrostatic analogue of what is known as human aura. At least the ability to observe mind–body–environment interactions would be improved, and we could become more aware of how the mind affects the body through emotional effects on the electrochemical balance. One potential approach for a more rapid and dynamic imaging system (utilizing hints from work on Kirlian effects reported in Russia) would be to investigate the ultraviolet components of high-frequency, high-intensity electrical corona discharge. The subject under test would be coated with a conductive material and the high-intensity field applied to a potential just below the arcing point. Ultraviolet corona characteristics can then be observed by a low-light-level-image vidicon television camera tube of high sensitivity, using ultraviolet transmission filters to replace the tube front (41, p. 1453). Sophisticated electronic color enhancement can be used to provide a color readout of changes in applied field caused by amplification of electrochemical and dielectric biosystem changes (modulation of applied field).

Preliminary investigations into body-field variations (since 1920) indicate that the natural body field is positively charged, while certain types of malignancies are negatively charged. Other pathologies produce drastic changes in body potential of an identifying nature (8, 13, 15). Further work remains to be done with interpretation of the data and development of suitable equipment. Consideration of many factors is required for the very minute signals of interest to be sifted from all the internal, external, and emotional background noise present. A standardized series of conditions is required that must consider environmental, geophysical, and astrophysical factors, as well as control of psychological attitudes and physiological factors reflecting body and mind states. Studies are now under way at Yale, Syracuse, and Queen's College in Kingston, Ontario, to determine which of the multitude of variables are most important to replication of experiments.

The magnetic field of the earth averages about 0.5 gauss and has continuous pulsations of low magnitude at frequencies ranging from 0.1 to 100 hertz, peaking around 10 hertz. This is known as the Schumann resonance, where the earth–ionosphere cavity acts as a natural resonator. This was much more powerful during primitive earth development and may have played an important part in the origin and evolution of life (12, 21). The typical 8–13-hertz alpha brain-wave pattern for sleep and dreaming falls precisely in this range, and a relationship between these phenomena has been suggested by many investigators. This is known as biological entrainment of the human brain by low-frequency radiation (16, p. 21). Note that similar frequencies of light and sound pulses can trigger epileptic attacks, induce altered states of consciousness, and cause nausea. The step from external sensory stimuli to subconscious electromagnetic stimuli in entraining cerebral rhythms is not a radical concept (12, 21, 23, 27). For example, approaching storm fronts appear to have a local electrical field variation of 3–5 hertz; the ion balance of the atmosphere and the electrostatic-field polarity are also affected by the storm front. In addition to reaction-time reductions, weather-sensitive individuals suffer headaches, general depression, and lethargy; paranormal abilities and events decrease. Accident rates of automobiles and aircraft seem to increase when warm fronts and solar activity coincide.

The possibilities of bioentrainment for enhancement, training, or supression of psychic ability are already present when you consider that medical equipment for treatment of hearing loss is now available for inducing sound into the cochlea electrically and without contact by use of audio-signal modulation of the 100-kilohertz carrier frequency. Although those in the vicinity hear nothing, the subject near the antenna perceives sound as if through earphones.* The ability of many individuals to "hear" radar waves as a "buzzing like bees" is well documented, as are sporadic reports of "hearing" aurora displays and meteors passing overhead (22, p. 57). As one might expect, these reports have until recently been dismissed as unfounded. After all, the effects were subjective and not everyone "heard" them. Nurses who work in mental institutions describe patients who are always trying to get away from "the terrible noise." Certain rooms or areas seem more quiet for them (electrical-field null points?). How many people are now in mental institutions or psychologically afflicted because of hypersensitivity to electric fields (48)? Russian investigators report that damage to hypothalamus activity greatly increases the sensitivity to electromagnetic fields (25, p. 41).

A flickering light sensation known as the "phosphene" effect can be induced by (alternating magnetic field [200 gauss, 30 hertz]) electrical frequencies, chemicals, fasting, meditation, or fatigue. It is not known why, but a person under hypnosis or in a state of mescalin intoxication

* Companies doing research in electrical stimulation of hearing include Laser Sound System, Inc., 438 West Cypress, Glendale, Calif. 91204; and Intelectron Corporation, 432 West 45th Street, New York, N.Y. 10036.

The research reported in this chapter was supported in part by grants from the Parapsychology Foundation in New York City and from Scientific Unlimited Research Foundation of San Antonio, Texas.

can often perceive a static magnetic field (20, p. 38). This is confirmation of Reichenbach's research with ill psychic sensitives in Europe about 1850. Their extreme sensitivity to magnetic field—pain and visual effects in a completely dark room—was well documented. It appears that there may be some potential clues for electronic stimulation (or simulation) of vision in the above areas for aid to the blind (26).

Viewed as a minute, but extremely elaborate, electrochemical system, the living cell is subject to the influence of electromagnetic fields, both static and dynamic. And these fields may induce not just one but a complex system of currents, as well as act as indicators of environmental conditions. Small wonder, therefore, that reported field effects at the cellular level (and psi at the mind level) are diverse and debatable. The effects will depend upon the field orientation, components of the system, its organization, its energy, and other variable factors. Indeed, effects are often more apparent in living systems that are *not* healthy. Schizophrenia may be an example of this, and familial periodic disease, a type of periodic paralysis (with preponderant 4–6-hertz brain waves) shows evidence of psychic ability in a large number of cases (46).

The bioelectric-field effects described briefly and inadequately above are not to be construed as the cause behind psychotronic and paranormal phenomena. They may only serve, at best, as weak indicators or precursors of some of the higher system effects or patterns being generated by living systems. As Julius Stulman, president of the World Institute Council, observes, "Suffice it to say that we are dealing in a new science, the *methodology of pattern*, which . . . should be the direction of our search. We must learn its laws and relationships as it exists in irregular pulsating reference frames in integrated systems so that we may emerge to new understandings in all our concerns" (42, p. 37). We are all a product of, and are "tuned in" to, cosmic patterns, and our biorhythms react accordingly to electromagnetic and electrostatic fields, low-frequency radiation, ions, and other unknown factors (29).

RECOMMENDATIONS FOR THE DEVELOPMENT OF PARAPHYSICS

What can be done to advance paraphysics and thereby help society? Certain considerations seem important.

Identify Researchers and Institutions to Handle Problems

A need exists for an organization to investigate the electromagnetic nature of man—the psychological, physiological and external environmental interactions—and to bring together all the studies, data, and references for dissemination to those with a need to know. Centers should be identified where existing data and equipment are available. A large number of individuals and groups around the world are making contributions, but difficulties in communication exist. The best approach may be to survey the worldwide literature and make decisions from that material. This function is now underway by individual researchers but needs coordination and support.

Develop Suitable Equipment, Evaluation Techniques, and Facilities

Data about methods and techniques of evaluation of effects and results obtained should be made more widely available. Identification and description of signal processing in high- and low-noise environments would be most helpful.

Means for determination of electrostatic and electromagnetic fields, preferably simultaneously, over an area of a biological system are needed. The optimum would be high signal-to-noise ratio and spatial resolution, and a fast response with readout similar to the infrared camera (IR thermography) or Schlieren system. Solid-state portable electrostatic- and electromagnetic-field measurement equipment already exist, but they are primarily point-measurement systems and would require excessive time for an X–Y high-resolution area scan. Dynamic area readouts in real time, which would indicate spatial and temporal variation of field potentials generated by living systems (and affected by environmental and psychophysiological factors), should have significant value for medical and psychological diagnosis and understanding of psi. The Kirlian equipment developments are presently showing great promise in these areas. However, in terms of biological safety and potential side effects, it would be desirable to monitor passively the living system rather than "drive" it at high potential and frequencies. A review of the extensive reports of Burr and Ravitz and the instruments they used to measure accurately the magnitude and polarity of body potentials is recommended (8; 37, p. 120).

As equipment is developed, the range of spatial and temporal variations of electrical, ionic, magnetic, and other "influence" fields generated by man, technology, animals, plants, and the geophysical environment must be established. Development of a standard environment for psychophysiological enhancement in the laboratory and in the field is recommended. Mechanisms by which such fields are generated and influenced must receive more study.

It is beyond the scope of this chapter to attempt to list the equipment required, but the types to be considered would be the usual environmental and electromagnetic–electrostatic-field monitors, detectors, and recorders, plus electromagnetic and electrostatic shielded rooms, sensory stimuli devices, environmental control or simulation equipment, and safety monitors. Biofeedback equipment is needed also and as much psychophysiological monitoring (preferably nonintrusive) as is comfortable to the subject. Biosensors of environmental changes, emotional states, and living-system hazards of unknown origin should be considered. Placebo devices can serve as training aids by the psychological transfer mechanism. Psychotronic devices may serve as psi "talent filters," which work best for the person who is most "tuned in." In their own way they serve as biofeedback devices when used as detectors of complex energy patterns but can also be used to store, enhance, or suppress energy.

During the evaluation or training of the subject, certain psychophysiological factors are recommended for consideration. These include facility environment; attitudes toward equipment used, the experiment conductor, and any other subjects; emotional, mental, and health state of the subject; and other factors such as the subject's biological rhythm schedule, personal values, cultural conditioning, and situation safety. In man and animals, we must look for behavior changes (individual and group, learned and instinctual), psychophysiological effects, biorhythm alterations, and navigation or homing errors. In plants we must consider effects on growth rate, biological rhythms, germination, mutation, orientation, and electrochemistry. For unicellular organisms, mobility, growth, mitotic effects, mutations, orientation, and rhythms may be affected.

Begin to Gather Detailed Information on Environmental Effects

Psychic and biological phenomena unique to unusual geophysical environments should be investigated. It must be clearly established whether there are psychic and/or biological effects that can be enhanced or suppressed by the application of our science and technology on the natural environment. We do not exist *in* our environments; we exist *by means of* our environments (30). The technology of the twentieth century finally presents an opportunity to control or change our immediate internal and external surroundings. Until now we have only had the natural electrostatic and electromagnetic fields (to which we have adapted) to contend with, largely undetectable by the senses but affecting mind and body in subtle ways.

It seems obvious that we should be studying how to evaluate and enhance psychic abilities in a controlled geophysical environment, complementing the internal body environment by the proper ties with the respiratory system, nerve network, blood chemistry, glandular chemistry, and body time. For example, possibilities seem to exist for effects on brain-wave frequency and bioentrainment of brain-wave rhythms with light, sound, and electromagnetic fields. Visual phosphene effects and sound can also be induced with suitable power and frequencies.

There is much qualitative data going back to the beginning of history about psi effects on people, domestic animals, plants, and inanimate things but little background data in terms of astrophysical, geophysical, psychological, and physiological conditions required to develop the effects. Such evidence as exists in arcane and ancient literature is clouded by dogma, ritual, theology, semantics, and secrecy. However, empirical evidence does exist that a number of ancient cultures knew about the vectorial relationship existing between the electromagnetic-field direction and the neuraxis and that the geomagnetic field appeared to effect the functioning of higher neuronal centers. The magnetic field orientation in tests of living systems is often overlooked in our present culture but was considered most important by the Chinese, for example, who felt that beneficial health, mental, and spiritual qualities could be obtained by proper geophysical orientation of homes and religious shrines in relation to the earth's magnetic polarity, geology, and topology. Thus, reappraisal of environmental effects in the historical and ancient literature in myths, legends, religious systems, and philosophies, where applicable in the field of psi, is warranted.

Consideration should be given to programs that examine and characterize phenomena having suspected effects. The phenomena may be natural or man-made (psychotronic generators or capacitors); the effects may be behavioral, physiological, pathological, or act upon inanimate objects; the occurrence may be in the present time or in history. Basic electrochemical mechanisms in living systems must receive more study. Simpler living systems should be used in tests and as biosensors.

Develop Models and Standards for Complex Interacting Variables and Synergistic Effects Associated with Living Systems

We need to develop specifications for producing and monitoring the optimum laboratory and field environments. The suitability of specific living systems as experimental models for best effects response must be more thoroughly established. Physiological-rhythm effects must be considered, and we must look for implicit and explicit patterns. It may be possible that certain pathological conditions serve as amplifiers of effects. Many species of animals, plants, insects, and aquatic organisms have already been investigated in some detail and may serve as suitable experimental subjects. We should also remember that we cannot separate a living system from its environment; the environment is not an external entity.

Safety standards for mind and body are of the utmost importance and must be observed and developed relative to electrical-shock hazards, radiation exposure and dosimetry, and intrusive equipment applications to particular living systems. The use of selected biosensors should be considered here as insurance against unknown quantities.

Education and Communication Needs in Psychic Research

Expansion of choice in curriculum for college students in order to encourage interdisciplinary interests is needed. It is encouraging to see a steadily rising number of institutions of higher education offering courses of study and experimentation with altered states of consciousness (ASCS) and subjective experience.

Apprenticeship and/or intensive short courses in productive areas, programmed autogenic training, and meditational methods are often useful with proper guidance and follow-up with practical applications. A primary motivation of learning is the need to discover and understand what makes us possible. We must value, in order to care for, whatever makes us possible. We can best be moved to care about our environments when we see how they make us possible (30).

Publications are available on report-preparation techniques, measurement units, and technical definitions. These should be readily available for investigators to use so that replication by others can be made easier. Where standards or guidelines do not exist, the new era must be thoroughly defined.

Exploit and utilize existing technology as soon as possible. Get the new developments into circulation and to the investigators so that optimum results are obtained and "reinvention of the wheel" is kept to a minimum. It is important to remember that information about what cannot be done, mistakes commonly made, research blind alleys, and equipment limitations are very important information factors in any developing area of scientific inquiry.

Also our thinking has centered on observing evidence-that-is-there. We need to broaden our perspective and also observe the *absence* of evidence —the "holes," as well as the objects, that fill our awareness. Rhine's statistical studies of psi have long pointed out that it is almost as remarkable for someone to score 100 misses out of 100 tries in coin-flipping, for example, as to score 100 hits in 100 tries. We must recognize that such patterns of consistent nonappearance of what we would normally expect is as solid, substantial, and useful evidence as the holes in transistor electronics (9).

It seems at present that there are too many specialists in some areas but not enough persons skilled in interdisciplinary areas involving physics, electrical engineering, biology, behavior, and general systems. There is a need for "interpreters" or application teams of individuals who can interface as "generalists" between disciplines. This would be a means by which a scientist or student in one discipline could obtain information in another discipline—and understand it.

IMPLICATIONS FOR SCIENCE, TECHNOLOGY, PHILOSOPHY, AND CULTURE

We are in a world with the greatest total awareness potential ever known to man. As a synergistic, total-systems approach to the human being (mind–body–environment) becomes more generally known, far-reaching and rapid changes now beginning in the sciences and social order will emerge. It seems that the threshold point has been reached.

But it will not be an easy passage. At present, our knowledge of the universe is only measurable in units of energy, time, and space. These are mostly above or below the narrow dimensions that man is accustomed to detecting by direct sensing and by conscious awareness (19, p. 32). Recent extension of our perceptions to other areas such as radio, microwave, X ray, and beyond has shown that new information is gained wherever man looks without bias, whether it be inner or outer space.

As more data is gathered in fundamental studies involving the nature of subjective awareness, the how and why of psychic-field effects and other patterns should emerge. Of course, in seeking the patterns, we will have to apply more systems engineering, electronics, and computers than ever before. To this same end, spiritual arts such as meditation and the fine arts, as expressed in creative combinations of sensory inputs (audio, visual, kinesthetic), must also be considered for training and enhancement of human resources to eliminate the considerable external, internal, and emotional noise present. To quote William Carlos Williams, "A new world is only a new mind!"

There are two problems associated with this possible expansion of awareness. First, recent evaluations of psi demonstrated by sensitives such as Uri Geller (47), Ingo Swann (24), and the Russians Nelya Mikhailova and Alla Vinogradava show that the instruments of science cannot be trusted. The human mind makes them go up or down! Catalytic reactions can be enhanced or suppressed. The whole basis of modern instrumentation is jeopardized, and this is why psychic research and paraphysics evoke panic reactions from some people in the scientific establishment.

The second problem is this: People seldom relate science and technology to the everyday business of living, fighting the daily traffic, getting the children off to school, and buying the groceries. If they do, they are apt to curse it, particularly when it comes to new ideas to improve knowledge of self or quality of the environment. Far too many do not understand or care about the need for research into the subjective, extended nature of man. We can point in vain to biofeedback, control of autonomic processes, benefits from meditation, advances in psychoenergetics, and the like. People simply yawn—it doesn't affect them directly. So who needs any more science and technology? We've got too much already. Look at the shape the world is in—as seen on a new solid-state, color television by satellite transmission from 10,000 miles away (4).

Few seem to realize that civilized man cannot long survive on this planet without increased discovery of new knowledge and its enlightened use to handle the fantastically complex, interrelated, and synergistic challenge of the future. Our difficulty is that as short-term pragmatists, we are not geared mentally to long-range planning and to some of the cultural changes and benefits resulting from advanced science and technology programs, not to mention inner-space research effects.

Concepts of man, the universe, and man in the universe motivate our thinking and actions on earth. Are contributions to such concepts unimportant to the quality of life we strive for today? On the contrary, they are basic to the definition of what we mean about quality of life. Without a growing precision of our definition of the universe, external and internal, objective and subjective, material and spiritual, and the elements involved, we cannot hope to improve more than the physical aspects of day-to-day living. More likely, we will be able to do little more than cope with ever-increasing planetary problems, while the cost of coping (in human terms) makes living itself deteriorate in quality.

It used to be said that man the scientist brought order out of chaos. Scientists are now rapidly discovering that all that is chaotic is man's fearful ignorance and constrained perception–imagination. However, because paraphysics at its "far end" turns into metaphysics, it may be one of the future's most important vehicles for accomplishing what the mystic William Blake called "cleansing the doors of perception." With our minds freed from blinding beliefs masquerading as science, we may—to refer to William Blake again—find that our senses and abilities extend from the normal to the so-called paranormal and begin to relate to everything as it really is: infinite.

REFERENCES

1. Beal, James B. "Space—For All," Paper presented at Mankind in the Universe Conference, Southern Illinois University, April 1971.
2. Beal, James B. "Electrostatic Fields, Electromagnetic Fields and Ions—Mind/Body/Environment Interrelationships." Paper presented at Neuro-

electric Society Symposium and Workshop, Snowmass-at-Aspen, Colorado, February 1973.

3. Beal, James B. "Paraphysics and Parapsychology." *Analog*, April 1973.

4. Beal, James B. "The New Biotechnology," in John White, ed., *Frontiers of Consciousness*. Julian: New York, 1974.

5. Bigú del Blanco, J., and Romera-Sierra, C. "Microwave Radiometry Techniques and Means to Explore the Possibility of Communication in Biological Systems." Paper presented at the Neuroelectric Society Symposium and Workshop, Snowmass-at-Aspen, Colorado, February 1973.

6. Brown, Frank A. "Living Clocks." *Science*, 4 December 1959.

7. Burr, Harold S. *Blueprint for Immortality*. Spearman: London, 1972.

8. Burr, H. S., and Langman, L. "A Technique to Aid in the Detection of Malignancy of the Female Genital Tract." *American Journal of Obstetrics and Gynecology*, 57, 2, February 1949.

9. Campbell, J. W. "Holes." *Astounding Science Fiction*, 1959.

10. Campbell, John W. "Sense of Security." *Analog*, February 1967.

11. Carson, R. W. "Anti-Fatigue Device Works by Creating Electric Field." *Product Engineering*, 13 February 1967.

12. Cole, F. E., and Graf, E. R. "Extra Low Frequency Electromagnetic Radiation as a Biocommunications Medium: A Protein Transreceiver System." Paper presented at Neuroelectric Society Symposium and Workshop, Snowmass-at-Aspen, Colorado, February 1973.

13. Cone, C. D., and Tongier, M., Jr. "Control of Somatic Cell Mitosis by Simulated Changes in the Transmembrane Potential Level." *Oncology*, 25 (1971).

14. Cope, Freeman W. "Biological Interfaces Behave Like Electrode Surfaces," Summary of Discussion at Workshop in Bioelectrochemistry. Princeton, New Jersey, October 1971 (unpublished).

15. Crile, G. W.; Hosmer, H. R.; and Rowland, A. F. "The Electrical Conductivity of Animal Tissues Under Normal and Pathological Conditions." *American Journal of Physiology*, 60 (1922).

16. Dewan, E. M. "Rhythms." *Science and Technology*, January 1969.

17. Eden, Jerome. *Orgone Energy*. Vantage: New York, 1972.

18. "Editorial Announcement." *Journal of Paraphysics*, 5, no. 3 (1971).

19. Fuller, R. Buckminster. *No More Secondhand God*. Anchor: New York, 1971.

20. Garrison, Webb. "Magnets and Human Life." *Science and Electronics*, August–September 1969.

21. Graf, E. R., and Cole, F. E. "Radiation Noise Energy and Human Physiology in Deep Space." American Astronautical Society National Symposium Document No. AAS67-322(EN-2)-1, June 1967.

22. Halacy, Dan. "Biological Radio—ESP." *Popular Electronics*, April 1967.

23. Hamer, J. R. "Biological Entrainment of the Human Brain by Low Frequency Radiation." Northrup Space Lab Technical Memo 532-65-45, January 1965.

24. "Ingo Swann in Interview." *Psychic*, April 1973.

25. Kholodov, Yu. A. "Effect of Electromagnetic and Magnetic Fields on the Central Nervous System." NASA Technical Translation TT F-465, June 1967. See also *Foreign Service Bulletin*, February 1967.

26. Knoll, M.; Kugler, J., Höfer, O., and Lawder, S. "Effects of Chemical Stimulation of Electrically Induced Phosphenes on their Bandwidth, Shape, Number and Intensity." *Confinia Neurologica*, 23, no. 3 (1963).

27. Konig, H. "Biological Effects of Extremely Low Frequency Electrical Phenomena in the Atmosphere." *Journal of Interdisciplinary Cycle Research*, 2, no. 3 (1971).
28. Lawrence, L. George. "Electronics and Parapsychology." *Electronics World*, April 1970.
29. Luce, Gay. *Biological Rhythms in Psychiatry and Medicine*. NIMH Public Health Service Publication 2088, 1970; see also *Body Time*. Pantheon: New York, 1971.
30. McInnis, Noel. *You Are an Environment—Teaching/Learning Environmental Attitudes*. Center for Curriculum Design: Evanston, Ill., 1972.
31. Mann, W. Edward. *Orgone, Reich and Eros*. Simon and Schuster: New York, 1973.
32. Mizusawa, Kiyoe. "The Effects of Atmospheric Ions on Visual Parameters." *Space-Optics*, September 1969.
33. Presman, A. S. *Electromagnetic Fields and Life*. Plenum: New York, 1970.
34. Puharich, A. *Beyond Telepathy*. Anchor: New York, 1973.
35. Puharich, A. "Protocommunication." In *Parapsychology Today: A Geographic View*. Parapsychology Foundation: New York, 1973.
36. *Radionic Quarterly*, all issues.
37. Ravitz, L. J. "Electromagnetic Field Monitoring of Changing State-Function, Including Hypnotic States." *Journal of the American Society of Psychosomatic Dentistry and Medicine*, 17, no. 4 (1970). See also reprints listed in the *Yale Journal of Biology and Medicine*, 30, no. 3 (1970).
38. Rhine, J. B. *New World of the Mind*. Sloane: New York, 1953.
39. Schaffranke, Rolf. "Summary of Information on the Basic Causes of the Overall Beneficial Effects of Biological DC Applications" (unpublished, 1972).
40. Speeth, Sheridan D. "Alpha Wave Synchronizing and ESP" (unpublished, 1972).
41. Strong, N. G.; Davis, N. E.; and Melville, D. R. G. "Visual, Ultraviolet and Ultrasonic Display of Corona Fields in Air." *Proceedings of the Institute of Electrical Engineers Society*, 117, no. 7 (1970).
42. Stulman, Julius. "The Methodology of Pattern." *Fields Within Fields . . . Within Fields*, 5, no. 1 (1972).
43. Sugiyama, Sadao. "A Study on Cycling of the Critical Flicker Frequency by the Application of Electric Fields." Paper presented at the Neuroelectric Society Symposium and Workshop, Snowmass-at-Aspen, Colorado, February 1973.
44. "Superconductivity Observed at 60° K." *Machine Design*, 19 April 1973.
45. Tansley, David C. *Radionics and the Subtle Anatomy of Man*. Health Science: Rustington, Sussex, England, 1972.
46. Terhune, Neil C. Personal communication, March 1973.
47. Vaughan, Alan. "The Phenomena of Uri Geller." *Psychic*, Vol. 4, No. 5, May–June 1973. See also Best, Connie, "The Power of the Mind vs. Science: Uri Geller, Psychic," *And It Is Divine*, May 1973.
48. Wioske, C. W. "Human Sensitivity to Electric Fields." Laboratory for the Study of Sensory Systems, Tucson, Arizona, 1963.

Brendan O'Regan

BRENDAN O'REGAN, *M.S., has been a consultant to the Center for the Study of Social Policy at Stanford Research Institute in Menlo Park, California. He is also associate editor of the* International Journal of Psychoenergetic Systems.

After obtaining his bachelor's degree in 1967 from the National University of Ireland at University College, Cork, where he studied chemistry, mathematics, and physics, Mr. O'Regan went to Indiana University. In 1970 he was awarded a master of science degree for work in brain research and biochemistry. Following that, he took the post of research coordinator for R. Buckminster Fuller at Southern Illinois University. In 1972 he left for his present position but is still a consultant to Dr. Fuller's Design Science Institute in Philadelphia.

Mr. O'Regan's publications include Changing Images of Man, *co-authored with O. W. Markley et al. (Stanford Research Institute, Merlo Park, Calif., 1973); "Acupuncture, Kirlian Photography and the Human Aura: Summary Statement," in Stanley Krippner and Daniel Rubin, eds.,* Galaxies of Life *(Gordon and Breach, 1972) and a report on psychic research at Stanford Research Institute in* New Scientist *(12 July 1973).*

Mr. O'Regan can be reached through The Institute of Noetic Sciences, 575 Middlefield Road, Palo Alto, Calif. 94301.

19 The Emergence of Paraphysics: Theoretical Foundations

BRENDAN O'REGAN

SUMMARY

Success in the formal scientific investigation of phenomena has always required that man learn to speak formally about the phenomena under investigation. Psychic phenomena are considered in terms of the unresolved problem of the relation between mind and matter, with paraphysics being defined as the physics of paranormal processes.

This chapter explores why modern science has been unable to deal with highly complex systems and has therefore been able to address only certain kinds of problems. This is discussed in terms of the commitment of science to the paradigms of reductionism and objective knowledge. The limitations imposed by classical concepts of causality and time have also been instrumental in the rejection of psychic research by contemporary science. The limitations of these concepts are discussed in terms of recent developments in physics.

The need for a completely new framework in physics, based on the "undivided wholeness" of quantum physics, is outlined and the vital distinction between "explicate" and "implicate" order is discussed. The potential contribution of investigations into the effects of electromagnetic and electrostatic phenomena is outlined, as well as the importance of research into biofeedback and subliminal perception.

INTRODUCTION

Language is often the stage upon which man's battles about reality are fought. Wittgenstein's remark "The limits of my language are the limits of my world" and his proposition "Whereof one cannot speak, thereof one must remain silent" provide a penetrating insight into the task that must be faced when attempts are made to enlarge the boundaries around human perception. The extension of language is a serious business, for it is through language that we make explicit so many of the previously implicit webs of belief upon which we suspend our world, along with the events and processes we permit that world to contain.

The question at issue here is whether or not it is going to be possible for man to learn to speak formally about an aspect of the world about which there has long been silence. Or is man still at the point where he must remain silent, in the formal sense, about phenomena around which there already exists a rich linguistic subculture outside the mainstream of science? The transition to formal description and understanding requires the construction of a vast web of interconnecting strands, each of which must withstand rigorous examination. At the same time, however, we must be prepared to question whether the new situation is always capable of being represented in terms of the old form. As we shall see, major advances in thought have always involved some degree of basic reformulation of the languages of science. Since the topics inherent in our discussion involve some of the most difficult questions in existence, it is likely that the construction of an adequate language will also involve reformulations as great, if not greater, than those necessary at any time in the past.

Up to the present time, our language has served to encode very effectively the many decades of reaction against psychic research. Krippner (29) has noted how workers in Russia created a certain degree of freedom to pursue parapsychological investigation when they succeeded in inventing a new terminology suggestive of seemingly reasonable mechanisms of how something like telepathic communication might work. Here they used the term *biological radio communication*—a term that may be all wrong in its implication of a mechanism for telepathy but that serves a purpose if it opens up the possibility of inquiry where previously none was permitted. The progress of knowledge has always served to make the present, during each phase of history, seem like two-dimensional Flatland encountering its sphere. And just as for the inhabitants of Flatland, the sphere first appeared as a dot in their two-dimensional world and gradually passed through it as a circle of first increasing and then decreasing diameter, so today psi are being examined via an ever-widening range of techniques as we try to comprehend the intersection of our world by phenomena of more dimension and depth than our concepts can presently accommodate.

A simple definition of the term *paraphysics* is that it is the study of the physics of paranormal processes. It is assumed that this volume itself provides sufficient definition of what *paranormal* means. However, there is controversy embedded even within this simple definition, because it may seem to imply primacy of the physical in processes in which the metaphysical and its relationship to the physical is clearly what is actually at issue. In classical terms, this is the old problem of the relationship between mind and matter. Twentieth-century physics has brought about a revolution in our understanding of the physical world, in which the "solid" world of reality has been all but dematerialized. Margenau (31) describes this: "The hard and solid atom has become mostly empty space. Electrons . . . may indeed be points, mathematical singularities haunting space."

No comparable amount of effort has been directed toward the phenomenon of human consciousness; the only reference physics makes to the question is expressed in the polite euphemism "the problem of the observer," and even this is both recent and currently not a fashionable question in physics. In fact, as far as the physical sciences are concerned, we may simply have to "make do" with Eddington's (15) suggestion that "consciousness being a quality, cannot be a subject of scientific enquiry, but if this consciousness exhibits a *structure*, then any such structure is a proper subject for science." From the physicist's standpoint, Freundlich (22) has summarized what appear to be the current possibilities for considering the question of relationships between mind and matter. Within a deterministic framework of definition of knowledge, the four alternatives are as follows:

1. Mental states do not exist (as conceptually distinct entities).
2. They do exist, but they are correlates of physical states, which evolve according to laws formulated with respect to inanimate material.
3. Mental states are correlates of physical states, but the laws depicting their evolution are not such as to be discoverable from the behavior of inanimate matter.
4. Mental states are not correlates of physical states, and a full description of nature would require laws depicting the evolution of mental and physical states from other mental and physical states.

While it remains to be seen which of these will finally emerge as ultimately closest to the truth, it may be said that the present state of our knowledge tends to contain at least some evidence for all four. Contemporary scientific thought seems attached to a combination of the first two, with the second being perhaps as radical as most established scientists are prepared to become. However, this second view, as we shall see, is the natural product of the reductionist orientation in science, and so, the implicit acceptance of this paradigm by most scientists makes this view all but inevitable.

That the third postulate has begun to receive some attention is an important event. Some physicists, notably Wigner (52), have begun to suggest that a full description of reality must include principles, not necessarily physical, that describe the conditions under which any act of measurement is completed by entering the mental process of our conscious being. Wigner (52, p. 287) points out that "*all* the information which the laws of physics provide consists of probability connections between subsequent impressions that a system makes on one if one interacts with it repeatedly, i.e., if one makes repeated measurements on it." Wigner (52, p. 289) then points out:

> The impression which one gains at an interaction, called also the *result of an observation,* modifies the wave function of the system. The modified wave function is, furthermore, in general unpredictable before the impression gained at the interaction has entered our consciousness: it is the entering of an impression into our consciousness which alters the wave function because it modifies our appraisal of the probabilities for different impressions which we expect to receive in the future. It is at this point that the consciousness enters the theory unavoidably and unalterably.

Freundlich (22) and Walker (49) have discussed this view in some depth. It is of interest that from this standpoint, questions concerning the ultimate existence of anything become irrelevant; all that the statement "It exists" means is that (a) it can be measured and hence uniquely defined, and (b) its knowledge is useful for understanding past phenomena and in helping to foresee further events.

The fourth postulate expresses the notion of mind and matter being autonomous and is construed by skeptics as the obviously "extreme" position of proponents of psychic research. As yet there is nothing in physics that can account for those circumstances obtaining when consciousness appears to operate independently of (and at a location remote from) the physical body. Reports of such phenomena tend to be rejected out of hand, even though recent work by Osis and Schmeidler, as well as Puthoff and Targ (now in press), seems to indicate that subjects can retrieve written information from remote locations with good accuracy. Clearly, paraphysics must concern itself with exploration of the claims of all four positions if it is to provide illumination in the search for concepts of order and measure that will eventually make possible a unified description of the most fundamental duality in Western thought—that between mind and matter.

It is logical to inquire: How are such concepts of order and measure reached? Ever since man first attempted to organize his perceptions of the world around him, there have been a multiplicity of approaches considered as the "proper" way to construct models of reality. A brief look at some of these may help in understanding how the questions permissible during different periods in history have been shaped. With the advent of literacy, integrated cosmological myths emerged, and these were among man's earliest attempts to piece together a pattern of meaning in the myriad events that attend human consciousness. Such myths, viewed as large-scale patterns of organization of knowledge, are important here because our contemporary ways of viewing the world have been modified by them. Although formally only models of reality, myths have been actively employed by man to facilitate four main functions. Campbell (10) gives these as follows:

1. *Mystical.* Myths function to inspire the individual toward a sense of the mystery of the universe and his own existence.
2. *Cosmological.* Myths form and present images of the world and life in accord with existent knowledge and experience.
3. *Sociological.* Myths are used to support and validate the local social order, representing it as one of accord with the universe.
4. *Pedagogical.* Myths serve to guide and support the individual "through the archetypal crises of his life, from the mystery of birth through childhood to maturity, and on through old age to the mystery door of death."

Throughout the centuries, myths were the basis of all the major religions, some of which used them to reinforce their authority by representing themselves as being "in accord with the universe." Following the Copernican revolution, a gradual shift away from religion and toward science as the major belief system occurred. The word *myth* itself gradually acquired a derogatory connotation. Science, of course, does not normally consider itself a belief system in view of its commitment to empirically *verifiable* knowledge. However, study of the history of science confronts present-day historians of science with what Kuhn (30) terms "growing difficulties in distinguishing [in retrospect] the 'scientific' component of past observation and belief from what their precedessors readily labelled 'error' and 'superstition.'" This leads to the question that if "myths can be produced by the *same sorts of methods* and held for the same sorts of reasons that now lead to scientific knowledge" (30, p. 2), then what are we to conclude about the so-called absolute proofs achieved by the methods of verification in science at any given time?

THE IMPACT OF PARADIGMS ON SCIENCE

One thing it tell us is that current derogatory usage of the word really indicates that the methods whereby myths were once "proved" to be true are no longer respected. Of course, from the standpoint of science, mythic ideas were never actually proved anyway. Kuhn's point is that within science itself, one can also find difficulty in distinguishing past observation from belief, since the criteria of rigorous observation, and hence verification, change with time. In the best sense, this is because science continuously becomes aware of variables that were previously thought to be unimportant, and so, past observations no longer stand as sufficient evidence for the "proof" of an explanation of a phenomenon. As Kuhn (30) points out, "In the absence of a paradigm or some candidate for paradigm, all the facts that could possibly pertain to the development of a given science are likely to seem equally relevant. As a result, early fact-gathering is a far more nearly random activity than the one that subsequent scientific development makes familiar."

Of course, as a paradigm forms relative to the organization of facts, that paradigm determines the subsequent methods of investigation to a large degree. This highlights the important role of *methods of verification* in defining the acceptable content of science. It indicates that at any given time, our science is only as broad as prevailing methods of verification allow it to become. Therefore, there will always be phenomena that seem to be outside the ability of science to verify. Clearly this will be even more true in cases where the prevailing scientific paradigm is threatened by a new organization of facts previously thought to be irrelevant.

In the absence of a compelling new paradigm, attempts to explain new discoveries in terms of classical concepts can run into several kinds of problems. The first of these is what Stent (44) terms "prematurity," which means that a discovery's implications "cannot be connected by a series of simple logical steps to canonical or generally accepted knowledge." An example of this was Polanyi's 1916 theory of the absorption of gases onto solids. Since there was no theory suggesting that gas molecules could behave in the way Polanyi's theory postulated, the model seemed to be without a conventional causal basis, and so the theory was rejected as crackpot until it was discovered as essentially correct in the 1950s. Although not every piece of surprising new data can be made respectable by regarding it as premature, it is tempting to observe that this phenomenon seems to describe the situation of psychic research today with some accuracy. Indeed Stent himself suggests that psychic research *is* in fact an example of the prematurity problem in modern science.

Another difficulty that a new theory or reports of a new kind of phenomenon can encounter is well described by Polanyi (36) himself:

A hostile audience may in fact deliberately refuse to entertain novel conceptions such as those of Freud, Eddington, Rhine or Lysenko, precisely because its members fear that once they have accepted this framework they will be led to conclusions which they—rightly or wrongly—abhor.

Proponents of a new system can convince their audience only by first winning their intellectual sympathy for a doctrine that they have not yet grasped. Those who listen sympathetically will discover for themselves what they otherwise would never have understood.

In this case, it is as though the clash is not just about opposing scientific theories but instead about opposing images of man himself and the kind of universe he is supposed to inhabit (32).

On a deeper level, Bohm (5) has elegantly illustrated how our prevailing concepts of order and measure serve to exert a very direct influence on the nature and course of our science:

> Beginning with immediate perception of an actual situation, we develop the fact by giving it further order, form and structure with the aid of our theoretical concepts. For example, by using the notions of order prevailing in ancient times, men were led to "make" the fact about planetary motions by describing and measuring in terms of epicycles. In classical physics, the "fact" was "made" in terms of the order of planetary orbits, measured through positions and times. In general relativity, the fact was "made" in terms of the order and measure of Riemannian geometry, and of the measure implied by concepts such as "curvature of space." And in quantum theory, the fact was made in terms of the order of energy levels, quantum numbers and symmetry groups etc., along with appropriate measures.

At any given time in science, the "facts" seem quite irrevocable and they appear to exclude opposing sets of data. Of course, what seems like an "impossible" result during one period can often simply be the result of an encounter with the closure that has been built into the total system we have created—a system consisting of our current concepts of order, the instruments that these concepts have allowed us to create, and the kind of perception or pattern recognition within ourselves that initiated the loop in the first place. Thus, science is state-specific, not only in terms of the consciousness of the observer but also in terms of the natural complementarity that exists between the idea of order in the observer's consciousness and the instruments that it creates.

CAUSALITY, TIME, REDUCTIONISM, AND OBJECTIVITY

It is generally important to understand what it is about the nature of science that makes it capable of effectively examining only certain kinds of questions because the problems raised by psi require a fundamental reconsideration of current notions of causality and time, as well as the commitment of modern science to a paradigm of objectively based knowledge and its organization within a reductionist framework.

One of the major reasons why modern science has rejected the data of psychic research, whatever the quality of the work, is that it appears to violate completely our normal concept of causality. In the classical sense, this means adherence to the idea that all subsequent events are caused by certain previous ones (i.e., cause precedes effect). Terletskii (45) however, has pointed out that

> although the "causality principle" is implicitly considered by most authors as some absolute and universal law of nature, there does not exist, however, a clear-cut physical and rigorous mathematical formulation of it.

Terletskii points out that our concept of causality actually stems from our sense of the direction of physical processes in time; if classical causality were indeed a "law," then we would be asserting an absolute direction of all physical processes in time. But, as Terletskii (45) reminds us,

> The fact that there is *no* preferential direction of the flow of time for phenomena of the microworld is firmly established. . . . The contradiction between macroscopic irreversibility and microscopic reversibility is removed, as is well known, by statistical physics, in which the 2nd Law is considered only as a statistical law, valid almost absolutely for macroprocesses and being only a purely probabilistic tendency for microprocesses.

It is now being realized that general relativity embodies causality violation also. This has caused Carter (11) to wonder if this signals a breakdown of the theory. However, since causality need only hold in the macroscopic mean, Sarfatt (39) has pointed out that causality can be violated in fluctuations without actual violation of the second law. Stapp (43) has suggested that if Bell's (4) hidden variable theory is true, then we should actually expect to find violation of causality on *both* the microscopic and macroscopic scale. This naturally leads to the question: What if we discover that consciousness itself also undergoes fluctuations, which manifest themselves in our experience as macroscopic examples of the causality violation which is already part of contemporary physics?

Ideas of causality in turn are intimately connected with our sense of time in ways that are only beginning to become apparent. Recent research by Aaronson (1) and Zimbardo (53) into our subjective perception of time has begun to elucidate a corollary of the relativity suggested by Einstein for objective time. Thus, the notion of the "external" frame of reference of the observer, which determines the rate at which objective time passes in the Einsteinian examples, is being explored and extended toward a description of those sets of conditions characterizing the "internal" frame of reference that determines the observer's subjective experience of time. Zimbardo (53) points out that these conditions define for us not only our sense of temporal perspective but also "a time sense of personal tempo, which involves both the estimation of the rate at which events are *(or should be)* occurring and affective reactions to different rates of stimulus input" (italics added). Fischer (21) has indicated an inverse relationship between time sense and metabolic rate. As the historical importance of geometry indicates, we have nearly always considered it important to specify the assumptions about space that underlie our theories (e.g., Bohm's description of order and measure). Einstein asserted the connection between space and time; this recent work is demonstrating that our assumptions about how things "ought" to be are deeply influenced by our innate (and varying) sense of time in previously unsuspected ways. Thus, a language to specify the time sense underlying any theory becomes an obvious need. Put another way, if the history of changing concepts of geometry can be thought of as a form of "space travel," then perhaps we need to become equally familiar with the related idea of "time travel."

Biofeedback research has provided a recent example of how our sense of time and causality are intimately bound together. The assertions by Indian yogis that voluntary control could be gained over autonomically controlled bodily functions were completely rejected in the West until it was discovered via biofeedback technology that the learning process involved could be accelerated into the kind of time frame that the West considers normal. The Indian thinkers precisely described the techniques whereby such skills could be learned, the only problem being that these techniques required periods ranging from several years to whole lifetimes to achieve results. When biofeedback techniques accelerated the learning process, the "impossible" suddenly became "possible," and their assertions then coincided with the Western sense of time.

Recent results in physical research are raising questions about many of the same fundamental principles that become problematic if the data of psychic research are true. Einstein indicated the connections between space and time through the definition of the space–time continuum. Now Wheeler (51) suggests that we need to transcend the notion of space–time in favor of the concept of superspace, which incorporates whole complexes of different space–time continua. In Russia, Kozyrev (28) has interpreted results of his experiments to indicate time as having objectively measurable properties such as "density" and differing flow rates in different geographical locations. Although it is too soon to indicate what the empirical effects of this research will be, it does support the notion that our ideas of the nature of time are undergoing radical change. Similarly, the second law of thermodynamics, which rests on our classical notions of time, is under reexamination. Defined for closed equilibrium systems, the second law cannot be said to describe the properties of open nonequilibrium biological systems. Until recent work by Eigen (16) on the "self-organization of matter" and Progogine (37) on the thermodynamics of evolution, some writers—for example, Huxley (27)—thought that biological systems violated the second law. This recent work has helped us to understand the limitations of the law. It remains to be ascertained whether the full range of causal processes occurring in self-organizing systems will fall within the classical definitions.

There is another way of looking at the seeming restrictions imposed by our limited concepts of causality and time. It seems that we presently wish to limit the occurrence of reversible causality in the microworld to the specimen end of the microscope. However, our ability to observe these processes depends on our measuring instruments, which, as Elsasser (19) points out, are a particular class of amplifying devices. Bohr (7) frequently emphasized that one can speak of a measurement only when a process has been amplified to the extent of providing a macroindication. In the broadest sense, however, biological systems themselves (including those of human observers) are amplifiers and transducers of multiple aspects of the physical world. It is just possible that we may have to begin considering them as the amplifiers through which classes of events we already acknowledge as existing in the microworld reach the realm of macroscopic indication.

However, modern science is not in a good position to approach either this type of question or the general class of problems raised by the behavior of highly complex systems. This is largely caused by the problem of reductionism in science. Goodfield (25) has emphasized that there are many meanings to this term, and just as fish cannot discern the water they swim in, so some scientists—for example, Monod (33)—find the term hard even to understand. Others capable of more vision—for example, Elsasser (17), Von Bertalanffy (47), and Weiss (50)—find it possible to see the logic in Skolimowski's (42) suggestion that reductionism may well be "science's ideological straitjacket."

A common form of reductionism assumes that all of the natural sciences will eventually be subsumed under the principles of physics. This leads to such statements as "life is *nothing but* physics and chemistry," and hence the second of Freundlich's (22) four postulates mentioned earlier. Dijksterhuis (13) suggests that this is the result of the "mechanization of the world picture" and that it directly revolves around the assumption that the universe is to be regarded as analyzable into separately existing parts or objects. In this "clockwork universe," the parts can of course work together in interaction, more or less like the parts of a machine, but it is asserted that they cannot function "in response to ends determined by an 'organism as a whole' "(5).

The prediction content of modern science depends on the discernment of the kind of order that is visible when a system is organized in accordance with a few principles. Ever since Newton showed the simple laws governing celestial mechanics and Dalton the essential simplicity in chemistry with the law of simple proportions, science has experienced its growth in modern times almost solely by the exploitation of these simplicities. Indeed, as Schlegel (40) has pointed out, "Progress in understanding the functions of biological organisms has in large part been achieved by discerning the physical–chemical mechanisms involved." This success has led to a concept of progress that has tended to set the trend in scientific investigation almost exclusively in the direction described by Ashby (3):

> Faced with a system, the scientist responded automatically by taking it to pieces. Animals were anatomized to organs, organs microscoped down to cells, cells studied as collections of molecules, and molecules smashed to component atoms. This method of analysis [has] tended to become dogma; and in fact, the reductionists tend to assert that all of science is to be advanced in this way alone. "Get to know the properties of the parts, and you only have to put the parts back together again to know the whole."

The trouble is that science in the past two centuries has "paid only lipservice to the putting together. Everywhere its triumphs were in the taking apart; the putting together was evaded"(3), and as long as it was possible for science to confine itself to those systems that are in fact reducible, a very strong case could be made for reductionism.

What characterizes reducible systems? Ashby provides a simple way of looking at this. Reducible systems exhibit what is called superposition. This means that if cause A evokes effect A' and cause B evokes B', $(A + B)$ evokes only the arithmetic sum $(A' + B')$ as an effect. Interaction between the component parts of the system is then only at the lowest level. Classic science has actively sought to find ways to explain all systems in such terms; it is, of course, this kind of analysis that permits the continued extension of classical causality also.

However, all biological systems are *non*superpositional systems that contain rich interactions between their parts, and it is in systems such as these that the vital property of synergy plays its role. According to Fuller (23), "Synergy means behavior of integral aggregate systems unpredicted by behaviors of any of their components or subassemblies of their components." So the behavior of the *whole* system is not predictable from the behavior of any of the parts. Ashby (3) gives as an example of this the case where if one takes a spring-driven watch apart to discover why the timekeeper usually ticks at five beats per second, one can find no trace of this 5. The balance spring by itself vibrates far faster and the balance wheel alone will not move at all: "The fact is that the '5 per second' belongs neither to the spring nor to the wheel, but to the *relation between them*."

This simple example gives some hint of what must be faced when dealing with highly complex systems. As Arbib (2) has so aptly pointed out, "When we consider that physics is as yet unable to explicitly solve highly simplified equations that describe a 3-dimensional magnet we see that even if the ordinary laws of the physical scientist were adequate to account for all aspects of what we consider to be intelligent or conscious behavior, we would still have a long way to go before we could explain such phenomena as intelligence and consciousness from those physical laws."

Large systems involve large amounts of information; these quantities are significant either as the quantity that an observer would have to receive from the system (if he is to study it) or as the quantity he would have to transmit to the system (if he is to control it). Biological systems present vast complexity, and it would seem that it will remain impossible to analyze them in terms of the reductionist framework. In this context, Arbib (2) suggests:

> We found that we needed to modify Newtonian mechanics to get to relativity when we entered the domain of the very fast; and we needed to modify them to get to the laws of quantum mechanics when we entered the domain of the very small. Thus we must not be unprepared to have to find new laws of physics when we enter the domain of the very complex.

Clearly some of these laws, if they exist, will be laws of matter, energy, and physics as we know them. What is *not* clear is whether some of them will apply to some kind of prephysical domain—for example, Wheeler's (51) "superspace," aspects of Everett's (20) "multiple universe," or O'Hanlon's (35) suggestion that the amount of mass and energy in the universe is determined by the geometry of space-time. Elsasser (19) suggests that it will *not* prove possible to derive principles of the kind with which we are familiar in modern science for the behavior of biological systems, because they are so radically inhomogeneous that there is no inductive scheme that can be meaningfully applied to them. In this connection, it is worth noting Goodwin's (26) point: "Created by Newton and Leibnitz in response to the necessity for a quantitative rendering of the Copernican model, the differential calculus was not intended to deal with discontinuity and structure but with continuous, smooth planetary motions." But discontinuity and structure are primary considerations in biological systems, and it is only with the recent work of Thom (46) that we may be beginning to acquire the necessary formal language to deal with such systems.

We can see therefore that reductionism in science makes it unable to make definitive statements limiting the "possible" processes in systems as complex as the human. However, psychic research also challenges yet another major paradigm of contemporary science. This is its commitment to objective knowledge. Until Heisenberg defined the uncertainty principle, it was assumed that the act of measurement would always allow the continued extension of knowledge in terms of stable space–time structures. This premise also assumed that it would always be possible to separate the observer from his act of measurement and that real knowledge was to be found only by maintaining that separation. As a result, in Western science it has been almost completely forgotten that *to describe experience completely, one must describe the consciousness that is looking outward as well as the universe seen when it looks outward.* It is of this point that Wigner (52) is trying to remind us.

However, even the notion of corresponding, and therefore somehow separate, descriptions of the observer and the observed implies the continuance of the kind of dualistic model that is an important part of our problem with psychic research. In some sense, the data on psi are telling us the same message as modern quantum physics. In the words of David Bohm (5), "A centrally relevant change in descriptive order required in the quantum theory is thus the dropping of the notion of analysis of the world into relatively autonomous parts, separately existent but in interaction. Rather, the primary emphasis is now on *undivided wholeness*, in which the observing instrument is not separable from what is observed." Psychic research, however, goes further and suggests that the observer himself cannot be separated from his instruments in this whole process either. Thus, Bohm suggests that the classical idea of the "separability of the world into distinct but interacting parts is no longer valid or relevant." In fact he goes further and suggests that even "division into particles *or into particles and fields* is only a crude approximation" (6; italics added). So science has reached the point where the business of taking the world apart to find out how all the "pieces" can be "fitted" back together again has become an obsolete way of thinking.

TOWARD A NEW ORDER IN SCIENCE

Clearly we require some new concepts of order and measure to begin to see the world anew. Here Bohm points out (6):

As we go on to develop new notions of order going beyond those of relativity and quantum theory, it will thus not be appropriate to try immediately to apply these notions to current problems that have arisen in the consideration of the present set of experimental facts. . . . This means that we do not *always* try to force the theory to fit the kinds of facts that may be appropriate in currently accepted general orders of description, but that we are also ready when necessary to consider changes in what is to be meant by fact, which may be required for assimilation of such fact into new theoretical notions of order.

In reaching for some articulation of such new orders, Bohm makes the distinction between "implicate" and "explicate" order. To develop this idea we can consider the difference between the way the world can be seen through an optical lens and a hologram. The lens brings objects into sharp relief and reinforces the tendency to think in terms of analysis and synthesis by strengthening awareness of various parts and their relationships. This way of seeing generates the search for explicit sets of relationships between things. Our senses are capable of picking up only explicate order in the world. The laws of physics thus far generally refer to this kind of order, making use of the idea of coordinate systems to aid in the precision of explicate description.

However, the hologram operates in quite a different way. Every point on the surface of the hologram is somehow relevant to the *whole structure* that was stored on it. Thus, it can be cut into smaller and smaller pieces and yet features of the complete structure can be seen. Bohm (6) suggests that "there is the germ of a new notion of order here. This order is not to be understood in terms of a regular arrangement of *objects* (e.g., in rows) or as a regular arrangement of events (e.g., in a series). Rather a *total order* is contained, in some *implicit* sense, in each region of space and time."

It is a common assumption that the true test of a scientific theory is its ability to suggest future experiments and predict at least some aspects of the results. This assumes a connection between our ability to discern order and as a result apprehend the operation of causality so that we can predict an anticipated "chain of events." As we are beginning to see, even the nature of our sense of prediction can be subtly conditioned into a certain form. The ideas outlined here remind us that "predictability is a property of a special kind of order such that a few steps determine the whole order (i.e., as in curves of low degree). But there can be complex and subtle orders which are not in essence related to predictability (e.g., a good painting is highly ordered and yet this order does not permit one part to be predicted from another)" (5).

The new order brought into physics by Einstein had to do with the notion of the signal, for the speed of light had to do not with the possible speed of an object but with the "maximum speed of propagation of a signal" (5). A signal is a kind of communication, and so, for the first time, significance, meaning, and communication became important in the general order of physics. Part of the problem in contemporary psychic research is the tendency to think of information in terms of "signals" (which must travel from "here" to "there," even if they can move faster than the speed of light—for example, tachyons). In the new implicate order enfolded throughout all of space and time, the notion of the signal also ceases to be relevant. "This means that where implicate order is involved, the descriptive language of special relativity will, in general, no longer be applicable" (6).

Thus, what is being invoked is a major reformulation of the entire context of physics (classical and quantum) that "will have to be assimilated in a different structure, in which space, time, matter, and movement are described in new ways" (5). Interestingly, then, psychic research is not alone in its request for a new vision, for the above statements stem from the forefront of contemporary physics. Rather, it is likely that when the prematurity gap between current psychic research and the physics of the near future is closed, psychic research, if it did not already exist, would have to be invented to fully explore the "new" experimental paradigm of "undivided wholeness." New ideas of order and measure result in new ways of doing experiments and the creation of new kinds of instruments. "New orders and measures evidently make possible the creation of new structures in music. We wish to enquire into how new orders and measures in physics may similarly make possible the consideration of new structures in physics" (5).

Although helpful, this analogy is weak to the extent that new structures in music tend to mean new forms in the *explicate* order of events. However, when we consider a shift to the notion of an implicate order, enfolded throughout all of space and time, even the notion of "event" must somehow be left behind. Instead, our attention must shift to the whole *pattern* involved, or toward what Fuller (23) would term the *synergy* of the observer, his instruments, and the observed.

In a deep sense, the Heisenberg uncertainty principle was perhaps our first manifestation of that synergy. Certainty has often been expressed by mystics and now by quantum physics that some universal order is somehow implicate in every point in space. Viewed in this way, psi might be regarded as "high synergy" occurring with an uncertainty delineated by our attachment to knowledge in the form of explicate order. Formally speaking, at present the uncertainty principle applies only to the observer's instruments. However, the work of Schmidt (41) and Puthoff and Targ concerning the effects of human subjects on a variety of scientific instruments by nonphysical means clearly implies that extension of the principle to include the observer, in some as yet unspecifiable fashion, must be considered (see Chapters 7 and 22). Attempts in this direction are being made by Walker (48), using the theory of hidden variables underlying events in space and time in a nonlocal and nontemporal way.

This kind of extension of the uncertainty principle, if successfully achieved, will naturally challenge the objective knowledge paradigm. We already know that the indefinite extension of knowledge in terms of stable space–time structures is untenable and modern physics expresses itself in terms of statistical description. However, just as it has not proved possible to draw any definite line between animate and inanimate matter (22), Elsasser (19) points out that "proceeding from [the macroscopic] toward the realm of microscopic phenomena, we can no longer assign numbers to an individual object; instead we must progress gradually and without a sharp boundary into the realm of statistical description, a description that refers to classes rather than identifiable objects." Rather it would seem that we must move away from the "epistemology of the other," discovered by the Greeks and now part of the foundation of modern science, toward the "epistemology of the self" to derive some sense of the inclusive paradigm required by psychic research (32).

Another approach to this search has been the tendency to look for more conceptual freedom to contain the phenomena of psychic research in the realms of hyperspace (i.e., dimensions above three in number). This approach is rather like an attempt to imagine a four- or five-dimensional Flatland. The direct application of the hyperspace idea to the study of consciousness seems to have been started over 50 years ago by Robert Browne in his volume *The Mystery of Space*, which he subtitled "A Study of the Hyperspace Movement in the Light of the Evolution of New Psychic Faculties." He suggested that mathematics is a true "biometer of intellectual evolution" and that the hyperspace movement represents "an actual seizure of a new domain of awareness by the mind" (9). Coxeter (12) has documented several cases of persons possessing the ability to express lucidly and mathematically the experience of hyperspace. Fuller (23) appears to operate quite freely in this domain. Musès (34) has carried out numerous investigations of the possible relationships between consciousness and hyperspace concepts, including some hints about a possible structure for the consciousness–matter continuum.

It is pertinent to ask: What other emerging trends in current research may aid our task? To begin with, the emerging body of research into the sensitivity of the biological system to magnetic and electromagnetic phenomena previously regarded as making no contribution to consciousness and human behavior will prove important. This work (see Chapter 18) will at least help to clarify the kinds of figure–ground relationships (to use an old-order distinction) between these phenomena and the "stream of consciousness." This research may also help to provide models for some phenomena now thought to require explanation in psychic terms. For example, the déjà vu experience bears of at least partial explanation in terms of a classical behaviorist paradigm involving a one-time learning situation with an unconscious conditioning stimulus, or set of stimuli, common to the initial (unconscious) conditioning and the environment of the déjà vu experience. Some of these stimuli may turn out to be electromagnetic in nature, although at the level of nonionizing strength (38).

Research into subliminal perception will also prove to be quite useful in that these experiments retain the conventional notions of information, although the transfer process seems to be psychic in at least some cases. For example, Dixon (14) has recently shown that "as a result of being tested in eight different contexts, subliminal stimulation has been shown to affect dreams, memory, adaptation level, conscious perception, verbal behavior, emotional responses, drive-related behavior and perceptual thresholds." This is the currently acceptable crossover point between the domains of conventional psychology and parapsychology, and no doubt the potential for remote conditioning implied by this work will stimulate further research.

Biofeedback research provides the technology for the exploration of new learning skills within the biological organism plus the possibility of exploring the phenomenon of resonance, or "biological entrainment" (discussed in Chapter 18), between different biological systems. Training to provide voluntary control of the magnetic and electrostatic fields around the body should prove particularly useful. Further research into the hypnotic induction of altered senses of space and time of the kind discussed earlier might be usefully included here.

However, it should be clear that the full development of new notions of order and measure is an equally vital part of the process of investigating psi. Without this concomitant effort, we are only likely to witness a buildup of contradictions of even more embarassing proportions than at present. It is no longer a matter of just new structures in physics but new structures in every discipline and the world as a whole. Just as the consciousness and instrumentation of contemporary science have changed the face of the earth in quite a literal sense, so too are the developments in the science of the near future likely to be just as radical. If, as Margenau (31) has pointed out, the physicists of 70 years ago were content simply with statistical proof of the existence of isotopes, achieved by traveling around with Geiger counters, which in certain places on earth naturally gave higher than normal readings, then the isotopes would still be in the ground and the world a nuclear virgin. We know only too well the dramatic result of their ability to isolate and concentrate the phenomenon of radioactivity.

Contemporary efforts to characterize the psychic event are likely to have, if anything, an even more radical impact on planetary consciousness. As has so often been pointed out, evolution depends on survival, but survival depends on evolution. Buckminster Fuller has suggested that man must evolve toward the "aesthetics of the invisible" and eventually live in more complete harmony with the universe around him. Such a cosmic charter seems appropriate not just for psychic research but for science as a whole.

REFERENCES

1. Aaronson, Bernard S. "Hypnotic Alterations of Space and Time." *International Journal of Parapsychology*, 10, no. 15 (1968).
2. Arbib, Michael. *The Metaphorical Brain.* Wiley: New York, 1972.
3. Ashby, W. Ross. Editorial. *Behavorial Science*, 18, no. 2 (1973).
4. Bell, J. S. "On the Problem of Hidden Variables in Quantum Mechanics." *Review of Modern Physics*, 38 (1966).
5. Bohm, David. "Quantum Theory as an Indication of a New Order in Physics, Part A." *Foundations of Physics*, 1, no. 4 (1971).
6. Bohm, David. "Quantum Theory as an Indication of a New Order in Physics, Part B." *Foundations of Physics*, 3, no. 2 (1973).
7. Bohr, Niels. *Atomic Physics and Human Knowledge.* Wiley: New York, 1958.
8. Bremermann, H. J. "Quantum Noise and Information." In *Proceedings of the Fifth Berkeley Symposium on Mathematical Statistics and Probability.* University of California Press: Berkeley, 1966.
9. Browne, Robert T. *The Mystery of Space.* Dutton: New York, 1919.
10. Campbell, Joseph. "Mythic Images of Man." Support document for O. W. Markley et al., *Changing Images of Man.* Stanford Research Institute: Menlo Park, Calif., 1973.
11. Carter, B. "Global Structure of the Kerr Family of Gravitational Fields." *Physical Review*, 2nd ser. 174, (1968).
12. Coxeter, H. S. M. "Cases of Hyperdimensional Awareness." In C. Musès and A. Young, eds., *Consciousness and Reality.* Outerbridge and Lazard: New York, 1972.
13. Dijksterhuis, E. J. *The Mechanization of the World Picture.* Clarendon: Oxford, 1961.
14. Dixon, N. F. *Subliminal Perception.* McGraw-Hill: London, 1971.
15. Eddington, Arthur. *The Philosophy of Physical Science.* University of Michigan Press: Ann Arbor, 1958, quoted in Elsasser (19, p. 117).
16. Eigen, Manfred. "Self-organization of Matter and the Evolution of Biological Macromolecules." *Die Naturwissenschaften*, 58 (1971).
17. Elsasser, Walter M. *Atom and Organism.* Princeton University Press: Princeton, N.J., 1966.
18. Elsasser, Walter M. "The Role of Individuality in Biological Theory." In C. H. Waddington, ed., *Towards a Theoretical Biology*, Vol. III. Aldine-Atherton: Chicago, 1970.
19. Elsasser, Walter M. "A Natural Philosophy of Quantum Mechanics Based on Induction." *Foundation of Physics*, 3, no. 1 (1973).

20. Everett, H. "A Relative State Formulation of Quantum Mechanics," *Review of Modern Physics*, Vol. 29, No. 3, 1957.
21. Fischer, Roland. "Biological Time." In J. Frazer, ed., *The Voices of Time*. Braziller: New York, 1966.
22. Freundlich, Yehudah. "Mind, Matter and Physicists." *Foundations of Physics*, 2, no. 2–3 (1972).
23. Fuller, R. Buckminster. *Synergetics* (in press).
24. Fuller, R. Buckminster. *No More Secondhand God*. Anchor: New York, 1972.
25. Goodfield, June. "The Problem of Reduction in Biology." *Nature*, 240 (1972).
26. Goodwin, B. C. "Mathematical Metaphor in Development." *Nature*, 242 (1973).
27. Huxley, Julian. "The Future of Man—Evolutionary Aspects." In Ronald Munson, ed., *Man and Nature*. Delta: New York, 1971.
28. Kozyrev, Nikolai. *Possibilities of Experimental Study of the Properties of Time*, JPRS Document No. 45238. Joint Publication Service, U. S. Department of Commerce, Washington, D.C., 1968.
29. Krippner, Stanley. Personal communication.
30. Kuhn, Thomas S. *The Structure of Scientific Revolutions*. University of Chicago Press: Chicago, 1962.
31. Margenau, Henry. "ESP in the Framework of Modern Science." *Journal of the American Society for Psychical Research*, 60, no. 3 (1966).
32. Markley, O. W., and Associates. *Changing Images of Man*. Stanford Research Institute: Menlo Park, Calif. 1973.
33. Monod, Jacques. *Change and Necessity*. Knopf: New York, 1971.
34. Musès, Charles. "Working with the Hypernumber Idea." In C. Musès and A. Young, eds., *Consciousness and Reality*. Outerbridge and Lazard: New York, 1972.
35. O'Hanlon, J. *Journal of Physics*, Sec. A. 5 (1972).
36. Polanyi, Michael. *Personal Knowledge*. Harper and Row: New York, 1964.
37. Progogine, Ilya. "Thermodynamics of Evolution." *Physics Today*, November 1972.
38. *Program for Control of Electromagnetic Pollution for the Environment: The Assessment of Biological Hazards of Non-ionizing Electromagnetic Radiation*, Research Program Proposal, Office of Telecommunications Policy, The White House, Washington, D.C.
39. Sarfatt, Jack, and Wolf, Fred A. "A Dirac Equation Description of a Quantized Kerr Space–Time" (unpublished).
40. Schlegel, Richard. *Inquiry into Science*. Anchor: New York, 1972.
41. Schmidt, Helmut. "PK Tests with a High-Speed Random Number Generator." *Journal of Parapsychology*, 37, no. 2 (1973).
42. Skolimowski, S. Quoted in Goodfield (25).
43. Stapp, H. P. "S-Matrix Interpretation of Quantum Theory." *Physical Review*, Pt. D. 3 (1971).
44. Stent, Gunther S. "Prematurity and Uniqueness in Scientific Discovery." *Scientific American*, December 1972.
45. Terletskii, Ya. P. "The Causality Principle and the Second Law of Thermodynamics." *Soviet Physics*, 5, no. 4 (1961).
46. Thom, René. *Structural Stability and Morphogenesis*. Benjamin: Reading, Mass., 1972 (in French).
47. Von Bertalanffy, Ludwig. *General Systems Theory*. Braziller: New York, 1968.

48. Walker, E. H. "The Nature of Consciousness." *Mathematical Biosciences*, 7 (1970).
49. Walker, E. H. "Consciousness Theory in the Quantum Theory of Measurement—Part 1." *Journal for the Study of Consciousness*, 5 (1972).
50. Weiss, Paul. "One Plus One Does Not Equal Two." In F. O. Schmitt, ed., *The Neurosciences*. Rockefeller University Press: New York, 1967.
51. Wheeler, John A. "Our Universe: The Known and the Unknown." *American Scholar*, Spring 1968; also "From Mendeleev's Atom to the Collapsing Star." *Transactions of the New York Academy of Sciences*, 11th ser. 33, no. 8 (1971).
52. Wigner, E. P. "Remarks on the Mind–Body Question." In I. J. Good, ed., *The Scientist Speculates*. Basic Books: New York, 1962; also "The Problem of Measurement." *American Journal of Physics*, 31, no. 1 (1963); and Wigner, E. P. *Foundations of Physics*, 1 no. 35 (1970).
53. Zimbardo, P. G., and Associates. "Objective Assessment of Hypnotically Induced Time Distortion." *Science*, 181 (1973).

Thelma Moss

THELMA MOSS, *Ph.D., is a medical psychologist and assistant professor at the Neuropsychiatric Institute, University of California at Los Angeles.*

Prior to entering the academic field in 1959, Dr. Moss spent 20 years as an actress, performing in theater, films, and television, as well as writing scripts. She began study at the University of California in Los Angeles in 1959 and was awarded a doctorate in psychology in 1966. Since then she has held her present position.

Dr. Moss has chaired psychic research symposia through the University of California Extension and has taught courses on parapsychology. Since 1961 she has published nearly three dozen professional papers and one book, My Self and I *(Coward-McCann, 1961), which is a case history of her own LSD therapy under the pseudonym of Constance A. Newland. Dr. Moss is a consultant on Kirlian photography, psychic research, and acupuncture research to various business and government agencies.*

Dr. Moss can be reached at the Neuropsychiatric Institute, University of California at Los Angeles, Los Angeles, Calif. 90024.

20 Psychic Research in the Soviet Union

THELMA MOSS

SUMMARY

This chapter is an anecdotal account of a personal voyage to the Soviet Union (Moscow, Leningrad, Alma-Ata) to investigate Russian research in telepathy, skin vision, psychokinesis, acupuncture, Kirlian photography, and psychic healing. After returning to the United States with a wealth of Soviet literature and some schematic diagrams, the author was able to replicate in the laboratory some of the Soviet claims, particularly in the areas of Kirlian photography, acupuncture, healing, and skin vision—all of which may be classified as exploration in "bioenergetics," or energy fields in and around the human body.

INTRODUCTION

Early in 1971, I was invited to lecture to UCLA medical students on the subject of parapsychology. This was an exceptional (and welcome) request, for I had just returned from a trip to the Soviet Union expressly to explore current Russian research into "biocommunication" (their term for ESP). En route to the UCLA lecture hall, I passed several bulletin boards that announced a discussion–demonstration on acupuncture to be held in the Department of Psychology. This was a synchronicity, since much of the Soviet research in biocommunication and bioenergetics is concerned with energy fields in and around the body—and consequently the concept of acupuncture had been repeatedly introduced. During the lecture, then, spontaneously the theme of acupuncture theory and therapy appeared, only to be met with puzzlement. One student inquired how the word was spelled, since he had never heard it. To repeat, this was early in 1971. Within the next months, Dr. Dimond and others reported on their visit to China (8) and *acupuncture* swiftly became an American household word. During that same period, the book *Psychic Discoveries Behind the Iron*

Curtain, by Ostrander and Schroeder (31), which had prompted by Soviet journey, became a best seller, and the topic of psychic research in the Soviet Union became notorious in this country—perhaps even somewhat threatening.

What is the true state of Russian knowledge in the areas of telepathy, clairvoyance, PK, and skin vision? Probably no one outside the Soviet Union—and very few persons inside it—can say with certainty. I claim no expertise and can only offer an anecdotal account of experiences with Soviet scientists, together with a survey of their literature, some of which our laboratory has attempted to replicate. In this report, therefore, errors both of omission and commission may be found.

TELEPATHY

A lucky prelude to my Russian visit had been an ESP symposium at UCLA in 1969, to which had been invited I. M. Kogan of Moscow's Scientific and Technical Society of Radio, Electronics, and Biocommunication. Kogan had accepted the invitation and had forwarded his paper, in Russian, in time to be translated into English for a simultaneous bilingual presentation. This proved unnecessary, because Kogan was unable to attend, and his paper, "The Informational Aspect of Telepathy" was read in absentia (21). This paper was both a delight and an astonishment, for independently—and from halfway around the world—Kogan had conducted short- and long-distance telepathic experiments that in some ways were remarkably similar in results to our own. For example, in one of our long-distance studies, we had attempted transmission of "emotional episodes" from transmitters in Los Angeles to receivers in New York and Sussex, England (24). One of the most successfully transmitted episodes was that of "space," in which a series of slides and sounds had been presented to the transmitters, showing satellites and rocket ships in flight, with astronauts walking in space. From Sussex had come one receiver's impression in writing: "I could see the world as if I were in a space ship." And from another receiver in Sussex: *"War of the Worlds*, H. G. Wells? Or the next war involving death by the use of satellites and flying platforms." From New York had come: "Dark edges, a centered pinpoint of light . . . a swinging weightlessness." And from Los Angeles, a receiver wrote of the impression of "twinkling stars versus a black night . . . universal fear of the unknown." As might be inferred from these (and numerous other) responses, there was an occasional direct hit, but much more frequently there were given symbolic representations of the episode, distorted presumably by the receiver's emotional reactions on an unconscious level—such distortions, condensations, and symbolic representations being very similar to what psychoanalytic literature has described as "primary process," so often found in dreams and fantasies. In Kogan's paper were reported studies by their two star telepaths, Nikolaev and Kamensky—one in Moscow, the other in Leningrad. On one occasion, the transmitter in Moscow was asked to send the image of a draftsman's compass to the receiver in Leningrad, who reported the impressions of "metallic luster . . . thin . . . chromium plated rod . . . rod is bifurcated . . . like a thin scissors." It can be seen that the attributes of the compass are well described, but the object has been incorrectly named as a scissors. (It is of interest to add that a second receiver was asked to intercept the message and he reported that it was "something that pricks the finger . . . a compass," achieving a direct hit and even picking up an action of the transmitter, who, to facilitate reception, had pricked his finger with the point of the compass!) Kogan suggests that the reception of the *name* of the transmitted object is rare and that what is being received seems to be the attributes of the object, together with the emotions of the receiver in relation to the object. This observation seems strongly to suggest the appearance of primary-process distortions and displacements. Thus, the similarity of experiments.

But Kogan's researches include far more sophisticated experiments, transcending anything that has been attempted in this country. For example, Kamensky and Nikolaev had been wired into electrophysiological equipment, exactly synchronized between Moscow and Leningrad. This equipment included a special kind of EEG apparatus—designed by the eminent Leningrad physiologist Sergeyev—that is capable of recording brain-wave activity at a distance from the scalp. In this study, the transmitter (Kamensky) was required to conduct a "boxing match" with the receiver, aiming in fantasy fierce blows to Nikolaev's body. There were both "long" and "short" bouts, the long bout lasting 45 seconds and the short one 15 seconds. Each long bout was to be translated in terms of Morse code as a dash and each short bout as a dot. A four-letter word was transmitted in this way, each dot and each dash being intricately coded so that the proper sequence of letters would be unknown to the participants. Each element—dot or dash—was transmitted 15 times, the redundancy considered necessary so that a majority vote could be obtained to determine the correct element. For example, if 8 or more of the 15 transmissions of one symbol were received as a dash, that element would be recorded as a dash. The word chosen for transmission was the name *Ivan*—and the word *Ivan* was decoded. In this extraordinary experiment, the Russians had successfully utilized brain waves as a carrier of information! It can, of course, be argued that this is neither an efficient nor practical way to transmit information (no competition for telephone or radio), but the promise inherent in this use of a known body energy can scarcely be denied or ignored.

More than a year after the UCLA symposium, Kogan reciprocated with an invitation to visit Moscow, and I accepted. Regrettably, for reasons that were never made clear, our meeting was canceled when I arrived in Moscow. But I was fortunate in being permitted to spend considerable time with Nikolaev and Kamensky, who had pioneered those long-distance telepathic experiments. Kamensky proved to be a young, intense biophysicist, not only immersed in microwave physics but also in Eastern meditative techniques; and Nikolaev was a dynamic character actor with reddish blond hair, a deep baritone voice, and a booming infectious laugh. Both men had had much practice in hatha yoga, particularly the breathing exercises, which they use in their telepathic experiments in an effort to synchronize their "vibrations." In commenting on the boxing experiment, Nikolaev boomed his characteristic laugh as he described one of his experiences, in which he felt so strongly the blow Kamensky had visualized to his stomach that he fell backward from the chair on which he was sitting, upsetting all the carefully placed electrodes on the surface of his body. Nikolaev added that he did not enjoy those "physical" telepathy experiments. Both men are dedicated to this infant science of biocommunication and expressed the wish that there were more interest and support for the research. Like similar research workers in the United States, their contribution is on a volunteer basis and performed as a hobby.

They reported that after their initial success from Leningrad to Moscow, a second experiment was made between Novosibirsk and Moscow, again successfully. These two studies evoked so much interest that a third was organized by a large, official publication. This study was to be conducted by impartial judges, which meant that the original experimenters could not participate. The results of this third study were not statistically significant, and as a result, the research was publicly decried. *Sic semper parapsychology!* It is not uncommon in American psychic research for an "unbiased" or skeptical investigator to try to repeat a successful ESP experiment, only to obtain negative results. The importance of the experimenter's *belief* in any psychological experiment has been extensively studied by Rosenthal (34), who has shown that the belief system of the experimenter can—often unconsciously—effect opposite results for the identical experiment.

Nikolaev and Kamensky had no explanation to offer for their failures, nor for their "near hits" (such as the compass transmission), but they are convinced that strong emotion facilitates good telepathic transmission. They also offered the interesting information that their transmission can go only in one direction: from Kamensky to Nikolaev. In their attempts to reverse the flow, making Kamensky the receiver of Nikolaev's messages, they have met with complete failure. (Subsequent work at UCLA has shown that on rare occasions, transmitter–receiver combinations can reverse roles, but this is the exception.)

During our last evening together, sipping coffee ice cream drinks in the hotel restaurant, our group became quietly sentimental, and we began to fantasize doing a long-distance experiment from Los Angeles to Moscow, wondering if the language barrier could be overcome. It was generally agreed it could, since the reception of telepathic messages usually appears as imagery rather than words (attributes rather than names, as in primary-process thinking). As the evening progressed, both Nikolaev and Kamensky described their early spontaneous psychic experiences—experiences very similar to those reported by gifted sensitives from any country in the world: a rare precognitive dream, a sudden impression to go to a particular place for no apparent reason, entering a room and seeing in fantasy a different environment with different people, and so on. Kamensky then described his early childhood, when he was reared with three families in one room of an apartment house, his space being under a table. He smiled, adding that now as a married man with a son, he knows the luxury of an apartment with three rooms, one room for each member of his family—largesse! Nikolaev interrupted with his booming laugh. "Uri. In twenty years from now, your children will think three rooms are too small!" And everyone at the table (except me) laughed at the absurdity of the idea. . . .

SKIN VISION AND PK

Another member of this Moscow group was Edward Naumov, who is the "PR man," the entrepreneur, of Soviet parapsychology. In addition to welcoming psychic researchers from all over the world, Naumov has developed an exhaustive bibliography of the extant Russian literature in parapsychology and bioenergetics (29). According to Naumov, one well-documented and accepted avenue of exploration among scientists in the Soviet Union is that of dermo-optical perception, or skin vision (30). In fact, Naumov's secretary, Larisa Vilenskaya, not only learned skin vision herself but also teaches it. She demonstrated her expertise one day, apologizing that she was out of practice and not as skillful as some of her pupils. She brought out demonstration cards on which had been printed letters of the Russian alphabet in large block letters about two inches high. I felt the letters and was assured that they had not been embossed. Under my fingertips, I could detect only a glossy surface. Then she asked that I blindfold her, which I did. And as a further precaution she turned her head away. Then I chose at random one and another of the letters for her to decipher, which she did by lightly running her fingertips over the surface of the cards. This was, of course, just an informal demonstration, not a controlled experiment, but it convinced me that information had been transferred into Larisa's awareness through her fingertips. For further elucidation, Larisa presented me with a technical publication, *Problems of Complex Investigation of Dermo-optical Sensitivity* (30), which describes some splendidly controlled experiments by Novomeisky and his colleagues and offers a large bibliography of research done in Soviet institutes and universities. That psychologists are interested in this phenomenon was given unexpected confirmation when, on leaving the Soviet Union, I was presented with a popular work, *Psychology: As You May Like It,* by the well-known Platonov (32). In this book, written in English, he reports: "In November, 1963, I chanced to meet Lena Bliznova, a nine-year-old very capable pupil of a Kharkhov music school, and to carry out several experiments with her [in skin vision]. Completely guaranteeing the elimination of telepathy, these experiments not only confirmed that Lena has this still mysterious ability, which nobody had developed in her, but also showed that she had it to an even greater extent than the other formerly investigated people." Platonov clearly believes that telepathy might be a factor that must be isolated—which can be interpreted to mean that at least some Russian psychologists accept this phenomenon as genuine.

Before leaving Moscow I was taken to see the Russian film *Seven Steps Beyond the Horizon,* one step of which was devoted to current Soviet research with skin vision as performed by Goldberg and his colleagues. The most dramatic of this series of filmed experiments showed the experimenter placing in one of six identical aluminum cassettes a strip of red gelatin paper and then covering each of the cassettes. The subject, a pleasant-faced young lady, was presented with the six covered boxes. She placed her hand about two inches *above* each of the boxes in turn and eventually stopped at one with a nod of her head. The cassette was opened to reveal the red paper. This study seemed much more than an exploration of skin vision: information was being conveyed at a distance from the skin. Was this some form of energy field receiving information?

Naturally I asked about the strange case of Rosa K., heralded in the world's headlines some years ago for her ability to detect colors—and even to read newspapers—with the tips of her fingers. Presumably Rosa had been strenuously tested at the Moscow Academy of Science and declared a genuine phenomenon—but was later, in the Russian press and then in newspapers around the world, discredited as a fraud. Naumov reported that Rosa had in fact been remarkably gifted but emotionally unstable and that after suffering a mental breakdown, she had lost her talent. There was no way to corroborate this story about Rosa K., but by a strange series of events, it has been possible to corroborate the reality of skin vision as a phenomenon through work in our laboratory.

About four months after returning from Russia, I received a phone call from Mary W., who said that she was totally blind but had recently "read" (by listening to tapes) *Psychic Discoveries Behind the Iron Curtain* and wanted to volunteer as a guinea pig in the laboratory to see if she could develop skin vision. Mary has come to the laboratory once or twice each week since then, for three- and four-hour sessions, doing grueling and often frustrating work. In the beginning she struggled to discriminate just two colors by touching the materials. Gradually, over the months, she was able to achieve great statistical success with five and six colors, at which time she began to try discriminating colors by *sensing* them at a distance of about an inch (23, 25). Mary has persisted in spite of repeated discouragements: after considerable effort she would acquire a color discrimination, only to lose it for no apparent reason. On certain days she would perform brilliantly, hardly making an error, while on other days she could scarcely achieve chance results—for reasons that we have not as yet been able to learn. Eventually, when she was able to perform consistently, she agreed to demonstrate at seminars and conferences—only to be challenged as to whether she really was totally blind, to be accused of using fraud in collaboration with the experimenter, or to be told that she was probably responding to textural cues or subliminal cues from the experimenter, perhaps on an unconscious level.

The topic of skin vision appeared again, unexpectedly, from Nina Kulagina in Leningrad. Kulagina is probably the most famous sensitive in the world today, for her extraordinarily rare capacity to move objects at a distance, either with gestures of her hands or by fixating the object with nothing more than her eyes. Kulagina has been studied intensively for more than 10 years by Professor Sergeyev of Leningrad University, who has reported only scantily of her work (35). As a result, Kulagina's films and demonstrations are subjects of unending controversy: sensitive or charlatan? The Ostrander–Schroeder book reports the controversy, and describes Kulagina's gift as having appeared unexpectedly one day when Kulagina, in an emotional turmoil, was working in her kitchen and noticed that a pitcher began to move more and more closely to the edge of the shelf, finally dropping off. I asked Kulagina if this was true, and learned that it was an oft-repeated, but apocryphal, account of her developing in PK. (This was one of only two errors I was to discover in the Ostrander–Schroeder book.) According to Kulagina, she had begun her explorations in psi with skin vision, under the pioneer Soviet parapsychologist, Vasiliev (38, 39). She said that one day while practicing at home, as she tried to sense what was beneath her fingers, she got the impression that the paper under her hand was moving. Then, deliberately, she tried to get the paper to move. After several abortive attempts she learned that she could, for a small percentage of the time, get lightweight objects to obey the movements dictated by her hands (and sometimes, to move in directions other than those dictated).

This discussion took place, as did almost all meetings with the Russians, in a hotel room. This Leningrad hotel was unusual in that it was an old and elegant establishment, preserved from czarist Russia and still boasting antique furniture with velvet draperies and Persian carpets—so much in contrast to modern Soviet architecture and decor. Into this hotel room came not only Kulagina and her engineer husband, M. Kulagin, but also Mme. Vasilieva, sister of the famous Russian parapsychologist with whom Kulagina had studied. Mme. Vasilieva was a beautiful companion piece for the hotel: elderly and faded but still elegant, delicate, and thoroughly charming. Mme. Vasilieva discussed her own abilities as a psychic, reporting that her distinguished brother had often made use of her talents on especially difficult occasions. (Like several scientists and professors, Vasiliev was famous for his absentmindedness.) One such occasion presented itself when he was scheduled to go abroad but at the last minute could not find his passport and other necessary documents, which he had carefully put away, forgetting where. In a panic he summoned his sister, who had had since childhood the capacity to locate missing objects (like the Dutch sensitive Croiset). Mme. Vasilieva described how, as she entered her brother's home, she felt herself directed toward his study. This sensation of being directed was a familiar one; and with it, she had learned to become very still and wait for spontaneous movement. Her previous experiences had taught her that her own ideas of where things might be were usually based on rational thinking and were generally incorrect. She found herself crossing directly to the desk, lifting several scientific journals from a large stack, to extract one particular journal—which then fell open to reveal the missing papers. On another occasion, Mme. Vasilieva had been able to retrieve a treasured diamond-and-sapphire tie pin from the muddy drive outside Vasiliev's home, using a similar technique of growing still and letting her instincts guide her footsteps.

In striking contrast to Mme. Vasilieva was the modish Mme. Kulagina, dressed in miniskirt and nylon hose and attractively made up to accentuate her beautiful eyes. Her conversation focused primarily on her laboratory experiments under Sergeyev and her husband, experiments that had demanded her being measured with sophisticated electrophysiological equipment. Only a fraction of this work has been published, unfortunately (22, 35). Kulagina's early studies with Vasiliev encouraged her to attempt moving a compass needle, encased in glass, by moving her fingers about three inches *above* the compass. She learned to do this successfully and still uses this technique for warming up before attempting to move other objects.

This ability to deflect a compass needle through manipulations of the fingers (and presumably the energy fields that emanate from them) was reported more than 100 years ago by the eminent German scientist Fechner. Fechner worked with a German woman, Mrs. Ruf, in his laboratory at the University of Leipzig, under stringently controlled conditions imposed by his colleagues and himself—and eventually published his account of the work, stating unequivocally that Mrs. Ruf possessed an "abnormal power" that could cause the "deflection of a magnetic needle by attractive and repulsive passes made merely in its vicinity by her fingers. . . . The fingertips of one hand held closely together deflected the needle (which was enclosed under glass in an ordinary compass box) from 40 to 50 degrees" . . . and Reichenbach, says Fechner, told him that he had seen her cause the needle to make a complete revolution through all 360 degrees of the circle (9). Kulagina has performed this exact experiment on numerous occasions before scientists and in a film that was presented over Soviet television in 1970.

It took years of intense work before Kulagina acquired a measure of control over her ability to move objects such as matches, cigarettes, cigar cases, fountain pens, and other light objects (usually no more than 5 grams in weight). Kulagina emphasized that it was the skin vision exercises that led the way toward PK, and again I was struck by the possibility of energy fields around the body being utilized in still another dimension of parapsychological exploration.

Kulagina did not perform for us that afternoon, nor did I regret the omission, for I had already seen several of the films made of her work (by Naumov, Sergeyev, and her husband). Two of these short films have been analyzed, frame by frame, by the physicist Benson Herbert (11, 12) and provide absorbing reading for those interested in the physical anomalies posed by Kulagina's PK talents. Her husband corroborated his report given at the Czechoslovakian Symposium of Psychotronics (22) in which he describes what to him is one of the most impressive of Kulagina's laboratory experiments: her ability to tilt a pair of scales, equally balanced with 30 grams of weight, simply by concentration of her eyes. She was able to hold the scale down, even after 10 additional grams had been added to the other side to make it heavier. But as soon as she stopped concentrating and moved her eyes, the heavier scale sank. Kulagina emphasized that she could not always command her gifts. Sometimes with skeptics present she is unable to perform at all. And even with friendly witnesses, it will sometimes take as long as three hours before she warms up sufficiently to move objects. She described a sensation that usually heralds success: a sensation like that of a hot stream of energy traveling from the base of her spine up to the back of her neck and remaining there as if waiting for her to direct it. She added ruefully that this hot current of energy often leaves her with a bad headache. I suggested that this "hot stream of energy" sounded like the yogic *kundalini,* which, when unleashed, generates great power. Kulagina seemed not to hear, but Mme. Vasilieva, sitting straight and proper next to me, leaned over to murmur in her elegant French, "But of course! Kundalini. These young people do not understand. . . ."

ACUPUNCTURE AND KIRLIAN PHOTOGRAPHY

Perhaps Kulagina did not understand kundalini, but back in Moscow it was my strong impression that many of the young scientists had studied yoga and knew of the power sources there described. Probably the most eloquent and gifted of these scientists is Viktor Adamenko, biophysicist, who has developed a transistorized "tobiscope," an instrument that he believes detects acupuncture points on the body. This device looks very much like a pocket flashlight. (The popular name for it is a "light pencil.") When touching an acupuncture point, the light bulb at its tip goes on, whereas when aimed at other body surfaces, the light bulb remains dark (4). Adamenko's interest in energy fields stems from his childhood, when he lived next door to Semyon and Valentina Kirlian, whose lives have been devoted to developing their special kind of electrical photography. They believe their photographs reveal energy fields in and around organic (and inorganic) materials (19, 20). Adamenko took up the study of physics in hopes of clarifying some of the important questions this photography raises: If it is an energy field being photographed, of what is it composed? Adamenko's theory, at that time, was "the cold emission of electrons," the patterning of which may reveal new information concerning life processes in animate objects (1). This hypothesis of Adamenko is in contrast to that of Inyushin at Kirov University, whom I was going to visit. Inyushin had published some provocative papers in which he claimed that the photographs reveal the "bioplasma body" of organisms, a patterning of electrons and photons that determines the structure of the physical body (14–17). When I mentioned this concept to Adamenko, he smiled, shrugged, and said softly, "Fantasy. . . ." It seems that Russian scientists disagree with each other as much as American scientists.

Adamenko's consuming interest in energy fields and Kirlian photography has led him to acupuncture, hypnosis, skin electricity, electrostatics, and PK (2, 3). He spoke enthusiastically of Kulagina's PK ability and claimed that he had been able to teach his wife, Alla, to move objects at a distance by employing some principles of electrostatic phenomena: dielectric surfaces, dry skin, friction, and the "ability to change the conductivity of acupuncture points" (3). On the night I was scheduled to fly to Alma-

Ata, Adamenko told me his wife was to appear on Russian television to demonstrate her PK. Unfortunately, at the airport (where color television was available) I learned that the program had been canceled. Subsequently I have seen a film of Alla's work, which appears to be similar to that of Kulagina but more limited. Herbert sums up his view of the difference between the ladies thus: "Around every human being there exists an electrical field, and Alla has learned how to master it. . . . But in the case of Kulagina . . . electrostatics plays at most a minor role" (13). Herbert's report continues with a digest of a paper by Adamenko presented at the 1972 International Congress of Psychology in Tokyo, in which Alla is said to "produce a voltage gradient of ten thousand volts per cm. in the neighborhood of an object without, apparently, giving any indication of an electrical field in the space between her and the object. A neon lamp glows near the object, but not near Alla." Electrostatics clearly play a part in this type of PK. In our own experiments at UCLA (as developed by Kendall Johnson), using a plastic surface and objects like Ping-Pong balls, cigar cases, and cigarettes, we obtain strong movement (always repulsion, unlike Kulagina but like Alla) by passing the hand an inch or two above the object. However, this movement is possible for us only after rubbing the table top with silk or wool, to produce a charge on the surface. In most cases, when the charge is dissipated after two or three minutes, the movement stops. Occasionally a subject with strong conductive (or some sort of electrical) properties can keep the objects moving for considerably longer periods of time. Apparently Alla is such a subject, for Adamenko admits that even though he trained his wife to develop these faculties, he has been unable to develop them in himself. It is possible, then, that the electrical properties of their respective skins may have something to do with this PK effect—which may account for Adamenko's particular interest in acupuncture and "skin electricity," about which he has written so provocatively (2).

BIOPLASMA, AURAS, AND PSYCHIC HEALING

Inyushin's interests, although similar to Adamenko's, derive from different origins. Inyushin is a native of Alma-Ata, the largest fruit-growing center of Russia and the capital of Kazakhstan, a recent addition to the Soviet Union. At the time of its joining the Soviet Union, Kazakhstan claimed but one university and an enormous illiteracy rate. In less than 30 years, it is averred, illiteracy has all but disappeared and the university has grown to be one of the finest and best equipped in the Soviet Union. I must take Inyushin's word for this because I never did see the inside of the university in spite of his cordial invitation. Permission had not been received from Moscow. As a result, our meetings were limited to personal appointments—which were exhilarating.

In spite of his impressive list of publications, Inyushin proved to be less than 30 years old, burly and rugged, with sideburns and longish hair, possessing an astonishing knowledge of American literature, art, and theater, as well as science. Furthermore, Inyushin, his chic and intelligent wife (an electrophysiologist), and their colleagues whom I was privileged to meet were all versed not only in modern technology but also in ancient mystical tradition. We discussed Eastern philosophy, yoga, gurus, Buddhism, and the astral body. After I participated in several such conversations, it occurred to me that the zeitgeist might not be manifesting itself in the hippie movement or the drug culture but in a return to ancient mystical philosophies by examining them with contemporary scientific methods.

Inyushin, like Adamenko (with whom he has collaborated on several research projects) is keenly interested in Kirlian photography, acupuncture, and energy fields. His basic training, though, has been in biology, and his thinking has been influenced by the field concepts of Presman (33), Gurvich (10), and "your great American scientist, Szent-Gyorgyi" (36, 37). (I confessed that until we had exchanged letters, I had been ignorant of the brilliant work of our Nobel Prize winner in bioenergetics and bioelectronics, subjects with which Inyushin is strenuously engaged.)

Inyushin's concept of "bioplasma" derives from the work of the Soviet engineer and physicist Grishenko. In an article (17), Inyushin proposes that plasma exists throughout the universe and is the substance of which the sun is composed. But currently, as studied by Soviet physicists, plasma is considered to be "a collective of elementary particles devoid of atoms," which is being discovered to exist at normal temperatures in metals, air, and so forth. "Plasma physicists are interested in an unusual reservoir and generator of plasma—living organisms." Going beyond plasma, "*bio*plasma consists of electrons and photons woven into definite structures, e.g., in bioplasma as opposed to plasma; harmony and order reign [and] it is only at the organism's death that bioplasma loses its stability and gives off its energy in the form of heat and other electro-magnetic oscillations."

In discussing bioplasma with Inyushin in Alma-Ata, I asked the question that had intrigued me ever since reading the Ostrander–Schroeder book: Did Inyushin conceive of bioplasma, the emanations appearing in his Kirlian photographs around leaves and fingers, to be the equivalent of the aura, as described in mystical literature? When I propounded this question, we were in the hotel, making do with basic Russian and English, without benefit of translator. When I began to ask about the aura, I suddenly realized I had no idea what the Russian word would be. And, as so often before, I took the chance of pronouncing the English word with Russian sounds: "ah-oó-rah." I was greeted with a shout of recognition from Inyushin who repeated, "Ah-oó-rah, da da!" His knowledge of the aura stems from his interest in yoga, kindled by his father, who had, as an engineer, traveled extensively in India and had made a lifelong study and practice of that philosophy. In discussing the aura, Inyushin proceeded to describe his scientific research into the phenomena of "healing" and "laying on of hands." Apparently the Soviet medical profession accepts this form of therapy, as it does acupuncture treatment. Inyushin described the work that had been done in the laboratory with a healer named Krivorotov, whose son is a medical doctor. Apparently Krivorotov *père* sometimes helps his son with difficult cases.

Among the studies done with Krivorotov are Kirlian photographs taken of his thumb, magnified 500 times, first when in a state of rest and then when he was asked to act "as if he were healing someone." As can be seen in Figures 1 and 2, the difference between the two pictures is striking. Inyushin confirmed that the healer's emanations increase dramatically during the process of healing and added that patients would occasionally report feeling intense heat at the spot where his hands were directed, although frequently his hands made no contact with a patient's body (1). Again, the concept of energy fields emerged.

It was in this discussion with Inyushin and his young colleague Nikolas Shuisky that I learned in detail of their research into acupuncture. And it was only then that I began to realize the importance of acupuncture theory in relation to the study of energy fields in and around living organisms. They told of a remarkable investigation they had been able to conduct because of the odd fact that Alma-Ata lies scarcely 100 kilometers from the Chinese border. It seems that not infrequently a Chinese will escape from his country into the Soviet Union. One of the recent defectors had been a doctor, trained in medicine and acupuncture at the University of Peking (a course that takes 12 years to complete). This Chinese doctor had agreed to locate by manual exploration the 700-odd acupuncture points that are presumed to exist on the body. His markings were done independently of Shuisky and Inyushin, who in turn determined the locations of the points by Adamenko's tobiscope. In comparing the markings made by the Chinese doctor with their own, they found a remarkably high correlation. Adamenko's belief, then, that his electronic instrument is able to locate the traditional acupuncture system seems well founded, based on this laboratory evidence. Further research led them to believe that the acupuncture theory of an energy system in and around the body is eminently worthy of extensive investigation. For example, they have measured, electrically, the energy emitted at certain points in their normal resting state, and then, by manipulation of the points (either using traditional needles, electrical stimulation, or stimulation by laser beam), they have been able to alter dramatically the electrical measurements at these

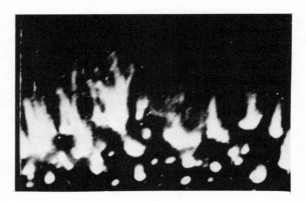

Figure 1.   Emanations from thumb of Russian
"healer"—normal state. (2× enlarged)

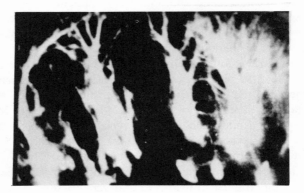

Figure 2.   Emanations from thumb of Russian
"healer" during healing. (2× enlarged)

points (5, 6). It is the use of the laser that particularly concerns Shuisky. He has been treating severely crippled arthritic patients who have not responded to any other form of therapy by focusing the laser directly on one point between the thumb and forefinger. (I learned subsequently that this point, "hoku," is considered a major one in the treatment of many illnesses, as well as in the alleviation of pain.) Shuisky had already treated eight patients, who had responded to the point of apparent remission, but he did not plan to publish until he had treated a far larger number of patients. (To my knowledge no paper has yet appeared about this research.)

In lecturing to the UCLA medical students in 1971 about this Soviet work with laser beams, acupuncture, and arthritis, I was met with incredulity and derision. Now, two years later, several laboratories in this country are doing basic research in acupuncture, with particular reference to pain control and anesthesia. In our laboratory, with the aid of a tobiscope (invented by Kendall Johnson) we have been able to replicate, in part, the Alma-Ata study with the Chinese doctor. We have compared presumed acupuncture points located by a traditional acupuncturist trained in Taiwan with those determined by Johnson's tobiscope and found a high correlation. We have also attempted electrical stimulation at some acupuncture points and obtained radically different readings with both skin resistance and current flow.

Furthermore, we are currently taking our version of Kirlian photography (with instrumentation again devised by Johnson) and have learned that emotional and physical changes in people are reflected in the photographs (26). We also have discovered that the electrical differences obtained by the stimulation at acupuncture points are revealed in these pictures (27).

Finally, intrigued by the Russian research with healers, we have been exploring the possible energy fields surrounding such persons who volunteer to come into the laboratory. The results of this work—premature for a full-scale report—seem genuinely encouraging, as revealed by the pre- and posthealing pictures in Figures 3–6 (28).

Thus, the long and frequently frustrating voyage to the Soviet Union provided a wealth of information into strange avenues of investigation that have already proved feasible in our laboratory, even though we are using different technology and instrumentation. The somber fact is that the Russians have had at least 15 years to do the basic explorations, which we have just begun.

And many basic questions remain shrouded in mystery. What is it that Nina Kulagina does that causes objects to move when she gestures or looks at them? Has this to do with unknown attributes of energy fields that she unconsciously has learned sometimes to control? Is the work with skin vision of Novomeisky and his colleagues similarly related to dimensions of energy fields and skin receptors, about which we still are ignorant? What is it that the Kirlian photographs reveal: corona discharge, the cold emission of electrons, bioplasma, electrical artifact, or the aura? Whatever it is, it has been demonstrated repeatedly that those emanations change dramatically when the organism is affected physically or emotionally. Why? Are these changes related to "bioenergetic" principles of which we are unaware? Is it possible that the acupuncture concept of energy flow (the meridians) may prove to be part of the energy fields that exist in and around the body, as those energy fields have been described by Burr (7) and Ravitz? Finally, is it not possible that some of these phenomena, now called parapsychological, may relate to a bioenergy field that interpene-

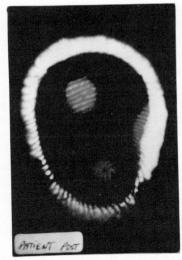

Figure 3.   Patient before healing.
(2× enlarged)

Figure 4.   Patient after healing.
(2× enlarged)

Figure 5.   "Healer" before healing.
(2× enlarged)

Figure 6.   "Healer" after healing.
(2× enlarged)

trates all things, making a unified field system throughout nature that helps to transmit thoughts through space, to move objects at great distances, and to render that which has been considered "paranormal" simply an extension of our normal faculties, as yet uncharted?

Clearly, we need to increase greatly our channels of communication with Soviet scientists and work cooperatively on these questions. And it also seems clear that Soviet scientists would like nothing better than that opportunity.

REFERENCES

1. Adamenko, V. "Electrodynamics of Living Systems." *Journal of Paraphysics*, 4 (1974).
2. Adamenko, V. G. "Living Detectors." *Journal of Paraphysics*, 6 (1972): 5–8.
3. Adamenko, V. G. "The Phenomenon of Skin Electricity." *Journal of Paraphysics*, 6 (1972).
4. Adamenko, V. "The Tobiscope: Its Uses in Hypnosis." *Journal of Paraphysics*, 6 (1972).
5. Adamenko, V. G. "Controlled Movements of Objects in Bioelectric Fields." Paper delivered at Moscow Parapsychology Conference, July 1972 .
6. Adamenko, V. G.; Kirlian, S.; and Kirlian, V. "The Biometer: Detection of Acupuncture Points." *Journal of Paraphysics*, 6 (1972).
7. Burr, H. S. *Blueprint for Immortality*. Spearman: London, 1972.
8. Dimond, E. Grey. "Acupuncture Anesthesia: Western Medicine and Chinese Traditional Medicine." *Journal of the American Medical Association*, 218 (1971).
9. Fechner, G. "Memories of the Last Days of Odic Theory and Its Originator." Breitkopf und Hartel: Leipzig, 1876, as reported in *Reichenbach's Letters on Od and Magnetism*, F. O'Byrne, trans. Repr. Health Research: Mokelumne Hill, Calif., 1964.
10. Gurvich, A. M. "Electrical Activity of the Brain During Death and Resuscitation." *Meditsina Leningrad*, 1966 (English summary).
11. Herbert, B. "Kulagina Cine Film A." *Journal of Paraphysics*, 4, (1970): 89–95.
12. Herbert, B. "Kulagina Cine Film B." *Journal of Paraphysics*, 5, (1971): 16–24.
13. Herbert, B. "Nina Kulagina: Demonstrations in Leningrad." *Journal of Paraphysics*, 6 (1972).
14. Inyushin, V. M. "The Biological Plasma of Human and Animal Organisms." *Proceedings of Symposium on Psychotronics*, Prague, 1970, pp. 50–53.
15. Inyushin, V. M.; Dombrovsky, B.; and Sergeyev, G., eds. *Problems of Bioenergetics: Materials of a Scientific Methods Seminar*, G. Shepak, trans. Kirov University: Alma-Ata, 1969.
16. Inyushin, V. M.; Grishenko, V. S.; et al. *The Biological Nature of the Kirlian Effect*, J. Krieger, trans. Kirov University: Alma-Ata, 1968.
17. Inyushin, V. M., and Kireeva, L. "Laser Beams and the Resonances of Life." M. Flier, trans. *Prostor*, (1971): 93–106.
18. Ivanov, A. "Soviet Experiments in Eyeless Vision." *International Journal of Parapsychology*, 6 (1964).
19. Kirlian, S. D., and Kirlian, V. Kh. "Photographic and Visual Observations

by Means of High Frequency Currents." *Journal of Applied Photography and Cinemaphotography* (Moscow). 6 (1961).

20. Kirlian, S. D., and Kirlian, V. Kh. "In the World of Wonderful Discharges." *Znanie*, Moscow, 1964.
21. Kogan, I. M. "The Informational Aspect of Telepathy." Paper presented in absentia at the UCLA symposium "A New Look at ESP," 1969.
22. Kulagin, Ing. V. "Nina S. Kulagina." *Proceedings of Symposium of Psychotronics*, Prague, 1970, pp. 54–62.
23. Moss, T. "That the Blind May See." *Osteopathic Physician*, 39 (1972).
24. Moss, T.; Chang, A.; and Levitt, M. "Long-Distance ESP: A Controlled Experiment." *Journal of Abnormal Psychology*, 76 (1970).
25. Moss, T.; Gray, J.; Hubacher, J.; and Bush, B. "Skin Vision and Telepathy in a Blind Subject." *Proceedings of Parapsychology Association*, Edinburgh (in press).
26. Moss, T., and Johnson, K. "Bioplasma or Corona Discharge?" In Stanley Krippner and Daniel Rubin, eds., *Galaxies of Life*. Gordon and Breach: New York, 1973.
27. Moss, T., and Johnson, K. "The Body as Energy Field." *Harper's*, January 1973.
28. Moss, T.; Johnson, K.; Gray, J.; and Hubacher, J. "Photographic Evidence of a Healing Energy." Paper delivered at UCLA Symposium "The Dimensions of Healing," October 1972.
29. Naumov, E. K., and Associates. *Bibliographies on Parapsychology (Psychoenergetics) and Related Subjects*. Joint Publications Research Service: Washington, D.C., 1972.
30. Novomeisky, A. C.; Chetin, F. E.; and Yakovlev, V. I. *Problems of Complex Investigations of Dermo-optical Sensitivity*. Sverdlovsk, 1968 (in Russian).
31. Ostrander, S., and Schroeder, L. *Psychic Discoveries Behind the Iron Curtain*. Prentice-Hall: Englewood Cliffs, N.J., 1970.
32. Platonov, K. *Psychology: As You May Like It*. Progress: Moscow, 1965 (in English).
33. Presman, A. S. *Electro-magnetic Fields and Life*, F. A. Brown, ed. Plenum: New York, 1970.
34. Rosenthal, R., and Associates. "Data Desirability, Experimenter Expectancy, and the Results of Psychological Experiments." *Journal of Personality and Social Psychology*, 3 (1966).
35. Sergeyev, G. A. "The KNS Phenomena." *Proceedings of Symposium of Psychotronics*, Prague (1970): 47–50.
36. Szent-Gyorgyi, A. *Bioenergetics*. Academic: New York, 1957.
37. Szent-Gyorgyi, A. *Bioelectronics*. Academic: New York, 1968.
38. Vasiliev, L. L. *Experiments in Mental Suggestion*. Galley Hill: Hampshire, England, 1963.
39. Vasiliev, L. L. *Mysterious Phenomena of the Human Psyche*. University: New Hyde Park, N.Y., 1965.

William A. Tiller

WILLIAM A. TILLER, Ph.D., is professor of materials science at Stanford University in Stanford, California. He is also a consultant to government and industry in the fields of metallurgy, chemistry, and solid-state physics.

Dr. Tiller earned his doctorate at the University of Toronto in 1955 and then took a research position with Westinghouse Electric Company. In 1964 he joined the materials science department at Stanford. He became chairman in 1966, a post he held until 1971. He is a member of several honorary societies and is associate editor of two scientific journals, Journal of Crystal Growth and Journal of Materials Science and Engineering. In addition, he is a director of the Academy of Parapsychology and Medicine in Los Altos, California, and of the Institute of Noetic Sciences in Palo Alto, California.

Among Dr. Tiller's publications are more than 100 scientific papers and two books that he co-edited, Atomic and Electronic Structure of Metals and An Introduction to Computer Simulation in Applied Science. He has two more books in preparation: a text on the science of crystallization and another on the subject of concepts and models for understanding the transformation of man.

Dr. Tiller can be reached at the Department of Materials Science, Stanford University, Stanford, Calif. 94305.

21 Devices for Monitoring Nonphysical Energies

WILLIAM A. TILLER

SUMMARY

Significant advances in the psychoenergetics field will be delayed until devices and techniques are developed for monitoring nonphysical energies. One general category of useful devices is that of a conventional electromagnetic nature that responds to such energies via interaction with an intermediary living transducer—human, animal, or plant. This paper is largely devoted to a discussion of two such devices: a high-voltage (Kirlian) photography device and an acupuncture-point monitoring device. The final portion of the paper deals with an expanded model of substance that seems sufficient to circumscribe known psychoenergetic phenomena so that one can gain some idea of how nonphysical energies may give rise to physical effects.

INTRODUCTION

The flux of worldwide investigation and activity in the area of psychoenergetic fields and phenomena has been such that mankind has now exceeded the "critical-mass" condition for a self-sustaining reaction. We can therefore anticipate a continued growth of awareness and perception about this domain of nature. Such an activity does not deny the validity of our present knowledge of the universe, nor does it pose a threat to what I shall call conventional physics. Rather, it calls for an extension, or expansion, of present laws to reliably model behavior in the expanded domain of variable space that circumscribes psychoenergetic fields (since we presently have some small ability to monitor this aspect of nature). Here, one should reflect on the example of Newton and Einstein. Newton's work on gravitation was not shown to be wrong by Einstein but merely limited to a domain of variable space in nature far removed from speeds approaching

488

the velocity of light. The laws of Einstein reproduce the laws of Newton in the appropriate limit of small velocities.

In the decades and centuries ahead, we would hope to follow and extend Einstein's example and develop quantitative laws that reliably model nature in the psychoenergetic domain and that reduce, in the appropriate limit, to our present physical laws of nature. To reach this goal, we shall need a supply of devices that can respond directly to such new energies.

We may liken conventional scientific understanding of the universe to the visible tip of an iceberg. We have come to know that exposed tip fairly well. However, most of nature is still hidden from us, and we know it not. History contains references and speculation on many aspects of the hidden iceberg, and very recent research, especially that fine work being carried out in the Soviet Union, suggests some fascinating characteristics. Let us touch briefly on some of these.

From experiments on telepathy, PK, psychic healers, and the like (18), we seem to be dealing with energy fields completely different from those known to us via conventional science.

The universe organizes and radiates information in other dimensions than the physical frame. From experiments on PK (18), radionics (24), materialization–dematerialization (19), and the like, the cause–effect relationships seem to follow a different path, or "field line," than we are used to dealing with in the conventional space–time frame of reference.

At some level of the universe, we are all interconnected. This can be deduced from the Soviet telepathy experiments on rabbits (18) and the Backster experiments on plants, eggs, and cells (4).

Time and space are not as immutable and confining as we ordinarily think. Experiments on precognition (22), materialization and dematerialization (19), and the like point to this.

From Slater's experiments (20) on the "upside-down glasses" and modern information theory (7), it seems clear that we do not perceive reality directly but only gain some bits of information about reality from our sensory system, which the brain then interprets in terms of what is in its memory picture book. The brain often does signal processing to squeeze the available information into the closest facsimile in the picture-book records (and usually causes considerable distortion in the process).

A wide range of exotic nonphysical functioning devices have been investigated over the course of this century. These devices include radionics (11), homeopathy (11), dowsing (18), Cayce appliances (25), Eemans's relaxation circuit (10), and many others. However, work on these exotic devices is limited by our inability to monitor nonphysical energies reliably.

By nonphysical energies, the author means (a) energies of a nonelectromagnetic, nonsonic, or nongravitational variety as we know them, (b) energies that do not directly stimulate our five physical senses as we know them, and (c) energies that do not propagate in the four-dimensional space–time continuum as we know it. An expanded model of substance dealing with nonphysical energies will be presented later. I feel that the devices just enumerated fall into this category.

In general, there seem to be three types of monitoring devices: (a) a completely human device such as a clairvoyant who "sees" with extended vision and gives a verbal readout of observations, (b) an electronic or mechanical device connected to a living system that responds to the energy via its effect on an intermediary transducer, human, animal, or plant, and (c) a totally inanimate device based on a unique logic system (different from that associated with the physical aspect of reality) that responds to these energies directly. The first type of device is in daily use by some investigators. Some devices of the second type exist, but they suffer from the variability of the intermediate living transducer. With respect to the third category, no direct readout devices, except perhaps the Sergeyev detector (23), exist at present.

Significant advance of this field will be held up until the third class of devices are available; however, some meaningful progress can be made in the near future using devices of the second variety. This paper is largely devoted to a discussion of two such devices: high-voltage (Kirlian) photography and acupuncture-point monitors. The final portion of the paper deals with an expanded model of substance that seems sufficient to circumscribe known psychoenergetic phenomena so that we can gain some idea of how nonphysical energies may give rise to physical effects.

HIGH-VOLTAGE PHOTOGRAPHY

Review of Some Soviet Work (26)

In this section, the important features fall into three categories: (a) the operating characteristics of the electrical power source and the postulated mechanism of device functioning, (b) the configuration and components of the information display and recording devices, and (c) the general experimental results obtained.

Adamenko (3) has indicated that the power source should be a pulsed high-frequency field, somewhat similar to a radar power source. The pulse characteristics are given in Figure 1 and are a pulse height of 20–100kV, a pulse width of 10^{-4} sec to 2×10^{-3} sec generally (as small as 10^{-6} sec in some cases), a pulse repetition rate of 60/sec and an AC frequency of 75–3000kHz. This electric field is applied to a device, such as illustrated in Figure 2, producing a discharge phenomenon

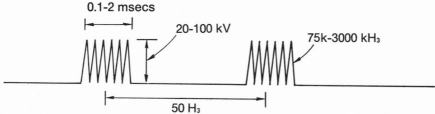

KIRLIAN POWER SUPPLY CHARACTERISTICS
Figure 1.   Electrical output properties of the energy source.

that appears to be cold electron emission from living systems (because the current–electric-field relationship follows the Fowler–Nordheim plot). The term *cold electron emission* is used to distinguish it from thermionic emission, which occurs at a high temperature. Cold emission occurs at low temperatures under the stimulus of an applied electric field. It is felt that

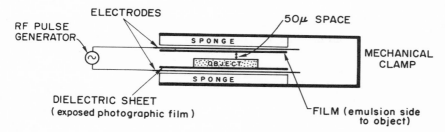

Figure 2.   Simple electrode device for taking Kirlian photographs.

the electron work function varies over the surface being photographed, and in air, the picture of the discharge channel occurs as a result of the positive ions clustering around the channel, providing a focusing effect to the electrons.

The Soviet experience was that a single DC pulse would not be effective in producing the desired effect and that it would be rather dangerous to use DC rather than high-frequency AC inside the pulse envelope. Although a static electric field of the same value as used in the AC system ($\sim 10^7$ V/cm) would also yield cold electron emission, the situation is not straightforward, as strong polarization of the electrodes would occur (electrolysis). The Soviets feel that it is necessary to have a discharge spacing between the specimen and the film in order for proper channel formation to occur (as a result of positive ions clustering around the electron stream). The electrons exit from the surface with different velocities, and this includes information about the object. If one uses a DC power source, equilibration of electrons seems to occur and the image is absent. With DC, in the first few moments an image appears but then disappears later as equilibration occurs. The high-frequency signal is also used in the pulse so that one can decrease the size of the equipment. The use of different frequencies allows one to obtain quite different pictures, presumably associated with different resonances from different cells, and so on—that is, the electrons can come from different parts of the skin.

Actually, one need use only one pulse to obtain a photograph. The slow pulse repetition rate is to provide low average power. It seems that a pulse duration of about 2×10^{-3} sec is maximum and, if pulse width (τ) is much larger, the image is poor. On the other hand, if τ is too small, the channel discharge process does not have time to develop. (For contact photography, one can use $\tau \sim 2 \times 10^{-6}$ sec.) The total current drawn from the entire surface is less than $1 \mu A$, so that the actual current in a discharge channel is much less. They suggest that this is the reason for the stability of the cold electron emission (3).

The average power of a generator is about 1 W (pulse power is much larger, of course). Thus, quite small generators using batteries, transformers, or transistors can be built and taken out into the field. However, such small generators generally do not have as much stability as one would like.

It has been stated (3) that any discharge includes photons but that only discharges in a strong field produce an image. This seems to relate to electron acceleration that leads to photon emission. Of course, even the radiation damage effect of the electrons hitting the photographic grains can be expected to produce massive exposure of such grains.

In the simplest Kirlian device, shaped like a sandwich or parallel-plate condenser, the object is placed between the two plates to which voltage is applied. If the condenser plates are too close to the object, there will be no effect on the film. In order to get good pictures, there must be a dielectric gap between the object and the film. The exposure time depends on the film speed and on the power density of the electric field.

To improve the effect and augment it, a fine screen (such as a silk screen) may be placed between the object and capacitor plate (and film). The film is between the condenser plate and the screen. This screen enhances the effect, probably by its serving as a dielectric. One type of effective screen material is film itself that has been completely exposed and developed.

The device can be placed in a clamp arrangement as illustrated in Figure 2, the clamp being used to apply a slight, but even, pressure via the paralon (or sponge) pads. The electrodes are developed X-ray film (AgBr → Ag), and the leads are fastened to them as indicated. The dull matt finish of these electrodes provides poor reflectivity of light, and thus, is an aid to producing a good image. The spacing between object and film is about 50 μ (it can be 10–100 μ).

To improve the resolution, a layer of saline water or other conductive liquid is sometimes placed between the object and the film. In this case, the film is placed with the emulsion facing away from the object so that the emulsion will not be disturbed. The capacitor plate is then placed outside of the film. A further improvement can be made by using the conductive liquid as one of the capacitor plates, thereby permitting better resolution and faster work with the film.

For taking pictures of a section of human skin or other part of the body, only one electrode is needed. In this case, the body acts as ground —that is, only one half of the device, presented in Figure 2, is needed. This same electrode procedure is used for the Kirlian microscope, illustrated in Figure 3, when it is applied to the body.

A simple rolling device, which has the advantage of operating at an average power of less than 1 watt, was also described. It is illustrated in

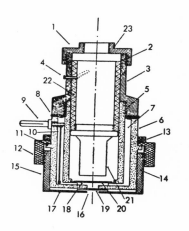

1. Transitional nut (to microscope tube)
2. Thread
3. Upper half of housing
4. Pin for focusing
5. Thread
6. Lower half of housing
7. Two orifices (ϕ 4mm) disposed one in front of the other
8. Rubber washer
9. Contact to power source
10. Metallic wire (for protection against circuit disruption because of water evaporation)
11. Thickening in form of a ring
12. Pressing nut, freely revolving
13. Collars
14. Thread
15. Traverse
16. Orifice ϕ 5mm
17. Bottom of the traverse
18. Glass with thickness 0.6-1.0mm
19. Glass with thickness 0.13-0.14mm
20. Chamber (cell), flooded by water through orifice 7
21. 8-12 times objective
22. Bushing which carries objective
23. Thread (in accordance with microscope tube thread)

Figure 3.   Microscope objective lens housing for direct observation of energy patterns.

Figure 4. In this device, no discharge occurs at points A or C but does occur at point B, where the spacing is about 10 μ. The cylinder is rolled at about 10 cm/min and gives a moving line discharge to expose the film in sequence. A device for taking moving pictures is illustrated in Figure 5. It utilizes the arrangement of Figure 2. Controlled weights are applied to the device, and the film is pulled through at some particular speed while the

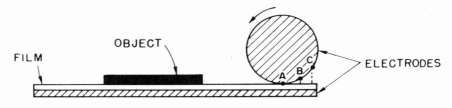

Figure 4.   Rolling-cylinder discharge device.

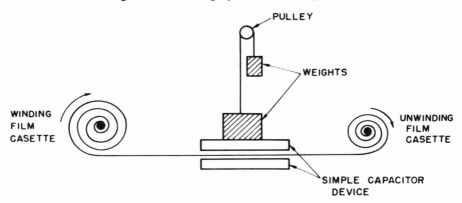

Figure 5.   Cinematographic discharge device.

discharge process is going on. The film is rolled in the usual way, and all is contained within a cassette.

In Figure 6, an extremely useful device idea is illustrated. The previous methods utilized rigid capacitor plates, which do not allow one to take pictures of objects having irregular profiles. In the new method (3), the device takes the shape of the body. The transparent electrode is a silicon organic film; however, many other possibilities exist. With this device, any portion of the body can be photographed directly. In fact, one could make a snug-fitting vest or garment of the material, which could then be monitored photographically from a distance or displayed continuously via closed-circuit TV.

This new method grew out of an earlier idea of Kirlian's (12) that utilized a conductive transparent material as part of the capacitor, to which a

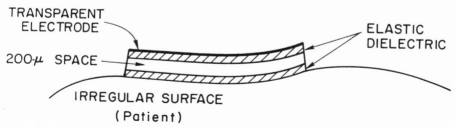

EYE OR CAMERA

TRANSPARENT
ELECTRODE

ELASTIC
DIELECTRIC

200μ SPACE

IRREGULAR SURFACE
(Patient)

Figure 6.   Transparent electrode device for continuous
monitoring of energy patterns.

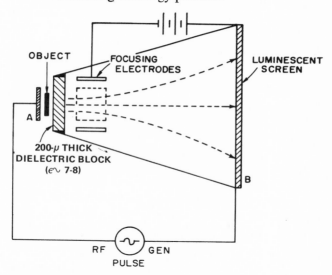

OBJECT

FOCUSING
ELECTRODES

LUMINESCENT
SCREEN

A

200-μ THICK
DIELECTRIC BLOCK
(ε∼ 7-8)

B

RF   GEN
PULSE

SCHEMATIC KIRLIAN CRT

Figure 7.   Cathode-ray-tube device for taking Kirlian photographs.

hinged mirror was attached, and a flexible conductive material laid upon
the object to be photographed. The mirror is concave and acts as a lens,
enlarging the object to be studied. The mirror is apparently used for visual
examination when not taking photographs. Between the object and the
flexible, transparent condenser plate is placed a dielectric net. A photographic plate is placed over the front or top of the conductor, so that the
prints are merely contact prints without focusing.

The foregoing devices all operate in air at 1 atm pressure. If the pressure is reduced to 10^{-5} mmHg, the image is still retained, provided the electrode separation is increased to 20–30 cm. At a pressure of 10^{-6} mmHg, the image disappears. A visual display system using something like a television tube is illustrated in Figure 7. In this cathode-ray tube (CRT) device, electrons from the object impinge on a $200 = \mu$ thick dielectric film, and their charge pattern induces charge polarization on the other side of the film, which, in turn, affects the preferential geometry of electron emission from the film. Thus, the eventual image on the screen is indeed that of the object. This is a very important phenomenon, for it allows many interesting modifications of device design.

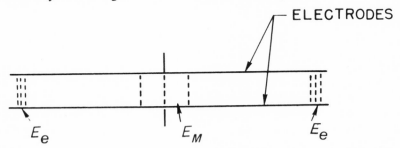

Figure 8.   Magnification technique by using different electric fields at the edges, E_e, and at the middle, E_M, in the device of Figure 2.

The methods have been developed for image amplification (magnification). In the first case, they use cold emission obtained in the small spacing device (50 μ) of Figure 2 with a high electric field at the edges, $E_e \sim 10^6$ V/cm. However, E is caused to decrease in the middle to $E_M \sim 10^4$ V/cm (see Figure 8). Thus, the magnification, μ, is given by

$$\mu = \frac{E_e}{E_M}$$

They have obtained values of $\mu \sim 340$. The second method is carried out in a CRT-type device as illustrated in Figure 9. The short electrode (cathode) has a field E_1, and the larger electrode (anode) has a field E_2 ($E_1 \sim 10^6$V/cm, E_2 is smaller). In this case, the magnification, μ, is given by

$$\mu = \frac{E_1}{E_2} = \frac{S_2}{S_1}$$

where S_1 and S_2 are the tension of the two electrodes ($S_1E_1 = S_2E_2$ from Gauss's law and charge conservation).

Using the TV-tube type of device, one might expect that the use of

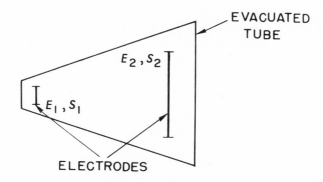

Figure 9.   Magnification technique using electrodes of area
in cathode-ray-tube device.

electron lenses would allow one to build an electron microscope with very
high magnification ($\sim 10^4 \times$). However, because of a high vacuum needed
in such a device, a severe limitation exists. At $10^{-7} - 10^{-8}$ mmHg pressure,
one gets no image because of the loss of channeling ions, but at $10^{-4} - 10^{-3}$ mmHg, one does not even need a lens.

It is generally quite inconvenient to be performing these experiments in
a dark room. This procedure can be avoided by utilizing an aspect of the
technique illustrated in Figure 7. Since an image of the object's energy
pattern can be transferred through a thin dielectric film, it should be
possible to use either a nontransparent envelope enclosing the sample or a
nontransparent envelope enclosing the film. This is illustrated in Figure
10. This technique is in common use in the Soviet Union and greatly
increases the practicality of the device for use in air under normal illumination.

On the Kirlian photographs one sees an image of the structure of the
surface plus a surrounding halo caused by a high-frequency discharge.

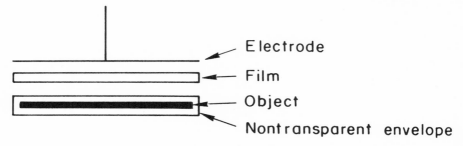

Figure 10.   Schematic illustration of the envelope technique
for taking photographs in a lighted room.

Both the dimensions of the halo and the overall brightness of glow change in accordance with changes in the physiological state of the organism. Different sections of skin surface are found to emit radiation in characteristically different colors: the heart area shows as dense blue; the hip shows as an olive; the forearm shows as greenish light blue. As a result of sudden emotional excitement (fear, pain, etc.), the color of the related section changes.

Using a high magnification system, one sees discharge channels arranged on the background configuration of the skin, and they exhibit a variety of energy-emission characteristics (2). They may be pointlike, crownlike, flarelike, or clotlike. They may have different coloring such as sky blue or various shades of lilac or yellow, and they may be bright or faded. Some of the channels glow constantly, some are twinkling, some flare up periodically, some are stationary, and some are always moving from place to place. In certain sections of the skin, one sees immobile flareup points that exhibit a definite rhythm and are light blue or golden. Besides these points, there are faded clots of indefinite form, taking from time to time a spherelike form. Some clots are continually spilled out from one point of the skin onto another where they are absorbed. The spilling out of one clot does not take place until the previous clot has been absorbed. In certain cases the luminous clots are not oriented in their movement. They slowly move between the flares and finally are extinguished with a little burst and seem to dissolve into space. The colors of the clots are generally milk-light blue, pale lilac, or grayish orange. In many respects these flares and clots resemble the plasma behavior often observed in observations of the sun.

They have found that a withered leaf shows almost no flares and that the clots barely move. As the leaf gradually dies, its self-emissions also decrease correspondingly until there is no emission from the dead leaf. Likewise, the finger of a human body, dead for several days, exhibits no distinctive self-emissions. The self-emission of living things seems to be a direct measure of the life processes occurring within their system.

The structure and emission characteristics of these discharge channels can be utilized for an objective evaluation of the physiological state of the living organism, for diagnosis of body health or pathology, for registration of the emotional state, and also for the control of the system's response to various radiations. For example, during the radiation of living objects with a laser ($\lambda = 6328$ Å), one observes a sharp increase in the intensity of discharge flaring. However, daylight radiation (incoherent radiation) of the same intensity does not cause any changes in the discharge process.

A special investigation of the high-frequency discharge glow from the leaves of plants revealed the existence of a series of peaks (4200 Å, 4250 Å, 4550 Å, 4750 Å) and several small peaks in the red part of the spectrum. If the plants were irradiated by a laser with λ-6328 Å, then the glow spectrum from the leaves was altered in the blue and green regions, so that characteristic peaks appeared at 5100 Å and 4800 Å and the spectrum shifts in the range 4400 Å–4500 Å. However, the number of peaks in the blue part of the spectrum remained unchanged. With the skin of animals (mainly rabbit), the peaks were found in the range 4950 Å–5000 Å, and the short-wave portion exhibits a peak structure coinciding with that from leaves.

If one photographs on the same film at the same time the fingers of two different people, then a crown discharge is seen around each finger. As the two fingers are brought closer together, the crowns of discharge deform and leave a small gap between them rather than interpenetrate. Using the fingers of three people, one again sees crown deformation and no penetration.

When observing the palm of a psychic healer as he begins a healing session, one initially sees many points flaring and then fewer points, but the area of discharge around the remaining points is larger (greater flare intensity) and eventually an area the size of a dime in the center of the palm becomes luminously brilliant. At this point, the healer is optimally attuned and the patient feels what is usually described as "heat" in the area of his body to which the healer is directing energy. By careful study of the location of the major flare points on the body, the Soviets have shown them to correspond to the active points marked on the Chinese maps of acupuncture points.

In concluding this section we should mention perhaps the most interesting and exciting experimental observation. In Figure 11a a photograph of a whole leaf is given showing the edge halo and inner light structure. It has been claimed that if 2–10% of a leaf has been cut away from one edge, the photograph shows not only the portion of the leaf remaining but also an energy pattern from the portion of the leaf that has been physically removed. In Figure 11b, we see such a cut-leaf photograph with the right-hand edge of the leaf removed and we note the remaining radiation pattern (albeit altered in contrast). It has been suggested (3) that the number of radiation sources in the leaf may be so numerous as to produce sufficient redundancy of information that when a portion of the leaf is removed, the lost sources do not significantly disrupt the multiple array pattern. It is also found that when one erases a person's fingerprint (by sanding it off), the Kirlian photograph clearly reveals the fingerprint (probably because the energy flare points are located only along the dactyloscopic design of the skin).

The Soviet scientist Inyushin has suggested that in living systems there is a single system of elementary charged particles that is dominant in all biodynamic relationships of the living organism. He has called this hy-

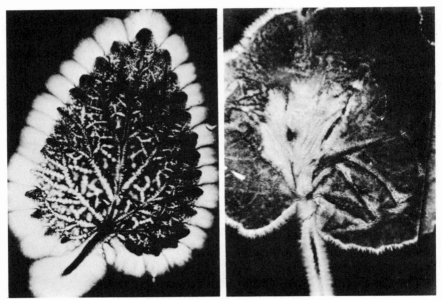

Figure 11.   (a) Kirlian photograph of a whole leaf (courtesy of
V. Adamenko). (b) Kirlian photograph of a cut leaf
(courtesy of V. Adamenko).

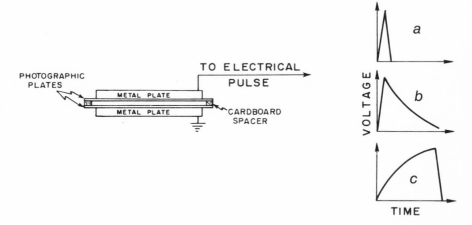

Figure 12.   The method of exposing the photographic plates to a pulse of
electricity with three of the types of pulse employed: (a) a rapid rate of
pulse increase and decrease, (b) a rapid increase and slow decrease, and
(c) a slow increase and rapid decrease.

pothesized system of elementary particles, "biological plasma." This biological plasma, or "bioplasma," as distinguished from nonorganic plasma, is a structurally organized system and the chaotic thermal randomization force is reduced to a minimum—that is, the entropy is minimal. Bioplasma is found to be strongly influenced by changes in temperature and other environmental factors.

Review of Some English and American Work

Milner and Smart (14) have for some years been experimenting with high voltage photography using a sandwich-type device similar to Figure 2. However, their work differs significantly from the Soviet work in that they use a DC pulse technique and control the process by controlling the slope of the leading and trailing edges of the pulse as illustrated in Figure 12. They are unable to detect any energy in the visible range; however, there is abundant new information to be found in the far ultraviolet. The pulse voltage used with their technique is in the range 5000–20,000 V, and great care must be exercised during the course of experimentation, because of the significant electrical power involved.

Using the arrangement of Figure 12, during application of the voltage across the empty cell, nothing visible occurs in the air gap during the voltage pulse, but one finds that the photographic emulsion has been exposed on both the positive plates and the negative plates, as illustrated in Figures 13a and 13b. The energy patterns on these complementary

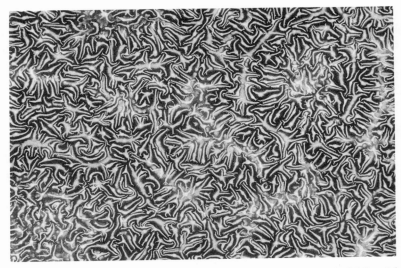

Figure 13.   (*a*) Photographic result on positive side of "sandwich" with intermediate rates of pulse increase and decrease. (*b*) Photographic result on negative side of "sandwich" (courtesy of Milner and Smart).

plates are quite different even though they were located only 75 μ apart. Steepening the rate of field decrease on the trailing edge of the pulse leads to Figures 14 and 15 for the positive plates, where Figure 15 had a much more rapid rate of decrease than Figure 14.

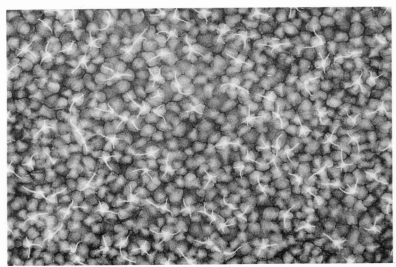

Figure 14.   Photographic result on positive side with steeper rate of pulse decrease than in Figure 13*a* (courtesy of Milner and Smart).

Figure 15.   Photographic result on positive side with still steeper rate of pulse decrease than in Figure 13*a* or 14 (courtesy of Milner and Smart).

Inserting a leaf or spray of leaves into the sandwich leads to Figure 16*a* for the positive plates. Here, using a rapid pulse, the leaves are hardly registered and are separated by a type of void space from the surrounding empty-sandwich pattern. With a more prolonged pulse, areas of the leaves become luminous and bright balls of plasma gather at the tips of the leaf serrations and begin to become detached and freed into the surrounding atmosphere (see Figure 16*b*). Maintaining the voltage for increasingly longer periods of time leads to the formation and detachment of more of these bright balls until the flow becomes exhausted and the leaf reverts to its original "dark" state (see Figure 16*c*). In Figure 17, we see an example of an energy transfer interaction between a freshly picked privet leaf (right) and a dying leaf picked 24 hours earlier.

Obviously, we are dealing, here, with a very complex phenomenon. Some of these results are at considerable variance with those of Soviet researchers; however, they will eventually help us to understand the phenomena involved in this process more completely.

From this work, we can begin to suspect that dielectric breakdown between heterogeneities in the plates may be playing an important role. In addition, bombardment of the two plates by different types of ions (positive and negative) may be playing a role in the different photographic effects produced on opposite plates. This would be accentuated by surface irregularities. (Soviet studies have shown that a surface roughness of 3.2 μ can be observed on exposed film with the unaided eye.)

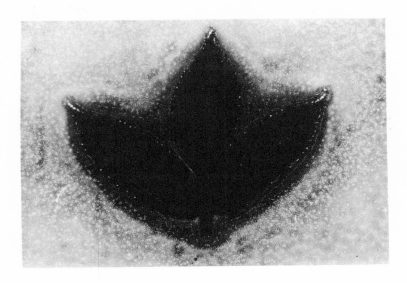

Monteith (15) has built what is perhaps the simplest and cheapest high-voltage device for illustrating the photographic effect. The circuit diagram is illustrated in Figure 18. From such a simple device one cannot anticipate much stability or controllability of device operation.

Monteith (15) found that a live leaf gave beautiful and varied emissions

Figure 16. (*a*) Result on positive side with a rapid pulse for a spray of leaves in sandwich (courtesy of Milner and Smart). (*b*) Result with more prolonged pulse (courtesy of Milner and Smart). (*c*) Result with still more prolonged pulse (courtesy of Milner and Smart).

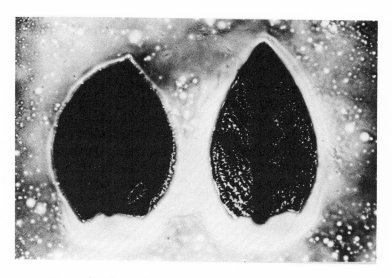

Figure 17. Example of transfer interaction between a freshly picked privet leaf (on right) and a dying leaf picked 24 hours earlier (courtesy of Milner and Smart).

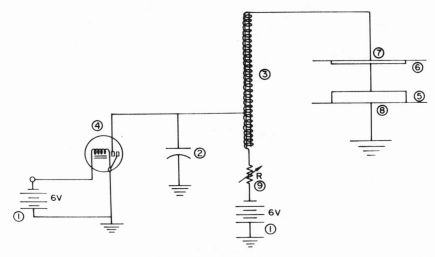

Figure 18.   Simple autoinduction-coil discharge system. (1) any 6-V source that can deliver at least 4 A; (2) a capacitor used in conjunction with the autoignition coil; (3) an autoignition coil; (4) a 6-V vibrator used to power autoradios (only one set of contacts need be used); (5) the object being photographed; (6) photographic film (Land type 58 is one of the best to use with this simple circuit; this is color film, but it is slow and seems to be relatively insensitive to voltage breakdown across the capacitor but very sensitive to emission from the object); (7) a capacitor plate at the high side of the emission coil (about 34,000 V placed on the plate); (8) grounded capacitor plate; (9) a variable resistor to give some control of the output voltage.

but that a dead leaf gave, at most, only a uniform glow (generally, it did not expose the film at all). Even when a dead leaf was thoroughly wet with water, in no way was the self-emission increased.

In the high-voltage device designed by Johnson and used by Moss and Johnson (16), the AC field was of low frequency ($\sim 10^2-10^4$ Hz) in contrast to the Soviet work ($\sim 10^5-10^7$ Hz), and yet good photographs have been obtained. They find that, with the same object, a change in the frequency leads to alternate zones where pictures appear and do not appear, depending on the frequency range. This suggests that some type of harmonic or wave diffraction effect is operative here. The Soviet cut-leaf effect has not yet been reproduced anywhere in the United States.

The Stanford device (6) was designed to approximate the Russian technique. The equipment is presented in Figure 19 and was used to carefully study metallic electrodes. Using short (~ 100 μsec) pulses of RF (1 MHz) applied to parallel electrodes in air at small electrode spacings (~ 250 μ) and at an applied field of $\sim 10^6$ V/cm, discharges from both biological

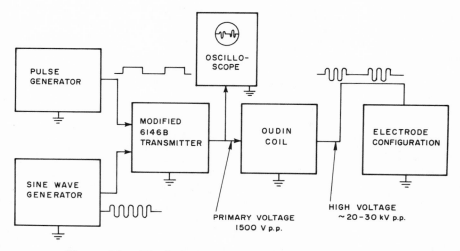

Figure 19.   Block diagram of equipment built by authors.

and metallic electrodes occurred from a network of points in the electrode surface. These discharges were recorded photographically and are illustrated in Figures 20 and 21. Multiple pulses led to a superposition effect such that a uniform corona exposure appeared on the film. The results were found to be completely explicable in terms of the streamer phenomenon of corona discharge. In fact, *the wide variety of color effects observed in Kirlian photography can be accounted for by this mechanism.* These results (6) illustrate that future Kirlian photography experiments must be done more carefully than those in the past if we are to use this as a tool truly to learn new information about changes in energy states of living systems. Certainly, the standard ionic processes discussed by Loeb (13) and others (5, 8, 17) are intimately involved here, and it is probably more appropriate to use the name "corona-discharge photography." Any new energies that may also be involved here must be determined by the careful experiments of the future.

In air at high field strengths, the normal color of the streamers is a bright blue, since the most frequently excited radiation is from highly excited nitrogen molecules. Rare yellow flashes in the streamer corona are thought to be due to the presence of sodium from salt.

The main reason for the presence of color other than blue and white, in the contact photographic process, is that it is associated with film buckling, so that streamers form between the electrode and the back side of the film and blue light enters the film from the back side to expose the red and green layers as well as from the front to expose the blue layers. However, the film buckling appears to be a nonrandom event.

A review of conventional DC-streamer studies with point-to-plane configuration illustrates the different discharge morphologies associated with (*a*) positive or negative points, (*b*) the presence of electropositive or electronegative gases, (*c*) film spacing, and (*d*) pulse shape to substantiate the streamer mechanism as the responsible physical mechanism for the generation of light in high-voltage photography (27).

Finally, there appear to be five ways in which psychoenergetic effects

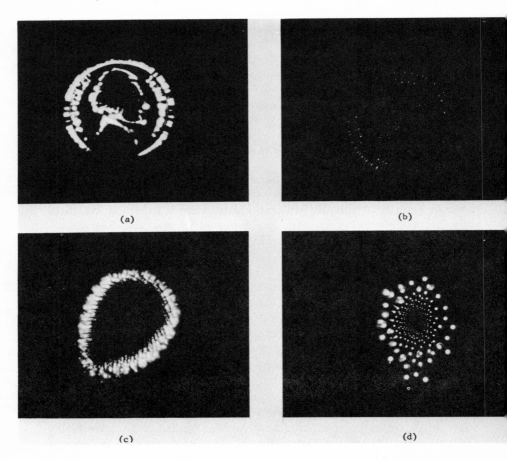

Figure 20.   (*a*) Photograph of coin (U.S. nickel): multiple pulses, pulse width = 100 μsec, rep. rate = 20 Hz, duration ~ 2 sec (2×). (*b*) Photograph of coin (U.S. nickel): single pulse, pulse width = 100 μsec, rep. rate = 1 Hz (2×). (*c*) Photograph of fingertip: multiple pulses, pulse width = 100 μsec, rep. rate = 20 Hz, duration ~ 2 sec (4×). (*d*) Photograph of fingertip: single pulse, pulse width = 100 μsec, rep. rate = 1 Hz (3×).

can alter the details of the streamer process: (a) by alteration of the electrostatic potential of the biological electrode that influences streamer length, (b) by a change in surface chemistry giving rise to electronegative-ion effects and perhaps weak direct color radiation, (c) by polarization-induced diffraction effects due to both shape effects and dielectric-phase-angle effects of the electrode material, (d) by emission of resonant frequency radiation from the cells (bioplasma may possibly enter here), and (e) by altered electrical impedance of the electrode material that controls the discharge current and thus the streamer intensity (plus film buckling).

ACUPUNCTURE-POINT MONITORING

As is now fairly well known, acupuncture is an ancient Chinese art of preventive medicine. The old practice was that people would go to their doctor about once every quarter and pay him to have their "circuits" checked and balanced using acupuncture techniques and stimulation. Because of this, they were supposed to be free from illness. If they happened to become ill, folklore tells us, the doctor paid them by treating them free of charge.

The early theory, at a fairly simple level, indicated that there were 12 main meridians in the body (very much like electrical wiring, figuratively speaking) which acted as prime energy circuits for the body. There was thought to exist a deep inner circuitry connected in some way to the inner organs and body systems and a shallow subsurface circuitry connected to the acupuncture points. It was felt to be essential for the health and well-being of the body that there be sufficient energy in these circuits and that they all be balanced with respect to each other—that is, that there be an equalization of energy between the various meridians of the overall system. The energy flowing in the circuits was thought to be a fluid called "chi" ("qi" and "ki" are variant spellings). The function of the acupuncture stimulation was primarily to take energy out of one limb of a circuit and put it into another. By shifting these energies around, one obtained a balanced system with continuously flowing energy.

Disease was thought to arise as a result of any major imbalance in what one might naively think of as an irrigation principle. Thus, if there was not enough energy flowing in one meridian, the body systems associated with that circuit had an altered energy terrain, and the environmental energy fields were such that the soil became more favorable as a nutrient for bacteria to grow and thrive. This altered energy condition led inevitably to manifestations of disease at the physical level.

In more recent times, we have become aware of the rather remarkable application of acupuncture to anesthesia and perhaps the even more re-

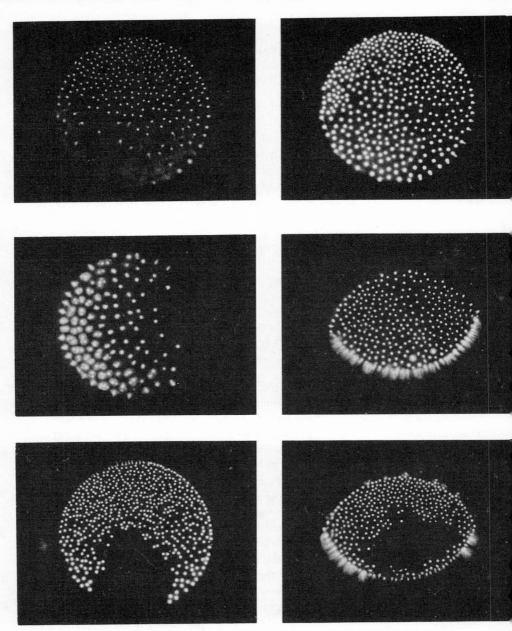

Figure 21. Photographs of single-pulse discharge between flat, polished brass electrodes under conditions of different pulse exposure, electrode spacing, and orientation (4×). (a) Pulse width = 100 μsec. (b) Pulse width = 500 μsec. (c) Pulse width = 500 μsec; nonparallel d, slight increase in discharge spacing d. (d) Pulse width = 500 μsec; electrode areas nonconcentric. (e) Pulse width = 500 μsec; local film buckling. (f) Pulse width = 500 μsec; local film buckling for nonconcentric areas.

markable observation that the patient can even eat food while undergoing a major operation. This latter seems to be in gross violation of presently accepted ideas of necessary sterilization conditions in an operating room. Because of the Western focus on applications to anesthesia, models of structure and functioning of the meridian system have begun to localize around equation with the nervous system. However, it has also been postulated that this meridian system of the body is a fourth circulatory

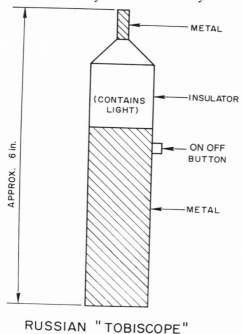

RUSSIAN "TOBISCOPE"
(1971)
Figure 22.   Schematic drawing of Adamenko tobiscope.

system of the physical body distinct from, and on a level equal with, the blood, the lymph, and the nerve systems. We should keep our minds open to this larger possibility rather than relegating all the emerging data to the more limited model of another behavior characteristic of the nervous system.

Using a special resistance-measuring device, the tobiscope (3), the Soviets have located a network of low-resistance points on the surface of the body which is in 1:1 correspondence with the acupuncture points on the Chinese charts. The device, illustrated in Figure 22, consists internally of a bridge circuit so arranged as to be balanced by the normal skin resistance and unbalanced when making contact with an acupuncture point. The electrical signal due to the imbalance is applied to a DC amplifier, which boosts the signal so as to activate a light bulb located in the front portion of the device (in other devices, the signal activates an audio speaker). This device is held in one hand (making contact with the metallic base) and the point is applied to the skin of the subject, while the other hand of the operator is in contact with a different portion of the patient's skin. Thus, an electrical circuit is made from the base of the tobiscope, through the body of the operator, along the body of the subject to the tip of the tobiscope, and, via internal connections, to the base of the device. Moving the point over the skin with light pressure, one can locate a network of points that cause the light to be activated in the device. A shift of the tip by about 1 mm removes the tip from these special points, which locate the low-resistance paths through the body. One also finds a network of such points in plants and animals.

The Adamenko (3) device operates on less than 1 μA at 4 V, with the 3-transistor DC amplifier being very stable over the range of 1.3–3.5 V. The input resistance is about 4–5 $\times$ 10^6 Ω, and the device needs dry skin to be effective in locating the acupuncture network points (wet, salty skin leads to surface shunt paths). Adamenko finds that a resistance of about 5 $\times$ 10^4 Ω exists between these network points and that the value increases by a factor of 2–3 during sleep. Over the same length of normal skin between two network points, the equivalent resistance is ~ 10^6 Ω. At present, the Soviets are investigating an AC device and are finding interesting results in the region of 10^3 Hz. Interestingly enough, this author finds the resistance ratio between normal skin and acupuncture points to also be 10:1; however, the value of the resistance is larger by a factor of about 5.

The DC resistance between any two acupuncture points on the body differs by less than a factor of 2, suggesting that almost all of the resistance is embodied in the thin layer of epidermis. A similar range of resistance variation occurs because of emotional change, mental concentration, light stimulus, and the like. In the case of emotional excitation, the points vary in diameter (as revealed by conductivity area) and there is the possibility of the areas overlapping one another to form high-conductivity regions.

An alternate circuit, for point location, is given by Devine (9, p. 117). Its major disadvantage is that it draws too much current and produces some polarization effects. A circuit that avoids this difficulty and also produces an audio signal is presented in Figure 23 (21). In this case, less than 1 μA of current is utilized and the frequency of the sound increases as the conductivity of the area increases.

Adamenko (3) has investigated the relationship between the conductivity of the network points and certain states of hypnosis of the patient. His results are given in Figure 24, in which the different states of conscious-

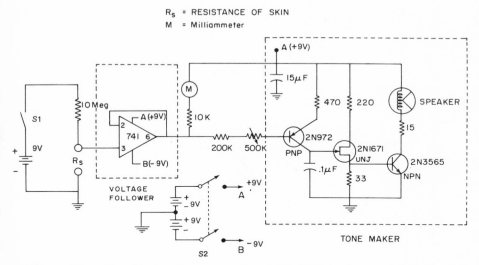

Figure 23. Circuit diagram for an audio-signal acupuncture-point locator.

ness are listed along the abscissa as (a) ordinary working state, (b) sleep with eyes closed, (c) sleep with eyes open, (d) suggestion of hallucinations, (e) "artificial reincarnation" (a particular hypnotic condition), and (f) work in the reincarnation state. The four graphs show variations in four groups of subjects ranging from control group A (those not hypnotizable) through B, C, and D in increasing order of hypnotizability. As seen from the graphs, there exists a certain relationship between the patient's hypnotizability and the character of the conductivity variations. In the control group, no conductivity variation has been recorded that indicates the absence of emotional reactions to the hypnotist's words. However, in the case of ordinary emotional states, these patients exhibit conductivity variations.

Adamenko has also discovered that a voltage signal can be detected between two network points if two different types of metals are used as electrodes. On dry skin using plated circular electrodes (5–7 mm in diameter), a nickel–silver combination yielded a potential difference of about 50 mV. At skin locations where such points are absent, the potential difference is close to zero. Likewise, using the same electrode material —say, nickel–nickel or silver–silver—the potential difference is again close to zero. The greater the work function difference between the two materials, the greater is the voltage developed. This suggests that we have a galvanic-cell effect operating here. The current drawn from this battery is about 10 μA. However, because this current level polarizes the elec-

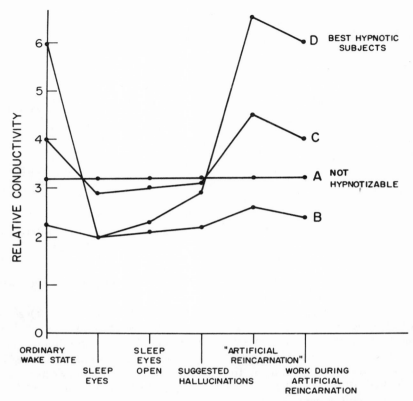

TOBISCOPIC INDICATIONS VS. HYPNOTIZATION

Figure 24.   Relative conductivity indications versus
hypnotic state of the subject.

trodes, one is advised to use an impedance in the measuring circuit to reduce the current to levels below 2 μA and then to amplify the signal for display purposes. In cases of emotional, volitive excitation, the potential difference may increase up to 100 mV. Further, using parallel connections between several network points, the voltage obtained may be as high as 0.5–1.0 V with a corresponding increase in saturation current.

The Soviets find that as the electrode area increases, the developed voltage increases. They also find that the amplitude of an AC pulse is diminished as the electrode area increases, which probably represents an averaging phenomenon wherein the AC signal arises only at the acupuncture point (less than 1 mm in diameter) in the central region of the electrode.

Adamenko performed an interesting healing experiment utilizing what the Soviets call the "semiconductor effect." When measuring the resistance between symmetrical points on the left and right sides of the body, one often finds that the resistance is different in the forward (R) from that in the reverse (R') direction (just like a semiconductor material that contains p–n junctions). If the person is healthy relative to that meridian or particular organ in that meridian, then the resistances will be the same ($R = R'$). However, if the person is ill relative to that organ or relative to an organ associated with that meridian, then one will find a difference in resistance ($R \neq R'$). This difference, ΔR, is called the semiconductor effect.

In the healing experiment Adamenko (1) used a manual healer who projected energy via his hands located a short distance from the patient. The semiconductor effect was measured on both the patient and the healer before the experiment and also after the experiment. The data given in Figure 25 was obtained. We can suspect that some energy was transferred from the healer to the patient because the value of ΔR had decreased for the patient. However, we note that the healer's circuits have become somewhat unbalanced in the process (temporarily). This suggests that the healer gave up a particular kind of energy in a particular location of his body in order to bring into closer balance the circuitry of the ill individual. *This appears to be a new type of energy that we have heretofore been unable to monitor in any numerical or objective way.* The author has tried a similar experiment with a patient and healer while monitoring the acupuncture points and found similar results except that there was only a small change in the healer, and ΔR for the patient changed over a period of a week after treatment eventually decreasing to zero. During this time period, both R and R' increased by a factor of 2.

It has been noticed that when a serious imbalance exists in the meridian circuitry and a needle is placed into the appropriate point, a force (almost like a suction force) holds the needle in the point, so that if one tries to withdraw it, the skin pulls up around the needle and it is not easily withdrawn. After the needle has remained in the point for a sufficient length of time to have brought about a temporary balance to the circuits, the needle may be withdrawn with no effort and the skin no longer pulls up around the needle. This suction force seems to be proportional to the degree of imbalance (i.e., to ΔR).

There are, at present, several ways in which one can produce point stimulation, and it appears that to bring about balance to the circuits, all one needs to do is stimulate the acupuncture points sufficiently. In increasing order of effectiveness, the various techniques are (a) chemical stimulation, (b) manual massage, (c) acupuncture needles, (d) electrical energy injection (requires sophisticated understanding), (e) laser beam

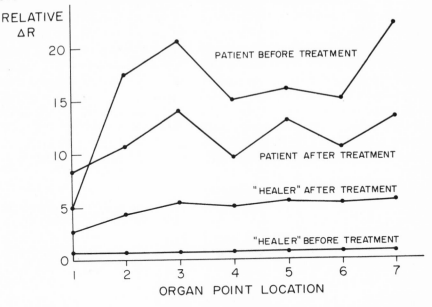

Figure 25.   Representation of the semiconductor effect observed
in paranormal healing.

(requires sophisticated equipment and understanding), and (*f*) an injection of "spiritual" energy from a psychic healer. This latter seems to be the best procedure for bringing about bodily balance (the energy does not need to be directed at a specific point or set of points). Using the laser-beam method, the Russians have found that when a mild-intensity laser beam is directed at the acupuncture point above the upper lip, it will immediately stop an epileptic seizure. Considerable possibility exists for the use of point monitoring in a biofeedback mode so that a patient can learn to stimulate various energy centers of his body or to control the development of pain.

A GENERALIZED MODEL OF SUBSTANCE

In order to make progress in the design of suitable sensing devices, we need a starting model. First, we should be clear about what is meant by a model. A model can be thought of as a working hypothesis. It is a conceptual framework from which we can start to try to understand some aspects of nature. It is a target at which we can start throwing experiments. In the beginning, it is the first discrimination of ideas within some format or structure that gives one a feeling he is starting to grapple meaningfully with the particular unknown area under consideration. As one begins to model the phenomenon, one is able to formulate the right kind of experiments for testing a hypothesis and then can perform the experiments and obtain feedback of new and pertinent information. This allows one to check out whether a particular aspect of the model is correct and to make corrective changes throughout the model as need requires. However, to do this, one must have a place to start. Thus, models are like the rungs of a ladder with which one climbs from one level of understanding to another. *All models are incorrect at some level of detail.* Their purpose is to present an idea that stimulates the thinking function—to move one into a new train of thought. They serve the tremendous function of allowing one to climb from one position of understanding of the universe to a more enlightened position of understanding.

Many phenomena seem to arise in the area of psychoenergetics that are not readily explicable in terms of electromagnetic or other familiar energies. This has caused the author to hypothesize a fundamental model of substance that leads to a variety of new forces and radiations capable of accounting for different psychoenergetic phenomena (24). It is postulated, following the yoga philosophies concerning the seven principles operating in man, that the human body is constituted of seven different types of substances that obey seven unique sets of natural laws and, based on the polarity principle, form atomic and other states of combination at each level of substance. From these different levels of substance, different types of radiations emanate. With this model we see in operation the metaphysical principle "as above, so below, as within, so without."

The seven substances, in an ascending scale of fineness and energy content, are the physical, the etheric (or the bioplasmic, as the Russians term it), the astral, the intuitive mind (M_1), the intellectual mind (M_2), the spiritual mind (M_3), and the spirit. There is probably nothing particularly important about this choice of names; it just happens to be that given in yogic philosophy. These substances are presumed to exist everywhere in nature and to interpenetrate within the human body—that is, they all exist within the energy construct of the physical atom and organize themselves in different macroscopic patterns within the body (but not in the same space–time frame as the physical). (As an analogy, think of seven transparent sheets containing seven different circuit patterns each in a different color. Put them together and you have the complete organization of the different levels of substance in the body.)

Although the different energy fields perturb each other normally in only a small way, they can be influenced to do so in a strong way by the agency of mind. It is presumed that waves of one type of mind field can be uniquely correlated so as to cause strong correlation, and thus energy transfer, with waves of a different level of substance. This means that a coherent mental image—for example, one concerning a physical change in the body—creates a coherent potential distribution in the etheric dimension that manifests ultimately as a coherent change in the energy patterns of certain spatial locations of the etheric body. This serves as a coherent potential distribution applied to the physical level that eventually causes specific changes in the energy patterns and atomic reorganization of the physical level of substance. We see here a characteristic pattern of cause-and-effect steps that I shall call the *ratchet effect*.

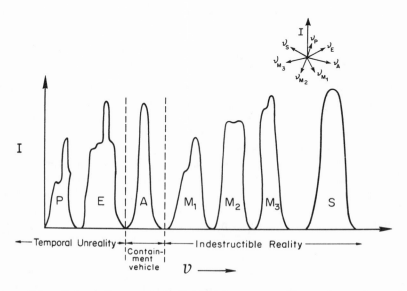

Figure 26.   Schematic spectral distribution curve illustrating, along one coordinate,   relative   radiation   characteristics   of   the   seven   postulated levels of substance.

This ratchet effect is a sequential mapping procedure (like mapping mathematical functions from the real to the complex plane and vice versa) via the following steps: (a) mind image generation to (b) etheric potential distribution to (c) reorganization of etheric substance to be in harmony with this potential distribution requiring time τ_E to (d) physical potential distribution changes during the reorganization of etheric substance so that a force exists for the reorganization of substance at that spatial location of the physical level. This reorganization on the physical level requires a time τ_P.

In Figure 26 a schematic diagram of possible spectral distribution curves (intensity versus frequency) is given for these different levels of substance. They should really be plotted on individual axes, as indicated on the insert, since we are discussing different kinds of radiations for each level of substance (and there may be more than one major type of radiation from a given level of substance). However, for pedagogical purposes, there is value in having them represented on one axis. It is from this diagram that we may see the basic radiation components that comprise the human aura.

Here, the first two levels deal with the temporal reality of physical man, and the fundamental waves of substance are characterized by a space–time frame of reference. However, the space–time frame for the etheric level is complementary to, but different from, the space–time frame for the physical level with which Einstein's name is so strongly associated. The third level, which is the structure of emotion, is primarily a containment vehicle for the indestructible reality of continuing man and, as such, is an envelope for holding the upper four levels of substance of an entity together between incarnations. The wave functions of the mind and spirit levels of substance are characterized by a frame of reference dealing with potential coordinates rather than space–time coordinates. In fact, it is proposed that space and time are properties of the mind and spirit waves, just as mass and charge are properties of electromagnetic waves in the space–time frame.

In the case of the physical dimension, we have the positive space–time frame or the Einsteinian frame with which we are fairly familiar. The etheric dimension is the conjugate-physical dimension and can be described as a negative space–time frame. These two are complementary frames; that is, as time goes on, for the physical, the potential decreases and entropy increases, whereas for the etheric, we have the reverse situation (the potential increases and entropy decreases). A characteristic of the physical frame is one of disorder. A characteristic of the etheric frame is one of order or the organization of substance. The physical is primarily characterized by electric effects. The etheric is primarily characterized by magnetic effects. In the physical, the arrow of time is in what we define as the positive direction; in the etheric, the arrow of time is in the reverse, or negative, direction. In the physical, both mass and energy are positive and the maximum signal velocity is the velocity of light. In the conjugate physical, both mass and energy must be considered to be negative and the minimum signal velocity is the velocity of light. Thus, that energy corresponding to mass moving at the velocity of light is a singular point on the energy scale wherein energies diverge to $\pm \infty$ on either side of the singular point. Rather than acting as an impenetrable barrier for substance at energies on either side of this point, it probably behaves like other mathematical singularities appearing in our description of nature—that is, tunneling is possible from one side to the other. This leads one to speculate on whether we have here the explanation for the "black holes" in space. As a final speculation, since conventional physics neglects the existence of energies beyond the physical, and the interaction of fundamental particles with same, we may ask if this is why we are chained to the use of an "uncertainty principle" and a statistical mode of description.

These factors and others will have to be taken into account in the designing of future devices for sensing nonphysical energies.

REFERENCES

1. Adamenko, V. G. *Journal of Paraphysics*, 4 (1970).
2. Adamenko, V. G. "Electrodynamics of Living Systems."
3. Adamenko, V. G. Private communication.
4. Backster, C. "Evidence of Primary Perception in Plant Life." *International Journal of Parapsychology*, 10:4 (1968).
5. Bandel, H. W. "Point-To-Plane Corona in Dry Air." *Physics Review*, 84 (1951).
6. Boyers, D., and Tiller, W. A. "On Corona Discharge Photography." *Journal of Applied Physics* (July 1973).
7. Brillouin, L. *Scientific Uncertainty, and Information.* Academic: New York, 1964.
8. Dawson, G. A., and Winn, W. P. "A Model for Streamer Propagation." *Zeitschrift für Physik*, 183 (1965).
9. Devine, R. E. *Electronic Experimenters Handbook.* Sporn: 1970.
10. Eemans, L. E. *Cooperative Healing.* Muller: London, 1947.
11. Gallert, M. *New Light on Therapeutic Energies.* Clarke: London, 1966.
12. Kirlian, S. Russian Patent No. 164906, 1963.
13. Loeb, L. B. *Electrical Coronas—Their Basic Physical Mechanisms.* University of California Press: Berkeley, 1965.
14. Milner, D. R., and Smart, E. F. "There Are More Things" (unpublished).
15. Monteith, H. C. Private communication, 1972.
16. Moss, T., and Johnson, K. "Bioplasma or Corona Discharge?" In Stanley Krippner and Daniel Rubin, eds., *Galaxies of Life.* Gordon and Breach: New York, 1973.
17. Nasser, E., and Loeb, L. B. "Impure Streamer Characteristics from Lichtenberg Figure Studies." *Journal of Applied Physics*, 34 (1963).
18. Ostrander, S., and Schroeder, L. *Psychic Discoveries Behind the Iron Curtain.* Prentice-Hall: Englewood Cliffs, N.J., 1970.
19. Puharich, A. Private communication.
20. Rock, I. *The Nature of Perceptual Adaption.* Basic Books: New York, 1967.
21. Royer, J. Private communication, May 1972.
22. Targ, R., and Hurt, D. "Learning Clairvoyance and Precognition with an Extra-Sensory Perception Teaching Machine." Institute of Electrical Engineering and Education Symposium on Information Theory, January 1972.
23. Sergeyev, G. A. "The Piezoelectric Detector of Bioplasma." *Journal of Paraphysics*, 6 (1972).
24. Tiller, W. A. "Radionics, Radiesthesia and Physics." *The Varieties of Healing Experience.* Academy of Parapsychology and Medicine: Los Altos, Calif. 1972.

25. Tiller, W. A. "Energy Fields and the Human Body, Part II." Paper delivered at the ARE Medical Symposium on Mind–Body Relationships in the Disease Process, Phoenix, Ariz., 1972.
26. Tiller, W. A. "Some Psychoenergetic Devices." *ARE Journal*, 7 (1972).
27. Tiller, W. A. "The Light Source in High-Voltage Photography," Proceedings of the Second Western Hemisphere Conference on Kirlian Photography, Acupuncture and the Human Aura, New York, February 1973.

Harold E. Puthoff
Russell Targ

HAROLD E. PUTHOFF, *Ph.D., is a senior research engineer at Stanford Research Institute. He joined the institute in 1971 as a specialist in laser physics, after working in research for eight years in the Microwave Laboratory at Stanford University.*

Dr. Puthoff holds bachelor's and master's degrees in electrical engineering from the University of Florida and in 1967 was awarded a Ph.D. from Stanford University. From 1960 to 1963 he served as an officer in the U.S. Navy at Fort Meade, Maryland, in a research capacity. He held the post of lecturer at Stanford University from 1969 to 1970.

Dr. Puthoff holds patents in the area of lasers and optical devices and has supervised research for doctoral candidates in electrical engineering and applied physics at Stanford University. In addition, he has initiated programs to study psychic phenomena from the standpoint of modern physics.

His publications include Fundamentals of Quantum Electronics, *as co-author with R. H. Pantell (John Wiley, 1969), a text bridging quantum mechanics with engineering and applied physics. He is also on the editorial advisory board of* Journal for the Study of Consciousness.

Dr. Puthoff can be reached at Stanford Research Institute, Menlo Park, Calif. 94025.

RUSSELL TARG *is a senior research physicist at Stanford Research Institute, having joined their electronics and bioengineering laboratory in 1972. Prior to that, he spent 10 years in laser and plasma physics research with Sylvania Corporation, developing gas lasers.*

Mr. Targ earned his bachelor's degree in physics at Queens College in 1954 and spent the next two years in graduate work in physics at Columbia University. During that time he taught physics as a research assistant. In 1959 he held the post of research associate at Polytechnic Institute of Brooklyn.

He is author of more than two dozen articles on lasers, plasma physics, and psychic research. He is also the inventor of the tunable plasma oscillator at microwave frequencies, the FM laser, and the high-power gas-

transport laser. With another inventor, he devised the ESP Teaching Machine, for training people in clairvoyance and precognition. He is also president of the Parapsychology Research Group, Inc., in Palo Alto, California.

Mr. Targ can be reached at Stanford Research Institute, Menlo Park, Calif. 94025.

22 Psychic Research and Modern Physics

HAROLD PUTHOFF and RUSSELL TARG

SUMMARY

This chapter describes the application of concepts of modern physics to the study of psychic functioning. Included are a discussion of an example of a theoretical model of precognition that is testable and is compatible with contemporary physics, and descriptions of recent experiments using instruments that have exceptional sensitivity.

Experiments are described in which (a) *a subject was able to control the electrical output of a well-shielded superconducting magnetometer,* (b) *a subject was able to deflect systematically a low-energy electron beam, and* (c) *a subject demonstrated an ability to enhance ESP functioning by the use of an automatic random generator that provided feedback and reinforcement.*

The primary aim of the chapter is to show that it is possible to construct and test hypotheses available in the frontier areas of physics as an approach to the explanation of parapsychological phenomena often thought to be incompatible with modern physics. Thus, this chapter presents an example of a physicist's approach to the problem involving the setting up of an hypothesis, and the design of an experiment toward the goal of comparison of theory and result.

INTRODUCTION

Throughout mankind's history there has existed a folklore that certain gifted individuals have been capable of producing physical effects by means of some agency generally referred to as psychic or psychoenergetic. Substantiation of such claims by accepted scientific methodology has been slow in coming, but recent laboratory experiments, especially in the Soviet Union and Czechoslovakia, and more recently in our own laboratory, have indicated that sufficient evidence does exist to warrant serious scientific investigation. From the evidence it would appear that experiments can be conducted with sufficient scientific rigor to uncover not just a catalog of interesting events but rather a pattern of cause–effect relationships of the type that lend themselves to analysis and hypothesis in the forms with which we are familiar in the physical sciences.

At the present time there is a very substantial literature describing carefully conducted experiments to demonstrate the existence of extraordinary human functioning. This includes both the perception of information not presented to any known sense and human influence exerted on physical systems without use of any known physical means. Many of these experiments have been examined, criticized, and verified by statisticians, biologists, and psychologists. We consider it important to examine various models describing the operation of these effects so that we can determine the relationship between extraordinary human functioning and the physical and psychological laws we presently understand. It is not the purpose of this chapter to add to the literature another demonstration of the statistical appearance of these phenomena in the laboratory. Instead, we are using techniques of feedback and reinforcement to train subjects to increase their ability so that it will be sufficiently reliable to allow us to achieve an understanding of the phenomenon, to make it more compatible with contemporary science, and ultimately more useful to mankind.

In this chapter we describe some of the new physical models and some of the new types of apparatus we have been using to achieve these goals.

PRECOGNITION AND PHYSICS

Psychic research studies three specific forms of so-called ESP. These are telepathy or mind-to-mind communication; clairvoyance, the perception of an event hidden from the ordinary senses; and precognition, the perception of a future event that could not be known through rational inference. Of these three phenomena, we believe that contemporary physics will find the least trouble in assimilating precognition. In order to understand this, one may want to reflect on the idea that "causality" is a fact observed in our lives or in the laboratory and not a law of the universe. The present concern of physics with the possibility of information from the future leaking into the present is set forth by Gal-Or (4):

> An old crisis in science is receiving renewed attention. . . . This crisis manifests itself most clearly when attempts are made to provide answers to such fundamental questions as: Is the origin of [time] irreversibility . . . local or cosmological? Is it in the laws or in the

boundary conditions? What might be the physical inter-relationships underlying the expansion of the universe, information theory, and the electromagnetic, biological and statistical arrows of time? What is the basic nature of the somewhat mysterious time coordinate system in which the very physical laws are embedded?

We agree with the author's conclusion that irreversibility appears to be more "factlike" than "lawlike." This says that although information usually propagates from the present to the future, we should not be shaken to our foundation if experiments are devised that show that sometimes information is found to be transmitted in the other direction. Indeed, it is the symmetry in the solutions to many physical equations that suggests the model presented here provides a working description of precognition. This model will be described, and some experiments to test its validity will be proposed.

We also will show that precognition is a natural phenomenon—not something invented in the laboratory. Precognition and its cousin, prophecy, have a long history of occurrence, well documented in spontaneously occurring recent cases collected by Louisa Rhine (9) and in laboratory experiments by Soal and Bateman (13).

The reason we believe physics will find precognition the easiest of psi to describe lies in this fact: in physics, everything that is *not* forbidden occurs. And, as we have suggested earlier, physics does not forbid the transmission of information from the future to the present. The difficulty that one has in dealing with this problem is more linguistic than physical.

The hypothesis presented here is that significant events create a perturbation in the space–time in which they occur, and this disturbance propagates forward and, to some small degree, backward in time.* Since precognitive phenomena are very rare, this disturbance must die out quite rapidly in the $-t$ direction. The wave traveling in the $+t$ direction is associated with causality as usually experienced.

Consider a coordinate system $-t$ to $+t$ perpendicular to the axis $-x$ to $+x$. Such a system is often used to describe the temporal character of events, where x is the spatial coordinate and t is the time axis. If these axes are superimposed on a pond of water, with the origin $(0,0)$ at here-and-now, future events will be at $+t$ and past events will be at $-t$, as shown in Figure 1. If this system is perturbed at the origin, a large effect will, of course, be created in the neighborhood of the perturbation. In other words, a rock thrown into the pond at $(0,0)$ will give rise to ripples that will be discernible at some small distance $+t$ to $-t$ and $+x$ to $-x$.

---

* This description was first proposed by Russell Targ in a paper "Precognition in Everyday Life: A Physical Model" read to the Fifteenth Annual Convention of the Parapsychological Association in Edinburgh, September 3–5, 1972.

Now if the pond is filled with a material that is more viscous than water, the ripples may be very small indeed. However, it is unreasonable within the framework of this model to imagine a medium so viscous that a point perturbation at the origin would have zero effect at some small $\pm t$. We are postulating that physical events are not delta-functions (instantaneous occurrences) in space and time. Moreover, if one is sufficiently close to an event, even though on the $-t$ side, there is no physical contradiction to its

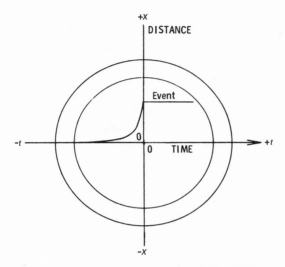

SPACE - TIME DIAGRAM SHOWING A PRECURSOR WAVE IN -t
BEFORE AN EVENT.

Figure 1.   Space–time diagram showing a precursor wave
in $-t$ before an event.

being perceived. The accuracy of the precognitive perception predicted from this model will increase with the "magnitude" of the event for the perceiver, and it will fall off with increasing temporal distance from the event.

From this model, which we recognize does not yet deserve to be called a theory, one would predict that the most common events to be perceived by precognition would be events occurring extremely close in time to the perception of them. Also, if one is going to perceive something before it happens, it should be an event of sufficient magnitude to catch one's attention—the larger, the better.

An example of such an event is the ringing of an alarm clock to awaken someone. It is a common occurrence for a person to awaken and look with surprise at his alarm clock, only to hear it click and then go off. We believe that one is awakened by the incipient occurrence of this large, timely, and unpleasant event.

We are aware that sleepers have a surprisingly good time sense when trained or motivated to do so. The most recent data of Tart (17) show that a person can awaken himself within 5 or 10 minutes of a desired time. However, the familiar occurrence is one in which a person awakens seconds before the alarm rings. We think this is an event of a different type.

A second event of this type is incorporating an alarm clock ringing into a dream. It is not unusual for some people to have a long and complicated dream terminated by the appropriately timed blowing of a bugle or ringing of an alarm clock that fits utterly into the continuity of the dream. Since we know that dreams happen in approximately real time (6), it is not the case that the dream is triggered by the alarm and then occurs in the fraction of a second between the onset of the alarm and one's awakening. We would again argue that this is an example of a dream being initiated by the incipient occurrence of an unpleasant event that is to take place in the very near future.

Advanced Potential Model

We want to introduce part of the physical basis for this model by making an analogy from the early days of the development of quantum theory.

In the early 1920s, when P. A. M. Dirac was developing his mathematical description of the relativisitic electron, his equations yielded a pair of solutions. This is usually the case with the homogeneous differential equations encountered in this type of problem. One of the solutions described a negatively charged particle with unit mass that was clearly the electron. However, a second solution gave a particle with positive charge and unit mass. This could not be a proton since the mass was wrong. So this solution was discarded as inapplicable. In 1932 C. D. Anderson discovered the positron in cloud-chamber experiments, and Dirac's discarded solution became applicable.

In our case we are concerned with the perception of an event occurring at a time in our future. A set of equations that might be used to describe this situation is that for the field at a distance r from a moving charge (corresponding to the perception, at a distance r and a time t, of an event). These equations also give two real solutions, one of which is conventionally discarded as not corresponding to any observable physical event.

Stratton (14) describes the choice of solutions for the moving-charge equations:

The reader has doubtless noted that the choice of the function (t + r/v) is highly arbitrary, since the field equation admits also a solution ($t - r/v$). This function leads obviously to an advanced time, implying that the field can be observed before it has been generated by the source. The familiar chain of cause and effect is thus reversed and this alternative solution might be discarded as logically inconceivable. However, the application of "logical" causality principles offers very insecure footing in matters such as these and we shall do better to restrict the theory to retarded action solely on the grounds that this solution alone conforms to the present physical data.

This seems to be an entirely appropriate course of action, and we therefore propose that there does exist some physical data that can make good use of the advanced-time or advanced-potential solution.

This model predicts the following general chain of events. One moves steadily along the time axis at the usual rate of one second per second, from $-t$ toward the origin where an event is about to occur. As one encounters the tail of an incipient event from the left, as shown in Figure 1, one is increasingly likely to perceive the event, until one finally reaches the origin and the event occurs. In terms of the advanced-potential model, an observer at $-t$ will be encountered by a wave of interference pattern caused by waves converging on the origin from the left (large values of $-t$). When these waves encounter the observer, he will perceive the event. Subjectively, he will believe he is remembering it. He will continue to do so until the packet of waves has passed him, at which point he will subjectively forget the event. The event will then happen, making the observer believe he had seen it all before, which indeed he had. We would therefore argue that the familiar déjà vu phenomenon is the most common form of precognition.

If the observer is to perceive the event a few seconds before it occurs, it is necessary that the information carried by these proposed precursor waves be propagated at a velocity less than c, the velocity of light. Since the waves themselves may travel at c, we assume that the information is carried as a traveling-wave interferogram or time-varying hologram. That is, the information propagates at the velocity of the interference pattern in the wake of the passing waves, rather than at the velocity of the waves themselves. The group velocity of this signal would, in this case, be slower than the phase velocity, c. This allows an extended interaction time that is more or less independent of the spatial distance between the observer and the event.

Verification of the Model

In order for a model such as that proposed here to be worth considering, it must be quantitatively testable. In the following we will describe the experiments that will be performed to determine the correctness of certain aspects of this model.

The most easily testable part of the hypothesis is the idea that the accuracy of precognition decreases with temporal distance from the event. It is important to note that this falloff is allowed but not required by the advanced-potential model. It is proposed as the most reasonable of the various choices.

We have already performed clairvoyance and precognition experiments with an ESP-teaching machine (15), whose purpose was the enhancement of ESP ability, which we assume to be latent to some extent in all people (16).* The enhancement is accomplished by allowing the user of the machine to become aware of his own mental state at those times when he is most successfully employing his extrasensory faculties. Only with increased reliability of ESP ability can we find the functional relationship between ESP and more familiar physical and psychoolgical variables— the psychic personality (see Chapter 3).

The teaching machine we used randomly selects one of four targets on each trial. These targets are chosen by the machine and are not presented to the subject until he has indicated to the machine what he believes the target to be. The targets are 35-millimeter color transparencies of San Francisco. The subject's task is to select the one the machine has chosen by means of its random-target generator.

An important feature of the machine is that the choice of a target is not mandatory. That is, the subject may press a *Pass* button on the machine when he wishes not to guess. Thus, with practice the subject can learn to recognize those states of mind in which he can correctly choose the target. He does not have to guess at targets when he does not feel that he "knows" which to choose.

When the *Pass* button is pushed, the machine indicates what its choice was and neither a hit nor a trial is scored by the machine, which then goes on to make its next selection. We consider this elimination of forced choice to be a significant condition for learning ESP.

When the user of the machine indicates his choice to the machine, he is immediately and automatically informed of the correct answer. The machine described here is being used in this instance to enhance clairvoyant perception in which experimenter and the subject both remain ignorant of the machine's state until the subject has made his choice.

---

* This machine is now commercially available from Aquarius Electronics, P.O. Box 627, Mendocino, Calif. 95460. *Editor*

Because the user obtains immediate information feedback about the correct answer, he may be able to recognize his mental state at those times when he has made a correct response. If the information feedback to the user were not immediate, we believe as much learning would not take place, and less or no enhancement would be achieved. The machine in this work is shown in Figure 2.

Figure 2.   ESP-teaching machine used in this experiment, with two of the four "encouragement lights" illuminated.

The machine has the following general properties. It generates random targets automatically and rapidly with the rate determined by the user. It automatically records and scores both the user's responses and the targets generated, and it displays for the user the current number of trials and hits. The all-solid-state machine has no moving parts and provides no sensory cue to the user about its internal state. Its randomness has also been carefully investigated.* The machine has 4 stable internal states (block diagram of the machine is shown in Figure 3). The 1.0-megahertz square-wave oscillator sends pulses to an electronic counter that counts from 1 to 4. On the fifth pulse, the counter returns to 1. This is called a "scale-of-4 counter." The machine therefore passes through each of its 4

---

* The distribution of targets with regard to singles, consecutive doubles, consecutive triples and sequential runs was analyzed for 2400 trials and was found to lie within one standard deviation of the expected value.

states at a rate of 250,000 times per second. The state in which the scale-of-4 counter resides is determined by the length of time the 1-megahertz oscillator runs. Once the machine is in a fixed state (not scaling), the user indicates his choice of which state he thinks the machine is in by pressing a button on the machine under the color slide of his choice. The correct slide will then be illuminated. The correct answer for the next choice is determined by the length of time the choice button was depressed in making the selection. There is no way for the user to control the final state of the machine because his reaction time is 4 orders of magnitude too slow for this and because the scaling rate is 250 kilohertz. In addition to the reward of having pushed the button under the slide that lights, a bell rings to indicate that a correct choice was made, and 4 lights carrying messages of encouragement are lit sequentially as the subject obtains 8, 10, 12, and 14 hits.

In the course of this work we have encountered three general classes of subjects. The majority of the 12 subjects working with the machine in this study did not show any significant improvement in their ESP ability. The subjects in this study were not prescreened but were chosen from the community at large on the basis of their interest in the investigation. They ranged in age from 8 to 35, with the younger subjects achieving higher scores but not necessarily greater learning. Three of the subjects gave indirect evidence of increased ESP by guessing at targets in a manner to cause their score distribution to become bimodal. Whereas chance scores should give a skewed binomial distribution with the probability of a hit at each trial equal to $\frac{1}{4}$, we observed that several subjects showed an increasing deviation from this distribution; that is, they generated a disproportionate number of high and low hits per run of 24. This variance of scoring patterns has been noted in the ESP literature (11). Among these subjects a particularly high score such as 12 out of 24 is often followed by a particularly low score such as 2 out of 24. We interpret this variance pattern as an indication of ESP, although it is not an effect that we set out to cultivate.

In the group indicating some improvement, one subject has shown an exceptional increase in ESP scores through more than 1600 trials. This subject has apparently learned to perceive the state of the machine clairvoyantly, to an extent providing a significant deviation from chance expectation. The hypothesis that this might be a PK effect will be the subject of a future investigation.

The protocol for the experiment was for the subject to make 4 runs of 24 trials. This was followed by a rest period and 4 more runs of 24.

The most successful subject in this experiment eventually reached a scoring level where on three occasions she scored more than 40 hits out of 96 trials in one of these sets of 4 runs, where only 24 hits would be

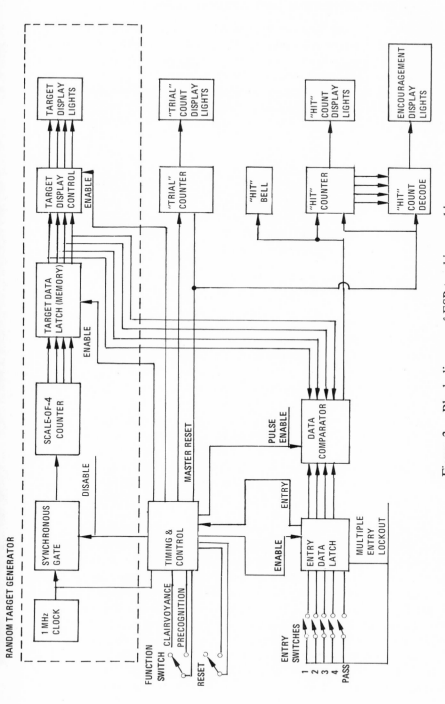

Figure 3. Block diagram of ESP-teaching machine.

expected. From the null hypothesis (no ESP), the probability of 40 or more hits out of 96 trials is less than 10^{-3}. This subject made a total of 64 runs of 24 trials with a mean score of 8.6 hits per run. The probability of this result occurring by chance alone is approximately 10^{-15}.

On the basis of the outcome of this work, we sought to determine if other phenomena in the ESP realm could be similarly enhanced. The machine was altered so that the target was not chosen by the machine

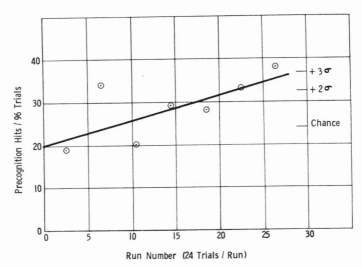

Figure 4.   Precognition experiment showing number of hits per run of 96 trials versus average trial number. Linear regression analysis of the data is also shown. 672 trials, $p < 0.005$.

until after the subject indicated his choice. The time delay was approximately 0.2 second, which is to say that subjects were asked to make a perception of an event that was to occur 0.2 second in the future. We chose this short delay time because, as stated earlier, we believe that the accuracy of precognition will be found to vary inversely with the temporal distance separating the perceiver from the event.

The subject, graduated to the precognitive experiment, reported at the beginning of her first run that "I don't feel anything anymore" about which picture would light and moreover that she was "just guessing." This was borne out in her early scores in the precognition experiment. However, in the course of 672 trials, her performance increased to a level approaching her scores in the clairvoyant test. For example, she obtained 19 hits out of her first 96 trials and 38 hits out of her last 96 trials. The results of the 28 precognitive runs of 24 trials each were subjected to a linear regression analysis and are plotted in blocks of 96, corresponding to experimental protocol. The grouped data for all precognitive trials are shown in Figure 4. A line drawn through these points has a positive slope of 2.24 hits per run of 96 trials. The correlation coefficient is 0.51, using the data from the 28 runs separately. This gives a probability of 1 in 200 (8) and is strongly suggestive that learning has taken place.

In order to verify the functional relationships between accuracy of precognition and time delay, it is necessary to alter the machine so that it makes its target selection some variable time Δt after the subject makes his selection. The time interval between the subject's choice of target and its occurrence should be randomly varied. A plot would then be made of precognition hits versus temporal distance in seconds or minutes.

This experiment must be performed using a gifted subject who has already demonstrated significant precognitive ability with this machine. With such a subject, the accuracy of precognition as a function of temporal distance from the event could be determined.

In a nondeterministic universe the probability is unity that an event that we are observing will occur. If we were at the same place but at a slightly earlier time, the most reasonable model would predict that we would have a slightly smaller probability of perceiving the event, because the probability of the event's occurring would be slightly less than unity (since it had not yet happened). Therefore, as we view a future event from ever-increasing temporal distances, we have a decreasing chance of perceiving it accurately. One reason for this must be because the event has a decreasing probability of occurring in a given manner or at all.

PSI AND PHYSICS

Although parapsychological literature exists that indicates some people can produce physical effects such as influencing the trajectory of falling cubes (2, 3, 10), this work has not attracted much attention in the scientific community. This is primarily because the results are of a statistical nature, the absolute magnitude of the forces involved are relatively small, and the work has not been replicated on a large scale by many laboratories.

However, in recent experiments in this country, in our own laboratory and elsewhere, some highly significant observations have been made. Charles Honorton, a research associate of the Division of Parapsychology and Psychophysics at Maimonides Medical Center, reported in a private communication that a subject was able to move large objects under a bell jar. Dr. Karlis Osis and Janet Mitchell of the ASPR reported observations concerning Ingo Swann, a New York artist, who appears capable of describing objects hidden from view in a remote location (1). Further work

with Swann by Gertrude Schmeidler at City College of New York indicated an ability to raise and lower temperatures at thermistors placed
some distance from his body (12).

Based on the success reported with Swann, it was arranged for him to
visit our laboratory at Stanford Research Institute. An experiment with
Swann and an experiment with another subject are described below.

Magnetometer Experiment

This is an anecdotal account of an observation with Swann in which he
attempted to change the magnetic field measured by a well-shielded
magnetometer. We wish to state at the outset that from a scientific point
of view it is important to discriminate between an observation as described here and the controlled experiments we propose to carry out in the
future. Nevertheless, we consider this observation significant.

In order to eliminate the possibility of trickery, it was decided that an
experiment should be performed in which the success of trickery would be
nearly as important as any direct effect that could be produced. Arrangements were made to use a superconductor-shielded magnetometer (5).
This magnetometer is located in a well under a building and is shielded by
μ-metal shielding, an aluminum container, copper shielding, and, most
important, a superconducting niobium shield. In previous tests no signals
have been induced in the shielded magnetometer from the outside. The
magnetometer is of the superconducting quantum interference device
(SQUID) variety, which has an output voltage whose frequency is a
measure of the rate of change of magnetic field present.

Before the experiment, a decaying magnetic field had been set up inside
the magnetometer, and its decay with time provided a background calibration signal that registered as a periodic output on an X–Y recorder, the
frequency of the output corresponding to the decay rate of the calibration
field ($\approx 10^{-6}$ gauss). The system had been running for about an hour with
no noise.

On the spur of the moment, Swann was shown the setup and told that if
he were to affect the magnetic field in the magnetometer, it would show up
as a change in the output recording. Then, to use his own description, he
"placed his attention" on the interior of the magnetometer, at which time
the frequency of the output doubled for about two of the cycles, or
roughly 30 seconds. This is indicated by A in Figure 5. Swann was next
asked if he could stop the field change being indicated by the periodic
output on the recorder. He then apparently proceeded to do just that, as
can be seen at B in the graph, for a period of roughly 45 seconds. He then
"let go," at which time the output returned to normal, as shown at C.

When we asked him what he had done, he explained that he had direct vision of the apparatus inside and that the act of looking at different parts seemed to him to be correlated with the different effects. As he described what he was doing, the recording again traced out a double-frequency cycle (shown at D), as had occurred before. An atypical dip (E) in the recording took place then, and on questioning him about what was happening, he said he was looking at a new part, the niobium ball sitting in a

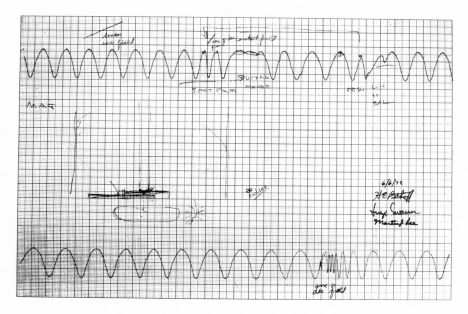

Figure 5.   Raw data, magnetometer test run.

cup. This ball was inert at the time, not being used in the magnetometer experiment. He was asked to refrain from thinking about the apparatus, and the normal pattern was then traced out for several minutes (continued on lower trace) while he was engaged in conversation on other subjects. At one point he started to discuss the magnetometer again, at which point the tracing went into a high-frequency pattern, shown at F. At our request he stopped, and the observation was terminated because Swann was tired from his effort. We then left the lab, while the apparatus was run for over an hour with no trace of noise or nonuniform activity, as indicated in Figure 6, where the top two traces show a continuing record following termination of the experiment. The third trace was taken some time later, the increase in the period indicating the reduced rate of magnetic-field decay. At various times during this and the following day, when similar

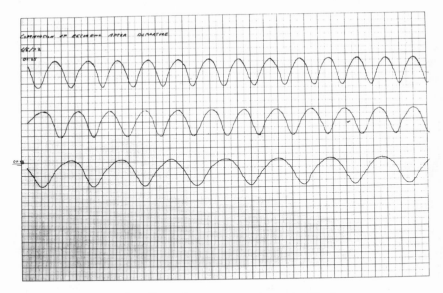

Figure 6.   Raw data, magnetometer control run.

data with Swann were taken, the experiment was observed by many other scientists.

An interesting sidelight of the experiment was that Swann was able to describe quite accurately what the interior of the device looked like, apparently with some form of direct observation. This tends to confirm the results obtained with Swann at the ASPR referred to earlier. Barring outright fraud and collusion, for which we looked but found no evidence, it appears unlikely that he would have had a chance to look at a diagram beforehand, since he did not know that this particular piece of apparatus was to be used until we arrived in the laboratory.

At this point, we wish to emphasize again that we consider this an observation, not a controlled experiment, and Swann was the only subject. There are variables to be checked, such as whether the recording device itself was affected rather than the field or field-associated apparatus. This could only be tested by random disconnects of the apparatus from the recording equipment to see if the recording would continue to change on command.

Electron-Beam Experiment

A second experiment performed by us with another subject entailed the deflection of a slow electron beam apparently by "willpower." The motivation for attempting to deflect electrons rather than the more traditional small cubes or balls lies in the fact that electrons should be much easier to move than the usual laboratory objects. The deflection one observes in trying to change the trajectory of a cube or an electron will be inversely proportional to the kinetic energy of the object. In addition, electrons are very easy to detect. In this experiment a slow electron beam (a few electron volts) was made to strike a divided collector consisting of inner

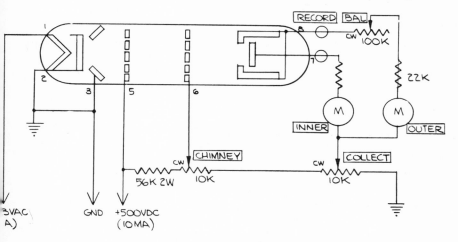

Figure 7.   Electron-beam apparatus.

and outer electrodes. A schematic drawing of the apparatus is shown in Figure 7. The electrodes were connected to ground through current-sensing resistors. A sensitive recording galvanometer was connected across the high-potential side of the resistors to measure any differential voltage between them.

At the beginning of the experiment the electron beam was balanced with respect to the collectors, so that equal currents flowed through the two resistors. This gave a null reading on the galvanometer. The experiment was designed to have great sensitivity, the galvanometer measuring the difference of two large numbers, since an electron current of several milliamperes flowed through the electron-beam tube.

After the electron beam was magnetically balanced to provide a null, the subject was asked to cause the beam to move. He was told that such movement would be indicated by the motion of the pen of the recording galvanometer. (The subject's attention was focused on both the beam tube and the chart recorder in front of him.) In our preliminary work we found a subject who could apparently cause the electron beam to move in accordance with his will. This experiment was performed in a screened room with the subject seated six feet from the beam tube. He was asked at three-minute intervals alternately to cause the beam to be deflected and then to

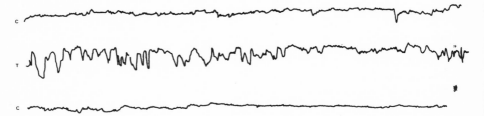

Figure 8.   Galvanometer output in divided-collector
electron-beam experiment.

remain still. Representative data are shown in Figure 8. The chart tracings marked C were control runs in which the subject was asked to refrain from exerting any influence over the beam. The trace marked T was one test in which he was told to move the beam. He described mentally "swirling the beam around inside the tube." The results of this experiment are very suggestive that this individual did indeed exert some influence over the position of the electron beam as indicated by the galvanometer potentials and the chart records.

The subject was seated during the entire experiment and great care was taken to prevent any other interference with the experiment through either accidental or deliberate means on the part of the subject.

As in the magnetometer experiment, the subject had direct feedback of success as shown on the chart recorder. He was thus able to determine what it felt like subjectively when he was able to produce even the slightest motion of the beam. Such feedback techniques allow the subject to learn to control what might otherwise be a fleeting or unconscious process. It is through this kind of direct feedback (biofeedback) and reinforcement that a variety of autonomic functions have already been taught to people who might benefit from such skills as the control of heart rate, the elimination of migraine headaches, and the like (7).

CONCLUSIONS

The main objective of this chapter has been to show that careful analysis of the frontier areas of physics can provide models for psi often thought to be incompatible with modern physics. In addition, we try to give examples of a physicist's approach to the problem, involving setting up a hypothesis, designing an experiment, and comparing theory and result.

We have given examples of new instrumentation being brought to bear on the question of psi. We believe that the introduction of the sensitive magnetometer and the electron-beam apparatus will allow observation of PK effects that have so far been observed only in statistical experiments. Furthermore, we believe that our subjects' success in these tasks was greatly facilitated by the fact that they received immediate and continuous feedback about their progress.

Since our first work with the ESP-teaching machine in 1965, we have continued to obtain encouraging results about the efficacy of enhancing ESP performance through feedback and reinforcement techniques. The work reported here is only one direction of many that may lead to fruitful results.

REFERENCES

1. *American Society for Psychical Research Newsletter*, No. 14, Summer 1972.
2. Cox, W. E. "A Comparison of Different Densities of Dice in a PK Task." *Journal of Parapsychology*, 35 (1971).
3. Forwald, H. *Mind, Matter, and Gravitation*. Parapsychological Monographs, Parapsychology Foundation: New York, 1969.
4. Gal-Or, Benjamin. "The Crisis About the Irreversibility and Time Anisotropy." *Science*, 7 April 1972.
5. Hebard, A. F. "Search for Fractional Charge Using Low Temperature Techniques." Ph.D. thesis, Stanford University, 1972.
6. Koulack, D. "Dream Time and Real Time." *Psychonomic Science*, 11 (1968).
7. Miller, N. E. "Learning of Visceral and Glandular Responses." *Science*, 31 January 1969.
8. Pearson, E. S., and Hartley, H. O., eds. *Biometrika Tables*. Cambridge University Press: Cambridge, 1962, Table 13.
9. Rhine, Louisa E. *Hidden Channels of the Mind*. Sloane: New York, 1961.
10. Rhine, Louisa E. *Mind Over Matter*. Macmillan: New York, 1970.
11. Rogers, D. P., and Carpenter, J. C. "Negative and Positive Affect and ESP Run-Score Variance." *Journal of Parapsychology*, 30 (1966).
12. Schmeidler, G. "Psychokinesis: Temperature Changes in a Distant Object Produced by 'Willing.' " Preprint, 1972.
13. Soal, S., and Bateman, F. *Modern Experiments in Telepathy*. Faber: London, 1954.
14. Stratton, J. A. *Electromagnetic Theory*. McGraw-Hill: New York, 1941.
15. Targ, Russell, and Hurt, David. "Learning Clairvoyance and Precognition with an ESP Teaching Machine." *Electronics*, 26 December 1966; repr. *Parapsychology Review*, 3, 4 (1972).

16. Tart, Charles. "Card Guessing Tests: Learning Paradigm or Extinction Paradigm." *Journal of the American Society for Psychical Research*, 60 (1966).
17. Tart, Charles. "Waking from Sleep at a Pre-selected Time." *Journal of the American Society for Psychosomatic Medicine and Dentistry*, 17 (1970).

Evan Harris Walker

EVAN HARRIS WALKER, *Ph.D., is a research physicist at the Ballistic Research Laboratories of the U.S. Army Aberdeen Research and Development Center.*

Dr. Walker obtained his doctorate degree from University of Maryland in 1964 and then became assistant professor and observatory director at University of Miami's Institute of Atmospheric and Space Physics. He left in 1967 to join NASA Electronics Research Center. The following year he obtained a post at the Ballistic Research Laboratories.

More than 40 technical papers by Dr. Walker have been published in physics and astrophysics journals. "The Nature of Consciousness" (Mathematical Biosciences, 7 [1970]) *presents his theory of consciousness.* "Consciousness in the Quantum Theory of Measurement" (Journal for the Study of Consciousness, 5 [1972] and 6 [1973]) *develops it further. Dr. Walker is a member of the editorial advisory board of* Journal for the Study of Consciousness.

Dr. Walker can be reached at the Ballistic Research Laboratories, U.S. Army Aberdeen Research and Development Center, Aberdeen, Md. 21005.

23 Consciousness and Quantum Theory

EVAN HARRIS WALKER

SUMMARY

This chapter presents a theory of consciousness. The relation of consciousness to, and its compatibility with, present quantum mechanics, particularly the so-called measurement problem in quantum theory, is presented. The neurophysiological basis for conscious experience is developed, and experimental data are given in its substantiation. In addition, a theory of paranormal phenomena is presented in which all the required properties arise out of the Copenhagen interpretation of quantum mechanics and the physical characteristics required of any hidden variable reinterpretation of that theory. Again, extensive experimental data stand in support of this theory of paranormal phenomena. The present chapter also presents a paradigm that provides a bridge between science and religion. Some of the religious implications of the theory are discussed.

INTRODUCTION

The question before us is the nature of man and the meaning of our existence. We live in an age that has developed a physicalistic paradigm—the underlying conception of reality on which we judge scientific ideas—which persuades us by its scope, precision, and acts that the universe consists only of physical bodies and the mechanics of their interaction. The concept of consciousness lies outside the domain of this paradigm. Why?

Science emerged from a part of philosophy that turned its attention to the nature of material bodies and set aside the difficult question of the nature of consciousness. The success of this "scientific approach" has been so great that philosophy has largely abandoned the pursuit of an answer to the question of the nature of consciousness. The residue of philosophy answers the question by saying that the question was never

544

valid. Consciousness is a "category mistake"; consciousness is a semantic error; consciousness is identical with the physical description of brain states.

But the time has now come to reexamine that difficult question of the nature of consciousness. Knowledge adequate to the task is at hand. A sound understanding of physical phenomena has been established. That base is sufficiently extensive for us to build on it and succeed. Moreover, certain physical phenomena indicate that the generally understood scientific paradigm, a physicalistic conception, is inadequate. The paradigm on which science presently stands must yield to an interpretation that incorporates the concept of consciousness, encompasses paranormal processes, and resolves factually the problem posed by the concept of God.

The mental compartmentalization in which religious and scientific thought are both held cannot endure. A common base must eventually be established or religion—which has been retreating for centuries—must fall. The search in science for a complete deterministic and finite representation of all processes occurring in all material bodies, if achieved within the present framework, would make the idea of God an unacceptable concept while dismissing the question of consciousness. Completeness in science demands that no construct be introduced into a physical equation that does not have its physical correlate. If one has a complete representation of all processes, there is no place at which a new concept— here, the concept of God—can be introduced. I will show here that science is not complete without the introduction of the concept of consciousness. I will also show that its scientific incorporation into the paradigm provides a foundation for understanding paranormal processes and that these form a bridge from science to religion.

The approach to the present problem will be basically from the point of view of physics, in which the objective world provides us with a reference point for our concept of reality as well as the basis for the language we use to talk about reality. Physicists generally have tended to disregard the question of the nature of consciousness. Those physicists who have an interest in this particular problem at all have felt that it should be dealt with after all the physical equations have been established. As a consequence, the problem has suffered indefinite postponement. However, the fundamental physical equations describing the processes involved in the brain are sufficiently established that such an argument against initiating a search for a solution to this problem is no longer justified.

The modification of the scientific paradigm, given in the form of postulates below, enlarges the scope of science to allow the study of this phenomenon as a natural process. At the same time, the solution of this problem, as it turns out, goes hand in hand with the solution of a basic problem in physics, the so-called measurement problem in quantum mechanics, which we will discuss later. The power of the new paradigm becomes apparent when it is used to solve the problem of paraphysical and parapsychological phenomena. The consciousness is our most obvious manifestation of an entity that possesses (as will be shown) distinctly nonphysical characteristics. As such, its study is the logical starting point for an understanding of the less frequently occurring paranormal events.

We will first consider new postulates to be introduced into the scientific paradigm and their use in approaching an understanding of consciousness.* This problem, however, does require some discussion of concepts in quantum mechanics. A brief treatment of these concepts allows us then to turn to the quantum theory of consciousness. With that theory in hand, we will discuss a newly developed theory of paraphysical and parapsychological phenomena as well as the present evidence in its support. These concepts provide solutions to the central problems of philosophy and have momentous consequence for religion.

THE POSTULATES

Let us now turn to the fundamental postulates. It might be thought that rather than base a theory of consciousness on postulates, it would be preferable to begin with a discussion of the question of consciousness on philosophical grounds. While the relationship of the philosophical arguments to the present treatment of the problem has been presented (21, 22, 26) such considerations do not lead to the solution of any of the basic issues. It is necessary to state postulates that will serve as a foundation for the scientific exploration of the problem.

Most of physics has been developed by starting with certain postulates, statements of laws, or statements of fundamental equations that are not derived from other principles. Perhaps the finest example of the use of postulates in physics is to be found in the theory of relativity. Based on certain simple principles, Einstein restructured the conception of the most fundamental physical constructs: mass, energy, space, and time. The proof of his postulates lies in their scope and power to expand our knowl-

* I am using the word *consciousness* in keeping with the philosophical concept of conscious being or experience, not as a name for physiological waking. The physiological processes are the *associable* quantities attendant to the occurrence of consciousness and should not be confused with the associated physiological events. As an example, dreams are a conscious experience, but are not associated with the wakeful state of the brain. Dreams occur in association with localized increases in brain activity that satisfy *locally* the conditions given here for the occurrence of consciousness. On the other hand, deep (nonrapid eye movement, or NREM) sleep is not associated with conscious experience. Although extensive brain activity is present during NREM sleep, this activity does not satisfy the condition for the occurrence of consciousness as given here.

edge. The basic postulates in the theory of consciousness serve a similar function.

Regardless of one's philosophy, it is possible to state, delineate, or describe what one means by consciousness well enough to establish that we have a real subject to talk about. The consciousness is a real entity. This is not to state whether the philosophical system in which it is embodied will ultimately prove to be monistic, dualistic, or something else, but just that there is something real that we are going to be talking about. But there exists at present no way of making a physical measurement that will show whether a state of consciousness exists in a given object; there is no way to establish its existence other than for our own personal consciousness. There is no piece of instrumentation, no meter, that can give a reading or measurement directly on the conscious experience. There is no means at present to demonstrate, using physical equipment, the presence or absence of consciousness itself in an object. Therefore, we are led to the following:

Postulate 1: Consciousness is a nonphysical, but real, entity.

The second postulate is derived from the fact that the consciousness clearly does incorporate or consist of data, a large portion of which concerns events in the physically real world. Therefore, the consciousness must allow of some connection with that world. Thus, *there exists at least one physical quantity that connects the consciousness to the physically real world.* For reasons of parsimony it will be assumed that only one quantity is involved in this interaction between the consciousness and the physical world. More than this, there appears to be a single carrier phenomenon on which pain, pleasure, red, C-sharp, and the like all ride. Thus:

Postulate 2: Physical reality is connected to the consciousness by means of a single physically fundamental quantity.

ASSOCIABLE QUANTITIES

Despite the fact that there is this nonphysical (i.e., not measurable in physical terms) aspect to consciousness, there are a number of "associable quantities" that can be related to the content of the consciousness. First of all, it has been known for 2,500 years, when Hippocrates first made the observation, that the consciousness is associated with the functions of the brain. The basis for this knowledge is the subjectively observable effects on the consciousness of actions taken against the normal functioning of the brain.

Second, the consciousness is an onset phenomenon. There are a number of phenomena of the onset type studied in physics. The condensation of a gas at a given critical temperature is an example. In the present case, as one goes from a state of sleep in which consciousness is absent, the increasing activity of the brain suddenly gives rise to the onset of the conscious state. We will come back to this point again to discuss the question of the subconscious.

The data that are incorporated in our conscious experience arise from spatially extended data-processing functions taking place throughout the brain. The data-processing events that structure sensory impulses from the skin, ears, and eyes into meaningful patterns take place throughout the brain, not in some minute part of it. As such, the consciousness must be associated with a physical process that is correspondingly extended.

Similarly, any theory of the nature of consciousness must also account for the temporal span of the consciousness. It requires some reflection to appreciate this point. One can imagine what the world might be like if our conscious experience were governed by a characteristic time interval of say 10^{-10} seconds. Under these conditions, the events of the world would appear totally static. Our bodies would still function in the same way, but the subjective time span for any experience would be enormously expanded. More easily visualized is the possibility of the consciousness extending for, say, 10 seconds, such that everything that occurs in the 10-second interval is essentially fused into one experience. It is, of course, a concept difficult to apprehend. (As an aid, recall that motion-picture film exposed and viewed at under 16 frames per second appears as a series of slow pictures.) Our consciousness is ourselves, our own personal being. It is difficult to have an experience of the existence of the consciousness and at the same time stand outside ourselves to observe this process objectively, as it relates to an overview of the phenomena in the external world. However, such understanding is required if one is to fathom this phenomenon.

THE LINK BETWEEN CONSCIOUSNESS AND PHYSICAL REALITY

The physical quantities that can serve as the connection between the consciousness and the events of the physical world are reasonably well delineated by physics. There are only a few forces that could conceivably be involved, and other than the forces, there is only the constraining equation that might be used to discover this link between the physical world and the consciousness. As for the force fields, neither the gravitational field, nuclear forces, nor weak interactions are involved with the appropriate data-processing events that occur in the brain. They do not give rise to a properly *adjoint* process. More specifically, the magnitudes of these quantities in the case of the brain are entirely too small to provide an interconnection of the events in the various regions of the brain.

On the other hand, the magnitude of the electromagnetic force is appropriate, and this in itself turns out to be something of a difficulty for ascribing consciousness to this force. Everything that goes on in the brain and throughout the body involves electromagnetic interactions; that is to say, all the chemical processes are electromagnetic in origin. Because of this, electromagnetic interactions are not properly adjoined to the unique set of processes that involve the data that enters our consciousness. We are not consciously aware of all the processes going on in our brain in spite of the fact that all these processes are really participating in the ongoing chemistry of the brain.

The notion that perhaps the consciousness is associated with electrical circuits in the brain is not satisfactory. The electrical currents in the brain are extremely localized; they are current loops interconnecting the inside to the outside of individual neurons. Currents do not flow along the axons and dendrites. They do not flow from one neuron to the next.

Brain waves per se suffer as a possible explanation because of the superposition principle for electromagnetic waves. Electromagnetic waves do not interact with one another (except for the rare photon–photon interaction). Finally, the level of electromagnetic activity in the brain does not satisfy the onset criterion previously mentioned. In the state of sleep the various electromagnetic processes are still being carried out by the brain; there is still brain activity; there are still various brain waves present; and the level of activity is only slightly reduced.

This leaves us with a single possibility: association by means of the fundamental equation, the Schrödinger wave equation. And that association must involve the data-processing functions of the brain—specifically, synaptic transmission. Thus, specific neurophysiological processes must be investigated.

Before proceeding into neurophysiology, however, we must consider quantum mechanics. Our examination will identify the means for adjointness between the consciousness and the data-processing functions of the brain. We will find that consciousness is a nonphysical entity connected to the physical world by means of the state vector for a quantum mechanical process linking the synapses of the brain. We will develop a theory that explains the nature of the interconnection and the nature of the onset of this process. The theory will also permit us to calculate the value of the associable quantities that serve as numerical tests of the theory.

QUANTUM MECHANICS AND
THE MEASUREMENT PROBLEM

Although quantum mechanics has dominated physics for half a century, many scientists and philosophers still conceive of physical processes in terms of classical or Newtonian pictures (involving local cause–effect deterministic mechanics). Of course, most appreciate that quantum mechanics is not deterministic, as was classical physics, but probabilistic. The profound picture of nature that lies behind this probabilistic conception is little appreciated outside the circle of physicists concerned with the details of the so-called measurement problem.

To discuss this problem we must begin by describing the character of classical physics. In classical mechanics it was thought that a knowledge of the initial conditions of all the bodies in the universe would allow one, in principle, to determine the whole future of the universe. Thus, classical mechanics is said to be deterministic. Had physics developed to completion along these lines—allowing the introduction of no concepts except motions of bodies and force fields—it would be difficult to conceive of consciousness except as a pseudonym for some force field, necessarily devoid of the features that distinguish conscious experience from physical descriptions.

However, classical physics was found to possess certain shortcomings. It had presupposed that the coordinate positions and velocities of bodies could be determined independently and simultaneously to any degree of precision. Heisenberg, however, showed this not to be the case. It is not possible to determine exactly the position and momentum of a body at a single instant in time. This fact by itself would not have been of major importance except that it indicated a change in the basic equations of physics would be required. The resulting changes led to the development of quantum mechanics, the equations of which involve a more profound change in our view of nature than could possibly have been suspected on philosophical grounds. Indeed, that the riddle of the nature of consciousness was never resolved despite centuries of philosophical scrutiny is attributable to this fact.

To clarify this, let us return again to the Newtonian mechanics. There we may refer to the system as being in a state, a single state, given by the solution to the classical equations of motion. If the initial conditions of the system are completely specified, the state of the system is calculable for any given time. Now in quantum mechanics there is not a single state but, in general, an infinite number of states that represent solutions to the basic equation for the same complete set of boundary conditions. Each state represents a solution to the Schrödinger equation. The collection of all these states is referred to as the *state vector*. Now the surprising thing is that in quantum theory the system is not in one of these states but in the totality simultaneously, and the state vector provides the complete representation of the system.

Of course, when we actually look at a physical system—carry out a measurement on it—we do not find each body simultaneously moving at several velocities, located in several positions. We find the system to be in a single state, one state out of the collection given by the state vector. Thus, the process of measurement of the system is said to "collapse" the state vector onto one of its component states. Which state the system goes into is determined only probabilistically (the exact probabilities, however, being calculable). Thus, before the measurement, the system is specified by the collection of possible states which develop in time, deterministically; upon measurement, the system is to be found in only one of these states, probabilistically. This probabilistic interpretation of quantum theory is called the Copenhagen interpretation. In physics, the Schrödinger equation is a generally applicable expression that completely specifies deterministically the state of a physical system. In that description the state vector Ψ (capital psi, to be distinguished from lower-case psi ψ, meaning psychic phenomena in general, although, ironically, we will find them to be related) incorporates simultaneously not one but many configurations of the physical system. Only when a measurement is performed —that is, when it is observed—does the physical system enter a single state. Quantum mechanics states explicitly that between observations of a system, the system is not in a single state but is in a combination of states, even though observationally these states are mutually exclusive.

Let me give an example. Suppose I have a radioactive atom that can lose its excess energy in one of two ways. It can decay to form atom A or atom B. After a suitably long period of time one can be rather certain that the decay has occurred. The atom has decayed into atom A with a given probability or into B with a given probability. Using the proper apparatus, one can demonstrate that the decay resulted in a transmutation to, say, a type-A atom. But—and this is the principal point—before the measurement the proper description would be that the atom is both an A atom with a given probability and at the same time a B atom with its appropriate probability. But on measurement only one state—that for the type-A atom—is found to occur, and the only feature of the measurement event distinguishing it from other physical processes is that it requires the introduction of a conscious observer for its specification.

This mathematical device, the collapse of the state vector, requires us to introduce the concept of an observer into quantum theory as an object not amenable to description by the Schrödinger equation. Since this equation specifies the properties of physical objects, the observer has properties that are "extraphysical," at least to this extent. The introduction of the observer as an entity distinct from physical processes has left much of the physics community in disquiet; this is the measurement problem in quantum mechanics. This Copenhagen interpretation presents to us a physics having a dualistic formulation.

The role of the observer in quantum theory has been given serious consideration by a number of authors in the physics literature, with specific reference to the function of the consciousness of the observer in securing the collapse of the state vector (27, 29). Certain of these papers show that the Copenhagen interpretation of quantum mechanics leads of necessity to a physical picture in which the consciousness plays a role. The primary objective of many of these papers has been to discredit the Copenhagen interpretation so that an interpretation free of this difficulty may be secured. These efforts, together with the ensuing counterarguments (1, 2, 6–9, 12, 13, 19, 20), have produced a sizable list of constraints that must be accommodated by any reinterpretation or extension of the present theory of measurement.

Bohm (2) proposed that new "hidden variables" might be discovered that would allow a reformulation of quantum mechanics. The introduction of hidden variables is allowed (8) but only if they meet certain quite surprising requirements. First of all, they must still interact physically only by means of the measurement process (9), making the observer or the apparatus carrying out the measurement something that cannot be described by the Schrödinger equation. To that extent, the measurement process remains dualistic, precisely the problem encountered in the Copenhagen interpretation. Second, it has been shown by Bell (1) that any new quantum theory that involved hidden variables would require these variables to be nonlocal;* experimental tests have failed to produce evidence to the contrary (4, 10, 14, 18). Here nonlocality means that these variables are not functions of space or time. They are thus not dependent on physical processes but do effect the collapse of the state vector.

It has also been found that, in order to satisfy the present experimental data, any new formulation of quantum theory involving hidden variables requires that these hidden variables remain true hidden variables—that is, that their insertion into the formulation does not make their state vector dispersion-free (8, 9)—and that they be infinite in number (29).

The fact that there must be an infinite number of nondegenerate hidden variables means that their complete interrelationships cannot be discovered by any finite sequence of experiments. However, the physical

---

* The protagonists have not realized that the proofs against dispersion-free formulations are based on arguments related to experiments of the double Stern–Gerlach type discussed by Wigner (27) while Bell's nonlocality proof stems from the Einstein-Podolsky-Rosen *Gedankenexperimente*.

variables of space and time are finite in number. As a consequence, their form can be determined by the observer to any desired accuracy by a finite set of measurements. Thus, an asymmetry exists between the physical processes and those of the hidden variables. It is in this manner that we can solve the ontological problem, the philosophical question over how a true duality could exist between mind and body or God and world while still allowing for an interaction between them.

Let us refer to these hidden variables as the c_i variables. Further, let us assume that as far as strictly physical measurements are concerned, the theory reduces to the Copenhagen interpretation of quantum theory. As such, the c_i variables must represent the mechanism responsible for state-vector collapse, which is the consciousness of the observer. There exists an even more surprising constraint that physics requires of them. Since the collapse of the state vector in the quantum theory of measurement occurs as a result of observation of the system and since we require that any two (ideal) observers yield the same result of the measurement, either the observation process must be coupled or there must exist a preferred, or first, observer. However, one can show, borrowing arguments from relativity theory, that it is not always possible to state which observer is the first observer. Such a consideration as to which is first depends on the selection of a preferred coordinate system, and relativity theory is founded on the premise that no preferred coordinate system exists. Thus, if the observers collapse the state vector and there is no preferred observer, the observers must be constrained collectively. This means that all the observers of any system or event must share one or several of these c_i variables. Observers of quantum mechanical processes are coupled.

It may be obvious at this point that the characteristics ascribed to the hidden variables are just those needed for a theory of consciousness, and moreover, the nonlocality of the c_i and the requirement that observers be coupled (or collectively constrained) are precisely the characteristics required for a theory of paraphysical processes.

We thus see that quantum mechanics in its most complete form, in which all physical objects are assumed to be governed by the Schrödinger equation, leads of necessity to the assumption of the existence of the consciousness of the observer, which has properties distinct from physically real objects subject to the Schrödinger equation. As a further comment, we find, physically speaking—that is, when we omit the c_i variables—the system is not deterministic. When we introduce the c_i variables, the system becomes causal. This enlarged interpretation makes the system causal yet physically indeterminable.

Since the c_i variables perform the task identified in the Copenhagen interpretation of quantum mechanics with the observer, these c_i must be representative of the consciousness of that observer. These quantities thus can be consistently introduced into quantum theory to serve precisely the same role enjoyed by the concept of the consciousness as a nonphysical entity associated with a neurophysiological quantum mechanical process to be discussed in the next section. It is this overall logical consistency provided by the present scientific paradigm that serves as the most compelling reason for the acceptance of the quantum theory of consciousness.

Finally, we may note that quantum theory, when it is restricted to physical measurements alone, is a statistical theory and, therefore, is not deterministic. When we introduce the c_i variables of the conscious observer, the system becomes causal. Thus, that part of the conscious state that is responsible for the collapse of the state vector representing a portion of the activity of the brain serves the function usually referred to by the philosophical concept of will.

THE CONSCIOUSNESS THEORY AND THE NATURE OF THE MIND–BRAIN INTERACTION

The justification for the introduction of true hidden variables into quantum mechanics can rest only on the value of such in securing agreement with experimental facts. The identification of such variables with the consciousness has given rise to a theory (21–23) concerning the operation of the brain that leads to several quantitative predictions supported by experimental evidence. This theory rests on the finding that quantum mechanical tunneling between macromolecules lying on either side of the synaptic cleft is capable of playing a role in synaptic transmission (16). It has further been shown that synaptic transmission events may be interrelated throughout the brain by means of a sequential tunneling from one synapse to another, using the soluble ribonucleic acid (RNA) molecules to form stepping-stone-like pathways in the manner of the so-called (3, 11, 15) hopping conduction mechanism in organic compounds.

To secure a satisfactory theory within the constraints of the postulates, it is necessary to show how a quantum mechanical process is involved in the data-processing functions of the brain, as carried out apparently by synapses. The process by which an impulse is transferred across the juncture between neurons that currently receives widespread acceptance among neurophysiologists is that of chemical transmission across the synaptic cleft. The chemical involved in transmission is carried in a large number of vesicles located at the synaptic cleft, on the presynaptic side. Upon arrival of the nerve impulse, some mechanism brings about vesicle release. Several characteristics of this process suggest (25) that a mechanism similar to that occurring in tunnel diodes is involved in an energy transfer between large molecules (which make up the so-called Gray's dense projections) on either side of the cleft, bringing about conformational changes in these molecules (proteolipids). The energy of excitation carried by the electrons across the cleft is capable of causing a size change in the molecule, opening macrogates for vesicle release. *Under the conditions existing at the synaptic cleft in which electric impulses propagate to within a mere 180 angstroms, it would be surprising if quantum mechanical tunneling did not occur.* If electron tunneling occurs at the synaptic cleft, the energy can bring about the opening of the vesicle macrogates to initiate the chemical transmission process.

Such a quantum mechanical phenomenon taking place at the synapse would explain some features of the brain's functions. However, although this process is important, it does not provide an adequate theory of consciousness, because it does not explain how the total brain system could be interconnected through a single physical process into one conscious experience, as required by Postulate 2. There must be an additional quantum mechanical process associated with the above process taking place at the synapse that allows transitions over long distances (several centimeters). The question for us to consider now is what kind of conditions would make possible an interaction connecting the transition at one synapse with the transition at another, distant synapse. The storage of information on molecules at the synapse, the involvement of soluble RNA in this process, and the quantum mechanical interconnection of the synapses must appear as factors in any satisfactory solution to the problem of the origin of consciousness.

Consider a volley of nerve impulses moving toward a synapse. As the pulses arrive, they bring about the excitation of successive energy levels of macromolecules located on the presynaptic membrane. Opposite these molecules, lying on the postsynaptic membrane, there are similar molecules. An appropriately formed molecular chain will have energy levels resonant to the presynaptic molecules. For these presynaptic molecules, the potential barrier will be depressed sufficiently for tunneling across the cleft to take place, leading to the opening of the macrogates as mentioned above and causing the synapse to fire.

If the excitation is not resonant, the tunneling probability is low and generally no impulse will be propagated across the synaptic cleft. However, in the presence of appropriate intermediary molecules distributed throughout the brain that the electron can use as stepping stones, a transition from one synapse to another can occur. If these "propagator" molecules lie within about 100 angstroms of one another, the transfer of the excitation energy during the period of time that both synapses are active becomes possible.

Now, if the brain as a whole is sufficiently inactive—that is, if the switching frequency for the synapses throughout the brain is sufficiently low—then the chance is small that two synapses meeting all the requirements for transmission will be activated at the same time. As the rate of synaptic switching in the brain increases, the probability for transmission by means of the propagator molecules improves. As the brain becomes more active, as the switching frequency rises, suddenly the condition for this interconnectivity of synapses throughout the brain is reached and one passes from sleep (or coma) into the state of waking consciousness.

Now, it is clear that this process entails the requirement that simultaneous synaptic activation be continually present if this process is to occur throughout the brain as a continuous (uninterrupted) process. In such a way, a single fundamental physical quantity, the state vector describing the tunneling process, can be identified with the data-processing events taking place throughout the brain yet excluding the many data reduction and chemical processes that do not form a part of the consciousness. It is found that for the consciousness to occur, the minimum synaptic transmission frequency for the entire brain v'_{min} must satisfy the relation (21)

$$v'_{min} = N^{2/3}/t, \tag{1}$$

where N is the total number of synapses in the brain and t is the synaptic transmission delay time.

This theory is consistent with the observed fact that the consciousness is an onset phenomenon. Theories that would identify the consciousness with the general electrochemical processes in the brain or with the brain waves are not consistent with this observation, inasmuch as such activity is not sufficiently reduced (only a factor of 2) to account for the absence of consciousness during the state of sleep.

A great deal of work on the physiology of the synapses has been carried out, making available the data needed to determine whether the conditions for such quantum mechanical processes exist at the synapses. The assumption of direct tunneling across the synaptic cleft leads to a calculated cleft thickness of 180 angstroms, substantially in agreement with the observed thickness. It has also been found that disklike areas of protein material are located and facing on either side of the synaptic cleft. The presence of such material was crucial to the theory, and its presence was inferred from the requirements of the theory.

Equation 1 gives the minimum average synaptic transition rate necessary to bring about consciousness. First of all, it is found that unconsciousness supervenes as soon as neuronal response activity is lowered below a critical level, as in anoxia, anesthesia, concussion, and sleep in keeping with Equation 1. Dreams are associated with bursts of electrical activity in the electroencephalogram. Further, substitution of experimental data into Equation 1 shows the theory to be in quantitative agreement with experiment.

Consideration of the sequential tunneling in which soluble RNA serves as propagator molecules shows that the spacing of these molecules allows the sequential tunneling to spread throughout the volume of the brain during the activation time of the synapse, as required by the theory.

An additional check on the theory involves a calculation of the data transference rate to the consciousness by this mechanism as compared with the data rate from the sensory channels. Essentially all the data transferred to the propagator molecules contribute to the conscious state. In order for the consciousness to contain all our sensory data, it is necessary that the number of sensory data channels (nerve fibers), S, multiplied by the (nominal) data load (bit rate) per channel, r, equal the rate at which activated synapses become connected to the ongoing quantum mechanical process associated with the consciousness. Thus, the data rate C into the consciousness is

$$C = Sr. \tag{2}$$

The experimental value of C from this expression is 9×10^8 bits per second as an upper limit. The present theory gives for the data rate of the conscious "stream"

$$C = nN/\tau M, \tag{3}$$

where n is the number of presynaptic excitation molecules in each synapse involved in the tunneling mechanism, about 2×10^5; N is the total number of synapses, 2.4×10^{13}; M is the total number of propagator molecules, 7.45×10^{20} soluble RNA molecules for the brain; and τ is the average time required to transfer the excitation energy from one propagator molecule to its nearest neighbor, 8.0×10^{-12} second. These values yield the data rate capacity of the consciousness to be 8×10^8 bits per second. Within the limits of the experimental data, these numbers are in agreement and provide a further check on the theory.

The subconscious activity of the brain entails all data-processing activity of the synapses not involved in the consciousness. The value for this data rate is about $S = 2.4 \times 10^{12}$ bits per second. There is a third data rate associated with the data transfer required to collapse the state vector moment by moment. This data rate is given by W, the number of bits of information in each complete transmission involving the propagator molecules per unit of time, and has a value of 3×10^4 bits per second.

This quantity, W, expresses the rate at which certain of the c_i variables, which we will call the w_i variables, in taking on values to bring about the collapse of the state vector to fire specific synapses, impress data onto the functioning of the brain. Their specific values, unlike the values for the rest of the c_i variables, are not specified by physical constraints. As such, the actual states of the brain leading to the behavior manifested by any individual are ultimately determined by the specific values of the w_i variables. Since the values are not specified deterministically by physical conditions, it is not appropriate to use the verb *to be constrained*, appropriate to physical systems, to describe the process whereby specific states occur. The verb *to choose* is more accurate. This term implies free will. This inference is necessitated by the fact that the w_i, a subset of the consciousness descriptors, are involved *essentially* in the collapse of the state vector —that is, in choosing which potentiality allowed by the Schrödinger equation is to be realized physically. As such, *will* has a proper designation represented in the theory by an expression for its associated data rate.

The preceding considerations constitute six independent checks on this theory of the nature of consciousness: width of the synaptic cleft; presence and nature of the structures located on the presynaptic and postsynaptic surfaces; the evaluation of v_{min}'; calculation of the characteristic value for the temporal extent of consciousness; a check on the adequacy of the propagator mechanism for excitation transfer; and the condition on the data rate to the consciousness. I will show below that even more significant verification of the theory is to be obtained from its application to explain paranormal phenomena.

THE PHENOMENON OF MEDITATION

Many altered states of consciousness have been reported. Some of these occur as a result of data-processing demands placed on the brain by an individual's environment. Others arise from the abnormal or spurious functioning of the brain due to a disruption of the brain's normal mode of functioning and do not merit special concern here. The mechanism of meditation, however, does warrant special consideration. It provides a significant and consistent body of information about conscious phenomena as well as a pertinence to the question of the will.

At present, however, the data are not adequate for us to develop a complete definitive theory of the phenomenon—indeed, meditation likely occurs in more than one form, each involving a distinct mechanism. Let us therefore discuss a possible mechanism and present information concerning its characteristics.

The above consciousness theory has been developed to explain the existence of a quantum mechanical interconnection of synaptic firing extended over the entire brain. This synaptic firing, being involved with the data processing of the brain as it responds to sensory excitation, is sufficiently unsynchronized that a very high rate of firing is required to meet the conditions set for the maintenance of the conscious state. It is easy to see that if the demands placed on the brain's data-processing capacity by the individual's environment were relaxed, it would be possible to select a brainwide pattern of firing of the synapses that would greatly enhance the quantum mechanical interconnection mechanism. Such a pattern would be provided by a rhythmical firing of the synapses, forming an in-phase wave of synaptic excitations traveling through the brain, as with the alpha and theta brain waves. Under these conditions, the consciousness could incorporate a large portion of the subconscious brain activity. The difference between this phase-locked state and the normal (environment interactive) state of the brain is in the degree to which the brain is dedicated to this single mode. The state, as described, is an enhanced restful state as expected from the similarity to the ordinary resting state of the brain in which alpha waves occur. There is, in addition, an enhanced or expanded conscious experience arising from the incorporation of a larger portion of the brain's activity into the ongoing conscious state. But the experience does not involve enhanced analytic perception but rather the experience of unity and oscillations, quite in keeping with this explanation.

We now ask if there is any significance to the meditative state beyond a purely physiologically induced experience. The channel capacity for the will previously calculated to be 10^4 bits per second may be enhanced. Under the conditions in which the consciousness interconnectedness is raised from a nominal 10^8 bits per second to some 10^{12} bits per second, there exist some four orders of magnitude of excess in the interconnectedness over and above that required to maintain the conscious state. As a consequence, the value of W will be increased by this factor of 10^4, giving for W in the meditative state $W_m = 10^8$. Interestingly enough, this raises the channel of the "collective will" to the level of normal consciousness. This is the basis of the religious "revelation" experience that occurs spontaneously in connection with various religious rituals and is reported to occur in certain states of meditation.

There is a fundamental significance to be attached to this concept. Its verification under the conditions of normal conscious perception, which provides the most highly developed analytic perception, objective consciousness, should allow us to establish that this state is not simply a vast illusion, an experience of things unreal, but a direct channel to an extensive nonphysical reality. (It may be noted in passing that the author is not a "meditator" and that the results of this study do not stem from a corresponding prejudice.)

APPLICATION TO PSI

At present the literature contains no theory capable of dealing with any portion of the problem of paraphysical or parapsychological phenomena in a quantitative manner. Pseudotheoretic language is frequently used: telepathy frequently is spoken of as "mental radio" (as a transmission on a force-field carrier), and PK as a "mind force." But the general characteristics of the phenomena are quite distinct from all force fields. A considerable departure from this mode of thought is required to achieve an understanding of paranormal processes.

In the absence of a physical device capable of demonstrating paranormal functions, any theory of psi must begin with an understanding of the nature of consciousness, the apparently unique factor presently required in any demonstration of these phenomena.

The consciousness theory discussed in this chapter identifies three processes involving data rates:

1. The data processing of the brain as a whole at the subconscious level having a rate
$$S = 2.4 \times 10^{12} \text{ bits/sec}$$
2. The rate at which data are impressed onto the consciousness by the physical processes of the brain
$$C = 8 \times 10^8 \text{ bits/sec}$$
3. The rate at which the state-vector collapse impresses data onto the functioning of the brain (or vice versa)
$$W = 3 \times 10^4 \text{ bits/sec.}$$

As already discussed, the interpretation of the process indicated by W may properly be identified with certain interpretations of the philosophical concept of will. This latter quantity, the will data rate W, provides the coupling or channel for paraphysical and psi phenomena. Its dilution in the much larger consciousness process accounts (24) for many of the characteristics of paranormal phenomena, especially their capricious occurrence.

THE NATURE OF PARAPHYSICAL PROCESSES

As we have seen, the collapse of the state vector concomitant with the process of observation (that is, the process of selection of allowable configurations of a physical system brought about by the observation of the system) is so constrained that observers of the process are not independent. The observers—indeed, the whole system—are coupled to the extent that agreement on the final state of the system is involved. This coupling, however, is immediate only as it depends on the determiners of the collapse of the state vector. In practical terms, this means that the content of the subconscious and the consciousness of the observers is not so constrained. However, the will, which maintains the continuity of the consciousness, is so coupled. This coupling of the observers is maintained by the c_i hidden variables. As hidden variables, they have the property of spatial and temporal independence, as already discussed, which means that these variables can determine the state of two systems, even though they are separated in both space and time.

Telepathy experiments require the subject to make calls and the experimenter ultimately to check these calls against a target list. These calls stem from a conscious act of selection addressed to the various subsequent potentialities of the physical system. This selection manifests itself in the record of calls, a "change of mind" about a call resulting in a different record; each possible record is a distinct potential state (i.e., component) of the state vector. Subsequently this record is checked for hits by the experimenter. But the experimenter, checking the calls against the target list, is also an observer and, as such, also serves to collapse the state vector. Both the subject (as one observer) and the experimenter (as a second observer) are constrained jointly to select the same state. Thus, the will of the subject and the experimenter act together to select the particular state into which the system is collapsed. Among these possibilities are those in which call-target records are correlated. The correlation is achieved by way of the c_i variables (actually the w_i subset) that are spatially independent. Therefore, telepathy is not affected by the distance separating the sender and caller. In like manner, the c_i are independent of time; the results are thus independent of temporal relationships (to the extent that the future states are not constrained by past events already consciously experienced). Thus, precognition is understood to be the same basic process encountered in telepathy, as experimental evidence already suggests (17).

We have pointed out that the subject and experimenter as observers must be constrained to choose the same state for the state-vector collapse. It does not of necessity follow that the state selected be one in which the call-target record results in a "hit." It appears, however, that failure to achieve either a correlation (or anticorrelation) arises from the dilution of the will data channel in the consciousness data channels and that, to the extent that correlation can occur on the W channels for subject and experimenter, it in fact does. The explanation for this ideal behavior of the W channels is that the channels correlate "emotional sets." So long as both subject and experimenter have the "same emotional set" toward a hit and provided the W channel is the basis for the call selection (i.e., aside from dilution effects), the correlated call-target state will occur.

Now it should be noted that there is no message in the usual sense transmitted between sender and receiver but rather the occurrence of a comparison of the record with the calls as consciously experienced by an observer that introduces a constraint on the system. As a result, it is the mental processes of the experimenter–observer that make intelligible in his brain the symbolic representation between the calls made and the target record. There is not a special part of the brain that has its own paranormal correlate to visual, auditory, and other sensory data reduction. As stated above, a message in the usual sense is not being transmitted, but a future state is being selected. For this reason, no sender is required, and therefore, clairvoyance is basically the same process as telepathy or precognition.

Now it might be asked why, if such constraints are imposed, the scores on such card tests are generally so near to the chance scoring rate. The reason is simple if we make reference to the theory of consciousness. There it is shown that only a small part of the data in the ongoing conscious experience is dictated by the state-vector collapse. The rate for this latter is given by W, while the total rate for the conscious experience is C. Further, the implementation of this link is largely fortuitous for most persons. Learning to implement this ability is limited in the population.

Finally, PK involves the same basic process as clairvoyance with one change. The system affected is not a quantum mechanical brain process that selects each call, but the selection effect is produced in a physical process that has the character of being divergent. The uncertainty in the initial state of the system as imposed by quantum mechanics leads to macroscopically (observably) different potential states. For example, the restrictions imposed by the Heisenberg uncertainty relations applied to the mechanics of a cube (die) bouncing on a flat surface involve an exceedingly small uncertainty in the initial conditions required for determining the subsequent orientation of the cube. Nevertheless, because the process is highly divergent, it is not possible to state the initial conditions with sufficient precision to allow a deterministic calculation of the final position of the cube where a large number of bounces is involved. The initial conditions specify a large number of potential final states of the system—that is, a state vector. The state vector is collapsed on observation of the cube. The coupling of the observer with the state vector for the cube (dependent on the initial quantum mechanical uncertainty) by means of the w_i variables entering into the conscious experience of the observer leads to the correlated collapse of the state vector. The fact that the physical process is divergent means that a small amount of input information by way of the w_i will lead to macroscopic effects.

The unique aspect to this phenomenon is the importance of the physical conditions of the material system being affected, specifically the composition and geometry of the cubes. This fact, together with the extensive experiments by Forwald (5), allowed a detailed test of the theory. The ability of the theory to account for the details of Forwald's experimental results provides compelling evidence for the present theory.

It has long been recognized that persons have ESP ability to various extents. The following treatment provides an understanding for this fact. From the consciousness theory we find that in an interval of time Δt during which the call choice (for the card-calling type of experiment) is made, a total of $C \times \Delta t$ bits of information will enter into the consciousness of the caller, while $W\Delta t$ of these bits, being the information measure on the state-vector collapse, will provide the channel by which call-agreement coincidence occurs. The call, however, is based on a finite sampling taken at random from the $C\Delta t$. These data then provide the input to the brain—that is, the subconscious data-processing functions of the brain where a further averaging of these data occurs and leads to the call.

This whole process is quite similar to that used by the psychologist to model mathematically the learning process of animals in maze-type experiments. There the animal, on each run, associates certain cues, sensory data related to choices in the maze, with the path to be taken to pass through the maze. Of course, until the animal learns to run the maze, it may make choices based on some valid cues and some spurious cues unrelated to the correct choice to be made. In the case of ESP, the valid cues are provided by the W channel, while the remainder of the consciousness contains data input from the physical world through the ordinary sensory channels. As a consequence, in a properly controlled ESP experiment, these sensory data are unrelated to the correct call to be made and so are like the spurious cues in maze experiments. Thus, since $W << C$, in general, the chance of a correct call on any given try is small.

This approach has allowed me to develop a detailed model of psi to account both for the average scoring (over and above that expected through chance) in the overall population and for the distribution of psi-performance ability in the human population that is in agreement with experimental data.

THE QUESTION OF DIRECT MENTAL ACTION

The foregoing discussion of paranormal phenomena has been limited to those phenomena that have been verified under laboratory conditions by various researchers over the years. There are other reported phenomena, rarer and more extraordinary than the usual ESP or PK phenomena.

These include reports of the translocation and deformation of material objects. It is usually quite difficult to subject these phenomena to laboratory scrutiny, and while the "conventional" physical scientist may humor the notion of telepathy, he has no tolerance for those who would seriously advocate the heresy that direct mental action might give rise to the displacement of material objects. The purpose of this section is to show that such phenomena, while requiring an extraordinary command of paraphysical ability, are not inherently impossible.

The paraphysical mechanism involved in direct mental action, while basically an example of the mechanism explained above for PK experiments, is nevertheless distinct. A divergent mechanism (carrying microscopic quantum mechanical uncertainties into various possible macroscopic effects) is not involved here. Instead, macroscopic effects arise from the selection (state-vector collapse) of a highly improbable state of the system that requires a sustained high level of control of the W data channel.

As has been pointed out, the channel capacity of the will has a data rate W of some 3×10^4 bits per second. If there is an indeterminacy in the position of an object (arising from the Heisenberg uncertainty relations) of magnitude δx, a single bit of information would be sufficient to specify or select a displacement of $\frac{1}{2}\delta x$ (on the average) toward the observer over the equally likely displacement away from the observer. As long as control can be maintained, displacements in the selected direction will accrue. Maintenance of this control for, say, one minute would lead to the selection of a state that ordinarily has a probability of occurrence of $10^{-60,000}$.

But how large is δx? The Heisenberg uncertainty relation allows us to place a lower limit on the value. If at some moment we check on the position and velocity of a body, then after an interval of time t, there will exist a minimum indeterminacy in that body's position, given by $\delta x = \sqrt{2ht/\pi m}$, where h is Planck's constant and m is the mass of the body. As I have mentioned already, this indeterminacy does not arise through a simple lack of information about the body's position; rather, until the observer interacts with the body, the exact position of the body is not physically defined. The value of this position uncertainty for ordinary masses and time intervals is exceedingly small.

However, the mass that is displaced need not be the entire body but various parts of the body, so long as energy conservation is not violated. The deformation of material bodies through direct mental influence would involve such a differential displacement, but the severe requirements on energy conservation during the process of deformation may not be achieved without some nominal outside energy. This fact may explain the necessity for some handling of bodies as the deformation develops, whereas the translocation phenomenon would generally not require such contact. The fact that small parts of the body may be displaced individually, rather than the entire body, increases the value of δx for that part of the body. The energy-conservation constraint requires the displacement nevertheless to be a collective displacement. That is to say, while individual elements of the body can be displaced, they cannot occur in isolation of the displacements of the various other elements of the body. As a result, energy-conservation limits the number of physically allowed displacements and thus reduces the total amount of data required to specify the state into which the whole body is displaced.* Calculations indicate that macroscopic displacement of bodies is possible by this mechanism and consistent with many of the reported aspects of such events. Such phenomena can no longer be dismissed out of hand.

There are other low-probability events that may be selected by an individual having sufficient control of the will channel. According to the theory, the willed selection of these low-probability states requires sufficient control of the W channel so that the desired state can be specified. Moreover, it is required that the individual acting as an observer be able to consciously recognize the state to be selected. No paranormal phenomenon is possible without both an adequate paranormal and a subsequent normal information link to the event.

However, it is only necessary that a conscious recognition of the desired state be possible. It is not necessary to have knowledge of the detailed events that lead to the desired state. The steps leading to the desired state can require mathematical calculations to select the target (as has been proved both for ESP and PK experiments), complex events to fulfill a prophecy, or physiological changes to heal, cure, or effect miracles.

SIGNIFICANCE OF THE QUANTUM THEORY OF CONSCIOUSNESS FOR RELIGION

From this work emerges a conception of reality in which, first of all, the familiar physical world is largely unchanged. Indeed, if we restrict ourselves to physically measurable quantities, all of the present formulation of physics is unchanged.

Coupled to that physical reality and involving the associable quantities that characterize states of consciousness lies an additional reality that we have shown can be dealt with by means of the tools of science. This domain of the c_i variables is not like the physical world in which all physical objects are placed in the same space. Instead, each physical

---

* I have derived an expression giving the magnitude of the displacement as $\delta x = Wt(ht/2\pi\rho)^{1/5}$, where ρ is the density (assumed homogeneous) of the body. This expression is approximate only. An exact expression would require complete state-vector specification for each case.

system (irreducible quantum mechanical process) has its own set of c_i variables. In more complex systems (as in the brain), the existence and content of the consciousness is primarily controlled by the physical system.

Entering into the consciousness, but extending beyond the limitation of the physical system, is a will. This will provides a link to all other conscious entities that interact at any time physically. To use more graphic language, the will arises from the pool of all consciousness—a pool formed by small contributions of each without spatial or temporal bounds. This collective will has the power to bring about events in the physical world that transcend the physical limits of information transfer or kinetic events, suggestive of (but much more complicated than) the ideas of omnipresence, omniscience, and omnipotence.

There is more. The prophetic and the miraculous occur. Such acts, recorded in the religious literature of the world, have provided man his principal knowledge of a greater reality. The treatment given here provides a basis for understanding these occurrences. In this way we may understand that many of the recorded events did occur, not thereby dismissing these events as natural phenomena that amazed a primitive people but in a way that bridges science and religion, allowing us to understand factually the reality that moved these people to their religious beliefs.

CONCLUSIONS

As I write, five centuries have passed since the birth of Copernicus. Less one decade, five centuries since Luther's birth. More than any others, these two struck the pattern for man's present conception of reality: for Copernicus, scientific reason that has cut away slowly, progressively the basis of religious faith; and for Luther, religion as faith that, in questions concerning God, must reject reason. This conflict between the rigorous scientific conception of nature and religious dogma is real; it is a profound cleavage. Its resolution can be achieved, is achieved, by the resolution of the problem of the nature of consciousness. It has been the purpose here to show the direction toward a solution to that problem, to show the way toward unifying religion and science, and to show emerging a new conception of science, of nature, and of God that lies beyond that solution.

But the theory is not the present; it is the future. The physical concepts that are presently common in physics do not incorporate the existence of consciousness, paraphysical processes, or the idea of a deity. The conception among many physicists is that the present form of quantum mechanics is a temporary phase in physics that embarrassingly does involve the concept of a conscious observer, a phase that will pass when a neoclassical deterministic formulation is found—an objective physics that holds no place for a consciousness and yields not to deities. It will not happen in that way.

It is essentially this failing in the objective rationale, predisposed as it is to a limited "mechanistic" interpretation of reality, that led Martin Luther to have such an antagonism toward reason whenever applied to the theological questions. He had a great deal more than distrust—almost a hatred —for the scholasticism that led to questionable theological concepts. As a consequence, he laid his emphasis on the concept of faith as the full basis for religion and the God concept. Indeed, since Martin Luther's time (and during the first four centuries of the Christian era), faith has been the foundation for religion; through faith, through grace, one is saved. But this strength for the fifteenth century is a weakness today.

Faith by itself is now an inadequate basis for religion. More and more people demand, intellectually, that their basis of religious knowledge be as sound and as factual as in any science. We must ask, Is this possible or does religion die?

We are now at a point in time for which certain knowledge, factual knowledge, can provide a basis for the God concept. Moreover, this basis for knowledge of God will have a dual character, incorporating both factual knowledge and experiential knowledge, a dualistic foundation for the understanding of religious concepts.

The present theory gives us only an inkling of the overall structure, the interaction of this agency, this collective will, this God, with the course of human events. In time, far more detail will, through research, be revealed. It is to be through efforts of this nature that the present basis of acceptance of God, faith, will come to an end and factual knowledge will become the basis for religion. That is to be the rock on which the new age is to be founded. That is the thesis I come to nail to your door.

REFERENCES

1. Bell, J. S. "On the Problem of Hidden Variables in Quantum Mechanics," *Review of Modern Physics*, 38 (1966).
2. Bohm, D. "A Suggested Interpretation of the Quantum Theory in Terms of 'Hidden' Variables, Parts I and II." *Physics Review*, 85, no. 2 (1952).
3. Bonniface, D. W.; Braithwaite, M. J.; Eley, D. D.; Evans, R. G.; Pathig, R.; and Willis, M. R. "Factors Affecting Conduction in Polymeric Complex TCNQ Salts." *Discussions of the Faraday Society*, No. 51 (1971).
4. Clauser, J. F.; Horne, M. A.; Shimony, A.; and Holt, R. A. "Proposed Experiment to Test Local Hidden-Variable Theories." *Physics Review* (Letters), 23 (1969).
5. Forwald, H. "An Experimental Study Suggesting a Relationship Between Psychokinesis and Nuclear Conditions of Matter." *Journal of Parapsychology*, 23 (1959).
6. Gleason, A. M. "Measures on the Closed Substances of a Hilbert Space." *Journal of Mathematical Mechanics*, 6 (1957).

7. Gudder, S. P. "Hidden Variables in Quantum Mechanics Reconsidered." *Review of Modern Physics*, 40 (1968).
8. Jauch, J. M., and Piron, C. "Can Hidden Variables Be Excluded in Quantum Mechanics?" *Helvetica Physica Acta*, 36, no. 7 (1963).
9. Jauch, J. M., and Piron, C. "Hidden Variables Revisited." *Review of Modern Physics*, 40 (1968).
10. Kocher, C. A., and Commins, E. D. "Polarization Correlation of Photons Emitted in an Atomic Cascade." *Physics Review* (Letters), 18 (1967).
11. McKellar, J. R.; Weighman, J. A.; and Williams, R. J. P. "Electrical Conductivity of Some Organic Materials Containing Metals." *Discussions of the Faraday Society*, No. 51 (1971).
12. Mackey, G. W. "Quantum Mechanics and Hilbert Space." *American Mathematics Monthly*, 64 (1957).
13. Misra, B. "When Can Hidden Variables Be Excluded in Quantum Mechanics?" *Il Nuova Cimento*, 47A (1967).
14. Papaliolios, C. "Experimental Test of a Hidden-Variable Quantum Theory." *Physics Review* (Letters), 18, 1967).
15. Pike, G. E. "AC Conductivity of Scandium Oxide and a New Hopping Model for Conductivity." *Physics Review*, 26 (1972).
16. Rosenberg, B. "Semiconductive and Photoconductive Properties of Bimolecular Lipid Membranes." *Discussions of the Faraday Society*, 51 (1971).
17. Schmeidler, G. "Respice, Adspice, Prospice." *Proceedings of the Parapsychological Association*, 8 (1971).
18. Shimony, A. Private communication. Preliminary data indicate an outcome favorable to true hidden variables.
19. Turner, J. E. "Violation of the Quantum Ordering of Propositions in Hidden-Variable Theories." *Journal of Mathematical Physics*, 9 (1968).
20. Tutsch, J. H. "Collapse Time for the Bohm–Bub Hidden-Variable Theory." *Review of Modern Physics*, 40 (1968).
21. Walker, E. H. "The Nature of Consciousness." *Mathematical Biosciences*, 7 (1970).
22. Walker, E. H. "Consciousness as a Hidden Variable." *Physics Today*, 24 (1971).
23. Walker, E. H. "Consciousness in the Quantum Theory of Measurement, Part I." *Journal for the Study of Consciousness*, 5 (1972).
24. Walker, E. H. "Application of the Quantum Theory of Consciousness to the Problem of Psi Phenomena." *Proceedings of the Parapsychological Association*, 9 (1972).
25. Walker, E. H. "Quantum Mechanical Processes in Synaptic Transmission." Paper presented at International Symposium on Quantum Biology and Quantum Pharmacology, Sanibel Island, Florida, January 1974. To appear in the proceedings in *International Journal of Quantum Chemistry*.
26. Walker, E. H. "On Problems Associated with the Copenhagen Interpretation of Quantum Mechanics." *Bulletin of the American Physics Society*, 2nd ser. 18 (1973).
27. Wigner, E. P. *Symmetrics and Reflections*. Indiana University Press: Bloomington, Ind., 1967.
28. Wigner, E. P. "Are We Machines?" *Proceedings of the American Philosophical Society*, 113 (1969).
29. Wigner, E. P. "On Hidden Variables and Quantum Mechanical Probabilities." *American Journal of Physics*, 38 (1970).

IV The Convergence

With Transpersonal Psychology

At the deeper levels of mind, boundaries and limitations drop away. Those who experience those levels emerge to build more encompassing disciplines. Transpersonal psychology, the study of man's ultimate development, is such a larger view. A blend of the best in science and religion, it provides a perspective in which the findings of psychic research are given significance *sub specie aeternitatis*. And in turn, transpersonal psychology takes its place within noetics, the general study of consciousness.

Lawrence L. LeShan

LAWRENCE L. LESHAN, *Ph.D., is chief investigator for the research project on paranormal phenomena sponsored by the Ayer Foundation. He has held the post since 1964. He also has held teaching positions at Roosevelt University, New School for Social Research, and Union Theological Seminary.*

Dr. LeShan spent five years in the U. S. Army as a clinical psychologist during World War II and the Korean War. He was chief investigator on the research project on psychosomatic aspects of neoplastic disease for the Ayer Foundation, after which he took his present post.

Besides more than 50 articles in professional journals, Dr. LeShan is the author of Toward a General Theory of the Paranormal *(Parapsychology Foundation, 1969) and* The Medium, the Mystic and the Physicist *(Viking, 1973).*

24 Psychic Phenomena and Mystical Experience

LAWRENCE L. LESHAN

SUMMARY

Mysticism and the paranormal have long been associated in two ways: in the repeated reports of mystically trained individuals acquiring paranormal abilities and in the warnings given in all serious mystical training schools that students who become interested in these abilities will cease to make progress. Modern studies of the special altered state of consciousness associated with the occurrence of paranormal events have shown that this altered state of consciousness is very similar to the altered state of consciousness that mystical training tends to develop and that the association between mysticism and the paranormal has a rational explanation.

But different uses

INTRODUCTION

Mysticism and the paranormal have long been associated with each other. The main reasons for this historically have been the widespread reports of individuals identified as mystics having paranormal powers. Both in the West and the East, a large percentage of those identified as mystics were frequently believed to have demonstrated ability at telepathy, clairvoyance, precognition, psychic healing, levitation, bilocation, and a variety of other such abilities. These reports have been so consistent that in any serious evaluation of the paranormal, it is not reasonable to ignore them.

Another factor which suggests a relationship between these two is the presence in serious mystical literature of constant warnings to the person who is working on the mystical path, against developing interest in the paranormal powers which sometimes appear as he continues his work. In Buddhist literature, Christian and Jewish mysticism, Sufism, and the Hesychast tradition, we find the same warnings. Again and again we are told that preoccupation with the miracles ("siddhis" in the Buddhist tradi-

571

tion) blocks the ability to develop oneself further (2, p. 186). It would seem unlikely that these warnings would be given so extensively and repeatedly if there were not a real danger involved.

More recently, as attention in psychic research has shifted from the description of paranormal events to the study of the conditions under which they occur, a second type of association has been revealed. It has become plain that if we view the mystic as training for, and entering, an altered state of consciousness, it is a very similar altered state that the sensitive appears to be using at the moment the paranormal perception occurs. (I use the term *perception* here as there has been no study so far of the state of consciousness in existence at the time physical paranormal activities take place.)

When the subject has been studied from the viewpoint of the "why," the goals for which the altered state of consciousness was entered, there appears to be little similarity between the ESP experience and the mystical experience (7). When the subject has been studied from the viewpoint of the "what," the formal analysis of the state of consciousness relating to the ESP and to the mystical experience, most students of the subject have found a real similarity.

The mystical approach is known in every country and time of which we have records. Basically it appears to be a search and training for an other than ordinary way of being at home in the world, of perceiving and relating to reality. No matter when and where the inspiration arises, the techniques developed and the disciplines followed, a very marked similarity emerges. "All mystics," wrote one of them, Louis Claude de St. Martin, "speak the same language and come from the same country." They agree that the most important goal for a man is to see more deeply into what is, to go beyond his ordinary perceptions, to *comprehend* rather than just *understand* the world. They agree further on the kinds of training and development techniques needed to move toward this goal. Further, they agree on what reality begins to look like when they have moved along the path. The overwhelming similarity in their conclusions as to the nature of the cosmos and the behavioral standards this implies for man have been remarked on by every serious student of mysticism.

All major schools of mysticism (and many of these appear to have arisen without roots in others) agree that there are two basic states of consciousness important for man. There is the everyday one, which we might call the way of multiplicity. Here objects and events are seen essentially as separate and individual (although they may be related causally, may influence each other, and may be considered in classes). The other state of consciousness is sometimes known as the way of the One. Here everything is considered as part of a great pattern of being, of a dynamic interacting field in which there is no possibility of anything being separate, of standing alone. In the first of these, we are well trained and expert.

From childhood we learn to function in the world of multiplicity. In the second of these, we are untrained and hardly function at all. From infancy this viewpoint of the world of the One is suppressed in us in all cultures in favor of the other with its higher potential for biological survival. (To get across a highway alive during the rush hour clearly demands strong functioning in the world of multiplicity.)

Although these two ways of perceiving and relating to the world are usually described, as I have done here, as if they were entirely separate, they are actually different points on a spectrum. As we progress from considering things as only separate (with no classes or interactions), to viewing only a contentless, flowing harmony, we go from one extreme of this spectrum to the other. The "world of multiplicity" is a view of reality near one extreme; the "world of the One," a view near the other.

It has gradually become clear that what we mean when we use the term *altered state of consciousness* is the full use of another metaphysical system. When we are perceiving and relating to reality as if it were put together and run on a different metaphysical system than the one we ordinarily use, we are in an altered state of consciousness and vice versa.

The implications of this seem to be greater than we have realized in the past. Each metaphysical system permits certain types of events to occur and does not permit others. We can legitimately state that what is "normal" (permissible) in one metaphysical system is "paranormal" (nonpermissible) in another.

This, however, seems to be trivial and hairsplitting until we come to a more basic question that immediately occurs to us. Given two metaphysical systems, two sets of descriptions of reality, which one is "right," or "correct," and which one is "incorrect"? It seems perfectly clear to us that only one of them can be valid. Science, after all, is the search for the correct and accurate description of reality. Obviously, then, there must be such a correct description and all others are wrong.

It is true that science and philosophy once were part of such a search and held the belief that man ultimately would find the correct solution to the question of the nature of reality. In the past 50 years, however, this search has been abandoned. We no longer look for the ultimate solution. We look for the implications of different descriptions of reality. How useful is a theory? "The question," wrote Henry Margenau, probably the leading theoretician of relativity physics of our time, "is not whether matter is continuous, but how theories succeed when they regard as a continuum the construct which they take to be their system" (6, p. 104). What can we do, accomplish, understand with a theory? This has been the question of modern science and not the search for the ultimate description of reality, which Max Planck has described as "theoretically unobtainable" (9, p. 15).

In these terms we must reevaluate the importance of the question of how significant it is that *an altered state of consciousness* and *a different metaphysical system* are two terms meaning the same thing. If there is no correct metaphysical system except in terms of your purpose (for example, if you wish to remain biologically alive, you had better retain some allegiance to the world of multiplicity), then when faced with apparently equally valid systems, you choose the one you wish in terms of your goals. If you choose correctly, you have a pretty good chance of attaining these goals because you have chosen a metaphysical system in which the particular type of process involved is permissible. To repeat, what is "normal" in one metaphysical system (a synonym for *state of consciousness*) is "paranormal" in another.

It is clearly not as simple as this. We know that there are limits as to what metaphysical systems are valid, even though we do not know what these limits are. You cannot choose a metaphysical system according to your whims and expect to be able to accomplish anything at all. The idea that you can is schizophrenia, not science.

About all we do know is that there are at least two altered states of consciousness within which human beings can operate effectively in terms of the processes permitted in those systems. The first is the everyday world of what we may loosely call "common-sense" reality—the world of multiplicity. The other is the world of the One.

Neither of these two systems is more valid than the other. Each has assets and liabilities. What you can do in one, you often cannot do in the other and vice versa. Which you choose depends on your goals, not on what is "out there." In the words of the old Spanish proverb, " 'Take what you want,' said God, 'take it and pay for it.' "

The specific metaphysical system known as the world of the One has been independently arrived at by three different groups of individuals using different starting points, training techniques, and goals. Two of these have used it as an altered state of consciousness, the third as a theoretical model. The three groups were the mystics, the serious sensitives, and the physicists. When members of each of these groups are asked, "What does the world look like when you are working?" (i.e., "What is the metaphysical system you are using?"), the answers—except for differences in language—are isomorphic. That is, they are identical in structure. I have explored and demonstrated this in detail elsewhere, and this has been independently studied by Osborn (8), by Crookall (1), and others. Therefore, I will not repeat it here. In one paper (4), I took 62 statements of "how the world works"—half from serious mystics and half from modern theoretical physicists—and, after removing the identifying tags, scrambled them. So far no one, whether trained in physics, mysticism, or neither, has been able to separate successfully the two groups of quotations without looking at the index at the end of the paper.

Three groups, then, independently arrive at the conclusion that there are two metaphysical systems viable for man. Furthermore, they agree on what these systems are. This means that there are available for man two sets of descriptions of how the world works and two sets of rules as to what is normal and what is paranormal in each.

From the viewpoint of this book, the most interesting aspect of this is that ESP is not "paranormal" in the record of these metaphysical systems. In a universe in which matter is conceptualized as continuous and in which all objects, entities, and events "flow" into each other; in which boundaries and dividing lines are illusory; and in which pastness, present-ness, and futurity are illusions, neither space nor time can act as prevent-ing information exchange within the great One, which comprises the cosmos. Telepathy, precognition, clairvoyance, and the like are expected and normal processes within this system.

If this formulation has validity, we can see why the mystics are so widely reported to have developed these abilities, for their training and long hard disciplines are, in the main, an attempt to be able to go into the altered state of consciousness known as the world of the One. We can also see the reasons for the warnings against too much interest in these abili-ties, for they can become status-gaining methods, can become an individ-ual's *raison d'être*, which brings him back to a focus on what he can attain in the world of multiplicity. He thus begins to bring the two systems into conflict and contradiction rather than expanding and purifying each of them in such a way that they can be ultimately fused in a constructive manner. The ultimate goal of serious mysticism is this purification of each so that they ultimately can be integrated in such a way that each is background music for the other, and from the mystic's viewpoint, the individual moves closer to his fullest potential as a human being.

We see from this also the reason why the serious sensitive typically replies to the question of how the world looks at the moment he is acquir-ing the paranormal information, with a description of reality that is the same as given by the serious mystics when asked how it looks in moments of "enlightenment" and by the modern physicist when asked how it looks from the viewpoint of relativity theory.

The theoretical model of the relationship of mystics and the paranormal I have presented in these pages has been explored in greater detail else-where (1, 3–5, 8). Further, I have demonstrated that the model can be used to predict that certain training techniques should, if followed, pro-duce the ability to perform certain activities usually called paranormal (5), that it implies a theory for training psychic abilities, and that this theory when tested was shown to be valid.

The exploration of parapsychological functions is incomplete without the parallel exploration of mystical understanding. On the other hand, the study of mysticism without the use of the tough-minded and elegant methods of modern science ignores our greatest tools for learning and developing and reduces our potential for growth and advancement as individuals and as a race.

REFERENCES

1. Crookall, R. *The Interpretation of Cosmic and Mystical Experiences.* Clark: London, 1969.
2. Huxley, A. *The Perennial Philosophy.* Meridian: New York, 1944.
3. LeShan, L. *Toward a General Theory of the Paranormal.* Parapsychology Foundation: New York, 1969.
4. LeShan, L. "Physicists and Mystics, Similarity in World View." *Journal of Transpersonal Psychology*, 1, no. 2 (1969): 1–20.
5. LeShan, L. *The Medium, the Mystic and the Physicist: Toward a General Theory of the Paranormal.* Viking: New York, 1973.
6. Margenau, H. *The Nature of Physical Reality.* McGraw-Hill: New York, 1950.
7. Murphy, G. *The Natural, the Mystical and the Paranormal*, The Second John William Graham Lecture on Psychic Science, Swarthmore College, Swarthmore, Pa., April 27, 1952.
8. Osborn, A. W. *The Expansion of Awareness.* Theosophical Publishing House: Wheaton, Ill. 1961.
9. Planck, M. *Where Is Science Going?* Allen and Unwin: London, 1933.

Jean Houston

JEAN HOUSTON, *Ph.D., is director of the Foundation for Mind Research near New York City.*

A graduate of Barnard College, Dr. Houston holds a doctorate in psychology and has served on the faculties of religion, philosophy, and psychology at Columbia, Hunter College, the New School for Social Research, and Marymount College. Since 1964 Dr. Houston and her co-workers at the foundation have pursued an extensive nondrug study of altered states of consciousness, accelerated learning, audiovisual environments, internal imagery processes, alternate cognitive modes, subjective time, biofeedback training, the psychology of the creative process and its induction, and the laboratory study of religious-type experiences. She defines this work as the potentiation of latent human capacities.

In recent years Dr. Houston has been active in setting up collegiate auxiliary programs in human-potentials development to help counteract drug usage among students and in developing an alternative style of education for women's colleges that is aimed at exploring and nurturing female potential. In addition to her work in human-potentials research, she is co-inventor of a number of machines and electronic devices and environments that serve to alter consciousness in unusual ways.

Dr. Houston was one of the pioneers in the scientific study of experimental effects of LSD on human personality. With her husband, Robert Masters, she has written several books on this and other research. These include The Varieties of Psychedelic Experience (*Holt, Rinehart and Winston, 1966*), Psychedelic Art (*Grove Press, 1968*), Mind Games (*Viking Press, 1972*), *and* New Ways of Being (*in press*).

25 Myth, Consciousness, and Psychic Research

JEAN HOUSTON

SUMMARY

This chapter explores the crisis of consciousness and its historical analogies and suggests that the mythic persona emerging from the crisis points toward a new image of man and a new possibility for humanity. It is additionally argued that the crisis of consciousness being experienced in our time holds both threat and promise for the future of mankind. The collapse of institutions, beliefs, and values systems imperils the motivations of men precisely at a time when countless problems of unparalleled urgency have to be dealt with. Yet the very collapse of old certainties has brought down the circumscribed boundaries of consciousness. Man is left without sheltering walls, but there are also new openings to see through, dramatic possibilities for growth, and new ways of being. Our time can be seen as uniquely favorable to the actualization of many latent and powerful human potentials and psychic capacities. Neither religion nor science, dogmatic theology nor dogmatic rationalism, any longer has the strength to impose arbitrary limits on reality and consciousness. Out of this uniquely free situation has already arisen the human-potentials movement and the great strides being made in psychic research, and there is emerging a new "science of consciousness," which in itself promises a revolution in the current scientific paradigm.

INTRODUCTION

In the beginning was the myth. The myth: that undefinable something that never was but is always happening—the coded DNA of the human psyche, calling us to citizenship in a universe and a reality larger than our aspiration and richer and more complex than all our dreams. Be it the myth of Gilgamesh or that of the Grail, of the many god-men who have died only to rise again, or even of the divine comedy of Don Quixote de la

Mancha, the myth is always the stimulus, the alarm clock, the lure of becoming. It quickens the heart to its potential and prepares the ground for society's transformation.

It follows then that to discern the emerging new forms of culture and consciousness, one should look to the myths and symbolic images that have begun to flower in the cultural mindscape of the past few years. What are these new archetypes that fascinate, these new myths that bypass ordinary critical consciousness and call to the deeps that lie within? What are the images of the more, or the less, than human that rise unbeckoned in modern man's dreams or waking fantasies? What or who makes the hair stand up on the head, the toes curl, and the breath come quicker? Think about it.

In ancient Greece on the occasion of the great dramatic festivals, the cosmic probings and lofty yearnings of the mythic tragedies were more often than not preceded by Dionysian satyr plays, grotesque and ribald revels, the pop myths and lowlife liturgies dealing out images of vulgarized sex and rascally violence. These lesser and more profane myths served to prepare the heart by degrees for the powerful and soul-charging tragic myths to come.

The same may be true today. A look into present-day consciousness reveals a veritable cornucopia of satyrs, Dionysiacs, grotesques—the whole peculiar crew that waits on the lesser mysteries. Some of their names? Dracula, Frankenstein's monster, the Mummy, the Blob, Unidentified Flying Objects, the Starship Enterprise, the chariots of the gods, Atlantis rising, California falling into the sea, the year 2000, LSD, DDT, FBI, NBC, the astrologers, witches, covens, and soothsayers coming at you from out of the national woodwork, the Loud family, the Partridge family, the entire city of Los Angeles. On the next wave there come those musicians whose music serves not to amuse but to mythologize. The Beatles were among the first and probably the best, and after them the Deluge: the Grateful Dead, Guess Who, Black Sabbath, Three Dog Night —many sporting primeval bearded faces and costumes fit for shamans. Lately, and right on schedule too, the Androgyne appears, still a creature of indeterminate sex, but this time electrified and amplified, a shrieking, frenetic, acoustical terror, gifted with some strange Dionysian alchemy to evoke the freak in all hearers, turning ballads into orgies and concerts into celebrations of *Walpurgisnacht*.

Outrageous and vulgar as they are, they serve their purpose. As with the ancient Greek theater, they profane and make less awesome the sacred way leading to the depths where lie the great and potent sacred myths that are about to be born again to bring new life to consciousness and culture.

What are these sacred emergent myths? I do not think we know as yet, but we have some powerful thematic clues that lie close to the heart, if not at the heart. I, for one, see these clues in three contemporary higher myths that have profoundly moved a multitude of people with a kind of shock of cosmic recognition. Using the words of Joseph Campbell, we could say that these three myths and symbols "touch and exhilarate centers of life beyond the reach of vocabularies of reason and coercion" (1). Each carries the intimation of things to come, the emotive thrust toward actualization. They are found in the figure of the Yaqui Indian sorcerer Don Juan as he is described in Carlos Castaneda's books (2–4); in the story of Michael Valentine Smith, the hero of Robert Heinlein's remarkable work of psychological science fiction, *Stranger in a Strange Land* (6); and finally, in the image of the star-child, the cosmic fetus that looms over Earth in the final moments of the film *2001.**

All three of these images share many of the same themes. Most important, they all tell of a mutation or change of consciousness. The reality felt and known by each of these three figures is not the everyday garden-variety reality that you and I know. Whereas many of us spend most of our days after our childhood ends looking out on a world circumscribed and severely restricted by psychological and sensory horse-blinders, these figures see reality as a dynamic flux, a flowing infinity of worlds within worlds within worlds. Two of the characters, Don Juan and Michael Smith, are adept in altering consciousness at will to perceive people and places with more profound understanding. Each has honed his senses to such acuity that colors, smells, sounds, and tastes become a revelation in themselves, intimations of immortality and not just some fleeting sensory binge. Nor are these figures limited to a paltry five senses. Their senses crisscross in an orchestral play of synesthesias, so that they hear color and see sound, touch light and taste God. With extended perceptions and heightened sensitivity to all subliminal cues it is not surprising that telepathy and clairvoyance are natural and ordinary faculties also, common ways of knowing in the uncommon reality in which each lives.

The two critical constructs of time and space are likewise perceived as fluid and creative. Each has the capacity to see infinity in a grain of sand and eternity in an hour. Neither is enslaved to the circadian shackles of clock time, but can experience subjective realities in which months occur in moments and moments in months. Having conquered the Euclidian geometric tyranny of clock time, they have the freedom of space and wander in their bodies or their minds through a wilderness of worlds, be they found in the aroma of some desert flower or 10 parsecs past Andromeda. All three of the figures have traveled over the horizon and then over that horizon to "the land of someplace else." Michael Smith was born on Mars and then returned to earth as an adult; the cosmic fetus was

* The film *2001: A Space Odyssey* was written by Arthur C. Clarke and Stanley Kubrick and directed by Kubrick. It was an MGM Production and released in 1968.

once a spaceman who journeyed to Jupiter and came back transformed; and Don Juan is a modern Ulysses of inner space. I might suggest that in the new emergent mythos Out There and In Here are analogues for each other.

What I have been suggesting is that each of these are myths that may, as myths do, prefigure a reality to come, myths of new ways of being. They tell of man acquiring potentials and capacities once thought of as belonging only to the gods. Thus, they are new Prometheus myths with the central characters again stealing fire from heaven, only this time the environs of heaven are extended to include inner, as well as outer, space. (But then, the ancient myth was probably just as suggestive of the inner as of the outer.) They tell, with a stirring poignancy, of man, for the first time in human history, becoming fully human. Not that this planet has not seen many thousands of richly actualized human beings. Obviously, it has, but only in the form of the random individual—never, so far as we know, with great numbers of mankind. What these myths portend is the democratization of the potentials of the human psyche. One notes, for example, that Don Juan does not pass on his secrets to another budding sorcerer. He tells all to an anthropologist from the University of California who then broadcasts it as three best sellers and a doctoral dissertation. For the past 40,000 years and more, characters like Don Juan and his acolyte Castaneda would have been spoken of only in whispers by the very few who had some dim inkling as to the nature and significance of their activities. But in our time they become the subjects of a cover story of *Time*.

Stranger in a Strange Land has been widely read, especially by college students, and the image of the cosmic fetus of *2001* has been imprinted on the minds of millions.

Most powerfully of all, these myths support and stimulate the emergence of a new image of man and of what it means to be human. Until very recently the dominant image governing man's self-identity had been that of *Homo laborans*, man the worker, man who defines and discovers himself in terms of what he does to put some food in his mouth and a roof over his head. Man in search of subsistence therefore became proficient at using only those potentials that enabled him to subsist. Thus, the consequent narrowing of his vision, the dissociation of himself from the body of nature and from the body of himself. Thus, too, the continued maintenance since prehistoric times of a manipulation psychology. Since the time when he dwelled in a cave, *Homo laborans* has looked outside of himself for the fulfillment of his needs. Today we persist in the same attitudes we had toward the world ages ago. Sophisticated technology is merely an extension of the ax, the stone, and the spear; it involves the same primitive materialism that has discouraged man for so long from discovering or exploring his own innate powers. And in his discovery of prosthetic extensions of his hands, his feet, his eyes, the material crutches of man were given priority over the more difficult to find inner resources. With the technological improvement and widespread deployment of these devices there has resulted the speeding up of the process of plundering the planet. According to some experts we may be on an exponential curve of environmental exploitation, so that there is a very real threat that we can drown in an apocalypse of garbage by the year 2000. The logic of *Homo laborans* and his prosthetic ravaging of the environment leads inevitably to the ecological holocaust.

It is enormously significant that the current crisis in consciousness, the loss of a sense of reality felt by so many, the rising tides of alienation, occurs concomitantly with the ecological destruction of the planet. We are forced into the realization that man is no encapsulated bag of skin. Rather man is organism–environment. And this fact brings us to the momentous point in human history where we have no choice if we are to survive but to reverse the ecological plunder, and that will mean discovering new forms of consciousness and fulfillment apart from the traditional ones of consumption, control, aggrandizement, and manipulation. It is time to take off of the psychological shelf all those potentials lying dormant there that were not immediately necessary to man in his role as *Homo laborans*. The ecological crisis is doing what no other crisis in history has ever done: it is challenging us to a realization of a new humanity.

Again, the modern myths of the new humanity tell us something about the nature and possibilities of these potentials. They also tell of a new reliance on body and mind quite apart from machines. Machines are curiously absent from the ambience of each figure even though the myth takes place in the present or the future. The star-child may have left the earth as an astronaut in a space ship (albeit a schizophrenic one), but returns wrapped in a luminous cosmic caul. Smith and Don Juan are able to accomplish their activities by drawing upon the energies and capacities of their own physical and mental storehouses.* Each, in fact, has a rather whimsical attitude toward machines. When they are around, large pieces of equipment tend to disappear, blow up, or go haywire.

Each of the figures lives in a state of ecological equilibrium with the planet, treating the things of nature as "presences" to be taken seriously

---

* With Don Juan's teachings especially, we may have guidelines for the learning and application of a metatechnology hitherto known only among shamans and other specialists in nonordinary realities who currently practice largely in tribal societies or in Third World countries. It would be a supreme, but delightful, irony if these alternate, but presently largely inexplicable, energy systems utilized by Third World shamans were to provide the dominant world governments with resources and energies sufficient to help them free themselves of their bondage to the now destructive and limited dynamics of the scientific–industrial paradigm, with its inevitable predilection toward Doomsday. Such, I suspect, is also the implication of the research described in this volume.

and attended to as *I* attends to *Thou*. The I–it syndrome that determines the quality of so many relationships in the modern world—to nature, to others, and even, to self—has no place in the world-set of these figures where *Thou* is the pervasive character of a reality in all points sentient and in all parts personal.

WHERE IS REALITY GOING?

The iconoclasm of these mythic figures is felt most seriously in their overt and covert critique of the current consensual understanding of the nature of reality.

In terms of this current understanding, it is generally assumed that there is a normal waking consciousness that is more or less the same from one person to the next; you and I are more or less seeing and experiencing the same things. And this consensus is what we call normal reality. It is recognized, of course, that with the individual within the limits seen as normal, there can be considerable variations in such areas as degrees of alertness, scope of attention to the environment, and the amount of concentration invested in a task. A hunter trying to be alert to every sound or movement around him certainly is not in the same state of consciousness as a man engrossed in a novel. And a woman paying attention to her knitting while also conducting a light conversation with her sister is obviously in yet another state. However, unless there is reason to think differently, each of these persons is assumed to be functioning within that range along the continuum of consciousness indicated by the term *normal consciousness*. It is also recognized that the normal consciousness of one individual may vary somewhat from the normal consciousness of another individual, but the consciousness of one is still sufficiently similar to the consciousness of the other for them to be able to have a consensus concerning their perceptions of the external world as well as other crucial perceptions that make up the boundaries of what we call reality. The problem then arises as to what to do with those people whose consciousness is sufficiently different from the majority as to cause them to reject the reality of the consensus.

In our culture those who reject the reality-consensus are sometimes considered to be psychotic or otherwise badly disturbed, while in some other cultures they may be acclaimed as divinely or demonically inspired. "Primitive" cultures are often much wiser than we are in dealing with those who reject the reality-consensus. A child in these so-called primitive cultures who shows a special facility for seeing visions or for having a psychic sensibility may be given rigorous training in different ways of seeing and being and then may grow up to be a critical member of the society—a priest, shaman, or prophet; a healer; or an artist. By contrast, too often in our society such children are intercepted by well-meaning "guidance counselors" and "delivered" from their curious talent by teachers, psychiatrists, and other executors of the "norm." Thus do we continually cut off at the root a dynamic vehicle for society's well-being, a vehicle of inspiration, of ecstasy, and of entrance into the larger reality in which we all live and breathe but are conditioned out of seeing.*

In the interests of what the public considers "sanity," the person of unusual perceptions is often disparaged or, what is worse, "adjusted" to society's norms. In many cases he is physically, surgically, and, most commonly, chemically removed from his possibilities, so that most of the powers of his inspiration and his novel sensibilities are thwarted or killed or go scurrying inward and become destructive or pathological. His visions are considered "bad trips" and not as breakthroughs to more varied and perhaps evolutionary modes of consciousness. In the case of psychic sensitives, one wonders how much happier and less neurotic would be their lives if they had not had to bear the stigma from childhood on of the "peculiar," the "crazy," the "not-to-be-tolerated."

Although such a student of these phenomena as R. D. Laing can be rightly challenged for a tendency to overromanticize madness, still his views are a welcome antidote to the prevailing tendency in our society to pathologize and derail those who have a different reality sense. In so doing, we merely uphold the level of psychological mediocrity that we call the norm and destroy or deflate our potential geniuses, artists, ecstatics, psychics, and visionaries.† Thus do we lose those very people who could project for us alternate possibilities and alternative futures.

We live in states of consciousness induced by our culture, our awareness and behavior limited and distorted by an elaborate prison network of environmental stimuli—of arbitrary belief systems, of reinforcing mechanisms of reward and punishment. This prison in which we ordinarily dwell is then deludedly described as "reality" or as "normal waking consciousness." Outside of its confines there lies the partially and the altogether unknown, the superstitiously feared and defended against by attitudes,

---

* There is a growing literature of reaction to current mental health standards of the "norm" and of the overt and covert methodologies employed in adjusting "deviants" to this "norm." The works of R. D. Laing are perhaps the best known representation of this point of view. A more intense and methodical analysis is to be had in the papers and books of Thomas S. Szasz (16–19).

† It is fitting, I think, to group these psychological types together, for investigation often reveals that they share many of the same proclivities to altered states of consciousness, have similar experiences of eidetic imagery and time distortion, and have easier access to unconscious and symbolic material. This suggests that they may be on a psychological continuum with each other and may be able to acquire easily the capacities of each other. Thus, the artist and the psychic may have interchangeable sensibilities, while the genius and the visionary mystic may apprehend the universe through psychological organs so similarly structured as to be almost identical.

taboos, laws, punishments. The maintenance of this "norm", requires, however, that the culture be relatively stable. The physical environment cannot change too drastically; the psychosocial environment has to be stable in the sense that the institutions that compose the cultural matrix preserve some authority, keeping confusion and conflict within those limits beyond which even the norms of consciousness tend to lose stability.

And now we find ourselves in the midst of perhaps the most radical and far-reaching crisis of consciousness in the known history of man. It would seem that in recent years the traditional norms have been shattered on almost every level, and with this, the reality consensus has been destroyed. No value, no social or political mandate, no reason for being has remained unshaken.

How did it happen? The exegetes of the decline and fall are many, and their commentaries are too well known to bear repetition here. From the perspective of the phenomenologist of consciousness and culture, it is important to suggest, however, that apart from the environmental stresses; the runaway technology; the hunger, crime, strife, and weapons of unprecedented destructiveness; the increasing withdrawal of human beings from their biorhythmic roots in nature; the sensory and existential overload; and the intensification of conflict as a way of life in practically every aspect of our social being—apart from these, we are faced with a shudder at the core of man's inwardness so profound that humanity seems threatened at its most basic level, that of the general consensus about what is real and what is not, perhaps the one consensus without which civilization is impossible.

Again, how did it happen? In part, it may have had much to do with the celebration of reason in Western culture since the eighteenth century. When reason rules, then dreams and prophecies, psychic insights and unconscious forces go underground and fester. Rationalism's success in cutting off access to our deep psychic and spiritual dimensions suppressed half our life. And suppression proverbially acts like the unrelieved pressure cooker. Sooner or later it blows up. It may well be that the holocausts of the twentieth century—the irrational rages of persons and nations, the closed and malevolent political systems, the "authorized" killing of millions—is partly the direct result of the rationalizing zeitgeist, which relegated one half of human nature to the subconscious stockpile where it spawned hothouse chimeras before emerging again through the back door onto the playing field of history, seeding the world with chaos and the demonic.* What we have been seeing in our times is the vengeance of the

---

* A poignant and brilliant analysis of the reasons leading to the holocaust is to be found in George Steiner's recent book, *In Bluebeard's Castle* (15). It is Steiner's belief that the devastation of World War I and II, and most particularly the destruction of the Jews, was the natural outcome of rationalism's rule over the nineteenth-

irrational, and what we are seeing in America today is one of its most recent and bizarre productions. It would seem as if an altered-states-of-consciousness syndrome were operative in American culture. The syndrome in several of its aspects is described in the well-known scriptural passage, "Your sons and daughters shall prophesy, and your young men shall see visions, and your old men shall dream dreams." Now this is nothing more nor less than a description of behaviors that always result when the norms of consciousness are massively transgressed and the reality-consensus breaks down.

I note the very remarkable, end-of-history, almost scriptural works of several young men who write of their *vision* of this culture. Robert Hunter in *The Storming of the Mind* (7), Theodore Roszak in *Where the Wasteland Ends* (13), and William Irwin Thompson in *At the Edge of History* (20) are like "hip" Hoseas, calling to their people and warning of an end but providing a promise for a new American Jerusalem if the heart and consciousness be changed. They are the prophetic chorus, celebrating and disseminating the intentions of the new myth but warning of the end if its possibilities are not explored. Yet they remain mindscape painters, applying metaphors of transformation of culture and consciousness—each finding his rallying point around the prayer of William Blake: "May God us keep/From single vision and Newton's sleep!"

And the sleep that is feared is not only the one that prevails with the technological heirs of Isaac Newton, but especially the one that involves the dream of a dreaming old man, B. F. Skinner, who, in a curiously medieval document entitled *Beyond Freedom and Dignity* (14), manages to achieve the epiphany of the mouse for our time. The deductive logic of the book, which solemnly, liturgically, and, yes, even benignly, turns man into machine, serves to remind us that in the past several hundred years we have abandoned the crude anthropomorphism of our senses only in favor of a more ambitious and pernicious anthropomorphism of our reason (12).

These visions and dreams of young and old men are symptomatic of those curious and tragic times in history when a whole culture was undergoing an ontological breakdown. Most of the structural and formal underpinnings of the society are either demythologized or disordered. And then,

---

century consciousness, which then generated a restlessness and an itch for chaos. "The collapse of revolutionary hopes after 1815, the brutal deceleration of time and radical expectation, left a reservoir of unused, turbulent energies." This, together with the immense growth of cities and the monetary–industrial complex effected the alienation and breakdown of consciousness on the part of nineteenth- and twentieth-century men, creating the necessary conditions for the coming debacle: "Outwardly brilliant and serene, 'la belle epoque' was menacingly overripe." An acutely perceptive and predictive statement about the genesis and pathology of the demonic in history is to be found in Paul Tillich's remarkable *The Interpretation of History* (21).

accompanying this breakdown, an extraordinary inward movement occurs. Psychological energy, which had been bound to social structures, is let loose. Moving inward, it breaches the unconscious, thus activating archaic and esoteric, as well as irrational and demonic, psychic contents. What occurs then is some of the phenomena being seen today—phenomena, in fact, reminiscent of the second and third centuries of the Roman Empire. It was during that period that the Pax Romana began to fail and the unwieldy structure of the empire came apart at the seams economically, militarily, politically, and religiously. Then, as now, consciousness escaped inward and there erupted a widespread fascination with the arcane, the occult, and with magic. Soothsayers abounded and standard-brand religions lost their followers while gnostic and Eastern cults of salvation and self-realization flourished. There was a premium on experience, ecstatic if possible, but extreme by all means. There arose a desire for more and more altered states of consciousness and for the tapping of some powerful mystical force that would give a new reality-consensus and bring order out of chaos. There was then, as there is now, a hope that in the return to subjective realities—to the green world within that belies the wasteland without—there would come a remythologizing, a revisioning of the world so that it would make sense again.*

This historical hypothesis can be applied to other periods of ontological breakdown. Most recently, let us consider what happened in Germany.† There, I believe, for a much briefer period all of the same tendencies appeared along the spectrum of the altered-states-of-consciousness syndrome leading to strife, chaos, the breakdown of the reality-consensus. After World War I, Germany was left devastated not only by the enormous loss of life and property but also by the loss or erosion of many of the ideals and cultural patternings that had given coherence to German culture for several hundred years. Then too, in addition to the breakdown of ontological structures and hierarchies, the devastation wrought by the economic depression completed the psychosocial atmosphere necessary for a complete loss of faith in traditional realities. With this came the breaching of a nation's consciousness. Carl Jung speaks of the reactivation of the Wotan symbols of pre-Christian Germanic mythology occurring in

* The psychohistorical analysis presented in this chapter is the result of my long-term interest and studies in the philosophy and psychology of history. These studies owe much to the work and theories of Eric Voeglin, Arnold Toynbee, and Lewis Mumford, with additional indebtedness to Karl Lowith, R. G. Collingwood, and Jacob Taubes. For a provocative analysis and comparison of the ontological crisis of ancient Rome and modern America, see Max Lerner (10). An excellent discussion of the generation of gnostic sects and philosophies from out of the dying body of the Roman Empire is given by Hans Jonas (8).

† The historical hypothesis that I suggest and its illustration with regard to the German scenario finds considerable resonance in Steiner (15) but also in Peter Gay's virtuoso study of the rise and fall of the Weimar culture (5).

many of his German patients. These archaic, undigested historical symbols of racial pride and dreams of conquest appeared to be ominously rising from the now seething layers of the collective psyche, looking for a social movement to attach themselves to. Coextensive with this, there occurred the eruption of strange and remarkable creative and visionary forms. The ecstatic but dissonant music of Berg, Weill, and others; the rise of the Bauhaus, whose work could almost be described as the unconscious become flesh, with its brilliant new forms of architecture and their influence on music, theater, and dance; the rise of surrealistic art; such extraordinary inner-space movies as *The Cabinet of Dr. Caligari*, which are supreme testimonials to the rise of deep psychic contents into consciousness.

Yet in the midst of the chaos and the ecstasy, the novelty and the invasion of the depths, we remember the words of Jung, who, writing around that time, said, "When such symbols occur in a large number of individuals and are not understood, they begin to draw these individuals together as if by magnetic force, and thus a mob is formed; and its leader will soon be found in the individual who has the least resistance, the least sense of responsibility, and because of his inferiority, the greatest will to power. He will let loose everything which is ready to break forth, and the mob will follow with the irresistible force of an avalanche" (9, p. xi).

If this is so, is it any wonder then that the charismatic Hitler arose to provide a hypnotic force and mystique, to forge a new consensual consciousness out of all this irrational and unleashed energy? It would appear that historically a profound crisis in consciousness has often led to one or both of two eventual disastrous consequences. One of these is chaos, bloody conflict, and the destruction of society through disintegration. These occurrences then frequently ensured a reinstitution of order imposed by an invader who comes and says, "I will give you peace. I will give you hope. I will make things real again."

The invading tyrant can be indigenous, someone rising up from within the culture as did Hitler, Cromwell, or some of the military Roman emperors. But then comes the awful denouement. The reinstitution of order in the society is accomplished by a countermovement of contraction of mass consciousness, the imposition of more limited norms of what is permissible to consciousness than those preceding the crisis, a consensus on a narrower and narrower reality, a constricted reality unable or unwilling to tolerate any deviation. Such a narrowing consensus is maintained by limiting and monotonizing stimuli of all sorts. The press is controlled, only permissible ideas are allowed dissemination, works of art are rigorously censored, architecture becomes monolithic (witness modern Peking or Speer's plans for Germania), and modes of dress are limited. Color, form, esthetic modalities—the entire spectrum of sensory and ideational input—

are severely limited. It amounts to the politicization of brain function. Brain function is restricted, stabilized, and maintained by a complex array of devices drastically limiting both inputs and outputs. One considers, for example, the flowing, fluid open dance forms of Mary Wigman in Germany in the 1920s, and then recalls that in the 1930s the geometric rigidities of the goose step became symbolic of the forms dominant in the national consciousness.

SOME STEPS ON THE WAY TO DISASTER

Before all this occurs, the consensus on disparate reality generates extremes of behavior and breakdown, as people frantically seek for a sense of what is real. Often, this search for a "tang" of reality is sought by means of intensities of sensation and emotion. Sexual excesses and intoxication states are cultivated to escape reality through obliteration, and to affirm reality through intensity of sensation, or to discern a new vision in the moments of intoxication that will make some sense of what is happening.

In such times, communication breakdown between groups of people becomes so extreme that in some cases, one group considers another group totally out of touch with reality—in fact, insane. The gap in our time between some older and some younger people is so deep and apparently unbridgeable because they do not share the norms of consciousness. Between these groupings yawn such great differences in their perception of reality that they hardly feel themselves to be living in the same world. One gets an eerie impression that we have a kind of epidemic borderline schizophrenia erupting. Many older people in increasing numbers complain that they can no longer recognize much that is familiar in the world around them. They claim to feel like aliens, visitors to their own cities and towns, as though the elements making for familiarity—the surroundings long perceived—had dissipated, leaving strange and ominous what ought to have been real and everyday, and what ought to have provided a sense of rootedness, continuity, reassurance.

In terms of the relationship between the young and the old, each tends to blame the other for the feelings each has of alienation, estrangement, unreality. The young blame the old for fashioning an unacceptable world; the old blame the young for destroying an acceptable world or making it unrecognizable. What is happening, then, is a shattering of the absolutely essential great chain of being between the generations, the chain that ensures continuity between one generation and the next. This, therefore, is no longer a generation gap. It is something immensely more profound. It is a reality gap in which there are no rights or wrongs—there are just totally different perceptions of reality. Even a historian of the stature of Arnold Toynbee suggests an extraordinary forbearance in dealing with the problem. He writes, "The destiny of the present rising wind of change in America is unforeseeable; so Gamaliel's advice to the Sanhedrin in the first century A.D. seems to me good advice today for present-day affluent American parents confronted by insurgent children, that is, 'Let them alone! For if this council or this work be of men it will come to naught, but if it be of God, ye cannot overthrow it' " (22, p. 26).

Deep as this wisdom is, I fear that it comes out of an age untouched by future shock and thus light years away in terms of slowness of pace and inability to control events. For if we should not be content to merely "let the wind bloweth where it listeth"—to play it by ear, so to speak—it may very well carry us toward destruction. And if our fate is now beyond our control, as many futurists and ecologists suggest, then Heidegger is right: the dreadful already has happened.

One of the principal dangers of a crisis of consciousness is that a fatalistic attitude will affect men generally. With the uncontrolled transgressions of the norms of consciousness occur regression, primitivization, superstition, a feeling that events are no longer subject to rational interpretation or controls, and apocalyptic fantasies of the end. This apocalyptic sense leads to excesses in practically every phase of life; people and environment assume increasingly bizarre aspects. Similarly, esoteric cults are embraced both as a diversion and as a hope of finding answers by means of which a re-visioning can be effected. The rise of the Jesus Freaks, and various forms of ecstatic fundamentalism, the following of a 15-year-old Indian boy as the "perfect master"—these are the pursuits of a simplistic esotericism, which, in my observation, frequently leads to emotional "highs" and a conviction of having attained "the Truth" but at the cost of the new ecstatic reacting to the larger field of the world around him as if he had undergone a psychological and social lobotomy.

Equally extreme and narrow-visioned are some of the political solutions that occur in these and similar times in the name of "holy" anarchy or "glorious" tyranny. These are often sought with an innocence so absurd as to become demonic. "Let's level the whole damn thing and then man will be free to be natural and good" or "What this country needs is just one good military leader to take over and put in some law and order."

In effect, an entire culture may be plunged into something very much like a bad psychedelic trip or a schizophrenic psychosis. Although individuals as such remain less affected than the collective, the collective society seems to possess a demented life of its own—swirling crazily along and steamrolling over people who observe it with a horror that is often a perverse fascination. There are degrees of this madness, and, of course, some civilizations went deeper into it than others. The Roman Empire went very far indeed, and Germany was "rescued" by Hitler, who then, however, managed to use the enfeebled collective consciousness of the Germans for his own psychotic purposes. Each nation will have its own variants because each nation and each people has its own ethnic and cultural tendencies, which become magnified. There are more similarities than differences between these cultures, since the behavior is shaped by the same basic phenomena: regression, primitivization, emotionalization, hypersuggestibility, fantasy vivified at the expense of reason, among many others. And, as we have seen from history, the powerful energies unleashed in these eras are likely to be extremely destructive.

As is apparent from my previous remarks, I believe that all of these elements are present in American society today, although they are not at the moment sufficiently widespread to insure that the United States will inevitably perish by disintegration, invasion, or despotism. They are surely at critical levels, though, and what we do in the next 10 years may determine our fate one way or another. For American civilization, this may be a watershed.

We have, however, a unique perspective that may save us—a perspective that most of the other cultures that succumbed to ontological breakdown did not really have.

Science?

No. Not entirely.

History!

The revealing of man's historic past over the last two centuries may well prove a more important, and indeed critical, contribution to man's survival than all his scientific knowledge. As Erich Neumann has emphasized, the reclamation of human history will involve the absorbing into man's conscious awareness of a perspective on chaos that, if unidentified and unrecognized, will otherwise continue to thwart and even to destroy him (11). By seeing parallels between our own process of cultural breakdown and that of others, we may be able to avoid the byways of unstructured psychological energy that have so often led to dark constraints and darker ages. Historiography teaches that history need not repeat itself, but the tendency in cultures for certain types of clusters of patterning to attend certain social phenomena is very strong. What we have in our time, and what the new myths tell us we have, is the opportunity to become the trustees of our own psychological and spiritual evolution. This insight gives us our uniqueness in that with it we may be the first age with the capacity to make a leap out of certain kinds of historical patterning.

The reasons for this are several. As suggested earlier, we are pushed in our time to the edge of survival—not just as a culture but as a planet. The ecology demands a radical change in how we deal with our problems lest all problems vanish and with them all humanity. As Willis Harman has clearly shown in his excellent discussion of the premises of the still dominant, but now failing, scientific–industrial paradigm (see Chapter 29), continued maintenance of this paradigm, with its emphasis on materialistic values, manipulative modalitites, and unlimited technological and economic growth, can only exacerbate the symptoms of disaster. If we are to continue as a species, we need a revolution in being and an evolution in cultural paradigm achieved by becoming what we have the demonstrable capacities to be.

The signs suggest that this is happening, first, in the emergent new myths and widespread metaphysical hunger and, second, in some remarkable attending phenomena. Chief among these are the signs indicating that we may be entering a golden age of brain and mind research, and with it a remarkably productive period for psychic research. We may well stand, with regard to our explorations of the mind–brain–psyche, where Einstein stood in the year 1904 with his discovery of the special theory of relativity, which helped accomplish the great revolution in physics. If I were to perceive (if only for whimsy's sake) the Freudian and Jungian analyses of human behavior as the Copernican revolution of the mind, then one might carry the analogy further and say that it appears that we now stand at the brink of the Einsteinian revolution of the mind, a quantum leap in the exploration and understanding of the nature and possibilities of man. The research in these areas is now apparently moving with a rapidity that may even outpace the momentum of the technology that poses such grave threats to us. The new explorations (and new interrelationships) in brain, mind, and psychic research increasingly allow us to view and probe the capacities of the human being and gradually to learn how to use our capacities more productively. For, as has been often noted, in the use of these capacities, we are literally operating along much the same lines as the iceberg, with most of our potential down there, out of sight, apparently inaccessible. Now, with the new advances in brain, mind, and psychic research it may be possible to raise the ice, lower the sea, or do both, especially in these times when the churning of the ocean gives us fleeting, phantasmagorical glimpses of what is really down there.

Writing again as a phenomenologist of culture and consciousness, a person who takes an intense interest in studying the nature of consciousness both in individuals and civilizations, I believe that we have a unique, but very feasible, opportunity to avoid the pitfalls of history by initiating a constructive mobilization and utilization of the very energies and phenomena that in their chaotic manifestations seem so very destructive and threatening.* We may be able to mobilize these energies in an entirely new

* For example, the energies that usually supply the impetus in times of reality crisis for the emergence of murky occultisms, zany superstitions, and pariah mystiques could, in our time, be directed instead toward the exploration and develop-

way in terms of what might be called a psychenaut program—the aim of which is to follow the initiative of the myths and put the first man on earth. This would be a project of inner-space exploration, aimed at mapping the mind and utilizing its vast untapped energies and capacities for a program of evolution now. It would involve a program of intensive mental and physical exploration and training aimed at enabling the psychenauts to use productively many capacities of mind and body that man has known about for centuries but access to which has never been sought systematically.

Nor, it may be added, has there ever been a major effort (apart from shamanistic societies) to orchestrate and integrate these capacities with each other. One of the problems with workers in psychic research, for example, is that they are so bemused and confounded by a subject's specific demonstrable capacity—be it for telepathy, PK, or whatever—that they tend to try to isolate and study the capacity apart from the much more important psychological matrix of the subject, in which the unusual capacity is embedded. Thus, for the psychic, the laboratory situation is proverbially the place to go to lose your skills or go sour. Again, the literature of the new myths suggest a differing, but highly pragmatic and successful, way of exploring and developing psychic abilities, to wit: treat them whimsically, as incidental skills that naturally and spontaneously emerge in the course of a training and development in a wide spectrum of human potentials.*

It is evident that as we are now, compared to what the new research suggests we could be, we live in a state of waste. The vastly greater part of every life is wasted: wasted time, wasted energy, wasted talent, leading to more waste—wasted food, wasted gadgets, wasted resources. We sleep too much, are too easily distracted, do not know how to think, to move, or even to breathe. We suffer needless pain, including such basic discomforts as those caused by temperatures and minor ailments that could just as well be ignored. Our minds move more slowly than need be and are constantly beset by petty concerns. Education neglects the basics of life: eating, breathing, movement, the utilization of mental and psychic capacities, states of consciousness—a thousand things. It also suffocates, imposes rigidities, squanders time and energies upon the obsolete, the superfluous,

---

ment of psychic abilities as natural and indigenous potentials that most people have and can be taught to utilize. In such a way, these potentials can be removed from the aristocratic darkness in which they have too long settled and be brought up to the democratic daylight, where everybody sees them for what they are: latent and subtle capacities of the human mind–body, probably more akin to the processes of art and creativity than to spooks, saucers, and schizoid spirits.

* At the Foundation for Mind Research, my husband, Robert Masters, and I have had some success in developing psychic abilities in subjects through just such an incidental approach. Some of the training is described in Chapter 26.

the banal. Waste—especially in negative emotions, self-destructive behavior, other-destructive behavior—whether by nations, groups, or persons, is the dominant factor in contemporary reality. It is for these reasons
that I find myself thinking that perhaps there is hope for man in the
current breakdown of educational, cultural, and psychosocial systems of
waste—systems generative of therapies that cannot heal and of images of
man now revealed as inadequate, distorted, sometimes flagrantly false,
and blatantly productive of damaging behaviors so numerous that we
cannot begin to count them.

And now, as in that once and future time, the walls have tumbled down
and what is revealed is a vastness, a perspective of human possibility, a
hopefulness that could not be seen when our vision was contained. It is for
this reason that the present time is uniquely favorable to explorations of
the mind and psychic sensibilities and to the effort to actualize and make
normative human potentials hitherto thought only as belonging to the
genius, the psychic, and the artist. That such an actualization is becoming
possible is evidenced also by the prodigious growth in recent years of
the human-potentials movement, of humanistic psychology, psychic research, and related or similar enterprises. Scientists, priests, psychics,
shamans, psychologists, mystics, artists, madmen, healers, yogis and
technicians are gathering together in conferences, in ashrams, and in laboratories all over. In a curious blending and interchange of the ancient
gnosis with present technical acumen, the future of man is in the process
of being engendered, as physical and mental capacities once only permitted to the few are enabled to function and experiences of a richer
reality beyond the consensual are given sanction and context in terms of
this new yeasting of East and West, science and ritual, the distant past and
the emergent future. Certainly, there are dangers, mainly from the eruption of the psychic technicians hawking the contents of their newly learned
bag of tricks but lacking the necessary wisdom, compassion, and selfless
dedication to mediate these techniques.

Timeo Danaan dona ferentes: I fear the Greeks bearing gifts. Be they
the ominous spiritual blackshirts and their clans, or the Chicken Delight-
type "mind-control" franchises, they contain the entropy factor, the
devolution in the midst of promise, the thirteenth fairy. Their tendency is
to pathologize or debilitate the possibilities inherent in consciousness.
There is no doing away with them. It's a free country and a relatively free
psyche, and Pandora's box has long since been opened and its contents
gone winging democratically past all and sundry. One can only effectively
counter such debasement with excellence. And that, hopefully, is what is
happening. Researchers and wise men and spiritual adepts of excellence
are drawing together and working together in ways that they have never
done before in order to answer the urgent need for a new image of man,

one that will energize human beings positively and constructively, give them faith in the human future, increase self-esteem, and provide directions in which to move and motivation to get there.

Thus, I project a psychenaut program as a feasible alternative to disaster. Its cultural aim is to take the psychological energy unleashed in our time that has been mobilized toward regression, superstition, and despair and redirect this energy to programs of human growth. Its psychological aim is to provide an environment in which human potentials and psychic abilities can be studied and worked with and realized in experimental subjects. The larger purpose of this is not just to gather knowledge and develop exemplars but to begin the introduction of the findings into the educational process so that the realization of potentials and innate psychic capabilities will become possible for almost anyone. If such were to happen, then I suspect that even the recalcitrant rigidities of the scientific–industrial paradigm would dissolve into a more holistic and ecologically sound paradigm, one that perceives, conceptualizes, and values in terms of an extended reality and an expanded sense of the possible.

Man unfolding, man emerging, man gaining access to the great latent powers of his body–mind–psyche: this must be the new image of man if we are to survive our time. Not man as something that has to be surpassed, not man the botched experiment, not man so hopeless that only psychopharmacology, behavioral conditioning, or genetic engineering can give him a structure capable of redeeming his baser nature, but man who already has the potentials to become fully human. This is the promise of the myth arising in our time. This is the hope of the paradigm of the possible humanity, the image that I believe can energize man to accomplish his transformation and so become the deserving trustee of his own evolution on this earth.

REFERENCES

1. Campbell, Joseph. *The Masks of God: Creative Mythology*. Viking: New York, 1968.
2. Castaneda, Carlos. *The Teachings of Don Juan*. University of California Press: Berkeley, 1968.
3. Castaneda, Carlos. *A Separate Reality*. Simon and Schuster: New York, 1971.
4. Castaneda, Carlos. *Journey to Ixtlan*. Simon and Schuster: New York, 1972.
5. Gay, Peter. *Weimer Culture*. Harper and Row: New York, 1968.
6. Heinlein, Robert. *Stranger in a Strange Land*. Putnam: New York, 1961.
7. Hunter, Robert. *The Storming of the Mind*. Anchor: New York, 1972.
8. Jonas, Hans. *The Gnostic Religion*. Beacon: Boston, 1963.
9. Jung, C. G. *Essays on Contemporary Events*. Kegan Paul: London, 1947.

10. Lerner, Max. *America As a Civilization*. Simon and Schuster: New York, 1967; see esp. chapter entitled "The Destiny of a Civilization."
11. Neumann, Erich. *The Origins and History of Consciousness*. Harper: New York, 1954.
12. Polanyi, Michael. *Personal Knowledge*. Torchbooks: New York, 1964.
13. Roszak, Theodore. *Where the Wasteland Ends*. Doubleday: New York, 1972.
14. Skinner, B. F. *Beyond Freedom and Dignity*. Knopf: New York, 1971.
15. Steiner, George. *In Bluebeard's Castle*. Yale University Press: New Haven, Conn., 1971.
16. Szasz, Thomas S. *The Myth of Mental Illness*. Hoeber-Harper: New York, 1961.
17. Szasz, Thomas S. "The Psychiatric Classification of Behavior: A Strategy of Personal Constraint." In L. D. Eron, ed., *The Classification of Behavior Disorders*. Aldine: Chicago, 1966, pp. 123–170.
18. Szasz, Thomas S. *New Republic*, 10 June 1967, pp. 21–23.
19. Szasz, Thomas S. *The Manufacture of Madness*. Delta: New York, 1970.
20. Thompson, William Irwin. *At the Edge of History*. Harper and Row: New York, 1971.
21. Tillich, Paul. *The Interpretation of History*, N. Razetski and E. Talmey, trans. Scribner's: New York, 1936; see esp. the chapter entitled "The Demonic in History."
22. Toynbee, Arnold. "As It Was in Rome. . . ." *Horizon*, 10, no. 2 (1968).

Robert Masters

ROBERT MASTERS *is director of research of the Foundation for Mind Research and director of the Sekhmet Institute for the Study of Images and Symbols. He is also general adjunct professor in the Union Graduate School and the author or co-author of 20 books in the areas of psychology, anthropology, psychedelic drugs, hypnosis, and sexual behavior. His books include* Eros and Evil (*Julian Press, 1963*) The Varieties of Psychedelic Experience (*Holt, Rinehart and Winston, 1966*), Psychedelic Art (*Grove Press, 1968*) *and* Mind Games (*Viking Press, 1972*).

26 Consciousness and Extraordinary Phenomena

ROBERT MASTERS

SUMMARY

Two cases are described in which extraordinary phenomena appear to have been elicited within the context of altered states of consciousness (trance) in a laboratory setting. In the first case, the research subject was given prolonged and elaborate training as a trance subject, including experiencing of trances of several days' duration. The subject then was able to demonstrate telepathic functioning repeatedly, as have a few other subjects who were participants in a similar training program. In the second case, the research subject, over a period of more than half a year, experienced herself as receiving training in "magic" from an Egyptian deity, the goddess Sekhmet. Her experiences are related in terms of the possible activation of an archetype, and it is suggested that those experiences are analogous to ones described by such historical visionary mystics as Swedenborg and Ibn 'Arabi.

INTRODUCTION

In the exploration of human potentials, consciousness is experimentally altered in order to uncover or disinhibit capacities of mind ordinarily more or less blocked. What is thought to obstruct these capacities, then, is *normal* consciousness—actually, a narrow range of states of consciousness within which most of our experience is fixed by accident, beliefs, and various other cultural conditionings. Alter consciousness to the necessary degree, and a particular capacity of mind, no longer obstructed, is enabled to manifest itself.

Among the capacities more or less obstructed by present norms of consciousness are the imageries of the several sensory modes; ongoing creative and other processes held by inhibiting mechanisms outside of awareness; quantities and qualities of memory materials; rates of thought far in excess of present normal ones; concentration well beyond the usual capacity; most of the data our sense organs receive; telepathic abilities; and many other materials and capacities, possibly including clairvoyance, psychometry, PK—the cluster of capacities that are commonly referred to as psychic or paranormal but that I am here calling *extraordinary*.

If these extraordinary capacities and their phenomena are indeed a part of the human potential, but obstructed, then it should be possible to effect their disinhibition by altering consciousness *in the manner and to the extent that is required*. The evidence accumulates that this can be achieved—evidence from experimental work and evidence from spontaneous manifestations when consciousness is altered by some stress originating either from within the person or without. There are also the cases of a few exceptional individuals who have gained access to these capacities and are able to apply them more or less at will in everyday life.

In this chapter I will describe the experiencing of extraordinary phenomena by two individuals with whom I have worked repeatedly and at great length. The first of these research subjects has, with training, become able to function telepathically on frequent occasions when in a rather deep trance. The other research subject has been enabled to enter into an archetypal world, or symbol system, that seems to give access to knowledge and experiences inaccessible to her by any other means.

My first subject (S-1), a female with a high school education in her mid-twenties, is one of a small number of research subjects who have participated in the first stages of what I call a psychenaut program of inner-space exploration. This subject (S) has been trained by me as a hypnotic subject for more than seven months, and several hundred hours have been spent by her in trance. This includes uninterrupted trances of more than two days' duration, the trance being maintained, I believe, during sleep, as well as in the waking state. That S is in trance upon waking from the sleep state has been repeatedly confirmed by observing responses to veiled suggestions and by observation of thought and perceptual processes characteristic of persons in deep trance. Trances have been induced by various instruments and devices, as well as by suggestion.

Before participation in this training program, S was tested for telepathy, precognition, clairvoyance, PK, imagery capacities, access to creative automatisms, and responses to suggestions of altered sensory perceptions, increased rate of thought and concentration capabilities. She was tested in her ordinary state of awareness and also with suggestions that she simulate trance. All testing for extraordinary capacities was negative. She also showed a very slight capability in the other areas mentioned.

In the early stages of psychenaut training, the subject first experiences a variety of trance induction and deepening procedures until it is considered that a maximum trance depth has been achieved. There is also a preliminary eliciting of the largest possible range of trance or altered-states-of-consciousness phenomena. Self-induction of trance and self-regulation of the depth of trance are taught. Later, S begins to learn to function in trance without suggestions from the experimenter (E). As time goes by, there is extensive training in several areas.

Imagery. S learns to experience visual, auditory, tactile, kinesthetic, olfactory, and gustatory images. Having vivid access to these imageries, S is able to experience subjective realities more completely.

Accelerated mental process. By *accelerated mental process*, or *time distortion*, is meant the capacity of the person to experience subjectively events that in the external world would require many hours or even days but to compress such lengthy experience into just a few minutes of clock time. Such acceleration is readily achieved in trance and occurs very often spontaneously in drug states, dreams, and life-threatening situations.

Creative automatisms. S is given access to ordinarily unconscious processes by means of which symbolic dramas, music, and literary productions become conscious without any kind of creative effort by the person. Such self-creating works of art are frequently accessible to highly creative individuals but have not often been experienced by other persons.

Energy systems in the body. S is enabled to experience various body energies or energy images of the kinds worked with in yoga and some other traditional spiritual and occult disciplines. For example, there are experienced powerful sensations of energy moving up the spine and reaching the brain, where explosions of colorful and white lights occur. The energy then is felt to surge over and stimulate the brain. Such phenomena have yet to be explained, but for S there is a subsequent impression of improved mental functioning, especially with respect to alertness, motivation to carry out necessary tasks, and a sense of being more creative.

Prolonged trances. As the training program progresses, S experiences increasingly longer trances, up to several days. S moves about in trance and engages in a variety of activities—sports, creative work, eating, reading, as well as experimental work eliciting the varieties of trance phenomena. Subjects, becoming accustomed to long trances, find themselves both more alert and more relaxed, with senses heightened and with an increased ability to concentrate and to remember. S is instructed to maintain the trance during sleep and to continue it then into the next day after waking from sleep. It is typically reported that dreams become richer, more orderly, and more vivid, with a greater amount of dream content recalled the next day. With the experiencing of prolonged trances, latent capacities, including telepathy, may begin to manifest themselves.

Belief systems programming. S is programmed, for the duration of the trance, to accept the validity of an image of the human being as a creature of very great and largely untapped resources. A large number of potentials are described, and S is told that these potentials are all her own and that she will have a productive access to them. Capacities latent until now will soon manifest, and there will be an even better access to potentials already uncovered and put into use. This programming concerning potentials includes extraordinary ones.

Personal problem-solving. A brief psychotherapy is undertaken to try to deal with neurotic and other problems of the subject. The life history of S is reviewed, and traumatic events may be revivified and desensitized.

Symbolic dramas. S is next enabled to participate in symbolic dramas in which the symbolization is a direct outgrowth of the preceding therapeutic work. S repeatedly returns to this symbolic realm, living out myths and rituals and sometimes finding and activating an archetype conducive to growth and liberation. Personifications of unconscious forces participate in these symbolic dramas, sometimes giving access to information not accessible to consciousness before. (I have described some early work with symbolic dramas, experienced in the context of psychedelic drug states, in previous writings (2, 3). Later work persuades me that trance is a more useful agent than was LSD for working with the symbolic dramas. With trance, S returns again and again to the archetypal world, interacting with symbols that gather power as time goes by. Of course, this means caution is warranted.)

Task-specific states. Subjects refine ability to self-regulate trance depth and work to determine states of consciousness most conducive to the performance of specific tasks. These include states most favorable to interpersonal relations, creativity, enhancement of pleasure and diminishment of pain responses, and extraordinary functioning.

Development of favored capacities. Capacities valued most highly by the particular subject are exercised to bring them to the highest possible level of application.

The foregoing is by no means a complete summary of the kinds of training included in the early stages of the psychenaut program. However, it does suggest the kinds of tools being made available to participants. All of this work, to be most productive, requires that S be engaged in an ongoing effort to bring her or his body to the highest possible degree of health and general perfection.

In regard to extraordinary capabilities, throughout the training program testing is done to measure improved performance, if any, and an effort is made to devise means whereby performance is improved. In the case of S-1, some telepathic ability began to emerge simultaneously with activation of "energy systems" and when duration of her average trance was at about four hours. She subsequently was allowed a portion of each experimental session for the exercise of this previously latent ability and special emphasis was placed, according to her need, on developing physical sensations serving to differentiate authentic telepathic transmissions from her own guesses and fantasies.

When the type of testing was to her liking, S would typically produce runs of six or seven responses considered correct by the experimenters and judges. Examples of successful performance are given here.

S, with her eyes closed and E positioned in back of her, was given the name of a woman but no additional information and was asked to say whatever she could about the person named. She described a dark-haired woman, probably in her mid-thirties, crippled and largely confined to a wheelchair. She next described an impression of frequent rages, of someone striking out to smash things, someone throwing objects and cursing, during childlike temper tantrums. Finally, she imitated a growling, almost animal voice that in fact was an excellent imitation of the person named. All of the other impressions were correct as well. Telepathy was considered to be the most likely explanation of S's performance.

In another typical experiment, S accurately described an event that had recently occurred in a shed on the laboratory's grounds. At first she reported anxiety, pain, and bewilderment and stated, "I believe a kid was hurt." She then declared there was something wrong with the word *kid*, which had seemed to her to mean a child. A visual image was forming where, at first, there had been only emotions and the word *kid*. She then reported accurately that it was not a kid but a large goat, that the goat had been injured in the shed, that the goat had been badly cut and lost considerable blood. In each of these tests, S experienced strong emotions and vivid images. Emotions and pain were felt with sufficient intensity to allow unmistakable identification. The visual images, seen with the eyes closed, were images of action, as if she were looking at a filmed version of what she then described. In the case of the woman in the wheelchair, there were also auditory images, allowing an excellent imitation of the distinctive voice. S also sometimes, although not in these instances, would feel herself briefly in the body of the person named. This would tend to happen in cases where the body of the individual was in some way unusual— crippled or deformed.

S could also successfully, in many instances, reconstruct important segments of the experiences of other research subjects. In making these reconstructions, S would very frequently give the most details concerning aspects of an experiment forgotten by me or not in my awareness at the moment mentioned. Parapsychologists have noted before that telepaths may find it easier to take information not presently in consciousness rather than from current awareness (4).

S's success in testing situations always was strongly dependent on her adequate motivation. An interesting personality or illness, some dramatic objective or subjective happening—these would invariably elicit her most successful performances. Performance fell off, although with definite successes, when S was asked to provide descriptions of works of art or photographs being looked at and "sent" by an experimenter. When Zener cards or numbers or letters were sent, S would make a few halfhearted, unsuccessful tries and then declare herself "too tired" or "too bored" or something of the sort. (LSD subjects used to respond in just the same way to telepathy tests that they considered insufficiently interesting.)

Apart from the experimental situations—in her personal life and work —S has not found the telepathic capacity to be spontaneously operative apart from trance. However, in a self-induced trance, she believes herself able to assess character, motives, and interests of other persons more quickly and accurately than she is able to do in her ordinary state. As with most individuals who have considered the matter, S would not at all want to have her awareness constantly flooded with telepathic impressions. Neither, in everyday life, would she want to be able to "read minds."

What is most significant about this case, which is typical of half a dozen such cases, is the emergence of a repeatedly demonstrable telepathic capacity in the course of a human-potentials training program, which alters consciousness and makes available tools—especially imageries— which extraordinary functioning usually requires. These cases seem to offer good evidence that telepathy is a capacity of the average person but is blocked by limitations on awareness and inhibition of specific mental tools. Telepathy, then, can be unblocked by altering consciousness sufficiently and by providing training of the kinds mentioned. However, a great deal of specifically telepathic practice undoubtedly is needed if the person is to achieve a fluency going beyond the minimally evidential performances seen in laboratories.

I am now working with research subjects toward trances eventually to be sustained for several weeks or even longer. This is an arduous labor, since it is a venture into unknown realms and the extensions of trance duration have to be made gradually to assure the well-being of research subjects. These experiments will aim at further unblocking, possibly of capacities that are more rare in the world than telepathy but that also may be a part of the human potential—clairvoyance, OOBE's, PK and others.*

LABORATORY INVESTIGATION OF THE MYSTERIES

It is my belief that the researcher investigating extraordinary phenomena must be willing to pass into the traditional domains of religion, mysti-

* Milan Ryzl, a Czech now working in California, has used hypnosis and imagery in a training program to develop ESP abilities. However, there are few other points of similarity between his reportedly successful training procedures and the system described here.

cism and the mysteries, art, mythology, magic, and the occult. These areas, if explored without credulousness, dogmatism, and undue anxiety, may be more fruitful pathways to follow than "science" on the road to understanding the phenomena being studied. After all, who is likely to be the more effective clairvoyant or telepath—the scientist or the shaman?

For over half a year now, with a female research subject (S-2), a recent university graduate in religion, I have carried out an experiment in what might be described as the activation of an archetype or symbol system—the Egyptian goddess Sekhmet and her "world." In this experiment S has followed in the footsteps of such predecessors as Swedenborg and Ibn 'Arabi, two of the most important visionary mystics of all time. She has returned again and again, as they did, to another reality, or "imaginal world," bringing back exhaustive accounts of her experiences. Being an artist, she has provided dozens of drawings in addition to her verbal descriptions.

This experiment has nothing to do with a regression to supposed past lives, with traveling back in time, or anything of that sort. It has to do with the intentional activation of, or awakening to, something that has its reality in present time; or perhaps it could better be said that it is from our own present time that we enter into its own nontemporal reality. It is my hope that the reader will suspend for a while any inclination to prejudge S's experience as "just fantasy." I have spent almost a quarter of a century exploring altered states of consciousness, the psychology of imagination, the creative process, and related areas, working with hypnosis, mind-altering chemicals, scientific instruments, and other tools, all with special emphasis on the study of the sensory imageries as alternate and supplemental ways of thinking and as sources of knowledge. S has had considerable firsthand experience of altered states and has devoted much thought and study to the criteria employed to differentiate fantasy about religious experience from authentic religious and mystical experiences. Before giving an account of the experiment, I would like to take note of some traditional beliefs about certain aspects of reality that need to be considered along with the more familiar ones of a Freudian psychiatry and a behaviorist psychology.

Some important Buddhist and Sufi approaches to consciousness and reality share with occultists and some mystics of the West a belief in the existence of realities that are the dwelling places of divine and other nonhuman, but intelligent, beings and affirm that humans may gain access to these realms, which are no less real and may be of a higher order of reality than our own familiar "objective" or "external" world. The question is not one of ontological status but of whether these realms and beings exist within or apart from human beings. If, as according to a Buddhist position, these realms and divinities are within the human body, this does not, of course, imply an existential dependency upon any person: they exist in *all* persons. The gods would then exist as Jung's archetypes exist, and it is said by some that the gods *are* archetypes and that their realms are the collective unconscious of humanity.

Some instructive statements about this have been made by the late Heinrich Zimmer, a professor of Indology who importantly influenced both Carl Jung and Thomas Mann. In an essay on tantric yoga (5), he writes:

> Tantric Yoga is directed toward man's own unconscious, the divine that is within us, which it conjures, awakens, and ritually worships. In the old cult of the Vedas, the gods come forth on their chariots externally though invisibly. Only the priest sees them corporeally, in an inner visualization effected by liturgical verses which describe them. . . . In Tantric Yoga the same occurs in the inner space of the body, in the inner field of vision, into which the figure of the deity rises from its—our—intangible depth.
>
> All the gods are in our body; nothing else is meant by the visual schema of the Kundalini Yoga, whose adept guides the world-unfolding, world-bearing life-serpent of the macrocosm out of its slumber in the depths, up through the whole body to its supraterrestrial opposite. . . . That all the gods and demons come from within us, even though they seem to approach us from without, is an open secret of Buddhism in its developed form, the "Great Vehicle," and is also taught in the Vedanta, which serves as the philosophical basis for the Tantras.

What happens, according to this teaching, when by skilled use of a ritual or mythic symbol, an archetype is brought into consciousness? It then may serve the person as a guide, source of knowledge, and vehicle of transformation. It can also possess the person, and this is the hazard of summoning forth the archetypal figure, whether it be goddess, figure of legend, or whatever. It is the business of the spiritual director, priest, psychotherapist, or experimenter to safeguard the student, patient, or research subject from the state of possession, while enabling him to accept what the guiding archetype has to offer.

Henry Corbin, professor of Islamic religion at the Sorbonne and an outstanding authority on Sufi mysticism, gives us a Sufi view of what may be involved in S's experimental exploration of the goddess Sekhmet's world. For the Sufis, there exist three worlds, each having its own organ of perception—the senses, imagination, and the intellect, corresponding with the triad body–soul–mind. Corbin writes (1):

We realize immediately that we are no longer confined to the dilemma of thought and extension, to the schema of a cosmology and a gnoseology restricted to the empirical world and the world of abstract intellect. Between them there is a world that is both intermediary and intermediate, described by our [Sufi] authors as the *'âlam al-mithâl*, the world of the image, the *mundus imaginalis*: a world that is ontologically as real as the world of the senses and that of the intellect. This world requires its own faculty of perception, namely, imaginative power, a faculty with a cognitive function, a *noetic* value which is as real as that of sense perception or intellectual intuition. We must be careful not to confuse it with the imagination identified by so-called modern man with "fantasy," and which, according to him, is nothing but an outpouring of "imaginings." This brings us to the heart of the matter and our problem of terminology.

What is this intermediary universe, i.e., the one we referred to earlier as the "eighth clime"? For all our thinkers the sensible world of space consists of the *seven climes* belonging to traditional geography. However, there is another clime represented by a world possessing extension and dimension, figures and colors; but these features cannot be perceived by the senses in the same manner as if they were the properties of physical bodies. No, these dimensions, figures, and colors are the object of imaginative perception, or of the "psycho-spiritual senses." This fully objective and real world with equivalents for everything existing in the sensible world without being perceptible by the senses is designated as the eighth clime. The term speaks for itself, since it signifies a clime *outside* all climes, a place *outside* all places, outside of *where*.

The *mundus imaginalis* of the Sufi mystics can probably, for practical purposes, be identified with the *mundus archetypus* of Jung, and the Sufi distinction between noetic imagination and fantasy has been stated in various ways by philosophers and mystics through the ages. Paracelsus doubtless meant the same thing when he cautioned against confusing the *imaginatio vera* of the alchemists with fantasy, "that cornerstone of fools." The imaginal world is the visionary world, the world of theophanic as of other visions, and it becomes perceptible to us only through a special cognitive imagination. This is a variety of imagination not accessible to those who remain in ordinary states of consciousness.

The gods appear in dreams and visions, rarely otherwise. The spiritual disciplines of mankind are always concerned with altering consciousness, whether by prayer, meditation, ascetic practices, drugs, trances, fasting, sexual intercourse—there are countless ways. But one must break out of the ordinary reality to become able to utilize the cognitive imagination, to attain to that consciousness in which it is possible for us to perceive what always is present but to which we are blind until our eyes have been opened, along with our other senses.

For my own part, I am not committed to the tantric, Sufi, or Jungian positions, any more than I am to the Freudian and behaviorist ("just fantasy") interpretations of visionary experience. But I have been interested in the firmness of the insistence by those who have had the most direct experience of visionary worlds that they are real and that it is possible to bring back from the experiencing of them information not accessible by other means. I have defined myself with regard to the materials of my experiments as explorer and phenomenologist. As phenomenologist, I do not have to, and must not, deal with questions such as that of ontological status. In this role, one does not evaluate—he only describes.

THE GODDESS SEKHMET

The extant images representing the goddess Sekhmet portray her with the powerful, but graceful, body of a human female and the head of a lioness. She is one of the most ancient of deities, having come into Egypt in times unrecorded and from a place unknown. Some of her titles refer to her very great antiquity: Lady of the Place of the Beginning of Time, and One Who Was Before the Gods Were. Sekhmet was a goddess of enormous power, defender of the gods against all forces of evil. This power is attested to by another of her names: Sovereign of Her Father, Ra. Among other titles of worship, the goddess was called Lady of Flame, Lady of the Lamp, and Great One of Magic. The first of these titles refers to her control of the sun, expressed by the solar disk, with uraeus, worn on her head. Lady of the Lamp appears to refer to the utilization of trance states by her priests.

The fascinating force of the Sekhmet image is expressed in her role as consort of her husband-brother Ptah, who is the creative process. Sekhmet is the one found most beautiful by art itself. Humans responded in a similar way, and no other Egyptian deity was represented by so many great statues. The priests of the goddess were for centuries the most potent magicians and healers of the ancient world.

The nature of the goddess is dual. By means of the sun, she makes the crops grow, but she also creates droughts and deserts. She is a goddess of both love and war, healing and pestilence, cursing and blessing, creation and destruction. All is well, so long as the positive side manifests itself. Always known as one of the most potentially dangerous of the Egyptian deities, it was also she who bestowed the greatest powers. The magicians

Robert Masters

The goddess Sekhmet (from the Temple of Karnak, Egypt).

and priests had nothing to fear so long as they, by their own misbehaviors, did not provoke her ferocious wrath.

My research subject and I did not deliberately set out to explore or activate the Sekhmet archetype. It was doubtless because of S's interest in a particular statue of the goddess that she found herself, while in trance, in a temple of Sekhmet on the occasion of our first working together. What we had intended to do was to utilize the trance state to elicit various images, which she would then draw. We intended to collaborate on a book about altered-states-of-consciousness imagery, for which I would provide the text.

The first trance, however, proved so exciting to S that she expressed a strong wish to return to the temple, if possible, on the occasion of her second trance. She already had had considerable trance experience and felt that the imagery of the Sekhmet temple was different from any she had encountered in the past, whether images of trance, dreams, meditation, or drug states. Everything was more vivid, more beautiful, more "real," and as a student of Jung's psychology, she felt that she possibly had entered into a world of archetypes.

I have found no reason to doubt S's statement that her knowledge of Egyptian myth and religion was very slight and that she knew virtually nothing about the goddess Sekhmet. Research concerning Sekhmet is difficult and requires fitting together small bits and pieces taken from a great many sources. These include papyrus sources and obscure, hard-to-obtain German, French, and other foreign-language volumes.

On the occasion of the second trance, S lived out, in an extremely vivid way and in a way that was personally relevant, one of the ancient Sekhmet myths having to do with the punishment of priests who had stolen objects of power. There was spontaneous time distortion, or acceleration of mental process, and the two-hour trance was experienced by S as lasting for more than a day.

We were now considerably interested in the experiences she was having. These seemed at least as real as any waking experiences and much more real than past trance experience. When she returned for a third time, she requested of Sekhmet that she be allowed to undergo training as a priestess or apprentice magician. She was told that this would be allowed but that the work would be long and exacting and would require her total commitment. She agreed to this and since then, over a period of more than half a year (to date), has experienced the unfolding of a course of instruction in an exceedingly rich and complex magical, religious, and philosophical system that seems perfectly coherent and logical. Existing scholarship does not allow us to say whether it is an authentic system in the historical sense. But it does seem consistent with the spirit of what we know of Egyptian magic and spiritual disciplines. Much of what she has been "taught" is also quite alien to the previous thinking of either S or myself. The system, at this writing, continues to emerge, with something new and significant added each time there is a trance, and the session transcripts already fill five volumes, with some 70 of S's drawings.

Several of the sessions have been extremely stressful. A kind of symbolic psychotherapy has taken place, removing many previously unconscious blocks, changing long-held values, and aiming at removing all impediments, whether physical or psychological, to S's ability to carry out the tasks she is instructed to perform. On one occasion, at S's request, Sekhmet "treated," by a kind of energy massage, a back injury of several years' duration. The injury had prevented S from making sudden movements (she had been obliged to wake up and change positions several times each night). After this particular trance, S bounded to her feet, as she had not done in years, and found herself to be quite free of all back pain. Four months later, the pain has not returned. Some of the psychotherapeutic work done has been similarly impressive in its positive results. In terms of Jungian psychology, this could be expected of a successfully activated archetype.

After a month, the trance sessions were spontaneously augmented by experiences occurring in dreams and hypnogogic states and in a kind of meditation that S had first learned about in trance. All of these experiences served the end of moving her toward a better understanding of the overall system, either by providing new information or by increasing motivation to practice what already had been learned.

Greatest and stern emphasis always was placed by Sekhmet upon S's mastering a special kind of concentration. This required becoming able to externalize images, projecting images onto a surface, or creating images in empty space. Concentration was, in fact, regarded as the most important element in the training of the magician in ancient Egypt, and it is also the foundation stone of mental training in yoga. Externalizing images is essential in the training of some Far and Middle Eastern spiritual adepts and artists. We do not have in the historical literature details of what concentration techniques were used in Egypt, but it seems exceedingly likely that the externalization of images was a requirement.

A great deal of the teaching has had to do with learning to experience body energy systems and with theoretical explanation of these and universal energies. Experiences in the body have included powerful energy surges up the spine, to the brain, with sensations of a boring out and opening of the "third-eye" area. Some have been like powerful doses of amphetamines, leaving the body highly energized but without any nervous agitation. Some have seemed to be working to effect a kind of restructuring of the nervous system. The teaching about universal energies has been elaborate and complex, providing a theoretical basis for practical applications of the teachings, to be taught later on. There has also been training in thinking and communicating with energies, which is described in the trance as a higher-level process than verbal or image thought. (Thinking experienced as energy or as motor or kinesthetic imagery has been described by individuals of genius as an important aspect of their creative process.)

It should be mentioned here that S, in trance, since the earliest sessions, has received very few suggestions from the experimenter. Often, I do not speak to her at all for an hour or more. During that time, I simply listen and record her intermittent reports of what she has been experiencing. Sometimes her silences last for an hour or even longer, when she cannot interrupt what she is doing to give verbal reports. The trances typically last from two to three and one-half hours, as measured by the clock. In terms of subjective, experiential time, trances seem to last for several days.

As an artist, S has been intensely interested in observing colors that she does not believe to exist in the external world. (This has also been reported to me by other trance and psychedelic-drug subjects, some of them artists.) There are also experiences of perspectives and "dimensions" that cannot be verbalized but that are described by S as unique. At one point in the experiments, S gave an instructive account of her experiences of the trance states up to that time:

> I had been curious as to where these experiences came from, whether from myself or without, and I had been very concerned with whether what was being taught made any sense. But the power of the energy, the lesson on concentration, after those I stopped asking that question. I realized that even though I was unable to make immediate sense of what was being taught, there was always an order to what was being shown. . . . Now I understood that while the experiences were received through my individual psyche, that I was experiencing something that transcended my personal experience. I could never have thought up the technique of concentration, and if I had, I would have dismissed it as impossible. I had been shown, however, how it works, and I had actually carried out the first step while still in trance.
>
> I became even more curious about trance. It seemed to me that what was happening was that through trance I was somehow able to bracket out a part of my conscious self and pass into either the personal or the collective unconscious. However, while this bracketing left me open and receptive, it also left me unable to reflect. In trance, I am never able to understand what is happening or even to think about it. This not only frustrated me but frightened me, for it seemed that the part of me that I know as me would fade away and be replaced by some other part. This other part seemed some sort of feeling guide who often would tell me what to do. After trance, I could see that the choices usually were good. But they were quite often very other than what I would ordinarily have done. For instance, taking part in bloody battles.
>
> It seemed in some trances that I was doing the action and in others it was being done to me. In some trances I was walking through a world, and the experiences and the world would unfold as I passed through it. But in other trances I have the feeling that the experiences come rushing down on me, it is being done to me. I feel completely contained and devoured by the experiences. . . .
>
> The images of the trances had been from the very beginning quite different from any I ever had experienced before. They were closer to dreams than to any kind of fantasy, but they were even far different from dreams. They always appear to be fully real, but they always have the quality of antiquity or of everlasting existence. I never have the feeling that these are my personal images, but they are there

waiting for anyone who chances to come along, and they are there even when I'm not looking for them.

After a while, there was a new kind of image that presented itself as energy. It would shoot from Sekhmet's eyes or thumbs, hang in the air, or crawl in my skin. There seemed to be three kinds of this energy: a misty, cloudy, smoky substance composed of minute particles; electric, luminous light lines of energy; and fluorescent pools of oscillating energy. I had experienced them all not just visually but also with my mind and body. Sekhmet told me that they all had meaning and that this was the way that I should learn to communicate, for it is more effective, economical, and powerful. I found them fantastically beautiful and enjoyed the experience of them on every level, but I didn't see how I was ever to understand them.

Image is not a good word, for *image* suggests a picture and two dimensionality. What I see in trance is very different from a picture. There seem to be three kinds of images, only the first two of which I think are images in the limited sense of the word. Both of them remind me of looking at the world, and I do not frequently see either one of them. One is a type of image that seems to pass before the eyes like a film on a screen and the second is a smoky formation that hangs in the air and suggests an object that never quite materializes. The other type of image doesn't appear to be an image at all but a real object in a three dimensional world. It is a moving world that I enter instead of looking at, and I can touch and act in it as fully as in ordinary reality. This world is experienced as completely and powerfully as the ordinary world and with the entire mind and body. It is because of this three-dimensional movement and personal involvement that the experiences are so powerful. If I were to look at a film of myself being born out of Sekhmet, it wouldn't begin to convey the feelings and the understanding of actual participation in the birth.

From the start, the personality of the goddess Sekhmet has been experienced as exceedingly rich, various, and powerful—also, in many ways, humanlike, as so many of the ancient gods were. Sekhmet is variously stern, loving, comical, tragic, ferociously angry, compassionate, wise, protective, punitive, whimsical, coldly logical, impatient, tolerant. Whatever facet manifests itself, however, there is no forgetting the gulf that separates the supernatural and godly being from the human one. At times, S has experienced very strong feelings of fear and dread, love, gratitude, awe, and ecstasy in her relationship with Sekhmet. Sometimes anxiety about becoming possessed has been almost as strong a motivating force as S's intense interest in what is occurring and as her desire to learn, if possible, what is experienced as Sekhmet's teachings. Ambivalence, however, has tended to diminish, albeit gradually, with the passage of time and additional experience.

On the whole, it seems likely that S's experience of Sekhmet must be not too different from an ancient Egyptian's experience of the goddess. What makes the difference, perhaps, is that Sekhmet's power no longer is nurtured or able to manifest itself throughout a culture. If this is true, then potentially any of the old gods is as powerful as ever and any potent archetype or symbol might under favorable conditions regain the full measure of its powers for a nation or even a world.

The authenticity of an archetype may perhaps be established in cases such as this by employing means used to validate religious experiences. For example, there should be definite changes in the thinking, behavior, and personality of the individual—there should be a transformation. The criteria for "authentic" religious and mystical experiences do not, however, take into account only those phenomena that are subsequent to the experience. There are elements of the experience itself that may tend to offer evidence that, if not conclusive, is at least supportive of experiential authenticity.

William James mentioned four universal characteristics of mystical experience, all of which are to be found in S's experiences of Sekhmet: ineffability; noetic quality (certainty that the knowledge gained is true); transiency of the mystical state; and passivity, the sense of being acted on. All of these characteristics apply to some portions of S's overall experience, although not to the whole of it. She has also experienced such common characteristics of mystical and religious experiences as encounter and union with a transcendent Other; ecstatic joy and bliss; loss of the sense of sin; a subjective death and rebirth; sense of objectivity or reality of the experience; being nonspatial and nontemporal; and paradoxicality. As a phenomenologist of altered states of consciousness and religious-type experiences, I cannot differentiate her experience from that of traditional mystics. Nor, speaking as a phenomenologist, do I find a basis for declaring the goddess Sekhmet to be any more or less real than any other deity past or present, as experienced by humans. Whether the gods are archetypes, whether they exist within or without human beings—these are matters about which I make no judgments here.

The instruction S is receiving contains a great deal about extraordinary phenomena. This includes teachings about levitation, telepathy, clairvoyance, PK, OOBE's, and dissolution and reconstitution of material objects. But she will have to accomplish much preliminary work before she will be able to attempt to implement these teachings, which in any case are as yet incomplete. What has definitely occurred is the healing of the back injury. That is, of course, not necessarily evidential of any extraordinary phenomenon. There have also been increasing instances of seeming telepathic and precognitive phenomena, but these have not been validated under strict conditions.

Personality and behavioral changes are more clear-cut. The experiences have not at all tended to separate her from other people. Rather, they have resulted in a broadening of her social contacts and in an increase of sociability. (She has, however, found it practically impossible to discuss the Sekhmet experiences with others, who are baffled and sometimes frightened by such a discussion.) With regard to S's creative work, there can be no doubt that it has become extremely prolific. In the opinion of our laboratory staff, there has also been a qualitative improvement in the areas of both drawing and writing. By her own judgment, S feels much more free, personally and creatively. She also feels that insights of great value have been had.

As a whole, then, it would appear that these experiences are, on one level, a process of integration. Where this process eventually will lead I will not attempt to predict. However, if S's experience is akin to that of yogis and some others who have embarked upon comparable journeys, then at some point the *siddhis* will appear: that is to say, the extraordinary capacities and phenomena will manifest themselves in definite and conclusive ways. For that, we will have to wait and see.

In any case, in the laboratory, we already have penetrated into regions of experience once thought to be reserved to the blessed—or unfortunate —few. Further explorations will make plain the possibilities and alter in one way or another our various present definitions of the real and the unreal.*

REFERENCES

1. Corbin, Henry. "Mundus Imaginalis, or the Imaginary and the Imaginal." In *Spring*. Spring: New York, 1972.
2. Masters, R. E. L., and Houston, Jean. *The Varieties of Psychedelic Experience*. Holt, Rinehart: New York, 1966.
3. Masters, R. E. L., and Houston, Jean. "Toward an Individual Psychedelic Psychotherapy." In Bernard Aaronson and Humphrey Osmond, eds., *Psychedelics*. Anchor: New York, 1970.
4. Osty, Eugene. *Supernormal Faculties in Man*. Methuen: London, 1923.
5. Zimmer, Heinrich. "On the Significance of the Indian Tantric Yoga." In *Spiritual Disciplines: Papers from the Eranos Yearbooks 4*. Pantheon: New York, 1960.

* This research subject and I are presently preparing a volume which will give a full account of the experiment here described. It is titled *Sekhmet: Dimensions of Mystery*. Pantheon Press: New York (in press).

Charles Honorton

CHARLES HONORTON *is director of research at the Division of Parapsychology and Psychophysics of Maimonides Medical Center in Brooklyn, New York. He also holds teaching positions at St. John's University and Brooklyn College.*

In 1965 Mr. Honorton became research coordinator for the Minnesota Society for Parapsychological Research. The next year he took the post of research fellow at the Institute for Parapsychology in Durham, North Carolina. In 1967 he assumed his present position at Maimonides.

Besides being a trustee of the American Society for Psychical Research, Mr. Honorton is on the board of directors of the Gardner Murphy Research Institute and is 1973 vice-president of the Parapsychological Association. He has published more than 50 professional papers and reviews dealing with psychic research.

Mr. Honorton can be reached at Maimonides Medical Center, Department of Psychiatry, Division of Parapsychology and Psychophysics, 4802 Tenth Avenue, Brooklyn, N.Y. 11219.

27 Psi-Conducive States
of Awareness *

CHARLES HONORTON

What if you slept, and what if in your sleep you dreamed, and what if in your dream you went to heaven and there plucked a strange and beautiful flower, and what if when you awoke you had the flower in your hand? Ah, what then?

—SAMUEL TAYLOR COLERIDGE

SUMMARY

Until recently, little systematic research has been directed toward examining the role of subjective state of awareness factors in psychic functioning. Historically, psi has been frequently associated with altered states of consciousness. The recent development of powerful psychophysiological tools and techniques for monitoring dreaming and other experiential states provides a new approach to the exploration of psi-conducive states. In this chapter recent experimental studies are described involving the elicitation of ESP through dreams, hypnosis, and meditation-type procedures. The findings are interpreted as indicating a relationship between successful psi functioning and the redistribution of attention toward internal processes such as thoughts, feelings, and images. This internalization of attention involves relaxation, mental passivity, and a reduction in sensory inflow. Studies of ESP in ordinary wakefulness are discussed that suggest individual differences in sensitivity to internal processes may be an important factor in psi success, particularly in studies involving attempts to train subjects to discriminate between correct and incorrect impressions. Points of convergence with yoga meditation systems invite more thorough examination of Eastern methods of consciousness expan-

* The preparation of this chapter was supported in part by U.S. Public Health Service Research Grant MH-21628-01, National Institute of Mental Health, and by the Foundation for Parasensory Investigation of New York City, Mrs. Judith Skutch, President.

sion and control as they may apply to the reliable production and under-standing of psi.

INTRODUCTION

The disparity between spontaneous human experience and its simulation in controlled laboratory experiments is nowhere more clearly evident than in the domain of parapsychology. The dramatic detail, vivid imagery, and feelings of conviction that so often characterize reports of spontaneous psi have seldom been encountered within the protective walls of the laboratory.

Psi has historically been closely identified with altered states of consciousness manifested in a variety of forms, both spontaneous and induced, including dream and reverie states, hypnosis, and meditation (9, 48, 52, 56). Despite the pervasiveness of this association, until recently there has been little systematic attention given to the role of internal state of awareness factors in psychic functioning. Most experimentally produced ESP effects have been obtained with subjects functioning in states of presumed "ordinary" wakefulness (54).

Before reviewing recent investigations of subjective state of awareness factors in psychic functioning, it will be useful to discuss some of the traditional problems that have been responsible for their neglect and some recent advances that provide us with new approaches for their investigation.

PUBLICIZING PRIVATE EVENTS

"Scientific psychology," according to a well-known saying, "having first lost its soul, then its consciousness, seems finally [through radical behaviorism] to have lost its mind altogether." Science has traditionally been ambivalent toward mental phenomena. The problem stated most simply is that states of consciousness and their contents (thoughts, feelings, and images) are essentially private. Since they are not directly observable, our knowledge of experiential processes is indirect and dependent upon introspection (in ourselves) and inferences from external behavior (in others).

From Introspection to Empty Organisms

Classical introspectionism involved analysis of experience through disciplined self-observation into elementary particles—sensation, feelings, and images—and delineation of their attributes, such as intensity and quality. The notorious unreliability of classical introspectionism led Sir Francis Galton, as early as 1883, to write sardonically, "Many persons, especially women and intelligent children, take pleasure in introspection, and strive their very best to explain their mental processes." Criticisms were numerous and severe, but the most damaging indictment of classical introspectionism was a pragmatic one: it did not lead anywhere (4).

Behaviorism sought to make a fresh, clean start in psychology through the exorcism of "subjective" subject matter and reliance on what, at the time, were considered to be thoroughly objective observations. J. B. Watson ushered in behaviorism with this declaration:

Our minds have been so warped by the fifty-odd years which have been devoted to the study of states of consciousness that we can envisage these problems only in one way. We should meet the situation squarely and say that we are not able to carry forward investigations along all of these lines by the behavior methods which are in use at the present time. . . . The topics have become so threadbare from much handling that they may well be put away for a time (78, p. 468).

Behaviorism became the psychology of the "empty organism." All lawful psychological statements according to this view were to be expressed in terms of stimulus and response (S–R). Events and processes occurring inside the organism were considered beyond the legitimate purview of science. Later variants of behaviorism, associated with names such as Tolman, Hull, and Spence, reintroduced mentalistic concepts in the guise of "intervening variables" and "hypothetical constructs."

Thus, for example, drinking behavior in water-deprived rats could be legitimized as "thirst." These neobehaviorists argued that intervening variables (thirst) were appropriate as long as they were firmly anchored with an observable stimulus (water deprivation) at one end and an observable response (drinking) at the other. This was not always as clear-cut as they believed.

In a penetrating critique of behaviorism, Sigmund Koch provided this appraisal:

If behaviorism is advanced as a *metaphysical* thesis, I do not see what, in final analysis, can be done for a truly obstinate disbeliever in mind or experience, even by way of therapy. If it is advanced as a *methodological* thesis, I think it can be shown that (*a*) the conception of science that it presupposes . . . does not accord with practice even in those sciences [e.g., physics] which it most wishes to emulate, and (*b*) that its methodic proposals have had extremely restrictive consequences for . . . problem selection and a trivializing effect upon the character of what are accepted as "solutions" by a large segment of the psychological community" (43, p. 6).

In parapsychology, the behavioristic influence is most clearly evidenced in the widespread popularity of the card-guessing paradigm and attendant lack of attention to the manner in which ESP responses are mediated into consciousness (79). It is perhaps understandable that early psi researchers should have chosen a methodological base that strayed as little as possible from methodological orthodoxy ("mainstream" psychology, circa 1930) in view of the excessive burden of criticism they had to bear.

Converging Operations

Today, however, the situation is different. Even the philosophers of science, who once provided the mainstay support for behaviorist doctrine, have abandoned it. Rudolph Carnap, a leading figure in the Vienna circle and former logical positivist, noted that "although many of the alleged results of introspection were indeed questionable, a person's awareness of his own state of imagining, feeling, etc., must be recognized as a kind of observation, in principle not different from external observation, and therefore a legitimate source of knowledge, though limited by its subjective character" (7, pp. 70–71).

The development, especially during the last decade, of powerful psychophysiological instrumentation and recording techniques has led to a renewal of scientific interest in states of consciousness and their systematic exploration (68).

Utilizing recent electrophysiological studies of dream recall as an illustration, Stoyva and Kamiya (67) have proposed a new strategy for the investigation of consciousness. They suggest that the combined use of physiological measures such as EEG and eye-movement recordings, *along with* introspective reports, represent "converging operations" that provide a more viable basis for inferring internal states (e.g., "dreaming") than has heretofore been possible. While physiological measures do not correlate perfectly with introspective accounts (dream reports, for example), to the extent that they do correlate, they may be said to converge upon a concept (such as "dreaming").

Terms such as *dreaming* and *altered states of consciousness* are useful ways of describing and categorizing complex psychophysiological relations or states.* The need for postulating unobservable entities is as great in modern physics as it is in psychology. For instance, we postulate the

* It must be remembered that state constructs are descriptive, *not* explanatory. They are helpful summary categories for complex interrelated processes (19).

existence of invisible elementary particles that possess neither mass nor spatial location yet which—in a manner understood only by physicists and their next of kin—constitute "solid matter," including our bodies, sense organs, and the "physical" stimuli that impinge upon them.

The strategy of converging operations can be extended to include states other than dreaming, and the armamentarium of the converging operationalist may be expected to expand to a wide range of objective instruments (e.g., physical and biological field detectors, chemical agents) as well as a greater variety of subjective measures (e.g., mood ratings, self-report scales, projective techniques). It may also be expected to utilize biofeedback techniques.

Biofeedback

Biofeedback may be thought of as a physiological mirroring technique in which normally inaccessible ("private") processes such as cortical activity, skin temperature, and muscle tension are externalized for the subject by means of electronic monitoring and filtering equipment. Biofeedback of specific brain waves may be accomplished by EEG monitoring with the addition of filters sensitive only to activity passing through a designated frequency range. Whenever such activity occurs, the filtering mechanism automatically and simultaneously provides the subject with an external signal (often a light or audible tone) of ongoing cortical activity. Utilizing these techniques for "on-line" self-monitoring, many persons are able to develop a degree of control over a wide range of somatic functions.

Self-monitoring of physiological processes has many important implications. For the converging operationalist, one of the greatest advantages of biofeedback is that it allows systematic comparisons to be made of subjective experiences accompanying varied levels of somatic activation. The subject learns to increase and decrease his physiological functions and to identify and describe subjective processes associated with his success in doing so.

The utility of biofeedback in converging operations may be illustrated by a recent EEG study (29). Subjects were trained via biofeedback to control a type of brain-wave activity known as the alpha rhythm (8–13 cycles per second). Alpha has been associated with relaxed, passive, inwardly focused awareness and with the absence of visual imagery. In terms of its relation to attentional processes, alpha displays a U-shaped function, desynchronizing and disappearing with both drowsiness and heightened arousal or complex cognitive tasks (66).

Whenever his brain produced alpha waves the subject heard a pleasant tone from a speaker connected to filters on an EEG machine. On alternate trials, the subject was asked to "keep the tone on as long as possible," and to "keep the tone off as long as possible." In order to assess changes in relaxation and attention during alpha generation (on) and suppression (off), eye movements and muscle tension levels were simultaneously monitored along with the EEG recordings.

Prior to beginning the training session, the subjects were instructed in the use of a "state-report scale" consisting of numbers from 0–4 and signifying their subjective assessment of changes in attentiveness and relaxation. Low state reports signified the type of active, externally oriented awareness associated with "ordinary" wakefulness, and high state reports signified increasing degrees of relaxation and internally directed awareness. The subjects were required to call out the first number that popped into their minds whenever an experimenter asked, "State?" State reports were elicited from the subjects near the end of both alpha-on and alpha-off trials, thereby representing an on-line assessment of subjective changes. At the end of the session, a postexperimental interview was conducted in order to elicit additional subjective material.

The converging operations in this study included three physiological measures (EEG, eye movements, muscle tension) and two subjective report measures (on-line state reports and retrospective interview responses). Although the three physiological measures did not correlate strongly with each other, each was significantly related to the state reports. High state reports were associated predominantly with alpha-on trials and low state reports with alpha-off trials. The amount of shift between alpha-on/alpha-off was reflected in concomitant state-report shifts. High state reports were also associated with reduced eye movement and muscle-tension activity, confirming earlier studies associating alpha with relaxation and reduced visual imagery, although suggesting the association to be more complex with alpha as one of several interacting components. Interview reports of unusual experiences during alpha-on periods, such as sensations of "floating in space," were related to strong internal shifts in awareness, according to state report and alpha density measures.

Based upon the convergence of physiological and experiential criteria such as these, it is possible to begin construction of an "alpha-state" model. It should be noted, however, that the converging measures utilized in this illustrative study were gross measures capable of finer refinement. For example, only one of several parameters of alpha (density or percent-time) was used. This study does, however, exemplify the development of a new methodology and conceptual approach to the scientific investigation of private experiential events and processes.

PSI-CONDUCIVE PSYCHOPHYSIOLOGICAL STATES

Stage-REM (Dream) Sleep

Dreaming is both the most familiar altered state of consciousness and the most frequently reported mediator of spontaneous ESP experiences. Through the discovery of major physiological correlates of dreaming, it became possible for the first time to monitor and arouse subjects during episodic dream periods, which consume a quarter of our normal sleep time. Known variously as *paradoxical sleep, ascending stage-1*, and, more recently, *"stage-REM,"* dream consciousness is associated with a low-voltage mixed-frequency EEG pattern; rapid eye movements (REM's), which correspond to some degree with visual activity in the dream; reduced muscle tonus; marked variability in pulse and respiratory rate; and penile erection (11).

Experientially, dreams contain vivid sensory imagery, a predominance of primary process (alogical) thinking, and continuation of daytime experiences, albeit in a distorted and often highly transformed manner. One of the most interesting findings to emerge from electrophysiological studies of dream recall is the relative imperviousness of the dreamer to external stimulation (11). The dreamer appears to be largely isolated from his external sensory environment.

Dreaming accounts for 37–65% of spontaneous ESP experiences in four international surveys (16, 53, 56, 58). In the largest survey (56), cases were divided on the basis of whether the paranormally acquired information was complete or fragmentary. Of the dream-mediated experiences, 85% were regarded as complete, compared to less than half of those occurring in the waking state. The difference is significant (31) and indicates a possible interaction between the percipient's state of consciousness and the quality of his psychic "perception."

A rather substantial clinical literature has also developed, focusing primarily on reports of telepathic dreams occurring during the course of psychotherapy (8). Often, striking "coincidences" have been observed between patients' dreams and contemporaneous events in the private lives of their therapists.

In 1960, Montague Ullman introduced electrophysiological monitoring techniques in a series of exploratory pilot studies in which telepathic stimuli were programmed in conjunction with subjects' dream (REM) periods (reviewed in 72). Through these exploratory efforts, an experimental analogue to the spontaneous psi dream was evolved that has now been applied in a series of carefully controlled investigations.

In these studies, tiny electrodes were affixed to the subject's scalp and face to permit continuous all-night electrophysiological monitoring of sleep stages. Whenever the polygraphic record indicated the onset of stage-REM activity, an experimenter signaled a distantly located agent ("sender") who then began to concentrate upon a randomly selected target picture, attempting to communicate telepathically the salient aspects of its contents to the dreaming subject. The distance between subject and agent has varied in these studies between 60 feet and 45 miles. At the end of each dream (stage-REM) period, the subject was aroused and asked for a dream report. Associations to each dream and other elaborative material were elicited in an interview conducted with the subject in the morning.

Upon completion of an experimental study (ranging from 7 to 32 nights), verbatim dream transcripts and copies of the target pictures were sent to a group of judges who did not know which target was used on a given night. Their task was to "blindly" rate the degree of similarity between each night's dreams and each of the potential target pictures. The results were then subjected to statistical analysis, which involved comparison of the average ratings given to the *correct* dream-target pairs (e.g., target 1 and dreams for night 1) with those given to the *incorrect* pairs (e.g., target 1 and dreams for nights 2, 3, etc). Significant differences between the correct and incorrect pair ratings indicated that the subjects were successful in telepathically incorporating salient aspects of the target pictures into their dreams.

Significant levels of success were obtained in seven experimental studies utilizing this methodology (32, 38, 40, 41, 71, 73). Three studies (37, 71) did not yield significant evidence of psi-dream incorporation. In addition to the formal experimental series, 83 pilot sessions were conducted for the purpose of screening potentially gifted subjects and assessing procedural innovations. The experimental precautions for these pilot sessions were identical to those employed in the formal experiments, and the results were highly significant (74).

This methodology was modified in two studies involving precognitive psi incorporation in dreams. Malcolm Bessent, an English psychic with a history of spontaneous precognitive experiences, participated in an eight-night series in which he attempted to dream about an experience that would be randomly determined and arranged for him on the following day. The results were highly significant (42). In a modified replication study, a series of target programs were utilized, consisting of color slides and coordinated sound effects structured around a common theme (e.g., "birds," "police," "2001"). On each odd-numbered (1, 3, 5, . . . , 15) night, Bessent attempted to dream about a target program that would be selected on a random basis and shown to him on the following even-numbered (2, 4, 6, . . . , 16) night. The results were highly significant for the precognitive nights. Bessent was successful in incorporating elements of target programs that, at the time of incorporation, had not yet been selected. He did not, however, incorporate the target material into his dreams on (even-numbered) nights following actual sensory exposure to the target programs (39). It appears at least for this subject that extra-sensory stimuli may be more easily incorporated into dreams than sensory stimuli.

These studies were all conducted in the Division of Parapsychology and Psychophysics of Maimonides Medical Center. Several attempts to in-vestigate experimentally induced psi effects in dreams have been reported from other laboratories. Globus (15) carried out a 17-night experiment with a single subject who claimed psychic ability. Evaluation of the judges' ratings did not yield significant results, although sessions that the judges rated with high confidence were significant. Calvin Hall (17) re-ported significant psi-incorporation in a pilot study with two subjects. Belvedere and Foulkes (2) and Foulkes and his associates (12) obtained insignificant results in two studies designed to replicate previously success-ful Maimonides series. Robert Van de Castle (76) obtained significant psi-incorporation with a group of subjects in an experiment utilizing sponta-neous dream recall.

Hypnosis

Hypnosis has traditionally been conceptualized as an artificially pro-duced altered state of consciousness that is brought about through a variety of "induction" techniques. Among the characteristics most fre-quently attributed to hypnosis are passivity, redistribution of attention, increased role-playing behavior, reduction in reality testing and increased tolerance for reality distortion, and hypersuggestibility (18). While a variety of somatic changes can be induced through hypnotic suggestion, the status of hypnosis as a distinctive psychophysiological state is contro-versial. There are presently no known physiological correlates that reliably distinguish hypnotic and nonhypnotic waking states. Studies comparing responsiveness to suggestions in hypnosis and in nonhypnotic motivated waking states appear to call into question many of the traditional assump-tions concerning the efficacy of hypnotic induction procedures (1).

While the nature of hypnosis remains controversial, there is no con-troversy over the historic association between hypnosis and ostensible psi (9). So close was this association for a time that ostensive psi phe-nomena were taken as criteria of deep "trance" and were known as the "higher phenomena of hypnotism."

The "higher phenomena" fell into four major categories: (a) com-munity of sensation, in which hypnotized subjects responded appropriately to stimuli presented to the hypnotist located at a distance; (*b*) transposition of the senses, including claims of eyeless vision and fingertip reading; (*c*) mental suggestion, involving ostensibly telepathic influence of the hypnotist on the subject's behavior while in "trance," posthypnotically, or by hypnotic induction at a distance; and (*d*) traveling clairvoyance, in which the hypnotized subject provided veridical information concerning a distant event or place unknown to him through normal channels.

Most of these early cases are of little value by contemporary standards of evidence. Rarely, for example, is it possible to feel confidence in the methods employed to eliminate sensory contact during eyeless-vision demonstrations. Experiments in community of sensation, although often impressive, were seldom conducted with sufficient distance between hypnotist and subject to eliminate sensory cues, particularly on occasions when olfactory stimuli were used.

Perhaps the most interesting and best controlled of the early claims was Gibert and Janet's experiment on the induction of hypnosis at a distance (48). Their subject, a peasant woman named Leonie, was reported to have entered hypnosis on 19 out of 25 attempts when the hypnotist and witnesses were located half a mile away. The time during which hypnotic induction was attempted was determined randomly by one of the witnesses. A number of cases of traveling clairvoyance in which hypnotized subjects provided specific information concerning a distant place or event are also difficult (although not impossible) to interpret on the basis of sensory leakage. One such case involved the well-known "somnambulist" Alexis Didier and was reported by the sitter, Rev. C. H. Townshend, who presented himself to Didier anonymously. It is described by Dingwall:

> Townshend asked Alexis if he would in thought visit his . . . house, to which the somnambule replied that, since his questioner had a house in London and in the country, which house should he go to first? Townshend said that he wanted him to visit his country house, and Alexis then said that he saw a house of medium size, surrounded by a garden, and on the left side of the same property there was a smaller house. Townshend was surprised at the accuracy of his description for the account could be applied to his house in Lausanne, where there was another small dwelling in which his landlady lived. Asked what kind of view Alexis was seeing, he replied that he saw water, plenty of water and trees opposite the house and quite near to it. All this was true. Townshend then suggested that he should go into the drawing room, which Alexis described as having many pictures on the walls, all of which were modern, except two, one of which was a sea-piece and the other a religious subject. As to the religious picture, Townshend had recently bought it from an Italian refugee and it had many

peculiarities which Alexis proceeded to describe. He stated that there were three figures in the picture, an old man, a woman and a child. The woman had a book upon her lap, and the child was pointing its finger to something in the book, while there was a distaff in the corner. All these details were correct, the picture representing St. Anne teaching the Virgin Mary to read. Asked on what was the picture painted, Alexis replied that it was neither on canvas nor metal, but on a curious substance which he finally stated to be of stone. The colour of the stone was something between black and grey: it was rough behind and was of curved shape. All this was true, since the picture was painted on a piece of curved marble (9, Vol. I, pp. 183–184).

more recently by a Swedish investigator, John Bjorkhem (3). Unfortunately,
Similar cases of apparent traveling clairvoyance have been reported
Bjorkhem's studies lack some of the controls necessary to eliminate non-psi interpretations. Successful confirmation of another nineteenth-century claim, telepathic hypnosis, was reported by the Soviet pioneer of parapsychological research, L. L. Vasiliev (77). In these studies, the hypnotist-agent attempted to influence a hypnotized subject's grasp on a rubber bulb (hand kymograph) at random intervals. Vasiliev reported only 6 failures in 260 attempts.

The effects of hypnosis on standard card-guessing ESP tasks have been explored in a dozen experimental studies (31). These studies compared ESP success in hypnotic and nonhypnotic waking states. Typically, subjects guessed ESP symbols while in hypnosis (or following posthypnotic suggestions) and in their normal waking state. Nine of the 12 studies demonstrated significant differences between the two conditions, indicating that hypnosis does affect ESP performance. Van de Castle (75) reported a pooled probability of 10 billion to 1 for the difference between hypnotic and waking ESP scores in these studies. Hypnosis appears to affect ESP magnitude rather than scoring direction (i.e., the sign of deviation, above or below chance), and it appears that hypnotic increments in ESP are not attributable to direct suggestions for high scores. Indeed, suggestibility is not highly correlated with ESP success (21, 63). These studies have been reviewed in greater detail elsewhere (31, 75).

Considerable interest was aroused by the recent claim by Ryzl (57) of a method for training ESP in unselected volunteer subjects by means of hypnosis. Ryzl describes the training technique as consisting of three interrelated phases. The first phase is characterized by intensive hypnotic training in which subjects learn to carry out increasingly complex suggestions, culminating in the development of complex and vivid visual hallucinations. ESP training proper begins in the second phase, with suggestions for veridical hallucinations of concealed target material and immediate feedback to the subject of success or failure. When initial success is achieved, attempts are made to sharpen the subject's psi faculties through the detection of psi-related internal cues. The final phase consists of gradual withdrawal of the subject's dependence upon hypnosis and the introduction of controlled quantitative tests. While one subject who underwent Ryzl's program has maintained impressive ESP scoring ability in a prolonged series of experiments with a number of different investigators, it is not clear what role—if any—hypnotic preparation may have played. A number of unsuccessful attempts to validate Ryzl's technique have been reported (31). None of these failures, however, incorporated the type of intensive hypnotic training emphasized by Ryzl and further exploration of his method should be encouraged.

Another potentially valuable application of hypnosis involves its use in simulating other states including anxiety, conflict and dreaming (44). Like biofeedback, hypnosis may provide an opportunity to examine extrasensory effects through the simulation of apparently psi-conducive states. A number of studies, for example, have been conducted utilizing hypnotically induced dreams as mediating vehicles for experimental psi incorporation. J. Stump and I (33) selected subjects falling in the upper range of a standard hypnotic susceptibility scale. Following induction of hypnosis, the subjects were given these suggestions: "You are going to have a dream. It will be a very vivid and realistic dream. You will dream about the target in the envelope. It will be as though you are walking right into the picture in the envelope. You will participate in whatever action is depicted, and you will observe the picture from that standpoint. You will see everything very clearly because you will be part of it."

The subjects each had four hypnotic dreams, and for each hypnotic dream, there was a randomly selected target picture enclosed in an opaque envelope. At the end of the experiment, the subjects were shown the four target pictures and asked to rate—on a blind basis—the similarity between each target picture and each of their four dreams. They succeeded to a significant degree, obtaining correct identification of the targets in 46% of the cases where chance expectation was 25%. This study was successfully repeated by Parker and Beloff (51), although a second study by these investigators provided only chance results. Two other independent confirmations of hypnotic dream psi incorporation have been reported with significant results (14, 35), and a further replication and extension of the Honorton–Stump findings has recently been reported in a study involving a nonhypnotized waking control group (25). Subjects with low hypnotic susceptibility ratings and subjects in the control group did not obtain significant ESP matchings, while highly susceptible hypnotized subjects did. Self-ratings of dream quality and state reports, similar to those utilized in the biofeedback study described earlier, were used as converging measures. High dream-quality ratings, indicating vivid, dream-like experiences, and high state reports, indicating subjects' assessment of being deeply hypnotized, were associated with more correct target–dream identification than low dream-quality ratings and low state reports. Subjects showing strong prehypnosis–hypnotic-dream shifts in state reports were more successful than those with relatively little shift in state.

Krippner (36) obtained significant ESP effects in a study involving hypnotically induced imagery, although in this experiment, nonhypnotic waking control subjects also produced significant psi incorporations. Krippner suggested that hypnosis may have speeded up the telepathic process.

Meditation and Protomeditative States

"Just as the pure crystal takes color from the object which is nearest to it," says Patanjali, in the ancient *Yoga Sutras*, "so the mind, when it is cleared, . . . achieves sameness or identity with the object of its concentration" (52). States of consciousness achieved through Eastern meditation techniques have been perennially associated with the concurrent manifestation of *siddhis*, or psychic powers.

The descriptions of these techniques bear striking similarities to those advocated by Western psychic-development practitioners and to the introspective strategies reported by gifted ESP subjects. Rhea White (79) inspected the introspective descriptions of a group of successful ESP percipients and found several consistent preparatory phases in their attempts to become psi-receptive. These include deep mental and physical relaxation, withdrawal of attention from external sensory stimuli, and development—through this preliminary elimination of distraction—of highly focused, "one-pointed" concentration. In Patanjali's schema, *siddhis* are manifest through a process called *samyama*, involving extended and relatively uninterrupted ("centered") concentration. The various "limbs" of yoga that precede *samyama* are viewed as preparatory purification. Purification involves the removal of impediments to concentration.

We have already discussed relaxation and redistribution of attention in relation to dreaming and hypnosis. The contribution of relaxation to ESP has been examined in other contexts as well. In an experiment with hospitalized patients, Gerber and Schmeidler (13) found that patients who were rated "relaxed and acceptant" produced significantly high ESP scores, while those rated "not relaxed and not acceptant" scored at a chance level. Significant ESP incorporation of pictorial targets was reported by Braud and Braud (5) in a series of experiments utilizing Jacobson's technique for deep muscle relaxation.

The withdrawal of attention from external stimuli, characteristic of dreaming and hypnosis, suggests that psi receptivity may be facilitated by a reduction in sensory input. Relatively weak psi impressions may be more readily detected and recognized during periods in which the sensory "noise level" (including somatic sensations) is minimized. Only one experimental study has so far been published concerning the effects of sensory deprivation on ESP (30). While confined in a suspended sensory isolation cradle, subjects gave intermittent state reports. A distantly located agent attempted to influence the subjects' spontaneous imagery with a randomly chosen target picture during the last 10 minutes of confinement. Subjects with high state reports (relaxed, inwardly focused attention) obtained significant psi incorporation with 76% hits, while subjects with low state reports (active, externally directed attention) obtained 46% hits. Chance expectancy was 50%.

As noted earlier, EEG alpha activity displays a U-shaped relation to attention and desynchronizes with sudden stimulation. Much of the current interest in alpha activity stems from research findings in psychophysiological studies with advanced practitioners of meditation disciplines. Strong increases in alpha density and amplitude have been found to occur during deep Zen and yoga meditation (reviewed in 69).

Consequently, research exploring the possible convergence between alpha density and ESP success has proliferated rapidly. The purpose, relationship between ESP and alpha density (6, 22, 47, 55), while others (27, 64) indicate a negative relationship. Still another (45) demonstrated both in the form of an interaction with two types of ESP tasks. The most reliable finding thus far is that an increase in alpha frequency (in cycles per second) from pretest to ESP-test periods is positively related to ESP performance (62, 64, 65); this the investigators tentatively interpret as evidence of a "stage-setting" mental quietude or passivity followed by a level of arousal adequate to attend to, and assimilate, the incoming psi information.

Inferences concerning subjective states in these studies were made exclusively on the basis of EEG criteria. Subjects in the biofeedback study, described earlier, returned for a subsequent session in which they completed ESP-card-guessing tasks while alternately turning their alpha on and off and giving state reports (28). The overall results were not significantly different for alpha-on and alpha-off ESP trials. However, only half of the subjects conformed to the "alpha state" model (i.e., high alpha—relaxed, internalized attention; low alpha—active, externalized attention). For these subjects, alpha-on trials were associated with significantly high ESP scores and were significantly higher than during the alpha-off trials.

This finding illustrates the inadvisability of inferring mental states exclusively from physiological criteria and argues strongly for a converging operations approach.*

Psychedelic Drugs

Tart (68) reported a questionnaire study of 150 frequent marihuana users. The respondents commonly described marihuana intoxication as involving vivid visual imagery, attention to normally ignored sensory qualities, time distortion, increased tolerance for logical inconsistencies, and reduced efficiency of short-term memory. They also frequently reported experiences that were interpreted as telepathic and a substantial number claimed OOBE's. There has been thus far no report of experimental research on the effects of marihuana on extrasensory functions. However, the phenomenological descriptions bear interesting similarities to the states surveyed above and controlled double-blind placebo studies seem warranted.

Much the same may be said of the major psychedelics such as LSD and psilocybin. A few experimental studies have been reported (50) to yield equivocal results. A major problem encountered in these studies involves the difficulty of structuring an appropriate psi task within the context of a powerful, overwhelming experience. More imaginative approaches must be evolved. At present, the association of ESP with psychedelic drug states is anecdotal.

PSI CUES

Conviction is a frequent attribute of spontaneous ESP experiences. It has been rare in experimental ESP-card-guessing studies and with good reason: few such studies have incorporated measures for detecting conviction. Card-guessing has dominated experimental psi research since the 1930s, and while the guessing paradigm has provided a simple, objective, and rapid basis of data collection, it has also been characterized by massed, unrewarded trials and severe limitations on response range. Thus, given a set to view his task as guessing, the subject is implicitly discouraged from attending to subtle internal cues that may be available to guide his response.

---

* K. Osis and E. Bokert (49) reported significant correlations between several measures of ESP and postmeditation questionnaire responses. Their studies involved a complex multivariate approach and must be interpreted with caution. A more straightforward finding, reported by G. Schmeidler (60), involved significant ESP-card-guessing scores following a swami's instruction on meditation and a breathing exercise.

Sooner or later, subjects confronted with such tasks begin to establish guessing habits that may interfere with comparably weak ESP impressions. While the evidence for this hypothesis is not yet compelling, there is no controversy over the fact that ESP guessing tasks are generally associated with scoring declines and eventual loss of ability (54).

In studies that have incorporated conviction measures, subjects have been instructed to give "confidence calls" on trials they believe most likely to be correct. Although confidence calls are usually associated with more hits than trials without them, there has been little development from this finding, because of the possibility that confidence calls are merely secondary ESP responses rather than the reflection of a weak, but genuine, discriminative function.

A recent series of studies suggests that confidence calls are more than secondary ESP impressions (23, 24, 46). In these studies subjects gave confidence calls during a clairvoyant guessing task. They were then given these instructions:

Now we're going to try something different. Rather than guessing "down through" the pack and making confidence calls, I'm going to turn each card over after you make your guess and I'll tell you whenever you're right. Pay special attention to your correct guesses and see if you can begin to discriminate between those that are right versus the ones that are wrong. In doing this, be sure to take note of any internal differences in feeling, attention, method of calling, etc. Feel free to modify your guessing strategy; freely explore the conditions associated with hits.

One group of subjects received immediate feedback for each correct guess. Another group received incorrect or false feedback. Subjects in both groups then completed another clairvoyant guessing task with confidence calls. In each study, subjects who received correct feedback obtained significant gains in the proportion of correct confidence calls. Subjects who were given false feedback did not. Of the subjects receiving correct feedback, 82% obtained postfeedback gains, compared to 44% of the subjects receiving false feedback.

In the most recent of these studies (46), postexperimental interviews were conducted to discover what—if any—internal cues were utilized by subjects in determining trials with confidence calls. The subjects fell into four categories: (a) those who reported relying on visual images of the targets, (b) intuitive (imageless) "feelings" of correctness, (c) multimode impressions involving two or more types of cues (e.g., "I could feel my heart beating faster and the impression was more persistent"), and (d) subjects who reported no discernible cues—for whom confidence calls were merely additional guesses. Subjects who reported multimode cues obtained significantly larger postfeedback increases in correct confidence calls than those who reported no discernible cues.

Cue utilization is a dimension of sensitivity to internal processes and has been found subject to wide individual differences. A consistent feature of the various states reviewed in this chapter is the shift of attention from external to internal stimuli, possibly providing greater access to psi-relevant cues through increased sensitivity to internal processes (see Chapter 9). Individual differences in internal sensitivity during normal wakefulness have also been found to interact with ESP scoring success. Schmeidler and LeShan (61) found that subjects who were rated as more internally responsive had significantly larger scoring fluctuations above and below chance in an ESP guessing task than subjects who were less internally responsive. Studies relating ESP with frequency of reported dream recall (26, 34) and creativity (20, 59) are consistent with this hypothesis, suggesting that subjects who in their normal waking state actively work with, and attend to, internal processes, may be more psi-sensitive than those who normally are inattentive to their internal states.

Various psychic-development claims, Ryzl's ESP "training" method, and yoga treatises consistently suggest an association between internalized, narrowly focused awareness and the detection (or development) of psi-relevant cues. Thus far, cue utilization in altered states of consciousness has been explored in only one published study. Fahler and Osis (10) hypnotized two subjects and had them perform a precognitive guessing task over a series of experimental sessions. The subjects were given suggestions that "on some trials they might have impressions of correctness or feelings that certain [guesses] were 'different' from the others." On such trials they were instructed to give confidence calls: 16% of the trials with confidence calls were correct, compared to 7% without confidence calls. The difference is a highly significant one, with a probability of 50 million to 1.

A PROVISIONAL FRAMEWORK

Explorations of ESP in dreams, hypnosis, sensory isolation, meditation, and protomeditative practices suggest that psychic communication (or perhaps the ability to detect and recognize psychic influences) is facilitated by an inward focus of awareness. This redistribution of attention to internal states is accompanied by a reduction in awareness of somatic and environmental stimuli. When sensory inflow and processing diminish, the number of irrelevant stimuli impinging upon the percipient as he tries to "tune in" a target may also diminish, thereby increasing his ability to detect, recognize, and respond appropriately to relevant extrasensory information.

In some of the waking-state studies, measures of attentiveness to internal processes—including dream recall, creativity, and instructional sets to "follow subjective cues"—were found to interact with ESP-card-calling success. The confidence-call experiments with immediate feedback suggest that external cues, such as feedback, may be more efficacious with subjects who have greater access to a variety of subjective cues. The incorporation of internal and external cue-detection devices (e.g., confidence calls and immediate feedback) with properly "tuned" subjects has not yet been reported experimentally. Ryzl's hypnotic "training" method embodies this in an informal, nonexperimental manner, and it is also suggested by Fahler and Osis's work with hypnotized subjects. It may also be recalled that in one of the hypnotic dream studies significantly more psi incorporation was obtained by subjects who reported especially vivid dreamlike experiences.

Elimination of internally generated distractions (e.g., daydreams and memories) through one-pointed concentration is a dominant feature of introspective reports by gifted psi percipients as well as of the meditation and psychic development traditions. Thus far, sustained concentration has not been directly studied in experimental psi investigations. However, in psi explorations with hypnosis, we have observed a facilitative effect that appears unrelated to suggestibility and direct suggestions for "success." The hypnotized subject literally "talks himself into it" through his undivided attention to an emotionally neutral (and, hence, minimally distracting) repetitious patter. Similarly, meditators are instructed to repeat their mantras (a subvocal sound) until there is "nothing left" except the mantra. When through concentration there is nothing left but the object of concentration and its reflection in consciousness, a state of mind-clearing –narrowing–focusing is achieved. This threefold process is Patanjali's *samyama*, concentration–meditation–absorption.

The points of convergence with yogic descriptions that have been suggested invite a more thorough examination of Eastern methods of consciousness alteration. The techniques described in Patanjali's *Yoga Sutras*, for instance, appear to be sophisticated and systematic and may well be fertile ground for parapsychological hypothesis-testing and conceptualization. The recent psychophysiological studies in voluntary control of autonomic processes by yogis illustrate the potential for cross-fertilization between Western technological science and Eastern self-regulatory practices.

The study of psi-conducive states is embryonic. Its development, as we have seen, has long been retarded by an almost exclusive preoccupation with objective measurements and elimination of nonpsi informational sources. The research presented in this chapter provides a provisional framework for a new and continuing inquiry into the nature of psi processing. Now as psychology regains consciousness we may begin, along with Coleridge, to press forward the query, "Ah, what then?"

REFERENCES

1. Barber, T. X. *Hypnosis: A Scientific Approach*. Nostrand Reinhold: New York, 1969.
2. Belvedere, E., and Foulkes, D. "Telepathy and Dreams: A Failure to Replicate." *Perceptual and Motor Skills*, 33 (1971): 783–839.
3. Bjorkhem, J. *Det ockulta problemet*. Lindblads: Uppsala, 1951.
4. Boring, E. G. "A History of Introspection." *Psychological Bulletin*, 50 (1953): 169–189.
5. Braud, W. G., and Braud, L. W. "Preliminary Explorations of Psi-Conducive States: Progressive Muscular Relaxation." *Journal of the American Society for Psychical Research*, 67 (1973): 26–46.
6. Cadoret, R. J. "An Exploratory Experiment: Continuous EEG Recording During Clairvoyant Card Tests. *Journal of Parapsychology*, 28 (1964): 226.
7. Carnap, R. "The Methodological Character of Theoretical Concepts." In H. Feigl and M. Scriven, eds., *Minnesota Studies in the Philosophy of Science*, Vol. I. University of Minnesota Press: Minneapolis, 1956.
8. Devereaux, G., ed. *Psychoanalysis and the Occult*. International Universities: New York, 1953.
9. Dingwall, E. J., ed. *Abnormal Hypnotic Phenomena*. 4 vols. Churchill: London, 1967–1968.
10. Fahler, J., and Osis, K. "Checking for Awareness of Hits in a Precognition Experiment with Hypnotized Subjects." *Journal of the American Society for Psychical Research*, 60 (1966): 340–346.
11. Foulkes, D. *The Psychology of Sleep*. Scribner's: New York, 1966.
12. Foulkes, D.; Belvedere, E.; Masters, R.; Houston, J.; Krippner, S.; Honorton, C.; and Ullman, M. "Long-Distance 'Sensory-Bombardment' ESP in Dreams: A Failure to Replicate." *Perceptual and Motor Skills*, 35 (1972): 731–734.
13. Gerber, R., and Schmeidler, G. "An Investigation of Relaxation and of Acceptance of the Experimental Situation as Related to ESP Scores in Maternity Patients." *Journal of Parapsychology*, 21 (1957): 47–57.
14. Glick, B., and Kogen, J. "Clairvoyance in Hypnotized Subjects: Positive Results." *Journal of Parapsychology*, 35 (1971): 331.
15. Globus, G. "An Appraisal of Telepathic Communication in Dreams." *Psychophysiology*, 4 (1968): 365.
16. Green, C. "Analysis of Spontaneous Cases." *Proceedings of the Society for Psychical Research*, 53 (1960): 97–167.
17. Hall, C. "Experiments with Telepathically Influenced Dreams." *Zeitschrift für Parapsychologie und Grenzgebiete der Psychologie* (Freiburg), 10 (1967): 18–47.
18. Hilgard, E. R. *Hypnotic Susceptibility*. Harcourt, Brace and World: New York, 1965.

19. Hilgard, E. R. "Altered States of Awareness." *Journal of Nervous and Mental Disease*, 149 (1969): 68–79.
20. Honorton, C. "Creativity and Precognition Scoring Level." *Journal of Parapsychology*, 31 (1967): 29–42.
21. Honorton, C. "A Combination of Techniques for the Separation of High- and Low-Scoring ESP Subjects: Experiments with Hypnotic and Waking-Imagination Instructions." *Journal of the American Society for Psychical Research*, 63 (1969): 69–82.
22. Honorton, C. "Relationship Between EEG Alpha Activity and ESP Card-Guessing Performance." *Journal of the American Society for Psychical Research*, 63 (1969): 365–374.
23. Honorton, C. "Effects of Feedback on Discrimination Between Correct and Incorrect ESP Responses." *Journal of the American Society for Psychical Research*, 64 (1970): 404–410.
24. Honorton, C. "Effects of Feedback on Discrimination Between Correct and Incorrect ESP Responses: A Replication Study." *Journal of the American Society for Psychical Research*, 65 (1971): 155–161.
25. Honorton, C. "Significant Factors in Hypnotically Induced Clairvoyant Dreams." *Journal of the American Society for Psychical Research*, 66 (1972): 86–102.
26. Honorton, C. "Reported Frequency of Dream Recall and ESP." *Journal of the American Society for Psychical Research*, 66 (1972): 369–374.
27. Honorton, C.; and Carbone, M. "A Preliminary Study of Feedback-Augmented EEG Alpha Activity and ESP Card-Guessing Performance." *Journal of the American Society for Psychical Research*, 65 (1971): 66–74.
28. Honorton, C.; Davidson, R.; and Bindler, P. "Feedback-Augmented EEG Alpha, Shifts in Subjective State, and ESP Card-Guessing Performance." *Journal of the American Society for Psychical Research*, 65 (1971): 308–323.
29. Honorton, C.; Davidson, R.; and Bindler, P. "Shifts in Subjective State Associated with Feedback-Augmented EEG Alpha." *Psychophysiology*, 9 (1972): 269–270.
30. Honorton, C.; Drucker, S.; and Hermon, H. "Shifts in Subjective State and ESP Under Conditions of Partial Sensory Deprivation." *Journal of the American Society of Psychical Research*, 67 (1973): 191–196.
31. Honorton, C., and Krippner, S. "Hypnosis and ESP Performance." *Journal of the American Society for Psychical Research*, 63 (1969): 214–252.
32. Honorton, C.; Krippner, S.; and Ullman, M. "Telepathic Transmission of Art Prints Under Two Conditions." *Proceedings*, 80th Annual Convention, American-Psychological Association, 1971, pp. 319–320.
33. Honorton, C., and Stump, J. "A Preliminary Study of Hypnotically Induced Clairvoyant Dreams." *Journal of the American Society for Psychical Research*, 63 (1969): 175–184.
34. Johnson, M. "Relationship Between Dream Recall and Scoring Direction." *Journal of Parapsychology*, 32 (1968): 56–57.
35. Keeling, K. "Telepathic Transmission in Hypnotic Dreams: An Exploratory Study." *Journal of Parapsychology*, 35 (1971): 330–331.
36. Krippner, S. "Experimentally Induced Telepathic Effects in Hypnosis and Non-Hypnosis Groups." *Journal of the American Society for Psychical Research*, 62 (1968): 387–398.
37. Krippner, S. "Investigations of 'Extra-Sensory' Phenomena in Dreams and

Other Altered States of Consciousness." *Journal of the American Society of Psychosomatic Dentistry and Medicine*, 16 (1969): 7–14.

38. Krippner, S.; Honorton, C.; and Ullman, M. "A Long-Distance ESP Dream Study with the Grateful Dead." *Journal of the American Society of Psychosomatic Dentistry and Medicine*, 19 (1972).

39. Krippner, S.; Honorton, C.; and Ullman, M. "A Second Precognitive Dream Study with Malcolm Bessent." *Journal of the American Society for Psychical Research*, 66 (1972): 269–279.

40. Krippner, S.; Honorton, C.; Ullman, M.; Masters, R.; and Houston, J. "A Long-Distance 'Sensory-Bombardment' Study of ESP in Dreams." *Journal of the American Society for Psychical Research*, 65 (1971): 468–475.

41. Krippner, S., and Ullman, M. "Telepathy and Dreams: A Controlled Experiment with EEG–EOG Monitoring." *Journal of Nervous and Mental Disease*, 151 (1970): 394–403.

42. Krippner, S.; Ullman, M.; and Honorton, C. "A Precognitive Dream Study with a Single Subject." *Journal of the American Society for Psychical Research*, 65 (1971): 192–203.

43. Koch, S. "Psychology and Emerging Conceptions of Knowledge as Unitary." In T. W. Wann, ed., *Behaviorism and Phenomenology*. University of Chicago Press: Chicago, 1964.

44. Levitt, E., and Chapman, R. "Hypnosis as a Research Method." In E. Fromm and R. Shor, eds., *Hypnosis Research Developments and Perspectives*, Aldine-Atherton: Chicago, 1972.

45. Lewis, L., and Schmeidler, G. "Alpha Relations with Non-Intentional and Purposeful ESP After Feedback." *Journal of the American Society for Psychical Research*, 65 (1971): 455–467.

46. McCollam, E., and Honorton, C. "Effects of Feedback on Discrimination Between Correct and Incorrect ESP Responses: A Further Replication and Extension." *Journal of the American Society for Psychical Research*, 67 (1973): 77–85.

47. Morris, R.; Roll, W.; Klein, J.; and Wheeler, G. "EEG Patterns and ESP Results in Forced-Choice Experiments with Lalsingh Harribance." *Journal of the American Society for Psychical Research*, 66 (1973): 253–268.

48. Myers, F. W. H. *Human Personality and Its Survival of Bodily Death*. 2 vols. Longmans: London, 1903.

49. Osis, K., and Bokert, E. "ESP and Changed States of Consciousness Induced by Meditation." *Journal of the American Society for Psychical Research*, 65 (1971): 17–65.

50. Pahnke, W. "The Use of Psychedelic Drugs in Parapsychological Research." In A. Angoff and B. Shapin, eds., *A Century of Psychical Research*. Parapsychology Foundation: New York, 1971.

51. Parker, A., and Beloff, J. "Hypnotically Induced Clairvoyant Dreams: A Partial Replication and Attempted Confirmation." *Journal of the American Society for Psychical Research*, 64 (1970): 432–442.

52. Prabhavananda, Swami, and Isherwood, C. *How to Know God: The Yoga Aphorisms of Patanjali*. New American Library: New York, 1973.

53. Prasad, J., and Stevenson, I. "A Survey of Spontaneous Psychical Experiences in School Children of Uttar Pradesh, India." *International Journal of Parapsychology*, 10 (1968): 241–261.

54. Rao, K. *Experimental Parapsychology*. Thomas: Springfield, Ill., 1967.

55. Rao, K., and Feola, J. "Alpha Rhythm and ESP in a Free Response Situation." *Proceedings of the Parapsychological Association* (1972).

56. Rhine, L. E. "Psychological Processes in ESP Experiences. I. Waking Experiences." *Journal of Parapsychology*, 26 (1962): 88–111.
57. Ryzl, M. "A Method of Training in ESP." *International Journal of Parapsychology*, 8 (1966): 501–532.
58. Sannwald, G. "Statistische Untersuchungen um Spontanphänomenen." *Zeitschrift für Parapsychologie und Grenzgebiete der Psychologie*, 3 (1959): 59–71.
59. Schmeidler, G. "An Experiment on Precognitive Clairvoyance." V. Precognition Scores Related to Feelings of Success." *Journal of Parapsychology*, 28 (1964): 109–125.
60. Schmeidler, G. "High ESP Scores After a Swami's Brief Instruction in Meditation and Breathing." *Journal of the American Society for Psychical Research*, 64 (1970): 100–103.
61. Schmeidler, G., and LeShan, L. "An Aspect of Body Image Related to ESP Scores." *Journal of the American Society for Psychical Research*, 64 (1970): 211–218.
62. Stanford, R. G. "EEG Alpha Activity and ESP Performance: A Replicative Study." *Journal of the American Society for Psychical Research*, 65 (1971): 144–154.
63. Stanford, R. G. "Suggestibility and Success at Augury—Divination from 'Chance' Outcomes." *Journal of the American Society for Psychical Research*, 66 (1972): 42–62.
64. Stanford, R. G., and Lovin, C. "EEG Alpha Activity and ESP Performance." *Journal of the American Society for Psychical Research*, 64 (1970): 375–384.
65. Stanford, R. G., and Stevenson, I. "EEG Correlates of Free-Response GESP in an Individual Subject." *Journal of the American Society for Psychical Research*, 66 (1972): 357–368.
66. Shagass, C. "Electrical Activity of the Brain." In N. Greenfield and R. Sternbach, eds., *Handbook of Psychophysiology*. Holt, Rinehart and Winston: New York, 1972.
67. Stoyva, J., and Kamiya, J. "Electrophysiological Studies of Dreaming as the Prototype of a New Strategy in the Study of Consciousness." *Psychological Review*, 75 (1968): 192–205.
68. Tart, C. *On Being Stoned: A Psychological Study of Marijuana Intoxication*. Science and Behavior: Palo Alto, Calif., 1971.
69. Tart, C., ed. *Altered States of Consciousness*. Wiley: New York, 1969.
70. Ullman, M. "Telepathy and Dreams." *Experimental Medicine and Surgery*, 27 (1969): 19–38.
71. Ullman, M., and Krippner, S. "A Laboratory Approach to the Nocturnal Dimension of Paranormal Experience." *Biological Psychiatry*, 1 (1969): 259–270.
72. Ullman, M., and Krippner, S. *Dream Studies and Telepathy*. Parapsychology Foundation: New York, 1970.
73. Ullman, M.; Krippner, S.; and Feldstein, S. "Experimentally Induced Telepathic Dreams: Two Studies Using EEG–REM Monitoring Techniques." *International Journal of Neuropsychiatry*, 2 (1966): 420–437.
74. Ullman, M.; Krippner, S.; and Honorton, C. "A Review of the Maimonides Dream ESP Experiments: 1964–1969." *Psychophysiology*, 7 (1970): 352–353.
75. Van de Castle, R. "The Facilitation of ESP Through Hypnosis." *American Journal of Clinical Hypnosis*, 12 (1969): 37–56.

76. Van de Castle, R. "The Study of GESP in a Group Setting by Means of Dreams." *Journal of Parapsychology*, 35 (1971): 312.
77. Vasiliev, L. L. *Experiments in Mental Suggestion.* Institute for the Study of Mental Images: Church Crookham, England, 1963.
78. Watson, J. B. "Psychology as the Behaviorist Views It." *Psychological Review*, 20 (1913): 158–177.
79. White, R. "A Comparison of Old and New Methods of Response to Targets in ESP Experiments." *Journal of the American Society for Psychical Research*, 58 (1964): 21–56.

Willis W. Harman

WILLIS W. HARMAN, *Ph.D., is director of the Center for Study of Social Policy at Stanford Research Institute and professor of engineering–economic systems at Stanford University.*

After receiving his doctorate in electrical engineering at Stanford in 1948, he taught at University of Florida until 1952, when he returned to Stanford as a professor of engineering. He has written several engineering texts and various professional papers on microwave electronics and communication theory.

For a period Dr. Harman was active in the newly formed Association for Humanistic Psychology, serving as a member of the executive board and a member of the editorial board of the Journal of Humanistic Psychology. *He has published several research papers in this field, including "Old Wine in New Wineskins" (in* The Challenge of Humanistic Psychology, *J. F. T. Bugental, ed. McGraw-Hill, 1967) and "The New Copernican Revolution" (in* Journal of Humanistic Psychology, *9 [1969]). These works have had a recognized effect upon the fields of humanistic and transpersonal psychology.*

Dr. Harman entered the field of social policy analysis and joined Stanford Research Institute in 1966, becoming director of the Educational Policy Research Center in 1967. In this work he has made various contributions to research on alternate futures and analysis of major societal problems. He has been consultant to the National Goals Research Staff of the White House and to the Conference Board in New York. He was a featured speaker at the 1972 White House Conference on the Industrial World Ahead: A Look at Business in 1990. His address, "Key Choices of the Next Two Decades," was published in Fields Within Fields . . . Within Fields *(5, no. 1 [1972]).*

Dr. Harman can be reached at the Center for Study of Social Policy, Stanford Research Institute, Menlo Park, Calif. 94025.

28 The Social Implications of Psychic Research

WILLIS W. HARMAN

SUMMARY

Psychic research, both as a formal discipline within the activity of science and as an informal fascination and exploration in the larger culture, is profoundly affecting habitual modes of thinking and perceiving, and thence social institutions and the culture itself. These habitual modes can collectively be termed paradigms. Both the scientific paradigm and the industrial-state paradigm spawned by the technology of science are being challenged. Thus, there is a powerful press for change arising in society.

That change apparently is occurring. Surveys and polls show increased emphasis on humanistic, transpersonal, and spiritual values in various areas of society. The characteristics of this paradigm shift are examined in terms of the Perennial Philosophy and the New Freemasonry, and the significance of this view of man in the universe if it were to become dominant is suggested.

INTRODUCTION

When Thomas Kuhn in *The Structure of Scientific Revolutions* (7) introduced the term *paradigm* to refer to the basic pattern of perceiving, thinking, valuing, and acting associated with a particular vision of reality, he was concerned with phenomena of radical change in scientific conceptual frameworks. In the decade that followed his publication, evidences of radical and fundamental change in the larger society prompted application of the term in a broadened sense, so that we began to hear references to a possible changing of the "dominant paradigm" within the society as a whole. The implication of this is profound. What it means is that a particular pattern of conceptualizing, valuing, and perceiving that has characterized all of what we consider to be "modern" industrial civilization may be giving way to a new order. Not only does this imply changed folkways and "new-age" values, it also means changed social institutions and power structures and an altered economic and political order. As the Reformation and the Copernican revolution were accompanied by a time of troubles and a century of religious wars, so we can expect (in this speeded-up age) that a fundamental paradigm change will bring with it at least a decade or two of tumultuous times and relative social disruption.

The activity known as psychic research will play a central role in all this. Until recently, peaks of interest in this area have threatened the prevailing paradigm in psychological science but have been suppressed by minor adaptations of that paradigm and the superior prestige of scientific orthodoxy. Thus, of the wealth of new territory surveyed in F. W. H. Myers's magnificent compendium *Human Personality and Its Survival of Bodily Death* (10), several important taboo topics—notably hypnosis, unconscious processes, and creativity ("inspiration")—passed over into the realm of legitimate inquiry without major disturbance to the basic scientific metaphors or methodological premises, while the main thrust of the work was successfully ignored. But the present situation is very different. Psychic research in the next few decades may be destined to have a social impact comparable to the impact, several centuries ago, of the astronomical investigations of Galileo and Copernicus, because, like those earlier inquiries, it is at the centroid of a powerful press for cultural paradigm change.

The social power of science through the technology it spawned was such that, by the middle of the nineteenth century, it was generally recognized as society's "official" truth seeking activity, displacing such less precise systematic inquiries as religion and philosophy. But it has also been in the name of science that the transcendental bases of humane values have been eroded, leaving this and other advanced nations with little guiding purpose beyond a growth and consumption ethic, which is increasingly leading to social and ecological crises. Thus, when the phenomena of psychic research challenge, as they do, the dominant scientific paradigm, they also threaten the dominant social paradigm.

In the discussion to follow we shall first look more thoroughly into this challenge. We will then examine the characteristics of an emergent paradigm that accommodates the data of psychic research. Finally, we will comment on the possible societal impact if this new paradigm should become dominant.

CHALLENGES TO PRESENT PARADIGMS

I am using the term *paradigm*, I repeat for emphasis, to refer to the basic pattern of perceiving, thinking, valuing, and acting associated with a particular vision of reality. As a part of the culture, the paradigm is communicated nonverbally and absorbed unconsciously and largely by example. Its role is primarily an invisible one; the vision of reality on which it is based is seldom reexamined, and the implicit premises it contains are generally unchallenged. By its very nature it is not easily identified, nor can it be concisely delineated. It is like "common sense"—no one can define it but everyone responds to it.

Table 1 attempts to list some of the premises implicit in the positivistic paradigm, which has been dominant in scientific activity at least until very recently. Of course, this is not to claim that all scientists accepted all these premises. But we can imagine that if they had been put forth in a college's basic science course, few would have risen to challenge them—at least up to about a decade ago. Yet each of these premises is directly challenged by a plenitude of data from the field of psychic research, and a large portion of those data have been available for more than half a century.

TABLE 1
IMPLICIT PREMISES OF POSITIVISTIC SCIENCE

1. The only conceivable ways in which we could come to acquire knowledge are through our physical senses and by inheritance of some sort of memory storage in the genes. Thus, the only way in which we can hope to extend our understanding of the nature of the universe is through fuller and more sophisticated use of such technological extensions of our senses as the electron microscope, radio telescope, electroencephalograph, magnetic-resonance spectrometers, and so on.

2. All qualitative properties are ultimately reducible to quantitative ones—that is, color is reduced to wavelength, thought to measurable brain waves, hate and love to the chemical composition of glandular secretions, and so on.

3. There is a clear distinction between the objective world, which is perceivable to anyone, and subjective experience, which is perceived by the individual alone, in the privacy of his own mind.

4. The concept of the free inner man is a prescientific substitute for the kinds of causes that are discovered in the course of scientific analysis—forces impinging upon the individual from the outside and internal tensions and pressures that are characteristic of the organism. In other words, freedom is only another name for the behavior for which we have not yet found a cause.

5. What we know as consciousness or awareness of our thoughts and feelings is really only a side effect of physical and biochemical processes going on in the brain.

6. What we know as memory is simply a matter of stored data in the physical organism, strictly comparable with the storage of information in a digital computer.

7. The nature of time being what it is, there is obviously no way in which

we can obtain knowledge of future events other than by rational prediction from known causes.

8. Since mental activity is simply a matter of altering states in the physical organism, primarily in the brain, it is completely impossible for this
mental activity to exert any effect directly on the physical world outside
the organism.

9. The evolution of the universe and of man has come about through
purely physical causes and there is no justification for any concept of
universal purpose, either in the evolution of consciousness or in the
strivings of the individual.

10. The individual does not survive the death of the organism, or if there
is any sense in which the individual exists after the death of this physical body, we can neither comprehend it in this life nor in any way
obtain knowledge regarding it.

On the other hand, it was on the basis of these premises, in effect, that
the increasingly prestigious scientific world view was able to dismiss as of
secondary consequence the religious, aesthetic, and intuitive experiences
of man and hence to erode the value postulates based in those subjective
experiences.

The transcendental component of human experience, which positivistic
scientists set out to debunk, formed an essential basis for American ideals
and institutions. "The very deepest goals for Americans relate to the spiritual health of our people . . . for ours is a spiritually based society" (12).
The symbolism of the Great Seal of the United States, on the back of the
dollar bill, is perhaps the most potent reminder that the structure (the
unfinished pyramid) is not complete unless the transcendent all-seeing eye
is the capstone position. It is clearly in a transcendental sense that all men
are created equal. The institutions of representative democracy are pre-
dicated upon a belief in spiritually free citizens possessed of a valid sense of
value. The free-enterprise market system assumes a transcendental "invisible
hand" to insure that the individual microdecisions in pursuit of self-interest
will add up to satisfactory social macrodecisions. Thus, much of high social
import hinges on the acceptance or nonacceptance of the premises of Table 1.

If we turn now to the dominant paradigm of the society as a whole, we
can see how it is challenged from another front, namely, the consequences
of its own successes. In Table 2 are listed a few salient characteristics of
the paradigm that has tended to dominate the industrializing world for at
least the last century and a half. The adequacy or suitability of each of
these characteristics is now held up for questioning The changing value
emphases as the industrially advanced nations acquire the ability to satisfy
their material needs relegate acquisitive materialism to a lower spot in the
value hierarchy. Technological and economic growth are pushing against
limits of the ecosphere. The thrust for economic efficiency has resulted in

boring and stultifying jobs and a scarcity of them at that. And a resurgence of religious and spiritual interests testify to a hunger for deeper understanding of man's place in the universe which is not satisfied by the utilitarian quest.

TABLE 2

CHARACTERISTICS OF THE INDUSTRIAL-STATE PARADIGM

1. Acquisitive materialism assumed as a dominant value; economic-man image implicit.
2. Efficiency sought through organization and division of labor; machine replacement of human labor.
3. Faith in unlimited material progress and technological–economic growth.
4. The dominant form of the search for knowledge is utilitarian—a wedding of scientific and technological advance.
5. Man seeking control over nature; positivistic theory of knowledge; manipulative rationality as a dominant theme.
6. Individual responsibility for one's own destiny; freedom and equality as fundamental rights; nihilistic value perspective, individual determination of the "good"; society as an aggregate of individuals pursuing their own interests.

The successes of the industrial-state paradigm have led to present social benefits but also to the present crisis, which is so intrinsic to the industrial-state system as to require extensive systemic change for its eventual resolution. We need to look at this crisis briefly and will summarize some of its most serious aspects under the three classical political–economic problems of employment, regulation, and distribution.

The Problem of Employment

One of the consequences of industrialization is the sharpening of the dichotomy between employment and unemployment. Those who are unemployed or underemployed constitute not only a national economic problem (which could be handled through supplying some combination of services and income) but, more important, a psychological–cultural problem of a shortage of satisfactory social roles. Without such opportunities for full and valued participation, individuals lack the affirming experiences that enable them to feel a sense of usefulness, self-esteem, and mastery over their own lives.

The basic technological–industrial thrust is toward economic efficiency through machine replacement of men and through division of labor to the point of unsatisfying segments. Thus, while the pursuit of efficiency has resulted in unneeded persons, advances in education and changing values have generated serious work dissatisfactions. The degree of actual unemployment and underemployment is hard to estimate, since various factors act to conceal the severity of the problem. Work opportunity is treated as a scarce commodity. It is rationed in a variety of ways—through raising work-entry age and lowering retirement age, inflating entry criteria, expanding compulsory schooling, "featherbedding," and "makework." But the problem remains, however well disguised. In the modern industrial state a growing group of citizens are defined as superfluous—kept on welfare or employed at unsatisfying and stultifying tasks, but unneeded for the mainstream activity of the society.

The Problem of Regulation

New technologies raise dramatically the question of how technological and industrial impact shall be regulated. Multiple effects of technological and economic growth on the physical and social environment (including the various ills of urbanization) represent one important aspect of the problem. Impact of cybernetic technology on unemployment is another. New informational–technological accomplishments have given rise to fears of infringements on individual rights to privacy and freedom. Faustian powers to change weather and topography, chemical content of air and rivers, natural cycles and ecological processes, and human psychology and genetic transmission have made regulating these powers for the common good a vastly more complex matter than ever before and have made painfully evident the inadequacy of the society's guiding ethic to support the necessary regulation.

Centralized planning and increased governmental regulation is one possible answer. Its demonstrated undesirable aspects are such as to prompt us to seek other resolutions.

The Problem of Distribution

The principle is well established that some form of redistribution of income and economic power is appropriate both among a nation's citizens and among nations. In regard to individuals, this redistribution is accomplished reasonably well in the socialized countries (although not without some highly undesirable side effects) and less well, in general, in the capitalist countries.

The gap in per capita gross national product (GNP) between the rich nations and the poor nations, on the other hand, continues inexorably to increase. The economic system itself contains within it no rationale for redistribution. That rationale has usually been provided within a nation by an altruistic ethic based in transcendental noneconomic values. These transcendentally based values are less compelling between nations and, in any event, have been seriously weakened in the advanced nations through the influence of positivistic science.

The three problems listed above are highly interrelated and interactive. For example, measures that might alleviate one problem (e.g., job enrichment and environmental protective measures) tend to exacerbate another (e.g., unemployment resulting from "exporting" jobs to low-wage countries). Moreover, they stem so directly from fundamental characteristics of the industrial-state paradigm that it appears questionable whether any satisfactory resolution is possible unless there is a change in the dominant paradigm.

THE PERENNIAL PHILOSOPHY AND THE NEW FREEMASONRY

Several sorts of indications substantiate the observation that a new paradigm may be ascending to dominance. Surveys and polls show significant value shifts in the direction of what Yankelovich terms the "New Naturalism"—increased emphasis on humanistic and spiritual values, oneness with fellow man and nature, community and quality of life, and decreased emphasis on materialistic values, status goals, and unqualified economic growth (13, 14). Numerous cultural indicators (e.g., books read, voluntary associations, new-age subculture) show greatly increased interest in, and tolerance for, transcendental, religious, mystical, and spiritual views. Particularly significant is the developing scientific interest in altered states of consciousness, which is resulting in a new legitimization of studies of religious beliefs, psi, mystical experience, and meditative states. Wherever the nature of man has been probed deeply, certain conclusions seem to be reached anew. We shall try to summarize these, introducing for convenience the terms *Perennial Philosophy* and the *New Freemasonry*.

There is, according to Aldous Huxley (among many other scholars), an identifiable view of man in the universe that he terms the "Perennial Philosophy" (5). This is a view which

is immemorial and universal. Rudiments of the Perennial Philosophy may be found among the traditionary lore of primitive peoples in every region of the world, and in its fully developed forms it has a place in every one of the higher religions. A version of this Highest Common Factor in all preceding and subsequent theologies was first committed to writing more than twenty-five centuries ago, and since that time the inexhaustible theme has been treated again and again, from the standpoint of every religious tradition and in all the principal languages of Asia and Europe.

The ethic deriving from the Perennial Philosophy, in its esoteric Western form, is an intermittently visible stream that in recent centuries has been associated with the movement termed Freemasonry. It has had a profound effect on Western civilization. Thales, Solon, Pythagoras, and Plato journeyed to Egypt to be initiated into its then ancient mysteries. Much of it is woven into the structure of Christianity. In its hermetic, cabalistic, Sulfic, and Rosicrucian forms it affected the history of the Middle East and Europe. Its symbolism in the Great Seal of the United States is testimony to the role it played in the lives and thought of many who helped found this country.

Use of the term *New Freemasonry* implies that the esoteric may be in process of becoming disclosed, the occult may be coming into public view. Whether or not this is happening is a question we cannot yet answer. However, there are indications, discussed below, that make it a plausible proposition. What we can do, and propose to do, is summarize the main characteristics of the Perennial Philosophy and of true Freemasonry and examine what it would mean *if* this view of man-in-the-universe were to become dominant.

The first important thing to be noted about the Perennial Philosophy is that its adherents have always insisted that it is *not* a philosophy or a metaphysic, *not* an ideology or a religious belief, although others have typically considered it so. Huxley speaks of it as the recognition of "a divine Reality substantial to the world of things and lives and minds; the psychology that finds in the soul something similar to, or even identical with, divine Reality; the ethic that places man's final end in the knowledge of the imminent and transcendent Ground of all being" (5).

The flavor of it can perhaps best be obtained from a selection of brief attestations by persons who have been held, in some cases for many generations, to be enlightened or supremely wise. The following excerpts are from such writers and sages of all ages. For convenience they are grouped into five categories: Being, Awareness, Motivation, Potentiality, and Attitude. Brief quotations are representative only, and typical of statements to be found in classical and modern writings on what Robert Browning in "Paracelsus" calls "this perfect, clear perception—which is truth" and in anthologies on the Perennial Philosophy (11).

Being

Central to all is the basic experimental proposition that man can under certain conditions attain to a higher awareness, a "cosmic consciousness."

This is a state in which he has immediate knowledge of a reality underlying the world of physical phenomena. In speaking of this state of consciousness, it seems appropriate to use such words as *infinite, eternal, divine ground of Being, Brahma, Godhead*. From this vantage point, one's own growth, creativity, and participation in the evolutionary process are seen to be under the ultimate direction of a higher center (the atman, the oversoul, the "self" of Vedantic writings, a transpersonal self).

Behold but One in all things.

Kabir

An invisible and subtle essence is the Spirit of the whole universe. That is Reality. That is Truth. Thou art That.

Upanishads

The *atman*, the Self, is never born and never dies. It is without a cause and is eternally changeless. It is beyond time, unborn, permanent and eternal. It does not die when the body dies. Concealed in the heart of all beings lies the *atman*, the Spirit, the Self; smaller than the smallest atom, greater than the greatest spaces.

Upanishads

The Ground of God and the Ground of the Soul are one and the same.

Meister Eckhart

[In the highest stages of consciousness] the conscious division and separation of the self from the divine being, the object from the subject, which is the normal condition of unregenerate humanity, is broken down. The individual surrenders to the object and is absorbed by it. He becomes what he beholds. The distinction between subject and object disappears. Tasting nothing, comprehending nothing in particular, holding itself in emptiness, the soul finds itself as having all.

Radhakrishnan, *Eastern Religions
and Western Thought*

Modern philosophy, science, and even religion seem to have lost hope and, all too often, interest itself in the possibility of metaphysical knowledge. By knowledge of this kind we mean neither religious belief, philosophical speculation, nor scientific theory. We mean actual experience or immediate realization of that ultimate Reality which is the ground and cause of the universe, and thus the principle and meaning of human life. There are many who think it proper humility for man to disclaim the possibility of this knowledge. Yet we shall try to show not only that such knowledge has existed among men, but also that the modern world's loss of contact with its sources is the chief reason for our culture's peculiar and dangerous disintegration.

Alan Watts, *The Supreme Identity*

Awareness

Man, the Perennial Philosophy asserts, goes through life in a sort of hypnotic sleep, feeling that he is making decisions, having accidents occur to him, meeting chance acquaintances, and so on. If he begins to see more clearly, he becomes aware of the direction of the higher self in this process. He becomes aware that decisions he felt he had come to logically or through intuition were really reflections of choices made on the higher level of the self, that experiences and relationships that he needed for his growth were attracted to him by the self and were by no means so accidental as he had assumed. What we know as "inspiration" or "creativity" is essentially a breaking through of these higher processes "as if a fountain of Mind were welling up, bubbling to expression within prepared spirits" (Thomas Kelly, *A Test of Devotion*). "When it breathes through his intellect, it is genius; when it breathes through his will, it is virtue; when it flows through his affection, it is love" (Ralph Waldo Emerson, "The Oversoul").

There is a traditional doctrine, usually associated with religion but now and then invading great literature, that our present waking state is not really being awake at all. . . . It is, the tradition says, a special form of sleep comparable to a hypnotic trance. . . . From the moment of birth and before, we are under the suggestion that we are not fully awake; and it is universally suggested to our consciousness that we must dream the dream of this world—as our parents and friends dream it. . . . Just as in night-dreams the first symptom of waking is to suspect that one is dreaming, the first symptom of waking from the waking state—the second awakening of religion—is the suspicion that our present waking state is dreaming likewise. To be aware that we are asleep is to be on the point of waking; and to be aware that we are only partially awake is the first condition of becoming and making ourselves more fully awake.

A. R. Orage, *Psychological Exercises and Essays*

Humanity is asleep, concerned only with what is useless, living in a wrong world.

Sanai of Afghanistan

If the doors of perception were cleansed, everything would appear to man as it is, infinite.

For man has closed himself up, 'til he sees all things thro' narrow chinks in his cavern.

William Blake, *The Marriage of*
Heaven and Hell

The prime characteristic of cosmic consciousness is, as its name implies, a consciousness of the cosmos, that is, of the life and order of the universe. . . . Along with the consciousness of the cosmos there occurs an intellectual enlightenment or illumination which alone would place the individual on a new plane of existence—would make him almost a member of a new species. To this is added a state of moral exaltation, an indescribable feeling of elevation, elation, and joyousness, and a quickening of the moral sense, which is fully striking and more important to the individual and to the race than is the enhanced intellectual power. With these come what may be called a sense of immortality, a consciousness of eternal life, not conviction that he shall have this, but the consciousness that he has it already.

R. M. Bucke, *Cosmic Consciousness*

Of all the hard facts of science, I know of none more solid and fundamental than the fact that if you inhibit thought (and persevere) you come at length to a region of consciousness below or behind thought and different from ordinary thought in its nature and character—a consciousness of quasi-universal quality, and a realization of an altogether vaster self than that to which we are accustomed. And since the ordinary consciousness, with which we are concerned in ordinary life, is before all things founded on the little, local self, and is in fact self-consciousness in the little, local sense, it follows that to pass out of that is to die to the ordinary self and the ordinary world.

It is to die in the ordinary sense, but in another sense it is to wake up and find that the I, one's real, most intimate self, pervades the universe and all other beings—that the mountains and the sea and the stars are a part of one's body and that one's soul is in touch with the souls of all creatures. It is to be assured of an indestructible immortal life and of a joy immense and inexpressible—"to . . . sit with all the Gods in Paradise."

Edward Carpenter, *Towards Democracy*

Because ordinary perception is only partial perception, any language built up from ordinary perception proves inadequate to describe the greater reality. Hence, such attempts sound paradoxical.

The self has the attributes of uniqueness and of occurring only once in time. Since the psychological self is a transcendental concept, expressing the totality of conscious and unconscious contents, it can be described only in antinomial terms (just as the transcendental nature of light can be expressed through the image of waves and particles); that is, the above attributes must be supplemented by their opposites if the transcendental situation is to be characterized correctly.

C. G. Jung, *Aion*

The more we understand the whole of Being, the more we can tolerate the simultaneous existence and perception of inconsistencies, of oppositions and of flat contradictions. These seem to be products of partial cognition, and fade away with cognition of the whole.

Abraham Maslow, *Toward a Psychology of Being*

True words always seem paradoxical but no other form of teaching can take its place.

Lao-Tse

Whoever seeks to gain his life will lose it; but whoever loses his life with preserve it.

Jesus of Nazareth

All things come from being,
And being comes from non-being.

Lao-Tse

I am in the Father and the Father is in me.

John 14:10

Having realized his own self as the Self, a man becomes selfless; and in virtue of selflessness he is to be conceived as unconditioned. This is the highest mystery, betokening emancipation.

Upanishads

That man is free who is conscious of being the author of the law he obeys.

Anonymous

Because the fundamental phenomenon is man hiding from himself, becoming aware—awakening, becoming dehypnotized—is a process of overcoming defenses, of realizing that which is already there.

If man wishes to gain a more inclusive world-view or to approach ultimate reality, it will be necessary for him to break through the several cocoons within which he is inevitably encapsulated. The first step in this process is to recognize that he is, in fact, encapsulated. Unfortunately, this first step is the most difficult.

Joseph R. Royce,
The Encapsulated Man

Man needs, in order to live his daily life, to be inwardly as if he had settled or eliminated the great questions that concern his state. Most men never reflect on their state because they are convinced, explicitly or implicitly, that they understand it. . . . Every man, whether he admits it or not, lives by a personal system of metaphysics which he believes to be true. . . . Man in general has faith in his system of metaphysics, explicit or implicit; that is to say, he is sure that he has nothing to learn in this domain. It is where he is most ignorant that he has the greatest assurance, because it is therein that he has the greatest need of assurance.

Hubert Benoit, *The Supreme
Doctrine*

Hold well in your mind this brief word: Forsake all things and you will find all things. . . . Print well in your mind what I have said, for when you have fulfilled it you will know well that it is true. Lord, this lesson is not one day's work, or play for children—in it is contained the full perfection of all religion.

Thomas à Kempis, *The
Imitation of Christ*

Oh, let the self exalt itself, not sink itself below: Self is the only friend of self, and self Self's only foe. For self, when it subdues itself, befriends itself. And so when it eludes self-conquest, is its own and only foe.

Bhagavad-Gita

Motivation

When man comes to know himself, according to the Perennial Philosophy, the pull of his material and ego needs is greatly lessened and he finds that his deepest motivation is to participate fully, with awareness, in the evolutionary process. (Maslow describes something similar in his comparison of deficiency-motivation with Being-motivation [9].)

Life is seen not to be a random matter but directed through evolution by a higher consciousness and characterized by purpose. This purpose includes the development of individual centers of consciousness with freedom of choice, gradually moving toward ever-increasing knowledge of oneself, of the self, and of the whole. Knowledge of and participation in this is the supreme value.

> Life does not need comfort, when it can be offered meaning, nor pleasure, when it can be shown purpose. Reveal what is the purpose and how he may attain it—the steps he must take—and man will go forward again hardily, happily, knowing that he has found what he must have—intentional living.
>
> Gerald Heard, *The Third Morality*

> All creatures seek after unity; all multiplicity struggles toward it—the universal aim of all life is always this unity.
>
> Johann   Tauler

> Know that, by nature, every creature seeks to become like God.
>
> Meister   Eckhardt

> [Our deepest] desire tells us to face reality, to be as human as possible, and that means going through time, through change, through death, keeping nothing, not even our life, giving everything, even our own will, being poor in spirit, being one with the universe, with our darkest enemy and with God. That is what we wish for most whether we know it or not.
>
> Fritz Kunkel, *The Choice*
> *Is Always Ours*

This unitive Being-motivation has sometimes seemed to Westerners to connote quietistic retreat. That it need not is made clear in Manly Hall's discussion (3) of true Freemasonry:

> There is but one Lodge—the Universe—and but one Brotherhood, composed of everything that moves or exists in any of the planes of Nature. . . . Man is given by Nature a gift—the privilege of labor. Through labor he learns all things. [The true] Mason is a builder of the temple of character. He is the architect of a sublime mystery—the gleaming, glowing temple of his own soul. . . . He best serves God when he joins with the Great Architect in building more noble structures in the universe below. . . . He seeks to learn the things which will make him of greater service in the Divine Plan. . . . His karmic responsibilities increase with his opportunities. . . . He realizes that all forms and their position in material affairs are of no importance to him compared to the life which is evolving within. . . . The true Mason has learned to be divinely impersonal in thought, action, and desire.

654   THE CONVERGENCE WITH TRANSPERSONAL PSYCHOLOGY

Potentiality

It follows from the foregoing that the human potentiality is limitless; that all knowledge and power is ultimately accessible to the mind, looking within itself; and that all limitations are ultimately self-chosen. Such supernormal phenomena as telepathic communication, clairvoyant perception, experiencing events that happened to others, "instant" diagnosis and healing, precognition, and levitation and other PK events are, in general, perfectly possible. At some deep level of the individual he understands them, and at some other deep level he chooses the ordinary "physical laws," which preclude them for the most part.

> Within yourself lies the cause of whatever enters into your life. To come into full realization of your own awakening powers is to be able to condition your life in exact accord with what you would have it.
>
> Ralph Waldo Emerson, "Self Reliance"

> I have no doubt whatever that most people live, whether physically, intellectually or morally, in a very restricted circle of their potential being. They make use of a very small portion of their possible consciousness, and of the soul's resources in general, much like a man who, out of his whole bodily organism, should get into a habit of using and moving only his little finger. . . . We all have reservoirs of life to draw upon, of which we do not dream.
>
> William James

> Man is made by his belief. . . . As he believes, so he is.
>
> *Bhagavad-Gita*

> [These experiences, during long days of imprisonment in the Spanish Civil War] had filled me with a direct certainty that a higher order of reality existed, and that it alone invested existence with meaning. I came to call it later on "the reality of the third order." The narrow world of sensory perception constituted the first order; this perceptual world was enveloped by the conceptual world which contained phenomena not directly perceivable, such as gravitation, electromagnetic fields, and curved space. The second order of reality filled in the gaps and gave meaning to the absurd patchiness of the sensory world. In the same manner, the third order of reality enveloped, interpenetrated, and gave meaning to the second. It contained "occult" phenomena which could not be apprehended or explained either on the sensory or on the conceptual level, and yet occasionally invaded them like spiritual meteors piercing the primitive's vaulted sky. Just as the conceptual order showed up the illusions and distortions of the senses, so

THE SOCIAL IMPLICATIONS OF PSYCHIC RESEARCH   655

the "third order" disclosed that time, space and causality, that isolation, separateness, and spatio-temporal limitations of the self were
merely optical illusions on the next higher level.

Arthur Koestler, The Invisible Writing

Attitude

Consequent to awareness of what has been discussed before comes a
new attitude toward life. One aspect of this has been noted under "Motivation," the desire to consciously participate, to labor and serve, in the
evolutionary process, the cosmic drama, the fulfillment of mankind. But
the reverse side of this is *acceptance*, the choosing of what is—since at
some deep level of the self it has already chosen this.

> To those who ask "What shall I do" we have finally one simple
> answer: "Accept yourself." To those who ask "But when I have
> accepted myself, what then?" we answer, "By your question you show
> that you have read without comprehension." To those who demur:
> "But you say nothing of man's duties—the world problems—peace or
> war—social reform—morality" we reply, "No, we say nothing of
> these things." His attitude to these things each man must let his
> accepted self determine. . . . What values a man will perpetuate, what
> values he can perpetuate, it is for himself to decide. We claim no more
> than perhaps to help him to a condition where these questions decide
> themselves with a different and higher authority than any imposed
> decisions of the unintegrated self could ever possess.
>
> John Middleton Murry, God

> It is of capital importance to understand this distinction between
> acceptance and resignation. To accept, really to accept a situation, is
> to think and feel with the whole of one's being that, even if one had
> the faculty of modifying it, one would not do it, and would have no
> reason to do it.
>
> Hubert Benoit, The Supreme Doctrine

> We cannot change anything unless we accept it. . . . I do not in the
> least mean that we must never pass judgement. . . . But if the doctor
> wishes to help a human being he must be able to accept him as he is.
> And he can do this in reality only when he has already seen and
> accepted himself as he is. . . . Perhaps this sounds very simple, but
> simple things are always the most difficult.
>
> C. G. Jung

Another important and related aspect is *nonattachment*—being "divinely impersonal," unattached to specific outcomes.

It is difficult to find a single word that will adequately describe the ideal man of the free philosophers and the founders of religions. "Non-attached" is perhaps the best. The ideal man is the non-attached man. Non-attached to his bodily sensations and lusts. Non-attached to his craving for power and possessions. Non-attached to the objects of these various desires. Non-attached to his anger and hatred; non-attached to his exclusive loves. Non-attached to wealth, fame, social position. Non-attached even to science, art, speculation, philanthropy. Yes, non-attached even to these.

Aldous Huxley, *Ends and Means*

Therefore, do thou ever perform without attachment the work that thou must do; for performing action without attachment man attains the Supreme.

Bhagavad-Gita

To die—for this into the world you came.
Yes, to abandon more than you ever conceived as possible:
All ideals, plans—even the very best and most unselfish—all hopes and desires,
All formulas of morality, all reputation for virtue or consistency or good sense; all cherished theories, doctrines, systems of knowledge.
Modes of life, habits, predilections, preferences, superiorities, weaknesses, indulgences,
Good health, wholeness of limb and brain, youth, manhood, age—nay life itself—in one word: to die—
For this into the world you came.
All to be abandoned, and when they have been finally abandoned,
Then to return to be used—and then only to be rightly used, to be free and open forever.

Edward Carpenter, *Towards Democracy*

Arjuna:

Krishna, how can one identify a man who is firmly established and absorbed in Brahman? In what manner does an illumined soul speak? How does he sit? How does he walk?

Sri Krishna:

He knows the bliss in the Atman
And wants nothing else.
Cravings torment the heart:
He renounces cravings.
I call him illumined.
Not shaken by adversity,

Not hankering after happiness:
Free from fear, free from anger,
Free from the things of desire.
I call him a seer, and illumined.
The bonds of his flesh are broken.
He is lucky, and does not rejoice;
He is unlucky, and does not weep.
I call him illumined.

The tortoise can draw in his legs;
The seer can draw in his senses.
I call him illumined.

The abstinent run away from what they desire
But carry their desires with them:
When a man enters Reality,
He leaves his desires behind him.

Bhagavad-Gita

The other side, as it were, of nonattachment is *impersonal love*, the most difficult to delineate, because the coinage has been so debased in all that has been written about other emotions that also go by the name of love.

The only way of full knowledge lies in the act of love: This act transcends thought, it transcends words . . . I have to know the other person and myself objectively in order to be able to see his reality, or rather, to overcome the illusions, the irrationally distorted picture I have of him. Only if I know a human being objectively, can I know him in his ultimate essence, in the act of love.

Erich Fromm, *The Art of Loving*

Love, which is the deification of persons, must become more impersonal every day . . . a love which knows not sex, nor person, nor partiality. . . . There are moments when the affections rule and absorb the man and make his happiness dependent on a person or persons. But in health the mind is presently seen again, its over-arching vault, bright with galaxies of immutable lights, and the warm loves and fears, that swept over us as clouds, must lose their finite character and blend with God, to attain their own perfection.

Ralph Waldo Emerson, "Love"

Conscious love . . . is the wish that the object should arrive at its own native perfection, regardless of the consequences to the lover. . . . It is rare among humans. . . . All people desire it, even the most cynical;

but since it seldom occurs by chance, and nobody has published the key to its creation, the vast majority doubt even its possibility.

A. R. Orage, *On Love*

When one at last contacts the true "Control Center" the awakening of the conscious to the spirit appears as a tremendous radiance, illuminating the mind and the body both from within and from without. . . . Once this has happened, one becomes as a child, having to learn of the world again in terms of the immanent God. . . .

He learns to live with people once again. He finds love for his family he never knew before. He finds friends that he never found before. . . . He lives, and loves, and acts, and thinks, just as he did before, but with this difference, selflessly.

He has to understand whom he can help, what help he can give, and how to give it in harmony with the law. But he lives as an ordinary person, making no show of his power, for it is not his, but God's, that he may use.

Anonymous

SIGNIFICANCE OF THE EMERGENT PARADIGM

We have argued, thus far, three points:

1. The real significance of the phenomena of psychic research is that they directly challenge the conventional scientific paradigm and hence the dominant social paradigm.

2. The most fundamental of contemporary societal problems appear to stem so directly from fundamental characteristics of the industrial-state paradigm that it is questionable whether any satisfactory resolution of them is possible unless there is a change in the dominant paradigm.

3. A new paradigm, a "new transcendentalism," appears to be emergent—one compatible with the data of psychic research. We have emphasized its millennia-old history in describing it with the terms *Perennial Philosophy* and *New Freemasonry*.

It remains to show that, on the one hand, the new paradigm challenges the present form and usage of many contemporary social institutions and, on the other hand, points the way to a transformed society in which the previously unresolvable problems of employment, regulation, and distribution become resolvable.

A New Guiding Ethic

Implicit in the new paradigm is replacement of the fragmented material-istic ethics (e.g., growth and consumption), which presently dominate the economic system and hence the society, with a new guiding ethic that is, in fact, two complementary principles—an "ecological ethic" and a "self-realization ethic."

Lynton Caldwell defines the *ecological ethic*, which, he argues, is essen-tial to the worldwide, fundamental, and pervasive change required to preserve the habitability of the earth (2). It involves recognition of the limited nature of available resources, including space, and recognition of man as an integral part of the natural world—hence inseparable from it and from its governing processes and laws. It fosters a sense of the total community of man and responsibility for the fate of the planet and relates self-interest to the interest of one's fellow man and of future generations. It implies movement toward a homeostatic (yet dynamic) economic–ecological system in which man acts in partnership with nature in modify-ing ecological relationships and in establishing satisfactory recycling mechanisms.

As Caldwell notes, this ethic implies behavior advocated in a variety of ethical systems extending through time, from the legendary Lao-Tse through St. Francis to Mahatma Gandhi. Its basic assumptions correspond to the prescientific assumptions of many so-called primitive peoples. Thus, the ecological viewpoint can find support not only in modern scientific knowledge of life on earth, but also in most known cultural or religious systems.

The same is true of the self-realization ethic, which holds that the proper end of all individual experience is the further evolutionary de-velopment of the emergent self and of the human species and that the appropriate function of social institutions is to create an environment that will foster that process. This too is supported not only by the emergence of modern psychotherapy and the recent emergence of "humanistic psy-chology" (1, 9) but is also found at the core of almost all the religious philosophies the world has known.

The self-realization ethic is the most satisfactory answer to the current alienation and anomie that surface in rebellions against industrial and bureaucratic practices that diminish man; in anxiety that we have some-how lost control of the management of our human affairs, of what our ancestors would have called our destiny; and in seeking (e.g., through return to handicrafts and home gardening) the satisfactions of a work life not excessively shaped by economic incentives. Its dominance is required for the restructuring of social institutions to satisfy the individual's basic need for full and valued participation. As corollaries to this ethic, the self-determination of individuals and of minority groups will be fostered, social decision making should be highly decentralized, and the mechanism of a strong but humanistic free-enterprise private sector should be preferred over public bureaucracy for the accomplishment of most social tasks.

The two ethics, the one emphasizing the total community of man-in-nature and the oneness of the human race and the other placing the highest value on development of selfhood, are not contradictory but complementary—two sides of the same coin. Together they leave room both for cooperation and for wholesome competition, for love and for individuality. Each is a corrective against excesses or misapplication of the other.

Short-Term Consequences

In the short term the effect of the new paradigm will be to a certain extent disruptive. We have already seen that the industrial age is running into trouble. The cultural premises and image of man-in-the-universe that fostered scientific, technological, industrial, and economic growth are proving to be maladapted to the humane use of the products of that growth, as well as to the necessary shift in emphasis from economic and material growth to human growth. The new paradigm, with its ecological ethic and self-realization ethic, points the way to resolution of the difficulties engendered by the industrial era. It might seem that we should welcome its coming with open arms. No more so than the Middle Ages welcomed Galilean science or than the neurotic welcomes the changes in perception and behavior necessary to extricate him from his unhappy condition.

The social structure involves behaviors, institutions, mores, and values —intrinsic cultural premises and ways of perceiving. When these are in flux they do not, in general, change at the same rate or in such a way that they remain compatible. If indeed we are correctly reading the signs and the cultural premises regarding the nature of man are changing rapidly, it seems clear that corresponding institutional changes are not keeping pace. Thus, the new beliefs and the new image of man will appear as a threat to the established order. The emphasis on inner exploration will look like escapism, and the new interest in psi and spiritual experience will be put down as a return to the superstitions of a less scientific and more gullible age. The increased reliance on intuitive processes will be interpreted as an abandonment of rationalism. The shift in priorities away from material and toward spiritual values will appear as a weakening of the work ethic and as a turning away from economic goals, both imperiling the state of the economy and the stability of economic institutions. The ethic of love and community will seem subversive to the national defense (somewhat realistically, since the world in general is a long way from being ready for love and community, so that partial moves in these directions are more likely to be interpreted as weakness).

At a more fundamental level, the implied responsibility (read response-ability) in the new paradigm, however dimly perceived, evokes a resistance to entertaining the new image of man. Maslow described this phenomenon succinctly in a chapter entitled "The Need to Know and the Fear of Knowing" (8):

> The great cause of much psychological illness is the fear of knowledge of oneself. . . . We tend to be afraid of any knowledge that could cause us to despise ourselves or make us feel inferior, weak, worthless, evil, shameful. We protect ourselves and our ideal image of ourselves by repression and similar defenses, which are essentially techniques by which we avoid becoming conscious of unpleasant or dangerous truths. . . . But there is another kind of truth we tend to evade. Not only do we hang on to our psychopathology, but also we tend to evade personal growth because this, too, can bring another kind of fear, of awe, of feelings of weakness and inadequacy. And so we find another kind of resistance, a denying of our best side, of our talents, of our finest impulses, of our highest potentialities, of our creativeness. . . . It is precisely the god-like in ourselves that we are ambivalent about, fascinated by and fearful of, motivated to and defensive against.

Thus, on the one hand, the new transcendentalism is, or may be, at both individual and societal levels, a means to wholeness and salvation. On the other hand, at both levels, its deepest complications are bound to develop strong resistance. This will contribute to the conflict, disruption, and chaos that inevitably accompany a period of rapid social change such as the present transition from industrial to postindustrial society. A paradoxical situation thus arises: Even if one argues that the new paradigm is essential to a satisfactory resolution of the problems of advanced industrialism, he will also have to observe that actions designed to hasten its emergence could be socially disruptive.

If, then, evidence mounts that this new image of man-in-the-universe is likely to become dominant in the next stage of history and that the transition period is upon us, what sorts of behavior will help to ease the strains and foster a smooth transition? We have argued that pushing the new image could add to the chaos and disruption. (Something like this seems to have taken place during the psychedelic period of the sixties, when Timothy Leary's advice to the young to "tune in, turn on, and drop out" added its bit to the disorder of the times.) It would be most desirable to establish a climate that encourages (*a*) diversity of individual choices (of life style, personal mores, etc.) and (*b*) experimentation with new forms of communities, institutions, and problem solutions. Perhaps the most important thing of all is to promote understanding of the need for, and nature of, the transition and to create a positive image of the kind of society that could lie on the far side of the transition, so as to keep the anxiety level as low as possible.

Long-Term Consequences

Let us turn now to the question of characteristics of the society in which the new paradigm has become established as the dominant image of man-in-the-universe. We shall look briefly at various aspects.

INDIVIDUAL AND SOCIAL GOALS

The goals are implicit in the two complementary guiding ethics, the ecological ethic and the self-realization ethic. The first dictates that the well-being of the whole human race, all of life on the planet, and future generations, is a paramount goal of the society and of all its institutions. The second is more explicit as to what that well-being implies—life, liberty, and the pursuit of self-realization.

The central activity of self-realization is work–play–learning. Thus, a central social goal could be considered to be full employment, where employment is taken to mean access to a satisfying work–play–learning role, performance in which earns affirmation by the society and thus contributes to development of a healthy self-image.

With material goals deemphasized, a steady-state economy, and cybernation of routine tasks (for both economic and humane reasons), it is clear that only a fraction of the work (–play–learning) force will be required to supply material and service wants. The remainder of the roles must satisfy the condition that the activities be meaningful, nonstultifying, and nonpolluting. Two primary areas of activity meet these conditions: learning, in the broad sense that includes exploration and research, and bringing about a still more desirable future.

Robert Hutchins (4) describes "the learning society" as one that will have transformed "its values in such a way that learning, fulfillment, becoming human, had become its aims and *all its institutions were directed to this end*. This is what the Athenians did. . . . They made their society one designed to bring all its members to the fullest development of their highest powers. . . . Education was not a segregated activity, conducted for certain hours, in certain places, at a certain time of life. It was the aim of the society. . . . The Athenian was educated by the culture, by *paideia.*" The central educational task fostered by paideia was "the search for the Divine Center" (6).

But the postindustrial society will differ from that of Athens in important respects. Its slaves will be cybernetic, and the Faustian powers of its technology will introduce a new level of responsibility. It will have to be a learning-and-planning society. Helping to choose the future will be a primary responsibility of its citizens.

SCIENCE

Science, under the new transcendentalism, will be clearly understood to be a moral inquiry. Having a balanced effort of systematic exploration of *both* the objective and subjective realms of human experience, it cannot be, as past science has tended to be, value-empty. It will deal with what is empirically found to promote wholeness—in much the same sense that present-day nutritional science deals with what foods are wholesome for man. It will place particular emphasis on the systematic exploration of various levels of subjective experience, the ultimate source of our value postulates. In this respect it will resemble the humanities and religion, and the boundaries between these three disciplines will become less sharp—as is already presaged in the recent writings of some psychotherapists. The models and metaphors used will be multileveled, corresponding to different levels or realms of experience, and no conflict will be perceived if, for example, mystical experiences are congenial to one of these metaphorical frameworks and operant conditioning to another.

New impetus will be given the biological sciences (with a whole-systems emphasis) and the psychology of consciousness. The latter will look strongly in the direction of new potentialities suggested by the newly appreciated powers of belief, imagination, and suggestion. To conscious and subconscious choice (repression, projection, sublimation, etc.) will be added what may be termed *supraconscious choice* (intuition, creative imagination, choosing "better than we know")—with as much impact on our policies regarding education, welfare, criminal rehabilitation, and justice as the Freudian concepts had some years earlier. Social science will be participative, in marked contrast to the "objective" observations of past social scientists. Experimenter and subject will explore together, in an atmosphere of mutual trust and with equal status. (The resulting science will be significantly different from the industrial-age social science based largely on manipulation and deception.)

Finally, the new science will become also a sort of "civil religion," supporting the humane value postulates of the culture rather than being neutral or undermining, as was the old science.

Institutions

Clearly the new transcendentalism would tend to support effective institutionalization of such values as society serving the self-fulfillment of the individual, individual fulfillment through community and meaningful vocation, human dignity and significance, honesty and trust, self-determination and diversity of choice for individuals and minority groups, equality of justice before the law, and responsibility for humankind and the planet. However, values do not become operative simply by being deemed "good." Let us look at some arguments that suggest these values might become operative because they work.

As the social system becomes more and more highly interdependent, the need becomes greater for accurate information to be available throughout the system. Just as the modern banking and credit system would not operate smoothly with the low-trust level of a warrior culture, so highly complex task operations (such as putting men in space or resolving the impending energy crisis) require a higher level of honesty, openness, and trust than have sufficed thus far in advertising and merchandising. For quite practical, as contrasted with moralistic, reasons, the demanded level of honesty and openness can be expected to increase.

Similarly, as the complexity of societal operations increases, autocratically and hierarchically organized bureaucratic structures tend to develop communication overloads near the top and discouragements to entrepreneurship and responsibility-taking lower down. Adaptive organic forms, with relatively autonomous subsystems, seem better adapted to complex tasks and provide more satisfying work roles to the people involved.

In general, the more significant a fraction of the whole is a subsystem, the more important it becomes that its goals be in close alignment with those of the overall system. Thus, as the large, multinational corporations become more powerful than the majority of nation-states, it becomes essential that their operative goals shift to become more like those of public institutions. This means, specifically, that prioritized corporate goals would become something like the following: (*a*) to carry on activities that will contribute to the self-fulfillment of the persons involved, (*b*) to carry on activities that contribute directly to satisfaction of social needs and accomplishment of societal goals, and (*c*) to earn a fair profit on investment, not so much as a goal in itself as a control signal monitoring effectiveness.

How might such a utopian-sounding situation come about? Does it not sound impractical and preposterous that corporations would be willing to relegate profit making to a third-priority goal? The social force that might bring about such a revolutionary change in operative goals is the subtle, but powerful (and poorly understood), influence of granting or withholding legitimacy. Governments have often felt the potency of legitimacy withdrawal (for instance, the post-Watergate Nixon administration, or the post–World War II colonial imperialisms). In the middle of the eighteenth century the suggestion would have seemed preposterous that autocratic monarchy would soon be declared not legitimate by contrast with governments "deriving their just powers from the consent of the governed." Giant corporations today are feeling the challenge put to the divine right of kings two centuries ago. It assumes many forms— consumerism, environmentalism, civil rights and women's liberation movements, truth-in-advertising pressures, worker demands for improved quality of work environment, stockholder revolts. Awareness is growing that the largest corporations, at least, are in an important sense public institutions. Directly or indirectly (through life insurance policies, annuities, mutual funds, etc.) they are owned by a large fraction of the public; they employ a large percentage of the public; the public uses the goods and services they produce and suffers the pollution and environmental degradation they cause. The wave of challenge is forming, demanding an end to the "divine right" of ownership and managership, and replacement by business "deriving its just powers from the consent of those impacted by it," business "of the people, by the people, and for the people." The capitalist structure remains ultimately most compatible with the growing strength of self-determination as a cultural value and with widespread disenchantment with monopolistic socialist bureaucracy. But if capitalism is to survive this challenge to legitimacy, the operative goals of corporations will have to undergo radical change.

ECONOMICS AND THE ECONOMY

The industrial-state paradigm underlying the present economic system includes the concepts of man as infinite consumer of goods and services (providing his appetites are properly whetted through advertising); profit maximizing and economic growth as preeminent goals; and government as master regulator of employment level, growth rate, wage and price stability, and a modicum of fair play. The new transcendentalism would remind that the root meaning of *economics* is "home management." Managing the planet earth, with its finite supplies of space and resources and its delicate ecological balance, and conserving and developing it as a suitable habitat for evolving man is a far different task from that for which the present economic system was set up.

Furthermore, an economic theory is inevitably based upon a theory of social psychology. If man is not "economic man" in a self-regulating free market nor an infinite consumer with manipulable motivations but an evolving spiritual being with unlimited potentialities and cosmic motivations, then a radical correction to economic theory will be needed.

One clear institutional need is for a network of citizen-participation policy and planning centers at local, regional, and national levels, linked together with a common understanding of the alternatives that lie before the society and some unifying agreement as to the futures to be desired and those to be avoided. These centers will have to combine two rather different activities—the technical activity of laying out alternatives with their anticipated costs and benefits, and the political activity of brokering "deals" between various participant institutions in order to bring about experiments and actions.

The new transcendentalism recognizes the key role of work in meaningful human existence as the main way in which persons contribute to the society and receive affirmation in return, thus developing a wholesome self-image, and as one of the main ways in which is satisfied the basic motivation to experience, confront, learn, and evolve. Thus, a primary function of all institutions in the society is structuring and facilitating such meaningful work. A basic anomaly in this regard has existed in the latter portion of the industrial era. An increasingly large fraction of the adult citizenry has been placed in a classic double bind. On the one hand, practically the only legitimated social roles have been to have a job (or be married to someone who has one or to be a student in training for one), whereas, on the other hand, there are not enough such satisfactory social roles to go around. As we saw earlier, the dilemma is an intrinsic one to the industrial state, since the central thrust of technology in pursuit of increased economic efficiency is the organization and subdivision of labor into more and more meaningless segments and the replacement of human work by machines. Two large groups of people emerge as a consequence: those low in self-definition ability (the unemployed and underemployed) who seek structured jobs and are offered income maintenance and those moderately in self-definition ability who tend to have jobs but seek income maintenance for sabbatical periods, educational leave, job retraining, social contributions, or initiation of entrepreneurial activities. The economic institutions that serve the goals of economic growth and exploitation of nature have not adequately served human beings. The new postindustrial society would take as one of its paramount priorities the restructuring of economic institutions to resolve the anomaly described above. It could not consider that it was adequately achieving its main reason for existence as long as persons desiring meaningful work roles were unable to obtain them.

EDUCATION

Even though, as argued above, every major institution in society will have an important educational function under the new transcendentalism, there will still no doubt be schools and colleges, institutions dedicated to education as a primary function. They will provide preparation for the learning-and-planning society and "recycling" preparation for undertaking a new career phase. They will emphasize self-understanding and interpersonal skills, ability to gain new skills (over acquisition of any particular skill), having access to knowledge (over having memorized any particular knowledge), dealing with wholes (rather than obtaining highly detailed knowledge of narrow specialties), and development of an evolutionary and future-oriented attitude. They will assume as one of their main functions the development and maintaining of a creative image of what man and society can be (recognizing that the future imagined tends to come into being, so that fostering the noblest image is of highest importance). Behavior-shaping, operant conditioning, and similar systematically manipulative approaches to learning may be used but only when they are specifically chosen by the learner. Choice of educational activities will be primarily on a basis of consumer choice from among options—placing trust in the ultimate ability of the learner to choose wisely and focusing evaluational activity on such forms as independent audits and "consumer reports."

Separation of church and state will be an abandoned doctrine, in part because the church is recognized as essentially another private educational enterprise and in part because it will be inconceivable that religion, education, and psychotherapy should be considered as separate activities, since they are in essence attempts to achieve the same goals.

One of the most serious pathologies of the late industrial-age culture will be pointed out as the way in which the social institutions conspired to instill and maintain two fundamental fears—the fear of psychosis and the fear of death—and through these to keep men prisoners of their social institutions. These two basic fears permeated and colored all aspects of life. In contrast to the fear of losing control through losing one's mind or through losing one's life, the basic new teaching will be that neither of these can possibly happen in the final analysis. Psychosis will be recognized as a particular form of confusion that is as much a function of the culture as of the individual. Death will be recognized as a major transition, no more to be feared than birth or rebirth. Neither psychosis nor death is "permanent," since existence is, in any event, eternal (as the person experiences for himself in the central task of his education, the search for the Divine Center). This changed attitude will especially affect the role of the aged in society (an area in which the failure of industrial-state society is particularly egregious). The latter period of life will be considered as much a period of learning as any other part of life, and the elderly will once again (as in many older or more primitive societies) be assumed to have a kind of wisdom of significant value to the younger members of society. Elimination of uncertainty about death and direct experience of the continuity between "normal" and "psychotic" (both accomplished by early adulthood, through removal of underlying fears and adding of meaning to both pleasure and adversity) will give a significance to postretirement years, which will keep them from having the stultifying effect that was typical in the late industrial age.

CONCLUSION

We have tried to suggest some of the more obvious consequences to societal goals and institutions if the new paradigm implied in the phenomena of psychic research were to become dominant. Among these major changes are the shift from a material growth orientation to a learning-and-planning society guided by an ecological ethic and a self-realization ethic; development of a participative science emphasizing exploration of subjective experience and above all moral inquiry; emergence of the corporation as one of the main institutional forms in which persons seek self-fulfillment, with a radically new basis for legitimacy; implementation of a full-employment policy in a wholly new sense, based on the human need for a satisfying vocation; assumption of education as a lifelong process intimately related to the carrying out of a life work, not to meet the demands of a growth-intoxicated economic system but as an integral part of life's search for the Divine Center; resolution of the problems of what had rapidly been becoming our largest deprived minority group—the aged. The first impression may be that these changes are too radical. To the contrary, they are probably too conservative. Our task is the equivalent of standing in the Middle Ages and extrapolating the culture and institutions after the Industrial Revolution, postulating only that materialistic values would gain sway and economic efficiency would be sought through organization and division of labor.

We can hardly claim to have demonstrated that a shift of the dominant paradigm in the society is underway—especially since such a fundamental shift is historically so improbable. We may have made the hypothesis plausible. If so, then the question raised here about the characteristics of a society dominated by the new paradigm is of extreme importance. The main reason has been mentioned earlier. The greatest hazard in such a transition is that the anxiety level rises to where the society responds with irrational and self-destructive behavior (e.g., the religious wars and inquisitions that accompanied the Reformation). The best safeguard is widespread understanding of why the transformation is taking place and reassurance that there is someplace good to get to on the other side.

REFERENCES

1. Bugental, J. F. T., ed. *Challenges of Humanistic Psychology.* McGraw-Hill: New York, 1967.
2. Caldwell, L. *Environment: A Challenge to Modern Society.* Indiana University Press: Bloomington, 1972.
3. Hall, Manly. *The Lost Keys of Freemasonry.* Macoy Publishing and Masonic Supply: Richmond, Va., 1923.
4. Hutchins, Robert. *The Learning Society.* Praeger: New York, 1968.
5. Huxley, Aldous. *The Perennial Philosophy.* Harper and Brothers: New York, 1945.
6. Jaeger, Werner. *Paideia: The Ideals of Greek Culture,* Gilbert Highet, trans. Oxford University Press: New York, 1965.
7. Kuhn, Thomas. *The Structure of Scientific Revolutions.* University of Chicago Press: Chicago, 1962.
8. Maslow, A. *Toward a Psychology of Being.* Van Nostrand: New York, 1962.
9. Maslow, A. *The Further Reaches of Human Nature.* Viking: New York, 1972.
10. Myers, F. W. H. *Human Personality and Its Survival of Bodily Death.* University Books: New York, 1961.
11. Phillips, Dorothy, ed. *The Choice Is Always Ours.* Smith: New York, 1957.
12. President's Committee on National Goals. *Goals for Americans.* Prentice-Hall: Englewood Cliffs, N.J., 1960.
13. Roszak, T. *Where the Wasteland Ends.* Doubleday: New York, 1972.
14. Yankelovich, D. *The Changing Values on Campus.* Washington Square: New York, 1972.

Conclusion: . . . And Back Again

EDGAR D. MITCHELL

> *To venture beyond the fantastic accomplishments of this physically fantastic age, sensory perception must combine with the extrasensory, and I suspect that the two will prove to be different faces of each other. I suspect it is through sensing and thinking about such concepts that great adventures of the future will be found.*
>
> —CHARLES LINDBERGH

THE OVERVIEW

We have just given you a comprehensive review of psychic research from its formal beginnings nearly 100 years ago in London, England, to its present world status. The authors presented here are among the leaders in presenting and interpreting this data. The evidence is now being examined in the laboratories of private and public scientific research institutions; in high schools, colleges, and universities; through the scholarly studies and reviews of the literature by organizations and individuals; and in the burgeoning number of periodicals, newspaper articles, radio and television programs, public lectures, symposia, and films. Psychic research is clearly a significant part of the contemporary scene.

But "significant" in what way? I trust it is apparent that those of us engaged in noetics, particularly psychic research, do not view our work as another fad to be recorded in the history of "pop" culture. In our view, we are dealing with deep levels of reality and human nature. The significance, as I indicated at the beginning of this book, may be quite simply the continued growth or the decline of the human race, depending upon our ability to understand and properly utilize all facets of human potential.

To be specific, the preceding chapters have done five things. First, they have convincingly demonstrated that *the psychic event is a reality and the work of psychic researchers is careful and credible.* That is not to say there is unanimity of opinion in the research community about the nature of psi and the special forms it takes. Poltergeists, for example: are they true survival phenomena or unconscious PK effects caused by someone living or a mixture of both? Precognition: is the advanced potentials theory from electrical engineering sufficient to explain the data or must we go to quantum mechanics or beyond for an adequate explanation? OOBE's: is the mechanism an "astral body" or is it an unusual form of clairvoyance? Is there a unitary process behind psi? To what degree are "normal" humans trainable as sensitives? Psychic researchers and parapsychologists have yet to agree on clear, unequivocal answers to these and many other questions.

Second, the chapters support the contention that *the consciousness of man has an "extended" nature, which enables him to surpass the ordinary bounds of space and time*—suggesting that there is another dimension (or dimensions) beyond the three-dimensional material world with which man interacts consciously and nonconsciously. Human will or intentionality can affect "objective" measuring instruments; attitudes can bias experimental data. The implications here are of enormous importance. The fact of man's participation in an unseen aspect of reality at once opens long-closed doors between the established compartments known as science, religion, philosophy, and the arts. The concept of soul is just one example of an apparently subjective belief that now seems to have some reasonable, objective basis.

Third, as the title states, *these chapters present a challenge for science that can no longer be ignored, avoided, or denied.* The very canons and processes of science—exact measurement, public verification, demonstrated repeatability, accumulations of unexplained empirical data—have been used by the authors to mount this test of the objective impartiality claimed by the community of science. Does the evidence prevail or does it not? We think it does and that the remaining resistance to acceptance of the evidence is strictly a matter of an entrenched belief structure. It is not the spirit of science that is in question. It is the materialist–reductionist paradigm associated with it. As C. C. L. Gregory and Anita Kohsen have put it, "Science as a discipline is magnificent and indispensable; as a belief system it is disastrous" (4).

Since the objective technique, as distinct from the present scientific world view, is indispensable from the viewpoint of noetic research, the fourth thing my associates and I have done in this book is *to offer suggestions for further research in both the laboratory and the field.* This is a pressing need. For the most part, advances in psychic research have been made by individuals or small teams of scientists who have been inadequately funded and without adequate facilities and manpower. They have often had to perform their work during spare time because it was necessary to work full time in some other area to support themselves. Despite these enormous handicaps, the resourcefulness, determination, and patience of these men and women have triumphed. Where establishment science once challenged psychic researchers to "put up or shut up," the researchers can now present their hard-won evidence with the assurance of a job well done. In my opinion, the case for the existence of many manifestations of psi is complete. It is now time to get on with the business of formulating, explaining, and testing a sufficiently broad hypothesis to allow the various manifestations to be understood in a more definitive way. And beyond that, we must find new modes of utilization that will result in beneficent application of the findings.

The fifth important contribution my colleagues have made in this volume is *to point out the scientific, philosophical, and social implications of psychic research.* This may eventually prove more important than the research itself. It has been the history of the acquisition of knowledge to ignore the impact of advances in science on value structures and ethical systems of society. Little effort is made beforehand to assure that new knowledge is used in appropriate ways for the betterment of mankind. The contributors to this volume have clearly shown that in utilizing the psychic dimension, we are dealing with mechanisms of great potential. The moral and social implications suggested here should not be lightly dismissed.

In his foreword to this volume Gerald Feinberg suggests there are three possible models for the mind–matter dilemma: the materialist model, the dualist model, and the idealist model. We must recognize that these represent fundamental assumptions about the nature of the universe and are presumed to be mutually exclusive. Even though the contemporary evidence does not permit us to choose between dualism and idealism, it is making the materialistic model quite difficult to support as an all-encompassing reality. Perhaps, however, there is an alternative that circumvents to some degree the need to consider these as mutually exclusive models. I will discuss this later. First let us examine the evidence that seems to challenge the materialist paradigm the most.

If research is able to show without equivocation the existence of OOBE or postmortem survival or psychic surgery or the bizarre PK effects called dematerialization and rematerialization, the materialist position would become absolutely unsupportable as a total description of reality. I term this class of events *greater* phenomena because of their implications for the materialist point of view. In the current absence of incontrovertible evidence for a particular event we can only suggest that the mounting data from the greater events as a class weakens the case for an all-inclusive materialistic hypothesis and requires that we look seriously at the other models.

For each individual, proof can become a very personal thing. The creative scientist will perceive truth that the plodding conservative will accept only after years of repetitious testing. If one were compelled to wait until proof satisfactory to all were obtained before taking the step beyond, science and knowledge in general could not move forward. I must assert that on the basis of my own observations, admittedly sometimes made under conditions less than ideal, I am now totally comfortable with the idea of OOBE, psychic surgery, and dematerialization. My observations of several gifted sensitives such as Uri Geller and Norbu Chen have been convincing. Either there is a massive conspiracy to deceive by a near-army of diverse, unrelated individuals, including sophisticated scientists, or the events I have observed are true phenomena of nature. Ockham's razor—the principle of parsimony in explanation—provides the test and resolves the question. The latter is much easier to accept.

In addition to the very spectacular and controversial phenomena of the greater class, the events called telepathy, clairvoyance, and precognition and some PK events such as teleportation (and which I will call *lesser* phenomena) also send reverberations through the materialist structure, although not sufficient to cause collapse. These types of functioning suggest the extended nature of man and imply sensory mechanisms and modes of information transfer that are poorly understood. It is quite conceivable that to explain these lesser phenomena, we might be able to propose a new "energy" concept and, to provide for precognitive phenomena, reshape our concepts of causality without abandoning the materialist hypothesis altogether. I am sure such an attempt will be made by those who become convinced of the need to deal with the class of lesser events but who are not yet ready to embrace the reality of the greater events.

It has always been this way in science—to pursue vigorously a piece of the puzzle by taking it methodically apart, oblivious to the subtle clues all around that our theories, based upon the parts, could not explain the whole. It is the old story of the blind men attempting to describe an elephant by individually feeling its legs, ears, and trunk. Such descriptions are rarely very useful unless one is only interested in legs, ears and trunks. To keep our investigations productive, we must occasionally pause in our analysis by reductionism and look from a greater perspective for the subtle clues. Thus, I suggest that we will arrive at an entirely different explanation for psychic functioning if we include events of the greater category in a working hypothesis rather than ignoring them until they have been subjected to more "proof." There is no need to wait for irrefutable proof when the evidence is so compelling.

The appeal of materialism is a commentary not only on the state of our science but on our social structure as well. From my experiences I have come to view life as a process of growth and change but a process with the *purpose* of evolving toward ultimate knowledge. I see individual humans as existing in fairly specific mental states along a spectrum of consciousness having field consciousness (FC, as suggested by W. G. Roll in Chapter 17) at one end and (drawing from Feinberg's foreword) what we might call a material consciousness at the other.

Human beings seem to exist during most of their life at the material-consciousness end of the spectrum. This state is characterized at its extreme by humans who exhibit no recognition of the spiritual nature of self and who respond exclusively and almost mechanically in accordance with the behavioral principle of operant conditioning. Since most of humanity exhibits this state of consciousness most of the time, it is not surprising that our model of nature is based on observations drawn largely from this state, while observations from the occasional shifts to other, more expanded states are dismissed as being aberrant and unworthy of serious consideration.

But once a person experiences a new state of consciousness that is either sufficiently different or of sufficient duration to be recognized as reality, he must of necessity begin to question the validity and completeness of the materialist world view. This becomes profoundly true when the individual begins to recognize that his physical self is not all there is to his real or total self.

Such an experience causes the person to start a movement along the spectrum of consciousness—a growth—in which the FC state can play a greater part. Here I offer support of Tart's concept of state-specific sciences (15). An individual cannot accurately understand and express that which he has not experienced. To do so causes gross errors in interpretation. For individuals who experience only the material consciousness, a materialist model is adequate to describe the nature of the universe. This has been the case for most of our scientific thought and has been the impetus behind the evolution of the prevailing paradigm.

From this point of view, it is reasonable to assert that an individual who describes an FC state as aberrant or hallucinatory has obviously not been there. In order for science to describe adequately the consciousness of human beings in terms other than the materialist model, scientists themselves must experience the reality of knowing that other models are required and then use that awareness in their search for a more adequate concept.

If you experience for any duration an FC state, not only is the materialist model inadequate to provide a description of nature, you are (to refer to Feinberg's foreword again) catapulted headlong into the idealist model that postulates consciousness as the essential ingredient of nature. The research in survival, OOBE, and other greater phenomena provide objective data in support of the subjective FC experience. Thus, for mystics who presumably spend a major portion of their existence in a state near the FC end of the spectrum, not only is the materialist paradigm trivial, it is mostly illusion, or *maya*, as the Hindus call it.

But one can build the case for *any* specific state on the spectrum of consciousness. Probably at some point between the ends of the spectrum of consciousness accessible to humans is a state in which the dualist model appears to be the best description of reality. If the concept proposed here is accepted as a working hypothesis, we can go on to suggest that events observed and interpreted in a particular state are more real and "physical" than events not readily dealt with in that state. Thus, as LeShan points out in Chapter 24, in a state of material consciousness, psychic things seem paranormal; in an FC state, physical things seem paranormal. We might deduce that our once-distinct boundaries between physical and non-physical must crumble, since the distinction may only be one of perception followed by interpretation. To illustrate, at an earlier age explanations for many physical phenomena such as gravitation and electromagnetism were unknown. Events arising from them were considered paranormal. As these effects were understood they ceased to be paranormal and were classified as physical, even though they do not exhibit the properties of matter and are not directly perceptible with our ordinary senses. The same pattern of perception and interpretation may hold as we become accustomed to different consciousness states.

Thus, as we shift from one state of consciousness to another, our perceptions of reality, physicality, normality, and even highly subjective matters such as personal fulfillment change along with our value systems and belief structure. The psychologist Abraham Maslow (9), one of the forces behind the development of transpersonal psychology (15), wrote cogently about higher values and higher motivations attending other conscious states. This is obviously an individual process that usually requires circumstances beyond the immediate perception and understanding of the individual for it to be set in motion. But once some bump on the road of life jars you into a new awareness, new growth patterns and a new facility at moving into other states of consciousness become available.

Only as a substantial segment of a society recognizes that other conscious states and other paradigms are not only possible but desirable will the movement toward new social realities take place.

The word *paradigm* has been used throughout the book to suggest an implicit belief structure. A paradigm often exists by a combination of spoken and unspoken agreement based upon a particular view of reality. We have seen how such a paradigm shapes the course of scientific investigation and in the social arena shapes the future events in that society (see Chapters 19 and 28).

Willis Harman (in Chapter 28) has suggested the nature of the goals and value system of future society should the paradigm of materialism be left behind in the dust of history. Even with the difficulties and trauma of transition to the Perennial Philosophy, which essentially uses an idealist model, this alternative is far preferable as a future for society to any other. There seems to be ample evidence from contemporary research (8, 11) that the materialist model and its resulting scientific and social paradigms will only lead to totally unacceptable futures for society.

I suggest that the prevailing materialist paradigm, which has gained strength over the past two centuries of Western history, if allowed to continue, will result in one of two possible alternative futures. The first leads to a fatalist point of view in which the social system will collapse because of its own instabilities. The second—equally noxious—is deliberate movement toward a materialistic power structure in which the physically strong will prevail.

Neither of these alternatives is necessary.

The more reasonable and desirable course is to recognize that other conscious states are accessible and then allow thought and experience derived from these states to shape a new paradigm, a new agreement about what the realities of nature are. Thus, it seems possible, simply by agreement that other alternatives exist, to redirect the entire course of science and the increasing social chaos it has spawned.

I trust that the foregoing discussion makes it clear that I think the evidence for both the greater and lesser psi phenomena is of sufficient weight and of such crucial importance to merit extensive research into formulating and testing new models of nature. The first step is to make explicit the characteristic of the models under consideration and point out with precision the differences from a materialist model. Thus, the talents of individuals who are trained in the intricacies of abstract mathematical and physical modeling could be well utilized in exploring the noetic sciences. It is not sufficient for the psychic researcher, whatever his discipline, to suggest a poorly defined idealist model when it is possible to construct an explicit model that is consistent with principles we now understand in physics.

This is now being done. In addition to the theoretical work presented in this volume, Robert Var (16) has presented a fluid mechanics approach and G. Spencer Brown a mathematics (2) that seem not only compatible with, but important to, the process of modeling beyond materialist concepts. Arthur Young (20) and Charles Musès (6) also offer penetrating insights and intriguing concepts that appear to embrace all experience from the creation of light and the vacuum of space to human and transhuman consciousness. The work in constructing suitable models of reality is only beginning, however, and requires much greater attention (17).

The suggestion that different realities can best be perceived and understood in other states of consciousness should be seriously considered, as Tart has suggested. The scientist may find it necessary to use himself as a laboratory to visit other states of consciousness before being able to adequately understand and explain the phenomenon he wishes to investigate. The pioneering work of Masters and Houston (10), Green and associates (3), and a host of other noeticians provide useful techniques for these investigations. However, these processes are still not understood as completely as we would like, and more effort is needed here too.

There seems to be need for special examination of the phenomenon called *kundalini*, referred to in several chapters. As noted by Masters and Moss, kundalini may be the causal basis for some psi. This ancient concept purportedly is also the source of enlightenment, genius, artistic creativity, and longevity with good health (7). The fact that kundalini is traditionally thought to be caused by a form of energy called *prana*, which is outside the forces recognized by science (electricity, magnetism, gravity, and the nuclear forces), makes the need for research all the more tempting, especially since many people in noetics see the kundalini concept reappearing in modern guise as orgone energy, odic force, bioplasma, and the like.

In the area of physical research, work to determine the applicability of physical principles to the psi events is necessary. In particular, to what degree and in what sense are the conservation laws of physics applicable? Are we dealing with phenomena describable by quantum concepts? Are there sensor systems, human or otherwise, that can measure the "energy" of consciousness?

The questions such as these that a physicist can ask and then conduct experiments to answer seem limitless. I feel confident, however, that within a few years a major portion of scientific effort will be directed to the study of these and related questions.

The research that is needed in the area of medicine and healing could prove to be the most beneficial of all during the immediate future, since psychic healers have repeatedly demonstrated their ability to aid in alleviating human suffering when orthodox medicine fails. This area is one I have examined extensively. But since I have also extensively felt the resistance the medical establishment makes here, this area is likely to be the slowest to progress.

This is understandable, of course. The caution required when conducting research with human subjects, especially those with illness, makes investigations into unorthodox healing methods an extremely sensitive subject. The history of fraud and religious fanaticism attendant to unorthodox healing practices does not contribute to making the investigation any easier. But I am confident that when careful study of processes such as acupuncture, psychic healing, and psychic surgery are integrated with knowledge from contemporary medical science, a new model for the health care of people will emerge.

In my opinion, the ultimate good of this work is this: it can provide an individual with new knowledge about himself and his environment and new techniques for interacting with that environment. We have said little in this book about the benefits and responsibilities accruing to individuals as a result of gaining that knowledge, but the implications are quite clear. The evidence cited by Masters (see Chapter 26) and Honorton (see

Chapter 27) suggests that most individuals can tap and develop deep resources within the psyche that lead to an expanded range of perception and capabilities for dealing with his outer daily life. If this is so, then we may be on the threshold of developing new methods of learning and teaching that will enormously increase the ability of individuals, and thus societies, to deal effectively with the complexities of the modern world.

Thus, in addition to the research in theoretical concepts, physics, and healing techniques, perhaps the most productive long-range research is likely to be in developing the processes and techniques in psychology that allow individuals to develop their latent capabilities and thereby acquire the tools to live more useful and fulfilled lives. I foresee that this latter area of concern will have the most profound influence on the ethics, value systems and paradigms of the society to come.

APPLIED PSI

Let us now look at the future. Assume for the moment that the mechanisms involved in the production of psi will be understood and harnessed in the same way we presently use electricity and magnetism. What might be part of our future?

One possible scenario would include any or all of the following:

1.   Scientific research aided by reliable psychic channels to evaluate various possibilities in vast, expensive experiments so as to avoid wasting time and money on fruitless directions

2.   Law enforcement agencies solving crimes and locating missing persons through psychic channels

3.   Historians and archeologists using psychic avenues to aid their research into the lives of historic figures and even entire cultures

4.   Psychiatry adopting psychic means as an aid for understanding the roots of an individual's neurotic or psychotic behavior and for making the much-needed distinction between psychic and psychotic problems (e.g., the difference between auditory hallucinations and an involuntary telepathic mode that results in hearing voices)

5.   Disaster-prediction agencies, forecasting accidents, earthquakes, and other unexpected events

6.   Management consulting and organizational development work taking into account the psychic aspect of human interaction and the need for a harmonious balance of forces.

These suggestions are only a very small number of the enormous beneficial applications that might be made. One of this book's contributors,

Alan Vaughan, has even predicted: "Even as we have music and art academies, we shall have specialized psi academies where each child will have an opportunity to explore his own inner self and to develop any latent psychic ability he may have" (17). This is not farfetched. My associates and I are looking with deep interest at the intriguing relation between intuition, creativity, and psychic powers, for these may all be facets of a unified process. It is vitally important that we also look at ways in which these faculties can be enhanced. I expect that before long we will see the widespread use of training courses and resource facilities developed for helping people "get in tune" with their subjective nature and deeper intelligence. A commendable effort in this direction has already been made by the practitioners of meditation in its various forms (5, 19). The proliferation of mind-development courses is another area where there appears to be some marginal value, although they presently include some dangerous practices and some highly misleading claims in their advertisements.

The evidence of psychic research suggests that mankind has a vast potential which is largely untapped. But unless that potential is guided by a moral purpose and an acceptable value system, there will undoubtedly be misuse of it. In fact, this is already happening. The less-serious aspect of it involves those confused individuals who are wandering through realms of mind in search of the meaning of life. Their quest for self-understanding is a good thing, of course. But along the way they frequently encounter occult subjects and unproductive esoteric practices that may have some nuggets of truth in them, but if so, they are usually buried in a matrix of nonsense and misdirection. The results are all too commonly visible: the show-off "psychic," who, if he has any genuine talent, uses it to impress rather than instruct people; the fortune teller who declares that certain disastrous events are inescapably coming to a person and thereby scares him out of his wits and perhaps even sets up a self-fulfilling prophecy; the "guru" who leads credulous disciples into a condition of mental dependency that amounts to enslavement; the swindler who promises financial success, instant healing, personal allurement, and so forth. In every one of these cases, people are being used, not helped. Ego games, sensationalism, and faddism in this area are unfortunately quite common, preying on those who are genuinely groping toward new understanding, new values, and new life styles based on transpersonal rather than personal development.

There is a more frightening aspect to this surging interest in flirting with psychic powers without consideration of an attendant moral basis. Some evidence has come to light recently that the governments of large nations both in the East and West have highly classified projects under way that could result in new weapons and techniques for thought probing and control. These projects, if successful, could take humanity far along the road to the Big Brother world of *1984*. The outcome of such work would best be described as psychic fascism.

The ominous fears this statement might raise in people are more than justified, in my opinion. Such a world is a prospect that I find heinous and anathema to every desirable alternative for the future. The specter of memory erasure, psychic assassination, clairvoyant eavesdropping, dematerialization of classified documents and devices, the telepathic induction of mass hypnosis, and other equally repugnant experimentation has been raised by many. To what extent these things are feasible no one knows, but they cannot be dismissed lightly. As Michael Rossman puts it, "We are dealing with the advent of a technology which has the most awesome and complicated potentials for liberation and for tyranny, in both the psychological and material domains" (13).

As always, tyranny must be resisted. The only defense I see is a well-informed public—one hopes, an enlightened public. In a confused state of mind such as we seem to be in today because of future shock, paradigm shift, the generation gap, and all the rest of the current cultural conflicts, we must be cautious against believing in too easy a fashion. On the other hand, dogmatic skepticism can be just as deadly. Noetics, especially psychic research, is one of our keys to bridging the chasm between daily living and ultimate meaning.

We will have to expect some misuses of psychic powers, of course (Rasputin may have been a good example of this), and unethical application of creativity (as in a well-planned bank robbery). But gross abuses of human dignity cannot take place en masse if people insist upon developing a growth pattern for society along the spectrum of consciousness toward the FC state. If we develop the value system of the FC state along with the technology to alter consciousness, these and other perversions of human ability are not likely to happen. The "power games" that are played with human lives on the national and international level can be negated at their place of origin—the mind of man—because ultimately power is a state of mind.

Psychic research indicates that people must learn to live in harmony with themselves, with others, with the planet, and with the universe. These "demands" are nonnegotiable. They are both ethical and biological—a universal value system seemingly inherent in the structure of the cosmos. They are ethical because experience has shown that harmony brings improved human functioning and fulfillment. They are biological because experience has shown that lack of harmony leads to stress, suffering, and death at all levels of human living. Moreover, continued disharmony of the present kind will surely lead to the destruction of mankind and perhaps the planet.

Principles being discovered in noetic research demonstrate the underlying unity of science and religion. It is the key to transforming human consciousness from narrow egotism to cosmic altruism, thereby providing the basis for solutions to the world's major problems. From the noetic point of view, man's existence takes on significance and psychic research becomes a significant tool in the quest for self-unnderstanding. The search for meaning involves regaining the self-knowledge that enlightened beings before us have had (12). "Who am I?" the saints and sages have asked throughout history. What is the nature of self, that it can be aware of being aware?

The question "Who am I?" may be restated as "What is consciousness?" Consciousness appears to be the essence of man and the universe. Man's purpose is to become more conscious, more aware of the nature of consciousness. Kathryn Breese-Whiting notes (1): "The ancients have stated that God sleeps in the mineral, awakens in the vegetable, walks in the animal and thinks in man." This beautifully summarizes my view. By expanding personal consciousness into transpersonal consciousness, we become a party by agreement to the functioning of the universe. Its existence becomes precious to us because it *is* us. The Bible says that in the beginning, God created the heavens and the earth. Since viewing earth from space, I have reconfirmed through personal experience what the ancient scriptures say. In a spirit of integration and harmony, then, between our rational, objective, experimental aspect and our intuitive, subjective, experiential aspect, perhaps we can restate that profound insight in modern idiom as the mark of a new age:

"In the beginning, Consciousness intended matter . . ."

REFERENCES

1. Breese-Whiting, Kathryn. *The Phoenix Rises*. Portal: San Diego, Calif., 1971.
2. Brown, G. Spencer. *Laws of Form*. Julian: New York, 1973.
3. Green, Elmer; Green, Alyce; and Walters, E. Dale. "Voluntary Control of Internal States: Psychological and Physiological." *Journal of Transpersonal Psychology*, 2, no. 1 (1970).
4. Gregory, C. C. L., and Kohsen, Anita. *Physical and Psychical Research*. Omega: Reigate, Surrey, England, 1954.
5. Griffith, Fred. "Meditation Research." In John White, ed., *Frontiers of Consciousness*. Julian: New York, 1974.
6. *Journal for the Study of Consciousness*. See various articles.
7. Krishna, Gopi. *The Biological Basis of Religion and Genius*. Harper and Row: New York, 1972. (See also his autobiography *Kundalini*. Shambala: Berkeley, Calif., 1971.)
8. Markley, O. W. *Changing Images of Man*. Stanford Research Institute: Menlo Park, Calif., 1973.

9. Maslow, Abraham. *Toward a Psychology of Being*. Van Nostrand: New York, 1968.
10. Masters, Robert, and Houston, Jean. *Mind Games*. Viking: New York, 1972.
11. Meadows, Dennis, and Meadows, Donella H. *Limits of Growth*. Universe: New York, 1972.
12. Merrell-Wolff, Franklin. *Pathways Through to Space*. Julian: New York, 1973.
13. Rossman, Michael. Personal communication, July 1973.
14. Sutich, Anthony. "Some Considerations Regarding Transpersonal Psychology." *Journal of Transpersonal Psychology* (1969).
15. Tart, Charles T. "States of Consciousness and State-Specific Sciences." *Science*, 16 June 1972.
16. Var, Robert E. "Considerations of a New Mathematical Physics for Fields and Particles" (unpublished).
17. Vaughan, Alan. "2001: A Psychic Odyssey." *Psychic*, September 1972.
18. White, John. "Considerations for a Science of Consciousness." *Journal of Altered States of Consciousness*, 1, no. 2 (1973).
19. John White, ed. *What Is Meditation?* Anchor: New York, 1974.
20. Young, Arthur. *The Reflexive Universe*. Privately printed, 1972. (See also *Consciousness and Reality*, Charles Musès and Arthur Young, eds. Outerbridge and Lazard: New York, 1972.)

Appendix:
Experiments with Uri Geller

EDGAR D. MITCHELL

I first met Uri Geller in August 1972 at the home of Dr. Andrija Puharich in Ossining, New York. Dr. Puharich, whom I had known for two years, had contacted me four months earlier to tell me of an extraordinarily gifted young psychic sensitive who had come to his attention. After listening to Dr. Puharich's claims about Uri's psychokinetic, telepathic and clairvoyant abilities, I felt we had the opportunity to bring psychic research into the laboratory in a way that had rarely, if ever, been done before. Uri was supposed to have very good control over his powerful abilities; he could give us the needed repeatability of effect that the scientific method often requires in checking observations. Therefore, I offered to raise funds for a scientific study of Uri and to manage the research effort. Dr. Puharich agreed and gave me the right to do the first U.S. research.

In the meeting at Dr. Puharich's home, Dr. Gerald Feinberg, of the physics department at Columbia, was present, along with Dr. Wilbur Franklin, dean of the graduate school at Kent State University. Also present were John White, a member of my staff, and some acquaintances of Dr. Puharich.

The three days I spent in observation, experimentation and talk with Uri and Dr. Puharich convinced me that we had a high degree of probability in attempting to validate the claims Dr. Puharich had made about Uri.

Accordingly, Dr. Puharich and I contacted officials at Stanford Research Institute in Menlo Park, California, with an offer to fund and monitor the research. Two scientists there, Dr. Harold Puthoff and Mr. Russell Targ, had previously indicated to us that they were both interested in psychic research and capable of conducting it competently. My offer stipulating that they were to conduct the research was accepted. Research began in November 1972 and continued for five weeks. Much of the time Dr. Franklin and I were present in the laboratory as part of the research team.

When the experiments had been completed, Dr. Puthoff and Mr. Targ presented their work in a preliminary form on March 9, 1973, at a colloquium sponsored by the physics department at Columbia University. The statement released by SRI's public relations department on that occasion gives an adequate summary of the work. The full text of it is as follows:

New York, New York—Two Stanford Research Institute (SRI) scientists said today (Friday, March 9) that they are conducting experiments to determine whether so-called psychic or psychoenergetic functioning can be observed under rigidly controlled laboratory conditions.

In a presentation to Columbia University's Physics Colloquium, Dr. Harold E. Puthoff and Russell Targ reported that they have been carrying out their work with two subjects.

"We do not claim that either of these men have psychic powers," they said. "We draw no sweeping conclusions as to the nature of these phenomena or the need to call them psychical.

"We have observed certain phenomena with the subjects for which we have no scientific explanation. All we can say at this point is that further investigation is clearly warranted. Our work is only in the preliminary stages," they said.

Research with the subjects—carried out last year in SRI's Information Science and Engineering Division—involved perception experiments as well as their alleged ability to interact with laboratory equipment.

Dr. Puthoff discussed research initiated in July, 1972, with a preliminary series of experiments with Ingo Swann, 39, a New York artist. Using a shielded magnetometer, Swann apparently demonstrated an ability to perturb the operation of the magnetometer, Puthoff said.

The scientist said that the magnetometer was shielded by one of the best known techniques—namely, a superconducting shield.

Targ, who spoke on the work with one of the subjects, Uri Geller, 25, an Israeli, showed a movie on the experimentation with Geller.

Before showing the movie, he explained that the experimenters were aware that many purported psychics have resorted to trickery to supplement claimed extraordinary capabilities. Therefore, he said, in order to minimize the possibility of fraud, the researchers set up the following ground rules:

• All experiments were under the design and control of the experimenters—not the subject.

• All experiments were designed to be as "cheat-proof" as possible. If in retrospect, the experimenters concluded that the subject could have achieved positive results in a particular experiment through trickery, the experiment was discounted even though there was no evidence that cheating actually had taken place.

• Whenever feasible, the experiments were performed on a "double-blind" basis—that is, neither subject nor experimenter would know the "right" answer beforehand.

• On any given repetition of an experiment, the subject was allowed to "pass"—that is, choose not to answer without being considered to have "failed."

The experiments performed with Geller are summarized below:

Dice Box. A double-blind experiment was performed in which a single die was placed in a closed metal box. The box was vigorously shaken by one of the experimenters and placed on a table. The orientation of the die inside the box was unknown to the experimenters at that time. The subject would then look at the box without touching it and call out which die face he believed was uppermost. He gave the correct answer each of the eight times the experiment was performed. The probability that this could have occurred by chance is approximately one in a million. The experiment was actually performed ten times, but on two occasions the subject said his perception was not clear and he was allowed to pass.

Hidden Object Experiment. Ten identical aluminum film cans were placed in a row. An outside assistant not associated with the research would place the cans in a random position and put the target object into one of them. He would then put caps on all the cans and leave the experimental area, notifying the experimenters that the experiment was ready. The experimenters, who were not aware which can contained the object, would then enter the room with the subject. The subject would either pass his hand over the row of cans or simply look at them. He would then call out the cans he felt confident were empty, and the experimenter would remove them from the row. When only two or three cans remained, the subject would announce which one he thought contained the target object. This task was performed twelve times, without error. The probability that this could have occurred by chance is about one in a trillion. On two occasions he declined to answer. One of the targets that apparently "stumped" him was a paper-wrapped metal ball bearing. The other was a sugar cube. He had no difficulty identifying water, steel ball bearings and small magnets.

Picture Drawing Experiment. In this experiment simple pictures were drawn on 3 × 5 file cards at a time when Geller was not at SRI. The pictures were put into double-sealed envelopes by an outside assistant not associated with the experiment. To conduct the experiment, the experimenters selected an envelope from a safe, opened it to identify the picture, sealed it again and went into the experimental room. The subject made seven almost exact reproductions of the target pictures, with no errors.

Two experiments to measure physical perturbation of laboratory apparatus were also carried out. One of these involved apparently exerting a force on a laboratory balance, and the other was the generation of an apparent magnetic field recorded by a magnetometer. Both of these experiments were performed several times with results improving with repetition, showing apparent evidence of learning taking place.

Laboratory Balance. A precision laboratory balance measuring weights from one milligram to fifty grams was placed under a bell jar. This balance, made by Scientech Corp., Boulder, Colorado, generates an electrical output voltage in proportion to the force applied to it. The balance had a one-gram mass placed on its pan before it was covered with a bell jar. A chart recorder then continuously monitored the force applied to the pan of the balance. On several occasions the subject caused the balance to respond as though a force were applied to the pan. This was evidenced by a corresponding displacement shown by the chart recorder. These displacements were ten to a hundred times larger than could be produced by striking the bell jar or the table or jumping on the floor.

Magnetometer Experiment. A Bell gaussmeter was used to determine if the subject could perturb an instrument sensitive to magnetic fields. The instrument was set to a full scale sensitivity of 0.3 gauss. The subject would move his empty hands near the instrument in an effort to cause a deflection of the chart recorder monitoring the magnetometer output. In carefully filmed experiments, the subject was able to perturb the magnetometer without touching the measuring head of the instrument.

The movie showed other experiments carried out with Geller that were labeled unsatisfactory or inconclusive by the scientists.

Among these were attempts to bend or manipulate objects such as rings and spoons without physical contact. In these cases, physical effects were observed but it was unclear without further instrumentation how Geller changed the physical appearance of the objects since he was permitted to touch them.

The experiments were carried out in November–December of last year.

Since the 1972 experiments, another week of laboratory research was carried out on Uri by Dr. Puthoff and Mr. Targ at Stanford Research Institute, with funding provided through The Institute of Noetic Sciences. The research was performed in December 1973. Details of the work should be available through publication in the scientific literature soon.

Glossary

ACUPUNCTURE. An ancient Chinese system of medicine that uses needles inserted in the body at prescribed sites to stimulate the flow of chi (life energy) and thereby allegedly restore balance to the energy system that is thought to determine health. Modern variants of the original system use sound, lasers, chemicals, and massage on the acupuncture points.

AGENT. In telepathy tests, the sender, or person whose mental states are to be apprehended by the percipient or receiver. In GESP tests, the person who looks at the target object. In spontaneous cases of ESP phenomena, the person who apparently initiates telepathic communication. In RSPK, the apparent initiator or focal point for poltergeist occurrences.

ALTERED STATE OF CONSCIOUSNESS (ASC). A pattern of awareness that is qualitatively different in overall mental functioning from one's ordinary waking pattern.

ANPSI. Psi in animals.

APPARITION. A visual paranormal appearance, generally spontaneous, that suggests the real presence of someone distant or dead.

APPORT. An object that purportedly appears in a closed area, indicating the apparent penetration of matter by matter—that is, dematerialization of an object that passes through obstacles such as walls and then rematerializes.

ASC. See ALTERED STATE OF CONSCIOUSNESS.

ASTRAL BODY. A hypothetical replica, or "double," of the individual's physical body that is exact but nonphysical. It is said to be the vehicle which leaves the physical body in OOBE.

ASTRAL PROJECTION. See OUT-OF-THE-BODY EXPERIENCES.

AURA. An envelope or field of colored energy or radiation(s) said by sensitives to surround the human body, with the color or colors indicative of different aspects of the person's physical, psychological, and spiritual condition. Some traditions hold that there is more than one aura within the total envelope, each having distinctive properties.

AUTOMATIC WRITING. Writing done as a motor automatism in a dissociated state—that is, not under conscious control of the writer.

AUTOMATISM.   Any sensory or motor activity carried out by a person in a dissociated state or without conscious muscular effort and mental direction.

BASIC TECHNIQUE (BT).   The clairvoyance-testing technique in which each card is laid aside by the experimenter as it is called by the subject. At the end of the run, the checkup is made.

BILOCATION.   The apparent simultaneous presence of a person in two different locations by paranormal means—generally thought to involve an astral double.

BIOCOMMUNICATIONS.   A Russian term for telepathy.

BIOENERGETICS.   A Russian term for psychokinesis.

BIOFEEDBACK.   An instrumental technique for self-monitoring of normally unconscious, involuntary body processes such as brainwaves, heartbeat rate, and muscle tension that can result in a degree of conscious, voluntary control of the process.

BIOINFORMATION.   A Russian term for extrasensory perception.

BIOLOCATION.   A Russian term for clairvoyance.

BIOPLASMA.   A hypothetical form of energy purportedly associated with living organisms, demonstrated by some Soviet researchers through Kirlian photography and termed by them "a fourth state of matter."

BT.   See BASIC TECHNIQUE.

CALL.   The specific guess made by the subject in trying to identify a target in an ESP test.

CHANCE.   The complex of undefined factors irrelevant to and uncorrelated with the purpose at hand.

CHANCE EXPECTATION (MEAN CHANCE EXPECTATION).   In testing for psychic phenomena, the most likely score if no information transfer is involved.

CHAKRA.   Sanskrit for "wheel." In yogic philosophy, a psychic center in the body, generally dormant, which can be activated by kundalini, resulting in the attainment of siddhis, or psychic powers. There are said to be seven major chakras from the base of the spine to the crown of the head, and various minor chakras. Some traditions maintain that the chakras are nerve ganglia in the physical body; others maintain they reside in the astral body and are associated with various glands or organs in the physical body.

CHI-SQUARE.   A statistical test derived from a sum of quantities, each of which is a deviation squared divided by an expected value. Also a sum of the squares of critical ratios (CR's).

CLAIRAUDIENCE.   Extrasensory data perceived as sound.

CLAIRSENTIENCE.   An archaic term meaning extrasensory awareness in a general sense as distinguished from the visual mode (clairvoyance), auditory mode (clairaudience), and other sensory modes.

CLAIRVOYANCE. ESP of physical objects or events as distinguished from telepathy, which involves ESP of thoughts.

COMMUNICATOR. An ostensible discarnate personality said to communicate with the living, usually through a medium or sensitive.

CONTROL. In trance mediumship, the ostensible discarnate personality of intelligence that habitually relays messages or originates communications through a medium to a sitter. Some researchers interpret this as a dissociation effect—that is, a secondary, repressed personality of the sensitive.

CONSCIOUSNESS. (1) A state of waking awareness. (2) The fundamental dimension or stratum of existence, through which all mental and physical activity (thoughts, feelings, sensations, dreams, volition, and behavior) is accomplished. Hence, consciousness is more than self-awareness. So-called unconscious activities also are dependent upon some degree of consciousness.

COSMIC CONSCIOUSNESS. Purportedly the highest state of consciousness known to humans. An awareness of the design and meaning of the universe and life is said to be obtained, along with a feeling of ecstasy, moral and intellectual illumination, and other characteristics generally exemplified by saints and enlightened spiritual teachers.

CRITICAL RATIO (CR). A statistical test used in limited choice tests to determine whether the observed deviation is significantly greater than the expected random fluctuation about the average. The CR is obtained by dividing the observed deviation by the standard deviation. (The probability of a given CR may be obtained by consulting tables of the probability integral.)

CROSS CORRESPONDENCE. A highly complex series of communications through two or more mediums unknown to each other that provide an understandable message only when the separate fragments are put together.

DEATHBED EXPERIENCE. An unusual state of exaltation or altered perception in a dying person, sometimes with apparent awareness of the presence of deceased loved ones.

DÉJÀ VU. French for "already seen." The experience in which a new event feels as if it had been experienced before.

DEMATERIALIZATION. The purported paranormal disappearance, usually quite rapidly, of an object.

DEVIATION. In quantitative testing, the amount an observed number of hits or an average score varies (either above or below) from mean chance expectation.

DIRECT VOICE. A phenomenon of mediumship in which an isolated voice without visible source is purportedly heard.

DISCARNATE. Disembodied. Used in mediumistic communications to refer to a soul, intelligence or personality of a deceased person. In a more general sense it includes the concepts of elementals, nature spirits and deities.

DISPLACEMENT.   ESP responses to targets other than those for which the calls were intended. Displacement may be either forward or backward. Displacement to the targets one, two, three, etc. places after the intended target are designated as $(+1)$, $(+2)$, $(+3)$, etc. Displacement to the targets one, two, three, etc. places before the intended target are designated (-1), (-2), (-3), etc.

DISSOCIATION.   A splitting of the mind so that one or more parts behave independently of the other, each functioning as a separate unit.

DOUBLE.   The purported astral or etheric counterpart of the physical body said to temporarily move about in space and appear in various degrees of density to others.

DOWSING.   A form of clairvoyance in which underground water, minerals, or hidden objects are located apparently by means of a divining (dowsing) rod, pendulum, or other instrument.

DOWN THROUGH (DT).   The clairvoyance technique in which the cards are called down through the pack before any are removed or checked.

ECTOPLASM.   A semiphysical substance alleged to issue from the body of a physical medium and out of which materializations are sometimes formed.

ESP.   See EXTRASENSORY PERCEPTION.

ESP CARDS (ZENER CARDS).   Cards that bear one of these symbols: star, circle, square, cross, and waves (three parallel wavy lines). A standard pack has 25 cards, 5 of each symbol.

EXTRA.   Images of people, supposedly deceased, that are said to appear paranormally on film through psychic photography or thoughtography.

EXTRACHANCE.   Not caused by chance alone.

EXTRASENSORY PERCEPTION (ESP).   The experience of, or response to, an external event, object, state, or influence without contact through the known senses. ESP is sometimes unconscious—that is, it occurs without awareness of it by the person or people involved, as in psi-mediated instrumental responses (PMIR).

FC.   See FIELD CONSCIOUSNESS.

FIELD CONSCIOUSNESS (FC).   An ASC in which an individual seems to experience an enlargement of the ordinary boundaries of self, so that part or all of the individual's environment becomes merged with his awareness of self.

GENERAL EXTRASENSORY PERCEPTION (GESP).   ESP that could be either telepathy or clairvoyance, or both.

GHOST.   The popular term for an apparition of a deceased person.

GUIDE.   A benevolent, protective supermundane influence alleged to continually watch over a person.

HALLUCINATION. A visual or auditory experience similar to sense perception but without sensory stimulation. It is termed veridical when it corresponds to a real event taking place outside the range of sensory awareness.

HAUNTING. Paranormal phenomena associated with a certain location, expecially a building. The phenomena are usually attributed to the activity of discarnate spirits.

HIGH-VOLTAGE PHOTOGRAPHY. Photography that characteristically uses a pulsed high-frequency electrical field and two electrodes, between which are placed the object to be photographed and an unexposed film plate. No optics are involved. It is also possible to gain this effect with direct current (DC) and/or low-frequency pulses. If a transparent electrode is used, the film may be placed outside the electrode system.

HIT. A correct response in a test for some aspect of psi.

HYPERESTHESIA. Unusual sensitivity of the skin or of a particular sense.

ILLUSION. An erroneous interpretation of sensory data obtained normally.

INTUITION. The ability of knowing, or the knowledge obtained, without conscious recourse to inference or reasoning.

KIRLIAN PHOTOGRAPHY. A type of high-voltage photography.

KUNDALINI. According to yogic philosophy, a nonphysical energy in the human body, derived from prana, which is capable of activating psychic centers called chakras. Its activation in individuals through practice of various spiritual disciplines is said to result in enlightenment, genius, creativity, and psychic powers. Thought by some modern investigators, such as Gopi Krishna, to be the psychophysiological mechanism by which the human race evolves toward higher consciousness.

LEVITATION. The purported raising of objects or bodies in the air by no apparent physical means.

MATERIALIZATION. A purported paranormal event in which some forms or objects become suddenly visible in solid form. Some physical mediums claim to use ectoplasm for materializations. Other types of psychics are said to materialize known physical objects such as coins or buttons that are indistinguishable from the genuine articles.

MEAN CHANCE EXPECTATION. See CHANCE EXPECTATION.

MEDIUM. A sensitive who apparently perceives and communicates with discarnates, or who acts as a channel for discarnates to communicate through direct voice. A *mental medium* receives messages from the deceased and transmits them to the living. A *physical medium* can, in addition, produce physical effects such as levitation and materialization.

MISS. An erroneous response in a test for some aspect of psi.

MYSTICISM. The doctrine or belief that direct knowledge of God or ultimate reality is attainable through intuition or insight and in a way differing from ordinary sense perception or the use of logical reasoning.

NEURAL. The adjectival form of *neuron*.

NEURON.   The fundamental functional unit of the nervous system.

NOETICS.   The general study of consciousness; from the Greek root *nous*, "mind."

OBJECT READING.   See PSYCHOMETRY.

OMEGA (Ω).   The symbol for consciousness and noetics.

OUT-OF-THE-BODY EXPERIENCE (OOBE).   Sometimes called astral projection, astral travel, or mobile center of consciousness, OOBE is an experience of seeming to be in a place separate from one's physical body while fully and normally conscious. The experience can be either spontaneous or induced.

P.   See PROBABILITY.

p.   See PROBABILITY.

PARAPHYSICS.   The study of the physics of paranormal processes—that is, phenomena that resemble physical phenomena but are without recognizable physical cause.

PARANORMAL.   As related to psychic research, faculties and phenomena that are beyond "normality" in terms of cause and effect as currently understood.

PARAPSYCHOLOGY.   The branch of science that deals with ESP and PK—that is, behavioral or personal exchanges with the environment that are extrasensorimotor (not dependent on the senses and muscles).

PERCIPIENT.   A subject in an ESP test or a person who has a spontaneous ESP experience.

PHANTASM OF THE DEAD.   An apparition or appearance suggesting the presence of a person or animal no longer living.

PHANTASM OF THE LIVING.   An apparition or appearance suggesting the presence of a living person or animal that is not there.

PK.   See PSYCHOKINESIS.

PLACEMENT TEST.   A technique for testing PK in which the subject tries to influence falling objects to land in a designated area of the surface on which they are thrown.

PMIR.   See PSI-MEDIATED INSTRUMENTAL RESPONSE.

POLTERGEIST.   German for "noisy spirit." Various paranormal manifestations involving the unexplained movement or breakage of objects. Poltergeist activity differs from a haunting in that it often seems to center around the presence of an adolescent. Now generally termed recurrent spontaneous psychokinesis (RSPK).

POSSESSION.   A state in which a person seems to be under the control in mind and body of another personality, generally thought to be a discarnate (and sometimes nonhuman) spirit.

PRANA.   A form of energy postulated in ancient Hindu texts as the basic life force. Prana is thought to exist outside the types of energy (electricity, magnetism, gravity, and the nuclear forces) known to Western science. It conceptually resembles the odic force (Reichenbach), orgone (Reich), chi (acupuncture theory), and bioplasma.

PRECOGNITION.   Prediction, or knowledge of future events that cannot be inferred from present knowledge.

PRIMARY PERCEPTION.   A hypothetical sensory system or perception capability allegedly existing in cell life that allows plants and animals low in the evolutionary scale to monitor their environment and communicate with other organisms, including humans.

PROBABILITY.   A mathematical statement of the likelihood of occurrence of a particular event, normally expressed as a decimal fraction. In parapsychology literature, probability (P) is a mathematical estimate of the a priori likelihood that chance alone could produce a particular result, while probability (p) is the statistically analyzed results of a particular test.

Psi (ψ).   A term to designate collectively paranormal events and/or faculties, including ESP, PK, and survival phenomena.

PSI FIELD.   The region in space in which psi are detectable.

PSI-MEDIATED INSTRUMENTAL RESPONSE (PMIR).   The production by the organism of one or more responses that are instrumental in serving the needs of the organism, when these responses are made possible by psi factors (ESP and/or PK). This can occur without the conscious intention or awareness of the organism.

PSI-MISSING.   Use of psi ability, so that the subject avoids the target he is trying to hit more often than would be expected if only chance were operating.

PSYCHE.   The Greek word for soul. In current English usage it can mean soul or mind.

PSYCHIC.   (1) A synonym for sensitive. (2) Describing paranormal events and abilities that cannot be explained in terms of established physical principles.

PSYCHIC PHOTOGRAPHY.   See THOUGHTOGRAPHY.

PSYCHIC RESEARCH.   A traditional term for the branch of science that studies psi in the laboratory and in the field.

PSYCHIC SURGERY.   A form of healing in which portions of diseased tissues are allegedly removed without the use of instruments.

PSYCHOENERGETICS.   A Russian term for parapsychology.

PSYCHOKINESIS (PK).   The direct influence of mind on matter without any known intermediate physical energy or instrumentation—that is, the extramotor aspect of psi. Also called telekinesis.

PSYCHOMETRY.   Object reading or the paranormal ability of some sensitives to obtain facts about the history of an object, including people and events connected with it, usually through touching or handling it.

PSYCHOPHYSIOLOGY.   The study of mental events as they relate to physiological changes in the body. Often called physiological psychology.

PSYCHOSPHERE.   In the philosophy of cosmic humanism, the hyperdimensional field of consciousness whereby the individual human psyche transcends egoism to achieve union and cosmic consciousness. There is a dual spiral wherein the individual reaches up to the Cosmic Imagination (God) and the universal spirit reaches down to man in synchronicity or resonance.

PSYCHOTRONICS.   The Czechoslovakian term for parapsychology.

RADIESTHESIA.   (1) Sensitivity to radiations throughout the spectrum of radiations from any source, living or inert. (2) A synonym for dowsing.

RAPID EYE MOVEMENT (REM).   Eye movement by a sleeping person that indicates he is dreaming.

RECURRENT SPONTANEOUS PSYCHOKINETIC PHENOMENA (RSPK).   The modern term for poltergeist.

REINCARNATION.   A theory of survival in which some aspect of a deceased person is reborn in another human body. Reincarnation is often confused with the transmigration of souls, which allows for rebirth of a human soul in the body of an animal.

REM.   See RAPID EYE MOVEMENT.

RSPK.   See RECURRENT SPONTANEOUS PSYCHOKINETIC PHENOMENA.

RUN.   A group of trials, usually the successive calling of a deck of 25 ESP cards or symbols. In PK tests, a run consists of 24 throws, regardless of the number of dice thrown at the same time.

SCORE.   The number of hits made in any given unit of trials, usually a run. *Total score* is the pooled score of all runs. *Average score* is the total score divided by the number of runs.

SÉANCE (SITTING).   A meeting of one or more persons with a medium, usually with the object of receiving communications from discarnates through the medium.

SENSITIVE.   A person who is psychic—that is, is often able to induce psychic experience at will.

SERIES.   Several runs in experimental sessions that are grouped in accordance with the stated purpose and design of the experiment.

SHEEP–GOAT EFFECT.   The relationship between belief in psi and scoring level. Believers (sheep) tend to score above chance and disbelievers (goats) below chance.

SIDDHI.   Sanskrit term for psychic power. In yogic philosophy, siddhis may awaken in the course of one's spiritual development but should be ignored because they are a hindrance to attaining enlightenment.

SIGNIFICANCE.   A numerical result is significant when it equals or surpasses some criterion of degree or chance improbability. The criterion commonly used in psychic research and parapsychology today is a probability value of 0.05, or odds of 20:1 against chance, or a deviation in either direction such that the CR is 2.33 or greater.

SITTER.   A person who consults or sits with a medium or sensitive.

SITTING.   See SÉANCE.

SPIRIT COMMUNICATION.   A communication, usually obtained through a medium or automatic writing, purporting to come from a deceased personality.

SPIRITUALISM.   A religious movement with doctrines and practices based on the belief that survival of death is a reality and that communication between the living and the deceased occurs, usually via mediumship.

SUBJECT.   The person who is tested in an experiment.

SUBLIMINAL PERCEPTION.   Nonconscious response to stimuli that are below the threshold of normal awareness.

SURVIVAL.   The concept of continued conscious existence for some time after death. Immortality (eternal existence) is neither implied nor ruled out.

SYNCHRONICITY.   A term coined by C. G. Jung for meaningful coincidences as an acausal connecting principle that could account for some psi.

TARGET.   In ESP tests, the objective or mental events to which the subject is attempting to respond. In PK tests, the objective process or object that the subject tries to influence (such as the face or location of a die). A *target card* is the card that the percipient is attempting to identify or otherwise indicate a knowledge of. A *target face* is the face of the falling die that the subject tries to make turn up by PK. A *target pack* is a pack of cards whose order the subject is attempting to identify.

TC.   See TRANSPERSONAL CONSCIOUSNESS.

TELEKINESIS.   A form of PK, the movement of stationary objects without the use of any known physical force.

TELEPATHY.   ESP of another person's mental state or thoughts.

TELEPORTATION.   A form of psychokinesis similar to telekinesis but generally used to designate the movement of objects (apports) through other physical objects or over great distances.

THETA (θ).   (1) The term that collectively designates survival phenomena, from the Greek word *thanatos*, "death." (2) A type of brain wave.

THOUGHTFORMS.   The purported creation of physical forms by mentally projecting an image that materializes in the visible world.

THOUGHTOGRAPHY.   The paranormal ability to produce images on photographic film.

TOBISCOPE.   A portable device for detecting acupuncture points through measuring skin resistance.

TRANCE.   An ASC, induced or spontaneous, that gives access to many ordinarily inhibited capacities of the mind–body system. These include imageries, accelerated mental processes, creative automatisms, enhanced concentration and perception, and other important phenomena. There are a variety of trance states, not just a single state.

TRANSPERSONAL CONSCIOUSNESS (TC).   Consciousness that extends or goes beyond the personal or individual.

TRANSPERSONAL PSYCHOLOGY.   A new major psychological approach to the study of the person that emphasizes humanity's ultimate development or transcendent potential as individuals and a species. Sometimes referred to as the "fourth force" in psychology (the others being psychoanalysis, behaviorism, and humanistic psychology).

TRAVELING CLAIRVOYANCE.   An older term used to describe hypnotized subjects' clairvoyance of distant scenes.

TRIAL.   In ESP tests, a single attempt to identify a target object. In PK tests, a single unit of effect to be measured in the evaluation of results.

VERIDICAL HALLUCINATION.   An hallucination corresponding with some degree of accuracy to an external object, person, place, or event.

WORLD SENSORIUM.   In the philosophy of cosmic humanism, the functional cybernetic system of human institutions and technologies whereby a holistic social synthesis culminates in an emergent world civilization. This is the "world-brain" basis for the psychosphere.

ZENER CARDS.   See ESP CARDS.

ndex

697

Schwarz, B. E., 124, 256, 257, 258, 260
Science magazine, 47, 117
Science Digest magazine, 298
Scientech Corporation, 686
Scientific and Technical Society of Radio, Electronics and Biocommunication (Moscow), 470
Secret of Yoga, The (Krishna), 48
Sekhmet, 604, 605, 607–14
Sekhmet: Dimensions of Mystery (Masters), 614 f.
"Self Reliance" (Emerson), 654
Sensitive personalities, 74–91
Sergeyev, G. A., 431, 475, 476, 477, 490
Serios, Ted., 317–28
Servadio, E., 254, 256, 257, 258, 260, 418
Seven Steps Beyond the Horizon (film), 474
SFF. *See* Spiritual Frontiers Fellowship
Shackleton, Basil, 66, 68, 89, 101, 116, 160
Shapin, Betty, 213, 218
Shepstone, Sir Theophilus, 277
Sherman, Harold, 33
Shuisky, Nikolas, 481, 482
Sidgwick, Eleanor, 60, 67, 161, 377, 385–86
Sidgwick, Henry, 60, 61, 64, 67, 69, 71, 113, 114
Sinclair, Mr. and Mrs. Upton, 114–15
"Six Theories About Apparitions" (Hart *et al.*), 381
Skinner, B. F., 586
Skolimowski, S., 457
Smart, E. F., 501
Smith, H. Justa, 339–40
Smith, Michael Valentine (fictional character), 580–82
Soal, Frank, 398–400
Soal, S. G., 33, 46–47, 66, 78, 116, 117, 118, 122, 159–60, 207, 398–401, 405, 526
Social Psychology (McDougall), 64
Società Italiana di Parapsicologia, 201
Society for Psychical Research (SPR), 38, 61, 62, 64, 96, 97, 114, 138, 158, 161, 197, 202, 203, 206, 210, 248, 249, 316, 376, 378, 379 f.; *Journal*, 203, 208, 218, 220, 221, 349; library, 209–10; *Proceedings*, 47, 203, 208, 217, 219, 220, 221, 252, 317
Society for Psychical Research in Finland, 201
Solomon Baba, 277
Solon, 647
Soomere, I., 164, 174
South African Society for Psychical Research, 201

Southern California Society for Psychical Research, 201
Southern Methodist University library, 210
Spearman, Mrs., 378
Speer, Albert, 588
Spence, K. W., 618
Spiritual Frontiers Fellowship (SFF), 71, 83, 202; library, 210
Spiritualist Association of Great Britain, 82
SPR. *See* Society for Psychical Research
Spraggett, Allen, 83
SRI. *See* Stanford Research Institute
Stanford, Rex, 165, 175, 198, 239, 419
Stanford Research Institute (SRI), 87, 89, 192, 536, 683–686
Stanford University, 211
Stapp, H. P., 455
Steiner, George, 587 f.
Steiner, Rudolf, 294
Stekel, W., 253, 256
Stent, G. S., 174, 453
Stepanek, Pavel, 89
Stevenson, Ian, 68, 121, 127, 164, 173, 195, 198, 239, 260, 318, 319, 392, 406, 419
Stewart, Gloria, 66, 68, 160
Storming of the Mind, The (Hunter), 586
Stoyva, J., 619
Stranger in a Strange Land (Heinlein), 580–81
Stratton, J. A., 172, 528
Stribic, Frances P., 140
Structure of Scientific Revolutions, The (Kuhn), 44, 640
Stuart, C. E., 119
Stulman, Julius, 438
Stump, John, 390, 627
Sturmann, Angelica, 294
Sudre, René, 382
Supreme Doctrine, The (Benoit), 652, 655
Supreme Identity, The (Watts), 649
Survival research, 397–422
Svengali (fictional character), 57
Swann, Ingo, 88–9, 365–67, 369, 443, 535–38, 712
Swedenborg, Emanuel, 56–57, 59, 62, 95–96, 98, 99
Szent-Gyorgi, A., 480

Tait, Mr., 377
Targ, Russell, 87, 165, 172–73, 174, 192, 451, 462, 526 f., 683–686
Tart, Charles T., 69, 205, 383 f., 392 f., 414, 419, 421, 528, 630, 674
Taubes, Jacob, 587 f.